Bed & Breakfast U.S.A.

1 9 9 8

B&Bs can be your home away from home!
Complete with hundreds of listings, all with
reasonable rates, this indispensable directory
gives you the keys to America's most popular
alternative to impersonal hotels and shows
you why B&Bs are the *only* way to travel.
Offering friendly, home-style places to stay for
business travelers, family vacationers, and
anyone looking for a way to really see the
country, this information-packed book will be
every traveler's constant companion.

◆

**"For those who have embraced the B&B way
to travel, there is no going back to hotel high-
rises and motel monotony."**—*Time*

◆

PEGGY ACKERMAN is the director of the Tourist House Association, Inc., a national association of over 1,100 members. She
lives in Greentown, Pennsylvania.

Bed & Breakfast U.S.A.

PEGGY ACKERMAN

Tourist House Association of America, Inc.

A PLUME BOOK

York, New York 10014, U.S.A.
W8 5TZ, England
oria, Australia
e, Toronto, Ontario, Canada

Penguin Books (N.Z.) Ltd, 182–190 Wairau Road, Auckland 10, New Zealand

Penguin Books Ltd, Registered Offices:
Harmondsworth, Middlesex, England

Published by Plume, an imprint of Dutton Signet,
a division of Penguin Putnam Inc.

First Printing, January, 1998

10 9 8 7 6 5 4 3 2 1

LC card number: 86-649303

Printed in the United States of America

Set in Palatino and Optima
Designed by Stanley S. Drate/Folio Graphics Co. Inc.

If you want to be listed in future editions of this guide, DO NOT WRITE TO
PLUME OR PENGUIN. See page 615 for a membership application, or write to:
   Tourist House Association of America, Inc.
   Greentown, PA 18426
Applications will be accepted until March 31, 1998.

The book you are holding is the result of one woman's hard work and big dreams. In 1974, my mother, Betty Revits Rundback, began thinking about how to celebrate the American Bicentennial in 1976. She decided to take her family of seven on a cross-country tour, but didn't like the idea of staying in motels night after night. She wanted her children to really see the country, and to get to know its people along the way. Remembering back to her own childhood, when the house down the road offered comfortable lodging and a bountiful breakfast to travelers, she set out to create a similar experience for us. She never expected to spend months at the New York Public Library doing it! But that's exactly what she did, going through every telephone directory in America to find listings of family-style guesthouses, contacting all the owners individually, and finally assembling them into a pamphlet in time for the Bicentennial. With the information Betty had gathered, she founded the Tourist House Association of America, which she ran enthusiastically and successfully until her death on July 4, 1990. My wife, Peggy, now continues her work of bringing together guests and hosts from around the world. We dedicate this book to her, in loving memory of her warmth, compassion, and spirit.

—Peggy and Michael Ackerman

Contents

Reservation service organizations appear here in boldface type.

Reservation service organizations appear here in boldface type.

Reservation service organizations appear here in boldface type.

Reservation service organizations appear here in boldface type.

Reservation service organizations appear here in boldface type.

Reservation service organizations appear here in boldface type.

Reservation service organizations appear here in boldface type.

Reservation service organizations appear here in boldface type.

Reservation service organizations appear here in boldface type.

Reservation service organizations appear here in boldface type.

Reservation service organizations appear here in boldface type.

Reservation service organizations appear here in boldface type.

Reservation service organizations appear here in boldface type.

Reservation service organizations appear here in boldface type.

Reservation service organizations appear here in boldface type.

Reservation service organizations appear here in boldface type.

Reservation service organizations appear here in boldface type.

Reservation service organizations appear here in boldface type.

Reservation service organizations appear here in boldface type.

Reservation service organizations appear here in boldface type.

Reservation service organizations appear here in boldface type.

Reservation service organizations appear here in boldface type.

Reservation service organizations appear here in boldface type.

Reservation service organizations appear here in boldface type.

Reservation service organizations appear here in boldface type.

Reservation service organizations appear here in boldface type.

Reservation service organizations appear here in boldface type.

Reservation service organizations appear here in boldface type.

Reservation service organizations appear here in boldface type.

Reservation service organizations appear here in boldface type.

Reservation service organizations appear here in boldface type.

Reservation service organizations appear here in boldface type.

Preface

If you are familiar with earlier editions of *Bed & Breakfast U.S.A.*, you know that this book has always been a labor of love. It is very gratifying to see how it has grown from the first sixteen-page edition, titled *Guide to Tourist Homes and Guest Houses,* which was published in 1975 and contained forty individual listings. Twenty-three years later, the twentieth revised edition lists 903 homes and 70 reservation agencies, giving travelers access to over 20,000 host homes. This spectacular success indicates how strongly the concept of the guesthouse has recaptured the fancy of both proprietors and travelers.

Although we do not list grand hotels, rental properties, or campground compounds, we do list an exciting amount of smaller bed and breakfasts and inns, and a small percentage of higher-priced inns. But make no mistake—we still dedicate most of this book to meeting the needs of our readers, which means listing only those B&Bs with reasonably priced accommodations. In the years of doing this book, we have found that you can pay a reasonable amount of money and enjoy the bed and breakfast experience just as much as a very chic inn, and in most cases enjoy more personal contact with your hosts. We have given a great deal of thought to what we feel a B&B should be and are focusing on our original definition: an owner-occupied residence with breakfast included at a fair rate, where a visitor is made to feel more like a welcome guest than a paying customer.

Because of personal experience and letters from our readers, *Bed & Breakfast U.S.A.* will not accept properties where the host does not reside on the premises, rental properties, B&Bs with more than fifteen guest rooms, rates exceeding $35 where six people or more share a bath, rates exceeding $45 where five people share a bath, or rates without breakfast included. Higher-priced B&Bs and inns will only be included according to space availability.

This is not a project for which listings have been compiled just for the sake of putting a book together; bigger isn't necessarily better. *Bed & Breakfast U.S.A.* is a product of a membership organization whose credo is "Comfort, cleanliness, cordiality, and fairness of cost." We solicit and rely on the comments of our readers. For this purpose, we include a tear-out form on page 625. We genuinely appreciate comments from guests—negative if necessary, positive when warranted—and we do follow up. We want to hear from you!

All of the B&Bs and inns described in this book are members of the Tourist House Association of America, Inc., Greentown, Pennsylvania 18426, phone: (888) 888-4068. THAA dues are $40 annually.

PEGGY ACKERMAN
Tourist House Association of America, Inc.

January 1998

Even after careful editing and proofreading, errors occasionally occur. We regret any inconvenience to our readers and members.

Acknowledgments

A special thanks to all the travel writers and reporters who have brought us to the attention of their audiences.

To my family, Mike Ackerman, Travis Kali, and Justin Ackerman, the three men in my life—thank you for all the encouragement and support you have shown; to Mary Kristyak Donnelly, a superb mother, grandmother, and best friend—I admire you so; to Bill Donnelly, dad and joke teller; to the grandmothers, Ann Revits and Helen Kristyak.

A final note of thanks to my editor, Leslie Jay, for her deeply appreciated assistance. Never too much, always a smile.

1

Introduction

Bed and breakfast is the popular lodging alternative to hotel high-rises and motel monotony. B&Bs are either private residences where the owners rent spare bedrooms to travelers, or small, family-operated inns offering a special kind of warm, personal hospitality. Whether large or small, B&Bs will make you feel more like a welcome guest than a paying customer.

The custom of opening one's home to travelers dates back to the earliest days of Colonial America. Hotels and inns were few and far between in those days, and wayfarers relied on the kindness of strangers to provide a bed for the night. Which is why, perhaps, there is hardly a Colonial-era home in the mid-Atlantic states that does not boast: "George Washington Slept Here!"

During the Depression, the tourist home provided an economic advantage to both the traveler and the host. Travelers always drove through the center of town; there were no superhighways to bypass local traffic. A house with a sign in the front yard reading "Tourists" or "Guests" indicated that a traveler could rent a room for the night and have a cup of coffee before leaving in the morning. The usual cost for this arrangement was $2. The money represented needed income for the proprietor as well as the opportunity to chat with an interesting visitor.

In the 1950s, the country guesthouse became a popular alternative to the costly hotels in resort areas. The host compensated for the lack of hotel amenities, such as private bathrooms, by providing comfortable bedrooms and bountiful breakfasts at a modest price. The visitors enjoyed the home-away-from-home atmosphere; the hosts were pleased to have paying houseguests.

The incredible growth in international travel that has occurred over the past 30 years has provided yet another stimulus. Millions of Americans now vacation annually in Europe, and travelers have become enchanted with the bed and breakfast concept so popular in England, Ireland, and other parts of the Continent. In fact, many well-traveled Americans are delighted to learn that we "finally" have B&Bs here. But, as you now know, they were always here—just a rose by another name.

Bed and breakfasts are for:

- **Parents of college kids:** Tuition is costly enough without the added expense of Parents' Weekends. Look for a B&B near campus.
- **Parents traveling with children:** A family living room, playroom, or backyard is preferable to the confines of a motel room.
- **"Parents" of pets:** Many proprietors will allow your well-behaved darling to come, too. This can cut down on the expense and trauma of kenneling Fido.
- **Business travelers:** Being "on the road" can be lonely and expensive. It's so nice, after a day's work, to return to a home-away-from-home.
- **Women traveling alone:** Friendship and conversation are the natural ingredients of a guesthouse.
- **Skiers:** Lift prices are lofty, so it helps to save some money on lodging. Many mountain homes include home-cooked meals in your room rate.
- **Students:** A visit with a family is a pleasant alternative to camping or the local "Y."
- **Visitors from abroad:** Cultural exchanges are often enhanced by a host who can speak your language.
- **Carless travelers:** If you plan to leave the auto at home, it's nice to know that many B&Bs are convenient to public transportation. Hosts will often arrange to meet your bus, plane, or train for a nominal fee.
- **Schoolteachers and retired persons:** Exploring out-of-the-way places is fun and will save you money.
- **History buffs:** Many B&Bs are located in areas important to our country's past. A number have the distinction of being listed on the National Register of Historic Places.
- **Sports fans:** Tickets to championship games are expensive. A stay at a B&B helps to defray the cost of attending out-of-town events.
- **Antique collectors:** Many hosts have lovely personal collections, and nearby towns are filled with undiscovered antique shops.
- **House hunters:** It's a practical way of trying out a neighborhood.
- **Relocating corporate executives:** It's more comfortable to stay in a real home while you look for a permanent residence. Hosts will often give more practical advice than professional realtors.
- **Relatives of hospitalized patients:** Many B&Bs are located near major hospitals. Hosts will offer tea and sympathy when visiting hours are over.
- **Convention and seminar attendees:** Staying at a nearby B&B is less expensive than checking into a hotel.

And everyone else who has had it up to here with plastic motel monotony!

What It Is Like to Be a Guest in a B&B

The B&B descriptions provided in this book will help you choose the places that have the greatest appeal to you. A firsthand insight into local culture awaits you; imagine the advantage of arriving in New York City or San Francisco and having an insider to help you sidestep the tourist traps and direct you to that special restaurant or discount store. Or explore the countryside, where fresh air and home-cooked meals beckon. Your choice is as wide as the U.S.A.

Each bed and breakfast listed offers personal contact, a real advantage in unfamiliar environments. You may not have a phone in your room or a TV on the dresser. You may even have to pad down the hall in robe and slippers to take a shower, but you'll discover that little things count.

- In Williamsburg, Virginia, a visitor from Germany opted to stay at a B&B to help improve her conversational English. When the hostess saw that she was having difficulty understanding directions, she personally escorted her on a tour of Old Williamsburg.
- In Pennsylvania, the guests mistakenly arrived a week prior to their stated reservation date and the B&B was full. The hostess made a call to a neighbor who accommodated the couple. (By the way, the neighbor has now become a B&B host!)
- In New York City, a guest was an Emmy Award nominee and arrived with his tuxedo in need of pressing. The hostess pressed it; when he claimed his award over nationwide TV, he looked well groomed!

Expect the unexpected, such as a pot of brewed coffee upon your arrival, or fresh flowers on a nightstand. At the very least, count on our required standard of cleanliness and comfort. Although we haven't personally visited all of the places listed, they have all been highly recommended by chambers of commerce or former guests. We have either spoken to or corresponded with all of the proprietors; they are a friendly group of people who enjoy having visitors. They will do all in their power to make your stay memorable.

Our goal is to enable the traveler to crisscross the country and stay only at B&Bs along the way. To achieve this, your help is vital. Please take a moment to write us of your experiences; we will follow up on every suggestion. Your comments will serve as the yardstick by which we can measure the quality of our accommodations. For your convenience, an evaluation form is included at the back of this book.

Cost of Accommodations

Bed and breakfast, in the purest sense, is a private home, often referred to as a "homestay," where the owners rent their spare bedrooms to travelers. These are the backbone of this book.

However, American ingenuity has enhanced this simple idea to include more spectacular homes, mansions, small inns, and intimate hotels. With few exceptions, the proprietor is the host and lives on the premises.

There is a distinction between B&B homestays and B&B inns. Inns are generally defined as a business and depend upon revenue from guests to pay expenses. They usually have six or more guest rooms, and may have a restaurant that is open to the public. The tariff at inns is usually higher than at a homestay because the owners must pay the mortgage, running expenses, and staff, whether or not guests come.

Whether plain or fancy, all B&Bs are based on the concept that people are tired of the plastic monotony of motels and are disappointed that even the so-called budget motels can be quite expensive. Travelers crave the personal touch, and they sincerely enjoy "visiting" rather than just "staying."

Prices vary accordingly. There are places listed in this book where lovely lodging may be had for as low as $40 a night, and others that feature an overnight stay with a gourmet breakfast in a canopied bed for $95. Whatever the price, if you see the sign ✪, it means that the B&B has guaranteed its rates through 1998 to holders of this book, so be sure to mention it when you call or write! (If there is a change in ownership, the guarantee may not apply. Please notify us in writing if any host fails to honor the guaranteed rate.)

Accommodations vary in price depending upon the locale and the season. Peak season usually refers to the availability of skiing in winter and water sports in summer; in the Sunbelt states, winter months are usually the peak season. Some B&Bs require a two-night weekend minimum during peak periods, and three nights on holiday weekends. Off-season rate schedules are usually reduced. Resorts and major cities are generally more expensive than out-of-the-way places. However, B&Bs are always less expensive than hotels and motels of equivalent caliber in the same area. A weekly rate is usually less expensive than a daily rate. Special reductions are sometimes given to families (occupying two rooms) or senior citizens. Whenever reduced rates are available, you will find this noted in the individual listings.

Meals

Breakfast: *Continental* refers to fruit or juice, rolls, and a hot beverage. Many hosts pride themselves on home-baked breads, homemade preserves, as well as imported teas and cakes, so their Continental breakfast may be quite deluxe. Several hosts have regular jobs outside the home, so you may have to adjust your schedule to theirs. A "full" breakfast includes fruit, cereal and/or eggs, breakfast meats, breads, and a hot beverage. The table is set family-style and is often the highlight of a B&B's hospitality. Either a Continental breakfast or full breakfast is included in the room rate unless otherwise specified.

Other Meals: If listed as "available," you can be assured that the host takes pride in his or her cooking skills. The prices for lunch or dinner are usually reasonable but are not included in the quoted room rate unless clearly specified as "included."

Making Reservations

- Reservations are a MUST or you may risk missing out on the accommodations of your choice. Reserve *early* and confirm with a deposit equal to one night's stay. If you call to inquire about reservations, please remember the difference in time zones. When dialing outside of your area, remember to dial the digit "1" before the area code.
- Many individual B&Bs now accept charge cards. This information is indicated in the listings by the symbols MC for MasterCard, AMEX for American Express, etc. A few have a surcharge for this service, so inquire as to the policy.
- Cash or traveler's checks are the accepted method of paying for your stay. Be sure to inquire whether or not tax is included in the rates quoted so that you will know exactly how much your lodging will cost.
- Rates are based on single or double occupancy of a room as quoted. Expect that an extra person(s) in the room will be charged a small additional fee. Inquire when making your reservation what the charge will be.
- If a listing indicates that children or pets are welcome, it is expected that they will be well behaved. All of our hosts take pride in their homes and it would be unfair to subject them to circumstances in which their possessions might be abused or the other houseguests disturbed by an unruly child or animal.

- Please note that many hosts have their own resident pets. If you are allergic or don't care to be around animals, inquire before making a reservation.
- In homes where smoking is permitted, do check to see if it is restricted in any of the rooms. Most hosts object to cigars.
- Where listings indicate that social drinking is permitted, it usually refers to your bringing your own beverages. Most hosts will provide ice; many will allow you to chill mixers in the refrigerator, and others offer complimentary wine and snacks. A few B&B inns have licenses to sell liquor. Any drinking should not be excessive.
- If Yes is indicated in the listings for airport/station pickup, it means that the host will meet your plane, bus, or train for a fee.
- Feel free to request brochures and local maps so that you can better plan for your visit.
- Do try to fit in with the host's house rules. You are on vacation; he or she isn't!
- A reservation form is included at the back of this book for your convenience; just tear it out and send it in to the B&B of your choice.

Cancellations

Cancellation policies vary from one B&B to another, so be sure to read the fine print on the reservation form. Many require a 15-day notice to refund the entire deposit, after which they will refund only if the room is rebooked. When a refund is due, most keep a processing fee and return the balance. A few keep the deposit and apply it to a future stay.

While these policies may seem harsh, please keep in mind that B&Bs are not hotels, which commonly overbook and where no-show guests can easily be replaced. Your host may have turned down a prospective guest, and may have bought special breakfast food in anticipation of your visit and should not be penalized. If you feel you've been unfairly treated in a cancellation situation, please do let us know.

B&B Reservation Services

There are many host families who prefer not to be individually listed in a book, and would rather have their houseguests referred by a coordinating agency. The organizations listed in this book are all members of the Tourist House Association. They all share our standards regarding the suitability of the host home as to cordiality, cleanliness, and comfort.

The majority do a marvelous job of matching host and guest according to age, interests, language, and any special requirements. To get the best match, it is practical to give them as much time as possible to find the host home best tailored to your needs.

Many have prepared descriptive pamphlets describing the homes on their rosters, the areas in which the homes are located, and information regarding special things to see and do. *Send a self-addressed, stamped, business-size envelope to receive a descriptive directory by return mail along with a reservation form for you to complete.* When returning the form, you will be asked to select the home or homes listed in the brochure that most appeal to you. (The homes are usually given a code number for reference.) The required deposit should accompany your reservation. Upon receipt, the coordinator will make the reservation and advise you of the name, address, telephone number, and travel instructions for your host.

A few agencies prepare a descriptive directory and *include* the host's name, address, and telephone number so that you can contact the host and make your arrangements directly. They charge anywhere from $2 to $11 for the directory.

Several agencies are *membership* organizations, charging guests an annual fee ranging from $5 to $25 per person. Their descriptive directories are free to members and many of them maintain toll-free telephone numbers for reservations.

Most reservation services have a specific geographic focus. The coordinators are experts in the areas they represent. They can often make arrangements for car rentals, theater tickets, and touring suggestions, and offer information in planning a trip best suited to your interests.

Most work on a commission basis with the host, and that fee is included in the room rates quoted in each listing. Some make a surcharge for a one-night stay; others require a two- or three-night minimum stay for holiday periods or special events. Some will accept a credit card for the reservation, but the balance due must be paid to the host in cash or traveler's checks.

All of their host homes offer a Continental breakfast, and some may include a full breakfast.

Many reservation services in the larger cities have, in addition to the traditional B&Bs, a selection of apartments, condominiums, and houses *without hosts in residence*. This may be appealing to those travelers anticipating an extended stay in a particular area.

Statewide services are listed first in the section for each state. City or regionally based organizations are listed first under the heading for that area. For a complete description of their services, look them up under the city and state where they're based.

NOTE: When calling, do so during normal business hours (for that time zone), unless otherwise stated. Collect calls are not accepted.

2

How to Start Your Own B&B

What It's Like to Be a Host

Hosts are people who like the idea of accommodating travelers and sharing their home and the special features of their area with them. They are people who have houses too large for their personal needs and like the idea of supplementing their income by having people visit. For many, it's a marvelous way of meeting rising utility and maintenance costs. For young families, it is a way of buying and keeping that otherwise-too-large house, as well as a way of furnishing it, since many of the furnishings may be tax deductible. Another advantage is that many state and local governments have recognized the service that some host families perform. In browsing through this book you will note that some homes are listed on the National Historic Register. Some state governments allow owners of landmark and historical houses a special tax advantage if they are used for any business purpose. Check with the Historical Preservation Society in your state for details.

If you have bedrooms to spare, if you sincerely like having overnight guests, if your home is clean and comfortable, this is an opportunity to consider. It is a unique business because *you* set the time of the visit and the length of stay. (Guesthouses are not boarding homes.) You invite the guests at *your* convenience, and the extras, such as meals, are entirely up to you. You can provide a cup of coffee, complete meals, or just a room and shared bath. Remember that your income may be erratic and should not be depended upon to pay for monthly bills. However, it can afford you some luxuries.

Although the majority of hosts are women, many couples are finding pleasure in this joint venture. The general profile of a typical host is a friendly, outgoing, flexible person who is proud of his or her home and hometown. The following information and suggestions represent a guideline to consider in deciding whether becoming a B&B host is really for you.

There are no set rules for the location, type, or style of a B&B. Apartments, condos, farmhouses, town houses, beach houses, vacation cottages, houseboats, mansions, as well as the traditional one-family dwelling are all appropriate. The important thing is for the host to be on the premises. The setting may be urban, rural, or suburban, near public transportation or in the hinterlands. Location is only important if you want to have guests every night. Areas where tourism is popular, such as resort areas or major cities, are often busier than out-of-the-way places. However, if a steady stream of visitors is not that important or even desirable, it doesn't matter where you are. People will contact you if your rates are reasonable and if there is something to see and do in your area, or if it is near a major transportation route.

Setting Rates

Consider carefully four key factors in setting your rates: location, private versus shared bath, type of breakfast, and your home itself.

Location: If you reside in a traditional resort or well-touristed area, near a major university or medical center, or in an urban hub or gateway city, your rates should be at least 40 percent lower than those of the area's major motels or hotels. If you live in an out-of-the-way location, your rates must be extremely reasonable. If your area has a "season"—snow sports in winter, water sports in summer—offer off-season rates when these attractions are not available. Reading through this book will help you to see what the going rate is in a situation similar to yours.

The Bath: You are entitled to charge more for a room with private bath. If the occupants of two rooms share one bath, the rate should be less. If more than five people must share one bathroom, you may have complaints, unless your rates are truly inexpensive.

The Breakfast: Figure the approximate cost of your ingredients, plus something for your time. Allow about $2 to $3 for a Continental breakfast, $4 to $5 for a full American breakfast, and then *include* it in the rate.

Your Home: Plan on charging a fair and reasonable rate for a typical B&B home, one that is warm and inviting, clean and comfortable. If your home is exceptionally luxurious, with king-size beds, Jacuzzi baths, tennis courts, or hot tubs, you will find guests who are willing to pay a premium. If your home is over 75 years old, well restored, with lots of antiques, you may also be able to charge a higher rate.

The Three Bs—Bed, Breakfast, and Bath

The Bedroom: The ideal situation for a prospective host is the possession of a house too large for current needs. The children may be away at college most of the year or may have left permanently, leaving behind their bedrooms and, in some cases, an extra bath. Refurbishing these rooms does not mean refurnishing; an extraordinary investment need not be contemplated for receiving guests. Take a long, hard look at the room. With a little imagination and a little monetary outlay, could it be changed into a bedroom *you'd* be pleased to spend the night in? Check it out *before* you go any further. Are the beds comfortable? Is the carpet clean? Are the walls attractive? Do the curtains or shades need attention? Are there sturdy hangers in the closet? Would emptying the closet and bureau be an impossible task? Is there a good light to read by? A writing table and comfortable chair? Peek under the bed to see if there are dust balls or old magazines tucked away. While relatives and friends would "understand" if things weren't perfect, a paying guest is entitled to cleanliness and comfort.

Equip the guest bureau or dresser with a good mirror, and provide a comfortable chair and good reading light. The clothes closet should be free of your family's clothing and storage items, and stocked with firm, plastic hangers, a few skirt hangers, and some hooks. Sachets hung on the rod will chase musty odors. Provide room-darkening shades or blinds on the windows. And, if your house is located on a busy street, it is wise to have your guest bedrooms in the rear. Paying guests are entitled to a good night's rest! If your tap water is not tasty, it is thoughtful to supply bottled water.

If the idea of sprucing up the room has you overwhelmed, forget the idea and continue to be a guest rather than a host! If, however, a little "spit and polish," replacement of lumpy mattresses and sagging springs, and freshening the room in general present no problem, continue!

Mattresses should be firm, covered with a mattress pad, attractive linens, and bedspread. Although seconds are OK, good-quality linens are a wise investment, since cheap sheets tend to pill. Offer a selection of pillows of various firmnesses—a choice of down or fiberfill is the ultimate in consideration! Twin beds are often preferred, since many people do not wish to share a bed. Sofa beds are really not comfortable and should be avoided. Is there a bedside lamp and night table on each side of the bed? Bulbs should be at least 75 watts for comfortable reading. A luggage rack is convenient for guests and keeps the bedspread clean. Provide a varied assortment of books, current magazines in a rack, a local newspaper, and some information on what's doing in your town along with a map. If yours is a shared-bath accommodation, do provide a well-lit mirror and convenient electric outlet for makeup and shaving purposes. It will take the pressure off the bathroom! A fresh thermos of ice water and drinking glasses placed on an attractive dresser tray is always appreciated. Put it in the room while the guest is out to dinner, right next to the dish of hard candy or fruit. A fancy candlestick is a pretty accessory and a useful object in case of a power failure. Dresser drawers should be clean and lined with fresh paper. A sachet, flashlight, and a pad and pencil are thoughtful touches. For safety's sake, prohibit smoking in the bedroom. Besides, the odor of tobacco clings forever. Always spray the bedroom with air freshener a few minutes before the guest arrives. On warm or humid days, turn on the air conditioner as well.

From time to time sleep in each guest room yourself. It's the best test.

The Breakfast: Breakfast time can be the most pleasant part of a guest's stay. It is at the breakfast table with you and the other guests that suggestions are made as to what to see and do, and exchanges of experiences are enjoyed. From a guest's point of view, the only expected offering is what is known as a Continental breakfast, which usually consists of juice, roll, and coffee or tea.

Breakfast fare is entirely up to you. If you are a morning person who whips out of bed at the crack of dawn with special recipes for muffins dancing in your head, muffins to be drenched with your homemade preserves followed by eggs Benedict, an assortment of imported coffees or exotic teas—hop to it! You will play to a most appreciative audience. If, however, morning represents an awful intrusion on sleep, and the idea of talking to anyone before noon is difficult, the least you should do is to prepare the breakfast table the night before with the necessary mugs, plates, and silverware. Fill the electric coffeepot and leave instructions that the first one up should plug it in; you can even hook it up to a timer so that it will brew automatically!

Most of us fall somewhere in between these two extremes. Remember that any breakfast at "home" is preferable to getting dressed, getting into a car, and driving to some coffee shop. Whether you decide upon a Continental breakfast or a full American breakfast, consisting of juice or fruit, cereal or eggs, possibly bacon or sausage, toast, rolls, and coffee or tea, is up to you. It is most important that whatever the fare, it be included in your room rate. It is most awkward, especially after getting to know and like your guests, to present an additional charge for breakfast.

With so many of us watching calories, caffeine, and cholesterol, be prepared to offer unsweetened and/or whole grain breads, oat-bran cereals and muffins, and brewed decaf coffee or tea. It is also thoughtful to inquire about your guests' dietary restrictions and allergies. Whatever you serve, do have your table attractively set.

Some Suggestions

- Don't have a messy kitchen. If you have pets, make sure their food dishes are removed after they've eaten. If you have cats, make sure they don't walk along the countertops, and be certain that litter boxes are cleaned without fail. Sparkling clean surroundings are far more important than the decor.
- Let guests know when breakfast will be served. Check to see if they have any allergies, diet restrictions, or dislikes. Vary the menu if guests are staying more than one night.
- Do offer one nonsweet bread for breakfast.
- Consider leaving a breakfast order sheet in each room with a request that it be returned before guests retire. It might read:

We serve breakfast between 7 AM and 10 AM. Please check your preference and note the time at which you plan to eat.

☐ Coffee ☐ Tea ☐ Decaf ☐ Milk ☐ Toast ☐ Muffins
☐ Sweet Rolls ☐ Orange Juice ☐ Tomato Juice ☐ Fruit Cup

The Bath: This really is the third B in B&B. If you are blessed with an extra bathroom for the exclusive use of a guest, that's super. If guests will have to share the facilities with others, that really presents no problem. If it's being shared with your family, the family must always be "last in line." Be sure that they are aware of the guest's importance; the guest, paying or otherwise, always comes first. No retainers, used Band-Aids, or topless toothpaste tubes are to be carelessly left on the sink. The tub, shower, floor, and toilet bowl are to be squeaky clean. The mirrors and chrome should sparkle, and a supply of toilet tissue, fresh soap, and unfrayed towels goes a long way in reflecting a high standard of cleanliness. Make sure that the grout between tiles is free of mildew and that the shower curtain is unstained; add nonskid tape to the tub. Cracked ceilings should be repaired. Paint should be free of chips, and if your bath is wallpapered, make certain no loose edges mar its beauty.

Although it is your responsibility to check out the bath at least twice a day, most guests realize that in a share-the-bath situation they should leave the room ready for the next person's use. It is a thoughtful reminder for you to leave tub cleanser, a cleaning towel or sponge, and bathroom deodorant handy for this purpose. A wastepaper basket, paper towels, and paper cups should be part of your supplies. Needless to say, your hot water and septic systems should be able to accommodate the number of guests you'll have without being overtaxed. Call the plumber to fix any clogged drains or dripping faucets. Make sure that there are enough towel bars and hooks to accommodate the towels of all guests. Extra bathroom touches:

- Use liquid soap dispensers in lieu of bar soap on the sink.
- Provide a place for guests' personal toilet articles; shelves add convenience and eliminate clutter.
- Give different colored towels to each guest.
- Supply each guest room with its own bath soap in a covered soap dish.
- Provide guests with one-size-fits-all terry robes.

The B&B Business

Money Matters: Before embarking upon any business, it's a good idea to discuss it with an accountant and possibly an attorney. Since you'll be using your home for a business enterprise there are things with which they are familiar that are important for you to know. For instance, you may want to incorporate, so find out what the pros and cons are. Ask about depreciation. Deductible business expenses may include refurbishing, furnishings, supplies, printing costs, postage, etc. An accountant will be able to guide you with a simple system of record keeping. Accurate records will help you analyze income and expense, and show if you are breaking even or operating at a profit or a loss.

Taxes: Contact your state department of taxation requesting specific written information regarding tax collection and payment schedules. Get a sales tax number from your county clerk. If you rent rooms less than 15 days a year, you need not report the B&B income on your federal return. Income after the fourteenth day is taxable, and you can take deductions and depreciation allowances against it. If the revenues from running the B&B are insignificant, you can call it "hobby income" and avoid taxes. However, you can't qualify as a business and may lose other tax advantages.

Record Keeping: Open a B&B checking account and use it to pay expenses and to deposit all income, including sales tax associated with the B&B. Write checks whenever possible for purchases; get dated receipts when you can. Estimate the cost of serving breakfast and multiply it by the number of guests you feed annually; keep track of extra expenses for household supplies and utilities.

The Case for Credit Cards: Many guests prefer to stay now and pay later; business travelers like the easy record keeping for their expense sheets. Even if you don't wish to accept them on a regular basis, credit cards give you the opportunity to take a deposit over the phone when there isn't time to receive one by mail. The cost is negligible, generally 4 percent.

If you do accept a last-minute reservation without a credit card number to guarantee it, make certain the caller understands that if they don't show up, and you have held the room for them, you will have lost a night's rent. You may also remind the caller that if they aren't there by a mutually agreed-upon time, you may rent the room to someone else. Needless to say, it is equally important for you to remain at home to receive the guests or to be on hand for a phone call should they get lost en route to your home.

Insurance: It is important to call your insurance broker. Some homeowner policies have a clause covering "an occasional overnight paying guest." See if you will be protected under your existing coverage and, if not, what the additional premium would be.

Every home should be equipped with smoke detectors and fire extinguishers. All fire hazards should be eliminated; stairways and halls should be well lit and kept free of clutter. If you haven't already done so, immediately post prominently the emergency numbers for the fire department, police, and ambulance service.

Safety Reminders: Equip guest bedrooms and bathrooms with nightlights. Keep a flashlight (in working order!) in each bedroom, in case of power failure. Bathrooms should have nonslip surfaces in the tub and shower, and handholds should be installed in bathtubs. Keep a well-stocked first aid kit handy and know how to use it. Learn the Heimlich Maneuver and CPR (cardiopulmonary resuscitation). Periodically test smoke detectors and fire extinguishers to make certain they are in working order.

Regulations: If you have read this far and are still excited about the concept of running a B&B, there are several steps to take at this point. As of this writing, there don't seem to be any specific laws governing B&Bs. Since guests are generally received on an irregular basis, B&Bs do not come under the same laws governing hotels and motels. And since B&Bs aren't inns where emphasis is on food rather than on lodging, no comparison can really be made in that regard either. As the idea grows, laws and regulations will probably be passed. Refer to the back of *Bed & Breakfast U.S.A.* to write to your state's office of tourism for information. The address and phone number are listed for your convenience. You might even call or write to a few B&Bs in your state and ask the host about his or her experience in this regard. Most hosts will be happy to give you the benefit of their experience, but keep in mind that they are busy people and it would be wise to limit your intrusion upon their time.

If you live in a traditional, residential area and you are the first in your neighborhood to consider operating a B&B, it would be prudent to examine closely the character of houses nearby. Do physicians, attorneys, accountants, or psychologists maintain offices in their residences? Do dressmakers, photographers, cosmeticians, or architects receive clients in their homes? These professions are legally accepted in the most prestigious communities as "customary house occupations." Bed and breakfast has been tested in many communities where the question was actually brought to court. In towns from La Jolla, California, to Croton-on-Hudson, New York, bed and breakfast has been approved and accepted.

Zoning boards are not always aware of the wide acceptance of the B&B concept. Possibly the best evidence that you could present to them is a copy of *Bed & Breakfast U.S.A.*, which indicates that it is an accepted practice throughout the entire country. It illustrates the caliber of the neighborhoods, the beauty of the homes, and the fact that many professionals are also hosts. Reassure the zoning board that you will accept guests only by advance reservation. You will not display any exterior signs to attract attention to your home. You will keep your home and grounds properly maintained, attractive, and in no way detract from the integrity of your neighborhood. You will direct guests to proper parking facilities and do nothing to intrude upon the privacy of your neighbors.

After all, there is little difference between the visit of a family friend and a B&B guest, because that is the spirit and essence of a B&B. Just as a friend would make prior arrangements to be a houseguest, so will a B&B guest make a reservation in advance. Neither would just drop in for an overnight stay. We are happy to share letters from hosts attesting to the high caliber, honesty, and integrity of B&B guests that come as a result of reading about their accommodations in this book. There are many B&Bs extending hospitality throughout the United States, and the number is increasing geometrically every day.

You should also bring along a copy of *Bed & Breakfast U.S.A.* when you go to visit the local chamber of commerce. Most of them are enthusiastic, because additional visitors mean extra business for local restaurants, shops, theaters, and businesses. This is a good time to inquire what it would cost to join the chamber of commerce.

The Name: The naming of your B&B is most important and will take some time and consideration because this is the moment when dreams become reality. It will be used on your brochures, stationery, and bills. (If you decide to incorporate, the corporation needs a name!) It should somehow be descriptive of the atmosphere you wish to convey.

Brochure: Once you have given a name to your house, design a brochure. The best ones include a reservation form and can be mailed to your prospective guests. The brochure should contain the name of your B&B, address, phone number, best time to call, your name, a brief description of your home, its ambience, a brief history of the house if it is old, the number of guest rooms, whether or not baths are shared, the type of breakfast served, rates, required deposit, minimum stay requirement if any, dates when you'll be closed, and your cancellation policy. Although widely used, the phrase "Rates subject to change without notice" should be avoided. Rather, state the specific dates when the rates will be valid. A deposit of one night's stay is acceptable, and the promise of a full refund if cancellation is received at least two weeks prior to arrival is typical. If you have reduced rates for a specific length of stay, for families, for senior citizens, etc., mention it.

The Rate Sheet should be a separate insert so that if rates change, the entire brochure need not be discarded. Mention your smoking policy. If you do allow smoking inside the house, do you reserve any bedrooms for nonsmokers? Don't forget to mention the ages of your children, and describe any pets in residence. If you don't accept a guest's pet, be prepared to supply the name, address, and phone number of a reliable local kennel.

If you can converse in a foreign language, say so, because many visitors from abroad seek out B&Bs; it's a marvelous plus to be able to chat in their native tongue. Include your policy regarding children, pets, or smokers, and whether you offer the convenience of a guest refrigerator or barbecue. It is helpful to include directions from a major route and a simple map for finding your home. It's a good idea to include a line or two about yourself and your interests, and do mention what there is to see and do in the area as well as proximity to any major university. A line drawing of your house is a good investment since the picture can be used not only on the brochure but on your stationery, postcards, and greeting cards as well. If you can't have this taken care of locally, write the Tourist House Association. We have a service that can handle it for you.

Take your ideas to a reliable printer for his professional guidance. Don't forget to keep the receipt for the printing bill since this is a business expense.

Confirmation Letter: Upon receipt of a paid reservation, do send out a letter confirming it. You can design a form letter and have it offset-printed by a printer, since the cost of doing so is usually nominal. Include the dates of the stay; number of people expected; the rate, including tax; the cancellation policy; as well as explicit directions by car and, if applicable, by public transportation. A simple map reflecting the exact location of your home in relation to major streets and highways is most useful. It is a good idea to ask your guests to call you if they will be traveling and unavailable by phone for the week prior to their expected arrival. You might even want to include any of the house rules regarding smoking, pets, or whatever.

Successful Hosting

The Advantage of Hosting: The nicest part of being a B&B host is that you aren't required to take guests every day of the year. Should there be times when having guests would not be convenient, you can always say you're full and try to arrange an alternate date. But most important, keep whatever date you reserve. It is an excellent idea at the time reservations are accepted to ask for the name and telephone number of an emergency contact should you have to cancel unexpectedly. However, *never* have a guest come to a locked door. If an emergency arises and you cannot reach your prospective guests in time, do make arrangements for someone to greet them, and make alternate arrangements so that they can be accommodated.

House Rules: While you're in the thinking stage, give some thought to the rules you'd like your guests to adhere to. The last thing you want for you or your family is to feel uncomfortable in your own home. Make a list of House Rules concerning arrival and departure during the guests' stay, and specify when breakfast is served. If you don't want guests coming home too late, say so. Most hosts like to lock up at a certain hour at night, so arrange for an extra key for night owls. If that makes you uncomfortable, have a curfew on your House Rules list. If smoking disturbs you, confine the area where it's permitted.

Some guests bring a bottle of their favorite beverage and enjoy a drink before going out to dinner. Many hosts enjoy a cocktail hour too, and often provide cheese and crackers to share with guests. B&Bs cannot sell drinks to guests since this would require licensing. If you'd rather no drinks be consumed in your home, say so.

Many hosts don't mind accommodating a well-behaved pet. If you don't mind, or have pets of your own, discuss this with your guests before they pack Fido's suitcase. Your House Rules can even be included in your brochure. That way, both host and guest are aware of each other's likes and dislikes, and no hard feelings are made.

Entertaining: One of the most appealing features of being a guest at a B&B is the opportunity to visit in the evening with the hosts. After a day of sightseeing or business, it is most relaxing and pleasant to sit around the living room and chat. For many hosts, this is the most enjoyable part of having guests. However, if you are accommodating several people on a daily basis, entertaining can be tiring. Don't feel you'll be offending anyone by excusing yourself to attend to your own family or personal needs. The situation can be easily handled by having a room to which you can retreat, and offering your guests the living room, den, or other area for games, books, magazines, and perhaps the use of a television or bridge table. Most guests enjoy just talking to one another since this is the main idea of staying at a B&B.

The Telephone: This is a most important link between you and your prospective guests. As soon as possible, have your telephone number included under your B&B name in the white pages. It is a good idea to be listed in the appropriate section in your telephone directory yellow pages. If your home phone is used for a lot of personal calls, ask the local telephone company about call-waiting service, or think about installing a separate line for your B&B. If you are out a lot, give some thought to using a telephone answering device to explain your absence and time of return, and record the caller's message. There is nothing more frustrating to a prospective guest than to call and get a constant busy signal, or no answer at all. Request that the caller leave his or her name and address so that you can mail a reservation form. This will help eliminate the necessity of having to return long-distance calls. If the caller wants further information, he or she will call again at the time you said you'd be home.

B&B guests don't expect a phone in the guest room. However, there are times when they might want to use your phone for a long-distance call. In your House Rules list, suggest that any such calls be charged to their home telephone. Business travelers often have telephone charge cards for this purpose. In either case, you should keep a telephone record book and timer near your instrument. Ask the caller to enter the city called, telephone number, and length of call. Thus, you will have an accurate record should a charge be inadvertently added to your bill. Or, if you wish, you can add telephone charges to the guest bill. A telephone operator will quote the cost of the per-minute charge throughout the country for this purpose.

Maid Service: If you have several guest rooms and bathrooms, you may find yourself being a chambermaid as part of the business. Naturally, each guest gets fresh linens upon arrival. If a guest stays up to three days, it isn't expected that bed linen be changed every day. What is expected is that the room be freshened and the bath be cleaned and towels replaced every day. If you don't employ a full-time maid you may want to investigate the possibility of hiring a high school student on a part-time basis to give you a hand with the housekeeping. Many guests, noticing the absence of help, will voluntarily lend a hand, although they have the right to expect some degree of service, particularly if they are paying a premium rate.

Keys: A great many hosts are not constantly home during the day. Some do "hosting" on a part-time basis, while involved with regular jobs. There are times when even full-time hosts have to be away during the day. If guests are to have access to the house while you are not on the premises, make extra keys and attach them to an oversize key chain. It is also wise to take a key deposit of $50 simply to assure return of the key. Let me add that in the 16 years of my personal experience, as well as in the opinions of other hosts, B&B guests are the most honest people you can have. No one has ever had even a washcloth stolen, let alone the family treasures. In fact, it isn't unusual for the guest to leave a small gift after a particularly pleasant visit. On the other hand, guests are sometimes forgetful and leave belongings behind. For this reason it is important for you to have their names and addresses so that you can return their possessions. They will expect to reimburse you for the postage.

Registering Guests: You should keep a regular registration ledger for the guest to complete before checking in. The information should include the full name of each guest, home address, phone number, business address and telephone, and auto license number. It's a good idea to include the name and phone number of a friend or relative in case of an emergency. This information will serve you well for other contingencies, such as the guest leaving some important article behind, an unpaid long-distance phone call, or the rare instance of an unpaid bill. You may prefer to have this information on your guest bill, which should be designed as a two-part carbon form. You will then have a record and the guest has a ready receipt. (Receipts are very important to business travelers!)

Settling the Bill: The average stay in a B&B is two nights. A deposit equal to one night's lodging is the norm; when to collect the balance is up to you. Most guests pay upon leaving, but if they leave so early that the settling of the bill at that time is inconvenient, you can request the payment the previous night. You might want to consider the convenience of accepting a major credit card, but contact the sponsoring company first to see what percentage of your gross is expected for this service. If you find yourself entertaining more business visitors than vacationers, it might be something you should offer. Most travelers are aware that cash or traveler's checks are the accepted modes of payment. Accepting a personal check is rarely risky, but again, it's up to you. You might include your preference in your brochure.

Other Meals: B&B means that only breakfast is served. If you enjoy cooking and would like to offer other meals for a fee, make sure that you investigate the applicable health laws. If you have to install a commercial kitchen, the idea might be too expensive for current consideration. However, allowing guests to store fixings for a quick snack or to use your barbecue can be a very attractive feature for families traveling with children or for people watching their budget. If you can offer this convenience, be sure to mention it in your brochure. (And be sure to add a line to your House Rules that the guest is expected to clean up.) Some hosts keep an extra guest refrigerator on hand for this purpose.

It's an excellent idea to keep menus from your local restaurants on hand. Try to have a good sampling, ranging from moderately priced to expensive dining spots, and find out if reservations are required. Your guests will always rely heavily upon your advice and suggestions. After all, when it comes to your town, you're the authority! It's also a nice idea to keep informed of local happenings that might be of interest to your visitors. A special concert at the university or a local fair or church supper can add an extra dimension to their visit. If parents are visiting with young children they might want to have dinner out without them; try to have a list of available baby-sitters. A selection of guidebooks covering your area is also a nice feature.

The Guest Book: These are available in most stationery and department stores, and it is important that you buy one. It should contain designated space for the date, the name of the guest, home address, and a blank area for the guest's comments. They generally sign the guest book before checking out. The guest book is first of all a permanent record of who came and went. It will give you an idea of what times during the year you were busiest and which times were slow. Second, it is an easy way to keep a mailing list for your Christmas cards and future promotional mailings. You will also find that thumbing through it in years to come will recall some very pleasant people who were once strangers but now are friends.

Advertising: Periodically distribute your brochures to the local university, college, and hospital, since out-of-town visitors always need a place to stay. Let your local caterers know of your existence since wedding guests are often from out of town. If you have a major corporation in your area, drop off a brochure at the personnel office. Even visiting or relocating executives and salespeople enjoy B&Bs. Hotels and motels are sometimes overbooked; it wouldn't hurt to leave your brochure with the manager for times when there's no room for their last-minute guests. Local residents sometimes have to put up extra guests, so it's a good idea to take an ad out in your local school or church newspaper. The cost is usually minimal. Repeat this distribution process from time to time so that you can replenish the supply of brochures.

Check the back of this book for the address of your state tourist office. Write to them, requesting inclusion in any brochures listing B&Bs in the state.

The best advertising is being a member of the Tourist House Association since all member B&Bs are fully described in this book, which is available in bookstores, libraries, and B&Bs throughout the United States and Canada. In addition, it is natural for THAA, Inc., members to recommend one another when guests inquire about similar accommodations in other areas. The most important reason for keeping your B&B clean, comfortable, and cordial is that we are all judged by what a guest experiences in any individual Tourist House Association home. The best publicity will come from your satisfied guests, who will recommend your B&B to their friends.

Additional Suggestions

Extra Earnings: You might want to consider a few ideas for earning extra money in connection with being a host. If guests consistently praise your muffins and preserves, you might sell attractively wrapped extras as take-home gifts. If you enjoy touring, you can plan and conduct a special outing, off the beaten tourist track, for a modest fee. In major cities, you can do such things as acquiring tickets for theater, concert, or sports events. A supply of *Bed & Breakfast U.S.A.* for sale to guests is both a source of income and gives every THAA, Inc., member direct exposure to the B&B market. Think about offering the use of your washer and dryer. You may, if you wish, charge a modest fee to cover the service. Guests who have been traveling are thrilled to do their wash or have it done for them "at home" rather than wasting a couple of hours at the laundromat.

Several hosts tell me that a small gift shop is often a natural off-shoot of a B&B. Items for sale might include handmade quilts, pillows, potholders, and knitted items. One host has turned his hobby of woodworking into extra income. He makes lovely picture frames, napkin rings, and footstools that many guests buy as souvenirs to take home. If you plan to do this, check with the Small Business Administration to inquire about such things as a resale license and tax collection; a chamber of commerce can advise in this regard.

Transportation: While the majority of B&B guests arrive by car, there are many who rely on public transportation. Some hosts, for a modest fee, are willing to meet arriving guests at airports, train depots, or bus stations. Do be knowledgeable about local transportation schedules in your area, and be prepared to give explicit directions for your visitors' comings and goings. Have phone numbers handy for taxi service, as well as information on car rentals.

Thoughtful Touches: Guests often write to tell us of their experiences at B&Bs as a result of learning about them through this book. These are some of the special touches that made their visit special: fresh flowers in the guest room; even a single flower in a bud vase is pretty. One hostess puts a foil-wrapped piece of candy on the pillow before the guest returns from dinner. A small decanter of wine and glasses, or a few pieces of fresh fruit in a pretty bowl on the dresser are lovely surprises. A small sewing kit in the bureau is handy. Offer guests the use of your iron and ironing board, rather than having them attempt to use the bed or dresser. Writing paper and envelopes in the desk invite the guest to send a quick note to the folks at home. If your house sketch is printed on it, it is marvelous free publicity. A pre-bed cup of tea for adults and cookies and milk for children are always appreciated.

By the way, keep a supply of guest-comment cards in the desk, both to attract compliments as well as to bring to your attention the flaws in your B&B that should be corrected.

Join the Tourist House Association of America, Inc.: If you are convinced that you want to be a host, and have thoroughly discussed the pros and cons with your family and advisers, complete and return the membership application found at the back of this book. Our dues are $40 annually. The description of your B&B will be part of the next edition of *Bed & Breakfast U.S.A.* Paid-up members receive a complimentary copy of *Bed & Breakfast U.S.A.* You will also receive the THAA, Inc.'s newsletter; regional seminars and conferences are held occasionally and you might enjoy attending. And, as an association, we will have clout should the time come when B&B becomes a recognized industry.

Affiliating with a B&B Reservation Agency: There are 70 agencies listed in *Bed & Breakfast U.S.A.* If you do not care to advertise your house directly to the public, consider joining one in your area. Membership and reservation fees, as well as the degree of professionalism, vary widely from agency to agency, so do check carefully.

Prediction of Success: Success should not be equated with money alone. If you thoroughly enjoy people, are well organized, enjoy sharing your tidy home without exhausting yourself, then the idea of receiving compensation for the use of an otherwise dormant bedroom will be a big plus. Your visitors will seek relaxing, wholesome surroundings, and unpretentious hosts who open their hearts as well as their homes. Being a B&B host or guest is an exciting, enriching experience.

3

B&B Recipes

The recipes that follow are B&B host originals. They've been chosen because of the raves they've received from satisfied B&B guests. The most important ingredient is the heartful of love that goes into each one.

We always have a good response to our request for favorite breakfast recipes. Although we could not publish them all this time, we will use most of them in future editions.

Old Thyme Inn Glazed Apple Bread

$^1/_2$ c. canola oil	$^1/_2$ tsp. cinnamon
1 c. sugar	$^1/_2$ tsp. salt
1 tsp. vanilla	2 tbsp. milk
2 large eggs	2 large baking apples, peeled, chopped
2 c. sifted unbleached all-purpose flour	$^1/_2$ c. raisins
2 tsp. baking powder	$^1/_2$ c. walnuts, chopped

Glaze

$^1/_2$ c. powdered sugar, sifted	1 tbsp. water
2 tbsp. melted butter	

Preheat the oven to 350°F. In a large bowl, cream together the oil, sugar, and vanilla until light and fluffy. Add the eggs and beat well. In a separate medium bowl, sift together the flour, baking powder, cinnamon, and salt. Add the flour mixture, milk, apples, raisins, and nuts to the oil mixture and stir until the flour is dampened. Transfer to a greased 9 × 5 × 4-inch loaf pan and bake for 50 to 60 minutes. Cool; remove from the pan. Combine the glaze ingredients, then pour over the loaf. Let the glaze set before wrapping loaf tightly. Best if made a day prior to serving. Serves 10.

Old Thyme Inn B&B, Half Moon Bay, California

Tea Scones

3 c. all-purpose flour
$1/2$ c. sugar
4 tsp. baking powder
$1/2$ tsp. salt
$1/2$ c. butter or margarine
1 tbsp. orange or lemon zest

$1/2$ c. raisins or currants
2 eggs
Approximately $1/4$ c. milk
Butter, strawberry jam, and Devon
 cream, for serving

Preheat the oven to 450°F. In a large bowl, combine the flour, sugar, baking powder, and salt. Cut in the butter or margarine to make a crumblike texture. Stir in the orange zest and raisins. Beat the eggs in a 1-cup measure, then add enough milk to reach 1 cup. Lightly stir the egg mixture into the dry mixture to form a soft dough. Roll out the dough to a $1/2$-inch thickness. Cut into 2-inch rounds with a cutter. Place on a lightly greased cookie sheet and bake for 15 minutes. Serve with butter, strawberry jam, and Devon cream. Makes 12–16 scones.

Dorrington B&B, White Rocks, B.C., Canada

Duck's Nest Eggs

$3/4$ c. crumbled corn bread
1 c. chopped ham
$1^1/2$ c. grated sharp cheese
$1^1/2$ c. milk
6 large eggs, lightly beaten

1 tsp. hot sauce
1 tsp. Pickapeppa sauce
$1/4$ tsp. salt
$1/4$ tsp. pepper

Preheat the oven to 375°F. Coat 6 individual baking dishes, 6 inches long, 3 inches wide, one inch deep, with nonstick cooking spray. Place a layer of cornbread in each dish, followed by a layer of chopped ham and a layer of cheese. Combine the remaining ingredients, then pour over the top of each dish. Bake for 20 to 25 minutes, until brown and puffy. Serves 6.

Bay Breeze Guest House, Fairhope, Alabama

Nancy's Cranberry Coffee Cake

1 c. sugar
1 tbsp. butter
1 large egg
1 c. milk
2 c. all-purpose flour
3 tsp. baking powder

$1/2$ tsp. salt
$1/2$ to $3/4$ of 16-oz. can whole cranberry
 sauce
$1/2$ cup chopped walnuts
1 tsp. cinnamon, and sugar, for
 topping

Preheat the oven to 350°F. In a large bowl, cream together the sugar, butter, and egg. Add the milk and dry ingredients. Pour the batter into 2 greased 8-inch cake pans. Spoon 1/2 cup of cranberry sauce over the top, then gently swirl it into the batter. Top with the leftover sauce and sprinkle generously with the nut topping. Bake for 20 to 25 minutes. Serve hot or cold. Serves 8–12.

Nancy's Auberge, Martha's Vineyard, Massachusetts

Pecan Pie Bars

3 c. all-purpose flour
1/2 c. sugar
1 c. margarine
1/2 tsp. salt
4 large eggs, lightly beaten

1 1/2 c. corn syrup
1 1/2 c. sugar
3 tbsp. margarine, melted
1 1/2 tsp. vanilla
2 1/2 c. chopped pecans

Preheat the oven to 350°F. Grease a 15 × 10 × 1-inch baking pan. In a large bowl with a mixer set at medium speed, beat the flour, sugar, margarine, and salt until the mixture resembles coarse crumbs; press firmly and evenly into the prepared pan. Bake for 15 to 20 minutes. While the crust is baking, prepare the filling. In a large bowl, stir the eggs, corn syrup, sugar, melted margarine, and vanilla until blended. Stir in the pecans. Spread evenly over the hot crust. Bake for 20 to 25 minutes or until set. Cool on a wire rack. Makes 48 bars.

Dear's Rest B&B, Ozark, Missouri

Sour Cherry Muffins

2 c. all-purpose flour
1/2 c. sugar
1 tbsp. baking powder
1/2 tsp. salt
1/2 tsp. nutmeg

1 1/2 c. pitted sour cherries
1 c. milk
2 medium eggs
1/3 c. vegetable oil
1/4 c. cinnamon sugar

Preheat the oven to 375°F. In a large bowl, combine the flour, sugar, baking powder, salt, and nutmeg. Gently stir in the cherries. In a separate bowl, combine the milk, eggs, and vegetable oil, then add to the dry mixture. Pour into greased muffin cups, then sprinkle with the cinnamon sugar. Bake for 20 minutes. Makes 18–20 muffins.

Woodshire B&B, Goodletsville, Tennessee

Pumpkin Chocolate Chip Muffins

1²/₃ c. all-purpose flour
1 c. granulated sugar
1 tbsp. pumpkin pie spice
¹/₄ tsp. baking powder
1 tsp. baking soda

¹/₄ tsp. salt
1 c. chocolate chips
2 large eggs
1 c. plain pumpkin puree
¹/₂ c. butter or margarine, melted

Preheat the oven to 350°F. In a medium bowl, combine the first 7 ingredients. In a separate bowl, beat the eggs, then add the pumpkin and butter or margarine and whisk until well blended. Pour over the dry ingredients and mix until moistened. Spoon into muffin cups and bake for 20 to 25 minutes. Makes 12 muffins.

Snow Goose Inn, Grove City, Pennsylvania

Almond Ham Croissants

4 croissants
6 tbsp. softened cream cheese
4 slices ham
9-oz. jar orange marmalade
¹/₃ c. orange juice
5 large eggs
1 c. half-and-half

1 tsp. almond extract (do not leave this out or substitute)
¹/₄ cup toasted almonds
Strawberries or raspberries and mandarin orange sections, for garnish

Cut the croissants in half lengthwise and spread the softened cream cheese over the bottom halves. Place a slice of ham on each one, then transfer to a 12 × 9-inch ovenproof dish. Combine the marmalade and orange juice and spread over the ham, reserving enough to be used as a glaze for the tops of the croissants. Place the tops on the croissants. In a medium bowl, beat the eggs, half-and-half, and almond extract until well blended, then pour over the croissants. Refrigerate overnight. Remove the croissants from the refrigerator 30 minutes before baking and preheat the oven to 350°F. Bake the croissants for 15 minutes, then spoon the remaining marmalade mixture on top and sprinkle with the toasted almonds. Continue baking for an additional 5 to 10 minutes, until the egg mixture is set. Serve hot, garnished with strawberries or raspberries and mandarin orange slices. Serves 4.

Austin's Wildflower Inn, Austin, Texas

Grand Marnier Soufflé Pancakes

6 large eggs, separated
2 c. small-curd cottage cheese
1/4 c. canola oil
5 tbsp. freshly squeezed orange juice
   (must be fresh)
1 tbsp. grated orange zest
1 tbsp. Grand Marnier

1 1/2 tbsp. sugar
4 tsp. baking powder
1/2 tsp. salt
1/4 c. finely chopped pecans
Pure maple syrup or fresh strawberry
   sauce, for serving

Place the egg yolks and all of the remaining ingredients except for the egg whites and pecans in a food processor and blend until smooth. Transfer the batter to a large bowl and set aside to rest for at least 30 minutes. In another large bowl, beat the egg whites until stiff. Fold in the pecans and egg whites. Spoon about 1/4 cup batter per pancake onto a hot buttered griddle and cook until browned on both sides, watching carefully to avoid burning. If desired, finished pancakes can be held in a warm oven for a few minutes. The texture will become a bit firmer upon standing. Serve with pure maple syrup or fresh strawberry sauce. Serves 6.

Sampson Eagon Inn, Staunton, Virginia

Sweet Tomato Chutney

1 whole bulb garlic, peeled and
   chopped
2 1-inch pieces fresh ginger, peeled and
   chopped
1 1/2 c. red wine vinegar
2 lbs. fresh tomatoes, skinned, or 1 lb.
   12 oz. canned whole tomatoes

1 1/2 c. sugar
1 1/2 tsp. salt
1/4–1/2 tsp. cayenne pepper, to taste
2 tbsp. golden raisins
2 tbsp. blanched slivered almonds
Cream cheese and crackers, for serving

Put the garlic, ginger, and 1/2 cup of the vinegar in a food processor and process until smooth. In a large, heavy-bottomed pot, combine the tomatoes (with their liquid if using canned tomatoes), the remaining 1 cup vinegar, the sugar, salt, and cayenne pepper. Bring to a boil. Add the puree from the food processor and simmer, uncovered, for 2 to 3 hours, until the chutney thickens and a film clings to a spoon when dipped into it. Stir occasionally at first and more frequently as it thickens; you may need to lower the heat as the liquid diminishes. Add the raisins and almonds. Simmer, stirring, for another 5 minutes. Turn off the heat and let cool. The chutney should be as thick as honey. Bottle in clean containers and refrigerate. Makes about 2 cups. Serve with cream cheese and crackers.

A B&B at Llewellyn, Lexington, Virginia

Rhubarb Muffins

1/2 c. buttermilk
1 medium egg
1/2 c. vegetable oil
2 tsp. vanilla
2 1/2 c. all-purpose flour
1 1/4 c. brown sugar

1 tsp. baking soda
1 tsp. baking powder
1/4 tsp. salt
1 1/2 c. diced rhubarb
1/2 c. chopped pecans

Topping

1 1/4 tsp. melted margarine
1/3 c. white sugar

1 heaping tbsp. all-purpose flour
1 tsp. cinnamon

Preheat oven to 400°F. Beat together the buttermilk, egg, oil, vanilla, flour, brown sugar, baking soda, baking powder, and salt. Add the rhubarb and nuts. Spoon into greased muffin cups about 2/3 of the way to the top. Combine the melted margarine, sugar, flour, and cinnamon, and sprinkle over the muffins. Bake for 18 to 20 minutes. Makes 24 muffins.

Rummel's Tree Haven B&B, Sebewaing, Michigan

Kahlúa Spiced Peaches

2 28-oz. cans peach halves in heavy syrup
1/4 c. tarragon wine vinegar
1/2 c. Kahlúa

zest of 1 lemon and 1 orange, coarsely grated
2 cinnamon sticks
Fresh mint leaf, for garnish

Drain the peaches, reserving the juice. Combine the peach juice, vinegar, and Kahlúa in a medium saucepan and bring to a boil. Add the lemon and orange zest and cinnamon sticks and boil for 5 minutes. In a large bowl, combine the reserved peaches and the juice mixture. Refrigerate until ready to serve. Garnish with a fresh mint leaf before serving. Serves 12.

The Atrium B&B, Eau Claire, Wisconsin

Blueberry Banana Muffins

1 egg
1/2 c. buttermilk
1/2 c. vegetable oil
1 ripe banana
2 c. all-purpose flour

1/3 c. sugar
2 tsp. baking powder
1 tsp. baking soda
1 tsp. salt
1 1/2 c. frozen blueberries

Preheat the oven to 400°F. In a blender, combine the egg, buttermilk, vegetable oil, and banana until smooth. Sift the dry ingredients into a medium bowl. Add the frozen blueberries and the banana mixture and stir until the flour is moistened (batter will be lumpy). Fill 12 greased muffin cups about 3/4 of the way to the top. Bake for about 20 minutes, until golden brown. Immediately remove the muffins from the pan. Makes 12 muffins.

The Blue Door B&B, Del Mar, California

Cornmeal Soufflé

3 tbsp. butter
2 tbsp. chopped green onion
1 1/4 c. milk
3/4 c. Monterey Jack cheese

1/4 c. yellow cornmeal
1/2 tsp. oregano
4 large eggs, separated

Preheat the oven to 350°F. In a medium saucepan, melt the butter. Add the green onion and sauté until softened. Add the milk, cheese, cornmeal, and oregano, and stir until the cheese is melted. Remove from the heat and stir in the egg yolks to blend. In a medium bowl, beat the egg whites to soft peaks, then fold them into the cornmeal mixture. Pour into 2 pint-size soufflé dishes. Set the soufflé dishes in a pan and add enough water to reach 1 1/2 inches up the sides. Bake for 45 minutes or until the top is dry. Serves 4.

The Heirloom Circa 1863 B&B Inn, Ione, California

Creamed Beef on Toast

1 lb. ground round beef
1 tsp. oregano
1 tsp. dried basil
salt and pepper, to taste
4 tbsp. chopped onion

1 stick margarine or butter
1/4 cup all-purpose flour
2 c. hot milk
1 tbsp. Worcestershire sauce
Toast or biscuits, for serving

In a heavy 10 to 12-inch skillet over medium heat, cook the beef with the oregano, basil, salt, and pepper until browned. Remove the meat from the skillet. In the same skillet, sauté the onion in the margarine for about 5 minutes. Add the flour and stir with a wooden spoon for about 1 minute. Heat the milk until just hot but not boiling, then pour into the skillet all at once, stirring constantly with a whisk until thickened. Remove the skillet from the heat and add the Worcestershire sauce and meat mixture. Serve over toast or biscuits. Creamed beef can be kept warm on a low setting in the oven for 2 hours. Serves 4.

Papaya Paradise B&B, Kailua, Oahu, Hawaii

Sour Cream Pancakes with Blueberry Sauce

4 large eggs
1 pint sour cream
6 heaping tbsp. all-purpose flour

2 tbsp. sugar
1 tsp. baking soda
$1/2$ tsp. salt

Blueberry Sauce

2 c. fresh or frozen blueberries
$1/2$ c. light corn syrup
1 tbsp. water
2 tbsp. cornstarch

$1/4$ tsp. pumpkin pie spice
salt to taste
1 tbsp. lemon juice

To make the pancakes, in a medium bowl, beat the eggs. Add the remaining ingredients and beat well. Spoon about $1/4$ cup batter per pancake on a lightly greased griddle and cook at 325°F until browned on both sides. If desired, hold the pancakes in a warm oven while preparing the sauce.

To make the sauce, in a medium saucepan, combine the blueberries and light corn syrup. Add the water, cornstarch, pumpkin pie spice, and salt. Bring to a boil over medium heat, stirring constantly. Boil 1 minute. Remove from the heat and stir in the lemon juice. Spoon the warm sauce over the pancakes. Serves 4.

Juniper Hill Farm, Dubuque, Iowa

Beef and Bean Round-Up

$1^1/2$ lb. ground beef
$1/4$ c. chopped onion
1 c. barbecue sauce
1 tbsp. brown sugar

16-oz. can baked beans
10-oz. can refrigerated flaky biscuit
   dough
$1/2$ c. shredded Cheddar cheese

Preheat the oven to 375°F. In a large skillet over medium heat, brown the ground beef and onion, then drain. Stir in the barbecue sauce, brown sugar, and beans, and heat until bubbly. Pour into a 2¹/₂-quart casserole. Separate the dough into 10 biscuits, then cut each biscuit in half crosswise. Place the biscuits over the hot meat mixture, cut side down and in spoke fashion around the edge of the casserole. Sprinkle the cheese over the biscuits. Bake for 22 to 25 minutes or until the biscuits are golden brown. Serves 6.

Oak Square Plantation, Port Gibson, Mississippi

Sampler's Steamy Apple Pudding

1¹/₂ c. sifted all-purpose flour
1 tsp. baking soda
¹/₄ tsp. salt
¹/₂ tsp. cinnamon
¹/₂ tsp. nutmeg
¹/₄ tsp. cloves
¹/₄ c. softened butter

1 c. sugar
2 large eggs, beaten
4 medium apples, pared and shredded
¹/₂ c. raisins
boiling water
Light cream, for serving

Grease a 1¹/₂-quart heatproof bowl. Into a small bowl, sift flour, baking soda, salt, and spices; set aside. In a large bowl, beat the butter, sugar, and eggs until smooth and light. Stir in the apples and raisins. Stir the flour mixture into the fruit mixture and mix well. Turn into the prepared bowl. Cover the surface of the pudding with a double thickness of wax paper. Cover the top of the bowl completely with aluminum foil and tie the edge securely with twine. Place the bowl on a trivet in a Dutch oven. Pour the boiling water around the bowl to come halfway up the side. Cover the Dutch oven and bring the water to a boil. Reduce the heat and simmer for 2 hours. Remove the bowl to a wire rack and let stand for 5 minutes. With a spatula, gently loosen the edge of the pudding from the side of the bowl. Invert onto a serving dish. Serve warm with cream. Serves 6–8.

Williamsburg Sampler Bed & Breakfast, Williamsburg, Virginia

4
Wheelchair Accessible Listings

Although this chapter is small, within a few years *Bed & Breakfast U.S.A.* hopes to have listings from all fifty states and Canada. The requirements are fairly simple. To be listed in this section, all B&Bs must have easy-access entrances and exits. Doorways must be wide enough to admit a wheelchair—36 inches should be wide enough. Toilets and tubs must have reach bars. If the bathroom has a shower, reach bars and a built-in seat are preferable. Wheelchairs should be able to fit under the breakfast table; 26 inches is high enough. It's also a good idea to check to see what kind of activities are available. Many parks, restaurants, shopping areas, museums, beaches, etc. have wheelchair accessibility. If you or someone you know has a B&B that is wheelchair accessible, please turn to page 615 for further details.

Kern River Inn Bed & Breakfast ✪
P.O. BOX 1725, 119 KERN RIVER DRIVE, KERNVILLE, CALIFORNIA 93238

Tel: **(760) 376-6750; (800) 986-4382**	Open: **All year**
Best Time to Call: **8 AM–8 PM**	Reduced Rates: **Available**
Hosts: **Jack and Carita Prestwich**	Breakfast: **Full**
Location: **50 mi. NE of Bakersfield**	Credit Cards: **AMEX, MC, VISA**
No. of Rooms: **1**	Pets: **No**
No. of Private Baths: **1**	Children: **Welcome**
Double/pb: **$89–$99**	Smoking: **No**
Single/pb: **$79–$89**	Social Drinking: **Permitted**

Stay in a charming riverfront B&B in a quaint Western town within Sequoia National Forest. Jack and Carita specialize in romantic, relaxing getaways. Their accessible room has a queen bed and a Piute-style, wood-burning fireplace. (Your hosts provide the wood.) Native American pictures and macramé wall hangings accent the room's Southwestern color scheme of beige, mauve, and sage green. The bathroom has grab bars; the full-size, mirror-doored closet has shelving that can be reached from a wheelchair.

San Francisco Bay Area B&B ✪
1636 CENTER ROAD, NOVATO, CALIFORNIA 94947

Tel: **(415) 892-9069**
Best Time to Call: **7–10 PM**
Hosts: **Russell and Joyce Woods**
Location: **25 mi. N of San Francisco**
Guest Apartment: **$55–$75**
Open: **April–mid-November**
Reduced Rates: **Available**

Breakfast: **Continental**
Pets: **Sometimes**
Children: **Welcome, crib & high chair**
Smoking: **No**
Social Drinking: **Permitted**
Minimum Stay: **2 nights**

Located in a garden setting with an easy-access private entrance, this bed and breakfast offers a queen bed, kitchenette, living room, cable TV, and a bath equipped with grab bars for wheelchair users. It's near downtown Novato, Muir Woods, and Marine World Africa USA, and 25 miles from Napa-Sonoma wine country. Russell and Joyce are retired, native to San Francisco, and enjoy guiding guests to the many interesting places in the beautiful Bay Area.

Redwood Reflections ✪
4600 SMITH GRADE, SANTA CRUZ, CALIFORNIA 95060

Tel: **(408) 423-7221**
Best Time to Call: **Evenings**
Hosts: **Ed and Dory Strong**
Location: **70 mi. S of San Francisco**
No. of Rooms: **1**
No. of Private Baths: **1**
Suite: **$100**
Open: **All year**

Reduced rates: **10% Seniors, Disabled**
Breakfast: **Full**
Credit Cards: **MC, VISA**
Pets: **No**
Children: **Welcome**
Smoking: **No**
Social Drinking: **Permitted**

Nestled on 10 private acres of giant redwoods, Redwood Reflections offers one wheelchair-accessible room with a private bath and patio. A romantic Roman tub for two has a transfer seat and adjustable shower head. Grab bars for toilet and tub, 36-inch doors, and a roll-in vanity provide accessibility and safety. Guests are invited to concoct favorite goodies and listen to old-time piano music in an ice cream parlor featuring 1920s collectibles and a 100-year-old potbelly stove. A full breakfast is served and dietary restrictions can be observed. Santa Cruz is a wheelchair-friendly town and offers an amusement park, wharf with fine restaurants, and a 2-mile coastline sidewalk. The Monterey Bay Aquarium and two state parks are great accessible day excursions.

Bed & Breakfast Honolulu Statewide ✪
3242 KAOHINANI DRIVE, HONOLULU, HAWAII 96817
bnbshi@aloha.net

Tel: (800) 288-4666; (808) 595-7533;
  fax: (808) 595-2030
Best Time to Call: 8 AM–5 PM
  Mon.–Fri., 8 AM–Noon Sat.
Coordinator: Mary Lee
States/Regions Covered: Hawaii
  Statewide

Rates (Single/Double):
  Modest: $45–$55/$45–$60
  Average: $55–$70/$55–$75
  Luxury: $75 up/$75 up
Credit Cards: MC, VISA

This home-based family service, started in 1982, pays careful attention to visitors who want to be more than tourists. That's made it Hawaii's largest statewide agency, listing more than 700 rooms, 10 wheelchair-friendly, on all islands. Many agencies have membership fees and directories; this one doesn't! When you call the 800 number, use the E-mail address, or fax Bed & Breakfast Honolulu, Mary Lee can match your needs, desires, and pocketbook to her computerized listings. This service's size lets her offer very favorable rates on rental cars and inter-island air.

Beautiful Dreamer ✪
440 EAST STEPHEN FOSTER AVENUE, BARDSTOWN, KENTUCKY 40004

Tel: (800) 811-8312
Host: Lynell Ginter
Location: 30 mi. SE of Louisville
No. of Rooms: 1
No. of Private Baths: 1
Double/pb: $85

Open: All year
Breakfast: Full
Credit Cards: MC, VISA
Pets: No
Children: Welcome, over 8
Smoking: No

Decorated with antiques and cherry furniture, this Federal-style home, circa 1995, is located in the historic district. Relax on the porch and enjoy a breathtaking view of My Old Kentucky Home, or show off your talent on the baby grand piano. The Stephen Foster Room is wheelchair accessible, featuring a shower with rails and a double sink that can accommodate a wheelchair, air-conditioning, and queen-size bed. A hearty breakfast is included.

Trinity Hills Farm B&B—Stained Glass Studio ✪
10455 OLD LOVELACEVILLE ROAD, PADUCAH, KENTUCKY 42001

Tel: (800) 488-3998
Best Time to Call: After 5 PM
Hosts: Mike and Ann Driver, Jim and
  Nancy Driver
Location: 12 mi. W of Paducah

Suites: $70–$90
Open: All year
Reduced Rates: Available
Breakfast: Full
Credit Cards: DISC, MC, VISA

Pets: **Sometimes**
Children: **Welcome**
Smoking: **No**

Social Drinking: **Permitted**
Airport Pickup: **Yes**

Share the serenity of the Drivers' 17-acre retreat. This three-story home offers amenities for romantic getaways and family retreats, and features one room for guests with disabilities. Your hosts have installed a chair-lift on both staircases to provide access to your suite. There is also an outdoor ramp. The room was specifically designed to meet your needs. Breakfast may include strawberry pecan waffles, blueberry pancakes, strata, and quiche.

Amanda's B&B Reservation Service ✪
1428 PARK AVENUE, BALTIMORE, MARYLAND 21217

Tel: **(410) 225-0001; fax: (410) 728-8957**
Best Time to Call: **8:30 AM–5:30 PM Mon.–Fri.**
Coordinator: **Betsy Grater**
States/Regions Covered: **Annapolis, Baltimore, Delaware, District of**

Columbia, Maryland, New Jersey, Pennsylvania, Virginia, West Virginia
Descriptive Directory of B&Bs: **$5**
Rates (Double):
  Modest: **$85**
  Luxury: **$100–$150**
Credit Cards: **AMEX, DISC, MC, VISA**

The roster of this reservation service includes eight sites designed for visitors with disabilities—five in downtown Baltimore, two in Annapolis, and one in Chesapeake City.

The Wildwood Inn ✪
121 CHURCH STREET, WARE, MASSACHUSETTS 01082

Tel: **(413) 967-7798; (800) 860-8098**
Best Time to Call: **After 10 AM**
Hosts: **Fraidell Fenster and Richard Watson**
Location: **8 mi. N of Mass. Pike (I-90), Exit 8**
No. of Rooms: **1**
No. of Private Baths: **1**
Double/pb: **$60–$90**

Open: **All year**
Reduced Rates: **Weekly**
Breakfast: **Full**
Credit Cards: **AMEX, DC, MC, VISA**
Pets: **No**
Children: **Welcome, over 6**
Smoking: **No**
Social Drinking: **Permitted**

This Queen Anne Victorian is furnished with American Primitive antiques, heirloom quilts, and early cradles. The first-floor bedroom is easily accessible from a roofed ramp leading directly to the accommodation. The beds can be arranged as twins or a king-size to meet most personal living styles. Both the room and the shower of the bath have grab bars for easy access. The shower is also equipped with a seat. For the hearing-impaired there is a strobe smoke detector. All the doors are equipped with lever-style handles. The room and bath are themed in birds and waterfowl, with air conditioning in summer. All the first-floor common areas are easily reached from this room, including the romantic fireplaced parlor, and spacious dining room overlooking a lovely garden, bird feeders, and birdbaths. Start off your day with a hearty New England breakfast before you venture out to Old Sturbridge Village, Old Deerfield, the Basketball Hall of Fame or the 100-acre park behind the Inn with its paved roads and rustic pathways. Abundant information about recreational activities is kept at the Inn to meet the varying needs of our guests. Your comfort and relaxation are your hosts' most important goals.

Market Sleigh Bed & Breakfast ✪
BOX 99, 57 SOUTH MAIN STREET, LOGANVILLE, PENNSYLVANIA 17342

Tel: **(717) 428-1440**
Best Time to Call: **3–6 PM**
Hosts: **Judy and Jerry Dietz**
Location: **7 mi. S of York**
No. of Rooms: **1**
No. of Private Baths: **1**
Suite: **$55–$100**
Open: **All year**
Reduced Rates: **Corporate travelers; Mon.–Thurs.**

Breakfast: **Full**
Credit Cards: **MC, VISA**
Pets: **No**
Children: **Welcome, over 12**
Smoking: **No**
Social Drinking: **Permitted**
Minimum Stay: **2 nights, convention weekends**

This bed and breakfast takes its name from the large 19th-century sleigh parked by the main entrance, as if stranded when the snow melted. Guests are encouraged to sit on the back porch with a good book or enjoy the many local attractions, ranging from parks and wineries to museums and malls. Judy serves a hearty farmer's breakfast of fruit, homemade breads, eggs, cheese, bacon, and French toast or pancakes. The suite is wheelchair-friendly, complete with handrails in the bath.

The Jam N Jelly Inn Bed and Breakfast ✪
1310 INDIAN RIDGE ROAD, JOHNSON CITY, TENNESSEE 37604

Tel: **(423) 929-0039**; fax: **(423) 929-9026**
Best Time to Call: **After 5 PM**
Host: **Walter D. Kidner**
Location: **5 mi. S of I-181, Exit 35**
No. of Rooms: **1**
No. of Private Baths: **1**
Double/pb: **$65**
Single/pb: **$55**
Suites: **$75**
Open: **All year**

Reduced Rates: **Available**
Breakfast: **Full**
Credit Cards: **AMEX, DISC, MC, VISA**
Pets: **No**
Children: **By arrangement**
Smoking: **No**
Social Drinking: **Permitted**
Minimum Stay: **2 nights special events weekends**
Airport Pickup: **Yes**

The Jam N Jelly Inn, Johnson City's newest bed & breakfast, offers a unique lodging experience. The Inn is a custom-built log home that offers comfort and privacy to guests. The decor is a tasteful blend of casual elegance in a homelike atmosphere. Guest rooms all have queen beds and reproduction antiques. Amenities include a well-stocked book and video library, snacks and beverages, an eight- to-ten person hot tub, a spacious front porch, and a covered rear deck for quiet reflection. Inside, you'll find a centrally located VCR, fax machine, air conditioning, and TV; three rooms have private telephones. One room is accessible to disabled visitors.

The Iris Inn ✪
191 CHINQUAPIN DRIVE, WAYNESBORO, VIRGINIA 22980

Tel: (540) 943-1991
Best Time to Call: 10 AM–8 PM
Hosts: Wayne and Iris Karl
Location: 25 mi. W of Charlottesville
No. of Rooms: 1
No. of Private Baths: 1
Double/pb: $75–$95
Single/pb: $65
Open: All year

Reduced Rates: Corporate; Sun.–Thurs.
Breakfast: Full
Credit Cards: MC, VISA
Pets: No
Children: Welcome, by arrangement
Smoking: No
Social Drinking: Permitted
Minimum Stay: 2 nights weekends
Airport Pickup: Yes

Southern charm and grace in a totally modern facility overlooking the historic Shenandoah Valley from the Blue Ridge Mountains' wooded western slope—that's what awaits you at The Iris Inn. It's ideal for a weekend retreat, a refreshing change for the business traveler, and a tranquil spot for tourists to spend a night or more. The wheelchair-accessible room is comfortably furnished and delightfully decorated with nature and wildlife motifs. The bathroom has a lavatory without a vanity, for easier use. There are grab bars at the toilet and on the sides of the shower, which also has a seat. A pocket door connects the bathroom and bedroom. For your convenience, a ramp leads from the parking lot level to the porch. Eight other rooms are available.

Connors Bed & Breakfast ✪
ROUTE 1, BOX 255, CABLE, WISCONSIN 54821

Tel: (715) 798-3661; (800) 848-3932
Hosts: Alex and Mona Connors
Location: 1.7 mi. N of Cable
No. of Rooms: 1
No. of Private Baths: 1
Suites: $85
Open: All year

Breakfast: Full
Credit Cards: MC, VISA
Pets: No
Children: Welcome
Smoking: No
Social Drinking: Permitted
Airport/Station Pickup: Yes

Located 40 miles south of Lake Superior, Connors Bed & Breakfast offers one wheelchair-accessible room with a private bath. The room is spacious and has a gas fireplace, wood floors for easy mobility, king-size bed, pedestal table with plenty of space to accommodate a wheelchair, a large sofa, and an armoire that can be reached from a seated position. The bath features a Kohler shower with a bench and built-in grab bars, a wall-mounted sink, and a taller toilet with adjacent grab bars. Next to your room is the parlor with hardwood floors, a piano, chess set, and fireplace—a perfect spot for a chat with other guests. From this room it's easy access to the dining area and the ramp leading outside. The region boasts many activities; in particular, the Cable-Hayward area hosts a fishing weekend called "Fishing Has No Boundaries" for the disabled in mid-May at the Chippewa Campground.

For key to listings, see inside front or back cover.

✪ This star means that rates are guaranteed through December 31, 1998, to any guest making a reservation as a result of reading about the B&B in *Bed & Breakfast U.S.A.*—1998 edition.

Important! To avoid misunderstandings, always ask about cancellation policies when booking.

Please enclose a self-addressed, stamped, business-size envelope when contacting reservation services.

For more details on what you can expect in a B&B, see Chapter 1.

Always mention *Bed & Breakfast U.S.A.* when making reservations!

We want to hear from you! Use the form on page 625.

5

State-by-State Listings

ALABAMA

Montgomery

Mobile
Fairhope

Bay Breeze Guest House ✪
P.O. BOX 526, 742 SOUTH MOBILE STREET, FAIRHOPE, ALABAMA 36532

Tel: **(334) 928-8976**
Best Time to Call: **9 AM–9 PM**
Hosts: **Bill and Becky Jones**
Location: **20 mi. E of Mobile**
No. of Rooms: **3**
No. of Private Baths: **3**
Double/pb: **$95**
Guest Cottage Suite: **$100**
Open: **All year**

Breakfast: **Full**
Credit Cards: **AMEX, MC, VISA**
Pets: **Sometimes**
Children: **By arrangement**
Smoking: **No**
Social Drinking: **Permitted**
Minimum Stay: **2 nights weekends Apr.–Oct.**
Airport/Station Pickup: **Yes**

This unique bay-front stucco was built in the early 1930s and has been lovingly restored throughout the years. The house is decorated with family heirlooms, wicker, stained glass, hooked and oriental rugs, and period antiques that date back five generations. The guest rooms all have queen beds. The cottage suite features a living room and a minikitchen. Within walking distance you will find excellent restaurants, shops, and a sidewalk that follows the beach for an afternoon or evening stroll. Bill and Becky have their quarters upstairs, but are always available to cater to your needs or answer any questions you may have about the area.

Towle House ✪

1104 MONTAUK AVENUE, MOBILE, ALABAMA 36604

Tel: **(334) 432-6440**
Best Time to Call: **8 AM–8 PM**
Hosts: **Felix and Carolyn Vereen**
No. of Rooms: **3**
No. of Private Baths: **1**
Max. No. Sharing Baths: **4**
Double/pb: **$70–$85**
Double/sb: **$70–$85**

Open: **All year**
Breakfast: **Full**
Credit Cards: **MC, VISA**
Pets: **No**
Children: **No**
Smoking: **No**
Social Drinking: **Permitted**
Airport/Station Pickup: **Yes**

Towle House, circa 1874, is located in the heart of the historic district. This Italianate-style home is constructed of heart pine and cypress, and sits on a large lot surrounded by azaleas, dogwoods, and seasonal flowers. The house, originally used as a boys' school, has been recently restored and is furnished with turn-of-the-century antiques. Towle House is only 10 minutes away from the Convention Center, Mobile Auditorium, historic homes, antique shopping, and the revitalized downtown area. The Vereens' location is within easy access to the City of Mobile Museum, Fort Conde, and the USS *Alabama*.

Red Bluff Cottage ✪

551 CLAY STREET, MONTGOMERY, ALABAMA
(MAILING ADDRESS: P.O. BOX 1026, MONTGOMERY,
ALABAMA 36101)
redblufbnb@aol.com

Tel: **(334) 264-0056**; fax: **(334) 263-3054**
Best Time to Call: **9 AM–10 PM**
Hosts: **Anne and Mark Waldo**
No. of Rooms: **4**
No. of Private Baths: **4**
Double/pb: **$75**
Single/pb: **$60**

Suite: **$85**
Open: **All year**
Breakfast: **Full**
Pets: **No**
Children: **Welcome (crib)**
Smoking: **No**
Social Drinking: **Permitted**
Airport/Station Pickup: **Yes**

This raised cottage is high above the Alabama River in Montgomery's historic Cottage Hill District, close to the State Capitol, Dexter Avenue King Memorial Baptist Church, the First White House of the Confederacy, the Civil Rights Memorial, and Old Alabama Town. The Alabama Shakespeare Festival Theatre, the Museum of Fine Arts, and the expanded zoo are also nearby. The bedrooms are downstairs. Guests come upstairs to read or relax in the living rooms, to enjoy the front porch view, and to have breakfast in the dining room. Many interesting antiques and a music room, complete with harpsichord, add to the charm of this home.

For key to listings, see inside front or back cover.

✪ This star means that rates are guaranteed through December 31, 1998, to any guest making a reservation as a result of reading about the B&B in *Bed & Breakfast U.S.A.—1998* edition.

Important! To avoid misunderstandings, always ask about cancellation policies when booking.

Please enclose a self-addressed, stamped, business-size envelope when contacting reservation services.

For more details on what you can expect in a B&B, see Chapter 1.

Always mention *Bed & Breakfast U.S.A.* when making reservations!

We want to hear from you! Use the form on page 625.

ALASKA

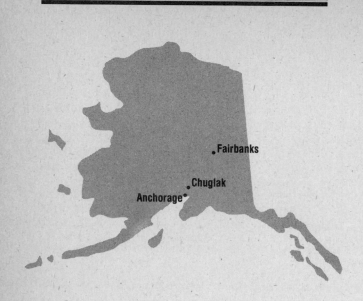

Fairbanks

Chuglak

Anchorage

Alaska Private Lodgings ✪
P.O. BOX 200047, ANCHORAGE, ALASKA 99520–0047

Tel: **(907) 258-1717**; fax: **(907) 258-6613**
Best Time to Call: **9 AM–6 PM**
Coordinator: **Mercy Dennis**
States/Regions Covered: **Anchorage, Denali, Fairbanks, Girdwood, Homer, Hope, Kenai, Palmer, Seward, Southeast Regions, Talkeetna, Valdez, Wasilla, Willow, Yukon**

Descriptive Directory of B&Bs: **$5**
Rates (Single/Double):
 Modest: **$55–$65**
 Average: **$66–$85**
 Luxury: **$86 up**
Credit Cards: **AMEX, MC, VISA**

Alaskan hosts are this state's warmest resource! Mercy's accommodations range from an original log house of a pioneer's homestead, where the host is in the antique-doll business, to a one-bedroom apartment with a view of Mt. Denali. Many are convenient to the University of Alaska and Alaska Pacific University.

Elderberry B&B ✪
8340 ELDERBERRY STREET, ANCHORAGE, ALASKA 99502

Tel: **(907) 243-6968**
Hosts: **Norm and Linda Seitz**
No. of Rooms: **3**
No. of Private Baths: **2**
Max. No. Sharing Bath: **4**
Double/pb: **$75**
Double/sb: **$50**
Open: **All year**

Reduced Rates: **10% seniors; Sept. 15–Apr. 15 all rooms $50**
Breakfast: **Full**
Credit Cards: **MC, VISA**
Pets: **Sometimes**
Children: **Welcome**
Smoking: **No**
Social Drinking: **Permitted**

Elderberry B&B is the perfect place to stay while visiting Anchorage—it's located close to the airport, bike and walking trails, and the bus route, and within a short walking distance to many local restaurants. The Seitz home is a yellow two-story tastefully decorated with oak furnishings using Alaskan accents. Each guest room has matching furnishings, one with a queen, one with a double, and one with twin beds. Guests can enjoy two common rooms. One is for reading and relaxing, and the other has a big-screen TV and many videos to choose from. Linda considers Norm one of their best amenities, as he loves to tell guests all about Alaska. They both take special pride in their beautiful summer flowers, which have won blue ribbons at the state fair.

The Green Bough ✪
3832 YOUNG STREET, ANCHORAGE, ALASKA 99508
76015.3514@compuserve.com

Tel: **(907) 562-4636; fax: (907) 562-0445**
Best Time to Call: **10 AM–9 PM**
Hosts: **Jerry and Phyllis Jost**
Location: **15 min. from airport/train**
No. of Rooms: **4**
Max. No. Sharing Bath: **4**
Double/pb: **$75–$85**
Single/pb: **$50**

Double/sb: **$60**
Open: **All year**
Reduced Rates: **Families; off-season**
Breakfast: **Continental, plus**
Pets: **No**
Children: **Welcome**
Smoking: **No**
Social Drinking: **No**

Since 1981, Anchorage's oldest bed and breakfast has been offering a special blend of gracious, unpretentious hospitality. Guest rooms are spacious and reflect a country atmosphere, featuring freshly ironed sheets, king, full, or twin beds, phones and TVs, and private bathrooms. The aromas of coffee and cinnamon will start you off to a full day of sightseeing, shopping, fishing, or hiking. You can expect to meet guests from around the world, including the backyards of Alaska. The Green Bough is centrally located, near buses, hospitals, universities, and bike trails. Freezer and storage are available for your fish and extra gear. Jerry and Phyllis have been transplanted Alaskans since 1967, and want to share their experience and enthusiasm about the area with you.

"K" Street Bed & Breakfast ✪

1443 "K" STREET, ANCHORAGE, ALASKA 99501
KSSTBB@Alaska.net

Tel: **(907) 279-1443**
Best Time to Call: **Mornings**
Host: **Kate Warrick**
No. of Rooms: **3**
No. of Private Baths: **1**
Max. No. Sharing Bath: **4**
Double/sb: **$85**
Suite: **$90**

Open: **All year**
Reduced Rates: **Available**
Breakfast: **Full**
Pets: **No**
Children: **Welcome, over 12**
Smoking: **No**
Social Drinking: **No**

This contemporary cedar home is located in downtown Anchorage. Guests can walk to restaurants, shopping, the Natural History Museum, a Saturday market, or a deli. Drive a short distance to Chugach State Park, the airport, or the mountains. The interior of the bed and breakfast boasts hardwood floors, tile, and Alaskan art, plus a solarium. Outside you'll find large trees and a garden. Breakfast is made from natural wholesome foods, accompanied by gourmet coffee.

Peters Creek Bed & Breakfast ✪

22626 CHAMBERS LANE, CHUGIAK, ALASKA 99567

Tel: **(907) 688-3465; (888) 688-3465;**
     fax: (907) 688-3466
Best Time to Call: **After 10 AM**
Hosts: **Bob and Lucy Moody**
Location: **17 mi. N of Anchorage**
No. of Rooms: **3**
No. of Private Baths: **3**
Double/pb: **$85**
Single/pb: **$75**

Open: **All year**
Reduced Rates: **10% seniors**
Breakfast: **Full**
Credit Cards: **AMEX, DISC, MC, VISA**
Pets: **No**
Children: **Welcome, crib**
Smoking: **No**
Social Drinking: **No**
Foreign Languages: **Spanish**

Newly built Peters Creek Bed & Breakfast is located on the north shore of Peters Creek, in the middle of two and a half acres of park-like terrain. The decor is predominantly Victorian antiques; each guest room has cable TV, VCR, and refrigerator. After a hearty Alaskan breakfast, take a hike at the nearby Thunderbird Falls, fish at Fire Lake, or swim at Mirror Lake. Boating, canoeing, kayaking, dogsled rides, horseshoes, horseback riding, and skiing are just a few of the other activities you can enjoy.

A Bed & Breakfast on Minnie ✪

345 MINNIE STREET, FAIRBANKS, ALASKA 99701
minniebb@mosquitonet.com

Tel: **(907) 456-1802**
Hosts: **Marnie and Lambert Hazelaar**

Location: **In Fairbanks**
No. of Rooms: **9**

No. of Private Baths: **4**
Max. No. Sharing Bath: **4**
Double/pb: **$85–$110**
Double/sb: **$75**
Suites: **$150 for 4**
Open: **All year**
Reduced Rates: **Winter**

Breakfast: **Full**
Credit Cards: **AMEX, MC, VISA**
Pets: **No**
Children: **Welcome**
Smoking: **No**
Social Drinking: **Permitted**

This bed and breakfast is located within walking distance of the train depot and only five minutes from downtown, where you will find the post office, banks, gift shops, and restaurants. En route you will cross the beautiful Chena River. The cozy, comfortably decorated guest rooms have queen-size beds. Ample parking is provided; rental cars are available next door. Marnie's sumptuous breakfasts include homemade breads, omelettes, and fruit salad.

7 Gables Inn ✪
P. O. BOX 80488, FAIRBANKS, ALASKA 99708

Tel: **(907) 479-0751; fax: (907) 479-2229**
Best Time to Call: **9 AM–10 PM**
Hosts: **Paul and Leicha Welton**
Location: **2 mi. W of Fairbanks**
No. of Rooms: **9**
No. of Private Baths: **9**
Double/pb: **$50–$120**
Single/pb: **$50–$110**
Suites: **$75–$180**
Open: **All year**

Reduced Rates: **50%, Oct.–Apr.**
Breakfast: **Full**
Other Meals: **Available**
Credit Cards: **AMEX, DC, DISC, MC, VISA**
Pets: **Sometimes**
Children: **Welcome**
Smoking: **No**
Social Drinking: **Permitted**
Airport/Station Pickup: **Yes**
Foreign Languages: **Spanish**

The Weltons' large Tudor-style home is central to many city attractions—Riverboat Discovery, Cripple Creek Resort, University Museum, Alaskaland, Gold Dredge #8—and within walking distance of the University of Alaska's Fairbanks campus. Paul designed and built the house, a worthy destination in its own right. You'll enter through a floral solarium, which leads to a foyer with antique stained glass and indoor waterfall. Party planners take note: 7 Gables has a wine cellar and a wedding chapel. Guests can use the laundry facilities, library, Jacuzzis, canoe, and bikes. All rooms have telephones, cable TV, and VCR, and 8 rooms have private Jacuzzi baths. Ample breakfasts feature dishes like salmon quiche, crab casserole, and peachy pecan crepes.

ARIZONA

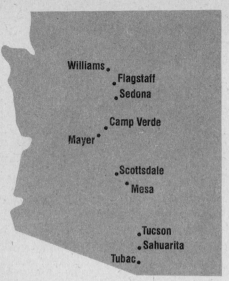

Mi Casa–Su Casa Bed & Breakfast ✪
P.O. BOX 950, TEMPE, ARIZONA 85280-0950

Tel: **(602) 990-0682; (800) 456-0682;**
    fax: (602) 990-3390
Best Time to Call: **8 AM–8 PM**
Coordinator: **Ruth T. Young**
States/Regions Covered: **Arizona—Ajo,**
    Bisbee, Cave Creek, Flagstaff,
    Fountain Hills, Mesa, Page, Phoenix,
    Prescott, Scottsdale, Sedona, Tempe,
Tucson, Wickenburg, Yuma;
Nevada—Las Vegas; New Mexico;
Utah
Rates (Single/Double):
    Modest: **$45–$55**
    Average: **$55–$65**
    Luxury: **$75–$200**
Descriptive Directory: **$9.50**

Ruth's guesthouses are located statewide; the cities listed above are only a partial listing. They are located in cities, suburbs, and rural settings, all of which are within easy driving range of canyons, national parks, Indian country, Colorado River gem country, the Mexican border area, historic mining towns, and water recreation areas. Send $9.50 for her detailed directory. Arizona State University and the University of

Arizona are convenient to many B&Bs. There is a $5 surcharge for one-night stays.

B's B&B ✪

94 COPPINGER STREET, P.O. BOX 2019, CAMP VERDE,
ARIZONA 86322

Tel: **(520) 567-6215**
Host: **Beatrice Richmond**
Location: **90 mi. N of Phoenix**
No. of Rooms: **2**
No. of Private Baths: **2**
Double/pb: **$60**
Single/pb: **$50**

Open: **All year**
Breakfast: **Full**
Pets: **No**
Children: **Welcome**
Smoking: **No**
Social Drinking: **Permitted**
Foreign Languages: **French, Spanish**

B's B&B sits on a hillside; a huge redwood deck has a panoramic view. Set on an acre of natural landscaping, this bed and breakfast seems isolated, but is very close to the center of town. Things to do include excursions to Fort Verde State Park, Captain King's boat rides, outback tours, horseback riding, and much more. Breakfast may feature B's blintzes, homemade granola, and yogurt. Beatrice is a retired elementary school teacher and teaches English as a second language one evening a week. She also enjoys foreign languages and travel.

Dierker House

423 WEST CHERRY, FLAGSTAFF, ARIZONA 86001

Tel: **(520) 774-3249**
Host: **Dorothea Dierker**
No. of Rooms: **3**
Max. No. Sharing Bath: **4**
Double/sb: **$50**
Open: **All year**

Breakfast: **Full**
Pets: **No**
Children: **Welcome, over 12**
Smoking: **No**
Social Drinking: **Permitted**

This lovely old home in Flagstaff's historic section is located high in the mountains, at an elevation of 7000 feet. Flagstaff is the hub of wonderful day trips to the Grand Canyon, Native American ruins and reservations, Lake Powell, Monument Valley, and many more sites. The second-floor accommodations are extremely comfortable and include many amenities. In the morning, Dorothea serves an excellent and sociable breakfast in the dining room.

Serenity House ✪

P.O. BOX 1254, THIRD STREET AND MAIN, MAYER, ARIZONA 86333

Tel: **(520) 632-4430**
Host: **Sue Ward**
Location: **25 mi. E of Prescott; 65 mi. N of Phoenix**
No. of Rooms: **2**

Max. No. Sharing Bath: **4**
Double/sb: **$50**
Open: **All year**
Breakfast: **Continental**
Pets: **No**

Children: **Welcome, over 12**   Social Drinking: **Permitted**
Smoking: **No**   Airport/Station Pickup: **Yes**

This comfortable, country Victorian home is located in an old mining town north of Phoenix and east of Prescott. Built around 1905 by one of the Mayer brothers, who gave this town its name, the home has twelve-foot gabled ceilings, two fireplaces, hardwood floors, original copper and brass door and light fixtures, stained glass, a front porch swing, many large trees, and a pool. One guest room has a private entrance to the pool area. There are many antique shops and historical buildings both in Mayer and Prescott. Popular pastimes include gold panning, hiking, rock hounding, and horse racing at Prescott Downs. Special sugar-free diets can easily be accommodated. Locally grown vegetables and fruits are a summer treat.

Casa Del Sol
6951 E. HOBART, MESA, ARIZONA 85207

Tel: **(602) 985-5956**   Open: **All year**
Hosts: **Ray and Barb Leo**   Reduced Rates: **Available**
Location: **20 mi. E of Phoenix**   Breakfast: **Full**
No. of Rooms: **2**   Pets: **Sometimes**
Max. No. Sharing Bath: **4**   Children: **Welcome**
Double/sb: **$50–$55**   Smoking: **No**
Single/sb: **$45**   Social Drinking: **Permitted**

This luxurious Southwestern home sits on an acre of property with desert landscaping, fruit trees, and a solar-heated swimming pool. The guest rooms emphasize comfort with queen-size beds and Southwest decor. The word for breakfast is fresh, from ground coffee and fresh-squeezed juice to home-baked breads, muffins and croissants, special omelettes, and waffles. Guests are welcome to enjoy the pool, Jacuzzi, fireplace, and VCR. Nearby attractions include beautiful state parks, the Salt River recreation area, Cactus League spring training, great shopping, golf, and restaurants.

Mi Gatita Bed & Breakfast ✪
**14085 AVENIDA HALEY S. (MAILING ADDRESS: HCR 70, BOX 3401),
SAHUARITA, ARIZONA 85629**

Tel: **(520) 648-6129**   Open: **All year**
Best Time to Call: **2–4 PM**   Reduced Rates: **Available**
Hosts: **Jean and Bentley Pace**   Breakfast: **Full**
Location: **15 mi. SW of Tucson**   Pets: **No**
No. of Rooms: **2**   Children: **Welcome, over 14**
No. of Private Baths: **2**   Smoking: **No**
Double/pb: **$68–$85**   Social Drinking: **Permitted**
Suites: **$85**

Carved out of land from the old Navarro Ranch—which still runs cattle close by—this adobe-hued hacienda sits on a high rise overlooking the mountains surrounding Tucson. On cool evenings, warm yourself at one of the fireplaces in the Great Room or on the Hogan Patio. If you are staying in San Blas, the other little house, you have your own private fireplace. Jean and Bentley offer many amenities, including plush bathrobes, fresh fruit, candies in your room, and a tray of coffee left at your door as a pleasant wake-up before you enjoy a healthy Southwestern breakfast. During warm weather you are invited to use the pool. Indoors or out the decor features Southwestern, Mexican, and Native American artifacts. A fifteen- to forty-minute drive takes you to Tucson, Madera Canyon, the Arizona Sonoran Desert Museum, Saguaro National Park, Tubac, and Tumacacori and San Xavier missions. There are three cats on the premises.

Bed & Breakfast Southwest Reservation Service—Arizona ☉

2916 NORTH 70TH STREET, SCOTTSDALE, ARIZONA 85251
b&bsw@juno.com

Tel: **(602) 945-9704; (800) 762-9704;**
  fax: **(602) 874-1316**
Best Time to Call: **8 AM–8 PM**
Coordinators: **Jo Cummings and Joan Petersen**
States/Regions Covered: **Arizona, New Mexico, Southern Colorado, Southern California**

Descriptive Directory: **Free**
Rates (Single/Double):
  Modest: **$40–$75**
  Average: **$80–$100**
  Luxury: **$105–up**

This service offers Southwestern travelers unique homestays in suites, guesthouses, ranches, and inns. All host facilities are personally inspected and provide the three C's of bed and breakfasts: cleanliness, cordiality, and convenience. Jo and Joan's specialty is finding the perfect B&B for you. They can plan your trip to include many of the historical and natural wonders in the great Southwest, such as the San Diego Zoo, Durango Historic Railroad, Scottsdale golf courses, Sedona's Red Rock formations, and the Santa Fe opera. You will be awed by the spectacular scenic beauty and legendary Western hospitality.

Valley o' the Sun Bed & Breakfast ☉

P.O. BOX 2214, SCOTTSDALE, ARIZONA 85252

Tel: **(602) 941-1281; (800) 689-1281**
Best Time to Call: **After 5:30 PM**
Host: **Kay Curtis**
Location: **Tempe**
No. of Rooms: **3**
No. of Private Baths: **1**

Max. No. Sharing Bath: **4**
Double/pb: **$50**
Double/sb: **$40**
Single/sb: **$30**
Open: **All year**
Reduced Rates: **Seniors; weekly**

Breakfast: **Continental, plus**
Pets: **No**
Children: **Welcome, over 10**
Smoking: **Restricted**

Social Drinking: **Permitted**
Minimum Stay: **2 nights**
Airport/Station Pickup: **Yes**

The house is ideally located in the college area of Tempe, but is close enough to Scottsdale for guests to enjoy its fine shops and restaurants. From the patio, you can enjoy a beautiful view of the Papago Buttes and McDowell Mountains. Local attractions include swimming at Big Surf, the Phoenix Zoo, and the Scottsdale Center for the Arts.

Moestly Wood Bed & Breakfast ✪
2085 UPPER RED ROCK LOOP ROAD, SEDONA, ARIZONA 86336

Tel: **(520) 204-1461**
Best Time to Call: **8 AM–8 PM**
Hosts: **Roger and Carolyn Moe**
Location: **110 mi. N of Phoenix**
No. of Rooms: **2**
No. of Private Baths: **2**
Suite: **$85–$95**
Open: **All year**

Breakfast: **Full**
Other Meals: **Available**
Credit Cards: **MC, VISA**
Pets: **No**
Children: **Welcome**
Smoking: **No**
Social Drinking: **Permitted**
Minimum Stay: **2 nights on weekends**

This contemporary home is located in the beautiful Arizona red rock country. Just 4 miles out of town you can enjoy spectacular views of Cathedral Rock and the surrounding area, or take a short hike to Red Rock Crossing, one of the state's most photographed sites. Roger and Carolyn enjoy visitors and are happy to help with touring plans, hiking, golfing, or just browsing through Sedona's many shops and galleries. Their large redwood deck is very inviting. Relaxing by the fire is also a comfy, cozy way to spend the evening.

Tubac Country Inn ✪
409 BURRUEL STREET, P.O. BOX 1540, TUBAC, ARIZONA 85646

Tel: **(520) 398-3178**
Best Time to Call: **Anytime**
Hosts: **Ruth and Jim Goebel**
Location: **41 mi. S of Tucson**
No. of Rooms: **4**
Suites: **$80**
Open: **Closed August**

Breakfast: **Continental**
Pets: **No**
Children: **Welcome**
Smoking: **No**
Social Drinking: **Permitted**
Airport Pickup: **Yes**

This adorable two-story Inn located in the center of Tubac will steal your heart away. Choose a one- or two-bedroom suite; two units have full kitchens for longer stays. Tubac, founded in 1752, is the oldest European settlement in Arizona. Today Tubac is the place where art and history meet. Visit galleries, boutiques, and restaurants all within walking distance of the Inn. Within a few minutes you can drive to shopping in Old Mexico, or see missions, museums, and national parks. The area boasts six outstanding golf courses.

Advance Reservations Inn Arizona
P.O. BOX 13603, TUCSON, ARIZONA 85732
http://www.azres.com

Tel: (800) 333-9776; (520) 790-0030;
   fax: (520) 790-2399
Best Time to Call: 8 AM–8 PM
   weekdays, 1 PM–5 PM weekends
Coordinator: William A. Janssen
States/Regions Covered: Statewide:
   Bisbee, Dragoon, Flagstaff, Florence,
   Page, Phoenix, Scottsdale, Sedona,
   Tombstone, Tucson, Williams

Descriptive Directory of B&Bs: $3 SASE
Rates (Single/Double):
   Modest: $45–$60
   Average: $65–$85
   Luxury: $90–$340
Credit Cards: DISC, MC, VISA

This service features accommodations in private homes, inns, and guest ranches that are located near Arizona cities, suburbs, mountains, and country areas. Sites range from the very modest to the very luxurious and include Continental to ultra-gourmet breakfasts. Many offer easy access to national parks, historic towns, universities, and the Mexican border.

Bienestar Bed and Breakfast ✪
10490 EAST ESCALANTE ROAD, TUCSON, ARIZONA 85730

Tel: (520) 290-1048; fax: (520) 290-1367
Best Time to Call: Mornings
Hosts: Peggy Muller and Angela Telfer
Location: 10 mi. from I-10, Exit 275
No. of Rooms: 2
No. of Private Baths: 2
Double/pb: $85
Single/pb: $75
Suites: $125
Open: All year

Reduced Rates: 25% June 1–Sept. 30;
   weekly; monthly
Breakfast: Full
Credit Cards: DISC, MC, VISA
Pets: No
Children: Welcome, over 10
Smoking: No
Social Drinking: Permitted
Minimum Stay: 2 nights weekends,
   Dec. 15–Mar. 15
Airport Pickup: Yes

This lovely hacienda is situated on six acres of Sonoran desert just off Saguaro National Park East. Peggy is a registered nurse and will provide you a stress-free, relaxing stay with panoramic mountain views, a large pool, spa, afternoon tea, and a natural gourmet breakfast. The decor is Southwestern, featuring king beds, private baths, and gorgeous views. The suite has two fireplaces, TV, stereo, and a private entrance. The common areas have beamed ceilings, a fireplace, a grand piano, and an extensive library. Complimentary horse facilities are available at the stables.

Casa Tierra Adobe Bed and Breakfast Inn
11155 WEST CALLE PIMA, TUCSON, ARIZONA 85743

Tel: **(520) 578-3058; fax: (520) 578-3058**
Best Time to Call: **Mornings**
Hosts: **Karen and Lyle Hymer-Thompson**
Location: **15 mi. W of Tucson**
No. of Rooms: **3**
No. of Private Baths: **3**
Double/pb: **$75–$105**
Open: **Sept.–May**

Reduced Rates: **10% after 7 days**
Breakfast: **Full**
Pets: **No**
Children: **Welcome, over 3**
Smoking: **No**
Social Drinking: **Permitted**
Minimum Stay: **2 nights**
Foreign Languages: **Spanish**

Casa Tierra is located on five acres of beautiful Sonoran desert thirty minutes from downtown Tucson. This secluded desert area has hundreds of saguaro cactus, spectacular mountain views, and brilliant sunsets. Built and designed by owners Lyle and Karen, the all-adobe house features entryways with vaulted brick ceilings, an interior arched courtyard, Mexican furnishings, and a Jacuzzi. Each guest room has a private bath, queen-size bed, microwave, small refrigerator, and private patio and entrance. Nearby attractions include the Desert Museum, the Saguaro National Park, and Old Tucson. Karen is an artist/photographer; Lyle is a designer/builder who takes tours into Mexico.

Ford's Bed & Breakfast ✪
1202 NORTH AVENIDA MARLENE, TUCSON, ARIZONA 85715

Tel: **(520) 885-1202**
Best Time to Call: **Anytime**
Hosts: **Sheila and Tom Ford**
Location: **In Tucson**
No. of Rooms: **2**

No. of Private Baths: **1**
Double/pb: **$60**
Single/pb: **$45**
Suites: **$100–$120; sleeps 4**
Open: **All year**

Breakfast: **Full**
Pets: **No**
Children: **No**

Smoking: **No**
Social Drinking: **Permitted**

A warm welcome awaits you at this air-conditioned ranch-style home in a quiet residential cul-de-sac on Tucson's northeast side. Walk through your private entrance and enjoy a bird's-eye view of the mountains from your own garden patio. Your English-born hostess, a retired nanny and dog breeder, has lived here since 1957 and can direct you to the attractions of the area: Sabino Canyon, Mount Lemmon, Saguaro National Monument, hiking trails, and the like. For easy access, city bus lines run nearby. Guests have use of a microwave, a refrigerator, and the sitting room with a TV.

The Gable House ✪
2324 NORTH MADELYN CIRCLE, TUCSON, ARIZONA 85712

Tel: **(520) 326-1150; (800) 756-4846**
Host: **Albert Cummings**
Location: **6 mi. from I-10, Exit Grant Road**
No. of Rooms: **3**
No. of Private Baths: **2**
Max. No. Sharing Bath: **4**
Double/pb: **$85**
Double/sb: **$55–$60**

Open: **All year**
Reduced Rates: **10% seniors; 7th day free**
Breakfast: **Continental, plus**
Pets: **No**
Children: **Welcome, over 10**
Smoking: **No**
Social Drinking: **Permitted**
Minimum Stay: **2 nights Feb.–Mar.**

This Santa Fe pueblo-style home is named for its most famous resident—Clark Gable—who lived here in the early 1940s, some twelve years after the house was built. Centrally located on a one-acre lot in a quiet residential neighborhood, this B&B is within walking distance of shops, restaurants, and a bus stop. It's one mile to Tucson Botanical Gardens and three miles to a large city park with golf, tennis, and other recreational facilities. Albert is a semi-retired real estate broker. One-night stays have a $10 surcharge.

Hideaway B&B ✪

4344 EAST POE STREET, TUCSON, ARIZONA 85711

Tel: **(520) 323-8067**
Best Time to Call: **After 5 PM**
Hosts: **Dwight and Ola Parker**
No. of Rooms: **1**
No. of Private Baths: **1**
Guest Cottage: **$45–$60**
Open: **Oct.–June; special arrangements for the rest of year**

Reduced Rates: **Weekly**
Breakfast: **Continental**
Pets: **No**
Children: **No**
Smoking: **No**
Minimum Stay: **3 nights**
Airport/Station Pickup: **Yes**

A cozy bungalow with its own entrance, Hideaway B&B is located in the hosts' backyard in central Tucson, just minutes from two major shopping centers. One mile away, a city park provides lots of diversions, with two golf courses, a driving range, tennis courts, and a zoo. Pima Air Museum, Davis Monthan Air Force Base, the University of Arizona, Colossal Cave, the Old Tucson movie set, and Mt. Lemmon Ski Resort are among the many sites of interest. The air-conditioned accommodations include a private bath, a bedroom, and a sitting room equipped with a TV, VCR, and stereo. Your hosts, a retired art teacher and an engineer/insurance man, enjoy big band music, gardening, and their clown ministry.

Katy's Hacienda ✪

5841 EAST 9TH STREET, TUCSON, ARIZONA 85711

Tel: **(520) 745-5695**
Host: **Katy Gage**
Location: **8 mi. from Rte. 10, Grant or Kolb exit**
No. of Rooms: **2**
No. of Private Baths: **1**
Max. No. Sharing Bath: **3**
Double/pb: **$55**
Single/pb: **$45**
Double/sb: **$55**

Single/sb: **$45**
Open: **All year**
Reduced Rates: **10% weekly**
Breakfast: **Full**
Pets: **No**
Children: **Welcome, over 8**
Smoking: **Permitted**
Social Drinking: **Permitted**
Minimum Stay: **2 nights**
Airport/Station Pickup: **Yes**

An ornamental iron guard protects this adobe brick house filled with charming antiques and glass. Guests can unwind in the backyard and the patio area, or come inside and enjoy the living room and television room. Katy's Hacienda is within walking distance of the bus line, fine restaurants, theaters, and a hospital. The El Con shopping area, the Randolph Golf Course, and the zoo are three miles away.

Llama Lee Ranch ✪

15415 NORTH LAGO DEL ORO PARKWAY, TUCSON, ARIZONA 85739

Tel: **(520) 825-0422**
Best Time to Call: **Evening**
Host: **Carolee Clopton**

Location: **14 mi. N of Tucson**
No. of Rooms: **2**
No. of Private Baths: **1**

Max. No. Sharing Bath: **4**
Double/pb: **$65**
Double/sb: **$75**
Open: **All year**
Breakfast: **Continental**

Pets: **No**
Children: **No**
Smoking: **No**
Social Drinking: **Permitted**

Carolee invites you to enjoy the luxurious comforts of a clean country setting with mountain views, wildlife, and tranquility. The interior boasts antiques, French provincial furniture, and large windows with views of the Catalina Mountains. Evenings can be spent on the patio enjoying the spectacular sunsets, playing horseshoes, or relaxing in the hot tub. In the winter enjoy the fireplace, play cards, watch TV, or read a good book.

Natural Bed and Breakfast ✪
3150 EAST PRESIDIO ROAD, TUCSON, ARIZONA 85716

Tel: **(520) 881-4582**
Best Time to Call: **7 AM–8 PM**
Host: **Marc Haberman**
No. of Rooms: **4**
No. of Private Baths: **2**
Max. No. Sharing Bath: **2**
Double/pb: **$65**
Single/pb: **$55**
Double/sb: **$65**

Open: **All year**
Reduced Rates: **5% seniors**
Breakfast: **Full**
Other Meals: **Available**
Pets: **Sometimes**
Children: **Welcome**
Smoking: **No**
Social Drinking: **Permitted**

Marc Haberman is a holistic health practitioner, and his B&B is natural in all senses of the word: it's a simply furnished, water-cooled home that provides a nontoxic, nonallergenic environment. The grounds are landscaped with palm and pine trees. Only whole-grain and natural foods are served here and the drinking water is purified. Soothing professional massages are available by request.

Quail's Vista Bed & Breakfast ✪
826 EAST PALISADES DRIVE, TUCSON, ARIZONA 85737

Tel: **(520) 297-5980**
Host: **Barbara Jones**
Location: **10 mi. NW of Tucson**
No. of Rooms: **3**
No. of Private Baths: **2**
Double/pb: **$65–$85**
Open: **All year**

Reduced Rates: **10% weekly**
Breakfast: **Continental**
Pets: **No**
Children: **No**
Smoking: **No**
Social Drinking: **Permitted**
Airport/Station Pickup: **Yes**

Native American artifacts and Mexican tile make this modern, solar-heated adobe on 2 acres of desert an attractive blend of the local cultures. Fiestaware dishes and grandmother's furniture in the guest room evoke memories of an older generation. From a seat on the redwood deck you can watch the gorgeous sunset and stargaze in the evening. The swim-stream hot tub is available for swimming or soaking. Breakfasts include a cereal buffet with several toppings, coffee, tea, juices, and baked goods. Light snacks may be put in the refrigerator. Your hostess, a professional Tucson tour guide, can help you discover the area's highlights, and maps, brochures, and restaurant menus are always on hand.

Redbud House Bed & Breakfast
7002 EAST REDBUD ROAD, TUCSON, ARIZONA 85715

Tel: **(520) 721-0218**	Open: **Sept.–May**
Hosts: **Ken and Wanda Mayer**	Breakfast: **Full**
Location: **7 mi. from Rte. 10**	Pets: **No**
No. of Rooms: **1**	Children: **No**
No. of Private Baths: **1**	Smoking: **No**
Double/pb: **$50**	Social Drinking: **Permitted**
Single/pb: **$40**	

The Mayers' comfortable ranch-style brick home is on a residential street bordered by tall pines and palm trees. There is a view of the Catalina Mountains from the porch. Local attractions are the Saguaro National Monument, the Arizona Sonora Desert Museum, Kitt Peak National Observatory, and Sabino Canyon. You are welcome to use the bicycles, barbecue, and TV, or to just relax on the patio. Several fine restaurants and a recreation complex with Olympic-size swimming pool are nearby.

The Johnstonian B&B ✪
321 WEST SHERIDAN AVENUE, WILLIAMS, ARIZONA 86046

Tel: **(520) 635-2178**	Double/sb: **$55–$60**
Best Time to Call: **Anytime**	Single/sb: **$50–$55**
Hosts: **Bill and Pidge Johnston**	Suites: **$115**
Location: **55 mi. S. of Grand Canyon National Park**	Open: **All year**
	Breakfast: **Full**
No. of Rooms: **4**	Pets: **No**
Max. No. Sharing Bath: **4**	Children: **Welcome**
Double/pb: **$70**	Smoking: **No**
Single/pb: **$65**	Social Drinking: **Permitted**

As old as the century, this two-story Victorian has been carefully restored and decorated in period style. You'll admire the antique oak furniture and the lovely floral wallpapers. In the winter, guests cluster around the wood-burning stove. Pidge's breakfast specialties include Ukrainian potato cakes, blueberry pancakes, and homemade breads.

ARKANSAS

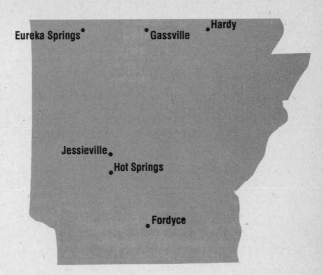

Eureka Springs •   • Gassville   • Hardy

Jessieville •
   • Hot Springs

• Fordyce

Crescent Cottage Inn
211 SPRING STREET, EUREKA SPRINGS, ARKANSAS 72632
raphael@ipa.net

Tel: **(501) 253-6022; fax: (501) 253-6234**
Best Time to Call: **10 AM–8 PM**
Hosts: **Ralph and Phyllis Becker**
Location: **On Rte. 62B, Historic Loop**
No. of Rooms: **4**
No. of Private Baths: **4**
Double/pb: **$95–$130**

Open: **All year**
Breakfast: **Full**
Credit Cards: **DISC, MC, VISA**
Pets: **No**
Children: **Welcome, under 1, over 13**
Smoking: **No**
Social Drinking: **Permitted**

Crescent Cottage Inn, built in 1881 for Arkansas' first post–Civil War governor, is listed on the National Register of Historic Places. This celebrated B&B has wonderful views of the mountains. All guest rooms are furnished with antiques and have double Jacuzzi spas; two have fireplaces. Ralph and Phyllis serve a full breakfast each morning. Then you'll be ready for the short walk to historic downtown Eureka Springs on a route that leads past lovely springs, shade trees, and a trolley stop.

Harvest House ✪
104 WALL STREET, EUREKA SPRINGS, ARKANSAS 72632

Tel: (501) 253-9363; (800) 293-5665
Best Time to Call: 9 AM–9 PM
Hosts: Bill and Patt Carmichael
No. of Rooms: 4
No. of Private Baths: 4
Double/pb: $79–$119
Open: All year

Breakfast: Full
Credit Cards: DISC, MC, VISA
Pets: Sometimes
Children: Welcome, over 12
Smoking: No
Social Drinking: Permitted

Located in the historic district of Eureka Springs, Harvest House is a step off the beaten path, yet close to the bustle of downtown. This turn-of-the-century Victorian house is filled with antiques, collectibles, and family favorites. All guest rooms have private entrances. Breakfast is served in the dining room or, weather permitting, in the screened-in gazebo overlooking pine and oak trees. Bill is a native Arkansan and knows all the hidden treasures of the area. Patt is a shopper with a particular interest in antiques and the local attractions.

Singleton House Bed and Breakfast ✪
11 SINGLETON, EUREKA SPRINGS, ARKANSAS 72632

Tel: (501) 253-9111; (800) 833-3394
Host: Barbara Gavron
No. of Rooms: 5
No. of Private Baths: 5
Double/pb: $65–$80
Single/pb: $55–$65
Suites: $75–$95
Open: All year

Reduced Rates: After 3rd night
Breakfast: Full
Credit Cards: AMEX, DISC, MC, VISA
Pets: No
Children: Welcome
Smoking: No
Social Drinking: Permitted

You'll find a hidden garden, winding stone paths, and more than fifty birdhouses at this "old-fashioned place with a touch of magic." This historic district Victorian inn with its light and airy rooms is whimsically decorated with antiques, folk art, and eclectic treasures. Breakfast is served on a balcony that overlooks the fantasy wildflower garden and lily-filled goldfish pond. After breakfast take a one-block scenic walk or ride the old-time trolley to Eureka's shops and galleries.

Wynne Phillips House ✪
412 WEST FOURTH STREET, FORDYCE, ARKANSAS 71742

Tel: (501) 352-7202
Best Time to Call: Morning

Hosts: Colonel and Mrs. James H. Phillips

Location: **60 mi. S of Little Rock**
No. of Rooms: **4**
No. of Private Baths: **4**
Double/pb: **$55**
Open: **All year**
Breakfast: **Full**

Credit Cards: **MC, VISA**
Pets: **No**
Children: **Yes**
Smoking: **No**
Social Drinking: **Permitted**

A gracious Colonial Revival mansion listed on the National Register of Historic Places, the Wynne Phillips House is filled with antiques and oriental rugs. Mrs. Phillips grew up here, and the bedrooms are furnished with family heirlooms. This is a place where you can enjoy old-fashioned pleasures, such as singing around the piano, or watching the sunset from the wraparound porch. A swimming pool is on the premises; tennis courts are nearby. The generous, Southern-style breakfasts feature fresh fruit, homemade biscuits, eggs, sausage, and grits.

Lithia Springs Bed & Breakfast Lodge ✪
RT. 1, BOX 77-A, HIGHWAY 126, GASSVILLE, ARKANSAS 72635

Tel: **(501) 435-6100**
Best Time to Call: **After 1 PM**
Hosts: **Paul and Reita Johnson**
No. of Rooms: **5**
No. of Private Baths: **3**
Max. No. Sharing Bath: **4**
Double/pb: **$55–$70**

Double/sb: **$55–$70**
Open: **All year, Dec.–Jan. special reservation only**
Breakfast: **Full**
Pets: **No**
Children: **Welcome, over 7**
Smoking: **No**

This 100-year-old former health lodge has been lovingly restored with an additional gift shop featuring many of the hosts' own fine handcrafts. The rooms are furnished with many antiques and period furniture. Breakfast is served in the dining room or on the large screened front porch. Lithia Springs is on 39 acres of meadows and woods. It is near the White and Buffalo Rivers, famous for fishing and canoeing, and between Bull Shoals and Norfork Lakes. It's 10 minutes from Mountain Home and a scenic drive to Blanchard Spring Caverns and Mountain View Folk Center.

Olde Stonehouse Bed & Breakfast Inn ✪
511 MAIN STREET, HARDY, ARKANSAS 72542

Tel: **(501) 856-2983; (800) 514-2983;**
  fax: **(501) 856-4036**
Best Time to Call: **10 AM–8 PM**
Host: **Peggy Johnson**
No. of Rooms: **7**
No. of Private Baths: **7**
Double/pb: **$65–$69**
Single/pb: **$55–$65**
Suites: **$99**
Open: **All year**

Reduced Rates: **10% Sun.–Thur.**
Breakfast: **Full**
Credit Cards: **AMEX, DISC, MC, VISA**
Pets: **No**
Children: **Welcome, over 13**
Smoking: **No**
Social Drinking: **Permitted**
Minimum Stay: **2 nights, holiday**
  weekends and special events
Station Pickup: **Yes**

Recapture the romance of times past at the Olde Stonehouse. Unwind in lovely air-conditioned rooms decorated with period antiques, quilts, and old lace, plus a ceiling fan and queen-size bed. Curl up in the large rocking chairs on the front porch or take a walk to Old Hardy Town's antique and crafts shops. Stroll along the river or join other guests for conversation and games. Awaken to the aroma of freshly brewed coffee and bread baking. After breakfast, canoeing, golfing, shopping, and horseback riding are among the many activities to choose from. The Inn is listed on the National Register of Historic Places.

Stillmeadow Farm ✪
111 STILLMEADOW LANE, HOT SPRINGS, ARKANSAS 71913

Tel: **(501) 525-9994**
Hosts: **Gene and Jody Sparling**
Location: **4 mi. S of Hot Springs**
No. of Rooms: **4**
No. of Private Baths: **2**
Max. No. Sharing Bath: **4**
Double/pb: **$65**
Single/pb: **$55**

Suites: **$90**
Open: **All year**
Breakfast: **Full**
Pets: **No**
Children: **Welcome, over 12**
Smoking: **No**
Social Drinking: **Permitted**

Stillmeadow Farm is a reproduction of an 18th-century New England saltbox, set in 75 acres of pine forest with walking trails and an herb garden. The decor is of early country antiques. Your hosts provide homemade snacks and fruit in the guest rooms. For breakfast, freshly baked pastries and breads are served. Hot Springs National Park, Lake Hamilton, the Mid-America Museum, and a racetrack are nearby.

Vintage Comfort B&B Inn ✪
303 QUAPAW AVENUE, HOT SPRINGS, ARKANSAS 71901

Tel: **(501) 623-3258; (800) 608-4682**
Host: **Helen Bartlett**
No. of Rooms: **4**

No. of Private Baths: **4**
Double/pb: **$65–$90**
Single/pb: **$55–$75**

Open: **All year**	Children: **Welcome, over 6**
Breakfast: **Full**	Smoking: **No**
Credit Cards: **AMEX, MC, VISA**	Social Drinking: **Permitted**
Pets: **No**	Airport/Station Pickup: **Yes**

This handsome turn-of-the-century Queen Anne–style home has been faithfully restored, attractively appointed, and air-conditioned. The theme here is comfort and Southern hospitality. Breakfast treats include biscuits and sausage gravy, grits, and regional hot breads. Afterwards, enjoy a short stroll to the famed Bath House Row or a brisk walk to the park, where miles of hiking trails will keep you in shape. Helen will be happy to direct you to the studios and shops of local artists and craftspeople. You are welcome to relax in the old-world sitting room and parlor or on the lovely veranda shaded by magnolia trees.

Mountain Thyme Bed & Breakfast Inn
10860 SCENIC BYWAY 7 NORTH, JESSIEVILLE, ARKANSAS 71949

Tel: **(501) 984-5428**	Reduced Rates: **$10 less after 3rd night**
Best Time to Call: **10 AM–10 PM**	Breakfast: **Full**
Hosts: **Rhonda and Michael Hicks**	Credit Cards: **MC, VISA**
No. of Rooms: **8**	Pets: **No**
No. of Private Baths: **8**	Children: **Welcome, over 10**
Double/pb: **$80–$120**	Smoking: **No**
Open: **All year**	Social Drinking: **Permitted**

Mountain Thyme Bed & Breakfast Inn was built from the ground up by innkeepers who are B&B travelers. They know from experience what makes a comfortable and luxurious inn; great beds, expensive linens, ample light, individual temperature control, fireplaces, whirlpool tubs, and varied, delicious breakfasts served in the dining room. Mountain Thyme Bed & Breakfast Inn is the perfect spot for a romantic weekend or an extended stay in the Hot Springs area. Rhonda and Michael welcome you to their little bit of heaven, and look forward to helping you plan the vacation of your dreams.

CALIFORNIA

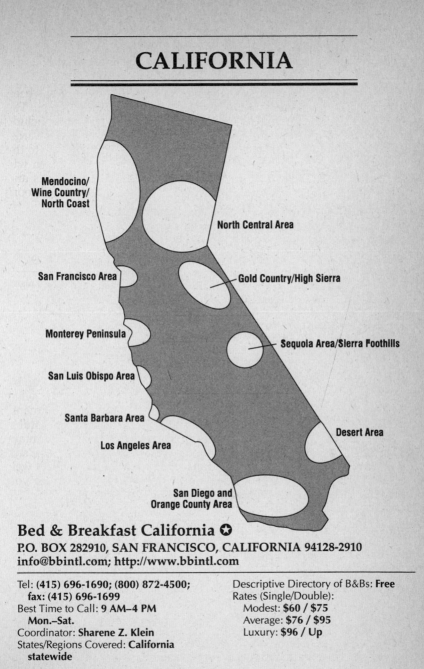

Mendocino/
Wine Country/
North Coast

North Central Area

San Francisco Area

Gold Country/High Sierra

Monterey Peninsula

San Luis Obispo Area

Sequoia Area/Sierra Foothills

Santa Barbara Area

Desert Area

Los Angeles Area

San Diego and
Orange County Area

Bed & Breakfast California ✪
P.O. BOX 282910, SAN FRANCISCO, CALIFORNIA 94128-2910
info@bbintl.com; http://www.bbintl.com

Tel: **(415) 696-1690; (800) 872-4500;**
 fax: (415) 696-1699
Best Time to Call: **9 AM–4 PM**
 Mon.–Sat.
Coordinator: **Sharene Z. Klein**
States/Regions Covered: **California**
 statewide

Descriptive Directory of B&Bs: **Free**
Rates (Single/Double):
 Modest: **$60 / $75**
 Average: **$76 / $95**
 Luxury: **$96 / Up**

Bed & Breakfast California, one of the oldest services in the U.S., represents over 300 B&Bs, private homes, inns, separate units, and long-term stays throughout California, with emphasis on San Francisco, Berkeley, the wine country, and Los Angeles. The website for this service is one of the very few that actually has real-time, up-to-date availability checks, not just inquiries. This function is ideal for international travelers or any guest who wants instant information because it eliminates the need to fax, e-mail, leave messages on voice mail, or send written requests asking about availability. Karen is also the president of The National Network. You can reach this network at (888) TNN-4BNB [866-4262], or http://www.tnn4bnb.com.

Eye Openers Bed & Breakfast Reservations ✪
P.O. BOX 694, ALTADENA, CALIFORNIA 91001
eobb@loop.com

Tel: **(818) 398-0529**	Descriptive Directory: **$2**
Best Time to Call: **9 AM–5 PM Mon.–Fri.**	Rates (Single/Double):
Coordinator: **Mary Gardner**	Modest: **$40–$50 / $40–$60**
States/Regions Covered: **Cambria,**	Average: **$50–$85 / $55–$95**
Laguna Beach, Los Angeles, Napa	Luxury: **$85–$175 / $95–$250**
Valley, Palm Springs, Pasadena, San	Credit Cards: **MC, VISA**
Diego, San Francisco, Santa Barbara,	
Santa Monica, Yosemite	

Eye Openers Bed & Breakfast Reservations offers a wide variety of accommodations in beautiful homes and inns with warm friendly hosts. Its staff pride themselves on personal attention to your comforts in reserving the bed and breakfast closest to your request.

DESERT AREA

Travellers Repose ✪
P.O. BOX 655, 66920 FIRST STREET, DESERT HOT SPRINGS, CALIFORNIA 92240

Tel: **(619) 329-9584**	Reduced Rates: **Weekly; 10% families**
Host: **Marian Relkoff**	**on 2nd room**
Location: **12 mi. N of Palm Springs**	Breakfast: **Continental**
No. of Rooms: **3**	Pets: **No**
No. of Private Baths: **3**	Children: **Welcome, over 12**
Double/pb: **$65–$85**	Smoking: **No**
Single/pb: **$59–$77**	Social Drinking: **Permitted**
Open: **Sept. 1–June 30**	

Bay windows, gingerbread trim, stained glass windows, and a white picket fence decorate this charming Victorian home. The warm look of oak predominates in floors, wainscoting, and cabinetry. Guest rooms are decorated with hearts, dolls, and teddy bears everywhere. There's a rose bedroom with antiques and lace, a blue-and-white room with a heart motif, and a green room decorated with pine furniture handcrafted by Sam Relkoff. A patio and spa complete the amenities. Golf, tennis, museums, galleries, and posh Palm Springs are nearby. Marian graciously serves tea at 4 PM.

Hotel Nipton ✪
72 NIPTON ROAD, NIPTON, CALIFORNIA 92364

Tel: **(760) 856-2335**
Best Time to Call: **8 AM–6 PM**
Hosts: **Jerry and Roxanne Freeman**
Location: **10 mi. from I-15**
No. of Rooms: **4**
Max. No. Sharing Bath: **4**
Double/sb: **$55**
Open: **All year**
Reduced Rates: **Group**

Breakfast: **Continental**
Other Meals: **Available**
Credit Cards: **DISC, MC, VISA**
Pets: **No**
Children: **Welcome**
Smoking: **No**
Social Drinking: **Permitted**
Foreign Languages: **Spanish**

The population of Nipton is 30! The recently restored hotel, with its foot-thick adobe walls, was built in 1904 and is located in the Mojave National Preserve. Nipton is in the heart of gold-mining territory, 30 minutes from Lake Mojave's Cottonwood Cove. You are welcome to relax on the porch or in the outdoor Jacuzzi. Continental breakfast is served in the lobby at your convenience.

GOLD COUNTRY/HIGH SIERRA

Silver Spur Bed & Breakfast ✪
44625 SILVER SPUR TRAIL, AHWAHNEE, CALIFORNIA 93601

Tel: **(209) 683-2896**
Best Time to Call: **After 3 PM**
Hosts: **Patty and Bryan Hays**
Location: **50 mi. N of Fresno**
No. of Rooms: **2**
No. of Private Baths: **2**
Double/pb: **$50–$60**
Open: **All year**

Reduced Rates: **Nov. 1–May 1**
  Sun.–Thurs. $45, Fri.–Sat. $55
Breakfast: **Continental**
Credit Cards: **DISC, MC, VISA**
Pets: **Sometimes**
Children: **Welcome**
Smoking: **No**
Social Drinking: **Permitted**

Silver Spur Bed & Breakfast is nestled in the Sierra Nevadas, just off historic Highway 49—key to the California Gold Country near the south and west gates of Yosemite National Park and minutes from many outdoor sports. This contemporary log home was built by Bryan and features beautiful clean rooms with private entrances, comfortable beds, and tasteful Southwestern decor. Outdoor resting and dining areas boast outstanding Sierra views. A healthy Continental breakfast is served daily. Patty is a part-time paralegal and gardening enthusiast and Bryan is a builder. Come enjoy Yosemite, and be treated to old-fashioned hospitality.

Tin Roof Bed & Breakfast ✪
24741 FORESTHILL ROAD, FORESTHILL, CALIFORNIA 95631

Tel: **(916) 367-4466**
Hosts: **Clyde and Judith Larrew**
No. of Rooms: **3**
No. of Private Baths: **1**
Max. No. Sharing Bath: **4**
Double/pb: **$85**
Double/sb: **$85**
Open: **All year**

Reduced Rates: **Available**
Breakfast: **Full**
Credit Cards: **AMEX, MC, VISA**
Pets: **Sometimes**
Children: **By arrangement**
Smoking: **No**
Social Drinking: **Permitted**
Airport/Station Pickup: **Yes**

Visit the Tin Roof Bed & Breakfast and experience the mountain air and friendly people. Enjoy white-water rafting, fishing at a nearby mountain lake, hiking, gold-panning tours with Clyde, or relax in the oak rocking chairs on the porch. Winter sports include snowmobiling, cross-country skiing, snowshoeing, and snowplay at the China Wall Recreation Area. The house was built in 1875 and the charm of days gone by is still evident from the tin roof, wraparound porch, and creaky stairs. Inside, you'll find a wood stove in the kitchen, knotty pine walls, antique furniture, and interesting memorabilia throughout.

The Heirloom ☉
P.O. BOX 322, 214 SHAKLEY LANE, IONE, CALIFORNIA 95640

Tel: **(209) 274-4468**
Hosts: **Melisande Hubbs and Patricia Cross**
Location: **35 mi. E of Sacramento**
No. of Rooms: **6**
No. of Private Baths: **4**
Max. No. Sharing Bath: **2**
Double/pb: **$75–$92**
Single/pb: **$65–$82**
Double/sb: **$60–$75**

Single/sb: **$55–$70**
Open: **All year**
Reduced Rates: **Weekly**
Breakfast: **Full**
Credit Cards: **AMEX, MC, VISA**
Pets: **No**
Children: **Welcome, over 10**
Smoking: **No**
Social Drinking: **Permitted**
Airport/Station Pickup: **Yes**

Nestled in the Sierra foothills, yet close to the historic gold mines, wineries, antique shops, and museums, this 1863 mansion, with its lovely balconies and fireplaces, is a classic example of antebellum architecture. It is furnished with a combination of family treasures and period pieces. Patricia and Melisande's hearty breakfast includes such delights as quiche, crepes, soufflé, and fresh fruits. Afternoon refreshments are always offered.

LOS ANGELES AREA

El Camino Real Bed & Breakfast ☉
P.O. BOX 5598, SHERMAN OAKS, CALIFORNIA 91403-5598

Tel: **(818) 787-6862**
Best Time to Call: **Evenings**
Coordinator: **Lisa Reinstein**
States/Regions Covered: **Beverly Hills, Burbank, Hollywood, Malibu, San Diego, San Fernando Valley; Studio City; Sun Valley, ID; Zion, UT**

Rates (Single/Double):
    Average: **$60–$100 / $55–$75**
    Luxury: **$60 / $115**
Credit Cards: **No**
Minimum Stay: **2 nights**

This service brings the tradition of California hospitality begun with the Franciscan missions to the present-day traveler. Homes are in beach communities conveniently located to such attractions as Disneyland, Knotts Berry Farm, and the movie studios. Average accommodations are in upper-middle-class homes with swimming pools/spas, except in hilly areas. Lisa offers modest apartments with simple furnishings and a luxurious private guesthouse on an estate with a hot tub and swimming pool. All hosts are longtime residents of California, familiar with the restaurants, tourist attractions, and the best ways of getting to them.

Marina Bed & Breakfast ☉
753 OXFORD AVENUE, MARINA DEL REY, CALIFORNIA 90292

Tel: **(310) 821-9862**
Best Time to Call: **5 PM–10 PM**
Hosts: **Peter and Carolyn Griswold**

Location: **15 min. N of Los Angeles International Airport**
No. of Rooms: **1**

No. of Private Baths: **1**
Suite: **$50–$80**
Open: **All year**
Reduced Rates: **Weekly**
Breakfast: **Continental**

Pets: **No**
Children: **Welcome, over 12**
Smoking: **No**
Social Drinking: **Permitted**
Minimum Stay: **2 nights**

Peter and Carolyn's two-story house has a spacious studio with a separate entrance, full kitchen, color TV, and queen-size bed. Have a leisurely breakfast in your room or on the large rooftop yard, then stroll across the street to admire the thousands of boats and yachts moored in the marina. Nearby, Fisherman's Village offers fine dining, shopping, and harbor cruises. Or you can borrow your hosts' bicycles and strike out for the bike path that runs from Malibu Beach in the north all the way down to San Pedro Harbor some 35 miles away.

Hideaway House ✪
8441 MELVIN AVENUE, NORTHRIDGE, CALIFORNIA 91324

Tel: **(818) 349-5421**
Best Time to Call: **6–10 PM**
Hosts: **Dean and Dorothy Dennis**
Location: **20 mi. NW of Los Angeles**
No. of Rooms: **1**
No. of Private Baths: **1**
Double/pb: **$55–$60**

Open: **All year**
Breakfast: **Full**
Pets: **Sometimes**
Children: **No**
Smoking: **No**
Social Drinking: **Permitted**
Airport/Station Pickup: **Yes**

Located in a beautiful Los Angeles suburb, this country ranch home on over an acre in the San Fernando Valley is a good base for exploring southern California. It's 30 minutes to the beach, and 50 minutes to Disneyland. Freeways, shops, and restaurants are nearby. Dean and Dorothy welcome you to their art- and antique-filled home, and will provide local guide service by prior arrangement.

The Whites' House ✪
17122 FAYSMITH AVENUE, TORRANCE, CALIFORNIA 90504

Tel: **(310) 324-6164**
Host: **Margaret White**
Location: **5 mi. S of Los Angeles Intl.
Airport**
No. of Rooms: **2**
No. of Private Baths: **2**
Double/pb: **$30–$35**
Single/pb: **$25**

Open: **All year**
Reduced Rates: **Weekly, monthly**
Breakfast: **Continental**
Pets: **No**
Children: **No**
Smoking: **No**
Social Drinking: **Permitted**

This contemporary home, with its fireplaces, deck, and patio, is located on a quiet street in an unpretentious neighborhood. The airport and lovely beaches are 15 minutes away. Disneyland, Knotts Berry Farm, Universal Studio Tours, and Hollywood are 30 minutes from the door.

Use the laundry facilities or kitchen; Margaret wants you to feel perfectly at home.

MENDOCINO/WINE COUNTRY/NORTH COAST

Hillcrest B&B ✪
3225 LAKE COUNTY HIGHWAY, CALISTOGA, CALIFORNIA 94515

Tel: **(707) 942-6334**
Best Time to Call: **After 8 PM**
Host: **Debbie O'Gorman**
Location: **2 mi. N of Calistoga**
No. of Rooms: **6**
No. of Private Baths: **4**
Max. No. Sharing Bath: **4**
Double/pb: **$60–$90**

Double/sb: **$45–$70**
Open: **All year**
Breakfast: **Continental**
Pets: **Welcome**
Children: **No**
Smoking: **Permitted**
Social Drinking: **Permitted**

Hillcrest has a breathtaking valley view of Mt. St. Helena, in an area famed for its wineries and spas. Without leaving the B&B's 36-acre property, guests can hike, swim, use the outdoor spa, fish, or stay indoors and play the Steinway grand piano and enjoy the cherished family heirlooms at every turn. The original house was built by Debbie's great-great-grandfather and burned to the ground in 1964. An elegant Continental breakfast of juice, coffee, fresh fruit, and baked goods is served on antique china and silver. For those of you who do not mind paying a higher rate, 6 rooms are available.

Sterling House ✪
1604 HARLEY STREET, CALISTOGA, CALIFORNIA 94515

Tel: **(707) 942-8402**
Host: **Jewell Sterling**
Location: **75 mi. N of San Francisco**
No. of Rooms: **1**
No. of Private Baths: **1**
Double/pb: **$85**
Single/pb: **$85**

Open: **All year**
Breakfast: **Full**
Pets: **No**
Children: **No**
Smoking: **No**
Social Drinking: **Permitted**
Minimum Stay: **2 nights**

Calistoga is known worldwide for its spas, mineral waters, award-winning restaurants, delightful shopping, and, of course, its wineries. Sterling House, located in a quiet residential neighborhood, is surrounded by flowers and trees. A fountain graces a spacious private terrace and welcomes guests to enjoy the tranquil outdoors. The guest room is furnished with antiques, wicker, a ceiling fan, and a New Orleans–style king-size bed. The house has central heat and air-conditioning. Jewell caters to special diets and preferences, such as vegetarian and health foods. Specialties may include pineapple pancakes, glorious granola, whole-grain breads, and muffins. Nearby activities include hiking, biking, golf, tennis, gliding, and hot-air ballooning. There is a $10 surcharge for one-night stays.

Muktip Manor ✪

12540 LAKESHORE DRIVE, CLEARLAKE, CALIFORNIA 95422

Tel: **(707) 994-9571**
Hosts: **Jerry and Nadine Schiffman**
Location: **101 mi. N of San Francisco**
No. of Rooms: **1 suite**
No. of Private Baths: **1**
Suite: **$65**

Open: **All year**
Breakfast: **Full**
Pets: **Welcome**
Children: **Sometimes**
Smoking: **Permitted**
Social Drinking: **Permitted**

Nadine and Jerry traded the often-frenzied San Francisco lifestyle for an uncomplicated existence by the largest lake in the state. They do not offer Victoriana, priceless antiques, or gourmet food. They do provide comfortable accommodations in an unpretentious beach house, a place to relax on the deck, and the use of their private beach and bicycles. They enjoy windsurfing and canoeing, and have been known to give instruction to interested guests. The motto of Muktip Manor is, "If you wish company, we are conversationalists; if you wish privacy, we're invisible."

Inn Oz ✪

13311 LAKESHORE DRIVE, P.O. BOX 1046, CLEARLAKE PARK, CALIFORNIA 95424

Tel: **(707) 995-0853**
Best Time to Call: **Between 8 AM and 6 PM PST**
Hosts: **Pauline and Charley Stephanski**
Location: **100 mi. N of San Francisco**
No. of Rooms: **1**
No. of Private Baths: **1**
Double/pb: **$60**

Open: **All year**
Reduced Rates: **10% seniors**
Breakfast: **Full, Continental**
Pets: **Yes**
Children: **Welcome**
Smoking: **Permitted**
Social Drinking: **Permitted**

On the shores of California's largest freshwater lake, two hours north of San Francisco by automobile (and faster by house in a cyclone), you'll find country so beautiful it could have inspired L. Frank Baum's tales of the land of Oz. Savor unsurpassed sunsets, full moons, and starry heavens over Clear Lake from your bed or on your private patio. Your spacious chamber has a private entrance, a wood-burning fireplace, and a fully equipped kitchenette; the bathroom has a shower and a tub with a portable whirlpool. Pianists are encouraged to tickle the ivories of the upright Steinway. For additional fun, ask your hosts to show you the doll's house Pauline's grandfather built in 1938.

Campbell Ranch Inn

1475 CANYON ROAD, GEYSERVILLE, CALIFORNIA 95441
http://www.campbellranchinn.com

Tel: **(707) 857-3476; (800) 959-3878;**
  fax: **(707) 857-3239**
Best Time to Call: **8 AM–8 PM**
Hosts: **Mary Jane and Jerry Campbell**
Location: **1.6 mi. from Rte. 101, Canyon
  Road exit**
No. of Rooms: **5**
No. of Private Baths: **5**
Double/pb: **$100–$145**
Guest Cottage: **$165**

Open: **All year**
Breakfast: **Full**
Credit Cards: **AMEX, MC, VISA**
Pets: **No**
Children: **Welcome, over 10**
Smoking: **No**
Social Drinking: **Permitted**
Minimum Stay: **2 nights weekends**
Airport/Station Pickup: **Yes**

"Spectacular!" and "Charming!" are expressions most often used when guests describe their stay at this picture-perfect hilltop home surrounded by 35 acres in the heart of the Sonoma County wine country. The spacious bedrooms, each with a king-size bed, are handsomely furnished; several have balconies where views of mountains and vineyards are a backdrop to the colorful flower gardens. Breakfast, beautifully served, features a selection of fresh fruit, choice of gourmet egg dishes, homemade breads and cakes, and a variety of beverages. You can burn off the calories on the Campbells' tennis court or in their swimming pool, or borrow a bike to tour the wineries. Water sports and fishing are less than four miles away. Jerry will be happy to make your dinner reservations at one of the area's fine restaurants, but leave room for Mary Jane's dessert, always served "at home."

Hilltop House B&B ✪

9550 ST. HELENA ROAD, ST. HELENA, CALIFORNIA 94574

Tel: **(707) 944-0880**
Hosts: **Annette and Bill Gevarter**
Location: **5 mi. from Rte. 29**
No. of Rooms: **3**
No. of Private Baths: **3**
Double/pb: **$105–$175**
Open: **All year**
Reduced Rates: **10% Jan. 1–Apr. 15**

Breakfast: **Full**
Credit Cards: **AMEX, MC, VISA**
Pets: **No**
Children: **Welcome**
Smoking: **No**
Social Drinking: **Permitted**
Minimum Stay: **2 nights weekends, Apr.
  15–Nov. 30**

Annette and Bill built their contemporary country retreat to follow the contours of the Mayacama Mountains. The house is surrounded by 135 acres at the top of the ridge separating the wine regions of Napa and Sonoma. The unspoiled wilderness includes a garden of native plants, shrubs, and the sounds of hummingbirds and other wildlife. A 2000-square-foot deck with hot tub provides the perfect spot for enjoying the panoramic views. The airy guest rooms are comfortably decorated with a combination of antiques and contemporary pieces, and each has spectacular views and a private entrance onto the deck. Your hosts serve a generous breakfast of fresh fruit, eggs, cheese, and yogurt, with fresh-baked breads and muffins. They also welcome you for afternoon snacks and a glass of sherry in the evening. Hilltop House is 12 minutes from St. Helena, and 30 minutes from Napa. The historic town of Calistoga, popular for its restorative hot mineral water, mud baths, massages, and fine restaurants, is located nearby.

MONTEREY PENINSULA

Happy Landing Inn ✪
P.O. BOX 2619, CARMEL, CALIFORNIA 93921

Tel: **(408) 624-7917**
Best Time to Call: **8:30 AM–9 PM**
Hosts: **Robert Ballard and Dick Stewart**
Location: **120 mi. S of San Francisco**
No. of Rooms: **7**
No. of Private Baths: **7**
Double/pb: **$90–$155**
Open: **All year**
Breakfast: **Continental**

Credit Cards: **MC, VISA**
Pets: **No**
Children: **Welcome, over 12**
Smoking: **No**
Social Drinking: **Permitted**
Minimum Stay: **2 nights weekends**
Foreign Languages: **Japanese, Portuguese, Spanish**

Located on Monte Verde between 5th and 6th Streets, this Hansel and Gretel–style Inn is a charming and romantic place to stay. Rooms with cathedral ceilings open onto a beautiful garden with gazebo, pond, and flagstone paths. Lovely antiques and personal touches, including breakfast served in your room, make your stay special.

Inn Laguna Creek ✪
2727 SMITH GRADE, SANTA CRUZ, CALIFORNIA 95060
inncreek@aol.com

Tel: **(408) 425-0692; (800) 730-5398;** fax: **(408) 426-9331**
Best Time to Call: **9 AM–8 PM**
Hosts: **Jim and Gay Holley**
Location: **8 mi. N of Santa Cruz**
No. of Rooms: **3**
Double/pb: **$95–$125**
Suite: **$155**

Open: **All year**
Breakfast: **Full**
Credit Cards: **AMEX, MC, VISA**
Pets: **No**
Children: **Welcome**
Smoking: **No**
Social Drinking: **Permitted**

A distinctive modern residence with a curved roof, this B&B nestles in the redwood forests of the Santa Cruz Mountains. The large rooms have queen-size beds, down comforters, a private deck overlooking the creek, and a private entrance. The sitting room boasts a wet bar, stereo, VCR, and games. A sunning deck with a spa, picnic area, and acres of gardens are yours to enjoy. There are lots of things to do, from hiking, biking, surfing, and beachcombing to whale watching, wine tasting, and antiquing. Sightseers will want to add Roaring Camp and Big Trees Railroad, Mystery Spot, Redwood State Parks, Lighthouse Point, and Mission Santa Cruz to their itineraries. A country-style breakfast is served with special attention to dietary restrictions. Herbal tea, cookies, fresh fruit, and popcorn are always available. A vegetarian breakfast is available with advance notice.

Redwood Croft ✪
275 NORTHWEST DRIVE, BONNY DOON, SANTA CRUZ, CALIFORNIA 95060

Tel: **(408) 458-1939**	Reduced Rates: **Available**
Best Time to Call: **8 AM–8 PM PST**	Breakfast: **Full**
Hosts: **Sitah, Dale, and Zoë Cummings**	Other Meals: **Available**
Location: **9 mi. N of Santa Cruz**	Pets: **Sometimes**
No. of Rooms: **2**	Children: **Welcome**
No. of Private Baths: **2**	Smoking: **No**
Double/pb: **$85–$125**	Social Drinking: **Permitted**
Open: **All year**	Foreign Languages: **Spanish, French**

The sentiment at Redwood Croft is quality for guests; no shortcuts are taken in the kitchen or amenities. Guest rooms are designed with an artist's eye and a grandmother's heart, complete with snuggly goose down, line-dried linen, fireplaces, and large tubs. The Garden Room has its own entrance, private deck, and a seven-foot spa under the country stars. The West Room has a king-size bed and a large tiled bathroom with a Roman tub and bidet. Breakfasts are lavish, with the freshest Croft ingredients. Special dietary needs can be accommodated. Afternoon tea is a cherished tradition. The guidebooks bring you to Santa Cruz; Redwood Croft's hospitality brings you back.

Redwood Reflections ✪
4600 SMITH GRADE, SANTA CRUZ, CALIFORNIA 95060

Tel: **(408) 423-7221**	Open: **All year**
Best Time to Call: **8–9 AM; 3–8 PM**	Reduced Rates: **Available**
Hosts: **Ed and Dory Strong**	Breakfast: **Full**
Location: **70 mi. S of San Francisco**	Credit Cards: **MC, VISA**
No. of Rooms: **3**	Pets: **No**
No. of Private Baths: **3**	Children: **Welcome**
Double/pb: **$80–$90**	Smoking: **No**
Suite: **$100**	Social Drinking: **Permitted**

Nestled in the Santa Cruz Mountains, Redwood Reflections offers ten unspoiled acres of giant redwoods and trails. The rambling, rustic home is paneled throughout, with lots of windows, and furnished in country antiques. Each secluded room provides a sitting area, private bath, TV, queen-size bed, down comforters, and a romantic fountain and fireplace. Guests may enjoy the spa and fulfill childhood fantasies concocting delicious treats from the antique soda fountain. Things to do include hiking, wine tasting, and exploring nearby beaches and numerous state parks in the area. A country-style breakfast is prepared on an antique wood stove. Waffles piled high with fresh berries and country hash browns are favorites of guests.

NORTH CENTRAL AREA

The Inn at Shallow Creek Farm ✪
4712 ROAD DD, ORLAND, CALIFORNIA 95963

Tel: **(530) 865-4093; (800) 865-4093**
Best Time to Call: **Evenings**
Hosts: **Mary and Kurt Glaeseman**
Location: **3 mi. from I-5**
No. of Rooms: **4**
No. of Private Baths: **2**
Max. No. Sharing Bath: **4**
Double/pb: **$65**
Double/sb: **$55**
Guest Cottage: **$75; sleeps 2–4**

Open: **All year**
Reduced Rates: **$10 less after 3rd night**
Breakfast: **Continental**
Pets: **No**
Children: **Sometimes**
Smoking: **No**
Social Drinking: **Permitted**
Airport/Station Pickup: **Yes**
Foreign Languages: **French, German, Spanish**

The orchards of Shallow Creek Farm are known for mandarin and navel oranges and sweet grapefruit. Luscious berries, fresh garden produce, and a collection of exotic poultry, including rare silver guinea hens and African geese, are quite extraordinary. The Inn, a gracious turn-of-the-century farmhouse, offers airy, spacious rooms furnished with carefully chosen antiques and family heirlooms, combining nostalgia with country comfort. Breakfast features homemade baked goods and jams, and a generous assortment of fresh fruits or juices and hot beverages.

The Feather Bed ✪
542 JACKSON STREET, QUINCY, CALIFORNIA 95971

Tel: **(530) 283-0102; (800) 696-8624**
Hosts: **Bob and Jan Janowski**
Location: **70 mi. NW of Reno, Nevada**
No. of Rooms: **7**
No. of Private Baths: **7**
Double/pb: **$75**
Single/pb: **$70**
Suite: **$85**
Separate Cottages: **$120**

Open: **All year**
Reduced Rates: **10% less on 3rd night**
Breakfast: **Full**
Credit Cards: **AMEX, DC, MC, VISA**
Pets: **No**
Children: **Welcome**
Smoking: **No**
Social Drinking: **Permitted**
Airport/Station Pickup: **Yes**

This charming Queen Anne was built in 1893. The rooms feature vintage wallpaper, antique furnishings, and charming baths; most have clawfoot tubs. Enjoy a glass of cider in the parlor, or a cool iced tea on the front porch. A full three-course breakfast is served on the patio or in the dining room. The inn is convenient to water sports, snowmobiling, hiking, tennis, and skiing. Your hosts offer complimentary bicycles to help you explore beautiful Plumas National Forest and historic downtown Quincy. Restaurants and the county museum are close by.

Palisades Paradise B&B ✪
1200 PALISADES AVENUE, REDDING, CALIFORNIA 96003

Tel: **(916) 223-5305**	Open: **All year**
Best Time to Call: **10 AM–2 PM**	Reduced Rates: **Available**
Host: **Gail Goetz**	Breakfast: **Continental, plus**
Location: **1¼ mi. from Rte. I-5 exit**	Credit Cards: **AMEX, MC, VISA**
Hilltop Dr.	Pets: **No**
No. of Rooms: **2**	Children: **Welcome, by arrangement**
Max. No. Sharing Bath: **4**	Smoking: **No**
Double/sb: **$65–$85**	Social Drinking: **Permitted**
Single/sb: **$60–$75**	

Enjoy breathtakingly beautiful views from the patio and spa deck of this contemporary riverside home near Shasta College and Simpson College. Stay in either the Cozy Retreat or the Sunset Suite, both aptly named. In the morning, Gail serves ample breakfasts, with gourmet coffee, pastries, and her own Palisades fruit puffs.

Clementine's ✪
200 HANFORD STREET, P.O. BOX 1537, SUTTER CREEK, CALIFORNIA 95685

Tel: **(209) 267-9384**	Breakfast: **Full**
Hosts: **Sharon F. and Kit L. Meitinger**	Other Meals: **Available**
Location: **42 mi. E of Sacramento**	Credit Cards: **AMEX, MC, VISA**
No. of Rooms: **1**	Pets: **Yes**
No. of Private Baths: **1**	Children: **Welcome**
Double/pb: **$75**	Smoking: **No**
Single/pb: **$70**	Social Drinking: **Permitted**
Open: **All year**	Airport/Station Pickup: **Yes**
Reduced Rates: **10% 5 days**	

Clementine's is located near the Gold Country in northern California. This B&B is 1 hour from Kirkwood, a popular skiing area, and 1½ hours from Lake Tahoe. This Mediterranean-style house was built in 1939. The interior is tastefully decorated with stenciling, pictures, antiques, and memorabilia. Guests have their own private entrance and sitting room. The town has many boutiques and antique stores to explore. Amador County's excellent wineries offer tours and private tastings. There are enough restaurants to satisfy many a palate. Other things to see include Daffodill Hill, museums, mine sites, and summer festivals. Sharon and Kit do woodworking and sewing in their spare time; some of their handiwork is for sale.

SAN DIEGO AND ORANGE COUNTY AREA

Bed & Breakfast Southwest Reservation Service—Southern California ✪
2916 NORTH 70TH STREET, SCOTTSDALE, ARIZONA 85251
b&bsw@juno.com

Tel: **(602) 945-9704; (800) 762-9704;** fax: **(602) 874-1316**	Descriptive Directory: **Free**
Best Time to Call: **8 AM–8 PM**	Rates (Single/Double):
Coordinators: **Jo Cummings and Joan Petersen**	Modest: **$40–$75**
States/Regions Covered: **Arizona, New Mexico, Southern California, Southern Colorado**	Average: **$80–$100**
	Luxury: **$105–up**

This service offers travelers unique homestays in suites, guesthouses, ranches, and inns. All host facilities are personally inspected and provide the three C's of bed and breakfasts: cleanliness, cordiality, and convenience. Jo and Joan's specialty is finding the perfect B&B for you. They can plan your trip to include many of the historical and natural wonders of the great Southwest, such as the San Diego Zoo, Durango Historic Railroad, Scottsdale golf courses, Sedona's Red Rock formations, and the Santa Fe opera. You will be awed by the spectacular scenic beauty and legendary Western hospitality.

Coronado Village Inn ✪
1017 PARK PLACE, CORONADO, CALIFORNIA 92118

Tel: **(619) 435-9318; (619) 435-9934**	Reduced Rates: **Winter $50–$70; 7th night free**
Best Time to Call: **8 AM–10 PM PCT**	
Hosts: **Tony and Leanne DiFulvio**	Breakfast: **Continental**
No. of Rooms: **15**	Credit Cards: **AMEX, MC, VISA**
No. of Private Baths: **15**	Pets: **No**
Double/pb: **$70–$80**	Children: **Welcome**
Single/pb: **$60–$70**	Smoking: **Permitted**
Open: **All year**	Social Drinking: **Permitted**

This quiet, European-style bed and breakfast is located one-half block off Coronado's main street, Orange Avenue, and one block from the Pacific Ocean. Each room is decorated in a different decor, some with canopy beds and step-up stools, and some with small Jacuzzi tubs. This charming, quaint Inn is perfect for honeymoons, anniversaries, retreats, or that special getaway vacation. Come join Leanne and Tony for a memorable step-back-in-time stay.

The Blue Door ✪
13707 DURANGO DRIVE, DEL MAR, CALIFORNIA 92014

Tel: **(619) 755-3819**
Best Time to Call: **Anytime**
Hosts: **Bob and Anna Belle Schock**
Location: **20 mi. N of San Diego**
No. of Rooms: **1 suite**
No. of Private Baths: **1**
Suite: **$60–$70**

Open: **All year**
Breakfast: **Full**
Pets: **No**
Children: **Welcome, over 16**
Smoking: **No**
Social Drinking: **Permitted**

Enjoy New England charm in a quiet southern California setting over-looking exclusive Torrey Pines State Reserve. A garden-level two-room suite with wicker accessories and king or twin beds is yours. The sitting room has a couch, a desk, and a color TV. Breakfast is served in the spacious country kitchen or in the dining room warmed by the fire on chilly days. Anna Belle prides herself on creative breakfast menus featuring homemade baked goods. Breakfast specialties include blueberry muffins, Swedish oatmeal pancakes, and Blue Door orange French toast. Your hosts will gladly direct you to the nearby racetrack, beach, zoo, or University of California at San Diego. There is a $10 surcharge for one-night stays.

At Your Leisure Bed and Breakfast ✪
525 SOUTH THIRD STREET, EL CAJON, CALIFORNIA 92019

Tel: **(619) 444-3124**
Best Time to Call: **Evenings**
Hosts: **Ron and Joan Leasure**
Location: **18 mi. E of San Diego Airport**
No. of Rooms: **2**
Max. No. Sharing Bath: **4**
Double/sb: **$58**
Single/sb: **$55**

Open: **All year**
Reduced Rates: **10% seniors; weekly**
Breakfast: **Continental**
Credit Cards: **MC, VISA**
Pets: **No**
Children: **Welcome**
Smoking: **No**
Social Drinking: **Permitted**

A warm welcome awaits you at this comfortable and historic 1928 home, decorated with antiques and vintage clothing. Guests can enjoy a glass of iced tea or a cup of hot chocolate in the game room, by the swimming pool, or on the front porch or patio. At Your Leisure Bed and Breakfast is located on the bus route, only one mile from the major freeways, and just minutes from the airport and train station. Places of interest include San Diego Zoo, Balboa Park, universities, golf courses, convention centers, stadium, beaches, mountains, deserts, and many sites in between, including fine restaurants and shopping.

Sea Breeze B&B ✪

121 NORTH VULCAN, ENCINITAS, CALIFORNIA 92024
http://www.compuvar.com/internet/seabreeze

Tel: **(760) 944-0318**	Open: **All year**
Host: **Kirsten Richter**	Reduced Rates: **10% weekly; seniors;**
Location: **23 mi. N of San Diego**	**families**
No. of Rooms: **5**	Breakfast: **Continental**
No. of Private Baths: **5**	Pets: **No**
Double/pb: **$75–$150**	Children: **Welcome (playpen)**
Double/sb: **$90**	Smoking: **Permitted**
Suite: **$150**	Social Drinking: **Permitted**

Choose among a separate apartment, three queen bedrooms, and a penthouse with a private spa, whirlpool tub, and shower in this contemporary two-story home filled with custom, one-of-a-kind furnishings. Sunbathe in privacy on the deck overlooking the Pacific, or stroll down to Moonlight Beach for a refreshing ocean dip. It's a short walk to downtown Encinitas, which boasts many fine restaurants. Mt. Palomar Observatory, Sea World, Del Mar Race Track, and the Mexican border are about a half hour away by car. Guests have use of a kitchenette. Continental breakfasts consist of muffins, fresh fruit, yogurt, and coffee, tea, or hot chocolate.

Hidden Village Bed & Breakfast ✪

9582 HALEKULANI DRIVE, GARDEN GROVE, CALIFORNIA 92641

Tel: **(714) 636-8312**	Single/sb: **$40**
Best Time to Call: **8 AM–9 PM**	Suites: **$90**
Hosts: **Dick and Linda O'Berg**	Open: **All year**
Location: **3 mi. S of Anaheim**	Breakfast: **Full**
No. of Rooms: **4**	Pets: **Sometimes**
No. of Private Baths: **2**	Children: **Welcome**
Max. No. Sharing Bath: **2**	Smoking: **No**
Double/pb: **$65**	Social Drinking: **Permitted**
Single/pb: **$50**	Airport/Station Pickup: **Yes**
Double/sb: **$55**	

Linda has decorated this large Colonial home with lacy draperies and handmade quilts; she's a professional weaver, and guests are welcome to browse in her studio. When you're done looking at fabrics, Disneyland, the Anaheim Convention Center, and Orange County's lovely beaches are just minutes away. Couch potatoes can watch tapes on the VCR, while the energetic can borrow the O'Bergs' bicycles and go for a spin. In the mornings, you'll savor a full breakfast of fresh fruit, homemade apple muffins, and quiche or omelettes.

Country Comfort Bed and Breakfast ✪

5104 EAST VALENCIA DRIVE, ORANGE, CALIFORNIA 92669

Tel: **(714) 532-2802, 532-4010**
Best Time to Call: **6–9 PM**
Hosts: **Geri Lopker and Joanne Angell**
Location: **5 mi. E of Anaheim**
No. of Rooms: **2**
No. of Private Baths: **2**
Double/pb: **$65**
Single/pb: **$65**

Open: **All year**
Reduced Rates: **10% less after 5th night**
Breakfast: **Full**
Other Meals: **Available**
Pets: **By arrangement**
Children: **Welcome**
Smoking: **No**
Social Drinking: **Permitted**

Geri and Joanne have furnished their home with your comfort and pleasure in mind. Located in a quiet residential area, it is disabled-accessible with adaptive equipment available. Amenities include a swimming pool, cable TV and VCR, an atrium, fireplace, and the use of Jacuzzi for two. Breakfast often features delicious Scotch eggs, stuffed French toast and hash, along with fruits and assorted beverages. Vegetarian selections are also available. Disneyland and Knotts Berry Farm are less than seven miles away.

The Cottage ✪

3829 ALBATROSS STREET, SAN DIEGO, CALIFORNIA 92103

Tel: **(619) 299-1564**
Best Time to Call: **9 AM–5 PM**
Hosts: **Robert and Carol Emerick**
Location: **1 mi. from Rte. 5**
No. of Rooms: **2**

No. of Private Baths: **2**
Double/pb: **$59–$80**
Guest Cottage: **$85–$95**
Open: **All year**
Breakfast: **Continental**

Credit Cards: **AMEX, MC, VISA**
Pets: **No**
Children: **Welcome**

Smoking: **No**
Social Drinking: **Permitted**

Located in the Hillcrest section, where canyons and old houses dot the landscape, this private hideaway offers a cottage with a king-size bed, full bath, and fully equipped kitchen. Decorated with turn-of-the-century furniture, the wood-burning stove and oak pump organ evoke memories of long ago. It's two miles to the zoo, less to Balboa Park, and it is within easy walking distance of restaurants, shops, and theater. The University of California and the University of San Diego are nearby.

Villa Serena Bed & Breakfast ☉
2164 ROSECRANS STREET, SAN DIEGO, CALIFORNIA 92106

Tel: **(619) 224-1451**
Best Time to Call: **Early AM, after 6 PM**
Hosts: **Alex and Kae Schreiber**
No. of Rooms: **2**
Suites: **$95**
Open: **All year**
Breakfast: **Full**

Pets: **No**
Children: **Welcome**
Smoking: **No**
Social Drinking: **Permitted**
Minimum Stay: **2 nights**
Airport/Station Pickup: **Yes**
Foreign Languages: **Spanish**

Villa Serena is a two-story Mediterranean-style Italian villa with tropical gardens, a large pool with three fountainheads, and a delightfully relaxing spa. Breakfasts are abundant, with fresh fruit compote, muffins or pastries, granola, yogurt, and a main entree. Located in the coastal area of San Diego, this B&B is in close central proximity to most major tourist attractions, beaches, convention sites, and the harbor. The bus runs in front of the house. Kae and Alex delight in sharing their home with you and will be happy to help you with directions, suggestions, reservations, and making a special occasion even more special. They have four outside cats.

SAN FRANCISCO AREA

Bed and Breakfast San Francisco ☉
P.O. BOX 420009, SAN FRANCISCO, CALIFORNIA 94142

Tel: **(415) 479-1913**
Best Time to Call: **9:30 AM–5 PM Mon.–Fri.**
Coordinators: **Susan and Richard Kreibich**
States/Regions Covered: **Carmel, Marin County, Monterey, Napa, San Francisco, Sonoma (wine country)**

Descriptive Directory: **$2**
Rates (Double):
Modest: **$55–$65**
Average: **$75–$95**
Luxury: **$100–$125**
Credit Cards: **AMEX, DC, MC, VISA**
Minimum Stay: **2 nights**

The San Francisco locations are near all of the famous sights, such as Fisherman's Wharf and Chinatown. Many are historic Victorian houses. Some homes offer hot tubs and sundecks; a few are on yachts and houseboats.

Burlingame B&B ✪
1021 BALBOA AVENUE, BURLINGAME, CALIFORNIA 94010

Tel: **(415) 344-5815**
Hosts: **Joe and Elnora Fernandez**
Location: **½ mi. from Rte. 101**
No. of Rooms: **1**
No. of Private Baths: **1**
Double/pb: **$50**
Single/pb: **$40**
Open: **All year**

Breakfast: **Continental**
Pets: **No**
Children: **Welcome**
Smoking: **No**
Social Drinking: **No**
Airport/Station Pickup: **Yes**
Foreign Languages: **Italian, Spanish**

Located in a pleasantly quiet neighborhood, with San Francisco only minutes away by good public transportation, the house offers the privacy of upstairs guest quarters with a view of a creek and native flora and fauna. It's all very clean and cheerfully decorated. Joe and Elnora will direct you to restaurants and shops to suit your budget.

Old Thyme Inn ✪
779 MAIN STREET, HALF MOON BAY, CALIFORNIA 94019
oldthyme@Coastside.net; http://www.virtualcities.com

Tel: **(415) 726-1616; fax: (415) 726-6394**
Best Time to Call: **8 AM–10 PM**
Hosts: **Marcia and George Dempsey**
Location: **30 mi. S of San Francisco**
No. of Rooms: **3**
No. of Private Baths: **3**
Double/pb: **$65–$85**
Single/pb: **$60–$85**
Suites: **$145–$210**

Open: **All year**
Breakfast: **Full**
Credit Cards: **MC, VISA**
Pets: **No**
Children: **Welcome, over 12**
Smoking: **No**
Social Drinking: **Permitted**
Minimum Stay: **Holiday weekends**
Foreign Languages: **French**

The Old Thyme Inn is a restored Victorian house located on the Pacific coast just 35 minutes south of San Francisco. Some rooms have fireplaces, some have baths with double-size whirlpool tubs, and all are decorated with antiques. Your hosts invite you to stroll in George's herb garden; if you like, you can have a cutting kit and take samples home for your own use. George's breakfast includes his justly celebrated buttermilk scones. For those of you who don't mind paying a higher rate, 4 rooms are available.

Goose & Turrets B&B ✪
835 GEORGE STREET, P.O. BOX 937, MONTARA,
CALIFORNIA 94037-0937

Tel: **(415) 728-5451**	Reduced Rates: **Available**
Best Time to Call: **10 AM–9 PM**	Breakfast: **Full**
Hosts: **Raymond and Emily Hoche-**	Credit Cards: **AMEX, DC, DISC, MC,**
Mong	**VISA**
Location: **23 mi. SW of San Francisco**	Pets: **No**
No. of Rooms: **5**	Children: **Welcome**
No. of Private Baths: **5**	Smoking: **No**
Double/pb: **$85–$130**	Social Drinking: **Permitted**
Open: **All year**	Foreign Languages: **French**

Located only 20 minutes from San Francisco Airport and half a mile from the beach, Goose & Turrets B&B is a convenient headquarters for day excursions to San Francisco, Silicon Valley, Berkeley, Monterey Aquarium, and Carmel. Nearby are restaurants, galleries, tidepools, fishing, golf, hiking, horseback riding, shops, and remnants of the area's lurid past during Prohibition. Enjoy delicious four-course breakfasts, comfortable beds, quiet gardens with courting swing, hammock, fountains, bocce ball court, and meet the three mascot geese. English tea and tasty snacks are served every afternoon. Raymond and Emily are well-traveled pilots who have lived in the South and in Europe, at places whose customs and cuisines are reflected in the food and the hospitality provided at the inn.

Adella Villa B&B ✪
P.O. BOX 4528, PALO ALTO, CALIFORNIA 94309

Tel: **(415) 321-5195; fax: (415) 325-**	Breakfast: **Full**
5121	Credit Cards: **AMEX, DC, MC, VISA**
Host: **Tricia Young**	Pets: **No**
Location: **30 mi. S of San Francisco**	Children: **Welcome, over 12**
No. of Rooms: **5**	Smoking: **No**
No. of Private Baths: **5**	Social Drinking: **Permitted**
Double/pb: **$99–$129**	Airport/Station Pickup: **Yes**
Open: **All year**	Foreign Languages: **German, Spanish**

This gorgeous, restored 1920s Italian villa is located in an exclusive area near Stanford University and Silicon Valley. The B&B, a pink stucco mansion with white trim, stands on an acre of lush park-like grounds with a Japanese koi pond, an aviary, and a swimming pool. The music foyer boasts a Steinway grand piano crafted in the 1930s. Fans of antiques will find much to admire, including an English dining room set, a five-foot 19th-century Imari vase, and a French marble commode. But there's nothing old-fashioned about the guest room amenities, such as bathrobes, down comforters, cable TV, sherry and wine, and cooked-to-order breakfasts.

Casa Arguello ✪

225 ARGUELLO BOULEVARD, SAN FRANCISCO, CALIFORNIA 94118
103221.3126@Compuserve

Tel: **(415) 752-9482; fax: (415) 681-1400**	Double/sb: **$58.95–$59.95**
Best Time to Call: **8 AM–2 PM; 5–9 PM**	Open: **All year**
Hosts: **Pete McKenzie, Emma Baires, and Marina McKenzie**	Breakfast: **Continental, plus**
	Pets: **No**
	Children: **Welcome, over 7**
No. of Rooms: **5**	Smoking: **No**
No. of Private Baths: **3**	Social Drinking: **Permitted**
Max. No. Sharing Bath: **4**	Minimum Stay: **2 nights**
Double/pb: **$79.50–$87.50**	Foreign Languages: **Spanish**

This spacious duplex has an elegant living room, dining room, and cheerful bedrooms that overlook neighboring gardens. Tastefully decorated with modern and antique furnishings, it is convenient to Golden Gate Park, Golden Gate Bridge, Union Square, and fine shops and restaurants. The University of California Medical School is nearby. Excellent public transportation is close by.

Casita Blanca ✪

330 EDGEHILL WAY, SAN FRANCISCO, CALIFORNIA 94127

Tel: **(415) 564-9339**	Pets: **No**
Host: **Joan Bard**	Children: **No**
No. of Rooms: **1 cottage**	Smoking: **No**
No. of Private Baths: **1**	Social Drinking: **Permitted**
Guest Cottage: **$80; sleeps 2**	Minimum Stay: **2 nights**
Open: **All year**	Foreign Languages: **French, Spanish**
Breakfast: **Continental**	

Casita Blanca is a guest cottage perched high on a hill, not far from Golden Gate Park. In this delightful hideaway, nestled among giant trees, you'll find twin beds, a private bath with a stall shower, and a complete kitchen stocked for your convenience with all the necessary items. If you tire of sightseeing and shopping, then just curl up in front of the little fireplace, have a glass of wine, and listen to the birds singing outside. Joan also offers accommodations in Carmel-by-the-Sea, Lake Tahoe, Sonoma, Palm Desert, and Maui.

Rancho San Gregorio ✪

ROUTE 1, BOX 54, SAN GREGORIO, CALIFORNIA 94074

Tel: **(415) 747-0810; fax: (415) 747-0184**	No. of Rooms: **3**
Hosts: **Bud and Lee Raynor**	No. of Private Baths: **3**
Location: **35 mi. S of San Francisco**	Double/pb: **$85–$105**
	Suite: **$145**

Open: **All year**
Reduced Rates: **Available**
Breakfast: **Full**
Pets: **No**

Children: **Welcome**
Smoking: **No**
Social Drinking: **Permitted**
Airport/Station Pickup: **Yes**

Graceful arches and bright stucco characterize this Spanish Mission home set on 15 wooded acres. Rooms are decorated with American antiques and family pieces. Your hosts, Bud and Lee, are glad to share a snack and a beverage. A full feast features eggs or pancakes, fresh fruit and breads, and a variety of meats. The atmosphere is relaxing, and guests are welcome to borrow a book from the library, or play the organ. Rancho San Gregorio is close to the beach, horseback riding, and golf. San Francisco, Half Moon Bay, and a variety of state parks and recreational areas are within an hour's drive. For those of you who don't mind paying a higher rate, 2 rooms are available.

SAN LUIS OBISPO AREA

Baywood Bed & Breakfast Inn ○

1370 SECOND STREET, BAYWOOD PARK, CALIFORNIA 93402

Tel: **(805) 528-8888**
Best Time to Call: **8 AM–8 PM**
Host: **Trisha Chassé**
Location: **12 mi. W of San Luis Obispo**
No. of Rooms: **15**
No. of Private Baths: **15**
Double/pb: **$80–$140**
Suites: **$120–$150**
Open: **All year**
Reduced Rates: **Available**

Breakfast: **Full**
Other Meals: **Available**
Credit Cards: **MC, VISA**
Pets: **No**
Children: **Welcome**
Smoking: **No**
Social Drinking: **Permitted**
Minimum Stay: **2 days on holiday weekends**

This waterfront establishment lies on a tiny peninsula that projects into Morro Bay. Outdoor types will find plenty to do here; the options include kayaking, golfing, hiking, bicycling, and picnicking. Several shops and restaurants are right in town, and Montano De Oro State Park, San Luis Obispo, and Hearst Castle are only minutes away. Each Baywood suite has bay views, cozy seating areas, and a wood-burning fireplace. Guests are treated to afternoon wine and cheese, room tours, and breakfast in bed.

SANTA BARBARA AREA

Carpinteria Beach Condo ○

1825 CRAVENS LANE, CARPINTERIA, CALIFORNIA 93013

Tel: **(805) 684-1579**
Best Time to Call: **7 AM–9 PM**
Hosts: **Bev and Don Schroeder**
Location: **11 mi. SE of Santa Barbara**

Guest Condo: **$70–$85; sleeps 2 to 4**
Open: **All year**
Reduced Rates: **Available**
Breakfast: **Continental**

Pets: **No**
Children: **Welcome**
Smoking: **No**

Social Drinking: **Permitted**
Station Pickup: **Yes**

You may view majestic mountains from this one-bedroom condo across the street from the beach. If you tire of the ocean, there is also a swimming pool. Play a set of tennis at the local Polo and Racquet Club, visit your hosts' avocado and lemon ranch less than two miles away, or take a ten-minute drive into Santa Barbara. Breakfast is a do-it-yourself affair in the condo's complete minikitchen.

Long's Seaview Bed & Breakfast
317 PIEDMONT ROAD, SANTA BARBARA, CALIFORNIA 93105

Tel: **(805) 687-2947**
Best Time to Call: **Before 6 PM**
Host: **LaVerne Long**
Location: **1 1/2 mi. from Hwy. 101**
No. of Rooms: **1**
No. of Private Baths: **1**
Double/pb: **$75–$79**
Single/pb: **$75**

Open: **All year**
Breakfast: **Full**
Pets: **No**
Children: **No**
Smoking: **No**
Social Drinking: **Permitted**
Airport/Station Pickup: **Yes**

Overlooking Santa Barbara's prestigious north side, this ranch-style home is in a quiet, residential neighborhood. Breakfast is usually served on the patio, where you can see the ocean, Channel Islands, and the small family citrus orchard and garden. Convenient to the beach, Solvang, and Santa Ynez Valley, the large, airy bedroom is cheerfully furnished with antiques and king-size bed. The breakfast menu varies from Southern dishes to Mexican specialties.

SEQUOIA AREA/SIERRA FOOTHILLS

Kern River Inn Bed & Breakfast ○
P.O. BOX 1725, 119 KERN RIVER DRIVE, KERNVILLE, CALIFORNIA 93238

Tel: **(760) 376-6750; (800) 986-4382**
Best Time to Call: **10 AM–9 PM**
Hosts: **Jack and Carita Prestwich**
Location: **50 mi. NE of Bakersfield**
No. of Rooms: **6**
No. of Private Baths: **6**
Double/pb: **$89–$99**
Single/pb: **$79–$89**

Open: **All year**
Reduced Rates: **Available**
Breakfast: **Full**
Credit Cards: **AMEX, MC, VISA**
Pets: **No**
Children: **Welcome**
Smoking: **No**
Social Drinking: **Permitted**

Stay in a charming riverfront B&B in a quaint Western town within Sequoia National Forest. Carita and Jack specialize in romantic, relaxing getaways. Nearby activities include golf, hiking, biking, white-water rafting, downhill skiing, and year-round fishing in front of the Inn. It's an easy stroll to shops, restaurants, and parks, and a short drive to the giant redwood trees. Your hosts love to fish and hike and can direct you to some of their favorite locations.

Cort Cottage ✪

P.O. BOX 245, THREE RIVERS, CALIFORNIA 93271

Tel: **(209) 561-4671**
Best Time to Call: **Before 9 PM**
Host: **Catherine Cort**
Location: **5 mi. W of Sequoia National Park**
Guest Cottage: **$85; sleeps 2**
Open: **All year**

Breakfast: **Continental**
Pets: **No**
Children: **Welcome**
Smoking: **No**
Social Drinking: **Permitted**
Minimum Stay: **2 nights**

Hidden in the Sierra foothill village of Three Rivers, you will find this private guest cottage ten minutes away from the entrance to Sequoia National Park. Built by Gary and Catherine Cort as a house for Grandma, the cottage fits snugly into the hillside and has a panoramic view of mountains and sky. It offers an outdoor hot tub, a fully equipped kitchen, and full bath with step-down tub. The Corts work as an architect/artist and a part-time nurse, have interests in gardening, crafts, and photography, and own a local art gallery.

COLORADO

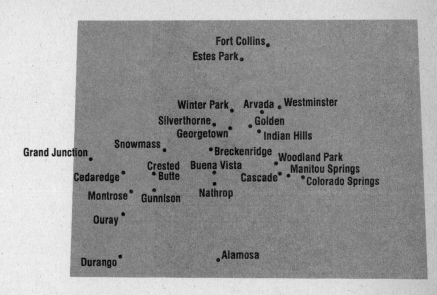

Bed & Breadfast Southwest Reservation Service—Southern Colorado ✪

2916 NORTH 70TH STREET, SCOTTSDALE, ARIZONA 85251
b&bsw@juno.com

Tel: **(602) 945-9704; (800) 762-9704;**
  fax: (602) 874-1316
Best Time to Call: **8 AM–8 PM**
Coordinators: **Jo Cummings and**
  Joan Petersen
States/Regions Covered: **Arizona, New**
  Mexico, Southern Colorado,
  Southern California

Descriptive Directory: **Free**
Rates (Single/Double):
  Modest: **$40–$75**
  Average: **$80–$100**
  Luxury: **$105–up**

This service offers travelers unique homestays in suites, guesthouses, ranches, and inns. All host facilities are personally inspected and provide the three C's of bed and breakfasts: cleanliness, cordiality, and convenience. Jo and Joan's specialty is finding the perfect B&B for you.

They can plan your trip to include many of the historical and natural wonders of the great Southwest, such as the San Diego Zoo, Durango Historic Railroad, Scottsdale golf courses, Sedona's Red Rock formations, and the Santa Fe opera. You will be awed by the spectacular scenic beauty and legendary Western hospitality.

Cottonwood Inn B&B ✪
123 SAN JUAN AVENUE, ALAMOSA, COLORADO 81101

Tel: **(719) 589-3882**
Host: **Julie Mordecai**
Location: **150 mi. SW of Colorado Springs**
No. of Rooms: **7**
No. of Private Baths: **7**
Double/pb: **$85–$125**
Single/pb: **$81**
Suites: **$85**
Open: **All year**
Reduced Rates: **10% Nov.–Feb. and families**

Breakfast: **Full**
Credit Cards: **AMEX, DC, DISC, MC, VISA**
Pets: **Sometimes**
Children: **Welcome**
Smoking: **No**
Social Drinking: **Permitted**
Minimum Stay: **2 nights on special weekends**
Airport/Station Pickup: **Yes**
Foreign Languages: **Spanish**

The Cottonwood Inn B&B is centrally located for guests visiting southern Colorado and northern New Mexico. The Inn is furnished with antiques and reproductions. Nearby are Adams State College, the Great Sand Dunes National Monument, wildlife sanctuaries, Cumbres Toltec Railway, three golf courses, horseback riding, and a variety of art classes and special weekends throughout the year. Julie is an ex-schoolteacher, avid outdoor person, and enthusiastic baker.

On Golden Pond Bed & Breakfast
7831 ELDRIDGE, ARVADA, COLORADO 80005

Tel: **(303) 424-2296**
Best Time to Call: **Anytime**
Hosts: **John and Kathy Kula**
Location: **15 mi. W of Denver**
No. of Rooms: **5**
No. of Private Baths: **5**
Double/pb: **$60–$70**
Single/pb: **$50–$60**
Suites: **$100–$120**

Open: **All year**
Reduced Rates: **10% weekly; seniors**
Breakfast: **Full**
Credit Cards: **AMEX, DISC, MC, VISA**
Pets: **1 room only**
Children: **1 room only**
Smoking: **No**
Social Drinking: **Permitted**
Foreign Languages: **German**

A secluded retreat tucked into the Rocky Mountain foothills, this custom-built, two-story brick home has dramatic views of mountains, prairies, and downtown Denver. Birds and other wildlife are drawn to the ten-acre grounds, which have a fishing pond and hiking trails. After a full breakfast, stroll along the garden path, bicycle by the creek, swim laps in the pool, or ride horses into the foothills. Then join John and

Kathy for a late afternoon kaffeeklatsch. Conclude the day with a soak in the hot tub.

Evans House Bed & Breakfast ✪

102 SOUTH FRENCH STREET, P.O. BOX 387, BRECKENRIDGE, COLORADO 80424
http://www.colorado-bnb.com/evanshse

Tel: **(970) 453-5509**	Open: **All year**
Hosts: **Peter and Georgette Contos**	Breakfast: **Full**
Location: **85 mi. W of Denver**	Other Meals: **Available**
No. of Rooms: **4**	Pets: **No**
No. of Private Baths: **1**	Children: **Welcome**
Max. No. Sharing Bath: **4**	Smoking: **No**
Double/pb: **$68–$95**	Social Drinking: **Permitted**
Double/sb: **$55–$85**	Foreign Languages: **Greek, French**

Get the feel of Breckenridge's mining days in this restored 1886 Victorian listed on the National Historic Register. Peter and Georgette can tell you about their town's past with the help of period photographs mounted on their walls. The common room—equipped with a TV, VCR, books, and games—is a favorite gathering place, but shopping, restaurants, and evening entertainments will lure you to Main Street, two blocks away. Breckenridge's stunning mountain setting is appealing throughout the year. Admire wildflowers in the spring, attend special summer events, see the aspens change color in the fall; higher rates apply in the winter, when you have access to cold weather activities from the free shuttle bus that stops at the B&B's front door.

Trout City Inn ✪

BOX 431, BUENA VISTA, COLORADO 81211

Tel: **(719) 495-0348**	Open: **June 15–Sept. 15**
Best Time to Call: **After 6 PM**	Breakfast: **Full**
Hosts: **Juel and Irene Kjeldsen**	Other Meals: **Available**
Location: **5 mi. E of Buena Vista on Hwy. 24**	Credit Cards: **MC, VISA**
	Pets: **No**
No. of Rooms: **4**	Children: **Welcome, over 10**
No. of Private Baths: **4**	Smoking: **No**
Double/pb: **$40**	Social Drinking: **Permitted**

Trout City Inn is a historic site on the famous South Park Narrow Gauge Railroad, and is located at the edge of a trout stream. It is an accurate reconstruction of a mountain railroad depot, with authentic private rail cars containing Pullman berths. The depot rooms feature Victorian decor, high ceilings, and four-poster or brass beds. Glass doors open onto a deck with views of the 14,000-foot peaks of the Continental Divide. Hiking, biking, panning for gold, and fly-fishing are within steps of the front door; white-water rafting is minutes away.

The Black Bear Inn of Pikes Peak
5250 PIKES PEAK HIGHWAY, CASCADE, COLORADO 80809

Tel: **(719) 684-0151**
Host: **Christi Heidenreich**
Location: **4 mi. W of Colorado Springs**
No. of Rooms: **9**
No. of Private Baths: **9**
Double/pb: **$75–$85**
Suites: **$90**
Open: **All year**

Reduced Rates: **Seniors 5%**
Breakfast: **Full**
Credit Cards: **DISC, MC, VISA**
Pets: **No**
Children: **Welcome**
Smoking: **No**
Social Drinking: **Permitted**
Airport Pickup: **Yes**

The Black Bear Inn of Pikes Peak is located between the North Pole and the Pikes Peak tollgate. Guests enjoy breathtaking mountain views from each bedroom. At the end of a wooded trail you are invited to enjoy the very private hot tub. Relax, read a book, or have special meetings or gatherings in the large common area. If you are feeling energetic, hiking and nature trails are right outside the Inn. Christi offers group rates and will be happy to arrange banquets.

Cedars' Edge Llamas Bed and Breakfast ✪
2169 HIGHWAY 65, CEDAREDGE, COLORADO 81413

Tel: **(970) 856-6836**
Hosts: **Ray and Gail Record**
Location: **50 mi. E of Grand Junction**
No. of Rooms: **4**
No. of Private Baths: **4**
Double/pb: **$50–$75**
Single/pb: **$40–$65**

Open: **All year**
Breakfast: **Full**
Pets: **No**
Children: **Welcome**
Smoking: **No**
Social Drinking: **Permitted**
Airport/Station Pickup: **Yes**

Nestled on the southern slope of the Grand Mesa, this modern cedar home offers a panoramic view of several mountain ranges, plus the unique opportunity to share life on a llama-breeding ranch. The accommodations are immaculate. Cheerful rooms are tastefully decorated in pastel shades, with exposed beams, hanging plants, and light streaming in from many windows. Sportsmen and sportswomen can fish for trout, hunt deer and elk, or go cross-country and downhill skiing. After a filling breakfast, guests can join Ray and Gail in feeding or grooming well-behaved four-footed friends—a rewarding experience for all.

Timberline Bed & Breakfast ✪
2457 U50 ROAD, CEDAREDGE, COLORADO 81413

Tel: **(970) 856-7379**
Best Time to Call: **Mornings or evenings**
Hosts: **Al and Shirley Richardson**
Location: **60 mi. E of Grand Junction**
No. of Rooms: **1**

No. of Private Baths: **1**
Double/pb: **$40**
Single/pb: **$30**
Open: **All year**
Breakfast: **Continental**

Pets: **Yes**
Children: **Welcome**
Smoking: **No**

Social Drinking: **Permitted**
Airport/Station Pickup: **Yes**

Set on a hillside at the foot of Grand Mesa, this B&B occupies the ground floor of a country home surrounded by pinyon, oak, and juniper trees. The three-room suite has a queen-size bed, living room, woodburning stove, and a fully equipped kitchen. Guests may while away the hours with fishing, hiking, boating, and cross-country and downhill skiing. Timberline lies within easy driving distance of Powderhorn Ski Resort, Black Canyon of the Gunnison, Colorado National Monument, and Curecanti National Recreation Area.

Holden House—1902 Victorian Bed & Breakfast Inn
1102 WEST PIKES PEAK AVENUE, COLORADO SPRINGS, COLORADO 80904
holdenhouse@worldnet.att.net

Tel: **(719) 471-3980**
Best Time to Call: **9 AM–9 PM**
Hosts: **Sallie and Welling Clark**
No. of Rooms: **5**
No. of Private Baths: **5**
Suites: **$110–$120**
Open: **All year**

Breakfast: **Full**
Credit Cards: **AMEX, DC, DISC, MC, VISA**
Pets: **No**
Children: **No**
Smoking: **No**
Social Drinking: **Permitted**

Built by Isabel Holden, this 1902 storybook Victorian, 1906 carriage house, and adjacent 1898 Victorian are centrally located near historic Old Colorado City. The Inn, lovingly restored by the Clarks in 1985, is filled with antiques and family heirlooms. Named for mining towns, guest rooms are furnished with queen beds, period furnishings, and down pillows. The Inn boasts five romantic suites with tubs for two, mountain views, fireplaces, and more! Gourmet breakfasts, served in the elegant formal dining room, might include carob chip muffins, Sallie's famous Southwestern Eggs Fiesta, fresh fruit, gourmet coffee, tea, and juice. Complimentary refreshments, homemade cookies, and turndown service are just some of Holden House's special touches, along with in-room phones and fax capability. Sallie and Welling will be happy to help in planning your itinerary around the many activities in the Pikes Peak region. Friendly resident cats Mingtoy and Muffin will greet you.

The Elizabeth Anne B&B ✪
P.O. BOX 1051, CRESTED BUTTE, COLORADO 81224

Tel: **(888) 745-4620**
Hosts: **Carl and Judy Jones**
Location: **225 mi. SW of Denver**
No. of Rooms: **4**
No. of Private Baths: **4**

Double/pb: **$73–$103**
Single/pb: **$68–$99**
Open: **May 25–Oct. 10; Nov. 15–Apr. 20**
Breakfast: **Full**

Credit Cards: **AMEX, MC, VISA**
Pets: **No**
Children: **Welcome (large room only)**
Smoking: **No**

Social Drinking: **Permitted**
Minimum Stay: **2 days winter weekends**
Airport Pickup: **Yes**

The Elizabeth Anne is in the National Historic District of Crested Butte, an 1880s mining town. This new Victorian home echoes the warmth and charm of Crested Butte's past. The common areas are decorated with Queen Anne furniture, and the bedrooms have a Victorian appeal of their own. Other amenities are a soothing hot tub, guest refrigerator, and bicycle and ski storage. Recreational opportunities abound, with Nordic and Alpine skiing in the winter. Summer offers mountain biking, hiking, fishing, golfing, and horseback riding. Crested Butte also has a myriad shops and gourmet restaurants. Your hosts, Carl and Judy, who recently retired from engineering and nursing careers, invite you to come and share their mountain experience.

Apple Orchard Inn ✪
7758 COUNTY ROAD 203, DURANGO, COLORADO 81301

Tel: **(800) 426-0751**
Hosts: **Celeste and John Gardiner**
Location: **8 mi. N of Durango**
No. of Rooms: **10**
No. of Private Baths: **10**
Double/pb: **$85–$125**
Guest Cottages: **$100–$150**
Open: **All year**
Reduced Rates: **10% AAA; after 3rd night; seniors**

Breakfast: **Full**
Other meals: **Available**
Credit Cards: **AMEX, DISC, MC, VISA**
Pets: **No**
Children: **Welcome**
Smoking: **Restricted**
Social Drinking: **Permitted**
Airport/Station Pickup: **Yes**
Foreign Languages: **Portuguese**

The Apple Orchard Inn is a newly constructed two-story farmhouse with six cottages on four-and-a-half acres of orchards and gardens surrounded by mountains and cliffs. The Inn has beautiful wood trim, cherrywood floors, and elegant country furniture, including featherbeds, armoires, and vanities. Each cottage has a special feature such as a fireplace and Jacuzzi tub, French doors leading to a private patio, or a cozy bay window. Enjoy a scrumptious breakfast while watching the Durango-Silverton Narrow Gauge Train pass by. Gourmet lunches and dinners are prepared by Celeste, who has European training.

Country Sunshine B&B ✪
35130 HIGHWAY 550 NORTH, DURANGO, COLORADO 81301

Tel: **(970) 247-2853; (800) 383-2853**
Best Time to Call: **9 AM–6 PM**
Hosts: **Beanie and Gary Archie**
No. of Rooms: **6**
No. of Private Baths: **6**
Double/pb: **$85**
Open: **All year**

Breakfast: **Full**
Credit Cards: **AMEX, DC, DISC, MC, VISA**
Pets: **No**
Children: **Welcome, over 5**
Smoking: **No**
Social Drinking: **Permitted**

Enjoy southwest Colorado's splendor and beauty while staying at this spacious ranch-style home. Indulge your senses and spirit with mountain views, river songs, abundant wildlife, and the aroma of the ponderosa pines. Awaken to the smell of a country breakfast. Nearby is Mesa Verde National Park, Durango-Silverton Narrow Gauge Train, and Purgatory Ski Area. After a busy day, relax in the hot tub under the star-filled sky.

The Leland House Bed & Breakfast Suites ✪
721 EAST SECOND AVENUE, DURANGO, COLORADO 81301

Tel: **(970) 385-1920; (800) 664-1920**
Best Time to Call: **8 AM–5 PM**
Host: **Kirk Komick**
Location: **350 mi. SW of Denver**
No. of Rooms: **10**
No. of Private Baths: **10**
Double/pb: **$95–$105**
Suites: **$125–$175**
Open: **All year**

Reduced Rates: **Available**
Breakfast: **Full**
Other Meals: **Available**
Credit Cards: **AMEX, MC, VISA**
Pets: **No**
Children: **Welcome**
Smoking: **No**
Social Drinking: **Permitted**

Originally built in 1927 as an apartment house, the Leland House was restored by the Komicks as a B&B in 1993. All rooms have cable TV and telephone service. Six suites have separate living rooms, bedrooms, and full service kitchens; four studios have kitchenettes. The interior is decorated with rustic antiques, accented by photos, memorabilia, and biographies of historic figures associated with the property. Leland House is steps away from Durango's historic downtown district and the

Durango-Silverton Narrow Gauge Railroad Station. Gourmet breakfasts consist of fresh-baked goods, homemade granola, and may include fruit-filled French toast or a Southwestern breakfast burrito.

Lightner Creek Inn Bed and Breakfast ✪
999 C.R. 207, DURANGO, COLORADO 81301
lci@frontier.net

Tel: **(970) 259-1226; (800) 268-9804;** fax: **(970) 259-9526**	Double/sb: **$85–$95**
Best Time to Call: **9 AM–9 PM**	Open: **All year**
Hosts: **Richard and Julie Houston**	Reduced Rates: **20% Nov. 1–Apr. 30**
Location: **4 mi W of Durango**	Breakfast: **Full**
No. of Rooms: **8**	Credit Cards: **DISC, MC, VISA**
No. of Private Baths: **5**	Pets: **No**
Max. No. Sharing Bath: **4**	Children: **Welcome, 10 and over**
Double/pb: **$95–$150**	Smoking: **No**
	Social Drinking: **Permitted**

Nestled among rugged peaks, shimmering streams, and grazing llamas and horses, Lightner Creek Inn's 20-acre pastoral setting deserves to be discovered. This 1903 French countryside home has been exquisitely renovated, providing a casual but elegantly romantic retreat. The Inn combines charming Victorian detail with antique furnishings and cozy fireplaces, gourmet breakfasts, and the warmth and hospitality of Julie and Richard. While only four miles from Durango (home of the Durango-Silverton Narrow Gauge Train) and an easy ride to Mesa Verde, Purgatory, Telluride, and Wolf Creek, the Inn offers excellent mountain trails, trout fishing, and spectacular vistas, making a stay here truly memorable.

Logwood—The Verheyden Inn ✪
35060 HIGHWAY 550, DURANGO, COLORADO 81301

Tel: **(970) 259-4396; (800) 369-4082**	Reduced Rates: **$10 less winter** single occupancy
Best Time to Call: **After 10 AM**	Breakfast: **Full**
Hosts: **Debby and Greg Verheyden**	Credit Cards: **MC, VISA**
Location: **212 mi. NW of Albuquerque, New Mexico**	Pets: **No**
No. of Rooms: **6**	Children: **Welcome, over 7**
No. of Private Baths: **6**	Smoking: **No**
Double/pb: **$75–$130**	Social Drinking: **Permitted**
Single/pb: **$55–$120**	Minimum Stay: **2 nights holidays**
Open: **All year**	

This luxurious red cedar log home is located on the Animas River. The house has a large wraparound deck with plenty of comfortable areas where guests can make themselves at home. Rooms are decorated with home-stitched quilts. A new suite has been added, complete with a fireplace, VCR, TV, and a view of the river. Guests can enjoy Purgatory

Ski Area, taking a sleigh ride, or relaxing by the fireplace with a cup of hot chocolate. A full country breakfast and award-winning desserts are served for your enjoyment.

Scrubby Oaks Bed & Breakfast ✪
P.O. BOX 1047, DURANGO, COLORADO 81302

Tel: **(970) 247-2176**
Best Time to Call: **Early mornings; evenings**
Host: **Mary Ann Craig**
Location: **4 mi. from junction 160 and 550**
No. of Rooms: **7**
No. of Private Baths: **3**
Max. No. Sharing Bath: **4**
Double/pb: **$75**

Single/pb: **$60**
Double/sb: **$65**
Single/sb: **$50**
Open: **Apr. 30–Oct. 31**
Breakfast: **Full**
Pets: **No**
Children: **Welcome**
Smoking: **No**
Social Drinking: **Permitted**

There's a quiet country feeling to this two-story home set on 10 acres overlooking the spectacular Animas Valley and surrounding mountains. Trees and gardens frame the patios where breakfast is apt to be served. All breads and preserves are homemade, and strawberry Belgian waffles are a specialty. On chilly mornings, the kitchen fireplace is the cozy backdrop for your wake-up cup of coffee or cocoa. You are made to feel part of the family and are welcome to play pool, take a sauna, read a book, watch a VCR movie, or simply take in the crisp air.

Eagle Cliff House
BOX 4312, ESTES PARK, COLORADO 80517

Tel: **(970) 586-5425**
Best Time to Call: **Early morning**
Hosts: **Nancy and Mike Conrin**
Location: **2½ mi. W of Estes Park**
No. of Rooms: **3**
No. of Private Baths: **3**
Double/pb: **$80**
Guest Cottage: **$115**

Open: **All year**
Breakfast: **Full**
Pets: **No**
Children: **Welcome**
Smoking: **No**
Social Drinking: **Permitted**
Minimum Stay: **2 nights, weekends**
Airport/Station Pickup: **Yes**

Nancy and Mike are dedicated hikers who live within walking distance of Rocky Mountain National Park, so don't be surprised if they invite you for an afternoon's exploration of their favorite "backyard" trails. Saturday evening get-togethers are commonplace, especially in the summer. Recreational opportunities abound throughout the year, from golf, tennis, and horseback riding to cross-country and downhill skiing. One guest room of this woodsy retreat is decorated with mementos of Mexico and the American Southwest; the cottage and the second guest room are furnished in Victorian style.

Elizabeth Street Guest House ✪
202 EAST ELIZABETH, FORT COLLINS, COLORADO 80524

Tel: **(970) 493-BEDS [2337]**
Best Time to Call: **8–10 AM; 5–7 PM**
Hosts: **John and Sheryl Clark**
Location: **65 mi. N of Denver**
No. of Rooms: **3**
Max. No. Sharing Bath: **4**
Double/pb: **$85–$90**
Single/pb: **$65–$70**
Double/sb: **$65–$70**

Single/sb: **$45–$50**
Open: **All year**
Breakfast: **Full**
Credit Cards: **AMEX, MC, VISA (for deposits only)**
Pets: **No**
Children: **Welcome, over 8**
Smoking: **No**
Social Drinking: **Permitted**

This completely renovated and restored 1905 brick American Four-square has leaded windows and oak woodwork. Family antiques, plants, old quilts, and handmade touches add to its charm. All of the bedrooms have sinks. It is close to historic Old Town Square, Estes Park, Rocky Mountain National Park, and a block away from Colorado State University. John and Sheryl will spoil you with their special brand of hospitality and homemade treats.

Hardy House ✪
605 BROWNELL STREET, GEORGETOWN, COLORADO 80444

Tel: **(303) 569-3388; (800) 490-4802**
Best Time to Call: **10 AM–8 PM**
Hosts: **Carla and Michael Wagner**
Location: **50 mi. W of Denver**
No. of Rooms: **4**
No. of Private Baths: **4**
Double/pb: **$73–$82**
Single/pb: **$63–$72**

Suite: **$82–$112**
Open: **All year**
Breakfast: **Full**
Other Meals: **Available**
Pets: **No**
Children: **No**
Smoking: **No**
Social Drinking: **Permitted**

Back in the 1870s this bright red Victorian, surrounded by a white picket fence, was the home of a blacksmith. Inside you can relax by the potbelly parlor stove, sleep under feather comforters, and wake up to candlelight gourmet breakfasts. Guest quarters range from a two-bedroom suite to rooms with queen beds. In the evening, the Wagners serve coffee and tea. Hardy House is located in the heart of the Historic District, half a block from the shops of Main Street. It is also close to hiking, skiing, and is walking distance from the Loop Railroad. Perhaps the best way to explore the town is on a six-speed tandem mountain bike, which your hosts will gladly lend.

The Dove Inn ✪
711 14TH STREET, GOLDEN, COLORADO 80401-1906

Tel: **(303) 278-2209**
Hosts: **Tim and Connie Sheffield**

Location: **10 mi. W of downtown Denver**

No. of Rooms: **6**
No. of Private Baths: **6**
Double/pb: **$75–$90**
Single/pb: **$65–$80**
Open: **All year**
Reduced Rates: **10% weekly**

Breakfast: **Full**
Credit Cards: **AMEX, DISC, MC, VISA**
Pets: **No**
Children: **Welcome (crib)**
Smoking: **No**
Social Drinking: **Permitted**

The Dove Inn is a charming Victorian on grounds beautifully land-scaped with decks, walkways, and huge trees. The house has many bay windows, dormers, and angled ceilings; each room is individually dec-orated with pretty wallpapers and Victorian touches. This delightful Inn is located in the foothills of Golden in one of the state's most beauti-ful valleys, yet it is just minutes from downtown Denver and many other Rocky Mountain attractions. Tim and Connie are sensitive to the needs of business travelers and international visitors.

The Cider House ✪
1126 GRAND AVENUE, GRAND JUNCTION, COLORADO 81501

Tel: **(970) 242-9087**
Host: **Helen Mills**
Location: **2 mi. from I-70**
No. of Rooms: **3**
No. of Private Baths: **1**
Max. No. Sharing Bath: **4**
Double/pb: **$50**
Single/pb: **$40**
Double/sb: **$45**
Single/sb: **$35**

Open: **All year**
Reduced Rates: **Available**
Breakfast: **Full**
Other Meals: **Available**
Credit Cards: **MC**
Pets: **Sometimes**
Children: **Welcome**
Smoking: **Permitted**
Social Drinking: **Permitted**
Airport/Station Pickup: **Yes**

Nestled in the heart of Grand Junction is this two-story frame house built at the start of the century. It is comfortably decorated with period furnishings, old-fashioned wallpapers, and nostalgic touches. Lace cur-tains and French doors add to the elegance of the living room. Sumptu-ous breakfasts of locally grown fruit, homemade breads, jams, special waffles, and beverages are served in the adjoining dining room. Nearby attractions include the Grand Mesa, river rafting, dinosaur digs, and some of the best winter skiing in the country.

Eagle's Nest Bed and Breakfast ✪
206 NORTH COLORADO, GUNNISON, COLORADO 81230

Tel: **(970) 641-4457**
Best Time to Call: **10 AM–5 PM**
Hosts: **Jane and Hugh McGee**
No. of Rooms: **1**
No. of Private Baths: **1**
Double/pb: **$45**

Open: **All year**
Breakfast: **Full, Continental**
Pets: **No**
Children: **By arrangement**
Smoking: **No**
Social Drinking: **Permitted**

Built in 1923, this early American former judge's home features stained glass and interior maple woodwork. The spacious guest room has a private entrance, queen-size bed, and a cheery reading and breakfast room. Gunnison is a beautiful place to visit in all four seasons. Nearby is skiing at Crested Butte, hunting in the fall, and fishing at Blue Mesa Lake or the Gunnison River. During the summer the attractions include the Gunnison Rodeo, the Crested Butte Wildflower Festival, rafting, and much more.

Mary Lawrence Inn
601 NORTH TAYLOR, GUNNISON, COLORADO 81230
http://www.gunnison.co.com/main/lodging/maryl.htm

Tel: **(970) 641-3343; (800) 445-3861**	Open: **All year**
Best Time to Call: **10 AM–10 PM**	Breakfast: **Full**
Hosts: **Pat and Jim Kennedy**	Credit Cards: **MC, VISA**
Location: **195 mi. W and S of Denver**	Pets: **No**
No. of Rooms: **5**	Children: **Welcome, over 6**
No. of Private Baths: **5**	Smoking: **No**
Double/pb: **$69–$74**	Social Drinking: **Permitted**
Single/pb: **$69–$74**	Airport/Station Pickup: **Yes**
Suites: **$85–$139; sleep 2–4**	

An Italianate frame house with spacious, antique-filled guest rooms, and comfortable common areas, the Mary Lawrence Inn is located in a well-kept neighborhood inside Gunnison's city limits. Surrounded by wilderness and Forest Service land, this B&B is a haven for sportspeople of all types; the Black Canyon of the Gunnison, the Alpine Tunnel, the town of Crested Butte, and many spectacular mountain vistas are all within an hour's drive.

Mountain View Bed & Breakfast ✪
4754 PICUTIS ROAD, P.O. BOX 631, INDIAN HILLS, COLORADO 80454

Tel: **(303) 697-6896**	Open: **All year**
Best Time to Call: **11 AM–3 PM**	Reduced Rates: **10% seniors**
Hosts: **Graham and Ortrud Richardson**	Breakfast: **Full**
Location: **20 mi. W of Denver**	Credit Cards: **AMEX, MC, VISA**
No. of Rooms: **4**	Pets: **No**
No. of Private Baths: **4**	Children: **Welcome**
Double/pb: **$80**	Smoking: **No**
Guest Cabin: **$135, sleeps 4**	Social Drinking: **Permitted**
Suites: **$105, sleeps 4**	Foreign Languages: **German**

Built in the 1920s as a writer's retreat, the Mountain View Bed & Breakfast is situated on $2^1/_2$ acres and offers a perfect romantic getaway. Guests can choose from three unique rooms or a private cabin, all with queen-size beds. Mountain View is located near Evergreen, which offers easy access to several mountain parks boasting many hiking trails and breathtaking views. Each afternoon, enjoy a cup of tea in the English tradition while sampling some Old Country delicacies. In the morning, wake to the aroma of freshly brewed coffee and a gourmet meal served by your European hosts.

Two Sisters Inn
TEN OTOE PLACE, MANITOU SPRINGS, COLORADO 80829

Tel: **(719) 685-9684; (800) 2 SIS-INN [274-7466]**
Best Time to Call: **Evenings**
Hosts: **Sharon Smith and Wendy Goldstein**
Location: **4 mi. W of Colorado Springs**
No. of Rooms: **5**
No. of Private Baths: **3**
Max. No. Sharing Bath: **4**
Double/pb: **$75**

Double/sb: **$63**
Guest Cottage: **$95**
Open: **All year**
Breakfast: **Full**
Credit Cards: **DISC, MC, VISA**
Pets: **No**
Children: **Welcome, over 10**
Smoking: **No**
Social Drinking: **Permitted**

Built in 1919 as a boardinghouse, this rose-colored Victorian bungalow has been lovingly restored with four bedrooms and a honeymoon cottage in the back garden. Family collectibles, antiques, and fresh flowers fill the sunny rooms. Your hosts, former caterers, set out a gourmet breakfast of home-baked muffins, freshly ground coffee, fresh fruit, and a hot entree. The Inn is located at the base of Pikes Peak, in Manitou Springs' historic district. Nearby attractions include the Garden of the Gods, the cog railway, the U.S. Air Force Academy, and the Olympic Training Center.

Maria's Bed & Breakfast ✪
20538 HIGHWAY 550 SOUTH, MONTROSE, COLORADO 81401

Tel: **(970) 249-8288; fax: (970) 240-8281**
Best Time to Call: **8 AM–9 PM**
Hosts: **Maria and Harold LaMar**
Location: **5 mi. S of Montrose**
No. of Rooms: **3**
No. of Private Baths: **3**
Double/pb: **$50**
Open: **Mar. 15–Dec. 31**

Breakfast: **Full**
Pets: **No**
Children: **Welcome**
Smoking: **No**
Social Drinking: **No**
Airport/Station Pickup: **Yes**
Foreign Languages: **French, German, Flemish**

Colorful flowers, trees, and a beautifully groomed yard surround this gambrel-roofed home. Summer evenings can be spent on the large comfortable porches enjoying the majestic views of the San Juan Mountains while indulging in one of Harold's homemade pies. A few things to do and see include hunting, hiking, fishing, and skiing. Black Canyon National Monument, Ouray Hot Springs, Ridegeway Recreational Area, and Telluride are famous for their summer festivals and skiing. Maria and Harold give all guests special attention and pamper them with home-cooked specialties, such as Belgian waffles with strawberries and whipped topping, eggs Benedict, Quiche Lorraine, blueberry muffins, breads, and jams.

Claveau's Streamside Bed and Breakfast ✪
18820 C.R. 162, NATHROP, COLORADO 81236

Tel: **(719) 395-2553**
Best Time to Call: **Anytime**
Hosts: **Denny and Kathy Claveau**
Location: **130 mi. SW of Denver**

No. of Rooms: **3**
No. of Private Baths: **3**
Double/pb: **$69–$74**
Open: **All year**

Breakfast: **Full**
Pets: **No**
Smoking: **No**

Social Drinking: **Permitted**
Minimum Stay: **Holiday weekends**

Located within San Isabel National Forest, Claveau's Streamside Bed and Breakfast is in the shadow of the Rockies' Collegiate Peaks. Mt. Princeton, Mt. Yale, Mt. Harvard, Mt. Oxford, and other challenging peaks beckon all to climb their glistening summits. Wildlife abounds here; deer, elk, bighorn sheep, and mountain goats are your hosts' neighbors. Winter offers downhill and cross-country skiing. Summer offers fishing, hiking, white-water rafting, horseback riding, or just relaxing by a stream. Kathy and Denny are environmentally active outdoor advocates. They look forward to helping guests plan their daily adventures, which may range from fine dining to visiting natural hot springs.

Ouray 1898 House ✪
322 MAIN STREET, P.O. BOX 641, OURAY, COLORADO 81427

Tel: **(970) 325-4871**
Best Time to Call: **After 5 PM**
Hosts: **Lee and Kathy Bates**
Location: **On Hwy. 550**
No. of Rooms: **3**
No. of Private Baths: **3**
Double/pb: **$68–$85**

Open: **May 25–Sept. 25**
Breakfast: **Full**
Credit Cards: **AMEX, MC, VISA**
Pets: **No**
Children: **Welcome**
Smoking: **No**
Social Drinking: **Permitted**

This 100-year-old house has been renovated to combine old-time elegance with modern amenities. Each guest room features antique furnishings, cable TV, and a deck where you can enjoy the view of the San Juan Mountains. You are also invited to use the hot tub and gazebo. A variety of foods is served at breakfast to tempt any appetite; coffee and tea are served at all times. Ouray, known as the "Jeep Capital of the World," is also famed for its natural hot springs and hiking trails.

Mountain Vista Bed & Breakfast ✪
P.O. BOX 1398, 358 LAGOON LANE, SILVERTHORNE, COLORADO 80498

Tel: **(970) 468-7700**
Best Time to Call: **Evening**
Host: **Sandy Ruggaber**
Location: **60 mi. W of Denver**
No. of Rooms: **3**
No. of Private Baths: **1**
Max. No. Sharing Bath: **4**
Double/pb: **$70–$75**

Double/sb: **$65–$75**
Open: **All year**
Reduced Rates: **10% seniors**
Breakfast: **Full, Continental**
Pets: **No**
Children: **Welcome, over 6**
Smoking: **No**
Social Drinking: **Permitted**

Mountain Vista offers something for everyone. Since it's surrounded by fine resorts like Keystone, Arapahoe Basin, Copper Mountain, Breckenridge, and Vail, guests can enjoy downhill skiing at its best. In the summer, try hiking, kayaking, cycling, golf, tennis, rafting, and fishing (an outdoor grill is available for you to cook your catch). Visit the factory outlet stores or go to the many concerts, festivals, and cultural events offered throughout Summit County. After a busy day, relax by the fireplace with your favorite drink, watch TV, read, do a puzzle, or retire to a warm comfortable room. You will awaken in the morning to the smell of a hearty homemade breakfast.

Starry Pines ✪
2262 SNOWMASS CREEK ROAD, SNOWMASS, COLORADO 81654

Tel: **(970) 927-4202; (800) 527-4202**
Best Time to Call: **7 AM–9 AM,
    4 PM–9 PM**
Host: **Shelley Burke**
Location: **200 mi. W of Denver**
No. of Rooms: **2**
Max. No. Sharing Bath: **4**
Double/sb: **$80–$95**
Single/sb: **$75–$90**

Apartment: **$100–$120, for two**
Open: **All year**
Reduced Rates: **Available**
Breakfast: **Continental**
Children: **Welcome, over 6**
Smoking: **No**
Social Drinking: **Permitted**
Minimum Stay: **2 nights ski season and
    weekends**

On 70 private acres with its own trout stream and a panoramic view of the Rockies, Starry Pines offers you year-round activities and hospitality. Enjoy the Aspen summer music festival, ballet, and theater. Try hotair balloon rides landing in the B&B's fields, or biking, hiking, jeeping, and riding in the back country. For quieter moments, there's a secluded picnic site with horseshoes and a hammock by the stream. Fall unveils spectacular aspen foliage. Winter and spring bring world-renowned skiing at four mountains only 25 minutes away, plus snowshoeing and cross-country skiing at Starry Pines's own door. At the end of the day, relax in the hot tub on the patio, then sit around the living room fireplace or watch a movie on the VCR.

The Victorian Lady ✪
4199 WEST 76TH AVENUE, WESTMINSTER, COLORADO 80030

Tel: **(303) 428-9829**
Best Time to Call: **Anytime**
Host: **Karen Sanders**
Location: **10 mi. NW of Denver**
No. of Rooms: **2**
Max. No. Sharing Bath: **4**
Double/sb: **$70**
Single/sb: **$60**

Open: **All year**
Breakfast: **Full**
Other Meals: **Available**
Pets: **No**
Children: **Welcome, over 8**
Smoking: **No**
Social Drinking: **No**
Airport/Station Pickup: **Yes**

You'll step back in time upon entering The Victorian Lady, where the rooms are filled with lovely reminders of another day. This B&B is ideally located for sightseers: just minutes from downtown Denver and public transportation, it's also near I-70, highway to some of the world's best skiing. Breakfast, served in the gazebo during the summer, may consist of cheese strata, almond poppyseed cake with warmed lemon sauce, or an old Western favorite, hearty biscuits and gravy. There's tea in the afternoon and, at bedtime, snacks that are sure to bring on pleasant dreams.

Engelmann Pines ✪
P.O. BOX 1305, WINTER PARK, COLORADO 80482

Tel: **(970) 726-4632; (800) 992-9512**	Open: **All year**
Hosts: **Heinz and Margaret Engel**	Breakfast: **Full**
Location: **67 mi. W of Denver**	Credit Cards: **AMEX, DISC, MC, VISA**
No. of Rooms: **7**	Pets: **No**
No. of Private Baths: **5**	Children: **Welcome**
Max. No. Sharing Bath: **4**	Smoking: **No**
Double/pb: **$75–$115**	Social Drinking: **Permitted**
Single/pb: **$65–$105**	Station Pickup: **Yes**
Double/sb: **$55–$75**	Foreign Languages: **German**
Single/sb: **$45–$65**	

From its Rocky Mountain perch, this spacious modern lodge offers spectacular views of the Continental Divide. Bathrooms are equipped with Jacuzzis, and there is a complete kitchen for guests' use. A free bus ferries skiers from the front door to some of Colorado's best ski slopes; cross-country ski aficionados will find a trail just across the road. When the snow melts, it's time to go golfing, hiking, fishing, and horseback riding. In the morning, eager sportsmen and -women can fill up on marzipan cake, muesli, and fresh fruit crepes.

Woodland Inn Bed & Breakfast ✪
159 TRULL ROAD, WOODLAND PARK, COLORADO 80863

Tel: **(800) 226-9565; (719) 687-8209**	Reduced Rates: **10% seniors; weekly;**
Best Time to Call: **8 AM–9 PM**	**groups booking 3 or more rooms**
Hosts: **Frank and Nancy O'Neil**	Breakfast: **Full**
Location: **18 mi. W of Colorado Springs**	Other Meals: **Available**
No. of Rooms: **6**	Credit Cards: **AMEX, DISC, MC, VISA**
No. of Private Baths: **6**	Pets: **No**
Double/pb: **$60–$80**	Children: **Welcome**
Suite: **$80–$120**	Smoking: **No**
Open: **All year**	Social Drinking: **Permitted**

Relax in the homelike atmosphere of this cozy country Inn located in the Colorado Rocky Mountains. Guest rooms are comfortably decorated, and some have spectacular views of Pikes Peak. A hearty breakfast is served in the dining room beside a warm fire or on the patio. Woodland Inn sits peacefully on twelve secluded acres, complete with a llama and a miniature donkey. On-site sports include badminton, volleyball, and ice skating. Or take a ride in a hot-air balloon with your host. Within minutes of the Inn, enjoy hiking, biking, cross-country skiing, trail riding, fishing, boating, golf, and many other tourist attractions in the Pikes Peak region.

For key to listings, see inside front or back cover.

✪ This star means that rates are guaranteed through December 31, 1998, to any guest making a reservation as a result of reading about the B&B in *Bed & Breakfast U.S.A.*—1998 edition.

Important! To avoid misunderstandings, always ask about cancellation policies when booking.

Please enclose a self-addressed, stamped, business-size envelope when contacting reservation services.

For more details on what you can expect in a B&B, see Chapter 1.

Always mention *Bed & Breakfast U.S.A.* when making reservations!

We want to hear from you! Use the form on page 625.

CONNECTICUT

B&B Bookings ✪
31½ SOUTH B STREET, TAFTVILLE, CONNECTICUT 06380

Tel: **(860) 823-1245**
Best Time to Call: **9 AM–6 PM**
Coordinator: **Scott Royce**
States/Regions Covered:
  Connecticut—Bozrah, Fitchville, Ledyard, Mystic, New London, North Stonington, Old Mystic, Preston, Salem; Rhode Island—Westerly

Rates (Double):
  Modest: **$100**
  Average: **$125–$185**
  Luxury: **$200–$250**
Minimum Stay: **2 nights weekends**

Experience Connecticut's country atmosphere in a cozy bed and breakfast. Scott's roster includes over forty listings and his service is without charge. B&B Bookings will help you plan a hassle-free vacation.

Covered Bridge Bed & Breakfast
P.O. BOX 447A, MAPLE AVENUE, NORFOLK, CONNECTICUT 06058

Tel: **(203) 542-5944**
Best Time to Call: **9 AM–6 PM**
Coordinators: **Hank and Diane Tremblay**
States/Regions Covered:
Connecticut—Statewide; New York—Amenia, Cherry Plains, Dover Plains; Massachusetts—The Berkshires; Rhode Island

Descriptive Directory: **$3**
Rates (Single/Double):
 Modest: **$85**
 Average: **$85–$95 / $85–$95**
 Luxury: **$100–$170 / $100–$195**
Credit Cards: **AMEX, MC, VISA**
Minimum Stay: **2 nights holidays, weekends**

If you enjoy historic homes, charming farmhouses, Victorian estates, picture-postcard New England scenery, unsurpassed fall foliage, music festivals, theater, antiquing, auto racing, skiing, white-water rafting, or hiking, call Diane.

Nutmeg Bed & Breakfast Agency ✪
P.O. BOX 271117, WEST HARTFORD, CONNECTICUT 06127

Tel: **(800) 727-7592; fax: (860) 232-7680**
Best Time to Call: **9:30 AM–5 PM**
Coordinator: **Michelle Souza**
States/Regions Covered:
Connecticut—Statewide; Coventry, Hartford, Litchfield, Madison, Mystic, New Haven, Salisbury, Simsbury, Stamford, Woodbury

Rates (Single/Double):
 Modest: **$45–$60**
 Average: **$70–$85**
 Luxury: **$90–$150**
Credit Cards: **AMEX, MC, VISA**
Minimum Stay: **2 nights, holiday weekends**

Nutmeg Bed & Breakfast is an exclusive member of Bed & Breakfast: The National Network, and has been serving travelers for over 12 years. With more than 105 B&Bs on her roster, Michelle can accommodate those traveling through the state, help to arrange a romantic getaway, house the business traveler, and assist those on a temporary assignment who may need a longer stay. Attractions include Mystic Seaport and Aquarium, wonderful theaters and museums in all cities, the beautiful coastline and fine beaches, and magnificent fall foliage.

Captain Dibbell House ✪
21 COMMERCE STREET, CLINTON, CONNECTICUT 06413

Tel: **(860) 669-1646**
Hosts: **Ellis and Helen Adams**
Location: **21 mi. E of New Haven**
No. of Rooms: **4**
No. of Private Baths: **4**
Double/pb: **$75–$95**
Single/pb: **$65–$85**
Open: **Apr.–Dec.**
Reduced Rates: **Weekly; 10% seniors; 3 or more nights**

Breakfast: **Full**
Credit Cards: **AMEX, DISC, MC, VISA**
Pets: **No**
Children: **Welcome, over 14**
Smoking: **No**
Social Drinking: **Permitted**
Airport/Station Pickup: **Yes**

Ellis and Helen fell in love with this piece of Connecticut shore years ago when they used to come from their home in New York to spend the weekend sailing. They liked it so much, in fact, that they bought this sea captain's home, located just one-half mile from the shore and marinas and a short drive from the town beach, and converted it into a B&B. Clinton is ideally situated for exploring the Connecticut coast; not far away you'll find Hammonassett State Beach, Mystic Seaport and Aquarium, Gillette Castle, the Goodspeed Opera House, the Essex Steam Train, Long Wharf Theater, and Yale. In order to help you enjoy the Connecticut shore they love so much, the Adamses are happy to lend you their bicycles and beach chairs.

Acorn Bed & Breakfast
628 ROUTE 148, KILLINGWORTH, CONNECTICUT 06419
acorn@connix.com; http://www.conix.com~acorn

Tel: **(860) 663-2214**	Breakfast: **Full**
Hosts: **Carole and Richard Pleines**	Credit Cards: **DC, DISC, MC, VISA**
Location: **8 mi. S/SE of Middletown**	Pets: **No**
No. of Rooms: **2**	Children: **No**
No. of Private Baths: **2**	Smoking: **No**
Double/pb: **$85**	Social Drinking: **Permitted**
Open: **All year**	Airport/Station Pickup: **Yes**

Acorn Bed & Breakfast offers a setting that is rural, yet convenient to fine restaurants, antique shops, summer and winter theater, biking, hiking, skiing, fishing, and beaches. Your hosts have an inground pool, two porches where you can sit and enjoy the wonderful array of birds, and a living room with a fireplace. Carole and Richard will do their best to ensure you a peaceful, relaxing, stress-free stay. Breakfast may consist of muffins, fresh fruit, cereal, toast, jams, and eggs donated by the resident chickens. Tea, coffee, and juice are available for early risers. Acorn is 30 to 40 minutes from New Haven and New London, one hour from Foxwoods Casino. The shoreline bustles with art, craft, and antique shows, shops, and art galleries. A cruise on the Connecticut River is a great way to spend the day.

Honeysuckle Hill B&B ✪
116 YANKEE PEDDLER PATH, MADISON, CONNECTICUT 06443

Tel: **(203) 245-4574**
Best Time to Call: **5–9 PM**
Host: **Linda Von Blon**
Location: **20 mi. E of New Haven**
No. of Rooms: **2**
Max. No. Sharing Bath: **3**
Double/pb: **$75**
Single/sb: **$65**
Suite: **$100**

Open: **All year**
Reduced Rates: **Available**
Breakfast: **Full**
Pets: **No**
Children: **Welcome, over 6**
Smoking: **No**
Social drinking: **Permitted**
Minimum Stay: **On holiday weekends**
Airport/Station Pickup: **Yes**

Honeysuckle Hill is a large raised ranch located between New Haven and Old Saybrook. This quiet shoreline retreat is close to a variety of activities. The suite, which is good for couples, has a fireplace, queen-size brass bed, sofa, cable TV, and VCR. The smaller room accommodates one guest. A short walk takes you to village boutiques, an art show on the green, and beaches. If you venture farther afield, you can cruise the Connecticut River, tour the Thimble Islands, take in a musical at Goodspeed, or bike to Hammonassett State Park.

Tucker Hill Inn ✪
96 TUCKER HILL ROAD, MIDDLEBURY, CONNECTICUT 06762

Tel: **(203) 758-8334; fax (203) 598-0652**
Best Time to Call: **9 AM–noon; after 4 PM**
Hosts: **Richard and Susan Cebelenski**
Location: **5 mi. W of Waterbury**
No. of Rooms: **4**
No. of Private Baths: **2**
Max. No. Sharing Bath: **4**
Double/pb: **$85–$120**

Double/sb: **$60–$75**
Open: **All year**
Reduced Rates: **Weekly**
Breakfast: **Full**
Credit Cards: **MC, VISA**
Pets: **No**
Children: **Welcome**
Smoking: **No**
Social Drinking: **Permitted**

Built in 1920, this large Colonial-style home, just down from the village green, exemplifies warm hospitality and charm. The spacious guest rooms are bright and airy, decorated with fine linens and pretty accessories. Breakfast features such caloric creations as pancakes, waffles, and omelettes. Facilities for antiquing, music, theater, golf, tennis, water sports, and cross-country skiing are nearby.

Pequot Hotel Bed and Breakfast
711 COW HILL ROAD, MYSTIC, CONNECTICUT 06355

Tel: **(860) 572-0390**
Best Time to Call: **8 AM–8 PM**
Host: **Nancy Mitchell**
Location: **135 mi. NE of New York**
No. of Rooms: **3**
No. of Private Baths: **3**
Double/pb: **$95–$145**
Suites: **$95–$135; sleeps 4**
Open: **All year**

Reduced Rates: **10% Jan.–Mar.**
Breakfast: **Full**
Other Meals: **Available**
Pets: **No**
Children: **Welcome, over 8**
Smoking: **No**
Social Drinking: **Permitted**
Airport/Station Pickup: **Yes**

The Pequot Hotel is an authentically restored 1840 stagecoach stop, in the center of the Burnett's Corners Historic District, just 2¹/₂ miles from the charming New England seacoast village of Mystic, Connecticut. This large, comfortable Greek Revival–style inn is situated on 23 wooded acres convenient to the Mystic Seaport Museum, the Mystic Aquarium, and the Foxwoods Gambling Casino. At the end of a busy day, guests are free to relax on the large screened porch or in one of the elegant fireplaced parlors. Recommendations and reservations for dinner at one of the area's fine restaurants are provided by the innkeeper, Nancy. In the morning a full country breakfast, including fresh local fruits and vegetables, is ready when you are. Nancy, a resident for 18 years, has 23 years' experience as an international flight attendant.

Weaver's House ✪
58 GREENWOODS ROAD, NORFOLK, CONNECTICUT 06058

Tel: **(860) 542-5108; (800) 283-1551**
Hosts: **Judy and Arnold Tsukroff**
Location: **39 mi. NW of Hartford**
No. of Rooms: **4**
Max. No. Sharing Bath: **4**
Double/sb: **$48–$58**
Single/sb: **$43–$53**

Open: **All year**
Breakfast: **Full**
Pets: **No**
Smoking: **No**
Social Drinking: **Permitted**
Foreign Languages: **German**

Weaver's House is a turn-of-the-century Victorian facing the Yale Summer School of Music and Art Estate. In the 1930s, it was used as an annex to the Norfolk Inn. The guest rooms are simply decorated with handwoven rag rugs. Your hostess is a talented weaver who will gladly display her loom for you. There are concerts and art shows in the summer, and two state parks are nearby with blazed hiking trails. Judy offers a simple hearty breakfast, including vegetarian choices.

Shelton House Bed & Breakfast ✪
663 MAIN STREET, ROUTE 6, PLYMOUTH, CONNECTICUT 06782

Tel: **(860) 283-4616**
Best Time to Call: **Evening**

Hosts: **Pat and Bill Doherty**
Location: **10 mi. N of Waterbury**

No. of Rooms: **4**
No. of Private Baths: **1**
Max. No. Sharing Bath: **4**
Double/pb: **$85**
Single/pb: **$75**
Double/sb: **$75**
Single/sb: **$65**

Open: **All year**
Breakfast: **Full**
Pets: **No**
Children: **No**
Smoking: **No**
Social Drinking: **No**

Enjoy a step back into time in this 1825 Greek Revival, elegantly furnished with antiques and period furniture. The grounds boast perennial gardens and a fountain. After a full day of shopping and sightseeing, enjoy afternoon tea and relax in the spacious parlor, complete with fireplace and TV. Shelton House is convenient to I-84, one mile to Route 8, 20 minutes to historic Litchfield, 30 minutes to Hartford. Nearby are antique centers, vineyards, nature preserves, and skiing.

The Charles R. Hart House ✪

1046 WINDSOR AVENUE, WINDSOR, CONNECTICUT 06095
harthous@ntplx.net; http://www.ntplx.net/~harthous

Tel: **(860) 688-5555**
Best Time to Call: **8–10 AM, 4–8 PM**
Hosts: **Dorothy and Bob McAllister**
Location: **6 mi. N of Hartford**
No. of Rooms: **4**
No. of Private Baths: **4**
Double/pb: **$75–$85**
Single/pb: **$65–$75**

Open: **All year**
Breakfast: **Full**
Pets: **No**
Children: **Welcome, over 12**
Smoking: **No**
Social Drinking: **Permitted**
Station Pickup: **Yes**

Hartford merchant Charles Hart added luxurious wallcoverings, ceramic tiled fireplaces, and an elegant Palladian window to this farmhouse in 1896, some thirty years after it was built. By the 1940s, the property was serving as a pheasant farm. The current owners have furnished it with exquisite period pieces. You can hear the past as well as see it, thanks to an antique music box. Local cultural sites span many eras, from the Mark Twain House and Old Newgate Prison to the New England Air Museum at Bradley International Airport. Modern distractions include shopping in Hartford and golf at the challenging Tournament Players Course, home of the Greater Hartford Open.

B&B by the Lake ✪
19 DILLON BEACH ROAD, WINSTED, CONNECTICUT 06098

Tel: **(860) 738-0230 May 15–Oct. 15;** **(914) 232-6864 Oct. 15–May 15**	Double/pb: **$85**
	Double/sb: **$85**
Best Time to Call: **Anytime**	Open: **May 15–Oct. 15**
Hosts: **Gayle Holt and Anastasio Rossi**	Reduced Rates: **5% May; 5% seniors**
Location: **25 mi. W of Hartford**	Breakfast: **Continental, plus**
No. of Rooms: **4**	Pets: **No**
No. of Private Baths: **1**	Smoking: **No**
Max. No. Sharing Bath: **4**	Social Drinking: **Permitted**

Guests will feel at home in this turn-of-the-century rustic lodge overlooking Litchfield County's West Hill Lake. The wraparound porch affords spectacular views of the encircling woods and Connecticut's cleanest lake, which is well-stocked with fish. Borrow the canoe, snooze on the private beach, or enjoy a country walk. Breakfast can be served on the large, lattice-covered dock. In the evening you can watch TV or a movie, unless you prefer to hear Anastasio play Gershwin or Chopin on the concert grand piano.

Taylor's Corner Bed & Breakfast ✪
880 ROUTE 171, WOODSTOCK, CONNECTICUT 06281-2930
tracyt@neca.com; http://www.neguide.com/taylors

Tel: **(860) 974-0490**
Hosts: **Peggy and Doug Tracy**
Location: **50 mi. NE of Hartford**
No. of Rooms: **4**
No. of Private Baths: **3**
Max. No. Sharing Bath: **3**
Double/pb: **$85**
Single/pb: **$80**
Single/sb: **$55**

Open: **All year**
Reduced Rates: **10% weekly**
Breakfast: **Full (weekends), Continental (weekdays)**
Pets: **No**
Children: **Welcome, over 12**
Smoking: **No**
Social Drinking: **Permitted**

This 18th-century Colonial is listed on the National Register of Historic Places and features eight working fireplaces. Common areas and spacious air-conditioned guest rooms are furnished with antiques. Originally a farmhouse, Taylor's Corner maintains a rustic setting surrounded by gardens, pastures, and towering trees. After experiencing a hint of Denmark at the breakfast table, guests are invited to meet Jessie Brown, the resident Scotch Highland cow. Nearby you can visit the Bowen House Museum on Woodstock's common, or do some antique shopping in Putnam. Old Sturbridge Village is 20 miles away. Peggy is a full-time innkeeper and Doug pursues a marketing career.

DELAWARE

Darley Manor Inn B&B ✪

3701 PHILADELPHIA PIKE, CLAYMONT, DELAWARE 19703

Tel: **(302) 792-2127; (800) 824-4703**
Best Time to Call: **11 AM–10 PM**
Hosts: **Ray and Judith Hester**
Location: **7 mi. N of Wilmington**
No. of Rooms: **5**
No. of Private Baths: **5**
Double/pb: **$79**
Suites: **$89–$99**
Open: **All year**
Reduced Rates: **Available**

Breakfast: **Full**
Credit Cards: **AMEX, DC, DISC, MC, VISA**
Pets: **No**
Children: **Welcome, over 9**
Smoking: **No**
Social Drinking: **Permitted**
Minimum Stay: **2 nights, weekends Apr., May, Oct., Nov., major holidays**

This 1790s National Register Colonial manor house was home to Victorian America's most famous illustrator, F.O.C. Darley. His work accompanied the writing of Hawthorne, Cooper, Irving, Poe, Longfellow, Charles Dickens, and others. Dickens stayed here for two weeks of rest in 1867. The seventeen rooms, including three parlors, are decorated in

1850s antiques and reproductions. All rooms have air-conditioning, TV/VCR, full or wall-canopied queen-size beds, and phones; one suite has a working fireplace. Breakfast is served in the dining room or on the large porch. The Victorian azalea garden, with small fountains, is great for relaxation. All Brandywine Valley attractions are nearby, including Winterthur, Longwood, Brandywine River Museum, Hagley, and historic Philadelphia. Many good restaurants are within five to ten minutes.

Becky's Country Inn ❂
401 MAIN STREET, DAGSBORO, DELAWARE 19939

Tel: **(302) 732-3953**	Open: **All year**
Best Time to Call: **Evenings**	Reduced Rates: **10% seniors**
Hosts: **Bill and Becky Madden**	Breakfast: **Continental, plus**
Location: **9 mi. W of Bethany Beach**	Pets: **No**
No. of Rooms: **3**	Children: **No**
No. of Private Baths: **3**	Smoking: **No**
Double/pb: **$65–$85**	Social Drinking: **Permitted**
Single/pb: **$55**	

The oldest home in Dagsboro, this Colonial house sits on the main street, just nine miles from the beaches—close enough to enjoy all the beach activities and just far enough away to enjoy country quiet. The library is a great place to be if you need to relax by the fireplace with a good book. In the summer, relax by the pool or on the fifty-foot deck. All the bedrooms are done in a warm country atmosphere. Breakfast is served in the dining room, on the deck, or by the pool. Your hosts can direct you to outlet stores, antiquing spots, and fine restaurants.

William Penn Guest House ❂
206 DELAWARE STREET, NEW CASTLE, DELAWARE 19720

Tel: **(302) 328-7736**	Single/sb: **$50**
Best Time to Call: **Anytime**	Open: **All year**
Hosts: **Mr. and Mrs. Richard Burwell**	Breakfast: **Continental**
Location: **2 mi. from I-95**	Pets: **No**
No. of Rooms: **4**	Children: **Welcome, over 10**
Max. No. Sharing Bath: **4**	Smoking: **No**
Double/pb: **$60–$90**	Social Drinking: **Permitted**
Double/sb: **$60–$90**	Foreign Languages: **Italian**

If you're a history buff, perhaps a stay in a 1682 house named for William Penn is what you've been seeking. Located in the heart of New Castle's historic district, the accommodations here are most comfortable. A lovely park for strolling and for the children to play in borders the Delaware shore, just two blocks away. The University of Delaware is 15 minutes from the house.

The Boulevard Bed & Breakfast ✪
1909 BAYNARD BOULEVARD, WILMINGTON, DELAWARE 19802

Tel: **(302) 656-9700**
Hosts: **Charles and Judy Powell**
Location: **¹/₂ mi. from I-95, Exit 8**
No. of Rooms: **6**
No. of Private Baths: **4**
Max. No. Sharing Bath: **3**
Double/pb: **$75–$80**
Single/pb: **$70–$75**
Double/sb: **$65**

Single/sb: **$60**
Open: **All year**
Reduced Rates: **Corporate**
Breakfast: **Full**
Credit Cards: **AMEX, MC, VISA**
Pets: **No**
Children: **Welcome**
Smoking: **No**
Social Drinking: **Permitted**

This beautifully restored city mansion was built in 1913 and has earned a place on the National Register of Historic Places. Upon entering, you'll be struck by the impressive foyer and magnificent staircase, leading to a landing complete with a window seat and large leaded-glass windows flanked by 15-foot-tall fluted columns. Breakfast is served in the formal dining room or on the screened-in porch. Although Baynard Boulevard is a quiet and peaceful street, it's just a short walk away from the downtown business district. Parks are close by, and it's just a short drive to Hagley, Winterthur, the Delaware Natural History and the Art Museum; or head for nearby Chadds Ford, Pennsylvania, and the famous Brandywine River Museum.

DISTRICT OF COLUMBIA

Bed & Breakfast Accommodations, Ltd.

P.O. BOX 12011, WASHINGTON, D.C. 20005

bnbaccom@aol.com

Tel: **(202) 328-3510; fax (202) 332-3885**
Best Time to Call: **10 AM–5 PM Mon.–Fri.**
Coordinator: **Wendy Serpan**
States/Regions Covered: **Washington, D.C.; Virginia and Maryland suburbs**

Rates: (Single/Double):
    Average: **$45–$150 / $55–$150**
Credit Cards: **AMEX, DISC, DC, MC, VISA**

This service has a network of 80 homes, apartments, guesthouses, and inns. Most of the accommodations are convenient to public transportation. Several of the homes are historic properties. There is a wide range of accommodations, from budget to luxury.

Bed & Breakfast League/Sweet Dreams and Toast ✪
P.O. BOX 9490, WASHINGTON, D.C. 20016
bandbwdc@erols.com

Tel: **(202) 363-7767; fax: (202) 363-8396**
Best Time to Call: **9 AM–5 PM Mon.–Thurs., 9 AM–1 PM Fri.**
Coordinator: **Millie Groobey**
States/Regions Covered: **Washington, D.C.**

Rates (Single/Double):
Modest: **$48–$58 / $58–$68**
Average: **$58–$73 / $68–$90**
Luxury: **$78–$120 / $88–$150**
Credit Cards: **AMEX, DC, MC, VISA**
Minimum Stay: **2 nights**

Bed & Breakfast League/Sweet Dreams and Toast reservation services were merged in 1988. They offer accommodations in privately owned homes and apartments. Many are in historic districts; all are in good, safe sections of the city within easy walking distance of an excellent public transportation system. Gracious hosts will cheerfully direct you to points of interest, monuments, museums, shops, and restaurants. The office of this service is closed on federal holidays, Thanksgiving, and Christmas. A $10 fee is charged for each reservation.

A Capitol Place ✪
134 12TH STREET SE, WASHINGTON, D.C. 20003

Tel: **(202) 543-1020;**
fax: **(202) 543-1734**
Best Time to Call: **Anytime**
Hosts: **Jim and Mary Pellettieri**
Location: **½ mi. E of U.S. Capitol Building**
Suite: **$95**

Open: **All year**
Breakfast: **Full**
Pets: **No**
Children: **No**
Smoking: **No**
Social Drinking: **Permitted**
Minimum Stay: **2 nights**

Stay in a newly renovated, "English basement" apartment, the entire lower level of a 100-year-old Victorian rowhouse in the historic district of Capitol Hill, 12 blocks from the U.S. Capitol. The light sunny quarters have a private entrance, a bay-fronted living room/dining room, a den with library bed, cable color TV, desk and telephone, a bedroom with queen-size bed, a modern bath with tub and shower, and a fully equipped kitchen. The refrigerator is filled with breakfast makings— juices, fruits, cheeses, homemade breads, and cookies. Located in a well-established, friendly neighborhood just off Lincoln Park, the guest apartment is a 7-minute walk from Eastern Market Metro and the historic Eastern Market with its cafes and antique stores. Off-street parking is accessible from the apartment's back door. Guests are invited to join their hosts for a complimentary beverage.

Hereford House ✪
604 SOUTH CAROLINA AVENUE, SE, WASHINGTON, D.C. 20003

Tel: **(202) 543-0102**
Host: **Ann Edwards**
Location: **In D.C.**
No. of Rooms: **4**
Max. No. Sharing Bath: **4**
Double/sb: **$65–$73**
Single/sb: **$50–$63**
Open: **All year**

Reduced Rates: **10% seniors; $5 less over 8 nights**
Breakfast: **Full**
Pets: **Sometimes**
Children: **Welcome, over 12**
Smoking: **No**
Social Drinking: **Permitted**

Hereford House is a 1915 brick town house with original parquet flooring and wood throughout. It is situated on a tree-lined street on historic Capitol Hill, one block from the subway. The U.S. Capitol, Congressional Library, Smithsonian Institute, and restaurants are all within easy walking distance, making Hereford House the perfect location for visitors to the nation's capital. Bountiful cooked English breakfasts are served by your full-time British hostess. Guests share the company of newly made friends (and resident dog) in the living room.

FLORIDA

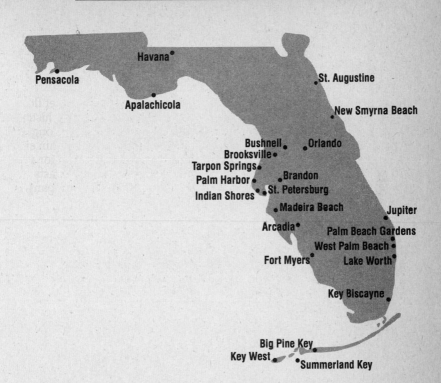

- Pensacola
- Havana
- St. Augustine
- Apalachicola
- New Smyrna Beach
- Bushnell
- Orlando
- Brooksville
- Tarpon Springs
- Brandon
- Palm Harbor
- St. Petersburg
- Indian Shores
- Madeira Beach
- Jupiter
- Arcadia
- Palm Beach Gardens
- West Palm Beach
- Fort Myers
- Lake Worth
- Key Biscayne
- Big Pine Key
- Key West
- Summerland Key

Coombs House Inn ✪
80 SIXTH STREET, APALACHICOLA, FLORIDA 32320

Tel: **(904) 653-9199**
Best Time to Call: **Anytime**
Hosts: **Marilyn and Charles Schubert**
Location: **75 mi. SW of Tallahassee**
No. of Rooms: **15**
No. of Private Baths: **15**
Double/pb: **$89–$99**
Single/pb: **$69–$89**

Suites: **$109–$119**
Open: **All year**
Breakfast: **Continental**
Credit Cards: **AMEX, MC, VISA**
Pets: **Sometimes**
Children: **Welcome**
Smoking: **No**
Social Drinking: **Permitted**

Elegantly restored, this 1905 Victorian mansion welcomes those special guests who appreciate the charm and historical authenticity of another era and an intimate homey atmosphere. The three-story mansion features high ceilings and nine fireplaces. Inside you'll admire antique furniture of the period, paintings, historical photographs, imported English chintz draperies that frame the large bay windows, and oriental carpets. Each guest room has a private bath and cable TV. Located only minutes from fishing, boating, the Apalachicola River, and the white beaches of St. George Island.

Historic Parker House ✪

427 WEST HICKORY STREET, ARCADIA, FLORIDA 34266

Tel: **(941) 494-2499; (800) 969-2499**
Best Time to Call: **8 AM–10 PM**
Hosts: **Bob and Shelly Baumann**
Location: **45 mi. E of Sarasota**
No. of Rooms: **4**
No. of Private Baths: **2**
Max. No. Sharing Bath: **4**
Double/pb: **$75**
Single/pb: **$75**
Double/sb: **$60**

Single/sb: **$60**
Open: **All year**
Reduced Rates: **10%**
Breakfast: **Continental**
Credit Cards: **AMEX, MC, VISA**
Pets: **No**
Children: **Welcome, over 10**
Smoking: **No**
Social Drinking: **Permitted**

Once you step inside the Historic Parker House you become acquainted with a much grander, yet simpler life. The 6000-square-foot home is chock full of antiques, old clocks, and Florida's past. The original section of the home dates to the mid 1890s; a large addition was put in in 1914 by the original owners, the Parkers, Florida cattle barons. Located in historic downtown Arcadia, recently named one of the one hundred best small towns in America, the home is close to antique and gift shopping and the Peace River for canoeing. Nearby are all of South Central Florida's attractions.

The Barnacle ✪
1557 LONG BEACH DRIVE, BIG PINE KEY, FLORIDA 33043

Tel: **(305) 872-3298; (800) 465-9100;**
  fax: **(305) 872-3863**
Best Time to Call: **10 AM–8 PM**
Hosts: **Jane and Tim Marquis**
Location: **Mile marker 33**
No. of Rooms: **4**
No. of Private Baths: **4**

Double/pb: **$105–$140**
Open: **All year**
Breakfast: **Full**
Pets: **No**
Children: **Welcome, over 16**
Smoking: **No**

Tim and Jane welcome you to their Caribbean-style home, where tranquility and leisurely breezes prevail. Enjoy the private beach, where you can scuba dive, snorkel, and swim. Then take a nature walk, soak in the hot tub, ride a bicycle or paddle boat, or nap in the hammock between the palms. Here, your time is your own. The ultimate in privacy is the self-contained cottage, a tropical treehouse with stained glass windows and a private terrace. The rooms overlook the ocean or open to the atrium, with a hot tub, waterfall, and lush plants. The Ocean room has a private entrance and opens to the patio on the beach. Special attention is given to the detail of the villa, decorated with artistic flair. The Barnacle puts emphasis on the sun and sea with warm hospitality.

Bed & Breakfast-on-the-Ocean "Casa Grande" ✪
P.O. BOX 378, BIG PINE KEY, FLORIDA 33043

Tel: **(305) 872-2878**
Host: **Kathleen Threlkeld**

Location: **30 mi. E of Key West**
No. of Rooms: **3**

No. of Private Baths: **3**
Double/pb: **$95**
Open: **All year**
Breakfast: **Full**

Pets: **No**
Children: **No**
Smoking: **Permitted**
Social Drinking: **Permitted**

This spectacular Spanish-style home, facing the ocean, was custom-designed to suit the natural beauty of the Keys. The large landscaped garden patio, with panoramic beach views, is where you'll enjoy Kathleen's bountiful breakfast. It is also the site of the hot tub/Jacuzzi for relaxing by day or under a moonlit sky. The large and airy guest rooms are comfortably cooled by Bahama fans or air-conditioning. Key deer and birds abound. From the private beach, you'll enjoy swimming, fishing, snorkeling, bicycling, and jogging. There's a picnic table, gas grill, hammock, and Windsurfer for guests to use, compliments of the gracious host.

Paradise Lodging ✪

31316 AVENUE J, BIG PINE KEY, FLORIDA 33043-4657

Tel: **(305) 872-9009**
Host: **Joan Thoman**
Location: **30 mi. E of Key West**
Guest Cottage: **$85, for two**
Open: **All year**

Breakfast: **Continental**
Pets: **Sometimes**
Children: **Welcome**
Smoking: **Permitted**
Social Drinking: **Permitted**

True to its name, Paradise Lodging is located six miles from Bahia Honda State Park (one of the best beaches in the country) and the famed Looe Key Reef. This spacious two-bedroom unit sleeps six and has a large kitchen and living room. Joan offers free dockage twenty feet from your door, a barbecue grill for cooking your dinner, and cable TV. Guests can enjoy fishing, scuba diving, snorkeling, and the great night-life in Key West.

Behind the Fence ✪

1400 VIOLA DRIVE AT COUNTRYSIDE, BRANDON, FLORIDA 33511

Tel: **(813) 685-8201**
Best Time to Call: 2–8 PM
Hosts: **Larry and Carolyn Yoss**
Location: **15 mi. E of Tampa**
No. of Rooms: **5**
No. of Private Baths: **3**
Max. No. Sharing Bath: **4**
Double/pb: **$69–$72**
Single/pb: **$49–$59**
Double/sb: **$59–$69**
Single/sb: **$49–$59**

Suites: **$72–$79**
Open: **All year**
Reduced Rates: **10% seniors;**
June–Aug.; weekly
Breakfast: **Continental, plus**
Pets: **Sometimes**
Children: **Welcome**
Smoking: **No**
Social Drinking: **Permitted**
Airport/Station Pickup: **Yes**

As the name suggests, this inn is nestled in the trees behind a fence on a quiet secluded lot. The ambiance of another era is reflected in the authentic country furnishings from the 1800s—you will feel as if you have entered another world. The house was built in 1976 in early saltbox style. The interior was finished in county salvage material from before the turn of the century. Art League tours of the house for groups interested in early lifestyles or antiques began in 1978 and are still available today. Nearby are restaurants, canoeing, fishing, horseback riding, golf, bike tours, and Florida's largest mall. Within driving distance is downtown Tampa, the Florida Aquarium, Florida State Fairgrounds, Busch Gardens, Adventure Island, Museum of Science and Industry, University of South Florida, west coast beaches, and Disney World.

Verona House ✪
201 SOUTH MAIN STREET, BROOKSVILLE, FLORIDA 34601

Tel: **(352) 796-4001**
Best Time to Call: **1–8 PM**
Hosts: **Bob and Jan Boyd**
Location: **50 mi. N of Tampa**
No. of Rooms: **4**
No. of Private Baths: **4**
Double/pb: **$65**
Single/pb: **$55**
Suites: **$80–$100**

Open: **All year**
Reduced Rates: **Available**
Breakfast: **Full, Continental**
Credit Cards: **AMEX, DISC, MC, VISA**
Pets: **No**
Smoking: **No**
Social Drinking: **Permitted**
Airport/Station Pickup: **Yes**

The Verona House is a unique 1925 Sears & Roebuck catalog house. The B&B is located among the rolling hills and oak tree–lined streets of this historical town, established in 1856. Guest rooms have queen-size beds and are furnished with antiques and collectible pieces. You'll enjoy true Southern hospitality at breakfast, which may include Jan's baked casseroles, muffins, nut bread, or quiche.

Cypress House Bed and Breakfast ✪
5175 SOUTHWEST 90 BOULEVARD, C.R. 476B, BUSHNELL, FLORIDA 33513

Tel: **(352) 568-0909**
Best Time to Call: **8 AM–10 PM**
Hosts: **Jan Fessler and Thelma Schaum**
Location: **50 mi. N of Tampa**
No. of Rooms: **6**
No. of Private Baths: **3**
Max. No. Sharing Bath: **4**
Double/pb: **$70**
Double/sb: **$50**

Suite: **$85**
Open: **All year**
Reduced Rates: **Available**
Breakfast: **Continental, buffet**
Other Meals: **Available**
Pets: **Horses ($10 per night)**
Children: **Welcome, over 5**
Smoking: **Restricted**
Social Drinking: **Permitted**

A new log home built in the gracious old Florida style, Cypress House is set on wooded farmland. From the oak rockers on the wide wraparound veranda, you can see oak trees draped with moss. The Webster Flea Market (Mondays only) and Brooksville's Christmas House are nearby, and Disney World and Busch Gardens are an hour away. You won't have to travel far to browse for antiques, fish, hike, or go canoeing. To bolster your energy, your hosts offer a generous breakfast buffet, plus afternoon snacks and evening dessert. Your hosts have seven horses and offer one- to six-hour trail rides. There's a pool 15 × 40 feet, long enough for lap swimming.

Windsong Garden & Art Gallery ✪
5570–4 WOODROSE COURT, FORT MYERS, FLORIDA 33907

Tel: **(813) 936-6378**	Breakfast: **Continental**
Host: **Embe Burdick**	Pets: **No**
No. of Rooms: **2**	Children: **No**
No. of Private Baths: **2**	Smoking: **No**
Double/pb: **$65**	Social Drinking: **Permitted**
Open: **All year**	Minimum Stay: **2 nights**

This modern clear-shake-and-brick town house has a private courtyard and balcony for your enjoyment. The spacious combination bedroom-and-sitting room is most comfortable. Embe's varied interests include arts, crafts, music, and her household cats. It's close to Sanibel and Captiva Islands, Ft. Myers Beach, fine shopping, good restaurants, and the University of Florida. You are welcome to use the pool.

Gaver's Bed & Breakfast ✪
301 EAST SIXTH AVENUE, HAVANA, FLORIDA 32333

Tel: **(904) 539-5611**	Open: **All year**
Hosts: **Shirley and Bruce Gaver**	Breakfast: **Full**
Location: **12 mi. N of Tallahassee**	Pets: **No**
No. of Rooms: **2**	Children: **Welcome, over 8**
No. of Private Baths: **2**	Smoking: **No**
Double/pb: **$75**	Social Drinking: **Permitted**

This B&B, situated on a quiet residential street two blocks from the center of town, is a likely stop for collectors—at last count, Havana had thirty antique shops plus many related businesses. Tallahassee, the state capital and home of Florida State University, is only fifteen minutes away by car. A restored 1907 frame house, Gaver's has a large screened porch, and guests are welcome to watch cable TV in the common area. For breakfast, your hosts will design a menu to suit your preferences.

Meeks B&B on the Gulf Beaches ✪
19418 GULF BOULEVARD, #408, INDIAN SHORES, FLORIDA 33785

Tel: **(813) 596-5424; fax: (813) 593-0065**	Hosts: **Greta and Bob Meeks**
Best Time to Call: **7 AM–10 PM**	Location: **35 min. from Tampa Airport**
	No. of Rooms: **7**

No. of Private Baths: **5**
Double/pb: **$60–$75**
Single/pb: **$50–$60**
Suites: **$75–$125**
Open: **All year**

Breakfast: **Continental, full**
Pets: **No**
Children: **Welcome**
Smoking: **No**
Social Drinking: **Permitted**

Beach! Pool! Sunsets! Enjoy your stay in this beach condo overlooking the Gulf of Mexico. A beach cottage is sometimes available. Choose your breakfast, then bask in the sun, swim in the gulf, and catch spectacular sunsets from your balcony. Dine at nearby seafood restaurants and visit the local seabird sanctuary, sunken gardens, and the Dali Museum. Other nearby attractions are Busch Gardens in Tampa and sponge diving in Tarpon Springs. This B&B is located between Clearwater and St. Petersburg Beach, only two hours from Walt Disney World. Your hostess is a real estate broker.

Innisfail ✪
134 TIMBER LANE, JUPITER, FLORIDA 33458

Tel: **(561) 744-5902**
Best Time to Call: **Evenings**
Hosts: **Katherine and Luke Van Noorden**
Location: **20 mi. N of Palm Beach**
No. of Rooms: **2**
No. of Private Baths: **2**
Double/pb: **$65–$75**
Open: **All year**

Reduced Rates: **10% weekly**
Breakfast: **Continental**
Other Meals: **Available**
Pets: **Welcome**
Children: **Welcome, over 7**
Smoking: **No**
Social Drinking: **Permitted**

A contemporary ranch framed by pine trees, Innisfail—Gaelic for "the abode of peace and harmony"—doubles as a gallery. The Van Noordens are sculptors, and guests are welcome to watch them work in their home studio. While you don't have to be an art lover to visit, it helps to be a pet lover; Katherine and Luke's four-footed family comprises three dogs and two cats. Jupiter has wonderful beaches, but you can get an equally good tan lounging by the Van Noordens' swimming pool. In the morning, a Continental breakfast of coffee or tea, fresh citrus fruit, and muffins or cereal is served.

Hibiscus House ✪
345 WEST ENID DRIVE, KEY BISCAYNE, FLORIDA 33149

Tel: **(305) 361-2456**
Best Time to Call: **9 AM–5 PM**
Hosts: **Bernice and Earl Duffy**
Location: **10 mi. SE of Miami**
No. of Rooms: **2**
No. of Private Baths: **2**
Double/pb: **$65**
Single/pb: **$60**

Open: **All year**
Reduced Rates: **May 1–Dec. 15**
Breakfast: **Full**
Pets: **No**
Children: **No**
Smoking: **Permitted**
Social Drinking: **Permitted**
Minimum Stay: **2 nights**

Welcome to an island paradise only 15 minutes from downtown Miami and 20 minutes from Miami International Airport. Key Biscayne features two lushly landscaped parks, a championship golf course, and miles of white sandy beaches; your hosts offer private beach privileges. Tennis courts and bicycle paths are in plentiful supply. Add to this the famous Miami Seaquarium and easy access to Greater Miami's many attractions and you have all of the ingredients for a very pleasant visit.

Center Court Historic Inn & Cottages ✪
916 CENTER STREET, KEY WEST, FLORIDA 33040

Tel: (305) 296-9292; (800) 797-8787
Best Time to Call: 9 AM–9 PM
Host: Naomi Van Steelandt
Location: 120 mi. S of Miami
No. of Rooms: 7
No. of Private Baths: 7
Double/pb: $118–$138
Guest Cottage: $138–$298, sleeps 2–6
Suites: $148
Open: All year
Reduced Rates: May 1–Dec. 15; 5% seniors

Breakfast: Continental, plus
Credit Cards: AMEX, DISC, MC, VISA
Pets: Sometimes
Children: Welcome in cottages, over 12 in main house
Smoking: No
Social Drinking: Permitted
Minimum Stay: 2 nights weekends, cottages

Center Court is located in the heart of Key West's Historic District, within walking distance to every major attraction. All rooms have been recently renovated with loving care and have lightweight comforters, feather pillows, hair dryers, TV, telephones, fans and air-conditioning. Amenities include private sundecks, an eight-person Jacuzzi, heated pool, exercise room, and a private courtyard with outdoor dining and barbecue grills. In the morning, enjoy breakfast at your leisure.

Mango Inn Bed and Breakfast ✪
128 NORTH LAKESIDE DRIVE, LAKE WORTH, FLORIDA 33460

Tel: (561) 533-6900
Best Time to Call: Evenings
Hosts: Erin Ehman and Bo Allen
Location: 5 mi. S of West Palm Beach
No. of Rooms: 8
No. of Private Baths: 8
Double/pb: $75–$120
Open: All year
Reduced Rates: 10% seniors; weekly
Breakfast: Full (weekends), Continental (weekdays)

Credit Cards: AMEX, DC, DISC, MC, VISA
Pets: No
Children: No
Smoking: No
Social Drinking: Permitted
Minimum Stay: 2 nights, weekends
Airport/Station Pickup: Yes

Built in 1915, this stucco home is nestled among the majestic Queen Palms shading the foot of the bridge that leads to the white sandy beaches of the Atlantic Ocean. The Inn is furnished with a mixture of antiques and updated pieces. Each guest room boasts down pillows, monogrammed designer bed linens, and central air. Breakfast can be served poolside or by the coral stone fireplace. The menu may consist of fresh-baked breads—such as mango-cashew muffins or orange scones with homemade blackberry butter—fresh-squeezed juices, and tropical fruit. Guests can enjoy the beach, water sports, golfing, parks, and shopping downtown in the Arts & Antiques District. Lunch or dine at eclectic restaurants and upscale coffeehouses, or take a day excursion to South Beach, Palm Beach, the Bahamas, and more.

Lighthouse Bed & Breakfast ✪
13355 2ND STREET, MADEIRA BEACH, FLORIDA 33708

Tel: **(813) 391-0015; (800) 241-0334**
Hosts: **Joyce and John Dickinson**
Location: **4 mi. W of St. Petersburg**
No. of Rooms: **5**
No. of Private Baths: **5**
Double/pb: **$45–$85**
Open: **All year**
Breakfast: **Full (winter), Continental (summer)**

Credit Cards: **MC, VISA**
Pets: **Sometimes**
Children: **Welcome, over 5**
Smoking: **Permitted**
Social Drinking: **Permitted**
Airport Pickup: **Yes**

Lighthouse Bed & Breakfast is located only 50 steps from the Intracoastal Waterway and 300 steps from white sand on the Gulf of Mexico's beaches. Guests enjoy the comfort of the Key West–style surroundings with a palm-filled courtyard, a gazebo for dining or relaxing, and a sundeck atop the lighthouse—for lying in the sun or watching the sunrise or sunset. If you want to cook your own supper, there's a barbecue grill. It's an easy walk to the famous John's Pass Boardwalk and village where shopping, restaurants, jet skiing, parasailing, chartered fishing boats, and casino cruises are available. St. Petersburg Pier, Dali Museum, and the Florida International Museum are within ten minutes. Busch Gardens in Tampa is approximately thirty minutes away. In 1995 St. Petersburg was awarded a major league baseball team. The Lighthouse is a quiet retreat from the city's traffic and commercial buildings, yet close enough to join in the rush if you want to. Breakfast specialties include pancakes, waffles, and omelettes. For those flying in, airport door-to-door service is available.

Night Swan Intracoastal Bed & Breakfast ✪
512 SOUTH RIVERSIDE DRIVE, NEW SMYRNA BEACH, FLORIDA 32168

Tel: **(904) 423-4940**
Best Time to Call: **9 AM–9 PM**
Hosts: **Martha and Charles Nighswonger**
Location: **15 mi. S of Daytona Beach**
No. of Rooms: **8**

No. of Private Baths: **8**
Double/pb: **$80–$95**
Suites: **$115–$150; sleeps 4**
Open: **All year**
Reduced Rates: **Available**
Breakfast: **Continental, full**

Credit Cards: **AMEX, DISC, MC, VISA**
Pets: **No**
Children: **Welcome**

Smoking: **No**
Social Drinking: **Permitted**
Airport/Station Pickup: **Yes**

Come sit on Night Swan's wraparound porch or by its windows and watch pelicans, dolphins, sailboats, and yachts ply the Atlantic Intracoastal Waterway. Then enjoy the waterfront yourself: surf, swim, fish, drive, or bicycle along the bathing beach two miles to the east. This spacious three-story home in New Smyrna's historic district has a central fireplace and intricate, natural woodwork in every room, and some rooms overlook the Indian River. Breakfast is served in the dining room; low-cholesterol dishes are a house specialty.

PerriHouse Bed & Breakfast Inn ✪
10417 CENTURION COURT, ORLANDO, FLORIDA 32836
http://www.shoppersmart.com/perrihse

Tel: **(407) 876-4830; (800) 780-4830;**
　fax: **(407) 876-0241**
Best Time to Call: **9 AM–9 PM**
Hosts: **Nick and Angi Perretti**
Location: **3 mi. N of I-4 Exit 27, Lake Buena Vista, on SR 535N**
No. of Rooms: **8**
No. of Private Baths: **8**
Double/pb: **$89–$109**
Single/pb: **$79–$99**

Open: **All year**
Reduced Rates: **Seniors; weekly**
Breakfast: **Continental**
Credit Cards: **AMEX, DISC, MC, VISA**
Pets: **No**
Children: **Welcome (crib)**
Smoking: **No**
Social Drinking: **Permitted**
Airport/Station Pickup: **Yes**

PerriHouse is a quiet, private country estate Inn secluded on 24 acres of land adjacent to the Walt Disney World Resort complex. Because of its outstanding location, Disney Village and Pleasure Island are only 3

minutes away; EPCOT center is only 5 minutes. It's the perfect vacation setting for families who desire a unique travel experience with a comfortable, convenient home away from home. An upscale Continental breakfast awaits you each morning, and a refreshing pool and spa relaxes you after a full day of activities. Each guest room features its own private bath, entrance, TV, telephone, ceiling fan, and central air/heat. The PerriHouse grounds are being developed and landscaped to create a future bird sanctuary and wildlife preserve. Come bird-watch on the peaceful, tranquil grounds of the PerriHouse estate and wake up to bird songs outside your window. Your hosts, Nick and Angi, instinctively offer their guests a unique blend of cordial hospitality, comfort, and friendship!

Things Worth Remembering ✪
7338 CABOR COURT, ORLANDO, FLORIDA 32818

Tel: **(407) 291-2127**	Open: **All year**
Hosts: **Lindsey Cunningham and James Johnston**	Reduced Rates: **10% seniors**
	Breakfast: **Continental**
Location: **6 mi. W of Orlando**	Pets: **Sometimes**
No. of Rooms: **1**	Children: **Welcome, over 10**
No. of Private Baths: **1**	Smoking: **No**
Double/pb: **$70**	Social Drinking: **Permitted**
Single/pb: **$65**	Airport/Station Pickup: **Yes**

Hidden within central Florida's busy city is Things Worth Remembering, with a unique decor of memorabilia from TV, movies, sports, and Broadway. There are more than 1000 signed autographs on display, plus movie props and clothing. You will awaken to the smell of fresh-baked goods and brewed coffee served in the dining room or on the patio with garden views. The room features a queen-size bed, cable TV, VCR, and unlimited access to your hosts' film library. Lindsey and James have worked for and with the local attractions, and can help you plan the perfect vacation.

Heron Cay ✪
15106 PALMWOOD ROAD, PALM BEACH GARDENS, FLORIDA 33410
heroncay@magg.net

Tel: **(561) 744-6315; fax (561) 744-0943**	Double/pb: **$85–$115**
	Suites: **$135–$185**
Best Time to Call: **10 AM–12 noon; after 7 PM**	Open: **All year**
	Reduced Rates: **Available**
Hosts: **Randy and Margie Salyer**	Breakfast: **Full**
Location: **15 mi. N of Palm Beach International Airport**	Pets: **Borzoi dogs only**
	Children: **By arrangement**
No. of Rooms: **9**	Smoking: **Restricted**
No. of Private Baths: **7**	Social Drinking: **Permitted**
Max. No. Sharing Bath: **4**	

At Heron Cay you'll think you're in Key West. This island-style home
is quietly nestled on two tropical acres overlooking the Intracoastal Waterway. Randy and Margie's private half-acre island is fun to explore—it protects their harbor, which accommodates boats to 55 feet,
plus a boat ramp for smaller water toys. All guest rooms open to a
balcony leading to the sundeck and several patio areas for relaxation
beside the 10-foot-deep pool or heated spa. Guests are provided with
refrigerators in rooms and may use the recreation room and barbecue
area poolside. Fine restaurants, major shopping, and miles of natural
ocean beaches are just minutes away. Margie and Randy are avid boaters who regularly invite longer-staying guests aboard their 48-foot
sportsfisherman, *Waterfront Lady,* for Palm Beach area cruises.

Bed & Breakfast of Tampa Bay ✪
126 OLD OAK CIRCLE, OAK TRAIL, PALM HARBOR, FLORIDA 34683

Tel: **(813) 785-2342**
Best Time to Call: **7–9 AM; 6–10 PM**
Hosts: **Vivian and David Grimm**
Location: **18 mi. W of Tampa**
No. of Rooms: **4**
No. of Private Baths: **2**
Max. No. Sharing Bath: **4**
Double/pb: **$60**
Single/pb: **$40**

Double/sb: **$45**
Single/sb: **$30**
Suite: **$75**
Open: **All year**
Breakfast: **Full**
Pets: **Sometimes**
Children: **Welcome**
Smoking: **No**
Social Drinking: **Permitted**

A premier facility in a premier location: this new Art Deco residence is
1½ miles from the Gulf of Mexico and 25 minutes from Busch Gardens,
Dali Museum, and Weeki-Wachee Springs. Shopping, restaurants,
churches, and public transportation are within easy walking distance.
The Grimms' home has an ivory stucco exterior, with front pillars, a tile
roof, and stained glass doors. Inside, artifacts from their world travels
are shown to advantage under 12-foot ceilings. Amenities include a
pool and Jacuzzi, a grand piano, and bicycles for local excursions.

Gulf Beach Inn ✪
10655 GULF BEACH HIGHWAY, PENSACOLA, FLORIDA 32507

Tel: **(904) 492-4501**
Hosts: **Fred and Lisa Krause**
Location: **50 mi. E of Mobile**
No. of Rooms: **2**
Guest Cottage: **$65**
Open: **All year**
Breakfast: **Full**

Pets: **No**
Children: **Welcome**
Smoking: **No**
Social Drinking: **Permitted**
Airport/Station Pickup: **Yes**
Foreign Languages: **German**

The Gulf Beach Inn is on the Intracoastal Waterway. Because it is located on your own private beach, it is the ideal spot for sunning, swimming, and watching sailboats, sunrises and sunsets. The Naval Aviation Museum, excellent seafood restaurants, and an outlet mall with over 100 stores are nearby. Perdido Key and the Emerald Coast of Florida are just minutes away.

Kenwood Inn
38 MARINE STREET, ST. AUGUSTINE, FLORIDA 32084

Tel: **(904) 824-2116**
Best Time to Call: **10 AM–10 PM**
Hosts: **Mark, Kerrianne, and Caitlin Constant**
Location: **40 mi. S of Jacksonville**
No. of Rooms: **14**
No. of Private Baths: **14**
Double/pb: **$85–$150**
Single/pb: **$65–$95**

Suite: **$115–$$150**
Open: **All year**
Breakfast: **Continental**
Credit Cards: **DISC, MC, VISA**
Pets: **No**
Children: **Welcome, over 8**
Smoking: **No**
Social Drinking: **Permitted**

If you are to discover a Victorian building in Florida, how appropriate that it should be in the historic section of St. Augustine, one of the oldest cities in the U.S. This New England–style inn is a rarity in the South; this one has old-fashioned beds with color-coordinated touches right down to the sheets and linens. Breakfast may be taken in your room, in the courtyard surrounded by trees, or by the swimming pool. Tour trains, waterfront shops, restaurants, and museums are within walking distance. Flagler College is three blocks away.

Bayboro House on Old Tampa Bay ✪
1719 BEACH DRIVE SOUTHEAST, ST. PETERSBURG, FLORIDA 33701

Tel: **(813) 823-4955**
Hosts: **Gordon and Antonia Powers**
Location: **¹/₂ mi. from I-275, Exit 9**
No. of Rooms: **4**
No. of Private Baths: **4**
Double/pb: **$85–$145**
Open: **All year**

Breakfast: **Continental**
Credit Cards: **MC, VISA**
Pets: **No**
Children: **No**
Smoking: **No**
Social Drinking: **Permitted**

Richly appointed in antiques and collectibles, the historic Bayboro House is what you would expect in a luxury waterfront bed and breakfast. All rooms have a water view, air-conditioning, TV, and VCR, and a morning paper is delivered to your door. Breakfast includes fresh fruits, juice, rolls, muffins, homemade breads, cereal, coffee and tea served in the formal dining room.

The Frog Pond Guesthouse
145 29TH AVENUE NORTH, ST. PETERSBURG, FLORIDA 33704

Tel: **(813) 823-7407**	Breakfast: **Continental**
Host: **Wendy Roberts**	Credit Cards: **MC, VISA**
Location: **2 mi. from Rte. I-275**	Pets: **No**
No. of Rooms: **1**	Children: **No**
No. of Private Baths: **1**	Smoking: **No**
Suites: **$55–$65**	Social Drinking: **Permitted**
Open: **All year**	Minimum Stay: **2 nights**

Located in the historical district of St. Petersburg's Old Northeast, the Frog Pond offers guests a relaxing atmosphere in a unique setting. The room features a queen bed, hardwood floors, French doors, cable TV, VCR, and a private entrance. Enjoy the spacious patio with garden pond, play billiards in the game room, take a sunset stroll along the water, or watch the sailboats at the Pier. Frog Pond is conveniently located near the Gulf beaches, Florida International and Dali museums, Busch Gardens, and Florida Aquarium in Tampa. It's just a 90-minute drive to Disney World and other major attractions in Orlando.

Florida Keys House ✪
P.O. BOX 41, SUMMERLAND KEY, FLORIDA 33042

Tel: **(305) 872-4680**	Pets: **No**
Best Time to Call: **8 AM–8 PM**	Children: **Welcome, over 10**
Hosts: **Capt. Dave and Camille Wiley**	Smoking: **Restricted**
Location: **27 mi. E of Key West**	Social Drinking: **Permitted**
Suites: **$89–$150**	Minimum Stay: **2 nights**
Open: **All year**	Foreign Languages: **French, Spanish**
Breakfast: **Continental**	

Set among an abundance of coconut palm trees, your private guest quarters can accommodate up to four people and consist of one or two bedrooms, a bathroom, living room, and large kitchen stocked with breakfast selections which you may prepare at your convenience. Florida Keys House is canal front with a dock where you can fish, barbecue, or just relax in the hammock under the shade trees. Snorkeling or diving at beautiful Looe Key Reef is just a short boat trip away. Ask about their specialty, "backcountry flats fishing" for Tarpon Bonefish, Permit Barracuda, and shark in the Great White Heron Wildlife Refuge.

Knightswood ✪
P.O. BOX 151, SUMMERLAND KEY, FLORIDA 33042

Tel: **(305) 872-2246; (800) 437-5402**
Hosts: **Chris and Herb Pontin**
Location: **26 mi. E of Key West**
No. of Rooms: **2**
No. of Private Baths: **2**
Double/pb: **$85**
Single/pb: **$70**

Open: **All year**
Breakfast: **Continental, plus**
Pets: **No**
Children: **No**
Smoking: **No**
Social Drinking: **Permitted**
Minimum Stay: **2 nights**

Knightswood boasts one of the loveliest water views in the Keys. The guest apartment is self-contained and very private. Snorkeling, fishing, and boating can be enjoyed right from the Pontins' dock. You are welcome to swim in the freshwater pool, relax in the spa, or sunbathe on the white sand beach. Trips to protected Looe Key Coral Reef can be arranged. Fine dining and Key West nightlife are within easy reach.

Fiorito's Bed & Breakfast ✪
421 OLD EAST LAKE ROAD, TARPON SPRINGS, FLORIDA 34689
littleflower@prodigy.com

Tel: **(813) 937-5487**
Best Time to Call: **8 AM–9 PM**
Hosts: **Dick and Marie Fiorito**
Location: **2 mi. E of US 19**
No. of Rooms: **1**
No. of Private Baths: **1**
Double/pb: **$40**
Single/pb: **$35**

Open: **All year**
Breakfast: **Full**
Pets: **No**
Children: **No**
Smoking: **Restricted**
Social Drinking: **Permitted**
Airport/Station Pickup: **Yes**

Just off a quiet road that runs along Lake Tarpon's horse country, this meticulously maintained home on two-and-a-half acres offers respite for the visitor. The guest room and bath are decorated in tones of blue, enhanced with beautiful accessories. Fresh fruit, cheese omelette, homemade bread and jam, and a choice of beverage is the Fioritos' idea of breakfast. It is beautifully served on the tree-shaded, screened terrace. They'll be happy to direct you to the Greek Sponge Docks, deep-sea fishing opportunities, golf courses, beaches, and great restaurants.

Heartsease ✪
272 OLD EAST LAKE ROAD, TARPON SPRINGS, FLORIDA 34689

Tel: **(813) 934-0994**
Best Time to Call: **After 7 PM**
Hosts: **Gerald and Sharon Goulish**
Suite: **$55–$60**
Open: **All year**
Reduced Rates: **Available**

Breakfast: **Continental**
Pets: **No**
Children: **No**
Smoking: **No**
Social Drinking: **Permitted**
Airport Pickup: **Yes**

You'll find plenty of "heartsease," meaning peace of mind and tranquility, at Gerald and Sharon's guest cottage. Wicker and pine furniture and a green and mauve color scheme create a light, airy feeling. Amenities include a private entrance, a mini-kitchen stocked with a microwave and breakfast fixings, cable TV, private bath, tennis court, and a deck overlooking the in-ground pool. Pluck an orange or a grapefruit from one of the many fruit trees and then settle in the gazebo, an ideal place for observing the bald eagles that nest nearby. Golf courses, Tampa's Old Hyde Park, Harbour Island, and Tarpon Springs' famed sponge docks are all within a short drive.

The Royal Palm House ✪
3215 SPRUCE AVENUE, WEST PALM BEACH, FLORIDA 33407

Tel: **(561) 863-9836**	Breakfast: **Continental**
Best Time to Call: **After 8 AM**	Other Meals: **Available**
Hosts: **Joe Pulvino and Kathie Mattson**	Credit Cards: **DISC, MC, VISA**
No. of Rooms: **5**	Pets: **Sometimes**
No. of Private Baths: **5**	Children: **No**
Double/pb: **$75–$95**	Smoking: **No**
Single/pb: **$70–$90**	Social Drinking: **Permitted**
Suites: **$105–$125**	Airport Pickup: **Yes**
Open: **All year**	

Built in 1952 during the Florida land boom by a local doctor, this rare Dutch Colonial was constructed using tropical techniques that introduce constant cooling breezes off the Atlantic Ocean. The house has been completely renovated and decorated with eclectic furnishings, including items from Kathie's extensive world travels. Joe's former occupation as a bakery owner is evident in the fresh breads and muffins baked every morning for breakfast. Royal Palm House is located in the heart of the Old Northwood Historic District and just minutes from Palm Beach, downtown West Palm Beach, the legendary shops of Worth Avenue, Fravis Cultural Center, Singer Island, West Palm Airport, and the Tri-Rail commuter train to Fort Lauderdale and Miami.

GEORGIA

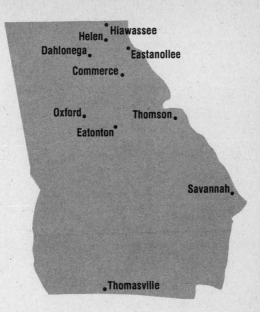

Magnolia Inn ✪
206 CHERRY STREET, COMMERCE, GEORGIA 30529

Tel: **(706) 335-7257**
Best Time to Call: **9 AM–noon; 6–9 PM**
Hosts: **Annette and Jerry Potter**
Location: **60 mi. N of Atlanta**
No. of Rooms: **4**
No. of Private Baths: **4**
Double/pb: **$60–$85**
Single/pb: **$50–$75**
Open: **All year**

Reduced Rates: **10% seniors; Dec.–Feb.**
Breakfast: **Full**
Credit Cards: **MC, VISA**
Pets: **No**
Children: **Welcome, over 10; under 10
   by arrangement**
Smoking: **No**
Social Drinking: **Permitted**
Airport/Station Pickup: **Yes**

Built in 1909, this restored Queen Anne Victorian is decorated with antiques and collectibles. In historic Commerce, you can browse through an antique mall, enjoy an old-fashioned soda at the local drugstore, or

visit the crafts and gift shops. Magnolia Inn is only minutes away from
the outlet malls, Atlanta Dragway, and Road Atlanta. It's twenty minutes to the University of Georgia and one hour to Atlanta. Take part in
a thrilling Murder Mystery Weekend or just relax in the porch swing
and rockers on the front veranda.

The Mountain Top Lodge
447 MOUNTAIN TOP LODGE ROAD, DAHLONEGA, GEORGIA 30533

Tel: **(706) 864-5257; (800) 526-9754**
Best Time to Call: **10 AM–6 PM**
Host: **Karen A. Lewan**
Location: **70 mi. N of Atlanta**
No. of Rooms: **13**
No. of Private Baths: **13**
Double/pb: **$70–$85**

Suites: **$115–$125**
Open: **All year**
Breakfast: **Full**
Pets: **No**
Children: **Welcome, over 12**
Smoking: **No**
Social Drinking: **Permitted**

Flanked by porches and decks, this gambrel-roofed, rustic cedar lodge
is a secluded rural retreat on 40 acres, with a 360-degree mountain
view. Decorated with art and antiques, the pine furniture and accessories made by mountain craftsmen add to the charm. Dahlonega was the
site of America's first gold rush, and nature buffs will appreciate the
Chattahoochee National Forest and Amicalola Falls State Park. Rafting,
hiking, and horseback riding are all nearby. Don't miss the "Alpine
village" of Helen, Georgia, only 30 minutes away. The Lodge now offers
deluxe rooms with in-bath Jacuzzi whirlpool tubs and gas-log fireplaces.

Royal Guard Inn
65 PARK STREET SOUTH, DAHLONEGA, GEORGIA 30533

Tel: **(706) 864-1713**
Best Time to Call: **10 AM–9 PM**
Hosts: **John and Farris Vanderhoff**
Location: **50 mi. N of Atlanta**
No. of Rooms: **5**
No. of Private Baths: **5**
Double/pb: **$70–$80**
Open: **All year**

Reduced Rates: **$5 seniors; Corp.
Sun.–Thurs.**
Breakfast: **Full**
Credit Cards: **AMEX, MC, VISA**
Pets: **No**
Children: **By arrangement**
Smoking: **No**
Social Drinking: **Permitted**

Located in the northeast Georgia mountains, Dahlonega is where the
first major U.S. gold rush occurred in 1828. Dahlonega Gold Museum,
Price Memorial Hall—on the site of one of the first U.S. branch mints—
and gold-panning areas are all in the heart of the historic downtown.
Royal Guard Inn, a half-block from the old town square, is a restored
and enlarged old home. John and Farris serve complimentary wine and
cheese on the great wraparound porch. Breakfast, served on fine china
and silver on crisp white linen, includes a casserole, pastries, or hotcakes from an old family recipe, and fresh fruit and whipped cream.

Apple Orchard Country Inn ✪
ROUTE 2, BOX 353, LIBERTY HILL ROAD, EASTANOLLEE, GEORGIA 30538

Tel: **(706) 779-7292; fax: (706) 779-7705**	Reduced Rates: **10% weekly**
Hosts: **Wade M. and Lu Loraine Lambert**	Breakfast: **Full**
Location: **90 mi. E of Atlanta**	Other Meals: **Available**
No. of Rooms: **4**	Credit Cards: **MC, VISA**
No. of Private Baths: **4**	Pets: **No**
Double/pb: **$75–$95**	Children: **Welcome, over 7**
Single/pb: **$75**	Smoking: **No**
Suites: **$125**	Social Drinking: **Permitted**
Open: **All year**	Station Pickup: **Yes**

Apple Orchard Country Inn is located sixty-five miles west of Greenville and Spartanburg, and thirty minutes from scenic Alpine Helen. Cleveland, home of the Cabbage Patch Dolls, is one hour away. There's gold mining in Dahlonega as well as quaint shops and antiques. Water sports are available at Lakes Hanier and Hartwell; golf, tennis, horseback riding, and other outdoor activities are at state and federal parks. Apple Orchard Country Inn's own attractions include a producing apple orchard, a pre–Civil War cemetery, and an old baptismal. This two-story home sits on twenty acres of wooded parklike land. The interior is furnished with a mixture of Oriental and traditional antiques.

The Crockett House
671 MADISON ROAD, EATONTON, GEORGIA 31024

Tel: **(706) 485-2248**	No. of Private Baths: **4**
Hosts: **Christa and Peter Crockett**	Double/pb: **$65–$95**
Location: **73 mi. E of Atlanta**	Open: **All year**
No. of Rooms: **6**	

Reduced Rates: **10% Nov.–Mar.;**
   extended stays; seniors; families
Breakfast: **Full**
Pets: **No**

Children: **Welcome, over 10**
Smoking: **No**
Social Drinking: **Permitted**
Airport Pickup: **Yes**

This stately and gracious turn-of-the-century home captures the history and charm of a bygone era. Guests receive a warm welcome and comfortable accommodations year-round. The home features seven bedrooms and eleven fireplaces. The large cozy bedrooms are thoughtfully decorated, some with private baths and fireplaces. Separate innkeepers' quarters insure the privacy of guests. Wander throughout the home and enjoy the principal rooms (equipped with telephones and TVs), balcony, wraparound porch, and tranquil setting of the three-acre yard.

Hilltop Haus ✪
P. O. BOX 154, 362 CHATTAHOOCHEE STREET, HELEN, GEORGIA 30545

Tel: **(706) 878-2388**
Best Time to Call: **9 AM–10 PM**
Hosts: **Frankie Allen and Barbara Nichols**
Location: **60 mi. from I-85**
No. of Rooms: **5**
No. of Private Baths: **3**
Max. No. Sharing Bath: **4**
Double/pb: **$60–$90**
Single/pb: **$50–$80**

Double/sb: **$50–$75**
Suites: **$80–$135**
Open: **All year**
Breakfast: **Continental, plus**
Credit Cards: **MC, VISA**
Pets: **No**
Children: **Welcome**
Smoking: **Restricted**
Social Drinking: **Permitted**

This split-level overlooks the Alpine town of Helen and the Chattahoochee River. It is near the foothills of the Smoky Mountains, six miles from the Appalachian Trail. Rich wood paneling and rooms with fireplaces create a homey atmosphere for the traveler. Guests may choose a private room or the efficiency with a separate entrance. A Continental breakfast is served in the bright, plant-filled sunroom. Your hostess will be happy to direct you to the many outdoor activities and sights.

Henson Cove Place ✪
3840 CAR MILES ROAD, HIAWASSEE, GEORGIA 30546-9585

Tel: **(800) 714-5542**
Best Time to Call: **After 10 AM**
Hosts: **Bill and Nancy Leffingwell**
Location: **2 hrs. N of Atlanta**
No. of Rooms: **2**
No. of Private Baths: **2**
Double/pb: **$60**
Suites: **$60**

Open: **All year**
Breakfast: **Full**
Credit Cards: **MC, VISA**
Pets: **No**
Children: **Welcome, over 10**
Smoking: **No**
Social Drinking: **Permitted**

Henson Cove Place has a warm homey atmosphere that will envelop you as you head for your room. The furniture and decorations are from Bill and Nancy's families and have stories behind them. You can browse through the magazine collection, read any of 2000 books, watch TV in the sitting room, and relax on the front porch. Or attend a festival, country music show, or hike or stop in the many small shops in the area. In the morning you'll be greeted with hot coffee and breakfast. A typical menu might be fruit cup, juice, muffins, rolled stuffed omelette, apple French toast with baby sausages, or sausage strata. Bill is a furniture maker specializing in reproductions. Nancy operates a business service above his workshop. Both like talking to guests and making their stay an enjoyable one.

The Hopkins House Bed & Breakfast ❂
1111 WESLEY STREET, OXFORD, GEORGIA 30267

Tel: **(770) 784-1010**	Reduced Rates: **10% seniors**
Best Time to Call: **8 AM–9 PM**	Breakfast: **Full (weekends), Continental**
Hosts: **Ralph and Nancy Brian**	**(weekdays)**
Location: **35 mi. SE of Atlanta**	Credit Cards: **AMEX, DISC, MC, VISA**
No. of Rooms: **5**	Pets: **Sometimes**
No. of Private Baths: **5**	Children: **Welcome**
Double/pb: **$85–$100**	Smoking: **No**
Suites: **$150**	Social Drinking: **Permitted**
Open: **All year**	

The Hopkins House Bed & Breakfast is in the historic district—the birthplace of Emory University, Georgia Tech, and a Methodist shrine.

Built in 1847, this Greek Revival–style home was spared during the Civil War on "Sherman's march to the sea." Guest rooms are exquisitely decorated in warm prints and handmade country quilts, set off by antiques, plates, dolls, and whimsicals. You are invited to enjoy the expansive screened porch with rocking chairs, overlooking acres of greens and gardens. To cool off from the warm Georgia days, take a dip in the pool.

R.S.V.P. Savannah—B&B Reservation Service ✪
9489 WHITFIELD AVENUE, BOX 49, SAVANNAH, GEORGIA 31406

Tel: **(912) 232-7787; (800) 729-7787**
Best Time to Call: **9:30 AM–5:30 PM Mon.–Fri.**
Coordinator: **Sonja Lazzaro**
States/Regions Covered: **Brunswick,**
Savannah, St. Simons Island, Tybee Island; South Carolina—Beaufort, Charleston
Rates (Single/Double): **$70–$225**
Credit Cards: **AMEX, DISC, MC, VISA**

Accommodations include elegantly restored inns, guesthouses, private homes, and even a villa on the water. They're located in the best historic districts as well as along the coast, from South Carolina's Low Country to Georgia's Sea Islands. A special blend of cordial hospitality, comfort, and services is provided. All are air-conditioned in the summer. Facilities for children and the disabled are often available. Please note that while some hosts accept credit cards, some do not.

Joan's on Jones ✪
17 WEST JONES STREET, SAVANNAH, GEORGIA 31401

Tel: **(912) 234-3863; (800) 407-3863; fax: (912) 234-1455**
Hosts: **Joan and Gary Levy**
Location: **140 mi. N of Jacksonville, FL**
Suites: **$115–$130; sleeps 2–4**
Open: **All year**
Reduced Rates: **Weekly**
Breakfast: **Continental**
Pets: **Sometimes**
Children: **Welcome**
Smoking: **No**
Social Drinking: **Permitted**
Minimum Stay: **3 days for St. Patrick's Day week only**

Clip-clopping along the brick streets of the city's historic district, horse-drawn carriages take you back to a more serene and elegant era. This bed and breakfast maintains the old-fashioned mood, with its original heart-pine floors, antique furnishings, and Savannah gray brick walls. (Note the late-19th-century documents that slipped behind one of the fireplace mantels.) All the historic places of interest, including the famous squares, are a short walk away. Joan and Gary, former restaurateurs, live upstairs and invite you to tour their home if you're staying at least two nights.

Lion's Head Inn ✪
120 EAST GASTON STREET, SAVANNAH, GEORGIA 31401

Tel: **(912) 232-4580**
Host: **Christy Dell'orco**
Location: **Downtown Savannah**
No. of Rooms: **5**

No. of Private Baths: **5**
Double/pb: **$90–$140**
Single/pb: **$85–$115**
Suites: **$125–$180**
Open: **All year**
Reduced Rates: **Available**

Breakfast: **Continental**
Credit Cards: **AMEX, DISC, MC, VISA**
Pets: **No**
Children: **Welcome**
Smoking: **No**
Social Drinking: **Permitted**

This elegant 19th-century mansion is tastefully adorned with pristine Empire furniture and accessories. A collection of European and American art, Italian marble, and French bronze sculptures and 19th-century lighting beautify each room. The Inn is located on Gaston Street, the prime residential street in the historic district. Stroll across the street to picturesque Forsyth Park and enjoy all the historic attractions and amenities within walking distance. The innkeeper, Christy, a retired sales manager, now is a registered Savannah tour guide and antiquarian. She'll help you enjoy gracious living at its best and experience true 19th-century grandeur at the Lion's Head Inn.

Serendipity Cottage Bed & Breakfast ✪
339 EAST JEFFERSON STREET, THOMASVILLE, GEORGIA 31792

Tel: **(912) 226-8111**
Hosts: **Kathy and Ed Middleton**
Location: **35 mi. N of Tallahassee, Florida**
No. of Rooms: **3**
No. of Private Baths: **3**
Double/pb: **$75**

Single/pb: **$70**
Open: **All year**
Breakfast: **Full**
Pets: **No**
Children: **Welcome, over 12**
Smoking: **No**
Social Drinking: **Permitted**

While it's only a 40-minute drive from Florida State University, Serendipity Cottage is located in a Victorian town, where a slower pace is the norm. Built in 1906, the house is decorated with a tasteful mix of Victorian antiques and comfortable country surroundings. Freshly starched and ironed bed linens greet you when you retire, and at wake-up call your choice of beverage is delivered to your room in the morning. People Hill Plantation, recently featured on A&E's *America's Castles*, is just south of town. Ed, a retired naval architect, and Kathy, a retired retail shop owner, share an interest in antiques, preservation of old homes, and counted cross-stitch.

Four Chimneys B&B
2316 WIRE ROAD SOUTHEAST, THOMSON, GEORGIA 30824

Tel: **(706) 597-0220**
Best Time to Call: **9 AM–10 PM**
Hosts: **Maggie and Ralph Zieger**
Location: **35 mi. W of Augusta**
No. of Rooms: **4**
No. of Private Baths: **3**
Double/pb: **$40–$60**
Single/pb: **$45**

Open: **All year**
Breakfast: **Continental, plus**
Credit Cards: **MC, VISA**
Pets: **No**
Children: **Welcome, over 12**
Smoking: **Restricted**
Social Drinking: **Permitted**
Foreign Languages: **German**

Escape from the modern world at this early 1800s country house with a rocking-chair porch. The old-fashioned landscape features a large herb garden and heirloom flowers. Antique and reproduction furniture complement the original heart-pine interior. A small library and a cozy parlor invite you to relax at your leisure. Guest rooms have four-poster beds and working fireplaces. Restaurants, golf courses, and antique shops are nearby. Fox hunts and other equestrian events take place throughout the year.

HAWAII

Bed & Breakfast Honolulu Statewide ✪
3242 KAOHINANI DRIVE, HONOLULU, HAWAII 96817
bnbshi@aloha.net

Tel: **(800) 288-4666; (808) 595-7533;**
  fax: **(808) 595-2030**
Best Time to Call: **8 AM–5 PM**
  Mon.–Fri., 8 AM–noon Sat.
Coordinator: **Mary Lee**
States/Regions Covered:
  Hawaii—statewide

Rates (Single/Double):
  Modest: **$45–$55 / $45–$60**
  Average: **$55–$70 / $55–$75**
  Luxury: **$75 up / $75 up**
Credit Cards: **MC, VISA**

This home-based family service, started in 1982, pays careful attention to visitors who want to be more than tourists. That's made it Hawaii's largest statewide agency, listing more than 700 rooms, on all islands. Many agencies have membership fees and directories; this one doesn't! When you call the 800 number, use the e-mail address, or fax Bed & Breakfast Honolulu, Mary Lee can match your needs, desires, and pocketbook to her computerized listings. This service's size lets her offer very favorable rates on rental cars and inter-island air.

Haikuleana B&B, Plantation House ✪
555 HAIKU ROAD, HAIKU, MAUI, HAWAII 96708
blumblum@maui.net

Tel: **(808) 575-2890;**
  fax: **(808) 575-9177**
Best Time to Call: **8 AM–8 PM HST**
Hosts: **Authors Ralph H. and**
  Jeanne Elizabeth Blum
No. of Rooms: **4**
No. of Private Baths: **4**
Double/pb: **$95–$110**
Single/pb: **$85–$110**
Open: **All year**

Reduced Rates: **Weekly**
Breakfast: **Full**
Pets: **No**
Children: **Welcome, over 7**
Smoking: **No**
Social Drinking: **Permitted**
Minimum Stay: **2 nights**
Foreign Languages: **French, Italian,**
  Russian, Spanish, German

Haikuleana is the gateway to upcountry Maui. Built in the 1850s, this plantation-style house is nestled among 100-year-old Cook Island pines and lush tropical foliage. Nearby are pools, secluded waterfalls, the world-famous windsurfing at Hookipa Beach, golfing, horseback riding, restaurants, and a health club. The house was completely renovated from 1990 to 1992. The original 12-foot ceilings and traditional fretwork of early Colonial architecture are enhanced by period Hawaiian and New England furniture. This is a perfect place for exploring the entire island, and it's convenient to the town of Hana and Haleakala Crater and Park. Rooms are furnished with ceiling fans, phones, and designer fabrics and bedding; dual-control electric blankets are provided for the winter months. Ralph and Jeanne can accommodate weddings and reunions.

Pilialoha Bed & Breakfast Cottage ✪
2512 KAUPAKALUA ROAD, HAIKU, MAUI, HAWAII 96708

Tel: **(808) 572-1440**
Best Time to Call: **9 AM–9 PM**
Hosts: **Bill and Machiko Heyde**
Location: **10 mi. E of Kahului**
Guest Cottage: **$95**
Open: **All year**
Reduced Rates: **Weekly**

Breakfast: **Continental**
Pets: **No**
Children: **Welcome**
Smoking: **No**
Social Drinking: **Permitted**
Minimum Stay: **2 nights**
Foreign Languages: **Japanese**

Located in cool upcountry Maui, this cozy cottage is surrounded by a rose garden overlooking a lush pasture and a eucalyptus grove. Accommodations are fully furnished with cable TV, phone, washer-dryer, and beach and picnic items. The kitchen is stocked with gourmet teas and coffees. Freshly baked muffins or bread, fruits, and juice are delivered daily to your door. The cottage is most comfortable for two people, but will house up to five. Pilialoha serves as a good central base for exploring the entire island of Maui. Bill and Machiko reside on the same property and are available for information and assistance.

Bev & Monty's Bed & Breakfast ✪
4571 UKALI STREET, HONOLULU, OAHU, HAWAII 96818

Tel: **(808) 422-9873**	Open: **All year**
Best Time to Call: **7 AM–9 PM HST**	Reduced Rates: **Weekly**
Hosts: **Bev and Monty Neese**	Breakfast: **Continental**
Location: **4½ mi. from airport**	Pets: **No**
No. of Rooms: **2**	Children: **Welcome**
Max. No. Sharing Bath: **4**	Smoking: **Permitted**
Double/sb: **$50**	Social Drinking: **Permitted**
Single/sb: **$40**	Airport/Station Pickup: **Yes**

This typical Hawaiian home is convenient to many of Hawaii's most popular attractions. Bev and Monty are just a mile above historic Pearl Harbor, and the Arizona Memorial can be seen from their veranda. They enjoy sharing a Hawaiian aloha for a convenient overnight stay or a long vacation when they can share their favorite places with you. This comfortable home is just off the access road leading east to Honolulu and Waikiki, or west to the North Shore beaches and pineapple fields. Good hiking country as well as city entertainment and shopping centers are located nearby.

Akamai Bed & Breakfast ✪
172 KUUMELE PLACE, KAILUA, OAHU, HAWAII 96734

Tel: **(808) 261-2227; (800) 642-5366**	Open: **All year**
Best Time to Call: **8 AM–8 PM**	Breakfast: **Full**
Host: **Diane Van Ryzin**	Pets: **No**
No. of Rooms: **2**	Children: **No**
No. of Private Baths: **2**	Smoking: **No**
Double/pb: **$65**	Social Drinking: **Permitted**
Single/pb: **$65**	Minimum Stay: **3 nights**

Guests at Akamai stay in a separate wing of the house; each studio has a private entrance, bath, kitchenette, private phone, cable TV, and radio. Honolulu and Waikiki are within a half-hour drive, but you may prefer to lounge by your host's pool or take the eight-minute stroll to the beach. No meals are served here, but your refrigerator is stocked with breakfast foods and the kitchen area is equipped with light cooking appliances, dishes, and flatware. Laundry facilities are also available.

Papaya Paradise ✪
395 AUWINALA ROAD, KAILUA, OAHU, HAWAII 96734

Tel: **(808) 261-0316; fax: (808) 261-0316**	Best Time to Call: **7 AM–8 PM HST**
	Hosts: **Bob and Jeanette Martz**

Location: **10 mi. E of Honolulu**
No. of Rooms: **2**
Double/pb: **$70–$75**
Open: **All year**
Breakfast: **Continental**

Pets: **No**
Children: **Welcome, over 6**
Smoking: **Permitted**
Social Drinking: **Permitted**
Minimum Stay: **3 nights**

The Martz paradise is on the windward side of Oahu, miles from the high-rise hotels, but just 20 miles from the Waikiki/Honolulu airport. Each guest room has two beds, a ceiling fan, air-conditioning, cable TV, and its own private entrance. Bob loves to cook, and serves breakfast on the lanai overlooking the pool and Jacuzzi. Kailua Beach, a beautiful white sandy beach 4 miles long, is within easy walking distance.

Anne's Three Bears Bed & Breakfast ✪
72-1001 PUUKALA STREET, KAILUA-KONA, HAWAII 96740

Tel: **(800) 765-0480; (808) 325-7563**
Best Time to Call: **AM**
Hosts: **Anne, Art, and Nanette Stockel**
Location: **7 mi. N of Kailua-Kona**
No. of Rooms: **2**
No. of Private Baths: **2**
Double/pb: **$75–$85**
Open: **All year**

Breakfast: **Full**
Credit Cards: **MC, VISA**
Pets: **No**
Children: **Welcome, over 2**
Smoking: **No**
Social Drinking: **Permitted**
Minimum Stay: **2 nights**
Foreign Languages: **German**

Anne's Three Bears Bed & Breakfast features comfortable, friendly accommodations and a spectacular view of the Kona coastline. This beautiful cedar home is close to Kailua town and the many beaches on the Kona coast. A terrific breakfast is served each morning on the lanai, and complimentary beach chairs, coolers, and boogie boards are provided.

Anne and Nanette also have a free reservation service specializing in bed and breakfast accommodations on all Hawaiian Islands. They charge no booking fee; all bed and breakfasts have been inspected. Accommodations range from $55 to $225 for two people.

Merryman's ✪
P.O. BOX 474, KEALAKEKUA, HAWAII 96750

Tel: **(808) 323-2276**
Hosts: **Don and Penny Merryman**
No. of Rooms: **4**
No. of Private Baths: **2**
Max. No. Sharing Bath: **4**
Double/pb: **$95–$125**
Double/sb: **$75**

Open: **All year**
Breakfast: **Full**
Credit Cards: **MC, VISA**
Pets: **No**
Children: **Welcome**
Smoking: **No**
Social Drinking: **Permitted**

Don and Penny left the snows of Alaska to settle in this lovely tropical retreat a few minutes from the Captain Cook Monument at Kealakekua Bay, where you'll also find an underwater sealife park. Your hosts' cedar home, situated on an acre of lush grounds, has open beams, wood floors, antique furniture, and wonderful ocean views. Breakfasts are highlighted by Kona coffee and fresh local fruit.

Eva Villa ✪
815 KUMULANI DRIVE, KIHEI, MAUI, HAWAII 96753
Pounder@maui.net

Tel: **(800) 884-1845;**	Open: **All year**
fax: **(808) 874-6407**	Reduced Rates: **Summer**
Hosts: **Rick and Dale Pounds**	Breakfast: **Continental**
Location: **5 mi. S of Kahalui**	Pets: **No**
No. of Rooms: **4**	Children: **Welcome, over 13**
No. of Private Baths: **4**	Smoking: **No**
Double/pb: **$95**	Social Drinking: **Permitted**
Guest Apartment: **$95**	Minimum Stay: **3 nights**
Cottage: **$100**	

Eva Villa is located at the top of Maui Meadows, just above Wailea on the dry side of the island. The islands of Lanai, Molokini, and Kahoolawe can be viewed from the rooftop deck. The grounds include many fruit and tropical trees and plants; there is also a koi pond with frogs, fish, and beautiful lilies. Amenities include a pool, Jacuzzi, barbecue facilities, outside table and chairs, and cable TV. Eva Villa has three guest sections. The main house has a studio that looks out on the pool and Jacuzzi. It contains a queen bed, kitchen, counter bar, and eating area. Also in the main house is the apartment, containing two bedrooms—one queen, one twin—living room, and kitchenette with a microwave oven and a two-burner hot plate. The cottage is separate from the house and has a kitchen, living room, queen-size bed, and a wraparound lanai with a barbecue.

Whale Watch House ✪
726 KUMULANI DRIVE, KIHEI, MAUI, HAWAII 96753

Tel: **(808) 879-0570; fax: (808) 874-8102**	Open: **All year**
	Reduced Rates: **10% less June, July, Sept., Oct.**
Best Time to Call: **8 AM–8 PM**	Breakfast: **Continental**
Hosts: **Patricia and Patrick Lowry**	Pets: **No**
No. of Rooms: **4**	Children: **No**
No. of Private Baths: **4**	Smoking: **No**
Double/pb: **$65**	Social Drinking: **Permitted**
Single/pb: **$60**	Minimum Stay: **2 nights**
Guest Cottage: **$95, sleeps 2; studio, $85**	

Whale Watch House is located at the very edge of Ulupalakua Ranch on Haleakala, Maui's 10,228-foot dormant volcano. At every turn there are wonderful views of the ocean, the mountains, and the neighboring is-

lands, Lanai and Kahoolawe. Your hosts' lush tropical garden is filled
with fruits and flowers, and the swimming pool is large enough for
laps. Sunbathe on the large decks around the house, cottage, and pool,
or drive down to the beach—you'll be there in five minutes.

Hale Ho'o Maha ✪

P.O. BOX 422, KILAUEA, KAUAI, HAWAII 96754
hoomaha@aloha.net; http://www.aloha.net/~hoomaha

Tel: **(800) 851-0291; (808) 828-1341;**
  fax: (808) 828-2046
Best Time to Call: **7 AM–7 PM**
Hosts: **Kirby B. Guyer and Toby Searles**
Location: **28 mi. N of Lihue Airport**
No. of Rooms: **4**
No. of Private Baths: **2**
Max. No. Sharing Bath: **4**
Double/pb: **$75–$80**

Double/sb: **$55–$65**
Open: **All year**
Reduced Rates: **10% after 5th night**
Breakfast: **Continental**
Pets: **No**
Children: **Welcome, over 10**
Smoking: **Permitted**
Social Drinking: **Permitted**
Foreign Languages: **Spanish**

Escape to a B&B that lives up to its name, which means "house of rest"
in Hawaiian. This single-story home is perched on the cliffs along Kauai's north shore. Sandy beaches, rivers, waterfalls, and riding stables are
five minutes away. Ask your hosts to direct you to "Queens Bath"—a
natural saltwater whirlpool. Guests have full use of the kitchen, gas
grill, cable TV, and boogie boards. When in Rome, do as the Romans:
Kirby will teach you to dance the hula and make leis, and Toby will
instruct you in scuba diving.

Kula Cottage ✪

206 PUAKEA PLACE, KULA, MAUI, HAWAII 96790

Tel: **(808) 871-6230, 878-2043**
Best Time to Call: **8 AM–5 PM**
Hosts: **Larry and Cecilia Gilbert**
Location: **16 mi. SE of Kahului**
Guest Cottage: **$85, sleeps 2**
Open: **All year**
Breakfast: **Continental**

Pets: **No**
Children: **Welcome, over 12**
Smoking: **Permitted**
Social Drinking: **Permitted**
Minimum Stay: **2 nights**
Foreign Languages: **Spanish**

Flowers and fruit-bearing trees surround this new, fully equipped one-
bedroom bungalow. There are wonderful views of the ocean and the
West Maui Mountains, plus loads of amenities: a wood-burning fireplace, washer and dryer, patio furniture, barbecue, cooler, beach towels,
and more. Nearby are restaurants, the beach, a national park, gardens,
and a winery. Your hosts can arrange sailing, snorkeling, and helicopter
trips for you. The Continental breakfast features home-baked breads,
fresh fruit, juice, and coffee or tea.

Kula View Bed and Breakfast ○
140 HOLOPUNI ROAD (MAILING ADDRESS: P.O. BOX 322), KULA, MAUI, HAWAII 96790

Tel: **(808) 878-6736**
Best Time to Call: **8 AM–6 PM**
Host: **Susan Kauai**
Location: **16 mi. E of Kahului**
No. of Rooms: **1**
No. of Private Baths: **1**
Double/pb: **$85**
Single/pb: **$85**

Open: **All year**
Reduced Rates: **10% weekly**
Breakfast: **Continental**
Pets: **No**
Children: **No**
Smoking: **No**
Social Drinking: **Permitted**
Minimum Stay: **2 nights**

The fragrances of island fruits and flowers fill the fresh mountain air at this B&B 2000 feet above sea level, on the slopes of the dormant volcano Haleakala. The upper-level guest room has its own private entrance and a spacious deck that faces majestic Haleakala Crater, where the sunrises are nothing short of magical. Breakfast is served at a sun-warmed wicker table overlooking a flower and herb garden. Kula View is surrounded by two acres of lush greenery, yet it is close to Kahului Airport, shopping centers, parks, and beaches.

Kuau Cove Plantation ○
2 WAA PLACE, PAIA, HAWAII 96779

Tel: **(808) 579-8988;**
  fax: **(808) 579-8710**
Best Time to Call: **10 AM–8 PM**
Host: **Frederick J. Fox, Jr.**
Location: **7 mi. E of Kahului Airport**
No. of Rooms: **4**
No. of Private Baths: **4**
Double/pb: **$85**
Single/pb: **$75**
Suites: **$95**
Open: **All year**

Reduced Rates: **Available**
Breakfast: **Full, Continental**
Credit Cards: **AMEX, DISC, MC, VISA**
Pets: **No**
Children: **Welcome, over 6; under 12 free**
Smoking: **No**
Social Drinking: **Permitted**
Minimum Stay: **2 nights**
Foreign Languages: **Swedish**

Nestled near a tropical ocean bay on the north shore of Maui, Kuau Cove has the charm of an old Hawaiian plantation home. Nearby are sandy beaches, Mama's Fish House, Kuau Food Mart and Deli, a world-class surfing and windsurfing beach, restaurants, entertainment, antique shops, and art and clothing boutiques. Kahului Airport, shopping malls, and the Maui Arts and Cultural Center are ten minutes away, en route to the town of Hana and Haleakala Crater, Maui's two top destinations. There are two large guest rooms in the main house with queen beds and ceiling fans. In addition, there are two studio apartments; one has an ocean view, the other overlooks a lovely shaded garden, and both have private lanais.

Hale Kilauea ✪
P.O. BOX 28, VOLCANO, HAWAII 96785

Tel: **(808) 967-7591; (800) 733-3839**
Best Time to Call: **8 AM–10 PM**
Hosts: **Maurice Thomas and Jiranan**
Location: **28 mi. NE of Hilo**
No. of Rooms: **5**
No. of Private Baths: **5**
Double/pb: **$55–$75**
Open: **All year**

Reduced Rates: **10% seniors**
Breakfast: **Continental**
Credit Cards: **AMEX, MC, VISA**
Pets: **Sometimes**
Children: **Welcome**
Smoking: **Permitted**
Social Drinking: **Permitted**

Hale Kilauea is a quiet place near the heart of Volcano Village, just outside Hawaii Volcanoes National Park, the world's only "drive-in volcano." Colorful, exotic native birds live in the towering pines and ohia trees that surround this B&B. After a day of climbing mountains and peering into craters, enjoy an evening of conversation around the living room fireplace. Your host Maurice, a lifelong Volcano resident, has neighbors and friends who know about volcano geology and the history and tradition of old Hawaii.

IDAHO

Post Falls
•Kingston
Lewiston
Salmon
Boise
Rigby
Fish Haven

Idaho Heritage Inn ✪
109 WEST IDAHO, BOISE, IDAHO 83702

Tel: **(208) 342-8066**
Best Time to Call: **9 AM–8 PM**
Hosts: **Phyllis and Tom Lupher**
No. of Rooms: **6**
No. of Private Baths: **6**
Double/pb: **$60–$75**
Suites: **$85–$95**

Open: **All year**
Breakfast: **Full**
Credit Cards: **AMEX, DISC, MC, VISA**
Pets: **No**
Children: **Welcome, over 5**
Smoking: **No**
Social Drinking: **Permitted**

The Idaho Heritage Inn is a traditional bed and breakfast located just six blocks from downtown Boise and a short walk from Boise's beautiful greenbelt, a paved river path leading to nature trails, historic museums, art galleries, and Zoo Boise. Many of the city's finest restaurants, shops, and movie theaters are just blocks away. The Inn's guest rooms are gracefully and comfortably appointed with antique furniture, giving each one its own special atmosphere in which to relax and enjoy. This

1904 Inn served as a former governor's mansion and home to the late Senator Frank Church and continues to host guests of political prominence, such as former First Lady Barbara Bush.

Bear Lake Bed and Breakfast ✪
500 LOVELAND LANE, FISH HAVEN, IDAHO 83287

Tel: **(208) 945-2688**
Best Time to Call: **Anytime**
Host: **Esther Harrison**
Location: **125 mi. N of Salt Lake City,** **Utah, on Bear Lake**
No. of Rooms: **4**
No. of Private Baths: **1**
Max. No. Sharing Bath: **4**
Double/pb: **$75**

Double/sb: **$65**
Open: **All year**
Breakfast: **Full**
Credit Cards: **MC, VISA**
Pets: **Sometimes**
Children: **Welcome, over 12**
Smoking: **No**
Social Drinking: **Permitted**

Make yourselves at home in this spacious secluded log home, hand built and designed by the owners. Sitting on the deck you can absorb the peace and beauty of the turquoise blue lake below. The national forest is half a mile behind the B&B and the colors are a sight to behold in the fall with the yellow aspens and red and orange maples mixed with the green pines. You will find total hospitality here. Each guest room is decorated in a different style, and yummy aromas come from the kitchen each morning. Take part in all lake activities, including boat rentals. Apart from the waterfront, there is a tour-guided cave, horseback riding, chuck wagon dinners, and mountain biking. Esther subs at local schools and makes items for the B&B gift shop. She has horses and loves the out-of-doors.

Kingston 5 Ranch Bed & Breakfast ✪
P.O. BOX 130-42, 297 SILVER VALLEY ROAD, KINGSTON,
IDAHO 83839

Tel: (208) 682-4862; (800) 254-1852;
  fax: (208) 682-4862
Best Time to Call: 8 AM–8 PM
Hosts: Walt and Pat Gentry
Location: 25 mi. E of Coeur d'Alene
No. of Rooms: 2
No. of Private Baths: 2
Double/pb: $85
Single/pb: $75

Suite: $85
Open: All year
Breakfast: Full
Credit Cards: MC, VISA
Pets: By arrangement
Children: No
Smoking: No
Social Drinking: Permitted
Minimum Stay: 3 nights suite

Kingston 5 Ranch is located in the heart of the Coeur d'Alene Mountains. The luxurious suite has spectacular views of the surrounding mountains and valley and an in-room jetted tub. This 4500-square-foot home offers guests many relaxing options, including an outdoor hot tub. The area is an outdoor paradise. In the winter enjoy skiing and snowmobiling. Summertime, choose from Silver Mountain outdoor concerts, mountain biking, tennis, golfing, hiking, fishing, canoeing and river float trips—all within ten minutes of the property. The biggest summer attraction is on-site horseback riding—your horse or your hosts'. Guests and their horses can be accommodated. A recently retired health care administrator, Walt is an expert horseman who truly enjoys the outdoors. Pat is currently working as a health care administrator and also does clinical research.

Shiloh Rose B&B ✪
3414 SELWAY DRIVE, LEWISTON, IDAHO 83501

Tel: (208) 743-2482
Best Time to Call: Before 10 AM
Host: Dorthy Mader
Location: 100 mi. S of Spokane, Wash.
Suite: $80
Open: All year
Reduced Rates: 10% seniors

Breakfast: Full
Credit Cards: MC, VISA
Pets: Sometimes
Children: Welcome, over 10
Smoking: No
Social Drinking: Permitted
Airport/Station Pickup: Yes

Shiloh Rose has one spacious suite. Lovely wallpapers, lace curtains, and fine bed linens give the bedroom a warm, country-Victorian feel. The cozy private sitting room has a wood-burning stove, overflowing bookshelves, and an upright grand piano, as well as a TV and VCR. Breakfasts feature fresh fruit, home-baked muffins, gourmet casseroles, and your choice of coffee or tea. On warm summer evenings, you'll share the backyard with quail and pheasant families. Golf and water sports are available much of the year. The surrounding area is a hunting and fishing paradise and the river levees provide eight miles of hiking and biking trails. But top priority should be given to a day-long jet-boat trip up Hells Canyon, the deepest gorge in the Northwest.

River Cove ✪

P.O. BOX 1862, POST FALLS, IDAHO 83854
http://www.nidlink.com/~rivercove

Tel/fax: **(208) 773-9190**	Open: **All year**
Best Time to Call: **After 5 PM**	Reduced Rates: **Available**
Hosts: **Eric and Rosalynd Wurmlinger**	Breakfast: **Full**
Location: **20 mi. E of Spokane,**	Pets: **Sometimes**
Washington	Children: **Welcome, under 5 by**
No. of Rooms: **3**	**arrangement**
No. of Private Baths: **3**	Smoking: **No**
Double/pb: **$99**	Social Drinking: **Permitted**
Suites: **$139**	Airport Pickup: **Yes**

At River Cove, guests enjoy a homey atmosphere with privacy. This new contemporary home is situated on a wooded lot overlooking the beautiful Spokane River. Guests can relax and take in the spectacular view from the patio, or stroll along the many scenic trails by the river. Each morning, breakfast is served in the main dining room or out on the terrace. Guests are often invited to join their hosts on a complimentary boat cruise.

BlackSmith Inn ✪

227 NORTH 3900 EAST, RIGBY, IDAHO 83442

Tel: **(208) 745-6208;** fax: **(208) 745-**	Reduced Rates: **20% Oct.–Mar.,**
0602	**weekly; 10% seniors**
Best Time to Call: **Before noon**	Breakfast: **Full**
Hosts: **Mike and Karla Black**	Credit Cards: **MC, VISA**
Location: **20 mi. N of Idaho Falls**	Pets: **No**
No. of Rooms: **2**	Children: **Welcome**
No. of Private Baths: **2**	Smoking: **No**
Double/pb: **$65–$75**	Social Drinking: **Permitted**
Single/pb: **$60–$70**	Airport/Station Pickup: **Yes**
Open: **All year**	

The BlackSmith Inn is a contemporary round Eagle's Nest home, cedar-sided for a unique Western flavor. Guest rooms feature Western murals and quilts; local artwork can be found in the common areas. Decking and patio areas allow you to enjoy pleasant cool evenings. The Inn is 85 miles from West Yellowstone, 20 miles from I-15, 2 miles from the local golf course, and within a short distance of distinctive shops, galleries, antique stores, and museums. Nearby, Ricks College offers plays and other activities throughout the year. There is plenty of winter and summer fun, including skiing, fly fishing, and much more. Mike and Karla are registered nurses. In their spare time, they raise and train Tennessee

Walking horses shown locally, and are in the process of building a greenhouse that will use hydroponics.

Heritage Inn ✪
510 LENA STREET, SALMON, IDAHO 83467

Tel: **(208) 756-3174**
Best Time to Call: **8 AM–8 PM**
Host: **Audrey Nichols**
Location: **½ mi. from Hwy. 93**
No. of Rooms: **5**
Max. No. Sharing Bath: **3**
Double/sb: **$40–$45**
Single/sb: **$30–$35**

Cottage: **$40**
Open: **All year**
Breakfast: **Continental, plus**
Credit Cards: **MC, VISA**
Pets: **No**
Children: **Welcome**
Smoking: **Restricted**
Social Drinking: **Permitted**

This 100-year-old Victorian farmhouse is set in a valley, surrounded by mountains and pine trees. In the old days, this was a cozy stopover for those traveling by stagecoach. The Heritage has since been lovingly restored and decorated with many antiques. Enjoy a cool drink on the glassed-in sunporch while you enjoy the quiet of this pretty neighborhood. The River of No Return is just half a mile away, and it's just a mile to the city park and swimming pool. Your hostess serves homemade muffins and jams in the sunny dining room or on the porch each morning. She is a native of Salmon and can gladly direct you to restaurants within walking distance, nearby ghost towns, and other places of historic or cultural interest.

Syringa Lodge ✪
2000 SYRINGA DRIVE, P.O. BOX 583, SALMON, IDAHO 83467

Tel: **(208) 756-4424**
Best Time to Call: **Before 9 PM**
Host: **Maxine Duncan**
Location: **150 mi. N of Idaho Falls**
No. of Rooms: **8**
No. of Private Baths: **6**
Max. No. Sharing Bath: **4**
Double/pb: **$60**
Single/sb: **$40**

Suites: **$85**
Open: **All year**
Reduced Rates: **5% seniors**
Breakfast: **Full**
Credit Cards: **MC, VISA**
Pets: **Sometimes**
Children: **Welcome**
Smoking: **No**
Social Drinking: **Permitted**

Built with large spruce logs, Syringa Lodge sits on 23 acres of an old homestead and has a 360-degree view. There is a great room with a seven-foot carved pine mantel over the fireplace, a library, and a large dining room for full breakfast and meetings. Each room is furnished with antiques and is named after living wildflowers. Maxine, a full-time hostess, is interested in painting and learning to speak French.

ILLINOIS

B&B Midwest Reservations ✪
2223 CRUMP LANE, COLUMBUS, INDIANA 47203

Tel: **(800) 34 B AND B [342-2632]**
Best Time to Call: **9 AM–5 PM Mon.–Fri.**
Coordinator: **Martha McDonald-Swan**
States/Regions Covered:
  Illinois—Antioch, Cairo, Danforth, Evanston, Franklin Grove, Galena, Geneva, Gurnee, Hinsdale, Morrison, Mundelein, Oakbrook, Oak Park, Oregon, Springfield, Taylorville, Wadsworth, West Dundee, **Woodstock, Yorkville; Indiana—Anderson, Bainbridge, Culver, Knightstown, Paoli**
Descriptive Directory: **Free**
Rates (Single/Double):
  Modest: **$45 / $55**
  Average: **$50 / $100**
  Luxury: **$110 / $179**
Credit Cards: **AMEX, DISC, MC, VISA**

B&B Midwest Reservations has expanded beyond northern Illinois to include southern Illinois and Indiana. Most homes are on historic registers. Hosts enjoy sharing beautiful antiques, handwork, and lots of TLC with their guests. Many also offer numerous special activities and theme weekends, available from suburban locations to country farms.

Curly's Corner ✪
425 EAST CR, 200 N, ARCOLA, ILLINOIS 61910

Tel: **(217) 268-3352**
Best Time to Call: **Anytime**
Hosts: **Warren and Maxine Arthur**
Location: **35 mi. S of Champaign; 5 mi.
  from I-57**
No. of Rooms: **4**
No. of Private Baths: **2**
Max. No. Sharing Bath: **3**
Double/pb: **$55–$60**

Single/sb: **$40**
Open: **All year**
Breakfast: **Full**
Pets: **No**
Children: **Welcome, over 10**
Smoking: **No**
Social Drinking: **No**
Airport/Station Pickup: **Yes**

This ranch-style farmhouse is located in a quiet Amish community. Your hosts are dedicated to cordial hospitality and will gladly share information about the area. They offer comfortable bedrooms with king- or queen-size beds. In the morning, enjoy a wonderful breakfast of homemade biscuits, apple butter, fresh country bacon, and eggs. Curly's Corner is a half mile from beautiful Rockome Gardens.

Vrooman Mansion—A Bed & Breakfast Hospitality Establishment ✪
701 EAST TAYLOR, BLOOMINGTON, ILLINOIS 61701

Tel: **(309) 828-8816**
Best Time to Call: **Evening**
Hosts: **John and Nanako McEntire**
Location: **150 mi. S of Chicago**
No. of Rooms: **5**
No. of Private Baths: **1**
Max. No. Sharing Bath: **4**
Double/pb: **$90**
Single/pb: **$80**
Double/sb: **$75**
Single/sb: **$65**

Open: **All year**
Reduced Rates: **5% seniors; 10%
  families**
Breakfast: **Continental, plus**
Credit Cards: **MC, VISA**
Pets: **No**
Children: **Welcome, over 10**
Smoking: **No**
Social Drinking: **No**
Airport/Station Pickup: **Yes**
Foreign Languages: **Japanese**

Built in 1869, Vrooman Mansion is listed on the National Register of Historic Places. It has 35 rooms and over 10,000 square feet of living space. The mansion's one-acre parklike setting will help you relax from the cares of modern life. Guest rooms are tastefully decorated with antique and period furniture. Each room has its own theme, drawn from the history of the prominent family that graced the home in years gone by. Breakfast is served in the red dining room on the same hand-carved table where former First Lady Eleanor Roosevelt, playwright Rachel Crothers, and many other famous dignitaries have dined.

The Golds
2065 COUNTY ROAD, 525 E, CHAMPAIGN, ILLINOIS 61821

Tel: **(217) 586-4345**
Best Time to Call: **Evenings**

Hosts: **Bob and Rita Gold**
Location: **6 mi. W of Champaign**

No. of Rooms: **3**
Max. No. Sharing Bath: **4**
Double/sb: **$50**
Single/sb: **$45**
Open: **All year**
Reduced Rates: **15% weekly**

Breakfast: **Continental**
Pets: **No**
Children: **Welcome**
Smoking: **No**
Social Drinking: **Permitted**

One of the most beautiful views in Champaign County is yours from the deck of this restored farmhouse. The house is set on six acres surrounded by prime central Illinois farmland. Inside you'll find country antiques, complemented by beautiful wainscoting. An open walnut stairway leads to bedrooms decorated with queen-size beds, handmade quilts, and oriental rugs. Guests can relax by the living room wood stove or enjoy a beverage on the deck. Bob and Rita offer garden fruits and cider for breakfast, served with homemade jams, muffins, and coffee cakes. The Golds is two miles from Lake of the Woods, and 20 minutes from the University of Illinois campus. Shopping and restaurants are also within easy reach.

A City Bed & Breakfast ✪

2150 NORTH LINCOLN PARK WEST, CHICAGO, ILLINOIS 60614

Tel: **(773) 472-0027**
Host: **Susan Barton**
No. of Rooms: **1**
No. of Private Baths: **1**
Double/pb: **$70**
Single/pb: **$60**
Open: **All year**

Reduced Rates: **Available**
Breakfast: **Continental**
Pets: **No**
Children: **Welcome, over 6**
Smoking: **No**
Social Drinking: **Permitted**

Nestled in a vintage apartment building in the heart of Lincoln Park, this bed and breakfast offers a charming yet sophisticated ambiance. Accommodations are spacious and comfortable. Guests are welcomed with a panoramic view of Lincoln Park, Lake Michigan, and Chicago's skyline. A breakfast buffet is Susan's specialty, with a selection of fruit juices, fresh-baked goods, fine jams, and the best coffee. Within walking distance guests can enjoy Lincoln Park's famous zoo, flower conservatory and gardens, jogging and cycling paths, and beaches. Shopping at Water Tower Palace, a visit to the John Hancock Center Observatory, or a tour of the Art Institute are only a short bus ride away. Ask Susan about dinner, theater, or the Chicago Symphony.

Lake Shore Drive Bed and Breakfast ✪
P.O. BOX 148643, CHICAGO, ILLINOIS 60614

Tel: **(773) 404-5500**	Open: **All year**
Best Time to Call: **9 AM–11 PM,**	Reduced Rates: **Available for extended**
weekdays	**stays**
Host: **Barbara Mark**	Breakfast: **Continental, plus**
Location: **2 mi. N of center Chicago**	Pets: **No**
No. of Rooms: **1**	Children: **No**
No. of Private Baths: **1**	Smoking: **No**
Double/pb: **$85**	Social Drinking: **Permitted**
Single/pb: **$75**	Minimum Stay: **3 nights**

Barbara welcomes you to her lovely home in the sky, featuring spectacular wraparound views of Lake Michigan, Lincoln Park, and the Chicago skyline. The romantic guest room features cable TV, air-conditioning, and a dazzling view of the city and the sailboats on Lake Michigan. In good weather, savor a glass of wine and the panoramic views from the rooftop garden. Lake Michigan's beaches, Lincoln Park Zoo, Wrigley Field, jogging and cycling paths, fine dining, jazz and blues clubs, theaters, and great shopping are all within walking distance of this neighborhood. Excellent public transportation at the corner provides easy access to downtown, Orchestra Hall, the Art Institute, architectural walking tours, Lake Michigan cruises, Northwestern Memorial Hospital, and McCormick Convention Center. Having hosted guests from all over the world, Barbara gives an extra-special welcome to visitors from abroad. Your gracious and charming hostess can update you on all there is to do and see in Chicago.

Old Town Bed & Breakfast ✪
1451 NORTH NORTH PARK AVENUE, CHICAGO, ILLINOIS 60610

Tel: **(312) 440-9268**	Breakfast: **Continental**
Best Time to Call: **Anytime**	Credit Cards: **AMEX, MC, VISA**
Host: **Michael Serritella**	Pets: **No**
No. of Rooms: **2**	Children: **No**
Max. No. Sharing Bath: **4**	Smoking: **No**
Double/sb: **$90**	Social Drinking: **Permitted**
Open: **All year**	

This modern town house is furnished with fine art and old family photographs. Each guest room has air-conditioning, a phone, and fully cabled TV. For your convenience there is both on-street and off-street parking. Restaurants, major museums, and public transportation are within walking distance. Enjoy breakfast indoors or, weather permitting, in the private, walled garden. Michael, a former teacher and university administrator, is knowledgeable about the city and surrounding countryside, and is eager to help guests make the most of their trip.

Avery Guest House ✪
606 SOUTH PROSPECT STREET, GALENA, ILLINOIS 61036

Tel: **(815) 777-3883**	Open: **All year**
Best Time to Call: **9 AM–9 PM**	Reduced Rates: **10% Sun.–Thur.**
Hosts: **Gerry and Armon Lamparelli**	Breakfast: **Full**
Location: **15 mi. E of Dubuque, Iowa**	Credit Cards: **DISC, MC, VISA**
No. of Rooms: **3**	Pets: **No**
Max. No. Sharing Bath: **4**	Children: **Welcome, over 12**
Double/pb: **$85**	Smoking: **Restricted**
Double/sb: **$75**	Social Drinking: **Permitted**

Built before the Civil War days and remodeled in the 1920s, the Avery Guest House is located within a few blocks of Galena's main shopping center and historical buildings. After a day of exploring, Avery Guest House is a homey refuge where you can share your experiences with your hosts or other guests. Enjoy the view from our porch swing, watch TV, or join in on a table game. Sleep will come easily on a comfortable queen-size bed in one of our three guest rooms. Breakfast is served in a sunny dining room with a bay window overlooking the Galena River Valley.

The Homeridge Bed and Breakfast
1470 NORTH STATE STREET, JERSEYVILLE, ILLINOIS 62052

Tel: **(618) 498-3442**	Reduced Rates: **Corporate rate $10 less Sun.–Thurs.**
Best Time to Call: **Anytime**	Breakfast: **Full**
Hosts: **Sue and Howard Landon**	Credit Cards: **MC, VISA**
Location: **45 mi. N of St. Louis, Mo.**	Pets: **No**
No. of Rooms: **4**	Children: **Welcome, over 14**
No. of Private Baths: **4**	Smoking: **No**
Double/pb: **$75**	Social Drinking: **No**
Single/pb: **$65**	Airport/Station Pickup: **Yes**
Open: **All year**	

The Homeridge, built in 1867, is a beautiful, warm, 14-room Italianate Victorian private home on 18 acres in a comfortable country atmosphere. You'll admire the original woodwork, 12-foot ceilings, and crown molding; a hand-carved, curved stairway leads to the third floor with its 12 × 12-foot cupola or watchtower room. Other details include a 20 × 40-foot swimming pool and an expansive, pillared front porch.

Once the estate of Senator Theodore S. Chapman (1891–1960), this B&B is being reviewed for listing in the National Historic Registry. Homeridge is conveniently located between Springfield, Illinois, and St. Louis, Missouri.

Corner George Inn ✪
CORNER OF MAIN AND MILL, P.O. BOX 103, MAEYSTOWN, ILLINOIS 62256

Tel: **(618) 458-6660; (800) 458-6020;** fax: **(618) 458-7770**	Open: **All year**
Best Time to Call: **9 AM–9 PM**	Breakfast: **Full**
Hosts: **David and Marcia Braswell**	Credit Cards: **AMEX, DISC, MC, VISA**
Location: **45 min. S of St. Louis**	Pets: **No**
No. of Rooms: **6**	Children: **Welcome, over 12**
No. of Private Baths: **6**	Smoking: **No**
Double/pb: **$67–$105**	Social Drinking: **Permitted**
	Foreign Languages: **German**

A frontier Victorian structure built in 1884—when it was known as the Maeystown Hotel and Saloon—the Corner George Inn has been painstakingly restored. In addition to the six antique-filled guest rooms, there are two sitting rooms, a wine cellar, and an elegant ballroom, where David and Marcia serve breakfast. Maeystown is a quaint 19th-century village; guests can tour it on a bicycle built for two or aboard a horse-drawn carriage. Nearby are St. Louis, Fort de Chartres, Fort Kaskaskia, and the scenic bluff road that hugs the Mississippi.

The Poor Farm Bed & Breakfast ✪
POOR FARM ROAD, MOUNT CARMEL, ILLINOIS 62863

Tel: **(800) 646-3276; (618) 262-4663;** fax: **(618) 262-8199**	Reduced Rates: **Available**
Hosts: **Liz and John Stelzer**	Breakfast: **Full**
Location: **1 mi. N of Mount Carmel**	Other Meals: **Available**
No. of Rooms: **5**	Credit Cards: **AMEX, DISC, MC, VISA**
No. of Private Baths: **5**	Pets: **No**
Double/pb: **$45–$55**	Children: **Welcome**
Single/pb: **$45–$55**	Smoking: **Restricted**
Suites: **$85–$95**	Social Drinking: **Permitted**
Open: **All year**	Airport Pickup: **Yes**

Named for its previous use—as a 19th-century shelter for the homeless—this stately, 35-room brick landmark is sure to enchant you with its quiet, country charm. Poor Farm is adjacent to a 25-acre county park and within sight of an 18-hole golf course. Red Hill State Park, Beall Woods Conservation Area and Nature Preserve, a swimming pool, driving range, tennis courts, boating, and fishing are only minutes away. These amenities, plus your hosts' Midwestern hospitality, make this B&B the "inn" place to stay.

Round-Robin Guesthouse ✪
231 EAST MAPLE AVENUE, MUNDELEIN, ILLINOIS 60060

Tel: **(800) 301-7664**
Hosts: **George and Laura Loffredo**
Location: **38 mi. NW of Chicago**
No. of Rooms: **6**
No. of Private Baths: **3**
Max. No. Sharing Bath: **4**
Double/pb: **$65**
Double/sb: **$45–$55**
Suite: **$115**

Open: **All year**
Reduced Rates: **10% seniors, families**
Breakfast: **Full**
Credit Cards: **MC, VISA**
Pets: **No**
Children: **Welcome**
Smoking: **No**
Social Drinking: **Permitted**

This handsome red Victorian with white trim takes its name from the letters circulated by your hosts' relatives for more than 70 years; to encourage you to write friends and family, George and Laura will provide you with paper, pen, and stamps. The many local diversions ensure that you'll have plenty to write about. Six Flags Great America, the Volo Auto Museum, and the antique village of Long Grove are barely fifteen minutes away by car, and you're never far from golf, swimming, and horseback riding. During the summer, the Chicago Symphony is in residence at nearby Ravinia Park. Or you can enjoy Laura's renditions of classical and ragtime music on the piano. You'll wake up to the aroma of fresh-brewed coffee; coffee cake, muffins, and homemade jam are served between 7:30 and 9 AM.

The Ancient Pines Bed & Breakfast
2015 PARLEY STREET, NAUVOO, ILLINOIS 62354

Tel: **(217) 453-2767**
Best Time to Call: **9 AM–9 PM**
Host: **Genevieve Simmens**
Location: **225 mi. SW of Chicago**
No. of Rooms: **3**
Max. No. Sharing Bath: **3**
Double/sb: **$45**
Single/sb: **$35**

Open: **All year**
Reduced Rates: **15% weekly**
Breakfast: **Full**
Pets: **Sometimes**
Children: **Welcome**
Smoking: **No**
Social Drinking: **Permitted**

This turn-of-the-century brick home is rich in detail inside and out, from the stained glass windows and etched-glass front door to the tin ceilings, open staircase, and carved woodwork. Wander through herb and flower gardens, play croquet on the lawn, or enjoy music or chess in the library. Local attractions include wineries (Nauvoo holds its own grape festival), Civil War reenactments, historic Mormon homes, and Nauvoo State Park. Whatever your itinerary, you'll wake to the aroma of baking bread, served with eggs and sausage or ham. Special low-cholesterol menus are available upon request.

The Gilbert Gaylord House ✪
1542 PLAINFIELD ROAD, OSWEGO, ILLINOIS 60543

Tel: **(630) 554-1865**
Best Time to Call: **8 AM–9 PM**
Hosts: **Robert and Candice Hadley Johnson**
Location: **45 mi. SW of Chicago**
No. of Rooms: **2**
No. of Private Baths: **2**
Double/pb: **$80–$90**
Single/pb: **$80–$90**
Suites: **$140**

Open: **All year**
Reduced Rates: **10% 2 nights or more; 5% seniors**
Breakfast: **Continental**
Pets: **Sometimes**
Children: **Welcome**
Smoking: **No**
Social Drinking: **Permitted**
Foreign Languages: **French**

The Gilbert Gaylord House is a stately brick Italianate built in 1865. This intimate B&B offers rural seclusion on an old farm. Nearby is southern Fox River Valley, antiquing, bicycling, cross-country skiing, hiking, fishing, golfing, canoeing, shopping, and riverboat gambling in Aurora and Joliet. Robert, Candice, and son Samuel will make you feel at home with the comfortable furnishings, including Victorian antiques. Breakfast is served either in front of a blazing fire or on the Victorian screen porch. Bob works in foreign exchange and Candice runs an advertising sales business from home.

The Kaufmann House ✪
1641 HAMPSHIRE, QUINCY, ILLINOIS 62301

Tel: **(217) 223-2502**
Best Time to Call: **Noon–9 PM**
Hosts: **Emery and Bettie Kaufmann**
Location: **100 mi. W of Springfield**
No. of Rooms: **3**
No. of Private Baths: **1**
Max. No. Sharing Bath: **4**
Double/pb: **$70**
Single/pb: **$65**
Double/sb: **$50–$60**

Single/sb: **$45–$55**
Reduced Rates: **10% 3 nights or more**
Open: **All year**
Breakfast: **Continental, plus**
Pets: **No**
Children: **Welcome (crib)**
Smoking: **No**
Social Drinking: **No**
Airport/Station Pickup: **Yes**

History buffs will remember Quincy, set right on the Mississippi River, as the scene of the famous Lincoln-Douglas debates, while architecture buffs will be attracted to the town's feast of Victorian styles—Greek Revival, Gothic Revival, Italianate, and Richardsonian. The Kaufmann House was built 100 years ago, and the owners have been careful to maintain its "country" feeling. Guests may enjoy breakfast in the Ancestor's Room, on a stone patio, or at a picnic table under the trees. They are invited to play the piano, watch TV, or enjoy popcorn by the fire. The Kaufmanns describe themselves as "Christians who have a love for God, people, nature, and life."

Top o' the Morning ✪
1505 19TH AVENUE, ROCK ISLAND, ILLINOIS 61201

Tel: **(309) 786-3513**
Best Time to Call: **After 5 PM**
Hosts: **Sam and Peggy Doak**
Location: **1½ mi. from Rte. 92, 18th Ave. exit**
No. of Rooms: **3**
No. of Private Baths: **3**

Double/pb: **$60–$80**
Open: **All year**
Breakfast: **Full**
Pets: **No**
Children: **Welcome**
Smoking: **Permitted**
Social Drinking: **Permitted**

Sam and Peggy welcome you to their country estate, set on a bluff overlooking the Mississippi River, near the center of the Quad Cities area. The 18-room mansion is situated at the end of a winding drive on three acres of lawn, orchards, and gardens. The guest rooms, graced with lovely chandeliers and oriental rugs, command a spectacular view of the cities and river. The parlor, with its grand piano and fireplace, is an inviting place to relax. Local attractions are Mississippi River boat rides, riverboat casinos, Rock Island Arsenal, Black Hawk State Park, Augustana College, and St. Ambrose University.

Country Charm Inn ✪
15165 QUIGLEY ROAD, SYCAMORE, ILLINOIS 60178

Tel: **(815) 895-4797**
Best Time to Call: **Anytime**
Hosts: **Howard and Donna Petersen**
Location: **55 mi. W of Chicago**
No. of Rooms: **3**
No. of Private Baths: **3**
Double/pb: **$55–$75**
Open: **All year**
Reduced Rates: **On a weekly basis**

Breakfast: **Continental, weekdays; full, weekends**
Pets: **No**
Children: **Welcome**
Smoking: **No**
Social Drinking: **No**
Minimum Stay: **Only for local weekend events**

On a tree-topped knoll in rich farming country stands this rambling, turn-of-the-century stucco home. Howard and Donna's comfortable accommodations blend understated elegance with casual warmth and friendliness. Enjoy a full country breakfast on the cozy front porch; house specialties range from egg-cheese dishes and designer pancakes to peach cobblers and pecan roll rings. Then lounge around the sunken fireplace, watch a movie on the large-screen TV with surround sound, borrow a book from the loft library, or roam around the farm. Champ, the trick horse, sends personal note cards to children telling about his barnyard pals, including llamas and another horse. For those planning to exchange vows, the Petersens have built a charming wedding chapel on the property.

Bed and Breakfast at Edie's ✪
233 EAST HARPOLE, P.O. BOX 351, WILLIAMSVILLE, ILLINOIS 62693

Tel: **(217) 566-2538**
Best Time to Call: **After 5 PM, weekends**

Host: **Edith L. Senalik**
Location: **10 mi. N of Springfield**

No. of Rooms: **3**
Max. No. Sharing Bath: **4**
Double/sb: **$50–$55**
Single/sb: **$40–$45**
Open: **All year**
Reduced Rates: **Available**

Breakfast: **Continental**
Pets: **No**
Children: **Welcome**
Smoking: **No**
Social Drinking: **Permitted**

Just ten minutes north of the state capital, Springfield, the friendly village of Williamsville offers the peace, quiet, and safety of a small town. Edie's is a 75-year-old Mission-style house where guests have use of a formal living room, dining room, and a TV room equipped with cable TV and a video library. Springfield offers the Abraham Lincoln attractions, Springfield Theater Centre, Old State Capitol, Lincoln Land Community College, and Sangamon State University. Historic Petersburg and New Salem, 20 miles to the west, are easily accessible.

For key to listings, see inside front or back cover.

✪ This star means that rates are guaranteed through December 31, 1998, to any guest making a reservation as a result of reading about the B&B in *Bed & Breakfast U.S.A.*—1998 edition.

Important! To avoid misunderstandings, always ask about cancellation policies when booking.

Please enclose a self-addressed, stamped, business-size envelope when contacting reservation services.

For more details on what you can expect in a B&B, see Chapter 1.

Always mention *Bed & Breakfast U.S.A.* when making reservations!

We want to hear from you! Use the form on page 625.

INDIANA

B&B Midwest Reservations ✪
2223 CRUMP LANE, COLUMBUS, INDIANA 47203

Tel: **(800) 34 B AND B [342-2632]**
Best Time to Call: **9 AM–5 PM**
  Mon.–Fri.
Coordinator: **Martha McDonald-Swan**
States/Regions Covered:
  Illinois—Antioch, Cairo, Danforth, Evanston, Franklin Grove, Galena, Geneva, Gurnee, Hinsdale, Morrison, Mundelein, Oakbrook, Oak Park, Oregon, Springfield, Taylorville, Wadsworth, West Dundee, Woodstock, Yorkville;
  Indiana—Anderson, Bainbridge, Culver, Knightstown, Paoli
Descriptive Directory: **Free**
Rates (Single/Double):
  Modest: **$45 / $55**
  Average: **$50 / $100**
  Luxury: **$110 / $179**
Credit Cards: **AMEX, DISC, MC, VISA**

B&B Midwest Reservations has expanded beyond northern Illinois to include southern Illinois and Indiana. Most homes are on historic registers. Hosts enjoy sharing beautiful antiques, handwork, and lots of TLC with their guests. Many also offer numerous special activities and theme weekends, available from suburban locations to country farms.

Gray Goose Inn ✪

350 INDIAN BOUNDARY ROAD, CHESTERTON, INDIANA 46304

Tel: (800) 521-5127; (219) 926-5781
Best Time to Call: 9 AM–10 PM
Hosts: Tim Wilk and Charles Ramsey
Location: 60 mi. E of Chicago
No. of Rooms: 8
No. of Private Baths: 8
Double/pb: $80–$108
Single/pb: $80–$108
Suites: $138–$156

Open: All year
Reduced Rates: 10% seniors
Breakfast: Full
Credit Cards: AMEX, DISC, MC, VISA
Pets: No
Children: Welcome, over 12
Smoking: Restricted
Social Drinking: Permitted

Elegant accommodations await you in this English country-style house overlooking a 30-acre lake. Guest rooms feature four-poster beds, fine linens, and thick, fluffy towels. Some rooms are decorated in Williamsburg style, some have fireplaces and Jacuzzi. Enjoy a quiet moment in the common rooms, or relax with a cup of coffee in the scenic wicker room. Take long walks beside shady oaks, feed the Canada geese and wild ducks. The Gray Goose is five minutes from Dunes State and National Lakeshore Parks. Swimming, hiking, and fishing sites on Lake Michigan are all within easy reach. Dining and weekend entertainment are within walking distance.

The Tranquil Cherub

2164 NORTH CAPITOL AVENUE, INDIANAPOLIS, INDIANA 46202-1251

Tel: (317) 923-9036
Best Time to Call: 8 AM–10 AM; 6 PM–10 PM
Hosts: Thom and Barbara Feit
Location: ½ mi. from I-65 exit 115
No. of Rooms: 4
No. of Private Baths: 4
Double/pb: $65–$75
Suite: $80–$85

Open: All year
Reduced Rates: Weekly
Breakfast: Full
Credit Cards: AMEX, MC, VISA
Pets: No
Children: Welcome, over 14
Smoking: Restricted
Social Drinking: Permitted
Airport Pickup: Yes

From the central location of this B&B, you are only minutes from downtown. As you enter the foyer, the beautifully crafted oak staircase and pier mirror will draw your eye. Lace curtains, Battenburg lace comforters, wicker furniture, Beardsley prints, and Art Deco furniture decorate the rooms. In the morning, the aroma of freshly brewed coffee—served from an English sideboard in the upstairs hall—will waft to your room. Ease into your day with juice and the paper in the upstairs sitting room. Breakfast is served in the dining room, where beveled glass and a sparkling chandelier accent the oak paneling and fireplace. Weather permitting, you may have your meal on the rear deck overlooking the lily ponds. There is a $5 surcharge for one-night stays.

Powers Inn
325 WEST 6TH STREET, JASPER, INDIANA 47546

Tel: **(812) 482-3018**
Hosts: **Alice and Larry Garland**
Location: **135 mi. S of Indianapolis, 1½
  hours from Louisville, Ky.**
No. of Rooms: **3**
No. of Private Baths: **3**
Double/pb: **$60**
Single/pb: **$55**

Open: **All year**
Breakfast: **Full**
Credit Cards: **MC, VISA**
Pets: **No**
Children: **Welcome, over 3**
Smoking: **No**
Social Drinking: **No**

Powers Inn is located within a few blocks of Indiana's Courthouse Square. This newly renovated Second Empire home offers original wood floors, a mansard roof, and a pleasant mix of antiques throughout. Breakfast is served in the dining room and may include homemade breads or muffins and other specialties. Nearby attractions include Holiday World Amusement Park, Abraham Lincoln's Boyhood Home and State Park, Patoka Lake, and Paoli Peaks.

Golden Oak Bed & Breakfast
809 WEST FOURTH STREET, MARION, INDIANA 46952

Tel: **(765) 651-9950**
Best Time to Call: **9 AM–9 PM**
Hosts: **Lois and Dave Lutes**
Location: **60 mi. N of Indianapolis**
No. of Rooms: **4**
No. of Private Baths: **4**
Double/sb: **$65**
Single/sb: **$60**

Open: **All year**
Breakfast: **Full**
Credit Cards: **AMEX, MC, VISA**
Pets: **No**
Children: **Welcome**
Smoking: **No**
Social Drinking: **Permitted**

Enjoy the elegance of this beautifully restored two-story home built in the 1890s. Inside, the rooms glow with the rich oak woodwork that inspires this B&B's name. Throughout the house, you'll see hand-crocheted items; similar ones are for sale in your hosts' gift shop. The James Dean Gallery and Historical Museum, the Mississinewa Battlefield, beaches, golf courses, and antique shops are among the area's attractions. For your dining pleasure, the Hostess House of Marion is within walking distance.

Big Locust Farm ✪
3295 WEST COUNTY ROAD 25 SOUTH, PAOLI, INDIANA 47454

Tel: **(812) 723-4856**
Best Time to Call: **8 PM**
Hosts: **Joe and Glenda Lindley**
Location: **50 mi. NW of Louisville,
  Kentucky**

No. of Rooms: **2**
No. of Private Baths: **2**
Double/pb: **$70**
Single/pb: **$60**
Open: **All year**

Reduced Rates: **$5 after first night**
Breakfast: **Full**
Credit Cards: **MC, VISA**
Pets: **No**

Children: **By arrangement**
Smoking: **No**
Social Drinking: **Permitted**

A warm country welcome awaits you at Big Locust Farm, a new brick country Victorian home that sits on 60 acres. Inside, the flooring and woodwork are made of oak, and central heat and air assure guests' comfort. The rooms are decorated with lace curtains, comfortable beds, and antiques. Your day will begin with a hearty breakfast that may include egg and meat dishes, breads or muffins, fruit, juice, and coffee. Enjoy a stroll in the herb, rose, and perennial gardens or rest on the large front porch while the world goes by. Wander along the limestone bottom creek or through the woods. Local attractions include antique shops, Frenck Lick Railroad and Winery, West Baden Dome, Patoka Lake, and much more.

Suits Us ✪

514 NORTH COLLEGE, ROCKVILLE, INDIANA 47872

Tel: **(317) 569-5660; (888) 4SUITS-US**
Hosts: **Marty and Bev Rose**
Location: **50 mi. W of Indianapolis**
No. of Rooms: **4**
No. of Private Baths: **4**
Double/pb: **$55–$75**
Suites: **$125, sleeps 2–6**

Open: **All year**
Breakfast: **Full**
Pets: **No**
Children: **Welcome**
Smoking: **No**
Social Drinking: **Permitted**

This classic plantation-style home, with its widow's walk and generous front porch, dates to the early 1880s. The Strausses, a locally prominent family, bought the house about 20 years later; their overnight guests included Woodrow Wilson, Annie Oakley, James Whitcomb Riley, and John Lewis. Today Marty and Bev extend their hospitality to you. All guest rooms have a TV and VCR. Guests are invited to choose a movie from the video library, or use one of the bikes to explore the area. Turkey Run Park is 10 miles away, while five universities—Indiana State, DePauw, Wabash, St. Mary-of-the-Woods, and Rose-Hulman—are within a 30-mile radius. Also, Rockville sponsors its own annual event, the Covered Bridge Festival.

IOWA

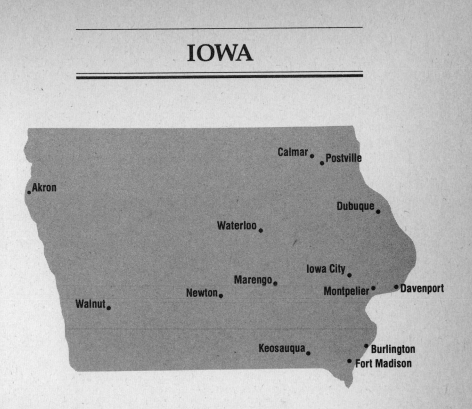

Wildflower Log Cabin Bed & Breakfast ✪
501 HIGHWAY 12, RR3, BOX 1, AKRON, IOWA 51001

Tel: **(800) 257-6642; (712) 568-2206**
Best Time to Call: **Evenings**
Hosts: **Jeanne and CJ Hinrichsen**
Location: **28 mi. N of Sioux City**
No. of Rooms: **3**
No. of Private Baths: **2**
Double/pb: **$45**
Double/sb: **$40**

Single/sb: **$35**
Open: **All year**
Reduced Rates: **10% after 2nd night**
Breakfast: **Full**
Pets: **No**
Children: **Welcome**
Smoking: **No**
Social Drinking: **Permitted**

This cozy log cabin on the prairie provides a delightful break for travelers. Jean and CJ welcome you to their handcrafted log home lovingly decorated with antiques and collectibles. Enjoy the porch swing in the living room, soak in the hot tub, stargaze around the backyard, or stroll among the abundant flowers. Breakfasts are country style, and guests are invited to help themselves to soft drinks and fresh baked cookies.

Wildflower Log Cabin Bed & Breakfast is located at the northernmost point of Iowa's Loess Hills Scenic Byway and adjoins a 29-acre prairie preserve, the only approved Volkswalk site in Western Iowa.

The Schramm House Bed & Breakfast ✪
616 COLUMBIA STREET, BURLINGTON, IOWA 52601

Tel: **(800) 683-7117; fax: (319) 754-0373**
Hosts: **Sandy and Bruce Morrison**
No. of Rooms: **3**
No. of Private Baths: **3**
Double p/b: **$65–$75**
Open: **All year**
Reduced Rates: **10% seniors**

Breakfast: **Full**
Credit Cards: **AMEX, DISC, MC, VISA**
Pets: **No**
Children: **Welcome**
Smoking: **No**
Social Drinking: **Permitted**
Airport/Station Pickup: **Yes**

Step into the past when you enter this restored 1870s Victorian home located in the heart of the historical district. Unique architectural features and antique furnishings create the mood of a bygone era. Experience Burlington hospitality while having lemonade on the porch or tea by the fire with your hosts. Walk to the Mississippi River, antique shops, restaurants, and more. A formal breakfast is served in the dining room. Weather permitting, the sunporch offers a bright and cheerful alternative for your morning meal.

Calmar Guesthouse ✪
103 NORTH STREET, R.R. 1, BOX 206, CALMAR, IOWA 52132

Tel: **(319) 562-3851**
Host: **Lucille Kruse**
Location: **10 mi. S of Decorah**
No. of Rooms: **5**
Max. No. Sharing Bath: **5**
Double/sb: **$40–$45**
Open: **All year**

Breakfast: **Full**
Pets: **No**
Children: **Welcome**
Smoking: **No**
Social Drinking: **Permitted**
Airport/Station Pickup: **Yes**

A recent guest reports that "The Calmar Guesthouse is a spacious, lovely, newly remodeled Victorian home located on the edge of town. The atmosphere is enhanced by the friendly, charming manner of Lucille, who made us feel right at home. The rooms were comfortable, private, and pretty. After a peaceful night's sleep, we were served a delicious breakfast of fresh farm eggs with ham and cheeses, croissants with butter and jam, homemade cinnamon rolls, and coffee. I would recommend it to anyone visiting the area." Nearby points of interest include Lake Meyer, the world's smallest church, and Spillville, home of hand-carved Bily Bros. Clocks.

Fulton's Landing Guest House ✪
1206 EAST RIVER DRIVE, DAVENPORT, IOWA 52803

Tel: **(319) 322-4069**
Hosts: **Bill and Pat Schmidt**
Location: **150 mi. W of Chicago**
No. of Rooms: **5**
No. of Private Baths: **5**
Double/pb: **$75–$85**
Suites: **$125**
Open: **All year**

Reduced Rates: **Available**
Breakfast: **Full**
Credit Cards: **AMEX, DISC, MC, VISA**
Pets: **No**
Children: **Welcome**
Smoking: **No**
Social Drinking: **Permitted**

Pat and Bill recently restored this house as a bed and breakfast, with cut-glass windows, wide hallways, carved woodwork, curved ceilings, and many of the original gas and electrical fixtures. Sixteen columns frame the front porch where guests can relax in comfortable chairs while enjoying the view of the Mississippi River. Guest rooms are furnished with antique walnut beds and floral wallcoverings, and terry robes are supplied. Breakfast specialties include juice, fruit, apple cinnamon French toast, and egg cheese sausage casserole. Bill and Pat have created a sophisticated yet comfortable environment from the beds to the meals.

Juniper Hill Farm Bed & Breakfast Inn ✪
15325 BUDD ROAD, DUBUQUE, IOWA 52002
JHBandB@AOL.COM

Tel: **(319) 582-4405; (800) 572-1449**
Best Time to Call: **8 AM–10 PM**
Hosts: **Bill and Ruth McEllhiney**
Location: **3.75 mi. NW of Dubuque**
No. of Rooms: **3**
No. of Private Baths: **3**
Double/pb: **$70**
Suites: **$90–$130**
Open: **All year**

Reduced Rates: **Available**
Breakfast: **Full**
Credit Cards: **MC, VISA**
Pets: **No**
Children: **Welcome, over 6**
Smoking: **No**
Social Drinking: **Permitted**
Minimum Stay: **2 nights, weekends**

Juniper Hill Farm Bed & Breakfast Inn is nestled in the Mississippi River Hills on 40 acres of woods, meadows, and hiking trails, with a fishing pond and a spectacular valley view enjoyed from the year-round outdoor hot tub. The shake-sided cottage has a modified country decor with white-painted wood walls showcasing the soft colors throughout. The Inn is near Heritage Train—a rails-to-trails path used for biking or cross-country skiing—and adjacent to Sundown ski area, making it the only Iowa B&B where you can ski to the front door. Ruth and Bill will gladly help plan your exploration of surrounding areas.

The Richards House
1492 LOCUST STREET, DUBUQUE, IOWA 52001

Tel: **(319) 557-1492**
Best Time to Call: **Anytime**
Host: **Michelle Delaney**
No. of Rooms: **6**
No. of Private Baths: **4**
Max. No. Sharing Bath: **2**
Double/pb: **$45–$75**
Single/pb: **$45–$75**
Double/sb: **$40–$55**
Single/sb: **$40–$55**
Suites: **$50–$85**

Open: **All year**
Reduced Rates: **10% Nov.–Apr.; 40% Sun.–Thurs.**
Breakfast: **Full**
Credit Cards: **AMEX, DC, DISC, MC, VISA**
Pets: **Sometimes**
Children: **Welcome (crib)**
Smoking: **Restricted**
Social Drinking: **Permitted**
Airport/Station Pickup: **Yes**

Inside and out, this four-story Victorian is a feast for the eyes, with its gabled roof, stained glass windows, gingerbread trim, and elaborate woodwork. Rooms are furnished in period style. Guests can continue their journey back in time with a ride on the Fenelon Place Cable Car, the shortest inclined railway in the country. Then it's time to pay respects to another form of transportation at the Woodward Riverboat Museum. You're welcome to use the kitchen for light snacks; in the morning, Michelle takes over, setting out fresh fruit, waffles, pancakes, sausage, and homemade breads.

Kingsley Inn ☼
707 AVENUE H, FORT MADISON, IOWA 52627

Tel: **(319) 372-7074; (800) 441-2327**
Best Time to Call: **Before 10 PM**
Host: **Mrs. Myrna Reinhard**
Location: **On U.S. Highway 61**
No. of Rooms: **14**
No. of Private Baths: **14**
Double/pb: **$70–$115**
Open: **All year**
Reduced Rates: **Available**
Breakfast: **Continental, plus**

Other Meals: **Available**
Credit Cards: **AMEX, DC, DISC, MC, VISA**
Pets: **No**
Children: **Welcome, over 12**
Smoking: **No**
Social Drinking: **Permitted**
Minimum Stay: **Holidays**
Station Pickup: **Yes**

Relax in 1860s Victorian luxury—these spacious rooms are furnished in period antiques with today's modern comforts. Awaken to the aroma of "Kingsley Blend" coffee and enjoy the specialty breakfast in the elegant morning room. Then stroll to the replica 1808 Fort, museum, parks, shops, antique malls, and Catfish Riverbend Casino. Historic Nauvoo, Illinois, is 15 minutes away. Treat yourselves to a unique lunch or dinner at Alpha's on the Riverfront. Amenities include private baths (some whirlpools), CATV, AC, and telephones.

Bella Vista Place Bed & Breakfast ✪
2 BELLA VISTA PLACE, IOWA CITY, IOWA 52245

Tel: **(319) 338-4129**
Host: **Daissy P. Owen**
Location: **1 mi. from Highway 80, Exit 244**
No. of Rooms: **4**
Max. No. Sharing Bath: **4**
Double/pb: **$75–$95**
Double/sb: **$58–$60**
Single/sb: **$45–$50**

Open: **All year**
Reduced Rates: **Available**
Breakfast: **Full**
Pets: **No**
Smoking: **No**
Social Drinking: **Permitted**
Airport Pickup: **Yes**
Foreign Languages: **Spanish**

Listed on the National Register of Historic Places, this lovely 1920s home is furnished with antiques and artifacts Daissy collected while traveling through Europe and Latin America. Guests can relax in a comfortable air-conditioned room, share the company of other guests in the living room or enjoy the view of the Iowa River from the deck. You will savor Daissy's hearty breakfast and delicious coffee. Downtown Iowa City and the University of Iowa are within walking distance. The Hoover Library, Amana Colonies, and the Amish center of Kalona are nearby.

The Golden Haug ✪
517 EAST WASHINGTON, IOWA CITY, IOWA 52240

Tel: **(319) 338-6452; 354-4284**
Best Time to Call: **Anytime**

Hosts: **Nila Haug and Dennis Nowotny**
Location: **2 mi. from I-80, Exit 244**

No. of Rooms: **4**
No. of Private Baths: **4**
Double/pb: **$68–$95**
Single/pb: **$68–$95**
Suites: **$84–$95**
Open: **All year**
Reduced Rates: **Available**

Breakfast: **Full**
Pets: **No**
Children: **Welcome**
Smoking: **No**
Social Drinking: **Permitted**
Airport Pickup: **Yes**

Nila and Dennis's 1920s Arts-and-Crafts house has been restored and updated to provide comfortable accommodations and modern conveniences. Guests can retreat to the comfort of their suites or enjoy the camaraderie of other visitors. With refreshments upon your arrival, and brunch-size breakfasts, you won't go away hungry. The convenient Iowa City location puts you within walking distance of the University of Iowa, restaurants, stores, and houses of worship.

Mason House Inn of Bentonsport ✪
ROUTE 2, BOX 237, KEOSAUQUA, IOWA 52565

Tel: **(319) 592-3133; (800) 592-3133**
Hosts: **Sheral and William McDermet**
Location: **40 mi. SE of Ottumwa**
No. of Rooms: **9**
No. of Private Baths: **5**
Max. No. Sharing Bath: **3**
Double/pb: **$74**
Single/pb: **$54**
Double/sb: **$54–$59**

Single/sb: **$44–$49**
Open: **All year**
Breakfast: **Full**
Other Meals: **Available**
Credlt Cards: **MC, VISA**
Pets: **Sometimes**
Children: **Welcome**
Smoking: **No**
Social Drinking: **Permitted**

Mason House Inn was built next to the Des Moines River by Mormon artisans en route to Salt Lake City. The three-story Georgian house contains 26 rooms. It is the only steamboat inn, built as such, still hosting persons in Iowa. The Inn has the only fold-down copper bathtub in the state. Sheral and Bill purchased the Inn in 1989 and have done extensive remodeling, allowing for ground-level rooms with private baths. Guests will find a full cookie jar in every room. The entire village is on the National Register of Historic Places. Iowa's oldest courthouse is six miles to the east. Bill served as a pastor for local congregations for

29 years, and Sheral was a manager for a deli before moving to Bentons-
port.

Loy's Farm Bed & Breakfast ✪
2077 KK AVENUE, MARENGO, IOWA 52301

Tel: **(319) 642-7787**
Best Time to Call: **7 AM–9:30 PM**
Hosts: **Loy and Robert Walker**
Location: **3 mi. from I-80, Exit 216 N**
No. of Rooms: **3**
No. of Private Baths: **1**
Max. No. Sharing Bath: **4**
Double/pb: **$55–$65**
Single/pb: **$45**

Double/sb: **$55–$65**
Single/sb: **$45**
Open: **All year**
Breakfast: **Full**
Other Meals: **Available**
Pets: **If caged**
Children: **Welcome**
Smoking: **No**
Social Drinking: **Permitted**

The Walkers invite you to visit their contemporary farm home in the
heartland of rural Iowa. Enjoy the peaceful surroundings of a large
lawn, gardens, and patio. The rooms are furnished in modern and refinished pieces. Guests are welcome to relax in the family room by the
fire or to stop by the recreation room for a game of shuffleboard or pool
and a treat from the snack bar. A farm tour gives you the chance to see
the farm facilities and operations, maybe even hold a baby pig. Each
morning enjoy a typical farm breakfast with a gourmet touch. Visit the
historic villages of the Amana Colonies, developed as a communal system. The Amana Colonies are Iowa's largest tourist attraction. Tanger
Mall, 64 designer outlet stores, and twelve restaurants (six that serve
German food) are all located nearby. Herbert Hoover's birthplace, the
Kalona Amish, Brucemore Mansion, and Iowa City are all just a short
drive away.

Varners' Caboose Bed & Breakfast ✪
204 EAST SECOND STREET, P.O. BOX 10, MONTPELIER, IOWA 52759

Tel: **(319) 381-3652**
Best Time to Call: **Afternoons**
Hosts: **Bob and Nancy Varner**
Location: **11 mi. W of Davenport**
No. of Rooms: **1**
No. of Private Baths: **1**
Double/pb: **$55**

Open: **All year**
Breakfast: **Full**
Pets: **Sometimes**
Children: **Welcome**
Smoking: **No**
Social Drinking: **Permitted**
Airport/Station Pickup: **Yes**

Bob and Nancy offer their guests the unique experience of staying in
a genuine Rock Island Line caboose. Their home, located close to the
Mississippi, was the original Montpelier Depot, and the caboose is a
self-contained unit with bath, shower, and kitchen set on its own track
behind the house. It sleeps four, with a queen-size bed and two singles
in the cupola. The rate is increased to $65 when more than two occupy
the caboose. A fully prepared egg casserole, fruit, homemade breads,

juice, and coffee or tea are left in the kitchen to be enjoyed at your leisure. Enjoy this quiet town while being a few minutes downstream from the heart of the Quad Cities.

LaCorsette Maison Inn ✪
629 FIRST AVENUE EAST, NEWTON, IOWA 50208

Tel: **(515) 792-6833**
Host: **Kay Owen**
Location: **25 mi. E of Des Moines**
No. of Rooms: **7**
No. of Private Baths: **7**
Double/pb: **$70–$175**
Suites: **$85–$175**
Open: **All year**

Breakfast: **Full**
Other Meals: **Available**
Pets: **Sometimes**
Children: **By arrangement**
Smoking: **No**
Social Drinking: **Permitted**
Airport/Station Pickup: **Yes**

Bringing a touch of Spanish architecture to the American heartland, this 21-room mansion has all the hallmarks of the Mission style, from its stucco walls and red-tiled roof to its interior oak woodwork. Certain nights of the week, Kay doubles as a chef, preparing elaborate five-course dinners for as many as 57 scheduled guests; the first caller to make reservations selects the entree, and a house tour precedes the meal. Overnight guests wake up to a full breakfast accented by the herbs and vegetables Kay grows in the backyard. If you want to work off the calories, tennis courts and a pool are in the area.

Old Shepherd House ✪
256 W. TILDEN STREET, BOX 251, POSTVILLE, IOWA 52162

Tel: **(319) 864-3452**
Best Time to Call: **10 AM–10 PM**
Host: **Rosalyn Krambeer**
Location: **25 mi. SE of Decorah**
No. of Rooms: **4**
No. of Private Baths: **4**
Double/pb: **$45–$50**

Single/sb: **$30**
Open: **All year**
Breakfast: **Full**
Pets: **Sometimes**
Children: **Welcome**
Smoking: **Restricted**
Social Drinking: **Permitted**

Postville, a town of 1500 with four quaint crafts shops and a fabulous antique emporium, is in northeast Iowa in an area known as the state's Little Switzerland. Within a thirty-mile radius you can canoe the Iowa River, or visit sites like the Vesterheim Museum, Effigy Mounds, Villa Louis, Spook Cave, and Bily Brothers clock museum. Shepherd House, built in the early 1880s, is furnished entirely with antique and Victorian pieces. Your hostess is an interior decorator, and she's filled her home with unusual window treatments, restored trunks, and crafts work.

Antique City Inn B&B ✪
400 ANTIQUE CITY DRIVE, P.O. BOX 584, WALNUT, IOWA 51577

Tel: **(712) 784-3722; (800) 714-3722**	Breakfast: **Full**
Host: **Sylvia Reddie**	Other Meals: **Available**
Location: **52 mi. E of Omaha, Nebraska**	Credit Cards: **MC, VISA**
No. of Rooms: **6**	Pets: **No**
No. of Private Baths: **2**	Children: **Welcome, over 12**
Max. No. Sharing Bath: **3**	Smoking: **No**
Double/pb: **$51.94**	Social Drinking: **Permitted**
Open: **All year**	

This 1911 Victorian residence has been restored to its original state and furnished in period style. You'll admire all the old-fashioned features, such as the wraparound porch, beautiful woodwork, French doors, butler pantry, and dumbwaiter. A block away, in a neighborhood of turn-of-the century brick streets and globed streetlights, you'll find antique shops with more than 200 dealers, plus the restored opera house—home of a country music museum and Iowa's Country Music Hall of Fame. Sylvia's full breakfasts typically consist of juice, fruit, fried potatoes, casseroles, and pecan rolls.

The Daisy Wilton Inn ✪
418 WALNUT STREET, WATERLOO, IOWA 50703

Tel: **(319) 232-0801**	Reduced Rates: **10% seniors; 10% families**
Best Time to Call: **Afternoons**	Breakfast: **Full**
Hosts: **Sue and Al Brase**	Pets: **No**
Location: **100 mi. NE of Des Moines**	Children: **Welcome, over 12**
No. of Rooms: **3**	Smoking: **No**
Max. No. Sharing Bath: **4**	Social Drinking: **Permitted**
Double/sb: **$55–$65**	Airport/Station Pickup: **Yes**
Single/sb: **$50–$60**	
Open: **All year**	

The Daisy Wilton Inn is a Queen Anne–style Victorian, rich in turn-of-the-century detail. Stained and beveled glass windows adorn the turreted home. Your hosts' cherished antiques and Victorian art nouveau decor complement the interior, which has oak woodwork and a dramatic winding staircase. The parlor, with its bookcase and fireplace, is an inviting room for conversation, music, reading, or games. Stately guest chambers offer luxurious accommodations. Savor the elegant surroundings and pleasant pastimes of the Victorian age.

For key to listings, see inside front or back cover.

✪ This star means that rates are guaranteed through December 31, 1998, to any guest making a reservation as a result of reading about the B&B in *Bed & Breakfast U.S.A.*—1998 edition.

Important! To avoid misunderstandings, always ask about cancellation policies when booking.

Please enclose a self-addressed, stamped, business-size envelope when contacting reservation services.

For more details on what you can expect in a B&B, see Chapter 1.

Always mention *Bed & Breakfast U.S.A.* when making reservations!

We want to hear from you! Use the form on page 625.

KANSAS

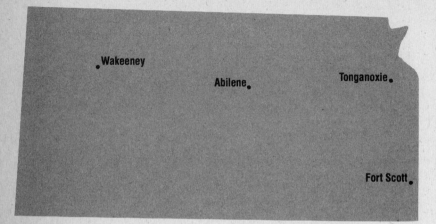

Wakeeney

Abilene

Tonganoxie

Fort Scott

Balfours' House
940 1900 AVENUE, ABILENE, KANSAS 67410

Tel: **(913) 263-4262**
Best Time to Call: **Anytime**
Hosts: **Gilbert and Marie Balfour**
Location: **2¼ mi. S of Abilene**
Suites: **$50–$150**
Open: **All year**
Breakfast: **Full**

Credit Cards: **AMEX, MC, VISA**
Pets: **Sometimes**
Children: **Welcome**
Smoking: **Restricted**
Social Drinking: **Permitted**
Airport/Station Pickup: **Sometimes**

Gilbert and Marie Balfour welcome you to their modern, cottage-style home, set on a hillside. The house is located on just over two acres, and has a spacious yard. Guests have their own private entrance into the family room, which includes a fireplace, piano, and TV. The main attraction of the house is a hexagonal recreation room that has a built-in swimming pool, spa, and dressing area with shower. A separate Southwestern-style bungalow is also available. Your hosts will gladly direct you to the Eisenhower Museum, Greyhound Hall of Fame, and old historic mansions.

Country Quarters ☉
ROUTE 5, BOX 80, FORT SCOTT, KANSAS 66701

Tel: **(316) 223-2889**
Best Time to Call: **After 5 PM**
Host: **Marilyn McQuitty**
Location: **2 mi. S of Fort Scott**
No. of Rooms: **2**
Max. No. Sharing Bath: **4**
Double/sb: **$30**

Open: **All year**
Breakfast: **Full**
Pets: **No**
Children: **Welcome**
Smoking: **Permitted**
Social Drinking: **Permitted**

Marilyn McQuitty welcomes you to a real working farm located outside a charming Victorian town. Her 100-year-old farmhouse is furnished with comfortable family pieces. While you're sitting by the fire, ask to hear the story behind the 100-year-old hearth and hand-carved mantelpiece. Guests are welcome to relax on the porch or visit the ceramic shop located on the premises. There is easy access to the Fort Scott Lake, Gunn Park, and the Fort Scott National Historic Site, an authentically restored military fort dating back to 1892. Downtown you can drive past the magnificent old homes, browse through antique stores, and visit a one-room schoolhouse.

Almeda's Bed and Breakfast Inn ☉
220 SOUTH MAIN, TONGANOXIE, KANSAS 66086

Tel: **(913) 845-2295**
Best Time to Call: **Before 9 AM;**
  evenings
Hosts: **Almeda and Richard Tinberg**
Location: **20 mi. W of Kansas City**
No. of Rooms: **6**
No. of Private Baths: **2**
Max. No. Sharing Bath: **4**
Double/pb: **$40**
Single/pb: **$35**

Double/sb: **$30**
Single/sb: **$25**
Suite: **$65**
Open: **All year**
Breakfast: **Continental, plus**
Pets: **No**
Children: **Welcome**
Smoking: **Restricted**
Social Drinking: **Permitted**

This small-town B&B has a tranquil, friendly atmosphere. An inn for decades—during World War I it attained coast-to-coast fame as the Myers Hotel—it was designated a historic landmark in 1983. The rooms are decorated with country flair, accented by antiques from Almeda's collection. Guests may sip a cup of coffee by the stone bar in the room used as a bus stop in the thirties; the movie *Bus Stop* was inspired by this site. A plaque outside the dining room tells the story of the hotel.

Thistle Hill
ROUTE 1, BOX 93, WAKEENEY, KANSAS 67672

Tel: **(785) 743-2644**
Hosts: **Dave and Mary Hendricks**
Location: **1¹/₂ mi. from I-70, Exit 120**
No. of Rooms: **3**
No. of Private Baths: **3**
Double/pb: **$55–$75**
Single/pb: **$45**
Open: **All year**

Breakfast: **Full**
Credit Cards: **MC, VISA**
Pets: **No**
Children: **Welcome**
Smoking: **Restricted**
Social Drinking: **Permitted**
Airport/Station Pickup: **Yes**

Thistle Hill bed and breakfast is a secluded cedar farmhouse located between Kansas City and Denver. Upon arrival you will see antique lanterns, wreaths, an early American bench, and a huge sign saying WELCOME TO THISTLE HILL. It's Dave and Mary's way of saying they're glad you came to visit. The Hendrickses are anxious to share the pleasures of rural life, which include restoring antiques, enjoying 60 acres of prairie wildflower restoration, and working the fields with their team of draft horses. A hearty country breakfast—which may include fresh-baked breads and hotcakes made from Dave and Mary's home-grown wheat—is served by the fireplace or on the summer porch overlooking the flower and herb garden. Thistle Hill is central to Castle Rock, Cedar Bluff Reservoir, the Sternberg Museum, and Cottonwood Ranch. A new hot tub and a gift shop have been added.

KENTUCKY

Florence
Augusta
New Castle Sulphur
Louisville
Georgetown Lexington
Bardstown Versailles
Nicholasville
Springfield
Hartford
Bowling Green
Somerset
Paducah
Murray

Augusta White House Inn B&B ✪
307 MAIN STREET, AUGUSTA, KENTUCKY 41002

Tel: **(606) 756-2004**
Best Time to Call: **9–11 AM**
Host: **Rebecca Spencer**
Location: **50 mi. SE of Cincinnati, Ohio**
No. of Rooms: **5**
Max. No. Sharing Bath: **4**
Double/sb: **$79**
Single/sb: **$59**
Guest Cottage: **$75**

Open: **All year**
Reduced Rates: **Available**
Breakfast: **Full**
Credit Cards: **AMEX, DISC, MC, VISA**
Pets: **No**
Children: **No**
Smoking: **No**
Social Drinking: **No**
Airport/Station Pickup: **Yes**

AWHIBB is located in the downtown section of historic Augusta, in a beautifully restored, two-story brick structure (the Buerger Tin Shop, circa 1840) that combines Victorian elegance and Southern hospitality. Comfortably sized rooms with flowered wallpaper and high, crown-molded ceilings may well remind you of your grandparents' home, albeit with all modern conveniences. In addition to their own room, guests have use of the parlor, formal dining and living rooms, and outside garden deck. Breakfast includes fresh-baked bread with an array of gourmet entrees and side dishes to please even the most discriminating palates. Antique shops and excellent restaurants are a short stroll away.

Beautiful Dreamer ✪

EAST STEPHEN FOSTER AVENUE, BARDSTOWN, KENTUCKY 40004

Tel: **(800) 811-8312**	Open: **All year**
Host: **Lynell Ginter**	Breakfast: **Full**
Location: **30 mi. SE of Louisville**	Credit Cards: **MC, VISA**
No. of Rooms: **4**	Pets: **No**
No. of Private Baths: **4**	Children: **Welcome, over 8**
Double/pb: **$85**	Smoking: **No**

Decorated with antiques and cherry furniture, this Federal-style home, circa 1995, is located in the historic district. Relax on the porch and enjoy a breathtaking view of My Old Kentucky Home, or show off your talent on the baby grand piano. The Beautiful Dreamer Room has a double Jacuzzi, the Captain's Room has a fireplace and a single Jacuzzi, and the Stephen Foster Room is wheelchair accessible, featuring a shower with rails and a double sink that can accommodate a wheelchair. All rooms are air-conditioned, have queen-size beds, and include a hearty breakfast. Music lovers will be happy to know that this B&B is within walking distance of the Stephen Foster Story.

Jailer's Inn ✪

111 WEST STEPHEN FOSTER AVENUE, BARDSTOWN, KENTUCKY 40004

Tel: **(502) 348-5551; (800) 948-5551**	Reduced Rates: **Available**
Best Time to Call: **10 AM–5 PM**	Breakfast: **Continental, plus**
Hosts: **Challen and Fran McCoy**	Credit Cards: **AMEX, DISC, MC, VISA**
Location: **35 mi. S of Louisville**	Pets: **No**
No. of Rooms: **6**	Children: **Welcome**
No. of Private Baths: **6**	Smoking: **No**
Double/pb: **$65–$100**	Social Drinking: **Permitted**
Open: **Mar.–Dec.**	Station pickup: **Yes**

For the ultimate in unusual experiences, spend the night in "jail" without having committed a crime. Built in 1819, this former jail originally housed prisoners upstairs, and has been completely remodeled and furnished with fine antiques and oriental rugs. An adjacent building, once used as the women's cell, has been transformed into a charming suite, where bunk beds are suspended from a brick wall and the decor is black-and-white checks instead of stripes. The town is famous for *The Stephen Foster Story*, an outdoor musical production. Take time to visit the Getz Museum of Whiskey History and a Civil War museum, and

take a tour of My Old Kentucky Home conducted by guides in antebellum costumes. Two guest rooms have Jacuzzi tubs.

Alpine Lodge ✪
5310 MORGANTOWN ROAD, BOWLING GREEN, KENTUCKY 42101

Tel: **(502) 843-4846**
Best Time to Call: **9 AM–9 PM**
Hosts: **Dr. and Mrs. David Livingston**
Location: **60 mi. N of Nashville, Tenn.**
No. of Rooms: **5**
No. of Private Baths: **3**
Max. No. Sharing Bath: **4**
Double/pb: **$50**
Single/pb: **$40**
Double/sb: **$45**
Single/sb: **$35**
Guest Cottage: **$150, sleeps 6**

Suites: **$75**
Open: **All year**
Reduced Rates: **Weekly**
Breakfast: **Full**
Other Meals: **Available**
Pets: **Dogs welcome**
Children: **Welcome**
Smoking: **Permitted**
Social Drinking: **Permitted**
Airport/Station Pickup: **Yes**
Foreign Languages: **Spanish**

The lush Bluegrass Region of Kentucky is the setting for this spacious
Swiss chalet–style home that's situated on four lovely acres and furnished with many antiques. A typical Southern breakfast of eggs, sausage, biscuits and gravy, fried apples, grits, coffee cake, and beverage
starts your day. If you can manage to get up from the table, stroll the
grounds complete with nature trails and gardens or take a swim in the
pool. Afterwards, take in the sights and sounds of Opryland, Mammoth
Cave, or the battlefields of historic Bowling Green. In the evening, relax
in the living room, where Dr. Livingston, a music professor, may entertain you with selections played on the grand piano.

Twin Pines ✪
28 LACRESTA DRIVE, FLORENCE, KENTUCKY 41042

Tel: **(606) 282-0456**
Best Time to Call: **8 AM–10 PM**
Hosts: **Coleen and Mike Detzel**
Location: **10 mi. S of Cincinnati, Ohio**
No. of Rooms: **3**
No. of Private Baths: **1**
Max. No. Sharing Bath: **4**
Double/pb: **$50**
Single/pb: **$40**
Double/sb: **$40**

Single/sb: **$30**
Open: **All year**
Reduced Rates: **10% seniors**
Breakfast: **Continental**
Pets: **Sometimes**
Children: **Welcome, over 10**
Smoking: **No**
Social Drinking: **Permitted**
Airport/Station Pickup: **Yes**

Twin Pines is a classic brick ranch, beautifully decorated with many
interesting collectibles and antiques. Enjoy reading or relaxing in the
living room, or try the 1950s-style lower level that features TV, games,
and a real pinball machine. Breakfast includes coffee, milk, tea, juices,
and your choice of pastries, bagels, and cereal. Twin Pines is conve-

niently located and easy to find. Coleen and Mike can tell you all about the great shopping, restaurants, and excellent attractions close by.

Jordan Farm Bed & Breakfast ✪
4091 NEWTOWN PIKE, GEORGETOWN, KENTUCKY 40324

Tel: **(502) 863-1944, 868-9002**
Best Time to Call: **Anytime**
Hosts: **Harold and Becky Jordan**
Location: **8 mi. N of Lexington**
Suites: **$75, sleeps 4**
Open: **All year**
Breakfast: **Continental**

Pets: **No**
Children: **Welcome**
Smoking: **No**
Social Drinking: **Permitted**
Minimum Stay: **2 nights weekends Apr. and Oct.**
Airport/Station Pickup: **Yes**

Derby fans will want to stay on this 100-acre thoroughbred farm in the middle of Kentucky's legendary horse country. Indeed, the Kentucky Horse Park is only five minutes away. From the guest room's private deck, you can watch the Jordans' horses cavort in the fields. Or drop a line into the fishing pond and try your luck. Separate guesthouse with two large Jacuzzi suites and mini-kitchens.

Ranney Porch Bed & Breakfast ✪
3810 HIGHWAY 231 NORTH, HARTFORD, KENTUCKY 42347

Tel: **(502) 298-7972**
Best time to Call: **After 4 PM**
Hosts: **Peggy Jo and Rance Ranney**
Location: **17.7 mi. S of Owensboro**
No. of Rooms: **1**
No. of Private Baths: **1**
Double/pb: **$50**

Single/pb: **$40**
Open: **All year**
Breakfast: **Full**
Pets: **No**
Children: **Welcome**
Smoking: **No**
Social Drinking: **No**

One of the unique features of this country B&B is the 57-foot porch spanning the length of the building, which is modeled after a Georgia tenant house. The exterior has blue trim, black shutters, and a candy apple red door. Inside, a Story and Clark piano sits on the foyer's red brick floor tiles, which came from the roof of a train depot. In the living room, cherry furniture complements the cherry wood floor. The bedroom's antique quilts and firm mattress assure you a good night's sleep. Numerous special events throughout the year, such as the Bar-be-que Festival, Yellow Banks Dulcimer Festival, and Bluegrass Music Festival, make this a place to visit often. Traditional and vegetarian meals are offered.

A True Inn ✪
467 WEST SECOND STREET, LEXINGTON, KENTUCKY 40507

Tel: **(800) 374-6151; (606) 252-6166**
Best Time to Call: **5–8 PM**
Hosts: **Bobby and Beverly True**

Location: **Downtown Lexington**
No. of Rooms: **5**
No. of Private Baths: **4**

Max. No. Sharing Bath: **4**
Double/pb: **$85**
Double/sb: **$65**
Suites: **$95–$125**
Open: **All year**
Breakfast: **Full**

Credit Cards: **AMEX, DC, MC, VISA**
Pets: **No**
Children: **Welcome, over 12**
Smoking: **No**
Social Drinking: **Permitted**
Airport/Station Pickup: **Yes**

Located in the heart of downtown Lexington, A True Inn is only two blocks from Rupp Arena, restaurants, antique and specialty shops, the opera house, and historic homes and churches. This large Victorian home, built in 1843, welcomes you to Lexington's past with stained and leaded glass, seven ornately carved Richardsonian and Victorian mantels, original chandeliers, and spacious formal rooms and gardens. All rooms are decorated with antiques and reproduction furnishings. Lovely quilts and afghans are in your room for afternoon naps and reading. A true Kentucky breakfast is served each morning, delightful refreshments in the afternoon. Bobby and Beverly and their families have been in Lexington for generations and are anxious to share their home and provide guests with true Southern hospitality.

Ashton's Victorian Secret Bed & Breakfast ✪
1132 SOUTH FIRST STREET, LOUISVILLE, KENTUCKY 40203

Tel: **(502) 581-1914; (800) 449-4691,
  Pin 0604**
Hosts: **Nan and Steve Roosa**
Location: **1 mi. S of downtown
  Louisville**
No. of Rooms: **3**
No. of Private Baths: **1**

Max. No. Sharing Bath: **3**
Double/pb: **$68–$89**
Double/sb: **$58–$68**
Open: **All year**
Reduced Rates: **Weekly**
Breakfast: **Continental**
Pets: **No**

Children: **Welcome** Social Drinking: **Permitted**
Smoking: **Permitted**

An elegant brick Victorian with lavish woodwork, this B&B has modern amenities like an exercise room with a bench press and a rowing machine, and color TVs in guest rooms. The Louisville area is rich in historic homes. Railbirds and would-be jockeys will want to make pilgrimages to the famous tracks at Churchill Downs (site of the Kentucky Derby) and Louisville Downs (home of harness races).

Diuguid House Bed & Breakfast ✪
603 MAIN STREET, MURRAY, KENTUCKY 42071

Tel: **(502) 753-5470**	Reduced Rates: **Seventh night free**
Best Time to Call: **4–10 PM**	Breakfast: **Full**
Hosts: **Karen and George Chapman**	Credit Cards: **MC, VISA**
Location: **45 mi. S of Paducah**	Pets: **No**
No. of Rooms: **3**	Children: **Welcome**
Max. No. Sharing Bath: **5**	Smoking: **No**
Double/sb: **$45**	Social Drinking: **Permitted**
Open: **All year**	Airport/Station Pickup: **Yes**

Upon walking into this 1890s Queen Anne, listed on the National Register of Historic Places, guests see an impressive sweeping oak staircase and unusual hallway fretwork. In addition to their rooms, visitors have use of the parlor, TV lounge, and dining room. Murray State University houses a local history museum, an art gallery, and the National Boy Scout Museum. The town, a top-rated retirement community, offers lots of theatrical and musical events. For outdoor activities, take the twenty-minute drive to Land Between the Lakes, where you can hike, hunt, fish, admire the resident buffalo herd, or see a working historical farm.

The Oldham House B&B and Antiques ✪
111 SOUTH MAIN STREET, P.O. BOX 628, NEW CASTLE, KENTUCKY 40050

Tel: **(502) 845-0103**	Reduced Rates: **Available**
Host: **Emmy Houweling**	Breakfast: **Full**
Location: **35 mi. NE of Louisville**	Pets: **No**
No. of Rooms: **2**	Children: **Welcome, over 12**
No. of Private Baths: **2**	Smoking: **No**
Double/pb: **$70**	Social Drinking: **Permitted**
Single/pb: **$65**	Airport Pickup: **Yes**
Suite: **$69**	Foreign Languages: **Dutch, French,**
Open: **All year**	**German**

A Federal period structure built in 1820, Oldham House is located a short distance north of the Bluegrass Region and convenient to Louisville, Lexington, and Cincinnati. The B&B is decorated in primitive antiques and accessories, most of which are for sale at Emmy's antique shop located on the property. The kitchen had once been the slave kitchen with separate quarters above. The original smokehouse still remains on the property. Things to do include horse racing twice a year in Louisville and Lexington horse farms, visiting scenic Ohio River towns and state parks, golfing, and of course, antiquing galore.

Sandusky House & O'Neal Log Cabin Bed & Breakfast ✪
1626 DELANY FERRY ROAD, NICHOLASVILLE, KENTUCKY 40356

Tel: **(606) 223-4730**
Best Time to Call: **8 AM–10 PM**
Hosts: **Jim and Linda Humphrey**
Location: **6 mi. SW of Lexington**
No. of Rooms: **3**
No. of Private Baths: **3**
Double/pb: **$75**
Guest Cabin: **$95**
Open: **All year**
Reduced Rates: **Available**

Breakfast: **Full; Continental plus in cabin**
Credit Cards: **MC, VISA**
Pets: **No**
Children: **Welcome, over 12 in house; no age restriction in cabin**
Smoking: **No**
Social Drinking: **Permitted**
Airport/Station Pickup: **Yes**

A tree-lined drive to the Sandusky House is just a prelude to the handsome Greek Revival residence built about 1850 with bricks fired on the premises. Once the property was a 1000-acre farm owned by Revolutionary War veteran Jacob Sandusky—he acquired the site in a 1780 land grant from Patrick Henry, then the governor of Virginia. Today the B&B sits on a ten-acre estate amid horse farms, yet is close to downtown Lexington, Keeneland Race Track, Kentucky Horse Park, and many other attractions. The 180-year-old authentic log cabin has been reconstructed and has two bedrooms, kitchen, living room with a fireplace, whirlpool tub, and air-conditioning.

Ehrhardt's B&B ✪
285 SPRINGWELL LANE, PADUCAH, KENTUCKY 42001

Tel: **(502) 554-0644**
Best Time to Call: **7–9 AM; 4–6 PM**
Hosts: **Eileen and Phil Ehrhardt**
Location: **1 mi. from I-24**
No. of Rooms: **2**
Max. No. Sharing Bath: **4**
Double/sb: **$45**
Single/sb: **$40**
Open: **All year**

Reduced Rates: **10% seniors**
Breakfast: **Full**
Other Meals: **Available**
Pets: **No**
Children: **Welcome, over 12**
Smoking: **Permitted**
Social Drinking: **Permitted**
Airport/Station Pickup: **Yes**

This brick Colonial ranch home is just a mile off I-24, which is famous for its beautiful scenery. Your hosts hope to make you feel at home in antique-filled bedrooms and a den with a fireplace. Homemade biscuits and jellies, and country ham and gravy are breakfast specialties. Enjoy swimming in the Ehrhardts' pool and boating at nearby Lake Barkley, Ky Lake, and Land Between the Lakes. Paducah features quarterhorse racing from June through November, and the National Quilt Show in April.

Trinity Hills Farm B&B—Stained Glass Studio ✪
10455 OLD LOVELACEVILLE ROAD, PADUCAH, KENTUCKY 42001

Tel: **(800) 488-3998**	Open: **All year**
Best Time to Call: **After 5 PM**	Reduced Rates: **Available**
Hosts: **Mike and Ann Driver, Jim and**	Breakfast: **Full**
Nancy Driver	Credit Cards: **DISC, MC, VISA**
Location: **12 mi. W of Paducah**	Pets: **Sometimes**
No. of Rooms: 5	Children: **Welcome**
No. of Private Baths: 5	Smoking: **No**
Double/pb: **$60**	Social Drinking: **Permitted**
Suite: **$70–$90**	Airport Pickup: **Yes**

Share the serenity of the Drivers' 17-acre country retreat. This three-story home features romantic upstairs suites with queen-size beds. Amenities include private whirlpools or spas, a treadmill, spacious common areas, and guest rooms ideal for family gatherings. You'll enjoy extras such as robes, soft music, and evening refreshments. Your hosts love to share the beauty of Nancy's stained glass windows and other unique creations. Things to do include fishing, hiking, boating, and bird-watching. Or just unwind in the large spa on the patio by the flower and water gardens. Kentucky and Barkley lakes, Columbus Belmont State Park, the National Quilt Museum, antiques, and shopping are all nearby. Trinity Hills is centrally located between Nashville, St. Louis, and Memphis.

Shadwick House ✪
411 SOUTH MAIN STREET, SOMERSET, KENTUCKY 42501

Tel: **(606) 678-4675**	Open: **All year**
Best Time to Call: **Anytime**	Breakfast: **Full**
Host: **Ann Epperson**	Credit Cards: **MC, VISA**
Location: **84 mi. S of Lexington**	Pets: **No**
No. of Rooms: 4	Children: **Welcome**
Max. No. Sharing Bath: 4	Smoking: **No**
Double/sb: **$50**	Social Drinking: **Permitted**
Single/sb: **$50**	

Shadwick House has been known for its Southern hospitality for more than seventy years—the home was built in 1920 by Nellie Stringer Shadwick, great-grandmother of the present owner. The first floor has been converted into an antique and crafts shop. Kentucky ham and biscuits are served for breakfast in the original dining room. This B&B is tucked into the Cumberland Mountain foothills, near Lake Cumberland. Other local attractions are Renfro Valley, Cumberland Falls State Park, Tombstone Junction, and Big South Fork National Park.

Maple Hill Manor B&B ✪
2941 PERRYVILLE ROAD, SPRINGFIELD, KENTUCKY 40069

Tel: **(606) 336-3075; (800) 886-7546**
Hosts: **Bob and Kay Carroll**
No. of Rooms: **7**
No. of Private Baths: **7**
Double/pb: **$65–$90**
Single/pb: **$55–$80**
Open: **All year**

Reduced Rates: **Available**
Breakfast: **Full**
Credit Cards: **MC, VISA**
Pets: **No**
Children: **Welcome (crib)**
Smoking: **No**
Social Drinking: **Permitted**

This hilltop manor house built in 1851 is situated on 14 tranquil acres in the scenic Bluegrass Region of Kentucky. Listed on the National Register of Historic Places, its Italianate design features 13-foot ceilings, 9-foot windows and doors, a profusion of fireplaces, and a solid cherry spiral staircase. The bedrooms are large, airy, and beautifully decorated with carefully chosen antique furnishings. The romantic honeymoon bed chamber has a canopy bed and Jacuzzi bath. In the evening, Bob and Kay graciously offer complimentary beverages and homemade dessert. Within an hour of Lexington and Louisville, you can visit Perryville Battlefield and Shaker Village and take a tour of distilleries. Murder mystery packages and gift certificates are available.

Sulphur Trace Farm B&B ✪
P.O. BOX 127, 8499 HIGHWAY 157, SULPHUR, KENTUCKY 40070

Tel: **(502) 743-5956**
Best Time to Call: **After 6 PM**
Hosts: **Penney Sanders and**
Francis Thiemann
Location: **32 mi. E of Louisville**
No. of Rooms: **2**
No. of Private Baths: **2**
Double/pb: **$70**
Single/pb: **$55**

Open: **Mar. 1–Oct. 31**
Reduced Rates: **10% seniors**
Breakfast: **Full**
Pets: **No**
Children: **Welcome**
Smoking: **No**
Social Drinking: **Permitted**
Airport/Station Pickup: **Yes**

Located at the edge of bluegrass country, Sulphur Trace Farm is 35 minutes from Louisville and 55 minutes from Cincinnati. Access either city or stay in the countryside to enjoy nearby antique shopping in Shelbyville, LaGrange, or Frankfort. Then visit the casino riverboat in Rising Sun, Indiana. Francis designed and built the contemporary house out of stone and wood. Breakfast is served in the great room, where you will look out over the farm. Birds are abundant, as are the sheep and goats who won't be far from the back door.

Shepherd Place ✪
31 HERITAGE ROAD (U.S. 60), VERSAILLES, KENTUCKY 40383

Tel: **(606) 873-7843; (800) 278-0864**
Hosts: **Marlin and Sylvia Yawn**
Location: **10 mi. W of Lexington**
No. of Rooms: **3**
No. of Private Baths: **3**
Double/pb: **$75**
Single/pb: **$65**

Open: **All year**
Breakfast: **Full**
Pets: **No**
Children: **Welcome, over 12**
Smoking: **No**
Social Drinking: **Permitted**
Airport/Station Pickup: **Yes**

Marlin and Sylvia encourage you to make yourself comfortable in their pre–Civil War home, built around 1815. Rest in a spacious, beautifully decorated bedroom or relax in the parlor. Enjoy the lovely scenery while sitting on the patio or the porch swing. You might even want to pet the resident ewes, Abigail and Victoria. Brochures, menus, and plenty of ideas will be available to help you plan the rest of your stay.

Tyrone Pike Bed and Breakfast ✪
3820 TYRONE PIKE, VERSAILLES, KENTUCKY 40383

Tel: **(800) 736-7722; (606) 873-2408**
Hosts: **Jean, Tim, Doug, and Carey**
Foreman
Location: **20 mi. W of Lexington**
No. of Rooms: **4**
No. of Private Baths: **4**
Double/pb: **$98**
Single/pb: **$89**

Suites: **$125**
Open: **All year**
Reduced Rates: **10% seniors,**
international students, AAA
members, Canadians
Breakfast: **Full**
Credit Cards: **MC, VISA**
Pets: **Sometimes**

Children: **Welcome**   Social Drinking: **Permitted**
Smoking: **No**   Airport Pickup: **Yes**

Tyrone Bed & Breakfast is located just three miles from historic down-town Versailles. Guests are treated like royalty in this peaceful country atmosphere. Upon your arrival your hosts will greet you with hors d'oeuvres. Accommodations include two guest rooms, a family suite, an efficiency suite complete with a kitchenette, soaking tub, private en-trance, and phone, and a game room. The location is enhanced by a neighboring horse farm and the Bluegrass Scenic Railroad, which can be seen from the backyard. For breakfast you can choose either a light or a hearty meal. If you have any special dietary requests, just let your hosts know when you make your reservation and they will do their best to accommodate you.

For key to listings, see inside front or back cover.

✪ This star means that rates are guaranteed through December 31, 1998, to any guest making a reservation as a result of reading about the B&B in *Bed & Breakfast U.S.A.*—1998 edition.

Important! To avoid misunderstandings, always ask about cancellation policies when booking.

Please enclose a self-addressed, stamped, busi-ness-size envelope when contacting reservation services.

For more details on what you can expect in a B&B, see Chapter 1.

Always mention *Bed & Breakfast U.S.A.* when making reservations!

We want to hear from you! Use the form on page 625.

LOUISIANA

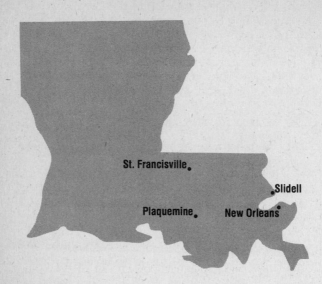

St. Francisville

Slidell

Plaquemine

New Orleans

Bed & Breakfast, Inc.—New Orleans ✪
1021 MOSS STREET, BOX 52257, NEW ORLEANS, LOUISIANA 70152-2257

Tel: **(504) 488-4640; (800) 729-4640;**
   fax: **(504) 488-4639**
Coordinator: **Hazell Boyce**
States/Regions Covered: **New Orleans**
Descriptive Directory: **Free**

Rates (Single/Double):
   Modest: **$36–$46 / $41–$51**
   Average: **$41–$76 / $41–$76**
   Luxury: **$71–$101 / $76–$101**
Credit Cards: **No**

New Orleans is called The City That Care Forgot. You are certain to be carefree, visiting the French Quarter, taking Mississippi riverboat rides, taking plantation tours, as well as dining in fine restaurants and attending jazz concerts. Hazell's hosts, many with historic properties along the streetcar line and in the French Quarter, will help you get the most out of your stay.

New Orleans Bed & Breakfast and Accommodations ✪
P.O. BOX 8163, NEW ORLEANS, LOUISIANA 70182-8163

Tel: **(504) 838-0071, 838-0072;**
  fax: **(504) 838-0140**
Best Time to Call: **8:30 AM–4:30 PM**
Coordinator: **Sarah-Margaret Brown**
States/Regions Covered:
  **Louisiana—Covington, Jeanerette,
  Lafayette, Mandeville, Natchitoches,
  New Iberia, New Orleans,
  Shreveport, St. Francisville**

Rates (Single/Double):
  Modest: **$55–$70**
  Average: **$75–$85**
  Luxury: **$95–up**
Credit Cards: **AMEX, DISC, MC, VISA
  (for deposit only)**
Minimum Stay: **5 nights Mardi Gras,
  Jazz Festival; 3 nights Sugar Bowl**

Since 1979 Sarah-Margaret has arranged accommodations for visitors in private homes, apartments, and condos. Tell her what you want and she will do her best to please you. Care is given to guests' safety, comfort, and special interests. Discount tickets are available for many attractions.

Beau Séjour ✪
1930 NAPOLEON AVENUE, NEW ORLEANS, LOUISIANA 70115

Tel: **(504) 897-3746**
Best Time to Call: **10 AM–8 PM**
Hosts: **Gilles and Kim Gagnon**
No. of Rooms: **5**
No. of Private Baths: **5**
Double/pb: **$95**
Single/pb: **$90**
Suites: **$130**
Open: **All year**

Breakfast: **Continental**
Pets: **No**
Children: **Welcome**
Smoking: **Permitted**
Social Drinking: **Permitted**
Minimum Stay: **2 nights special events
  and holidays**
Foreign Languages: **French**

Kim and Gilles recently restored their 1906 Beau Séjour house to its original character, with beautiful detailing and wood floors. It is decorated in the best New Orleans style, blending country and European antiques with Louisiana and New Orleans touches. Located in one of the most picturesque neighborhoods of New Orleans, surrounded by lush tropical plantings, and on the Mardi Gras parade route, the mansion is convenient to convention and tourist attractions. Kim and Gilles are dedicated to New Orleans preservation and enjoy sharing their knowledge of local restaurants, excursions, and the culture of the "Big Easy."

The Chimes Bed & Breakfast ✪
CONSTANTINOPLE AT COLISEUM, BOX 52257, NEW ORLEANS, LOUISIANA 70152-2257

Tel: **(504) 488-4640; (800) 729-4640**
Best Time to Call: **10 AM–5 PM
  Mon.–Fri.**

Hosts: **Jill and Charles Abbyad and
  Susan Smith**
Location: **In New Orleans**
No. of Rooms: **5**

No. of Private Baths: **5**
Double/pb: **$66–$79**
Suites: **$86–$126**
Open: **All year**
Reduced Rates: **Available**
Breakfast: **Continental, plus**

Pets: **Sometimes**
Children: **Welcome**
Social Drinking: **Permitted**
Minimum Stay: **Special events**
Foreign Languages: **French**

These quaint guest quarters sit behind a Victorian uptown home. Stained and leaded glass windows, French doors, cypress staircases, and a brick courtyard enhance the friendly, relaxed atmosphere here. Caring for a property of this magnitude is an ongoing commitment and truly a labor of love. Your hosts, who are coming to the end of a two-year renovation, typify Southern hospitality. Three blocks from St. Charles Avenue, the Chimes cottages are minutes away from major New Orleans attractions including the French Quarter, convention centers, Audubon Zoological Gardens with the walk-through Louisiana Swamp Exhibit, the Mississippi River, and universities. The historic St. Charles Avenue streetcar makes the famous restaurants, jazz clubs, art galleries, and antique shops accessible without an auto. Your hosts live on the second floor of the main house—their door is always open! They willingly share their vast knowledge of New Orleans, offering suggestions for tours and restaurants. For your convenience, each suite has a telephone, tea/coffeepot, television set, and stereo. Laundry facilities and use of a refrigerator are available.

The Glimmer Inn ✪
1631 SEVENTH STREET, NEW ORLEANS, LOUISIANA 70115

Tel: **(504) 897-1895**
Best Time to Call: **9 AM–9 PM**
Hosts: **Sharon Agiewich and Cathy Andros**
No. of Rooms: **6**
No. of Private Baths: **1**
Max. No. Sharing Bath: **4**
Double/pb: **$85**
Double/sb: **$70**

Single/sb: **$60**
Open: **All year**
Breakfast: **Continental, plus**
Pets: **No**
Children: **Welcome, by arrangement**
Smoking: **Permitted**
Social Drinking: **Permitted**
Minimum Stay: **2 nights**

This restored 1891 Victorian home has wonderful period elements: twelve-foot cove ceilings, cypress woodwork, side and front galleries, a wraparound front porch, and an enclosed brick patio. Public rooms are comfortably furnished for reading, TV viewing, and musical enjoyment. The main house's guest rooms are beautifully appointed, with antiques, ceiling fans, and individually controlled air-conditioning and heat. Also offered is a private carriage house with bath, refrigerator, and central air-conditioning and heating. The Glimmer Inn is across the street from the historic Garden District, a block from the trolley line and Mardi Gras parade route, and fifteen minutes from the French Quarter. Let Cathy and Sharon know your interests; they pride themselves on meeting guests' travel needs in a relaxed but attentive atmosphere.

Sun & Moon Bed & Breakfast
1037 NORTH RAMPART STREET, NEW ORLEANS, LOUISIANA 70116

Tel: **(504) 529-4652**
Best Time to Call: **Mornings**
Hosts: **Mary Pat Van Tine, owner; Kathleen Barrow, mngr.**
No. of Rooms: **2**
No. of Private Baths: **2**
Double/pb: **$75**

Open: **All year**
Breakfast: **Continental**
Pets: **No**
Children: **Welcome**
Smoking: **No**
Social Drinking: **Permitted**
Minimum Stay: **2 nights**

Sun & Moon Bed & Breakfast is located in the French Quarter and provides a warm homelike atmosphere to guests. Each guest room has a TV and a small refrigerator for midnight snacking, and all are air conditioned. Kathleen will make your stay a memorable one, and she can fill you in on all the local happenings, clubs, restaurants, and points of interest.

Old Turnerville B&B ✪
23230 NADLER STREET, PLAQUEMINE, LOUISIANA 70764

Tel: **(504) 687-5337**
Best Time to Call: **10 AM–4 PM**

Host: **Brenda Bourgoyne Blanchard**
Location: **20 mi. S of Baton Rouge**

No. of Rooms: **1**
No. of Private Baths: **1**
Double/pb: **$65**
Single/pb: **$60**
Cottage: **$75**
Open: **All year**

Reduced Rates: **10% seniors**
Breakfast: **Continental**
Pets: **No**
Children: **Welcome**
Smoking: **Permitted**
Social Drinking: **Permitted**

Old Turnerville is an 1800s village on the Mississippi in the heart of plantation country. Bed and breakfast accommodations are available at Miss Louise's House, built more than a century ago. The antique-furnished home includes a guest bedroom with private bath, TV, air-conditioning, and ceiling fan. Guests can enjoy the swing and rockers on the wide front gallery and stroll along the top of the Mississippi River levee. A separate guest cottage sleeps up to four. Restaurants and historic attractions are close by. Tariff includes a guided tour of Miss Louise's House and Marietta's House, an 1800s cottage across the street.

Butler Greenwood ✪
8345 U.S. HIGHWAY 61, ST. FRANCISVILLE, LOUISIANA 70775

Tel: **(504) 635-6312**
Best Time to Call: **Anytime**
Host: **Anne Butler**
Location: **25 mi. N of Baton Rouge**
Guest Cottages: **$90–$110, sleeps 2–6**
Open: **All year**
Reduced Rates: **Families**

Breakfast: **Continental, plus**
Credit Cards: **AMEX, MC, VISA**
Pets: **Sometimes**
Children: **Welcome**
Smoking: **Permitted**
Social Drinking: **Permitted**

Butler Greenwood offers six cottages on picturesque plantation grounds. Choose from the 1796 kitchen, with exposed beams and skylights; the nineteenth-century cook's cottage, with a fireplace and porch swing; the romantic gazebo with antique stained glass windows; the treehouse at the edge of a steep wooded ravine, with a wonderful 3-level deck and fireplace; the dovecote, three stories, sleeps six, with a fireplace and Jacuzzi; or the pond house on its own pond. All sites have private baths, partial kitchens, and cable TV. Rates include a tour of the main house—listed on the National Register of Historic Places—and the extensive grounds. A tour book is available, describing the area's history and attractions. Continental-plus breakfast is served; other amenities include a pool, nature walks, and ballooning.

Salmen-Fritchie House Circa 1895 ✪
127 CLEVELAND AVENUE, SLIDELL, LOUISIANA 70458

Tel: **(504) 643-1405; (800) 235-4168,**
   for reservations
Best Time to Call: **8 AM–9 PM**
Hosts: **Homer and Sharon Fritchie**
Location: **30 mi. N of New Orleans**

No. of Rooms: **6**
No. of Private Baths: **6**
Double/pb: **$75–$85**
Single/pb: **$75–$85**
Cottage: **$150 for 2**

Suites: **$115–$150**
Open: **All year**
Reduced Rates: **Available**
Breakfast: **Full**
Credit Cards: **AMEX, DISC, MC, VISA**

Pets: **No**
Children: **Welcome, over 12**
Smoking: **No**
Social Drinking: **Permitted**
Station Pickup: **Yes**

You'll feel the sense of history as you step inside this magnificent sixteen-room house listed on the National Register of Historic Places. From the front door to the back, the great hall measures twenty feet wide and eighty-five feet long! All the rooms are filled with beautiful antiques, reminiscent of days gone by. Hospitality is a way of life here. Arrive by 4 PM and you can join your hosts for tea in the parlor and afterward, a tour of the house and grounds. In the morning, you'll receive fresh hot coffee in your room. Then you'll enjoy a full Southern breakfast in the bright, cheery breakfast room. A cottage has been added, with a screened-in porch, living room, kitchen, and marble tub Jacuzzi.

MAINE

Dexter

Southwest Harbor
Ashville
Cherryfield
Addison
Belfast
Camden
Milbridge
Sorrento
Waldboro
Corea
Bath
Mt. Desert Island
Vinalhaven
Boothbay
Thomaston
Walpole (Damariscotta)
Fryeburg
Kennebunk
Kennebunkport
York
Kittery

Pleasant Bay Bed and Breakfast ✪
BOX 222 WEST SIDE ROAD, ADDISON, MAINE 04606

Tel: **(207) 483-4490**
Hosts: **Leon and Joan Yeaton**
Location: **42 mi. N of Ellsworth**
No. of Rooms: **3**
No. of Private Baths: **1**
Max. No. Sharing Bath: **4**
Double/pb: **$70**
Single/pb: **$60**
Double/sb: **$55**

Single/sb: **$45–$50**
Open: **All year**
Breakfast: **Full**
Credit Cards: **MC, VISA**
Pets: **No**
Children: **Welcome**
Smoking: **No**
Social Drinking: **Permitted**

The Yeatons' 110-acre llama farm rests on a knoll by the shores of Pleasant Bay and the Pleasant River. Watch shorebirds and seals play in the rising and falling tides. Explore the shoreline in seclusion or meander along rustic trails, accompanied by a gentle llama. Relax before the hearth at sunset. In the morning, you'll wake up to a full Down East breakfast made with farm-fresh eggs laid by your hosts' own chickens.

Green Hill Farm ✪

RR 1, BOX 328, ASHVILLE, MAINE 04607
nabunaba@aol.com

Tel: **(207) 422-3273**	Open: **Late May–late Oct.**
Best Time to Call: **Before 10 AM; after 4 PM**	Reduced Rates: **Available**
	Breakfast: **Full, Continental**
Hosts: **Ted and Nuna Cass**	Pets: **Sometimes**
Location: **17 mi. E of Ellsworth**	Children: **Welcome**
No. of Rooms: **2**	Smoking: **No**
Max. No. Sharing Bath: **4**	Social Drinking: **Permitted**
Double/sb: **$45**	Foreign Languages: **Spanish**
Single/sb: **$40**	

Stay in an 1820s home in a rural neighborhood, surrounded by fields, a large vegetable garden, and a small apple orchard on the edge of the forest. From its 35 acres, Green Hill Farm looks out over woods to the peaks of Acadia National Park. It's a convenient day trip to Campobello Island, and Bar Harbor is 45 minutes away.

Elizabeth's Bed and Breakfast ✪

360 FRONT STREET, BATH, MAINE 04530

Tel: **(207) 443-1146**	Single/sb: **$45**
Best Time to Call: **Anytime**	Open: **Apr. 15–Jan. 1**
Host: **Elizabeth Lindsay**	Breakfast: **Continental**
Location: **40 mi. up the coast from Portland**	Pets: **No**
	Children: **Welcome, over 12**
No. of Rooms: **5**	Smoking: **Restricted**
Max. No. Sharing Bath: **4**	Social Drinking: **Permitted**
Double/sb: **$55–$65**	

Elizabeth's Bed and Breakfast is a fine old Federalist house, painted a traditional white with green shutters. Each bedroom is furnished in country antiques. Bath is famed as a shipbuilding center, and the Maine Maritime Museum merits a visit. It's also fun to walk around the downtown area, which has been restored to its 19th-century glory. Breakfast includes juice, cereal, muffins, and jam. During the summer, Elizabeth prepares Sunday brunches.

Fairhaven Inn ✪

RR 2, BOX 85, NORTH BATH ROAD, BATH, MAINE 04530

Tel: **(207) 443-4391**	Double/sb: **$70–$80**
Hosts: **Susie and David Reed**	Single/sb: **$50–$60**
Location: **35 mi. N of Portland**	Open: **All year**
No. of Rooms: **8**	Breakfast: **Full**
No. of Private Baths: **7**	Pets: **No**
Max. No. Sharing Bath: **4**	Children: **Yes**
Double/pb: **$80–$120**	Smoking: **No**
Single/pb: **$50–$65**	Social Drinking: **Permitted**

An 18th-century Colonial mansion on a hill above the Kennebec River, Fairhaven Inn is furnished with antique and country pieces. Shaded by hemlock, birch, and pine trees, the 17-acre grounds lure cross-country skiers in the winter, and strollers year round. Around the bend, Bath Country Club is open to the public for golfing, and beaches are nearby. Bird-watchers can study migratory waterfowl at Merrymeeting Bay. You'll get stamina for the day's activities from ample breakfasts of juice, fresh fruit, home-baked breads, and main courses such as blintzes, eggs Benedict, and orange honey French toast.

The Galen C. Moses House ✪

1009 WASHINGTON STREET, BATH, MAINE 04530
http://www.bnbcity.com/inns/20028

Tel: **(207) 442-8771**	Credit Cards: **MC, VISA**
Hosts: **James Haught and Larry Kieft**	Pets: **No**
Location: **40 mi. N of Portland**	Children: **Welcome, over 12**
No. of Rooms: **3**	Smoking: **No**
No. of Private Baths: **3**	Social drinking: **Permitted**
Double/pb: **$65–$85**	Minimum stay: **2 nights weekends**
Open: **All year**	**June–Oct.**
Breakfast: **Full**	

Built in 1874 for Galen Clapp Moses, this Italianate structure has been draped in very vivid colors of plum, pink, and teal, and has been given the nickname "the Pink House." The large rooms are reminiscent of nineteenth-century Victorian style. There are many surprises throughout the house, including antiques, elegant gardens, and a full theater located on the third floor—during World War II, it was used to entertain officers from a nearby naval air station. The house also contains a number of assuredly friendly spirits, who make their presence known on a frequent basis. Breakfast varies according to the cook's mood, and may include blueberry pancakes, mushroom quiche, or sour cream chive omelettes. Coffee, juices, and muffins are available for early risers and late sleepers.

Belfast Bay Meadows Inn ✪

90 NORTHPORT AVENUE, BELFAST, MAINE 04915
bbmi@acadia.net

Tel: **(800) 335-2370**	Reduced Rates: **30% Nov.–April**
Best Time to Call: **7 AM–10 PM**	Breakfast: **Full**
Hosts: **John and Patty Lebowitz**	Credit Cards: **AMEX, MC, VISA**
Location: **100 mi. N of Portland**	Pets: **Welcome**
No. of Rooms: **12**	Children: **Welcome**
No. of Private Baths: **12**	Smoking: **No**
Double/pb: **$75–$125**	Social Drinking: **Permitted**
Open: **All year**	

Stroll winding, grassy paths through 17 bayside acres, flowered meadows, gardens, and forest to the cold blue waters of Penobscot Bay, where you'll see wheeling gulls, white-sailed schooners heeling to the breeze, and green-shadowed islands in bright morning mist. This breezy, bright blue bay is shaded by whispering, mottled forest. Experience cool summer mornings on the spacious breakfast deck with big green umbrellas. Enjoy sweet, fresh local fruit, fancy muffins, creamy eggs with tender lobster, and tasty sweet peppers. This exemplary, very large, shingled Down East cottage and renovated post-and-beam barn boasts wonderful international antique decor: fine paintings, colorful Persian carpets, and comfortable furnishings. Rooms have air-conditioning, phones, TV. Belfast Bay is a lot like grandma's house, not so much lavish as lived in and dearly loved.

Kenniston Hill Inn ❍
ROUTE 27, P.O. BOX 125, BOOTHBAY, MAINE 04537

Tel: **(207) 633-2159; (800) 992-2915**	Breakfast: **Full**
Best Time to Call: **10 AM–10 PM**	Other Meals: **MAP available**
Hosts: **Susan and David Straight**	Credit Cards: **MC, VISA**
Location: **50 ml. N of Portland**	Pets: **No**
No. of Rooms: **10**	Children: **Welcome, over 13**
No. of Private Baths: **10**	Smoking: **No**
Double/pb: **$69–$110**	Social Drinking: **Permitted**
Open: **All year**	

Kenniston Hill Inn is a center-chimney Georgian Colonial dating back to 1786. The house is warm and gracious, with a large front porch and open-hearth fireplace. The bedrooms, five with fireplaces, are tastefully decorated with antiques and fresh flowers. David and Susan offer sumptuous breakfast specialties such as peaches and cream French toast, or maple walnut pancakes with cinnamon butter. The Inn is surrounded by large, shady maples and fields of flowers, but is within easy reach of the harbor, shops, restaurants, boat rides, and the beautiful Maine coastline. Fireside dining is offered during the winter months, November–April.

Blue Harbor House, A Village Inn
67 ELM STREET, ROUTE 1, CAMDEN, MAINE 04843

Tel: **(207) 236-3196; (800) 248-3196;**	Open: **All year**
fax: **(207) 236-6523**	Breakfast: **Full**
Hosts: **Dennis Hayden and Jody Schmoll**	Credit Cards: **AMEX, DISC, MC, VISA**
Location: **85 mi. NE of Portland**	Pets: **By arrangement**
No. of Rooms: **10**	Children: **Welcome**
No. of Private Baths: **10**	Smoking: **No**
Double/pb: **$85–$135**	Social Drinking: **Permitted**

Camden is one of the prettiest coastal villages in New England. This 1835 Cape Cod house has been completely renovated and captures the essence of a bygone era. Each room is decorated in country antiques, stenciled walls, and handmade quilts. Guests enjoy visiting with each other in the common room, furnished with comfortable chairs and accented by antique stoneware, samplers, and folk art. The spacious dining room, with its views of Mt. Battie, is the setting for the generous breakfast that features homemade breads, delicious egg dishes, and Maine blueberries. It's a few minutes' walk to many fine restaurants, unique shops, and the famous Windjammer fleet.

Hawthorn Inn
9 HIGH STREET, CAMDEN, MAINE 04843

Tel: **(207) 236-8842; fax: (207) 236-6181**
Best Time to Call: **9 AM–9 PM**
Hosts: **Nick and Patty Wharton**
Location: **On Rte. 1, 190 mi. N of Boston**
No. of Rooms: **10**
No. of Private Baths: **10**
Double/pb: **$100–$195**

Reduced Rates: **$20 less daily Nov. 1–May 1**
Breakfast: **Full**
Credit Cards: **AMEX, MC, VISA**
Pets: **No**
Children: **Welcome, over 12**
Smoking: **No**
Social Drinking: **Permitted**

The airy rooms of this Victorian inn are an elegant mixture of the old and the new. Guests are welcome to coffee while relaxing on the deck or getting warm by the fire. Tea is served at 4 PM. All rooms overlook either Mt. Battie or Camden Harbor. A score of sports can be enjoyed in the area, and shops and restaurants are a short walk away. Rooms with fireplaces and Jacuzzis are available.

Ricker House ✪
PARK STREET, P.O. BOX 256, CHERRYFIELD, MAINE 04622

Tel: **(207) 546-2780**
Hosts: **William and Jean Conway**
Location: **32 mi. E of Ellsworth**
No. of Rooms: **3**
Max. No. Sharing Bath: **4**
Double/sb: **$50**
Single/sb: **$45**
Open: **All year**

Reduced Rates: **Available**
Breakfast: **Full**
Pets: **No**
Children: **Welcome (crib)**
Smoking: **No**
Social Drinking: **Permitted**
Airport/Station Pickup: **Yes**

Built in 1803, this comfortable Federal Colonial has grounds that border the Narraguagus River, one of the best salmon rivers in the States. The village is quaint and historic, and it is fun to tour it on foot or by bike. Reasonable restaurants offer great menus, and all feature fabulous local lobster. Your hosts will be pleased to direct you to a freshwater lake and the best places to canoe and mountain climb.

The Black Duck Inn on Corea Harbor
P.O. BOX 39, CROWLEY ISLAND ROAD, COREA, MAINE 04624

Tel: **(207) 963-2689**
Best Time to Call: **8 AM–9 PM**
Hosts: **Barry C. Canner and Robert Travers**
Location: **300 mi. NE of Boston, MA**
No. of Rooms: **4**
No. of Private Baths: **2**
Max. No. Sharing Bath: **4**
Double/pb: **$90**
Double/sb: **$70–$85**
Guest Cottage: **$99–$145**

Open: **All year**
Reduced Rates: **$10 less Oct. 15–May 30**
Breakfast: **Full**
Pets: **Sometimes**
Children: **Welcome, under 1, over 7**
Smoking: **No**
Social Drinking: **Permitted**
Minimum Stay: **3 nights cottage**
Foreign Languages: **Danish**

Guests enjoy casual elegance in this 100-year-old New England fisherman's home overlooking one of the most spectacular working harbors in Maine, the outer islands, and the open ocean. The rooms are filled with antiques, contemporary art, and the hosts' eclectic collections. You'll also meet their dog, two cats, and potbelly pig. There are a variety of common areas with a fireplace, TV, and a library. Outside is a large deck, over 12 acres of woods, harbor frontage, salt marshes, sub-Arctic plant species, and granite rock outcrops and ledge. Located nearby are the Schoodic section of the Acadia National Park, several beaches, wildlife areas, Bar Harbor, Campobello, restaurants, antique shops, and other attractions.

The Brewster Inn ✪
37 ZION'S HILL ROAD, DEXTER, MAINE 04930

Tel: **(207) 924-3130**
Best Time to Call: **9 AM–9 PM**

Hosts: **Michael and Ivy Brooks**
Location: **40 mi. NW of Bangor**

No. of Rooms: **7**
No. of Private Baths: **7**
Double/pb: **$59–$79**
Single/pb: **$49–$69**
Open: **All year**
Reduced Rates: **7th night free; 10% seniors**
Breakfast: **Full**

Other Meals: **Available**
Credit Cards: **MC, VISA**
Pets: **No**
Children: **Welcome**
Smoking: **No**
Social Drinking: **Permitted**
Airport/Station Pickup: **Yes**

Built for Governor Owen Brewster, this 1930s home is listed on the National Register of Historic Places, and embodies classic, comfortable elegance. Guests are invited to use the dining room, living room, and sunroom, which are furnished with a variety of antiques, reproductions, and family heirlooms. Books, arts and crafts, and an antique radio collection spill over to many of the rooms. Guest rooms feature original tile baths, fireplaces, or window seats, plus cozy quilts and special bath amenities. The Inn is close to Maine's coasts, mountains, and lake regions. Ivy is a graphic designer and former university professor and Michael is an expert in process control with photography and guitars.

Acres of Austria ✪
RR1, BOX 177, ROUTE 5, FIRELANE 48, FRYEBURG, MAINE 04037

Tel: **(800) 988-4391**
Hosts: **Candice and Franz Redl**
Location: **60 mi. W of Portland**
No. of Rooms: **4**
No. of Private Baths: **4**
Double/pb: **$75–$105**
Single/pb: **$59**
Open: **All year**
Reduced Rates: **Available**

Breakfast: **Full**
Other Meals: **Available**
Credit Cards: **MC, VISA**
Pets: **No**
Children: **Welcome**
Smoking: **No**
Social Drinking: **Permitted**
Airport/Station Pickup: **Yes**
Foreign Languages: **German, French**

Make yourself at home on the Redls' 65 acres. View the old Saco River, the White Mountains, or acres of forest from any room in the house. Browse through the library, test your billiard skills with a game of Carombol on a 1920s table from Vienna, or use a canoe to paddle the romantic river. Nearby, visit the outlet and antique shops, or enjoy golfing, scenic plane rides, skiing, or many other outdoor activities. Breakfast is served on the screen porch or by the warmth of a crackling fire. Make arrangements to try one of Franz's Austrian dinner specialties, including Kas'nockn, Wiener schnitzel, Sacher torte, and many more. Get a taste of Europe for a fraction of the price.

The Alewife House ✪
1917 ALEWIVE ROAD, KENNEBUNK, MAINE 04043
alewifehouse@lamere.net

Tel: **(207) 985-2118**
Best Time to Call: **8 AM–11 PM**
Hosts: **Maryellen and Tom Foley**

Location: **25 mi. S of Portland**
No. of Rooms: **2**
No. of Private Baths: **2**

Double/pb: **$95**
Open: **All year**
Breakfast: **Continental**
Credit Cards: **MC, VISA**

Pets: **No**
Children: **Welcome, over 12**
Smoking: **No**
Social Drinking: **Permitted**

Step back in time as you enter this 1756 farmhouse, located on six acres of rolling hills and gardens. Inside, the house is decorated with antiques; more are sold in the on-site shop. Awaken to the aroma of hot muffins, fresh fruit, and fresh-perked coffee served on the sunporch each morning. Then explore the area's coastline or the many nearby lakes.

Arundel Meadows Inn ✪
P.O. BOX 1129, KENNEBUNK, MAINE 04043
http://www.biddeford.com/arundel-meadows-inn

Tel: **(207) 985-3770**
Best Time to Call: **9 AM–9 PM**
Hosts: **Mark Bachelder and Murray Yaeger**
Location: **2 ml. N of Kennebunk**
No. of Rooms: **7**
No. of Private Baths: **7**
Double/pb: **$75–$95**

Suites: **$100–$125**
Open: **All year**
Breakfast: **Full**
Pets: **Sometimes**
Children: **Welcome, over 11**
Smoking: **No**
Social Drinking: **Permitted**

The Arundel Meadows Inn is situated on three and a half acres next to the Kennebunk River. Murray, a retired professor, and Mark, a professional chef, have always loved this area, and it is a dream come true for them to watch others enjoy it. They renovated this 165-year-old house themselves, and meticulously planned the decor. Several guest rooms have fireplaces and two suites sleep four. Mark's beautifully prepared breakfast specialties are the perfect start for your day. It's just three minutes to the center of town, and about ten to Kennebunk Beach. In the afternoon, come back to the Inn for tea and enjoy homemade sweets and beverages.

English Meadows Inn ✪
141 PORT ROAD, KENNEBUNK, MAINE 04043

Tel: **(207) 967-5766; (800) 272-0698**
Best Time to Call: **Mornings**
Host: **Charlie Doane**
Location: **35 mi. S of Portland**
No. of Rooms: **13**
No. of Private Baths: **13**
Double/pb: **$88–$108**
Guest Cottage: **$135; sleeps 4**
Suites: **$120**
Open: **All year**

Reduced Rates: **25% Nov.–Apr.; 10% May–June**
Breakfast: **Full**
Credit Cards: **AMEX, DISC, MC, VISA**
Pets: **No**
Children: **Welcome, over 10**
Smoking: **No**
Social Drinking: **Permitted**
Airport/Station Pickup: **Yes**

Inside this Victorian farmhouse, period antiques and reproductions transport visitors to a bygone time. But prominently displayed works of local painters and craftspeople demonstrate why Kennebunkport is known as a haven for artists, artisans, and authors. Your host is a native New Englander and retired naval officer; the specialty of the day, in addition to the sumptuous breakfasts, is sharing your experiences with Charlie and his family.

Lake Brook Bed & Breakfast ✪
P.O. BOX 762, KENNEBUNKPORT, MAINE 04043

Tel: **(207) 967-4069**	Open: **May–Feb.**
Best Time to Call: **9 AM–9 PM**	Breakfast: **Full**
Host: **Carolyn A. McAdams**	Credit Cards: **MC, VISA**
Location: **25 mi. S of Portland**	Pets: **No**
No. of Rooms: **4**	Children: **Welcome**
No. of Private Baths: **4**	Smoking: **No**
Double/pb: **$80–$95**	Social Drinking: **Permitted**
Single/pb: **$70**	Foreign Languages: **Spanish**
Suite: **$100**	

Lake Brook is an appealing turn-of-the-century New England farmhouse. Its wraparound porch is equipped with comfortable rocking chairs, and flower gardens stretch right down to the tidal brook that feeds the property. The shops and restaurants of Dock Square are within easy walking distance, and Kennebunk Beach is a little more than one mile away. Breakfasts include such main dishes as quiche, baked French toast, and Mexican chili eggs and cheese.

Gundalow Inn ✪
6 WATER STREET, KITTERY, MAINE 03904

Tel: **(207) 439-4040**	Open: **All year**
Hosts: **Cevia and George Rosol**	Breakfast: **Full**
Location: **50 mi. N of Boston**	Credit Cards: **DISC, MC, VISA**
No. of Rooms: **6**	Pets: **No**
No. of Private Baths: **6**	Children: **Welcome, over 16**
Double/pb: **$80–$125**	Smoking: **No**
Single/pb: **$80–$125**	Social Drinking: **Permitted**

Gundalow Inn is a wonderful brick Victorian overlooking Portsmouth harbor. Guest rooms are comfortably furnished with antiques; most have water views. Savor a hearty home-cooked breakfast by the fireplace or on the patio. Stroll over to Colonial Portsmouth, a town noted for its museums, theaters, restaurants, cafes, gardens, festivals, boat tours, and antique and craft shops. Strawbery Banke and Prescott Park are within walking distance. It's a ten-minute drive to beaches and factory outlets, and the White Mountains are two hours away. Of course, you can always relax with a book on the porch or patio or in the parlor.

Moonraker Bed & Breakfast
MAIN STREET, ROUTE 1, MILBRIDGE, MAINE 04658

Tel: **(207) 546-2191**
Best Time to Call: **9 AM–9 PM**
Hosts: **Bill and Ingrid Handrahan**
Location: **29 mi. N of Ellsworth**
No. of Rooms: **5**
Max. No. Sharing Bath: **4**
Double/pb: **$55–$60**
Double/sb: **$50**
Single/sb: **$45**

Open: **All year**
Breakfast: **Full**
Other Meals: **Available**
Credit Cards: **MC, VISA**
Pets: **No**
Children: **Welcome**
Smoking: **No**
Social Drinking: **Permitted**

This Queen Anne mansion offers an in-town location in a rural village setting. Rooms, on the second and third stories, have outstanding ocean views and turn-of-the-century mahogany furnishings. Restaurants, light shopping, and an inexpensive movie theater are a short walk from the doorstep. It's a pleasant stroll to the Narraguagus River, where you may see seals sunning themselves. Your hosts serve full breakfasts as well as four o'clock tea, so you'll have energy to explore the area.

Bed & Breakfast Year 'Round—the MacDonalds ✪
P.O. BOX 52, MT. DESERT, MAINE 04660

Tel: **(207) 244-3316**
Best Time to Call: **Anytime**

Hosts: **Stan and Binnie MacDonald**
Location: **45 mi. S of Bangor**

No. of Rooms: **3**
No. of Private Baths: **3**
Double/pb: **$75–$85**
Open: **All year**
Reduced Rates: **$15 less Oct. 16– June 14**
Breakfast: **Full**

Credit Cards: **MC, VISA**
Pets: **No**
Children: **Welcome, over 6**
Smoking: **No**
Social Drinking: **Permitted**
Minimum Stay: **2 nights**

Built in 1850 in Somesville, Mt. Desert's first permanent settlement, this B&B is listed on the National Register of Historic Places. The beautifully furnished home has views of the water and mountains from almost every window. In addition to having full use of the living and music rooms, guests may lounge on the screened porch, in the garden courtyard, or in the backyard. At this location, you'll have the pleasure of village living apart from summer crowds. There's much to enjoy on foot, notably Somes Harbor, historic Brookside Cemetery, a bookstore, a museum, and a summer theater. Somesville is surrounded by Acadia National Park and is nearly equidistant from the larger towns of Northeast Harbor, Southwest Harbor, and Bar Harbor. You'll be ready to go exploring after breakfasting on fresh fruit, blueberry pancakes or crepes, and homemade breads and muffins. Stan and Binnie enjoy reading and music—Stan plays a mean banjo!

Black Friar Inn ✪

10 SUMMER STREET, BAR HARBOR, MT. DESERT ISLAND, MAINE 04609

Tel: **(207) 288-5091**
Best Time to Call: **12–3 PM; evenings**
Hosts: **Perry and Sharon Risley and Falke**
No. of Rooms: **7**
No. of Private Baths: **7**
Double/pb: **$90–$140**
Single/pb: **$85–$135**
Open: **May 1–Nov. 30**
Reduced Rates: **Mid Oct.–mid June**

Breakfast: **Full**
Credit Cards: **DISC, MC, VISA**
Pets: **No**
Children: **Welcome, over 12**
Smoking: **No**
Social Drinking: **Permitted**
Minimum Stay: **2 nights June 15– Columbus Day**
Airport/Station Pickup: **Yes**

This uniquely restored Victorian incorporates beautiful woodwork, mantels, and tin from area churches and homes. Afternoon refreshments are served in the sunroom, which is paneled in cypress and embossed tin, or by the fireside in the intimate English pub. Full breakfasts include fresh fruit, juice, eggs, Belgian waffles, and homebaked breads, rolls, and muffins, served in the dining area, featured on the back cover of the 1992 edition of *Bed & Breakfast U.S.A.* Guests have a short walk to shops, restaurants, and the waterfront; it's an easy drive to Acadia National Park.

Hearthside B&B ✪
7 HIGH STREET, BAR HARBOR, MT. DESERT ISLAND, MAINE 04609
hearth@acadia.net

Tel: **(207) 288-4533**	Breakfast: **Full**
Hosts: **Susan and Barry Schwartz**	Credit Cards: **DISC, MC, VISA**
No. of Rooms: **9**	Pets: **No**
No. of Private Baths: **9**	Children: **Welcome, over 10**
Double/pb: **$85–$135**	Smoking: **No**
Open: **All year**	Social Drinking: **Permitted**
Reduced Rates: **Before June 15**	

On a quiet street, just a short walk to town, is this gracious home, recently redecorated in the manner of a country cottage. Breakfast is served buffet-style, featuring home-baked muffins and cakes, eggs, pancakes, hot cereal, a fresh fruit bowl, and beverages. You are invited to share the special ambience of a living room with a cozy fireplace and brimming with books. Some rooms have a balcony or a fireplace, and all rooms are air conditioned.

The Kingsleigh Inn 1904 ✪
P.O. BOX 1426, MAIN STREET, SOUTHWEST HARBOR,
MT. DESERT ISLAND, MAINE 04679

Tel: **(207) 244-5302**	Reduced Rates: **Available**
Hosts: **Ken and Cyd Champagne Collins**	Breakfast: **Full**
Location: **45 mi. E of Bangor**	Credit Cards: **MC, VISA**
No. of Rooms: **8**	Pets: **No**
No. of Private Baths: **8**	Children: **Welcome, over 12**
Double/pb: **$90–$120**	Smoking: **No**
Suite: **$105–$175**	Social Drinking: **Permitted**
Open: **All year**	

Built at the turn of the century, the Kingsleigh Inn is a shingled and pebble-dash Colonial revival. The house overlooks Southwest Harbor, where generations of boatbuilders and fishermen have earned their living. All guest rooms are tastefully decorated and many have beautiful harbor views. Afternoon refreshments are served on a wraparound porch overlooking the harbor or, on cooler days, by a crackling fire. For breakfast your hosts serve freshly brewed coffee, teas, juices, home-baked muffins and breads, fresh fruit, and a daily specialty, such as omelettes, blueberry and buttermilk pancakes, or French toast. Cyd and Ken take pleasure in welcoming you to Mt. Desert Island and will gladly direct you to swimming, hiking, fishing expeditions, whale-watching, restaurants, museums, and shopping.

The Lamb's Ear

P.O. BOX 30, CLARK POINT ROAD, SOUTHWEST HARBOR, MT. DESERT ISLAND, MAINE 04679
http://www.acadia.net/lambsear

Tel: **(207) 244-9828**	Open: **May–Nov.**
Host: **Elizabeth Hoke**	Breakfast: **Full**
Location: **45 mi. E of Bangor**	Credit Cards: **MC, VISA**
No. of Rooms: **6**	Pets: **No**
No. of Private Baths: **6**	Children: **Welcome, over 10**
Double/pb: **$65–$165**	Smoking: **No**
Suite: **$125**	Social Drinking: **Permitted**

A stately home that dates to the mid-19th century, The Lamb's Ear overlooks the waterfront of Southwest Harbor, a quaint fishing village. While swimming, sailing, and fishing are the primary activities here, you'll want to set aside time to explore nearby galleries, museums, and Acadia National Park. After a full breakfast of eggs, Belgian waffles, fresh fruit, and muffins, you'll be ready for the day's adventures.

Lindenwood Inn ✪

P.O. BOX 1328, SOUTHWEST HARBOR, MT. DESERT ISLAND, MAINE 04679

Tel: **(207) 244-5335; (800) 307-5335**	Reduced Rates: **Nov. 1–June 30**
Host: **James King**	Breakfast: **Full**
No. of Rooms: **15**	Pets: **No**
No. of Private Baths: **15**	Children: **Welcome, over 12 in Inn, any**
Double/pb: **$85–$145**	**age cottages and apartments**
Suites: **$165–$195**	Smoking: **No**
Cottages and Apartments: **$125–$195**	Social Drinking: **Permitted**
Open: **All year**	

Built at the turn of the century as a sea captain's home, the Inn derives its name from the stately linden trees that line the front lawn. Each room is individually decorated and many enjoy harbor views from sun-drenched private balconies. On cool mornings you'll be greeted by glowing fireplaces and a hearty full breakfast. Relax and unwind in one of the Inn's elegant sitting rooms or on the large shaded front porch, where you can hear the sounds of the working harbor. Acadia National Park and all the island's activities are only minutes away.

Penury Hall ✪

BOX 68, MAIN STREET, SOUTHWEST HARBOR, MT. DESERT ISLAND, MAINE 04679
http://www.acadia.net/penury-n

Tel: **(207) 244-7102; fax: (207) 244-5651**
Hosts: **Gretchen and Toby Strong**
No. of Rooms: **3**
Max. No. Sharing Bath: **3**
Double/sb: **$70**
Single/sb: **$65**
Open: **All year**
Reduced Rates: **Nov. 1–April 30**

Breakfast: **Full**
Pets: **No**
Children: **Welcome, over 16**
Smoking: **No**
Social Drinking: **Permitted**
Minimum Stay: **2 nights June 1– Oct. 30**
Airport/Station Pickup: **Yes**

This gray frame house is on the quiet side of Mt. Desert Island. Built in 1830, it is comfortably furnished with traditional pieces, antiques, and original art. Gretchen and Toby are cosmopolitan and cordial. Their motto is: "Each guest is an honorary member of the family," and you'll soon feel at home. Knowledgeable about the area's highlights, they'll direct you to special shops and restaurants and all of the best things to see and do. Breakfast often features eggs Benedict and blueberry pancakes or cinnamon waffles. You are welcome to use the canoe. After a day of hiking or skiing, relax in the sauna. There's a $10 surcharge for one-night stays.

Pointy Head Inn ✪

H.C.R. 33 BOX 2A, BASS HARBOR, MT. DESERT ISLAND, MAINE 04653

Tel: **(207) 244-7261**
Best Time to Call: **9:30 AM–3 PM**
Hosts: **Doris and Warren Townsend**
Location: **18 mi. S of Bar Harbor**
No. of Rooms: **6**
No. of Private Baths: **2**
Max. No. Sharing Bath: **4**
Double/pb: **$95**
Double/sb: **$70**

Single/sb: **$45**
Open: **May 15–Oct.**
Breakfast: **Full**
Pets: **No**
Children: **Welcome, over 10**
Smoking: **No**
Social Drinking: **Permitted**
Airport/Station Pickup: **Yes**

In Colonial times a sea captain made his home here, overlooking beautiful Bass Harbor. Today, this sprawling Inn is a haven for artists and photographers who appreciate the quiet side of Mount Desert Island. The house is decorated with nautical accents and homey furnishings. One of its special qualities is the beautiful sunsets that can be enjoyed from your room or the comfortable porch. The Inn is set in a quaint fishing village bordering Acadia National Park. Swimming, canoeing, nature trails, fishing, and mountain climbing are just a few of the activities that can be enjoyed locally. A variety of restaurants, shops, and galleries are within walking distance.

Bass Cove Farm B&B ✪

H.C. 32, BOX 132, ROUTE 185, SORRENTO, MAINE 04677
basscove@downeast.net

Tel: **(207) 422-3564**	Open: **All year**
Hosts: **Mary Ann Solet and Michael Tansey**	Reduced Rates: **10% less Nov.–Apr.; suite, weekly**
Location: **30 mi. NE of Bar Harbor**	Breakfast: **Full**
No. of Rooms: **3**	Credit Cards: **MC, VISA**
No. of Private Baths: **1**	Pets: **Sometimes**
Max. No. Sharing Bath: **4**	Children: **Welcome, over 12**
Double/sb: **$50**	Smoking: **No**
Single/sb: **$45**	Social Drinking: **No**
Suites: **$70–$80**	Minimum Stay: **2 nights for suite**

This 1840s farmhouse is located in a small coastal village—Bass Cove can be seen from the dining room. Outdoor enthusiasts can hike, bike, swim, boat, follow a nature trail, or visit the nearby shops and flea markets for antiques and treasures from local attics. Talk to the artists and craftspeople in their gallery/studio, or attend concerts by local and visiting musicians. Mary Ann does editorial work in her electronic cottage; she is a fiber craftsperson and herb and flower gardener. Mike, group home counselor and photographer, is a Harry S. Truman Manure Pitchoff champion at Maine's Common Ground Country Fair. He oversees the small greenhouse/rabbitry.

Harbour Woods Mount Desert Island ✪
P.O. BOX 1214, ROUTE 102, SOUTHWEST HARBOR, MAINE 04679

Tel: **(207) 244-5388**	Guest Cottage: **$65–$105**
Best Time to Call: **After 10 AM**	Open: **All year**
Hosts: **Joseph and Christine Titka**	Breakfast: **Full**
Location: **20 mi. S of Ellsworth**	Pets: **No**
No. of Rooms: **3**	Children: **Welcome, over 12**
No. of Private Baths: **3**	Smoking: **No**
Double/pb: **$65–$105**	Social Drinking: **Permitted**

This 1800s Maine home retains all the charm and character celebrating a bygone era. Family keepsakes, antiques, flowers, soft glowing oil lamps, warm tones, and subtle wallcoverings create an atmosphere of casual elegance. Guest rooms are attractively decorated with distinctive personalities. All boast queen beds piled with plump pillows, cozy crackling fireplaces, evening mints and candy, telephones, and private baths with luxurious towels and a selection of rich soaps. Each morning a candlelight breakfast becomes a dining experience. While listening to soft music, enjoy a variety of coffees, teas, juices, fruits, home-baked breads, muffins, and the entree of the day, prepared with the freshest ingredients. A refrigerator, tea, and cookies are provided on the house. And of course you may privately reserve the indoor spa to refresh and relax yourself after a full day of activities.

The Island House ✪
CLARK POINT ROAD, P.O. BOX 1006, SOUTHWEST HARBOR, MAINE 04679

Tel: **(207) 244-5180**	Carriage House: **$95–$165**
Best Time to Call: **AM**	Suites: **$140, sleeps 4**
Hosts: **Ann and Charles Bradford**	Open: **All year**
Location: **21 mi. S of Ellsworth**	Reduced Rates: **Available**
No. of Rooms: **4**	Breakfast: **Full**
No. of Private Baths: **2**	Pets: **No**
Max. No. Sharing Bath: **4**	Children: **Welcome, over 10**
Double/pb: **$60–$75**	Smoking: **No**
Single/pb: **$60–$65**	Social Drinking: **Permitted**
Double/sb: **$50–$70**	Minimum Stay: **2 nights in August**
Single/sb: **$50–$65**	

Launched in the mid-1800s as Mt. Desert Island's first summer hotel, The Island House retains its old-time charm as a gracious seacoast family home. Furnishings collected from Ann's childhood in Southeast Asia blend beautifully with the spacious, simply decorated rooms. Breakfasts, served in the dining room, may include eggs Florentine, blueberry coffee cake, and a sausage or cheese casserole. Your hosts know the island well and will be happy to help you plan your day. Acadia National Park is two miles away and Bar Harbor is 15 miles away.

Serenity on the Oyster ✪
ROUTE 1, BOX 5915, THOMASTON, MAINE 04861

Tel: **(207) 354-2063; (888) SERENE 1**	Single/sb: **$65**
Best Time to Call: **9 AM**	Open: **All year**
Hosts: **Chuck and Terry Fleming**	Breakfast: **Full**
Location: **1 1/2 hrs. NE of Portland**	Credit Cards: **MC, VISA**
No. of Rooms: **4**	Pets: **No**
No. of Private Baths: **1**	Children: **Welcome, over 12**
Max. No. Sharing Bath: **4**	Smoking: **No**
Double/pb: **$85**	Social Drinking: **Permitted**
Double/sb: **$75**	Airport/Station Pickup: **Yes**

Serenity overlooks the Oyster River from five acres of wooded land, including a quarter-acre pond. Guests will experience total relaxation in the spacious rooms. A New England–style breakfast is served in the formal dining room and may consist of fresh-baked breads, cakes, and ethnic delights. This B&B is conveniently located on Route 1, just before the historic town of Thomaston.

Fox Island Inn ✪
P.O. BOX 451, VINALHAVEN, MAINE 04863

Tel: **(207) 863-2122, Nov.–May;** **(904) 425-5059**	Single/sb: **$40**
	Open: **June–Sept.**
Best Time to Call: **Evenings**	Breakfast: **Continental**
Host: **Gail Reinertsen**	Pets: **No**
Location: **70 mi. N of Portland**	Children: **Welcome, over 8**
No. of Rooms: **6**	Smoking: **No**
Max. No. Sharing Bath: **4**	Social Drinking: **Permitted**
Double/sb: **$50–$65**	

This midcoast Maine island is the perfect getaway from tourist traffic and crowds. To get to the Inn, leave your car in the ferry parking lot in Rockland and enjoy the hour-plus cruise across island-dotted Penobscot Bay. Once there it's a short walk to the Inn. Guest rooms are simply decorated with quilts and flowers. In the morning enjoy a hearty homemade Continental breakfast. Things to do include hiking, biking, swimming in the ocean or spring-fed quarries, and enjoying the great little restaurants located a few blocks away.

Broad Bay Inn & Gallery ✪
1014 MAIN STREET, P.O. BOX 607, WALDOBORO, MAINE 04572

Tel: **(207) 832-6668; (800) 736-6769**
Host: **Libby Hopkins**
Location: **80 mi. N of Portland**
No. of Rooms: **5**
Max. No. Sharing Bath: **4**
Double/sb: **$40–$75**
Single/sb: **$35–$60**
Open: **All year**

Breakfast: **Full**
Credit Cards: **MC, VISA**
Pets: **No**
Children: **Welcome, over 12**
Smoking: **No**
Social Drinking: **Permitted**
Foreign Languages: **French**

The Inn, set in a charming midcoast village, is a classic Colonial, circa 1830, with light, airy, handsomely decorated rooms. Some guest rooms have canopy beds, and all have Victorian furnishings. There's a large deck on which to sip afternoon tea or sherry, and Libby's garden is lovely enough to be included in local Garden Club tours. This is a convenient base from which to enjoy the quaint fishing villages, the lighthouse, and the Audubon Sanctuary. Guests can swim at Damariscotta Lake, and morning or evening sailboat cruises are easily arranged. A sumptuous breakfast often includes crepes and herbed cheese omelettes. Libby is a theater buff and retired commercial artist; she has a gallery, which is located in the two-story barn behind the Inn. Watercolor workshops are offered in the summer.

Brannon-Bunker Inn ✪
349L STATE ROUTE 129, (DAMARISCOTTA) WALPOLE, MAINE 04543

Tel: **(207) 563-5941; (800) 563-9225**
Best Time to Call: **9 AM–9 PM**

Hosts: **Jeanne and Joseph Hovance**
No. of Rooms: **7**

No. of Private Baths: **5**
Max. No. Sharing Bath: **2**
Double/pb: **$70**
Single/pb: **$65**
Double/sb: **$60**
Single/sb: **$55**
Suites: **$75–$115**

Open: **Apr.–Dec.**
Breakfast: **Continental, plus**
Credit Cards: **AMEX, MC, VISA**
Pets: **No**
Children: **Welcome**
Smoking: **No**
Social Drinking: **Permitted**

The Brannon-Bunker Inn is an informal, relaxing inn, ideally situated in rural, coastal Maine. Guests may choose from accommodations in the 1900 converted barn or the carriage house across the stream. Each room is individually decorated in styles ranging from Colonial to Victorian. Hosts Jeanne and Joseph Hovance will help you plan your days over breakfast. Nearby activities include golf, ocean swimming at Pemaquid Beach Park, and fishing on the Damariscotta River.

The Cape Neddick House

1300 ROUTE 1, P.O. BOX 70, CAPE NEDDICK (YORK), MAINE 03902

Tel: **(207) 363-2500; fax (207) 363-4499**
Hosts: **John and Dianne Goodwin**
Location: **12 mi. N of Portsmouth, New Hampshire**
No. of Rooms: **5**
No. of Private Baths: **5**
Double/pb: **$70–$120**
Single/pb: **$65–$110**

Suites: **$100–$130**
Open: **All year**
Reduced Rates: **Weekly**
Breakfast: **Full**
Pets: **No**
Children: **Welcome, over 5**
Smoking: **No**
Social Drinking: **Permitted**

Replete with family treasures, this inherited 1885 Victorian farmhouse is located in the historic coastal town of York. Relax by a fireplace in the living room in fall or winter, or cool off on the deck overlooking gardens and woods in spring and summer. Shop till you drop at nearby factory outlets, boutiques, and antique shops, or observe Mother Nature's creations on rural roads, in wildlife sanctuaries, and on the beaches. Sleep in antique-filled bedrooms under handmade quilts and air-conditioning. The two-room suite has a fireplace. Awake to the scent of cinnamon popovers, strawberry scones, peach almond torte, or ham and apple biscuits—enough to sustain you for another day of exploring the Maine coast.

The Wild Rose of York B&B

78 LONG SANDS ROAD, YORK, MAINE 03909

Tel: **(207) 363-2532**
Best Time to Call: **6–10 PM**
Hosts: **Fran and Frank Sullivan**
No. of Rooms: **3**
No. of Private Baths: **3**
Double/pb: **$65–$75**
Single/pb: **$60**

Open: **All year**
Reduced Rates: **Oct. 16–May 31**
Breakfast: **Full**
Pets: **No**
Children: **Welcome, over 7**
Smoking: **No**
Social Drinking: **Permitted**

This handsome house, built in 1814, sits high on a hill within easy range of the ocean breezes. The bedrooms are cozy, with antique beds, patchwork quilts, fireplaces, and Fran's special artistic touches. Breakfast is special and may feature peach pancakes or nut waffles. In summer, an old-fashioned trolley will take you to the beach. Deep-sea fishing, golf, hiking, shops, galleries, and factory outlets are nearby diversions. In winter, sledding, skating, and cross-country skiing are all fun.

For key to listings, see inside front or back cover.

❂ This star means that rates are guaranteed through December 31, 1998, to any guest making a reservation as a result of reading about the B&B in *Bed & Breakfast U.S.A.*—1998 edition.

Important! To avoid misunderstandings, always ask about cancellation policies when booking.

Please enclose a self-addressed, stamped, business-size envelope when contacting reservation services.

For more details on what you can expect in a B&B, see Chapter 1.

Always mention *Bed & Breakfast U.S.A.* when making reservations!

We want to hear from you! Use the form on page 625.

MARYLAND

Bed & Breakfast of Maryland/The Traveller in Maryland, Inc. ✪

P.O. BOX 2277, ANNAPOLIS, MARYLAND 21404-2277

Tel: **(410) 269-6232; (800) 736-4667;**
  fax: **(410) 263-4841**
Best Time to Call: **9 AM–5 PM**
Coordinator: **Greg Page**
States/Regions Covered: **Annapolis,
  Baltimore, Central Maryland, Eastern
  and Southern Shore, Western
  Maryland; London, England, United
  Kingdom**

Descriptive Directory of B&Bs: **$5**
Rates (Single/Double):
  Modest: **$55 / $60**
  Average: **$60 / $70**
  Luxury: **$80 / $100**
Credit Cards: **AMEX, MC, VISA**

This reservation service is one of Maryland's oldest, representing fine-
quality, inspected accommodations throughout Maryland and the
United Kingdom. Greg will lead you to hosted and unhosted accommodations in interesting and exciting B&B homes, inns, yachts, apart-

ments, and guest cottages. Bed & Breakfast of Maryland offers you a variety of urban and rural locations. Professional staff will help you find just the right location for business, family vacation, relocation, interim housing, romantic getaway, and special occasions. All listings are held to a strict set of standards to ensure your comfort and enjoyment. Greg and his staff look forward to helping you with your travel requests.

College House Suites
ONE COLLEGE AVENUE, ANNAPOLIS, MARYLAND 21401

Tel: (410) 263-6124
Best Time to Call: 10 AM–4 PM
Hosts: Jo Anne and Don Wolfrey
Suites: $170
Open: All year
Breakfast: Continental

Credit Cards: MC, VISA
Pets: No
Children: No
Smoking: No
Social Drinking: Permitted
Minimum Stay: 2 nights

This brick town house is nestled between the U.S. Naval Academy and St. John's College. The Annapolitan suite has a fireplace, light Victorian decor, and a private entrance through the ivy-covered courtyard. The Colonial suite has superb oriental rugs, antiques, and views of the Academy. The hosts pay close attention to details such as fresh flowers, fruit baskets, and chocolates. College House Suites is a short walk to the city dock, Paca House and Gardens, fine restaurants, fascinating shops and boutiques, art and antique galleries, museums, historic buildings, churches, and theater. A "breakfast-out" option is available.

Amanda's B&B Reservation Service ✪
1428 PARK AVENUE, BALTIMORE, MARYLAND 21217

Tel: (410) 225-0001; (800) 899-7533;
fax (410) 728-8957
Best Time to Call: 8:30 AM–5:30 PM
Mon.–Fri.; 8:30 AM–noon Sat.
Coordinator: Betsy Grater
States/Regions Covered: Delaware,
District of Columbia, Maryland, New

Jersey, Pennsylvania, Virginia, West Virginia
Descriptive Directory of B&Bs: $5
Rates (Single/Double):
Modest: $60–$65
Luxury: $85–$150
Credit Cards: AMEX, DISC, MC, VISA

Amanda's is a regional reservation service for private homes, small inns and yachts. This service represents almost 200 properties throughout Maryland and the six surrounding states. Accommodations include everything from economical to luxury rooms with Jacuzzis and private baths.

Betsy's Bed and Breakfast ✪
1428 PARK AVENUE, BALTIMORE, MARYLAND 21217

Tel: (410) 383-1274
Best Time to Call: 9:30 AM–10 PM

Host: Betsy Grater
No. of Rooms: 3

No. of Private Baths: **3**
Double/pb: **$85**
Single/pb: **$65**
Open: **All year**
Breakfast: **Full**

Credit Cards: **AMEX, MC, VISA**
Pets: **No**
Children: **Welcome**
Smoking: **No**
Social Drinking: **Permitted**

A petite estate, this four-story row house is in Bolton Hill, a historic Baltimore neighborhood listed on the National Registry. The interior features 12-foot ceilings with center medallions, a hall floor inlaid with oak and walnut, crown moldings, and carved marble fireplaces. This charming old house is uniquely decorated with a large collection of original brass rubbings, heirloom quilts, and interesting wall groupings. Modern amenities include a hot tub. Betsy's B&B is just a few blocks from a new light-rail stop at "Cultural Station," and steps away from Meyerhoff Symphony Hall, the Lyric Opera House, Antique Row, and the Maryland Institute of Art. The Inner Harbor is seven minutes away by car.

Shady Oaks of Serenity ✪
P.O. BOX 842, BRYANTOWN, MARYLAND 20617-0842

Tel: **(800) 597-0924**
Best Time to Call: **4–11 PM**
Hosts: **Kathy and Gene Kazimer**
Location: **35 mi. from Washington, D.C.**
Suites: **$65**
Open: **All year**

Breakfast: **Continental**
Pets: **No**
Children: **Welcome, over 14**
Smoking: **No**
Social Drinking: **Permitted**

Shady Oaks of Serenity is a new Georgia Victorian situated on three acres and surrounded by trees. This secluded home is off the beaten path, yet within a 45-minute drive of the nation's capital and Annapolis, home of the U.S. Naval Academy. Just down the road is Amish country with antiques and unique shops, historic churches, the renowned Dr. Mudd Home, and Gilbert Run Park, a favorite county stop. Also, this retreat may be of interest to those visiting patients at the Charlotte Hall Veterans Home, only minutes away. Decorated with the Amish theme, the suite has a private bath. Visitors are welcome to gather in the sitting room or the front porch, or enjoy an evening on the deck. Your room has a king-size bed for a peaceful night's rest. Kathy and Gene cordially invite you to be a guest in their home and visit historic Charles County. The morning brings fresh coffee, homemade muffins or breads, and a variety of fresh fruits.

The Taylors' B&B ✪
P.O. BOX 238, BURTONSVILLE, MARYLAND 20866-0238

Tel: **(301) 236-4318**
Best Time to Call: **9–11 AM; 7–9 PM**
Hosts: **Ruth and Fred Taylor**

Location: **30 min. from Washington, D.C., and the Inner Harbor**
No. of Rooms: **1**

No. of Private Baths: **1**
Double/pb: **$60**
Open: **All year**
Breakfast: **Continental**
Pets: **No**

Children: **No**
Smoking: **No**
Social Drinking: **Permitted**
Foreign Languages: **French**

This gracious two-story Colonial home offers a breath of fresh country air just 30 minutes from Washington, D.C., and Baltimore's Inner Harbor district. Guests can enjoy the grand piano, the extensive collection of books in the library, and Ruth's paintings. In warm weather, cool drinks are served in the gazebo; in winter, guests gather by the fireplace in the family room. Both of your hosts are retired. Ruth likes to read, sew, paint, and cook; Fred enjoys reading, writing, history, and music. They've traveled extensively and know how to make guests feel welcome. Tennis courts, horseback riding, and nature trails are nearby.

Chevy Chase Bed & Breakfast
6815 CONNECTICUT AVENUE, CHEVY CHASE, MARYLAND 20815

Tel: **(301) 656-5867; fax (301) 656-5867**
Best Time to Call: **Anytime**
Host: **S. C. Gotbaum**
Location: **1 mi. N of Washington**
No. of rooms: **2**
No. of Private Baths: **2**
Double/pb: **$70**

Single/pb: **$60**
Open: **All year**
Reduced Rates: **Families**
Breakfast: **Continental, plus**
Pets: **No**
Children: **Welcome**
Smoking: **No**
Social Drinking: **Permitted**

Enjoy the convenience of being close to the transportation and sights of Washington, D.C., and Maryland's Montgomery County while staying at a relaxing, turn-of-the century, country-style house. Rooms have beamed ceilings and are filled with rare tapestries, oriental rugs, baskets, copperware, and native crafts from Mexico to the Mideast. The garden room has a cathedral ceiling and private deck. The gabled skylight room has a king-size bed. Your host is a sociologist with a private consulting business. Breakfast items include homemade breads, jams, pancakes, French toast, and a special blend of Louisiana coffee. When you want to take a break from touring, the lovely garden is there for you. There is a $5 surcharge for one-night stays.

The Garden Cottage at Sinking Springs Herb Farm ✪
234 BLAIR SHORE ROAD, ELKTON, MARYLAND 21921

Tel: **(410) 398-5566**
Best Time to Call: **9 AM–9 PM**
Hosts: **Ann and Bill Stubbs**
Location: **4¹/₂ mi. from Rte. 40**
No. of Rooms: **1**
No. of Private Baths: **1**

Guest Cottage: **$88 for 2; sleeps 3**
Open: **All year**
Reduced Rates: **5% seniors**
Breakfast: **Full**
Credit Cards: **MC, VISA**
Other Meals: **Available**

Pets: **No**
Children: **Welcome**
Smoking: **No**

Social Drinking: **Permitted**
Airport/Station Pickup: **Yes**

Guests frequently comment on the peaceful beauty of this 128-acre historic farm. The garden cottage has a sitting room and fireplace adjoining the bedroom. Breakfast features coffee ground from organically grown beans, herbal teas, homemade buns, fruit, and juice. A full country breakfast prepared with unprocessed food fresh from the farm is available at no extra charge. Lectures on herbs and craft classes are available, and a gift shop is on the premises. Longwood Gardens and the famed Winterthur Museum are close by. Historic Chesapeake City is five minutes away, with excellent restaurants.

Hayland Farm ✪
5000 SHEPPARD LANE, ELLICOTT CITY, MARYLAND 21042

Tel: **(410) 531-5593**
Host: **Dorothy Mobley**
Location: **Bet. Baltimore and D.C.**
No. of Rooms: **3**
No. of Private Baths: **1**
Max. No. Sharing Bath: **4**
Double/pb: **$60**
Single/pb: **$40**

Double/sb: **$40**
Single/sb: **$25**
Open: **All year**
Breakfast: **Full**
Pets: **No**
Children: **No**
Smoking: **No**
Social Drinking: **Permitted**

When you breathe the country-fresh air, it may surprise you that Baltimore and Washington, D.C., are only a short drive away. At Hayland Farm you will find gracious living in a large manor house furnished in a handsome, yet comfortable, style. Dorothy is retired and has traveled extensively. She enjoys sharing conversation with her guests. In warm weather, the 20- by 50-foot swimming pool is a joy.

Middle Plantation Inn ✪
9549 LIBERTY ROAD, FREDERICK, MARYLAND 21701

Tel: **(301) 898-7128**
Best Time to Call: **6–10 PM**
Hosts: **Shirley and Dwight Mullican**
Location: **5 mi. E of Frederick**
No. of Rooms: **4**
No. of Private Baths: **4**
Double/pb: **$95–$110**

Open: **All year**
Breakfast: **Continental**
Credit Cards: **MC, VISA**
Pets: **No**
Children: **Welcome, over 15**
Smoking: **No**
Social Drinking: **Permitted**

Dwight and Shirley have furnished their handsome stone and log home with antiques collected on their travels. Their charming B&B will appeal to Civil War buffs, since Gettysburg, Pennsylvania, Sharpsburg, Maryland, and Harpers Ferry, West Virginia, are all 40 minutes away by car. Closer to home, Frederick's 33-block historic district boasts a fascinating mix of museums, galleries, antique shops, and eateries. And for more antiquing, guests should head to nearby New Market.

Lewrene Farm B&B ✪
9738 DOWNSVILLE PIKE, HAGERSTOWN, MARYLAND 21740

Tel: **(301) 582-1735**
Hosts: **Lewis and Irene Lehman**
Location: **3½ mi. from I-70 and I-81**
No. of Rooms: **6**
No. of Private Baths: **3**
Max. No. Sharing Bath: **4**
Double/pb: **$79–$115**
Double/sb: **$62–$68**

Suites: **$115**
Open: **All year**
Breakfast: **Full**
Children: **Welcome**
Smoking: **No**
Social Drinking: **No**
Foreign Languages: **Spanish**

Lewis and Irene will help you discover the peaceful beauty of their 125-acre farm located in a historic area near the Antietam Battlefield. Guests are treated like old friends and are welcome to lounge in front of the fireplace or to play the piano in the Colonial-style living room. You're invited to enjoy snacks and a video in the evening. Harpers Ferry, Fort Frederick, the C&O Canal, and Gettysburg are nearby. Irene sells antiques and collectibles on the premises.

Sunday's Bed & Breakfast ✪
39 BROADWAY, HAGERSTOWN, MARYLAND 21740

Tel: **(800) 221-4828; (301) 797-4331**
Best Time to Call: **Anytime**
Host: **Bob Ferrino**
Location: **70 mi. NW of Washington, D.C.**
No. of Rooms: **4**
No. of Private Baths: **4**

Double/pb: **$75–$110**
Single/pb: **$55–$90**
Open: **All year**
Reduced Rates: **Available**
Breakfast: **Full**
Credit Cards: **DC, MC, VISA**
Other Meals: **Available**

Pets: **Sometimes**
Children: **Welcome, over 10**
Smoking: **No**

Social Drinking: **Permitted**
Airport Pickup: **Yes**

Built in 1890, this elegant Queen Anne Victorian is located in Hagerstown's historic north end, on a street lined with other grand old homes. Relax in your room or in the many public areas and porches. You may want to visit the area's numerous attractions, such as the National Historical Parks of Antietam, Harpers Ferry, Whitetails Ski Resort, and the C&O Canal. Or choose among the myriad other historic sites, antique shops, fishing areas, golf courses, museums, shopping outlets, and theaters.

The Wingrove Manor Inn ✪

635 OAK HILL AVENUE, HAGERSTOWN, MARYLAND 21740
http://www.interaccess.com/wingrove manor/index.html

Tel: **(301) 797-7769**; fax **(301) 797-8659**
Host: **Winnie Price**
Location: **70 mi. NW of Washington, D.C.**
Suites: **$85–$125**
Open: **All year**
Reduced Rates: **Available**

Breakfast: **Continental**
Credit Cards: **MC, VISA**
Pets: **No**
Children: **Welcome, off-season**
Smoking: **No**
Social Drinking: **Permitted**
Minimum Stay: **2 nights peak season**
Airport Pickup: **Yes**

The Wingrove Manor is a beautifully restored bed and breakfast on a street lined with Victorian mansions. Relax in the wicker rockers stretched across a large Southern porch surrounded by 23 white columns, ceramic tiled floors, and breathtaking beauty. Inside you will find magnificent turn-of-the-century craftsmanship, marble fireplaces, a winding staircase, oriental rugs, crystal chandeliers, and towering white columns—all reflecting the home's lineage. The common rooms are elegant. Featured on the first floor is the Canopy Suite with a queen-size bed, marble fireplace, private entrance, TV, VCR, and a full bath with a Jacuzzi, ideally suited for honeymooners. On the second floor are three spacious rooms all with TV, VCR, telephone, double-thick towels, fragrant sprays, sweet soaps, and queen beds that bid travelers welcome and promise a good night's sleep.

Currier House ✪
800 SOUTH MARKET STREET, HAVRE de GRACE, MARYLAND 21078

Tel: **(800) 827-2889; (410) 939-7886**
Best Time to Call: **8 AM–8 PM**
Hosts: **Jane and Paul Belbot**
Location: **35 mi. NE of Baltimore**
No. of Rooms: **4**
No. of Private Baths: **4**
Double/pb: **$85–$95**
Single/pb: **$75–$85**

Open: **All year**
Reduced Rates: **No**
Breakfast: **Full**
Credit Cards: **AMEX, DISC, MC, VISA**
Pets: **No**
Children: **No**
Smoking: **No**
Social Drinking: **Permitted**

Currier House, located in Havre de Grace's historic residential district at the top of the Chesapeake Bay, has been occupied by the Currier family since 1861. The B&B is furnished with antiques, family heirlooms, and mementos that have been passed from generation to generation. Just one block from the Currier House are the Decoy and Maritime museums and the Concord Point Lighthouse, the oldest lighthouse in continuous operation in this country. Numerous antique shops, galleries, boutiques, and restaurants are within walking distance; a water taxi operates from one end of town to the other. Currier House was always a waterman's home, and keeping the tradition alive, a waterman's breakfast is served in the morning.

The Mill House B&B ✪
102 MILL LANE, NORTH EAST, MARYLAND 21901

Tel: **(410) 287-3532**	Single/sb: **$60–$70**
Best Time to Call: **Before 9 AM; after 4 PM**	Open: **Mar. 1–Dec. 1**
Hosts: **Lucia and Nick Demond**	Breakfast: **Full**
Location: **40 mi. NE of Baltimore**	Credit Cards: **MC, VISA**
No. of Rooms: **2**	Pets: **No**
Max. No. Sharing Bath: **4**	Children: **Welcome, over 12**
Double/sb: **$65–$75**	Smoking: **No**
	Social Drinking: **Permitted**

A genuine mill house that dates to the early 18th century, this B&B is furnished entirely in antiques. You'll see picturesque mill ruins and wildflowers on the grounds, but you won't see the parlor's original Queen Anne paneling; that was purchased by Henry Francis Du Pont and installed in his Winterthur estate bedroom. The Winterthur Museum and the Brandywine River Museum are less than an hour's drive away, as is Baltimore's Inner Harbor. Sightseers will be sustained with a full breakfast, including homemade breads fresh from the oven.

Rocker Inn ✪
17924 ELGIN ROAD, POOLESVILLE, MARYLAND 20837

Tel: **(301) 972-8543**	Single/pb: **$40**
Best Time to Call: **After 5:30 PM**	Open: **All year**
Host: **Nancy Hopkinson**	Breakfast: **Continental**
Location: **25 mi. NW of Washington, D.C.**	Pets: **Sometimes**
No. of Rooms: **2**	Children: **Welcome**
No. of Private Baths: **1**	Smoking: **No**
Double/pb: **$45**	Social Drinking: **Permitted**

Built in 1915 as a local telephone house, Rocker Inn takes its name from the rocking chairs and two swings that fill its 48-foot front porch. Inside, the home is decorated in an informal country mode. Walking tours of Poolesville and Frederick, along with a hike on the C&O Canal, are minutes away. For more ambitious excursions, Harpers Ferry, Gettysburg Battlefield, and historic Leesburg are within an hour's drive.

St. Michael's Manor B&B ✪
ST. MICHAEL'S MANOR, SCOTLAND, MARYLAND 20687

Tel: **(301) 872-4025**
Hosts: **Joe and Nancy Dick**
Location: **9 mi. S of St. Marys City**
No. of Rooms: **4**
Max. No. Sharing Bath: **4**
Double/sb: **$70**
Single/sb: **$50**

Open: **All year**
Breakfast: **Full**
Pets: **No**
Children: **By arrangement**
Smoking: **Downstairs**
Social Drinking: **Permitted**

St. Michael's Manor was built in 1805 on land patented to Leonard Calvert during the 17th century. Today, the white stucco manor home on picturesque Long Neck Creek is included in the state's Pilgrimage Tour. The beautiful handcrafted woodwork has been preserved and is complemented by antiques and handcrafts. Your hosts offer you the use of a canoe, paddleboat, bikes, spa, and swimming pool. Estate wine tasting is also available. The manor house is near Point Lookout State Park, the Chesapeake Bay, and historic St. Marys City.

Blue Bear Bed & Breakfast ✪
13810 FRANK'S RUN ROAD, SMITHSBURG, MARYLAND 21783

Tel: **(800) 381-2292**
Best Time to Call: **After 4 PM**
Hosts: **Ellen Panchula and Marilyn
  Motter**
Location: **6 mi. from I-70, exit 35**
No. of Rooms: **2**
No. of Private Baths: **2**
Double/pb: **$60–$65**

Single/pb: **$50–$55**
Open: **All year**
Breakfast: **Continental**
Pets: **No**
Children: **Welcome, over 12**
Smoking: **No**
Social Drinking: **Permitted**

Ellen, a full-time schoolteacher, and her sister Marilyn, a professional dog groomer, have joined together at the Blue Bear Bed & Breakfast to offer guests year-round hospitality. Their home is decorated in an informal country mode, with several antiques and a charming collection of friendly-faced teddy bears throughout the house. Guests can relax and enjoy beautiful views from the front porch or tour nearby battlefields. Breakfast consists of fresh fruits, homemade breads, pastries, and coffee cake. Snacks are offered in the evening.

The Tavern House ✪
111 WATER STREET, P.O. BOX 98, VIENNA, MARYLAND 21869

Tel: **(410) 376-3347**
Hosts: **Harvey and Elise Altergott**
Location: **15 mi. NW of Salisbury**
No. of Rooms: **4**
Max. No. Sharing Bath: **4**
Double/sb: **$70–$75**
Single/sb: **$65–$70**

Open: **All year**
Breakfast: **Full**
Credit Cards: **MC, VISA**
Pets: **No**
Children: **Welcome, over 12**
Smoking: **Permitted**
Social Drinking: **Permitted**

Vienna is a quiet little town on the Nanticoke River, where one can escape the stress of the 20th century. Careful restoration has brought back the simple purity of this Colonial tavern. The stark white "lime, sand, and hair" plaster accents the authentic furnishings. This is a place for those who enjoy looking at the river and marshes, watching an osprey in flight, or taking a leisurely walk. Days begin with a special full breakfast that is always a social event. For the sports minded, there's tennis, boating, and flat roads for bicycling, all within easy reach. This is an excellent base for exploring the Eastern Shore, interesting small towns, and Blackwater National Wildlife Refuge.

MASSACHUSETTS

Bed & Breakfast Cambridge & Greater Boston
P.O. BOX 1344, CAMBRIDGE, MASSACHUSETTS 02238

Tel: **(617) 720-1492; (800) 888-0178**
Best Time to Call: **10 AM–5 PM**
  Mon.–Fri, 10 AM–3 PM Sat.
Coordinators: **Tally and Pamela**
  Carruthers
States/Regions Covered: **Boston,**
  Cambridge, Lexington, and
  surrounding areas

Rates (Single/Double):
  Average: **$55–$85**
  Luxury: **$85–$115**
Credit Cards: **AMEX, MC, VISA**
Minimum Stay: **2 nights**

Tally and Pamela can place you in host homes convenient to historic
Lexington and Concord, downtown Boston, or in Cambridge. Many are
close to Harvard and MIT, Lahey Clinic, historic Wright Tavern, Emer-
son's home, Walden Pond, and the Charles River. Unusual restaurants,
specialty shops, and cultural happenings abound. Just tell your host

about your interests and you will be assured of excellent advice. There's a $10 surcharge for one-night stays.

Bed & Breakfast Reservations North Shore ○

P.O. BOX 35, NEWTONVILLE, MASSACHUSETTS 02160
bnbinc@aol.com; http://www.bnbinc.com

Tel: (617) 964-1606; (800) 832-2632 in the U.S. outside Massachusetts and Canada; fax: (617) 332-8572
Best Time to Call: 8:30 AM–8 PM Mon.–Thurs., 9 AM–5 PM Fri., 9 AM–noon Sat., 7 PM–9 PM Sun.
Coordinator: Sheryl Felleman
States/Regions Covered:
Massachusetts—Beverly, Boxford, Danvers, Essex, Gloucester, Hamilton, Lynn, Lynnfield, Manchester, Marblehead, Middleton, Newburyport, Peabody, Rockport, Salem, Swampscott; Maine; New Hampshire; Vermont

Rates (Single/Double):
Modest: $50–$65 / $65–$70
Average: $65–$75 / $75–$95
Luxury: $100–$135 / $100–$195
Credit Cards: AMEX, MC, VISA

Come home to the history and culture of New England! Stay in one of the beautiful B&B homes, small inns, or furnished apartments in historic oceanside towns on Massachusetts's North Shore. This area is known for its rich past, beautiful beaches and harbors, recreational activities, wonderful restaurants, and friendly New England hospitality. Easy access by public transportation to Boston. Selected B&Bs in fall foliage and ski areas elsewhere in New England. Daily, weekly, or monthly rates. There is a $15 booking fee.

BOSTON AREA

B&B Host Homes of Boston ○

P.O. BOX 117, WABAN BRANCH, BOSTON, MASSACHUSETTS 02168

Tel: (617) 244-1308; (800) 600-1308; fax: (617) 244-5156
Best Time to Call: 9 AM–noon; 1:30–4:30 PM weekdays
Coordinator: Marcia Whittington
States/Regions Covered: Boston, Brookline, Cambridge, Hamilton, Lincoln, Lexington, Milton, Needham, Newton, Quincy, Scituate, Southborough, Sudbury, Waltham, Wellesley, Westwood, Weymouth

Descriptive Directory: Free
Rates (Single/Double):
Modest: $64–75 / $68–$85
Average: $68–$81 / $85–$95
Luxury: $90–$130 / $120–$150
Credit Cards: AMEX, MC, VISA
Minimum Stay: 2 nights

Since 1982, Marcia has culled a variety of select private homes in excellent areas near major hotels and institutions, historic sites, and good public transportation. Hosts offer free parking (except downtown), hearty breakfasts, and a cordial welcome to their city of colleges, universities, museums, and cultural life. To fax your reservation request, please use the form in the directory.

Bed & Breakfast Associates—Bay Colony, Ltd. ✪
P.O. BOX 57166, BABSON PARK, BOSTON,
MASSACHUSETTS 02157-0166
BnBBoston@aol.com; http://www.bnbboston.com

Tel: **(617) 449-5302; (800) 347-5088;**
  fax: **(617) 449-5958**
Best Time to Call: **9:30 AM–5 PM**
  Mon.–Fri.
Coordinators: **Arline Kardasis and**
  Marilyn Mitchell
States/Regions Covered: **Boston,**
  Brookline, Cambridge, Cape Cod,
Concord, Framingham, Gloucester,
Newton, North Shore, South Shore
Rates (Single/Double):
  Modest: **$50–$65 / $60–$75**
  Average: **$65–$100 / $75–$100**
  Luxury: **$100–$150 / $100–$175**
Credit Cards: **AMEX, CB, DC, MC, VISA**
Minimum Stay: **2 nights**

Bed & Breakfast Associates—Bay Colony is one of the original reservation services. Founded in 1981 by Marilyn and Arline, they provide a highly personalized service with a staff of six who together have accumulated 70 years of experience. Guest requests for specific amenities are carefully matched with over 150 B&B inns, homes, or unhosted apartments. Accommodations range from elegant Victorian brownstones and inns, located in the heart of Boston's best and most convenient neighborhoods, to suburban homes in 35 towns, including Cambridge and Brookline. Properties are fully inspected and are also available throughout Cape Cod and on the romantic islands of Martha's Vineyard and Nantucket. Most B&Bs are non-smoking. Requests for TV, phone, air-conditioning, canopy bed, Jacuzzi, or fireplaces can usually be met. They even offer swimming pools, oceanside settings, one kosher home, and an Arabian horse farm.

Bed & Breakfast Reservations Greater Boston & Cape Cod ✪
P.O. BOX 35, NEWTONVILLE, MASSACHUSETTS 02160
bnbinc.@aol.com; http://www.bnbinc.com

Tel: **(617) 964-1606; (800) 832-2632**
  (outside Massachusetts) in U.S.A. and
  Canada; fax: (617) 332-8572
Best Time to Call: **8:30 AM–8 PM**
  Mon.–Thurs., 8:30 AM–5 PM Fri.,
  9 AM–noon Sat., 7 PM–9 PM Sun.
Coordinator: **Suzanne Ross**
States/Regions Covered: **Arlington,**
  Boston: Back Bay, Beacon Hill,
  Waterfront, South End; Cape Cod:
Barnstable, Cambridge, Concord,
Eastham, Falmouth Heights, Harwich
Port, Onset, Orleans, Sandwich,
Sturbridge, Provincetown, West
Harwich, West Yarmouth
Rates (Single/Double):
  Modest: **$50–$65 / $65–$70**
  Average: **$65–$75 / $75–$95**
  Luxury: **$100–$135 / $100–$195**
Credit Cards: **AMEX, MC, VISA**

Explore the city and the many tourist attractions this region offers, then escape to the beautiful beaches of Cape Cod. Whether you choose an antique Victorian, restored inn, classic Colonial, charming ocean-view apartment, cozy carriage house, or contemporary condo, you will experience the finest New England hospitality. Many accommodations are close to area colleges and universities and public transportation. Furnished apartments in downtown Boston, Back Bay, waterfront and Beacon Hill for short or long term and re-location. Selected B&Bs elsewhere in New England, fall foliage and ski areas. There is a $15 booking fee.

George Fuller House ✪
148 MAIN STREET, ESSEX, MASSACHUSETTS 01929

Tel: **(508) 768-7766; (800) 477-0148**	Reduced Rates: **10% less Nov. 1–May 31**
Best Time to Call: **10 AM–10 PM**	Breakfast: **Full**
Hosts: **Cindy and Bob Cameron**	Credit Cards: **AMEX, DISC, MC, VISA**
Location: **3 mi. off Rte. 128, Exit 15**	Pets: **No**
No. of Rooms: **7**	Children: **Welcome, over 6**
No. of Private Baths: **7**	Smoking: **No**
Double/pb: **$89–$115**	Social Drinking: **Permitted**
Suites: **$135–$145**	Airport/Station Pickup: **Yes**
Open: **All year**	

This handsome Federalist home retains much of its 19th-century paneling and woodwork; four of the guest rooms have working fireplaces. The Camerons have decorated the house with antique beds, handmade quilts, braided rugs, and caned Boston rockers. Three hundred years ago, Essex was a shipbuilding center. Among landlubbers, Essex's main claim to fame is its antique shops. Whether you venture out on sea or on land, you'll be fortified by Cindy's versions of breakfast classics, such as her French toast drizzled with brandied lemon butter.

Williams Guest House ✪
136 BASS AVENUE, GLOUCESTER, MASSACHUSETTS 01930

Tel: **(508) 283-4931**	Guest Cottage: **$500 weekly for 2**
Best Time to Call: **8 AM–8 PM**	Open: **May 1–Nov. 1**
Host: **Betty Williams**	Reduced Rates: **Off-season, before June 17 and after Labor Day**
Location: **30 mi. N of Boston**	Breakfast: **Continental**
No. of Rooms: **7**	Pets: **No**
No. of Private Baths: **5**	Children: **Welcome, in cottage**
Max. No. Sharing Bath: **4**	Smoking: **No**
Double/pb: **$62**	Social Drinking: **Permitted**
Double/sb: **$54**	

Located five miles from Rockport, and one and a half miles from Rocky Neck, Gloucester is a quaint fishing village on the North Shore. Betty's Colonial Revival house borders the finest beach, Good Harbor. The guest rooms are furnished with comfort in mind. Betty will be happy to suggest many interesting things to do, such as boat tours, sport fishing, whale-watching trips, sightseeing cruises around Cape Ann, the Hammond Castle Museum, and the shops and galleries of the artist colony.

Diamond District Breakfast Inn
142 OCEAN STREET, LYNN, MASSACHUSETTS 01902-2007

Tel: **(617) 599-4470; (800) 666-3076;**
  (617) 599-5122
Hosts: **Sandra and Jerry Caron**
Location: **8 mi. NE of Boston**
No. of Rooms: **10**
No. of Private Baths: **6**
Double/pb: **$95–$140**
Double/sb: **$80–$110**

Open: **All year**
Reduced Rates: **Available**
Breakfast: **Full**
Credit Cards: **AMEX, DC, MC, VISA**
Pets: **Sometimes**
Children: **Welcome**
Smoking: **No**

This 17-room Georgian clapboard mansion was built in 1911 by P. J. Harney, a local shoe manufacturer. Features include a gracious foyer and a staircase winding its way up three floors; a spacious living room with Mexican mahogany, marble fireplace, and French doors leading to a large 36 × 14-foot veranda that overlooks the gardens and ocean, and a banquet-size dining room. The 44-page architect's specifications permitted only the best of materials to be used. Antiques and oriental rugs fill the house. Furnishings include an 1895 Rosewood Kanabe concert grand piano and custom Chippendale dining room table and chairs signed by Joseph Gerty, a 1940s Boston custom furniture maker. Bedrooms offer a custom 1870s Victorian bed and twin beds by Charak, another Boston custom furniture maker. Each room boasts the elegance of yesteryear.

The Thistle ✪
31 FAIRFIELD STREET, NEEDHAM, MASSACHUSETTS 02192

Tel: **(617) 444-5724**
Best Time to Call: **Anytime**
Hosts: **Leo and Susan Rainville**
Location: **10 mi. SW of Boston**
No. of Rooms: **2**
Max. No. Sharing Bath: **4**
Double/sb: **$60**
Single/sb: **$50**

Open: **All year**
Breakfast: **Continental**
Pets: **No**
Children: **No**
Smoking: **No**
Social Drinking: **Permitted**
Station Pickup: **Yes**

Relax in this peaceful setting on a tree-lined street just a few blocks off Route 128 and Interstate 95. The Thistle offers easy access to colleges, business districts, restaurants, and golf courses, not to mention the many historic tourist sites in Boston, Lexington, Concord, Quincy, and Plymouth. Ask your hosts to suggest activities; Leo enjoys woodworking and deep-sea fishing, while Susan likes sightseeing, walking, and swimming.

1810 House Bed & Breakfast ✪
147 OLD OAKEN BUCKET ROAD, NORWELL, MASSACHUSETTS 02061
tuttle 1810@aol.com

Tel: **(617) 659-1810**
Best Time to Call: **8 AM–9 PM**
Hosts: **Susanne and Harold Tuttle**
Location: **20 mi. S of Boston**
No. of Rooms: **3**
No. of Private Baths: **2**
Max. No. Sharing Bath: **4**

Double/pb: **$75–$85**
Open: **All year**
Breakfast: **Full**
Pets: **No**
Children: **Welcome, over 6**
Smoking: **No**
Social Drinking: **No**

The 1810 House is located in Norwell, a beautiful historic town halfway between Boston and Plymouth. The antique half-Cape boasts wide pine floors, stenciled walls, beamed ceilings, three working fireplaces, plus oriental rugs and lovely antiques. Harold is a woodworker who did extensive restoration in the house, while Susanne is a seamstress who created the custom window treatments. A tour of the area in their 1915 Model T depot hack adds to the feeling of a bygone era and is part of the fun of staying at the 1810 House.

The Allen House
18 ALLEN PLACE, SCITUATE, MASSACHUSETTS 02066

Tel: **(617) 545-8221**
Best Time to Call: **Mornings; evenings**
Hosts: **Christine and Iain Gilmour**
Location: **32 mi. SE of Boston**

No. of Rooms: **6**
No. of Private Baths: **6**
Double/pb: **$69–$149**
Open: **All year**

Breakfast: **Full**
Pets: **No**
Children: **Welcome, over 12**

Smoking: **No**
Social Drinking: **Permitted**
Airport/Station Pickup: **Yes**

With views of the village center, this white gabled Victorian overlooks the yacht harbor. When the Gilmours came to the United States in 1976, they brought along the lovely furniture of their native Great Britain. English antiques fill the house. They also imported British rituals: tea is a frequent celebration. For breakfast, Christine, a professional caterer, offers standards such as waffles and pancakes, as well as gourmet treats. The Allen House is distinguished by good music and good food. Iain, an accomplished musician, cheerfully shares the large library of classical music.

Marshall House ✪
11 EASTERN AVENUE, SWAMPSCOTT, MASSACHUSETTS 01907

Tel: **(617) 595-6544**
Hosts: **Pat and Al Marshall**
Location: **10 mi. N of Boston**
No. of Rooms: **3**
Max. No. Sharing Bath: **4**
Double/sb: **$75–$85**
Single/sb: **$65–$75**
Open: **All year**
Reduced Rates: **10% seniors**

Breakfast: **Continental**
Credit Cards: **AMEX, MC, VISA**
Pets: **No**
Children: **Welcome, over 6**
Smoking: **No**
Social Drinking: **Permitted**
Minimum stay: **2 nights, weekends**
Airport/Station Pickup: **Yes**

Marshall House, built circa 1900, is located just a short walk from the beaches of the North Shore. The many porches of this spacious home offer salty breezes and an ocean view. Inside, the rooms are decorated with country furnishings, some cherished antiques, and accents of wood and stained glass. The bedrooms have modern amenities such as color televisions and refrigerators. Guests are welcome to relax in the common room and warm up beside the wood stove. This B&B is located ten miles from Logan International Airport. Pat and Al will gladly direct you to nearby restaurants, historic seacoast villages, and popular bicycle touring routes.

Webb-Bigelow House
863 BOSTON POST ROAD, WESTON, MASSACHUSETTS 02193

Tel: **(617) 899-2444**
Hosts: **Mr. and Mrs. Robert C. Webb**
Location: **4 mi. from Rte. 90, Exit 15**
No. of Rooms: **3**
No. of Private Baths: **2**
Max. No. Sharing Bath: **1**
Double/pb: **$95**
Single/pb: **$90**

Double/sb: **$90**
Open: **Apr.–Nov. 30**
Breakfast: **Full**
Pets: **No**
Children: **Welcome, over 10**
Smoking: **Restricted**
Social Drinking: **Permitted**
Minimum Stay: **2 nights Sept.–Oct.**

Experience old New England in this historic 1827 house built by Alphaeus Bigelow Jr. The Webbs added to its charm, surrounding it with lawns and flowers. Today it sits on three acres in Weston's National Registered Historic District and remains one of the finest preserved residences on the Post Road. Explore a wooded trail, relax by the pool, admire the fall foliage, or just read by a cozy fire. Hearty breakfasts, featuring fruit from the Webbs' orchards, are served in the formal dining room or on the pool deck. This B&B is twenty minutes from Radcliffe, Harvard, Wellesley, MIT, Boston University, and Boston College. Area attractions include Longfellow's Wayside Inn, Faneuil Hall Market Place, Plymouth, Salem, and Concord.

CAPE COD/MARTHA'S VINEYARD

Bed & Breakfast Cape Cod ✪
P.O. BOX 341, WEST HYANNISPORT, MASSACHUSETTS 02672-0341
http://www.oneweb.com/bbcc

Tel: **(508) 775-2772; fax: (508) 775-2884; (800) 686-5252 for reservations**
Best Time to Call: **8:30 AM–6 PM**
Coordinator: **Clark Diehl**
States/Regions Covered: **Cape Cod, Martha's Vineyard, Nantucket**

Descriptive Directory: **Free**
Rates (Single/Double):
Modest: **$42 / $65**
Average: **$60 / $75**
Luxury: **$90 / $195**
Credit Cards: **AMEX, DISC, MC, VISA**
Minimum Stay: **2 nights in season**

It's a little over an hour's drive from Boston to the charm, history, and relaxation of Cape Cod and the islands. Choose from more than 100 of Clark's inspected restored sea captains' houses, host homes, or small inns. Enjoy the warm-water beaches on Nantucket Sound, golf, biking, and other recreational activities. Don't miss the discount shopping. Your hosts can direct you to things to do, including whale watches, antiquing, seafood restaurants, and evening entertainment at a wonderful summer theater. There is a $10 surcharge for one-night stays, subject to availability. Write, call, fax, or look for brochure information and pictures on Bed & Breakfast Cape Cod's Internet home page.

Orleans Bed & Breakfast Associates ✪

P.O. BOX 1312, ORLEANS, MASSACHUSETTS 02653
orleansbnb@capecod.net; http://www.capecod.net/bb

Tel: **(508) 255-3824; (800) 541-6226;**
  fax: (508) 240-0599
Best Time to Call: **8 AM–8 PM**
Coordinators: **Gilles and Susanne**
  Thibault
States/Regions Covered: **Cape**
  Cod—Brewster, Chatham, Eastham,
  Orleans, Truro, Wellfleet

Descriptive Directory: **Free**
Rates: **$70–$135**
Credit Cards: **AMEX, DISC, MC, VISA**
Minimum Stay: **2 nights**

Gilles and Susanne offer a variety of accommodations with a diversity of styles, and guests may choose from historic to contemporary houses, all compatible with the atmosphere of the Cape. The fine reputation this service enjoys is largely due to the attitude of the host to the guest. Each host is aware that a guest's experience reflects on the association as a whole. We applaud the professionalism of this organization! A $10 booking fee is charged per reservation.

Blowin' a Gale ✪

219 OLD HARBOR ROAD, ROUTE 28, CHATHAM,
MASSACHUSETTS 02633

Tel: **(508) 945-9716**
Best Time to Call: **After 10 AM**
Hosts: **Nancy and Bob Petrus**
Location: **90 mi. SE of Boston**
No. of Rooms: **2**
Max. No. Sharing Bath: **4**
Double/sb: **$85**
Single/sb: **$75**
Open: **June 15–Oct. 15**

Reduced Rates: **Available**
Breakfast: **Continental, plus**
Credit Cards: **MC, VISA**
Pets: **No**
Children: **Welcome, over 12**
Smoking: **No**
Social Drinking: **Permitted**
Minimum Stay: **2 nights**
Airport/Station Pickup: **Yes, prearranged**

If you are looking for restful, old-fashioned accommodations in a small homey atmosphere, Bob and Nancy invite you to this 1888 historic Victorian home. Blowin' a Gale is a charming guesthouse located one half-mile north of the downtown rotary on Route 28 and within walking distance of beaches, restaurants, and shops. Breakfast is served in the dining area or outside on the deck. A sitting area is provided for guests to enjoy TV. A phone and refrigerator are provided.

The Acworth Inn ✪
**4352 MAIN STREET, P.O. BOX 256, CUMMAQUID,
MASSACHUSETTS 02637**

Tel: **(800) 362-6363; (508) 362-3330**
Best Time to Call: **8 AM–10 PM**
Hosts: **Cheryl and Jack Ferrell**
Location: **5 mi. N of Hyannis**
No. of Rooms: **6**
No. of Private Baths: **6**
Double/pb: **$75–$95**
Open: **All year**

Reduced Rates: **Nov.–Apr.**
Credit Cards: **AMEX, MC, VISA**
Pets: **No**
Children: **Welcome, over 12**
Smoking: **No**
Social Drinking: **Permitted**
Minimum Stay: **2 nights holidays**

Acworth Inn sits quietly alongside the Old Kings Highway that winds through the historic, unspoiled north side of Cape Cod. Located near the town of Barnstable, Acworth Inn offers guests an opportunity to experience the gracious lifestyle of a bygone era. The Inn, circa 1860, is especially noted for the many hand-painted furnishings that decorate each of the bright, airy guest rooms. From its central location, day trips to Martha's Vineyard, Nantucket, and all points on the Cape are easily accomplished.

Isaiah Hall B&B Inn ✪
152 WHIG STREET, P.O. BOX 1007, DENNIS, MASSACHUSETTS 02638

Tel: **(508) 385-9928; (800) 736-0160**
Best Time to Call: **8 AM–10 PM**
Host: **Marie Brophy**
Location: **7 mi. E of Hyannis**
No. of Rooms: **10**
No. of Private Baths: **10**
Double/pb: **$85–$119**
Single/pb: **$75–$109**

Suite: **$142–$150**
Open: **Apr. 15–mid-Oct.**
Breakfast: **Continental, plus**
Credit Cards: **AMEX, MC, VISA**
Pets: **No**
Children: **Welcome, over 7**
Smoking: **No**
Social Drinking: **Permitted**

This Cape Cod farmhouse built in 1857 offers casual country living on the quiet, historic northside. The house is decorated in true New England style with quilts, antiques, and oriental rugs. Four rooms have balconies and one has a fireplace. Within walking distance are the beach, good restaurants, the Cape Playhouse, and countless antique and craft shops. It is also close to freshwater swimming, bike paths, and golf. All guest rooms have air-conditioning.

The Parsonage Inn
**202 MAIN STREET, P.O. BOX 1501, EAST ORLEANS,
MASSACHUSETTS 02643**

Tel: **(508) 255-8217**
Best Time to Call: **10 AM–9 PM**
Hosts: **Ian and Elizabeth Browne**

Location: **90 mi. SE of Boston**
No. of Rooms: **8**
No. of Private Baths: **8**

Double/pb: **$85–$105**
Suites: **$115**
Open: **All year**
Reduced Rates: **Oct.–May**
Breakfast: **Full**

Credit Cards: **AMEX, MC, VISA**
Pets: **No**
Children: **Welcome, over 6**
Smoking: **No**
Social Drinking: **Permitted**

This quiet, romantic Inn is housed in a charming 18th-century parsonage just one and a half miles from the sparkling waters at Nauset Beach. Bike trails, lakes, galleries, fine stores, and restaurants are all nearby. Delicious breakfasts are served in the morning; in the evening, your hosts set out complimentary hors d'oeuvres in the parlor. And fresh floral arrangements add a special touch to the comfortable, tastefully decorated rooms.

Captain Tom Lawrence House—1861 ✪
75 LOCUST STREET, FALMOUTH, MASSACHUSETTS 02540

Tel: **(508) 540-1445; (800) 266-8139;**
  fax: (508) 457-1790
Best Time to Call: **8 AM–noon**
Host: **Barbara Sabo**
Location: **67 mi. S of Boston**
No. of Rooms: **6**
No. of Private Baths: **6**
Double/pb: **$85–$145**
Open: **All year**

Reduced Rates: **Off-season**
Breakfast: **Full**
Credit Cards: **MC, VISA**
Pets: **No**
Children: **Welcome, over 11**
Smoking: **No**
Social Drinking: **Permitted**
Foreign Languages: **German**

Captain Lawrence was a successful whaler in the 1800s. When he retired from the sea, he built himself a town residence on Locust Street. Today, the house remains much as he left it, including the original hardwood floors, circular stairwell, high ceilings, and antique furnishings; central air-conditioning has been added. In the morning, Barbara serves a hearty breakfast of fruit and creative entrees. Her Black Forest bread and Belgian waffles are truly special. She grinds her own flour from organically grown grain. She will gladly help you get around town— it's half a mile to the beach, a short walk to downtown Falmouth, and four miles to Woods Hole Seaport.

Hewins House Bed & Breakfast ✪
20 HEWINS STREET, FALMOUTH, MASSACHUSETTS 02540

Tel: **(508) 457-4363; (800) 555-4366**
Best Time to Call: **9 AM–5 PM**
Host: **Virginia Price**
Location: **In Falmouth Village of Cape
  Cod**
No. of Rooms: **3**
No. of Private Baths: **3**
Double/pb: **$85–$90**
Single/pb: **$75–$85**
Open: **All year**

Reduced Rates: **10% after 4 nights or
  off-season**
Breakfast: **Full**
Pets: **No**
Children: **Welcome**
Smoking: **No**
Social Drinking: **Permitted**
Minimum Stay: **2 nights**
Station Pickup: **Yes**

Elegant accommodations, 19th-century charm, and warm hospitality await you at this gracious old Federal home on the historic Village Green. Queen-size beds, cotton sheets, feather pillows, and firm mattresses assure a good night's sleep. Feel free to play the Steinway or relax with a book in the living room. Breakfast is served in the elegant Federal dining room. Enjoy the attractions of Falmouth or use Hewins House as a base from which to explore the Cape as well as the surrounding area.

Palmer House Inn

81 PALMER AVENUE, FALMOUTH, MASSACHUSETTS 02540

Tel: **(508) 548-1230; (800) 472-2632;**
   fax: (508) 540-1878
Best Time to Call: **10 AM–10 PM**
Hosts: **Ken and Joanne Baker**
Location: **1 block from Rte. 28**
No. of Rooms: **13**
No. of Private Baths: **13**
Double/pb: **$88–$139**
Single/pb: **$78–$129**
Suite: **$165–$185**

Open: **All year**
Reduced Rates: **Nov.–Apr.**
Breakfast: **Full**
Credit Cards: **AMEX, DC, DISC, MC,**
   VISA
Pets: **No**
Children: **Welcome, over 10**
Smoking: **No**
Social Drinking: **Permitted**
Airport/Station Pickup: **Yes**

Warmth and charm are evident in this turn-of-the-century Victorian home, with its stained glass windows, soft warm wood, antiques, and collectibles. Centrally located within the Historic District, it is convenient to recreational diversions, miles of sandy beaches, ferries, and Woods Hole. Guests rave about breakfast entrees such as pain perdu with orange cream and Vermont maple syrup, Belgian waffles with honey butter, or Finnish pancakes and strawberry soup, served in the dining room on fine linen, china, and crystal. Return from your afternoon activities and enjoy a glass of lemonade in a rocker on the front porch. Spend your after-dinner hours relaxing before the fireplace or sampling theater offerings close by. Three of the guest rooms have whirlpool tubs.

Dunscroft-by-the-Sea ✪
24 PILGRIM ROAD, HARWICH PORT, MASSACHUSETTS 02646

Tel: (508) 432-0810; (800) 432-4345
Hosts: Alyce and Wally Cunningham
Location: 10 mi. E of Hyannis
No. of Rooms: 10
No. of Private Baths: 10
Double/pb: $95–$165
Honeymoon Cottage: $155–$195

Open: All year
Breakfast: Full
Credit Cards: AMEX, MC, VISA
Pets: No
Children: Welcome, over 14
Smoking: No
Social Drinking: Permitted

With its breathtaking, private mile-long beach, this romantic 14-room Colonial inn, its cedar shingles weathered a traditional waterfront gray, offers everything you'd expect from a Cape Cod bed & breakfast. The many amenities include flower gardens, spacious grounds, an enclosed sunporch, a piano in the living room, library, a king suite with a fireplace, and robes for lounging or for the beach. Located within easy walking distance are Harwich Port's shops, galleries, and restaurants. You'll awaken to the aroma of freshly ground coffee as Alyce prepares a generous breakfast.

1875 House ✪
36 SEVENTH STREET, NEW BEDFORD, MASSACHUSETTS 02740

Tel: (508) 997-6433
Best Time to Call: After 7 PM
Hosts: Cynthia Poyant and
    Steven Saint-Aubin
Location: 55 mi. S of Boston
No. of Rooms: 3
No. of Private Baths: 3
Double/pb: $55–$70
Single/pb: $35–$45

Open: All year
Reduced Rates: 10% family, seniors
Breakfast: Continental
Pets: Sometimes
Children: Welcome
Smoking: Permitted
Social Drinking: Permitted
Airport/Station Pickup: Yes

Located in the historic district, this 1875 Victorian home is within walking distance of downtown. Some of the local attractions include the Whaling Museum, art museum, Rotch Jones Duff Museum, and beaches. Cape Cod and Newport, R.I., are only 30 minutes away. The home has undergone thoughtful restoration, reflected in the tasteful decor throughout. Family photographs, books, and curio pieces are displayed in the sitting and dining rooms. Your hosts enjoy active exercise and sports. Cynthia is a social worker and Steven is an anesthetist. They welcome you to relax with them.

The Beach Rose ✪

COLUMBIAN AVENUE, BOX 2352, OAK BLUFFS,
MASSACHUSETTS 02557

Tel: **(508) 693-6135**	Breakfast: **Continental, plus**
Best Time to Call: **9 AM–9 PM**	Pets: **No**
Hosts: **Gloria and Russ Everett**	Children: **Welcome, over 5**
Location: **70 mi. SE of Boston**	Smoking: **No**
No. of Rooms: **3**	Social Drinking: **Permitted**
Max. No. Sharing Bath: **4**	Minimum Stay: **3 nights holiday**
Double/sb: **$60–$100**	**weekends; 2 nights summer**
Single/sb: **$60**	**weekends**
Open: **May–Oct.**	Airport/Ferry Pickup: **Yes**
Reduced Rates: **Off-season**	

The Beach Rose is named for the colorful island plant, *Rosa rugosa*, whose pink flowers and bright red rose hips punctuate the island dunes. This charming home, nestled in an oak and pine woodland on Martha's Vineyard, is decorated in country antique style. Greet the morning with a breakfast of fresh fruit, a delicious entree du jour, homemade muffins and jams, and freshly brewed beverages. Your hosts provide warm hospitality and personal attention. Guests will want to see the gingerbread cottages of the Methodist camp-meeting grounds, the Gay Head cliffs, and the historic whaling homes of Edgartown. The Vineyard has a myriad sightseeing and other activities to offer visitors: biking, sailing, nature trails, fishing, picturesque beaches, and much more.

Academy Place Bed & Breakfast ✪

8 ACADEMY PLACE, P.O. BOX 1407, ORLEANS,
MASSACHUSETTS 02653

Tel: **(508) 255-3181**	Reduced Rates: **Available**
Hosts: **Sandy and Charles Terrell**	Breakfast: **Continental**
Location: **25 mi. E of Hyannis**	Credit Cards: **MC, VISA**
No. of Rooms: **5**	Pets: **No**
No. of Private Baths: **3**	Children: **Welcome, over 6**
Max. No. Sharing Bath: **4**	Minimum stay: **2 nights all holidays and**
Double/pb: **$80–$90**	**weekends July–Aug.**
Double/sb: **$70**	Smoking: **No**
Open: **Memorial Day–Columbus Day**	Station Pickup: **Yes**

A quaint Cape Cod home on the village green with comfortable beds awaits you. This 1752 house with many antique charms and period antiques is on the edge of Orleans's shopping district. Many fine retail stores and restaurants are a short walk away. For swimming, sunbathing, and fishing, the Atlantic Ocean and Cape Cod Bay beaches are within 2¹/₂ miles. The Cape Cod National Seashore is 10 minutes by car or can be reached by a paved bike path, which is ¹/₄ mile from the house. A Continental breakfast of homemade hot tasty muffins and breads with chilled juices and fresh fruits, freshly brewed coffee, teas, or hot chocolate is served daily.

Morgan's Way Bed and Breakfast ✪
NINE MORGAN'S WAY, ORLEANS, CAPE COD, MASSACHUSETTS 02653
morgnway@capecod.net

Tel: **(508) 255-0831**	Open: **All year**
Best Time to Call: **11:30 AM–9 PM**	Reduced Rates: **Off season**
Hosts: **Page McMahan and Will Joy**	Breakfast: **Full**
Location: **90 mi. SE of Boston**	Pets: **No**
No. of Rooms: **1**	Children: **Welcome, over 12**
No. of Private Baths: **1**	Smoking: **No**
Double/pb: **$85**	Social Drinking: **Permitted**
Single/pb: **$85**	Minimum Stay: **2 nights; 1 week for**
Guest Cottage: **$700 weekly; sleeps 3**	**cottage**

This dramatic contemporary home, overlooking five acres of gardens and wooded land, offers guests a peaceful, romantic getaway. Soaring cathedral ceilings, oak beams, arched windows with panoramic views, oriental carpets, and porcelains give a feeling of luxury throughout. Specially appointed bedrooms have queen-size beds; those desiring extra privacy may prefer to stay in the poolside guest cottage. Relax on the massive, flower-filled deck or lounge by the large heated pool after a refreshing swim. Page's memorable breakfasts include creative fruit courses, delicious entrees, and homemade breads; she always has low-fat and low-cholesterol alternatives on hand. Morgan's Way is located just one mile from Orleans center and two miles from Nauset Beach; golf courses, lakes, bike trails, galleries, shops, and restaurants are all nearby. Page, an avid gardener, has a background in health administration, and Will is a civil engineer; they love sharing their property and Cape Cod, and will treat you as their special houseguest. For those of you who do not mind a higher rate, 1 room is available.

Foxglove Cottage Bed & Breakfast ✪
101 SANDWICH ROAD, PLYMOUTH, MASSACHUSETTS 02360

Tel: **(800) 479-4746; (508) 747-6576;**
 fax: **(508) 747-7622**
Hosts: **Charles and Michael Mary Cowan**
Location: **40 mi. S of Boston**
No. of Rooms: **3**
No. of Private Baths: **3**
Double/pb: **$80**
Single/pb: **$70**
Open: **All year**

Reduced Rates: **10% Jan.–Mar.**
Breakfast: **Full**
Pets: **No**
Children: **Welcome, over 12**
Smoking: **No**
Social Drinking: **Permitted**
Minimum Stay: **2 nights weekends June–Oct.**
Station Pickup: **Yes**

Foxglove Cottage is a charming restored Cape-style home, located in an unspoiled historic area in Plymouth. Guest rooms are tastefully furnished in English and American antiques, with original working fireplaces, woodwork, wide pine board floors and private baths. There is a common room where guests can relax, watch TV, read, or take advantage of the video library. Rolling fields, breakfast on the deck, and a lovely country setting make for a touch of tranquility. This B&B is within five minutes of downtown Plymouth, the Plimoth Plantation, beaches, historical houses and sites, major highways to Boston and Cape Cod, and the islands. It's also conveniently located for day trips to Nantucket and Martha's Vineyard. Daily whale-watching trips sail from Plymouth Harbor. Charles, an executive in the chemical industry, has interests in travel and general aviation, and Michael, a nurse, enjoys interior design and maintains a small antique shop in the house.

The Captain Ezra Nye House ✪
152 MAIN STREET, SANDWICH, MASSACHUSETTS 02563

Tel: **(800) 388-2278; fax: (508) 833-2897**
Best Time to Call: **10 AM–6 PM**
Hosts: **Elaine and Harry Dickson**
Location: **60 mi. SE of Boston**
No. of Rooms: **6**

No. of Private Baths: **6**
Double/pb: **$85–$110**
Single/pb: **$75–$100**
Suites: **$100–$110**
Open: **All year**
Reduced Rates: **Off season**

Breakfast: **Full**
Credit Cards: **AMEX, DISC, MC, VISA**
Pets: **No**
Children: **Welcome, over 6**

Smoking: **No**
Social Drinking: **Permitted**
Airport/Station Pickup: **Yes**
Foreign Languages: **Spanish**

The Captain Ezra Nye House is a stately 1829 Federal home built by a seafarer noted for his record-breaking North Atlantic crossings and daring ocean rescues. The house sits in the heart of Sandwich, the oldest town on Cape Cod, and is within walking distance of museums, shops, and fine restaurants. Guests rooms are tastefully decorated in soft pastel tones, antiques, and an eclectic art collection. Hearty homemade breakfasts are served in the dining room. A cozy den with fireplace and parlor with piano complete the common areas.

Dillingham House ✪
71 MAIN STREET, SANDWICH, MASSACHUSETTS 02563

Tel: **(508) 833-0065**
Best Time to Call: **6–8 PM**
Host: **Kathleen Kenney**
Location: **60 mi. S of Boston**
No. of Rooms: **3**
No. of Private Baths: **3**
Double/pb: **$85**
Open: **All year**

Reduced Rates: **$10 less Nov.–Mar.**
Breakfast: **Continental**
Pets: **Sometimes**
Children: **Welcome**
Smoking: **Permitted**
Social Drinking: **Permitted**
Minimum Stay: **2 nights off-season**

Dillingham House is named for its first owner, who helped to found Sandwich, Cape Cod's oldest town. The house has many of the hallmarks of 17th-century construction, such as wide pine floors, exposed beams and rafters, and cozy brick hearths. Kathy is a Cape native and loves to discuss local lore. A Continental breakfast of juice, fresh fruit, muffins, and coffee or tea will fortify you for your excursions, whether they occur on land or on sea.

Captain Nickerson Inn ✪
333 MAIN STREET, SOUTH DENNIS, MASSACHUSETTS 02660

Tel: **(508) 398-5966**
Best Time to Call: **10 AM–1 PM Mon.–Fri.**
Hosts: **Pat and Dave York**
Location: **90 mi. SE of Boston**
No. of Rooms: **5**
No. of Private Baths: **3**
Max. No. Sharing Bath: **4**
Double/pb: **$80–$90**
Single/pb: **$75–$85**
Double/sb: **$60–$75**
Single/sb: **$55–$65**

Open: **All year**
Reduced Rates: **Off season 15–20%, 10% after fifth night**
Breakfast: **Full**
Credit Cards: **DISC, MC, VISA**
Pets: **No**
Children: **Welcome**
Smoking: **No**
Social Drinking: **Permitted**
Minimum Stay: **2 nights July–Aug., 3 nights July fourth weekend**

This delightful sea captain's home was built in 1828 and changed to its present Queen Anne style in 1879. Guest rooms are decorated with period four-poster or white iron queen beds and oriental or handwoven rugs. Relax in the fireplaced living room complete with a TV and VCR, a small selection of video movies, and popular board games. The Inn is situated on a bike path and bicycles are available for a small fee. Breakfast is served in the dining room, which has a fireplace and stained glass windows. Area attractions include championship public golf courses, world-class beaches, paddleboats, horseback riding, museums, fishing, crafts and antique shops, and a local church which has the oldest working pipe organ in the country. Cape Cod's 20-plus-mile bike trail is only a half mile away.

Nancy's Auberge ❂
98 MAIN STREET, P.O. BOX 4433, VINEYARD HAVEN, MARTHA'S VINEYARD, MASSACHUSETTS 02568

Tel: **(508) 693-4434**
Best Time to Call: **Evenings**
Host: **Nancy Hurd**
Location: **7 mi. SE of Woods Hole**
No. of Rooms: **3**
No. of Private Baths: **1**
Max. No. Sharing Bath: **4**
Double/pb: **$108**
Double/sb: **$88–$98**
Open: **All year**

Reduced Rates: **Available**
Breakfast: **Continental**
Credit Cards: **MC, VISA**
Pets: **No**
Children: **Welcome**
Smoking: **No**
Social Drinking: **Permitted**
Minimum Stay: **Summer season; holiday weekends**

Nancy's Auberge is a 150-year-old island home with a harbor view, convenient location, and three fireplaces. Comfortable and inviting whatever the season, the antique-filled B&B offers as much privacy as you seek. One guest remarked, "It's so picturesque. It's like living on a postcard." Since it's just a block and a half from the ferry, a car is not necessary. However, off-street parking is available. Within a few blocks are some of the island's finest restaurants, the Vineyard Playhouse, the Katherine Cornell Theatre, artisans' shops, windsurfing, sailing, and tennis. Nearby are excellent golf courses, horseback riding, and world-famous beaches. The town beach is a block away. Nancy's passions are travel, music, sports, and cooking.

The 1720 House
130 MAINE STREET, VINEYARD HAVEN, MASSACHUSETTS 02568

Tel: **(508) 693-6407**
Best Time to Call: **7:30 AM–9 PM**
Host: **Abby Hirsch**
No. of Rooms: **6**
No. of Private Baths: **3**
Max. No. Sharing Bath: **4**
Double/pb: **$85–$150**
Single/pb: **$85–$135**
Double/pb: **$85–$145**
Suites: **$175**
Open: **All year**
Reduced Rates: **Available**

Breakfast: **Continental**
Credit Cards: **MC, VISA**
Pets: **No**
Children: **Welcome, over 6**
Smoking: **Restricted**
Social Drinking: **Permitted**
Minimum Stay: **3 nights holiday weekends**
Airport Pickup: **Yes**
Foreign Languages: **Dutch, French, German**

The 1720 House is located one and a half blocks from the beach, three blocks from the ferry, and three blocks from the town of Vineyard Haven, which is filled with quaint stores, restaurants, and a movie house. Rooms are tastefully decorated in Colonial style and offer the comfort of days gone by. Outside, the house is surrounded by land-scaped flower gardens allowing for peaceful and private afternoons. Activities include deep-sea fishing, horseback riding, boating, biking, swimming, theater, and arts. Breakfast specialties include fresh-baked muffins, cakes, and breads. Abby is a writer and TV producer.

Mulberry Bed and Breakfast ✪
257 HIGH STREET, WAREHAM, MASSACHUSETTS 02571

Tel: **(508) 295-0684**
Best Time to Call: **Before 9 AM, after 4 PM**
Host: **Frances Murphy**
Location: **52 mi. S of Boston**
No. of Rooms: **3**
Max. No. Sharing Bath: **4**
Double/pb: **$60–$65**
Double/sb: **$50–$55**

Open: **All year**
Reduced Rates: **15% weekly**
Breakfast: **Full**
Pets: **No**
Children: **Welcome, over 10**
Smoking: **No**
Social Drinking: **Permitted**
Airport/Station Pickup: **Yes**

Frances Murphy welcomes you to her vintage Cape Cod home, built in 1847. The house is one and a half stories and is painted white with red shutters. It is named for the mulberry tree in the yard that attracts many birds and provides shade from the summer sun. Frances has created a home-away-from-home atmosphere, where guests can relax in a small living room with a piano, or join her in a larger living-dining area with fireplace. Spend the night in an Early American–style bedroom and have breakfast on the spacious private deck. Home-baked breads and muffins, casseroles, and fresh fruit are served with jams and jellies made from Frances's fruit trees. In the afternoon, snacks and cool drinks are served. Mulberry Bed and Breakfast is located in the historic part of town, ten minutes from the beach.

The Marlborough ✪

320 WOODS HOLE ROAD, FALMOUTH, WOODS HOLE, MASSACHUSETTS 02543

Tel: **(508) 548-6218**
Best Time to Call: **10 AM–9 PM**
Host: **Al Hammond**
Location: **2¹/₂ mi. from Rte. 28**
No. of Rooms: **6**
No. of Private Baths: **6**
Double/pb: **$85–$125**
Single/pb: **$80–$120**

Open: **All year**
Breakfast: **Full**
Credit Cards: **AMEX, MC, VISA**
Pets: **No**
Children: **Welcome, over 2**
Smoking: **No**
Social Drinking: **Permitted**

This faithful reproduction of a full Cape house is beautifully decorated with antiques, collectibles, fabric wallcoverings, and matching bed linens. It is situated on a shaded half-acre with a paddle tennis court, swimming pool, and hammock. It's 1 mile to a private beach. Ferries to Martha's Vineyard are a mile away. Al serves a full gourmet breakfast year round.

One Centre Street Inn ✪

ONE CENTRE STREET, YARMOUTHPORT, MASSACHUSETTS 02675

Tel: **(888) 407-1653; (508) 362-8910**
Best Time to Call: **10 AM–8 PM**
Host: **Karen Iannello**
No. of Rooms: **6**
No. of Private Baths: **4**
Max. No. Sharing Bath: **4**
Double/pb: **$85–$95**
Double/sb: **$75**
Suites: **$110**
Open: **All year**

Reduced Rates: **10% seniors,**
   $10 Oct. 15–May 15
Breakfast: **Full**
Credit Cards: **MC, VISA**
Pets: **No**
Children: **Welcome, over 8**
Smoking: **No**
Social Drinking: **Permitted**
Minimum Stay: **2 nights, weekends in**
   summer

This 1824 parsonage offers understated elegance on the historic north side of Cape Cod. The Inn's walls are adorned with original prints and paintings by a local artist. Enjoy the piano in the parlor or take a ride to the beach on a bicycle provided by the Inn. A gourmet breakfast is served daily, including fruit, scones, muffins, yogurt, juice, freshly ground coffee, and such entrees as orange French toast with strawberry Grand Marnier sauce, the house specialty.

CENTRAL/WESTERN/SOUTHERN MASSACHUSETTS

Folkstone Bed & Breakfast Reservation Service ✪
51 SEARS ROAD, SOUTHBORO, MASSACHUSETTS 01772

Tel: **(800) 762-2751; (508) 480-0380**
Best Time to Call: **9 AM–5 PM,
7–9 PM**
Coordinator: **Abigail Miller**
States/Regions Covered: **Auburn, Barre,
Concord, Groton, Lancaster, Palmer,
Southboro, Stowe, Sturbridge,
Thompson, Worcester**

Descriptive Directory: **Free**
Rates (Single/Double):
Modest: **$55–$60**
Average: **$70–$75**
Luxury: **$90 / $95–$120**
Credit Cards: **AMEX, MC, VISA**

Abigail's service offers comfortable relaxed lodging in a wide variety of host homes, including convenient in-town locations and country hideaways throughout central Massachusetts and northeast Connecticut. Experience the wealth of cultural entertainment and recreational opportunities this area has to offer.

Allen House Victorian Inn ✪
599 MAIN STREET, AMHERST, MASSACHUSETTS 01002

Tel: **(413) 253-5000**
Hosts: **Alan and Ann Zieminski**
Location: **5 mi. from Rte. 91, Exit 19**
No. of Rooms: **7**

No. of Private Baths: **7**
Double/pb: **$55–$125**
Single/pb: **$45–$105**
Open: **All year**

Breakfast: **Full**
Pets: **No**
Children: **Welcome, over 7**
Smoking: **No**

Social Drinking: **Permitted**
Minimum Stay: **College and fall foliage weekends**

This 1886 Queen Anne Stick–style Victorian features period antiques, decor, and art wallcoverings by designers from the Aesthetic movement, which emphasized art in interior decoration; Charles Eastlake, Walter Crane, and William Morris are represented. Allen House Victorian Inn is located on three scenic acres in the heart of Amherst, within walking distance of Emily Dickinson House, Amherst College, the University of Massachusetts, and innumerable galleries, museums, theaters, shops, and restaurants. Free busing is available throughout the five-college area. A full formal breakfast is served.

Captain Samuel Eddy House ✪
609 OXFORD STREET SOUTH, AUBURN, MASSACHUSETTS 01501

Tel: **(508) 832-7282**
Best Time to Call: **10 AM–9 PM**
Hosts: **Diedre and Mike Meddaugh**
Location: **5 mi. S of Worcester**
No. of Rooms: **5**
No. of Private Baths: **5**
Double/pb: **$70**
Single/pb: **$55**

Suites: **$90–$120; sleeps 2–5**
Open: **All year**
Reduced Rates: **Available**
Breakfast: **Full**
Pets: **No**
Children: **Welcome, over 5**
Smoking: **No**
Social Drinking: **Permitted**

The Captain Samuel Eddy House, circa 1765, is a typical New England design. The center chimney Colonial home has three fireplaces, one in each parlor, and a Sturbridge fireplace in the keeping room—which now serves as a dining room. The house is decorated in period style with antiques, four-poster beds, Windsor and wing-back chairs, beautiful draperies, original wide-board floors, and hand stenciled walls. The sunroom, circa 1980, lets guests enjoy a view of the woods, garden, and Eddy Pond. The inn is conveniently located near the Mass Pike, Exit 10, south of Worcester and east of Sturbridge.

1797 House ✪
UPPER STREET, BUCKLAND, MASSACHUSETTS 01338

Tel: **(413) 625-2975**
Best Time to Call: **5 PM–9 PM**
Host: **Janet Turley**
Location: **13 mi. from Rte. 91, Exit 26**
No. of Rooms: **3**
No. of Private Baths: **3**
Double/pb: **$65–$80**

Single/pb: **$58**
Open: **Jan. 2–Oct. 31**
Breakfast: **Full**
Pets: **No**
Children: **No**
Smoking: **No**
Social Drinking: **Permitted**

This white, center-hall Colonial, circa 1797, has a lovely screened-in porch for summer enjoyment and four fireplaces and down quilts for cozy winter pleasure. Prestigious Deerfield Academy, Old Deerfield, Sturbridge Village, and the historic sights of Pioneer Valley are all close by. The University of Massachusetts, Smith, Amherst, and Williams are convenient to Janet's home. Sensational breakfast treats include stuffed croissants, French toast, and special casseroles, along with fresh fruit and breakfast meats.

The Seven Hearths Bed & Breakfast ✪

412 MAIN ROAD, ROUTE 143, CHESTERFIELD,
MASSACHUSETTS 01012
d7hearths@aol.com

Tel: **(413) 296-4312; fax: (413) 296-4599**
Best Time to Call: **Until 11 PM**
Hosts: **Doc and Denise LeDuc**
Location: **12 mi. W of Northampton**
No. of Rooms: **3**
No. of Private Baths: **1**
Max. No. Sharing Bath: **4**
Double/pb: **$75**
Single/pb: **$70**
Double/sb: **$65**

Single/sb: **$60**
Open: **All year**
Reduced Rates: **Available**
Breakfast: **Full weekends, Continental. plus, weekdays**
Credit Cards: **DISC, MC, VISA**
Pets: **No**
Children: **Welcome, over 12**
Smoking: **No**
Social Drinking: **Permitted**
Minimum Stay: **2 nights weekends**

Simple country elegance is the theme at the Seven Hearths. This theme is carried out by the homelike atmosphere, country decor, and wide range of antiques. Sit by the fire to read, relax, listen to music, or just converse. Enjoy the simple pleasure of rocking in one of many rocking chairs, or bask in the private hot tub. Wake in the morning to the aroma of fresh-ground coffee and savor a breakfast you're sure not to forget.

Windfields Farm O
154 WINDSOR BUSH ROAD, CUMMINGTON, MASSACHUSETTS 01026

Tel: **(413) 684-3786**	Open: **May 1–Mar. 1**
Best Time to Call: **Before 9 PM**	Reduced Rates: **10% midweek**
Hosts: **Carolyn and Arnold Westwood**	Breakfast: **Full**
Location: **20 mi. E of Pittsfield**	Pets: **No**
No. of Rooms: **2**	Children: **Welcome, over 12**
Max. No. Sharing Bath: **4**	Smoking: **No**
Double/sb: **$70**	Social Drinking: **Permitted**
Single/sb: **$50**	Minimum Stay: **2 nights most weekends**

Since 1983, the Westwoods have been welcoming guests to their secluded 19th-century homestead in the rolling Berkshire countryside. The hundred-acre estate includes organic gardens, flower beds, wild blueberry fields, and a brook and a pond. Hiking and skiing trails, a state forest, and the Audubon Wildlife Sanctuary are within walking distance. Arnold, a retired Unitarian minister, built his own sugarhouse and greenhouse and doubles as publisher of a local monthly newspaper. Carolyn is an award-winning gardener. Both are active in community affairs and conservation, and, during the late winter mud season, they make maple syrup from their property's 500 taps.

Bullard Farm Bed & Breakfast O
89 ELM STREET, NORTH NEW SALEM, MASSACHUSETTS 01364

Tel: **(508) 544-6959**	Reduced Rates: **Available**
Host: **Janet Kraft**	Breakfast: **Full**
Location: **75 mi. W of Boston**	Credit Cards: **MC, VISA**
No. of Rooms: **4**	Pets: **Sometimes**
Max. No. Sharing Bath: **4**	Children: **Welcome, over 3**
Double/sb: **$75**	Smoking: **No**
Single/sb: **$60**	Social Drinking: **Permitted**
Suite: **$90, sleeps 4**	Airport/Station Pickup: **Yes**
Open: **All year**	

Just half an hour from Amherst and historic Deerfield, you'll find this 200-year-old restored Colonial home with all the trimmings, like six working fireplaces, exposed beams, and treasured family antiques. Allow plenty of time for surveying the 300-acre property, with its rhododendron gardens, cultivated blueberries, hiking and cross-country ski trails, old swimming hole, and 18th-century mill sites. The renovated barn with an upper-level dance floor serves as a conference center offering occasional nature programs, jazz concerts, and other events. Sleigh rides and hayrides are available upon request.

Five Bridge Farm B&B ✪
154 PINE STREET, REHOBOTH, MASSACHUSETTS 02769

Tel: **(508) 252-3190**	Reduced Rates: **$10 less Sun.–Thurs.,**
Hosts: **Ann and Harold Messenger**	**Jan.–Feb.; 10% seniors, families**
Location: **35 mi. S of Boston**	Breakfast: **Full**
No. of Rooms: **5**	Other Meals: **Available**
No. of Private Baths: **3**	Credit Cards: **AMEX, DC, DISC, MC,**
Max. No. Sharing Bath: **4**	**VISA**
Double/pb: **$75**	Pets: **Sometimes**
Single/pb: **$65**	Children: **Welcome**
Double/sb: **$55**	Smoking: **No**
Single/sb: **$50**	Social Drinking: **Permitted**
Suites: **$85, sleeps 5**	Minimum Stay: **2 nights, weekends**
Open: **All year**	Airport/Station Pickup: **Yes**

Five Bridge Farm B&B inn is a unique Georgian Colonial secluded on 60 acres of forest and field. Enjoy the private tennis court, lap pool, jogging track, and hiking trails all on the property. Nearby are golf courses, restaurants, and a riding stable next door to the inn. Homemade breads, mushroom quiche, French toast, and farm-raised sausage are just a few breakfast treats you may be served in the dining room that overlooks open pastures, wooded trails and Duffy, the resident llama. Ann and Harold offer local attraction information and brochures upon request.

Historic Jacob Hill Farm Bed & Breakfast Inn ✪
120 JACOB STREET, SEEKONK, MASSACHUSETTS 02771

Tel: **(888) 336-9165; (508) 336-9165**	Credit Cards: **AMEX, DISC, MC, VISA**
Hosts: **Bill and Eleonora Rezek**	Pets: **Horses only**
Location: **3 mi. E of Providence, R.I.**	Children: **Welcome, over 12**
No. of Rooms: **5**	Smoking: **No**
No. of Private Baths: **5**	Social Drinking: **Permitted**
Double/pb: **$85–$150**	Minimum Stay: **2 nights holiday**
Single/pb: **$75–$85**	**weekends, 3 nights Memorial Day &**
Suites: **$135–$140**	**Labor Day**
Open: **All year**	Airport/Station Pickup: **Yes**
Reduced Rates: **Weekly**	Foreign Languages: **Polish**
Breakfast: **Full**	

Built in 1722, Jacob Hill Farm was once known as the Jacob Hill Hunt Club, where the legendary Vanderbilts once displayed their horses and coach. Today guests are entertained with the same old-fashioned hospitality. Rooms are spacious, with queen- and king-size beds. The Inn is furnished with antiques and charming fireplaces, an inground pool, and tennis court. The stable is still in use and riding lessons are available. After a busy day of shopping and sightseeing, relax at the Inn and enjoy the magnificent sunsets.

The Golden Goose ✪
MAIN ROAD, BOX 336, TYRINGHAM, MASSACHUSETTS 01264

Tel: **(413) 243-3008**
Best Time to Call: **8 AM–8 PM**
Hosts: **Lilja and Joseph Rizzo**
Location: **4 mi. from Mass. Tpk., Exit 2—Lee**
No. of Rooms: **7**
Max. No. Sharing Bath: **4**
Double/pb: **$90–$110**
Single/pb: **$90–$110**
Double/sb: **$80–$90**
Single/sb: **$80–$90**

Suites: **$110–$125**
Open: **All year**
Reduced Rates: **Available**
Breakfast: **Continental, plus**
Pets: **No**
Children: **Welcome, in suite**
Smoking: **No**
Social Drinking: **Permitted**
Minimum Stay: **2–3 nights weekends during Tanglewood season; 2 nights weekends during fall foliage**

The inn lies between Stockbridge and Lenox in the Berkshires. Antique beds with firm new mattresses, and washstands, are in each bedroom. Lilja and Joseph serve hors d'oeuvres and drinks by the fireside in the two common rooms. In warm weather, you may play croquet, volleyball, badminton, hike the Appalachian Trail, or fish for trout in the brook across the street and barbecue it at "home." In summer, the cultural attractions of Tanglewood and Jacob's Pillow are nearby. Skiing is popular in winter. A $5 surcharge is added for one-night stays.

The Wildwood Inn ✪
121 CHURCH STREET, WARE, MASSACHUSETTS 01082

Tel: **(413) 967-7798; (800) 860-8098**
Best Time to Call: **After 10 AM**
Hosts: **Fraidell Fenster and Richard Watson**
Location: **8 mi. N of Mass. Pike (I-90), Exit 8**
No. of Rooms: **9**
No. of Private Baths: **7**
Max. No. Sharing Bath: **4**
Double/pb: **$60–$90**

Double/sb: **$50–$70**
Open: **All year**
Reduced Rates: **10%, weekly**
Breakfast: **Full**
Credit Cards: **AMEX, DC, MC, VISA**
Pets: **No**
Children: **Welcome, over 6**
Smoking: **No**
Social Drinking: **Permitted**

Everything about this old-fashioned country home, with its rambling two acres, is designed to help you unwind. There's a swing on the porch, a hammock under the firs, a blazing fire in the winter, a Norman Rockwell–esque brook-fed swimming hole in the summer. Your host Fraidell has furnished her guest rooms with heirloom quilts and American primitive antiques, all of which work to spell welcome. Homemade bread and Wildwood's own peach butter and "country yummies" are included with breakfast. Sturbridge Village, Old Deerfield, and Amherst offer recreational activities that are all close by. You can stroll to the tennis court or borrow the canoe, or visit in the parlor for stimulating conversation. Fraidell does her best to spoil you.

NANTUCKET

Lynda Watts Bed & Breakfast ✪
30 VESTAL STREET, BOX 478, NANTUCKET, MASSACHUSETTS 02554

Tel: **(508) 228-3828; fax (508) 228-4162**
Hosts: **Lynda and David Watts**
No. of Rooms: **2**
Max. No. Sharing Bath: **4**
Double/sb: **$75**
Open: **All year**
Reduced Rates: **20% Jan. 1–Apr. 15**

Breakfast: **Continental**
Credit Cards: **MC, VISA**
Pets: **No**
Children: **Welcome**
Smoking: **Permitted**
Social Drinking: **Permitted**
Minimum Stay: **2 nights**

Lynda and David's 20-year-old saltbox house is located on a quiet street in a residential neighborhood, only a seven-minute walk to town. It is simply furnished and guest rooms are equipped with TVs. Weather permitting, breakfast is served on the sunny patio.

MICHIGAN

The Urban Retreat ✪
2759 CANTERBURY ROAD, ANN ARBOR, MICHIGAN 48104

Tel: **(313) 971-8110**
Best Time to Call: **5–10 PM**
Hosts: **Andre Rosalik and Gloria Krys**
Location: **40 mi. W of Detroit**
No. of Rooms: **2**
Max. No. Sharing Bath: **4**
Double/pb: **$60–$65**
Single/pb: **$50**

Double/sb: **$55–$60**
Single/sb: **$45**
Open: **All year**
Breakfast: **Full**
Pets: **No, cats on premises**
Children: **No**
Smoking: **Restricted**
Social Drinking: **Permitted**

This 1950s ranch-style house is located on a quiet, tree-lined street, 10 minutes from downtown and the University of Michigan campus. The home is decorated with antiques and collectibles from the early 1900s, with an abundance of bird's-eye maple furniture. Adjacent to the property is the County Farm Park, 127 acres of meadowland with walking and jogging paths and a 13-box bluebird trail. The Retreat has been designated as a Backyard Wildlife Habitat by the National Wildlife Federation. Andre and Gloria emphasize a quiet, relaxed atmosphere and assure their guests a peaceful visit and personal attention.

Pinewood Lodge ✪
P.O. BOX 176, M28 WEST, AU TRAIN, MICHIGAN 49806

Tel: **(906) 892-8300**
Best Time to Call: **9 AM–9 PM**
Hosts: **Jerry and Jenny Krieg**
Location: **24 mi. E of Marquette**
No. of Rooms: **7**
No. of Private Baths: **5**
Max. No. Sharing Bath: **4**
Double/pb: **$85–$125**
Double/sb: **$75**

Single/sb: **$65**
Open: **All year**
Breakfast: **Full**
Credit Cards: **DISC, MC, VISA**
Pets: **No**
Children: **No**
Smoking: **No**
Social Drinking: **Permitted**
Airport/Station Pickup: **Yes**

This B&B is a pine log home on the shores of Lake Superior. Pictured Rocks National Shoreline is right down the highway, and you can see the Grand Islands from the living room. Guests can enjoy activities year-round, from swimming, diving, and boating to ice fishing, snowmobiling, and downhill and cross-country skiing.

The Windermere Inn ✪
7723 CRYSTAL DRIVE, BEULAH, MICHIGAN 49617

Tel: **(616) 882-9000**
Best Time to Call: **8 AM–11 PM**
Hosts: **Anne Fitch-Clark and Cameron Clark**
Location: **35 mi. SW of Traverse City**
No. of Rooms: **4**
No. of Private Baths: **4**
Double/pb: **$69**
Single/pb: **$59**

Open: **All year**
Breakfast: **Continental**
Credit Cards: **MC, VISA**
Pets: **Sometimes**
Children: **Welcome**
Smoking: **No**
Social Drinking: **Permitted**
Minimum Stay: **2 nights on weekends June–Aug.**

Whether you sip lemonade on the porch in summer or enjoy a hot toddy by the fire in winter, The Windermere Inn on beautiful Crystal Lake makes comfort its top priority. Situated in scenic Benzie County, the Inn has Sleeping Bear National Lakeshore to its north, Crystal Mountain ski resort to its south, Interlochen Arts Academy to its east, Lake Michigan and its beaches to its west, and golf courses all around. Anne and Cameron can help make your stay as eventful or relaxing as you wish. Your day begins with native fruits and muffins in summer, breakfast casseroles and breads in winter.

Celibeth House ✪

ROUTE 1, BOX 58A, M-77 BLANEY PARK ROAD, BLANEY PARK, MICHIGAN 49836

Tel: **(906) 283-3409**
Host: **Elsa Strom**
Location: **60 mi. W of Mackinac Bridge**
No. of Rooms: **7**
No. of Private Baths: **7**
Double/pb: **$48–$53**
Single/pb: **$43–$48**
Open: **May 1–Dec. 1**

Reduced Rates: **10% after 2nd night**
Breakfast: **Continental**
Credit Cards: **MC, VISA**
Pets: **No**
Children: **Welcome**
Smoking: **No**
Social Drinking: **Permitted**

This lovely house, built in 1895, is situated on 85 acres overlooking a small lake. Many of the scenic attractions of Michigan's Upper Peninsula lie within an hour's drive. Guests may enjoy a cozy living room, a quiet reading room, a comfortably furnished porch, an outdoor deck, and lots of nature trails. Elsa is a retired personnel manager who enjoys reading, gardening, traveling, and collecting antiques.

Dewey Lake Manor Bed & Breakfast ✪

11811 LAIRD ROAD, BROOKLYN, MICHIGAN 49230

Tel: **(517) 467-7122**
Best Time to Call: **Before 11 PM**
Hosts: **Joe and Barb Phillips**
Location: **45 mi. SW of Ann Arbor**
No. of Rooms: **5**
No. of Private Baths: **5**
Double/pb: **$60–$78**
Single/pb: **$55–$73**
Open: **All year**
Reduced Rates: **Available**

Breakfast: **Full**
Other Meals: **Available, picnic baskets**
Credit Cards: **MC, VISA**
Pets: **No**
Children: **Welcome**
Smoking: **No**
Social Drinking: **Permitted**
Minimum Stay: **3 nights on race weekends, 2 nights holiday weekends**

This 1870s Italianate home sits on the shore of Dewey Lake in the Irish Hills of southern Michigan. Five spacious, airy rooms are furnished with antiques and old-fashioned wallpapers. Three have fireplaces. Guests may linger over breakfast in the formal dining room or on the porch overlooking the lake. Picnics, bonfires, volleyball, or croquet may be enjoyed on the large lawn. A paddleboat and canoe are provided for guests. Nearby is the Stagecoach Stop Dinner Theater, as well as golf courses, quaint towns, and many antique shops. Come experience the country with the Phillips family.

The Calumet House ✪

1159 CALUMET AVENUE, P.O. BOX 126, CALUMET, MICHIGAN 49913

Tel: **(906) 337-1936**
Hosts: **George and Rose Chivses**

Location: **10 mi. N of Hancock-Houghton**

No. of Rooms: **2**
Max. No. Sharing Bath: **4**
Double/sb: **$35**
Single/sb: **$30**
Open: **All year**
Breakfast: **Full**

Pets: **No**
Children: **No**
Smoking: **No**
Social Drinking: **Permitted**
Airport/Station Pickup: **Yes**
Foreign Languages: **Finnish**

The Calumet House is set in a historic old mining town known for its clean air and scenic vistas. Built in 1895, the house boasts its original woodwork and is filled with local antique furnishings. In the morning, you're in for a treat with Rose's home cooking. Breakfast specialties include English scones, pancakes, local berries in season, and homemade jam. Calumet House is within walking distance of the village, with its opera house, museum, and antique shops. Your hosts will also direct you to local hunting and fishing, as well as to places that any botanist would call paradise. It's 10 miles north of Michigan Technological University and Suomi College.

York House ✪
1141 NORTH YORK, DEARBORN, MICHIGAN 42128

Tel: **(313) 561-2432**
Best Time to Call: **Afternoons, evenings**
Host: **Joan Schnell**
Location: **15 mi. W of Detroit**
No. of Rooms: **2**
No. of Private Baths: **2**
Double/pb: **$65**
Single/pb: **$55**

Open: **All year**
Breakfast: **Continental**
Pets: **No**
Children: **Welcome**
Smoking: **No**
Social Drinking: **No**
Airport/Station Pickup: **Yes**

This unique 1927 yellow brick home with red tile roof is furnished in the period of the 1920s and 1930s, and is perfect for a getaway weekend. The Charles Lindbergh room and the Old Car room have been furnished by Joan with antiques and other mementos from the past, adding to the house's charm and your comfort. York House is located five minutes from the Henry Ford Museum, Greenfield Village, and Fairlane Town Mall with 220 stores. Sports fans will be close to the Detroit Tigers, Pistons, Red Wings, and Lions. For an international adventure, it's just twenty minutes to the casinos in Windsor, Ontario, Canada.

Bannicks B&B ✪
4608 MICHIGAN ROAD, M-99, DIMONDALE, MICHIGAN 48821

Tel: **(517) 646-0224**
Hosts: **Pat and Jim Bannick**
Location: **5 mi. SW of Lansing**
No. of Rooms: **2**
Max. No. Sharing Bath: **3**
Double/sb: **$40**
Single/sb: **$25**

Open: **All year**
Breakfast: **Full**
Pets: **No**
Children: **Welcome**
Smoking: **No**
Social Drinking: **Permitted**

This large ranch-style home features a stained glass entry, nautical-style basement, and a Mona Lisa bathroom. Guest accommodations consist of comfortable bedrooms and a den-TV room. Your hosts invite you to share a cup of coffee anytime. They will be happy to advise on the sights of Michigan's capital city, just five minutes away. Michigan State University is eight miles away.

Torch Lake Sunrise Bed and Breakfast ✪
BOX 52, EASTPORT, MICHIGAN 49627

Tel: **(616) 599-2706**	Open: **May 15–Dec. 15**
Host: **Betty A. Collins**	Breakfast: **Full**
Location: **35 mi. N of Traverse City**	Pets: **Sometimes**
No. of Rooms: **3**	Children: **Welcome**
No. of Private Baths: **3**	Smoking: **No**
Double/pb: **$75–$120**	Social Drinking: **Permitted**

This B&B overlooks what *National Geographic* calls the third most beautiful lake in the world. All rooms are furnished with antiques and have decks and private baths. Close at hand are several golf courses, tennis courts, gourmet restaurants, and ski resorts. For summer activities, a canoe, a rowboat, and paddleboards are available. In winter, cross-country skiing awaits you just outside. Wake up seeing the sunrise over the lake and smelling the wonderful aroma of fresh muffins baking! Perhaps you'll be served a frittata, or strawberry pancakes, or eggs Benedict, but always fresh fruit of the season.

The Kingsley House
626 WEST MAIN STREET, FENNVILLE, MICHIGAN 49408

Tel: **(616) 561-6425**	Reduced Rates: **10% seniors; AARP**
Hosts: **Gary and Kari King**	Breakfast: **Full weekends, Continental,**
Location: **8 mi. SE of Saugatuck**	**plus, weekdays**
No. of Rooms: **8**	Pets: **No**
No. of Private Baths: **8**	Smoking: **No**
Double/pb: **$80–$90**	Social Drinking: **Permitted**
Suites: **$110–$145**	Airport/Station Pickup: **Yes**
Open: **All year**	

This elegant Queen Anne Victorian takes its name from the locally prominent family who built it in 1886. Furnished and decorated in period style, the inn reflects the warmth and charm of a bygone era. Full family-style breakfasts are served in the formal dining room. Honeymoon suites with whirlpool baths and fireplaces are available. Saugatuck, Holland, and the sandy beaches of Lake Michigan are only minutes away.

Will O' Glenn Irish Bed & Breakfast ✪
P.O. BOX 288, GLENN, MICHIGAN 49416

Tel: **(616) 227-3045**
Best Time to Call: **9 AM–9 PM**
Hosts: **Shelley and Ward Gahan**
Location: **25 mi. S of Holland**
No. of Rooms: **4**
No. of Private Baths: **4**
Double/pb: **$89–$109**
Open: **All year**
Reduced Rates: **Available**
Breakfast: **Full**

Other Meals: **Available**
Credit Cards: **MC, VISA**
Pets: **No**
Children: **Welcome, over 8**
Smoking: **No**
Social Drinking: **Permitted**
Minimum Stay: **2 nights weekends May–Sept.**
Foreign Languages: **French**

Enjoy a warm Irish welcome upon arrival on this 17-acre estate. The house is full of Irish art, literature, and antiques. Guests are invited to enjoy the large common areas, decks, and gardens that are a part of this estate, or simply enjoy the sounds of nature through the wooded acreage. Tranquility is the order of the day. A full authentic Irish breakfast is served in the morning featuring imported Irish meats and homemade Irish brown bread.

The Brick Inn ✪
74 WEST 24TH STREET, HOLLAND, MICHIGAN 49423

Tel: **(616) 396-0401**
Hosts: **Ed and Freda Mott**
Location: **35 mi. W of Grand Rapids**
No. of Rooms: **2**
Max. No. Sharing Bath: **4**
Double/sb: **$70**
Open: **Apr. 1–Dec. 31**

Breakfast: **Full**
Pets: **No**
Children: **Welcome**
Smoking: **No**
Social Drinking: **Permitted**
Airport/Station Pickup: **Yes**

The Brick Inn is located in a unique neighborhood of homes in the city of Holland, famous for its Tulip Gardens, Wooden Shoe Factory, Dutch Village, Windmill Island, and Veldeer's Delft Factory. Guests will be within walking distance of Hope College and downtown Holland. Rooms are spacious, decorated with antiques and beautiful antique linens; each has a sitting area with a TV. Breakfast is served in the formal dining room and might include homemade muffins, apple dumplings, or chocolate crepes. After a busy day of sightseeing, you may want to enjoy the private patio garden or relax in the living room by the fireplace. Ed and Freda are retired and enjoy gardening and spending time with their guests.

Montgomery Place ✪
618 EAST LAKE STREET, PETOSKEY, MICHIGAN 49770

Tel: **(616) 347-1338**
Best Time to Call: **After 10 AM**
Hosts: **Ruth Bellissimo and Diane Gillette**
No. of Rooms: **3**
No. of Private Baths: **3**
Double/pb: **$95–$105**
Suite: **$135**

Open: **All year**
Breakfast: **Full**
Credit Cards: **MC, VISA**
Pets: **No**
Children: **Welcome, over 6**
Smoking: **No**
Social Drinking: **Permitted**
Airport/Station Pickup: **Yes**

From the beautiful veranda of Benson House, you can admire Lake Michigan's Little Traverse Bay, just as guests did in 1878 when this Victorian inn first opened its doors. Petoskey is in the heart of Michigan's Little New England; the town's Gaslight District offers excellent shopping and dining. Mackinac Island is just a short drive away, as are numerous beaches, lakes, and other points of interest. The area's scenic roads wind through forests, valleys, and upland meadows. Five major ski resorts provide the Midwest's best downhill and cross-country skiing. For those of you who don't mind paying a higher rate, one other room is available.

Serenity—A Bed & Breakfast ✪
504 RUSH STREET, PETOSKEY, MICHIGAN 49770

Tel: **(616) 347-6171**
Best Time to Call: **After 10 AM**
Hosts: **Ralph and Sherry Gillett**
No. of Rooms: **3**
No. of Private Baths: **3**
Double/pb: **$85**
Open: **All year**
Reduced Rates: **Jan. 1–May 1**

Breakfast: **Full Fri.–Sun., Continental, plus, Mon.–Thurs.**
Credit Cards: **MC, VISA**
Pets: **No**
Children: **Welcome, over 12**
Smoking: **No**
Social Drinking: **Permitted**

Serenity is a lovely Victorian home with two glass-enclosed porches, natural oak hardwood floors, antiques, lace, and soft music that create an ambience of tranquil beauty. This B&B lies within walking distance of the historic Gaslight District, where you can enjoy a special shopping experience and many fine restaurants overlooking Little Traverse Bay. Mackinac Island is only 35 miles from Petoskey. Also featured are three major ski resorts, lovely beaches, golfing, and breathtaking sunsets.

Sherwood Forest Bed & Breakfast ✪
938 CENTER STREET, P.O. BOX 315, SAUGATUCK, MICHIGAN 49453

Tel: **(800) 838-1246**
Best Time to Call: **9 AM–10 PM**
Hosts: **Keith and Sue Charak**
Location: **40 mi. SW of Grand Rapids**
No. of Rooms: **5**
No. of Private Baths: **5**
Double/pb: **$60–$140**
Open: **All year**
Breakfast: **Continental**

Other Meals: **Available**
Credit Cards: **DC, DISC, MC, VISA**
Pets: **No**
Children: **Welcome, over 12**
Smoking: **No**
Social Drinking: **Permitted**
Minimum Stay: **2 nights, weekends;
    May 1–Oct. 31**

This beautiful Victorian home offers inviting elegance, located in a wooded setting. Hardwood floors, leaded glass windows, and a wrap-around porch add to the ideal surroundings. Guest rooms are furnished with antiques, cozy wing chairs, queen&size beds, and air-conditioning. One room has a hand-painted mural that transforms the room into a canopied tree loft and is complemented with a gas fireplace. Another room has a Jacuzzi. Outside is a heated pool adorned with dolphins riding the ocean waves. If you would like to see a spectacular sunset, a Lake Michigan public beach is only half a block away. Winter offers cross-country skiing or hiking along wooded paths. A separate cottage is also available.

Rummel's Tree Haven ✪
41 NORTH BECK STREET, M-25, SEBEWAING, MICHIGAN 48759

Tel: (517) 883-2450	Open: All year
Best Time to Call: Afternoons; evenings	Breakfast: Full
Hosts: Carl and Erma Rummel	Pets: Sometimes
Location: 28 mi. NE of Bay City	Children: Welcome (crib)
No. of Rooms: 2	Smoking: Permitted
Double/pb: $50	Social Drinking: Permitted
Single/pb: $35	Airport/Station Pickup: Yes

A tree grows right through the porch and roof of this charming old home that was built by the Beck family in 1878. Guests can relax in large, airy rooms furnished with twin beds and comfortable family pieces. City dwellers are sure to enjoy the small-town friendliness and the quiet of the countryside. Saginaw Bay offers fine fishing, hunting, boating, bird-watching, or just plain relaxing. Carl and Erma offer color TV, videocassettes, and the use of the barbecue and refrigerator. They love having company and will do all they can to make you feel welcome and relaxed.

The Seymour House ✪
1248 BLUE STAR HIGHWAY, SOUTH HAVEN, MICHIGAN 49090
seymour@cybersol.com

Tel: (616) 227-3918;	Reduced Rates: Available
fax: (616) 227-3010	Breakfast: Full
Best Time to Call: 8 AM–10 PM	Other Meals: Available
Hosts: Tom and Gwen Paton	Credit Cards: MC, VISA
Location: 10 mi. S of Saugatuck	Pets: No
No. of Rooms: 5	Children: Welcome, in cabin
No. of Private Baths: 5	Smoking: No
Double/pb: $75–$119	Social Drinking: Permitted
Guest Cabin: $90–$120; $475–$595 weekly	Minimum Stay: 2–3 nights weekends May 1–Nov. 1 main house; 2 nights most weekends, 3–4 nights holidays in cabin
Suites: $108–$129	
Open: All year	

The Seymour House is a stately brick Italianate-style Victorian featuring original pocket doors and intricate carved wood trim on doors and windows. You will enjoy nature and ultimate relaxation on the Patons' 11 acres. The grounds feature maintained nature trails and a stocked one-acre pond. Relax on white wicker in the garden patio beneath giant oaks and weeping willows. The B&B is located half a mile from Lake Michigan; it's only minutes to the popular resort towns of Saugatuck and South Haven. Gwen's pottery and photography are featured in the gift shop.

Linden Lea, A B&B on Long Lake
279 SOUTH LONG LAKE ROAD, TRAVERSE CITY, MICHIGAN 49684

Tel: **(616) 943-9182**
Hosts: **Jim and Vicky McDonnell**
Location: **9 mi. W of Traverse City**
No. of Rooms: **2**
No. of Private Baths: **2**
Double/pb: **$95**
Open: **All year**
Reduced Rates: **$75 Nov.–Apr.**

Breakfast: **Full**
Pets: **No**
Children: **Welcome, by arrangement**
Smoking: **No**
Social Drinking: **Permitted**
Minimum Stay: **Holiday weekends**
Airport/Station Pickup: **Yes**

Linden Lea is an extensively remodeled and expanded 1900 lakeside cottage set on a private sandy beach surrounded by woods. The bedrooms are comfortably furnished in country style, accented with antiques. You are certain to enjoy the window seats and the panoramic views of Long Lake. The area offers the Interlochen Center for the Arts National Music Camp, a PGA golf course, and local wineries. Breakfast features local specialties, such as smoked bacon, maple syrup, and berries that make the home-baked muffins so delicious.

MINNESOTA

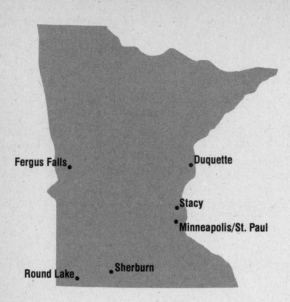

Fergus Falls

Duquette

Stacy

Minneapolis/St. Paul

Round Lake

Sherburn

Home in the Pines Bed & Breakfast ✪
P.O. BOX 688, HIGHWAY 23, DUQUETTE, MINNESOTA 55729

Tel: **(218) 496-5825**	Open: **All year**
Best Time to Call: **After 6 PM**	Breakfast: **Full**
Hosts: **Curtis and Julie Gunderson**	Credit Cards: **DISC, VISA**
No. of Rooms: **2**	Pets: **Sometimes**
No. of Private Baths: **2**	Children: **Welcome**
Double/pb: **$60–$75**	Smoking: **No**

A mounted moose head surveys guests as they enter this turn-of-the-century home, which was enlarged in the 1990s. Play boccie ball, croquet, badminton, or horseshoe games right on the five-acre grounds. Jackie Berger Memorial Park, next door, has a tennis court, softball diamond, and riverfront campsites. The Gundersons' hearty country breakfasts will give you energy for any activity.

Bergerud B's ✪
ROUTE 5, BOX 61, FERGUS FALLS, MINNESOTA 56537

Tel: **(218) 736-4720; (800) 557-4720**
Hosts: **James and Sylvia Bergerud**
Location: **12 mi. S of Fergus Falls**
No. of Rooms: **3**
Max. No. Sharing Bath: **4**
Double/pb: **$75**
Double/sb: **$40–$45**
Single/sb: **$30**

Open: **All year**
Breakfast: **Full**
Other Meals: **Available**
Pets: **No**
Children: **Welcome, over 8**
Smoking: **No**
Social Drinking: **Permitted**
Foreign Languages: **Norwegian**

This home was built by the host's grandfather in 1895, on the century farm homesteaded in 1881. Jim and Sylvia have modernized the house, but the original structure remains much the same. Located twelve miles from the city, Bergerud B's offers a peaceful night of rest and relaxation. Take a walk in the country, play a game of pool, or just sit by one of the two fireplaces on a cool night with a good book and a cup of hot cider. Awake to the smell of flavored coffee and a sumptuous hearty breakfast. Upon your departure Jim and Sylvia will fill your thermos and send you on your way with a baked goody. Your hosts enjoy meeting new people and will make your stay at Bergerud's a memorable experience.

Shingle Creek Bed & Breakfast ✪
5206 NORTH VINCENT AVENUE, MINNEAPOLIS, MINNESOTA 55430

Tel: **(612) 529-7063**
Hosts: **Dick and Wilma Sweere**
Location: **5 mi. NW of Minneapolis**
No. of Rooms: **1**
No. of Private Baths: **1**
Double/pb: **$55**
Single/pb: **$45**

Open: **June 1–Oct. 31**
Reduced Rates: **Weekly**
Breakfast: **Continental**
Pets: **No**
Children: **Welcome, over 4**
Smoking: **No**
Social Drinking: **Permitted**

This one-and-a-half-story Cape Cod Colonial home is located in a safe residential neighborhood within walking distance to a major shopping center, Metro bike trail, walking nature trail, and the Metro bus. Major sports facilities and downtown Minneapolis are 10 minutes away, the Mall of America 20 minutes, and the Minneapolis Zoo 30 minutes.

The Prairie House on Round Lake ✪
RR 1, BOX 105, ROUND LAKE, MINNESOTA 56167

Tel: **(507) 945-8934**
Hosts: **Ralph and Virginia Schenck**
No. of Rooms: **4**
No. of Private Baths: **1**
Max. No. Sharing Bath: **4**
Double/pb: **$55**

Single/pb: **$55**
Double/sb: **$45**
Single/sb: **$45**
Open: **All year**
Breakfast: **Full**
Pets: **Welcome**

Children: **Welcome**   Social Drinking: **Permitted**
Smoking: **No**   Airport/Station Pickup: **Yes**

Built in 1879 by a prominent Chicago businessman, this farmhouse is a retreat from the bustle of city life. It's a working horse farm: American paint horses roam the pasture, and three barns house both young stock in training and show horses that are exhibited all over the world. A cupola rising from the central stairway is circled by four dormer bedrooms on the second floor. Antique furniture accented with equine touches reflects the spirit of the farm. Fishing, hiking, swimming, boating, and tennis are at the doorstep.

The Garden Gate ✪
925 GOODRICH AVENUE, ST. PAUL, MINNESOTA 55105

Tel: **(612) 227-8430; (800) 967-2703**   Open: **All year**
Hosts: **Mary and Miles Conway**   Breakfast: **Continental**
Location: **1 mi. from I-94 exit Lexington**   Credit Cards: **No**
  Parkway   Pets: **Sometimes**
No. of Rooms: **3**   Children: **Welcome**
Max. No. Sharing Bath: **4**   Smoking: **No**
Double/sb: **$65–$75**   Social Drinking: **Permitted**
Single/sb: **$55**   Airport/Station Pickup: **Yes**

A garden of delights awaits you at this Victorian duplex in the heart of St. Paul's Victoria Crossing neighborhood, within easy reach of downtown, the airport, the capitol, and the Mall of America. The Gladiola, Rose, and Delphinium rooms are as beautiful as their namesakes. A typical breakfast may include fresh fruit, baked pastries, cereal, and yogurt. To pamper the body as well as the palate, guests may arrange to have a therapeutic massage.

Four Columns Inn ✪
RT. 2, BOX 75, SHERBURN, MINNESOTA 56171

Tel: **(507) 764-8861**   Single/pb: **$55–$75**
Best Time to Call: **Anytime**   Open: **All year**
Hosts: **Norman and Pennie Kittleson**   Breakfast: **Full**
Location: **150 mi. W of Minneapolis**   Pets: **No**
No. of Rooms: **4**   Children: **By arrangement**
No. of Private Baths: **4**   Smoking: **No**
Double/pb: **$55–$75**   Social Drinking: **Permitted**

Built as a guesthouse in 1884, this former stagecoach stop now welcomes the modern-day traveler. Lovingly remodeled by the Kittlesons during the last forty-five years, this Victorian mansion offers four rooms—including the very popular Bridal Suite. Throughout, the house is filled with antiques and musical instruments, including a player piano and a 1950s jukebox. A walnut-paneled den, two working fireplaces, circular stairway, and a library complete your home-away-from-home. A full breakfast served with warm hospitality rounds out your stay in the country. Four Columns is located in south central Minnesota, just two miles from I-90. Norman and Penny now have grand piano entertainment.

Kings Oakdale Park Guest House ✪
6933 232 AVENUE NORTHEAST, STACY, MINNESOTA 55079

Tel: **(612) 462-5598**
Hosts: **Donna and Charles Solem**
Location: **38 mi. N of St. Paul**
No. of Rooms: **3**
No. of Private Baths: **2**
Double/pb: **$32**
Single/pb: **$26**
Double/sb: **$30**
Single/sb: **$25**

Suites: **$35**
Open: **All year**
Breakfast: **Continental**
Pets: **Sometimes**
Children: **No**
Smoking: **Permitted**
Social Drinking: **Permitted**
Foreign Languages: **French**

This comfortable home is situated on four landscaped acres on the banks of Typo Creek. The picnic tables, volleyball net, and horseshoe game are sure signs of a hospitable country place. It is a serene retreat for people on business trips to the Twin Cities. The Wisconsin border and the scenic St. Croix River, where boat trips are offered, are minutes from the house. Charles and Donna will direct you to the most reasonable restaurants in town. For late snacks, refrigerators in the bedrooms are provided.

MISSISSIPPI

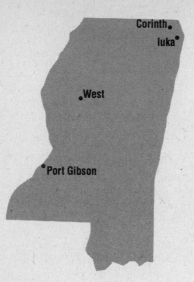

Lincoln, Ltd. Bed & Breakfast—Mississippi Reservation Service ✪
P.O. BOX 3479, 2303 23RD AVENUE, MERIDIAN, MISSISSIPPI 39303

Tel: **(601) 482-5483; resv. only: (800) 633-MISS [6477]; fax: (601) 693-7447**
Best Time to Call: **9 AM–5 PM**
Coordinator: **Barbara Lincoln Hall**
States/Regions Covered:
  Mississippi—Natchez to Memphis, Alabama

Descriptive Directory: **$3.50**
Rates (Single/Double):
  Average: **$65–$75 / $75–$85**
  Luxury: **$85–$125 / $95–$165**
Credit Cards: **AMEX, MC, VISA**

For the traveling businessperson or for the vacationer, a stay with one of Barbara's hosts offers a personal taste of the finest Southern hospitality. All rooms have private baths. Mississippi abounds with historic-house tours, called "pilgrimages," in March and April, and Natchez and Vicksburg have similar pilgrimages in autumn. In May, Meridian is host to the Jimmie Rodgers Festival. Accommodations range from a cozy, historic log cabin to an elegant antebellum mansion.

The Samuel D. Bramlitt House ✪
1125 CRUISE STREET, CORINTH, MISSISSIPPI 38834

Tel: **(601) 286-5370**
Hosts: **Cindy and Kevin Thomas**
Location: **80 mi. SE of Memphis, Tennessee**
No. of Rooms: **5**
No. of Private Baths: **5**
Double/pb: **$75**
Open: **All year**

Breakfast: **Full**
Other Meals: **Available**
Credit Cards: **AMEX, MC, VISA**
Pets: **No**
Children: **Welcome**
Smoking: **No**
Social Drinking: **Permitted**
Airport/Station Pickup: **Yes**

Starry skies, soft summer breezes, the fragrance of magnolia and roses, a good book, and the smell of fresh-baked bread are only a few of the pleasures you will enjoy at the Samuel D. Bramlitt House, circa 1892. This gracious and warm Victorian mansion is filled with antiques and is located in the historic district of Corinth. Guests are invited to sip iced tea on one of the four verandas or walk to one of Mississippi's oldest drugstores complete with soda fountain. Explore the historic homes and churches, attend one of the many colorful festivals and battle re-enactments, or visit nearby Shiloh National Military Park and Natchez Trace Parkway.

Eastport Inn Bed & Breakfast ✪
100 SOUTH PEARL STREET, IUKA, MISSISSIPPI 38852

Tel: **(601) 423-2511**
Best Time to Call: **8 AM–5 PM**
Host: **Betty Watson**
No. of Rooms: **7**
No. of Private Baths: **7**
Double/pb: **$50**
Single/pb: **$40**
Suites: **$50**
Open: **All year**

Reduced Rates: **Available**
Breakfast: **Continental**
Other Meals: **Available**
Credit Cards: **AMEX, DC, DISC, MC, VISA**
Pets: **No**
Children: **Welcome**
Smoking: **No**
Social Drinking: **Permitted**

This gracious home was built in 1864 and is decorated in period style, with four-poster beds and floral bedspreads. For swimming and boating, Pickwick Lake is six miles away; Shiloh National Park, Tishomingo State Park, Coleman State Park, and the Natchez Trace Drive are also nearby.

Oak Square Plantation ✪
1207 CHURCH STREET, PORT GIBSON, MISSISSIPPI 39150

Tel: **(601) 437-4350; (800) 729-0240**
Best Time to Call: **Anytime**
Hosts: **Mr. and Mrs. William D. Lum**

Location: **On Hwy. 61 between Natchez and Vicksburg**
No. of Rooms: **12**

No. of Private Baths: **12**
Double/pb: **$85–$95**
Single/pb: **$70–$75**
Open: **All year**
Breakfast: **Full**

Credit Cards: **AMEX, DISC, MC, VISA**
Pets: **No**
Children: **Welcome**
Smoking: **No**
Social Drinking: **Permitted**

Port Gibson is the town that Union General Ulysses S. Grant said was "too beautiful to burn." Oak Square is the largest and most palatial antebellum mansion, circa 1850, in Port Gibson, and is listed on the National Register of Historic Places. The guest rooms are all furnished with family heirlooms, and all have canopied beds. Guests will enjoy the courtyard, gazebo, and beautiful grounds. A chairlift for upstairs rooms is available. You will enjoy the delightful Southern breakfast and tour of the mansion. Your hosts offer complimentary wine, tea, or coffee, and will enlighten you on the many historic attractions in the area.

The Alexander House ✪
210 GREEN STREET, P.O. BOX 187, WEST, MISSISSIPPI 39192

Tel: **(800) 350-8034**
Hosts: **Ruth Ray and Woody Dinstel**
Location: **70 mi. N of Jackson**
No. of Rooms: **5**
No. of Private Baths: **3**
Max. No. Sharing Bath: **4**
Double/pb: **$65**
Double/sb: **$65**
Suites: **$110**

Open: **All year**
Breakfast: **Full**
Other Meals: **Available**
Pets: **Sometimes**
Children: **Welcome, over 10**
Smoking: **No**
Social Drinking: **Permitted**
Station Pickup: **Yes**

The Alexander House, which has been dated to the 1880s, opened as a bed and breakfast in March 1994. Located in the town historic district, the house has been carefully restored with authentic decor, but with added conveniences. A full breakfast is served each morning and may include hot biscuits, fruit compote, grits, eggs, or casseroles. The two-story home has three bedrooms and a suite.

For key to listings, see inside front or back cover.

✪ This star means that rates are guaranteed through December 31, 1998, to any guest making a reservation as a result of reading about the B&B in *Bed & Breakfast U.S.A.*—1998 edition.

Important! To avoid misunderstandings, always ask about cancellation policies when booking.

Please enclose a self-addressed, stamped, business-size envelope when contacting reservation services.

For more details on what you can expect in a B&B, see Chapter 1.

Always mention *Bed & Breakfast U.S.A.* when making reservations!

We want to hear from you! Use the form on page 625.

MISSOURI

Plattsburg

Hannibal

Kansas City

Arrow Rock

Marthaville St. Louis

Washington

Bland Bourbon

Cape Girardeau

Marshfield

Ozark

Branson

Bed & Breakfast Kansas City—Missouri & Kansas
P.O. BOX 14781, LENEXA, KANSAS 66285

Tel: **(913) 888-3636**
Coordinator: **Edwina Monroe**
States/Regions Covered:
Kansas—Lenexa, Overland Park,
Wichita; Missouri—Grandview,
Independence, Kansas City, Lee's

Summit, Parkville, St. Joseph,
Springfield, Warrensburg, Weston
Rates (Single/Double):
Average: **$35 / $40–$50**
Luxury: **$60 / $65–$130**
Credit Cards: **No**

You will enjoy visiting such places as the Truman Library and home, Crown Center, Country Club Plaza, Arrowhead Stadium, Royals Stadium, Kemper Arena, the Missouri Repertory Theatre, the American Heartland Theater, Nelson Art Gallery, New Theatre Restaurant, and Toy & Miniature Museum.

Borgman's Bed & Breakfast ✪
ARROW ROCK, MISSOURI 65320

Tel: **(816) 837-3350**
Best Time to Call: **7–9 AM**
Hosts: **Helen and Kathy Borgman**
Location: **100 mi. E of Kansas City**
No. of Rooms: **4**
Max. No. Sharing Bath: **4**
Double/sb: **$50–$55**
Single/sb: **$40**

Open: **All year**
Reduced Rates: **10% 3 nights**
Breakfast: **Continental**
Pets: **Sometimes**
Children: **Welcome**
Smoking: **No**
Social Drinking: **Permitted**

This 1860 home is spacious and comfortable, and it is furnished with cherished family pieces. Helen is a seamstress, artisan, and baker. Wait till you taste her fresh breads! Daughter Kathy is a town tour guide, so you will get firsthand information on this National Historic Landmark town at the beginning of the Santa Fe Trail. A fine repertory theater, the Lyceum, is open in summer. Crafts shops, antique stalls, and the old country store are fun places to browse in. Good restaurants are within walking distance.

Caverly Farm & Orchard
100 CEDAR RIDGE ROAD, BLAND, MISSOURI 65014

Tel: **(573) 646-3732**
Best Time to Call: **8 AM–10 PM**
Hosts: **David and Nancy Caverly**
Location: **85 mi. WSW of St. Louis**

No. of Rooms: **3**
No. of Private Baths: **3**
Double/pb: **$50**
Single/pb: **$45**

Open: **All year**
Breakfast: **Full**
Other Meals: **Available**
Pets: **Sometimes**

Children: **Welcome, crib**
Smoking: **No**
Social Drinking: **Permitted**

Caverly Farm & Orchard bed and breakfast is located on a 57-acre farm in central Missouri. The farm is in a colorful valley of grazing land, hay fields, and wooded hillsides. The renovated 1850 farmhouse has a new roof and siding and completely new bedrooms, decorated with a collection of antiques gathered over 35 years. Guests can enjoy fishing and hiking on the farm or floating on nearby rivers. Antique and craft shops, farm auctions, and five major Missouri wineries are within 30 to 45 minutes.

The Wildflower Inn ✪
ROUTE 2, BOX 101, BOURBON, MISSOURI 65441

Tel: **(573) 468-7975**
Best Time to Call: **4–7 PM**
Hosts: **Mary Lou and Jerry Hubble**
Location: **65 mi. from St. Louis**
No. of Rooms: **4**
No. of Private Baths: **4**
Double/pb: **$65–$75**

Open: **All year**
Breakfast: **Full**
Pets: **No**
Children: **No**
Smoking: **No**
Social Drinking: **Permitted**

The Wildflower Inn sits graciously on 42 acres in the foothills of the Ozarks. Surrounded by natural springs and abundant wildlife, the setting is private and relaxing. Amenities include color TVs, central heating and air-conditioning for year-round comfort. Guests are invited to relax in the gathering room in front of an old-fashioned fireplace. There, you can enjoy a book, games, or visit with other guests while sipping complimentary coffee or tea. Things to do include fishing, canoeing, rafting, antiquing, or visiting the wineries, Meramec Caverns, Meramec State Park, and Meramec Springs. A full country breakfast is served. Specialties include Belgian waffles, Western omelettes, orange muffins, angel flake biscuits, sausage gravy and apple quiche.

Ozark Mountain Country B&B Service
BOX 295, BRANSON, MISSOURI 65616

Tel: **(417) 334-4720; (800) 695-1546**
Best Time to Call: **10 AM–4 PM;
7–10 PM**
Coordinator: **Kay Cameron**
States/Regions Covered:
  **Missouri—Branson, Camdenton,
  Carthage, Hollister, Kimberling City,
  Marionville, Osage Beach, Shell**

  **Knob, Springfield; Arkansas—Eureka
  Springs**
Rates (Single/Double):
  Modest: **$35–$55**
  Average: **$60–$75**
  Luxury: **$80–$150**
Credit Cards: **AMEX, DISC, MC, VISA**

After receiving a stamped, self-addressed legal envelope, Kay will send you a complimentary copy of her descriptive listings of more than one hundred carefully selected small inns, private cottages, and luxurious suites. She will also include coupons. Discounts are available for groups and stays of more than three nights.

Cameron's Crag ✪
P.O. BOX 295, BRANSON, MISSOURI 65613

Tel: (417) 335-8134; (800) 933-8529
Host: Glen Cameron
Location: 3 mi. S of Branson
Suites: $75–$95; sleeps 2
Open: All year
Reduced Rates: $10 less Jan.–Mar., after 1st night

Breakfast: Full
Other Meals: Available
Pets: No
Children: Welcome, infants, over 6
Smoking: No
Social Drinking: Permitted
Airport Pickup: Yes

Enjoy your choice of three delightful accommodations in this striking contemporary home perched high on a bluff overlooking Lake Taneycomo. All three suites have private entrances, king-size beds, and a deck with a spa. You'll savor one of your host's hearty breakfasts before you explore area attractions like Silver Dollar City, Table Rock State Park, and Mutton Hollow Craft Village.

Bellevue Bed & Breakfast ✪
312 BELLEVUE, CAPE GIRARDEAU, MISSOURI 63701

Tel: (800) 768-6822; (573) 335–3302
Hosts: Fred and Jackie Hoelscher
Location: 100 mi. S of St. Louis
No. of Rooms: 4
No. of Private Baths: 4
Double/pb: $55–$90
Single/pb: $50–$85
Open: All year

Breakfast: Full
Credit Cards: MC, VISA
Pets: No
Children: Welcome
Smoking: No
Social Drinking: Permitted
Airport/Station Pickup: Yes

Built in 1891, this Second Empire Victorian home has been faithfully returned to its turn-of-the-century elegance. The original ceiling stencils have been restored in the dining room and parlor. Both bedrooms, furnished in antiques, have queen-size beds. A full breakfast served in the formal dining room features fresh breads and seasonal fruits. Guests may enjoy a leisurely stroll to the nearby riverfront and shopping at the many nearby antique and specialty shops. Fred is a retired salesman who will make you feel at home and tell you all you want to know about the area.

Garth Woodside Mansion
RR3, BOX 578, HANNIBAL, MISSOURI 63401

Tel: **(573) 221-2789**
Best Time to Call: **10 AM–7 PM**
Hosts: **Irv and Diane Feinberg**
Location: **99 mi. N of St. Louis**
No. of Rooms: **8**
No. of Private Baths: **8**
Double/pb: **$67–$107**

Open: **All year**
Breakfast: **Full**
Credit Cards: **MC, VISA**
Pets: **No**
Children: **Welcome, over 12**
Smoking: **No**
Social Drinking: **Permitted**

This Second Empire Victorian, built in 1871, has a three-story flying staircase, 14-foot ceilings, and eight hand-carved marble fireplaces. Many of the room furnishings date back to the original owners. Stroll the 39 country acres, then sit down for a leisurely afternoon beverage. Breakfast, served in the formal dining room, features peach French toast, fluted quiche cups, and eggs picante. This location is ideal for touring Mark Twain country or for a romantic getaway. What's more, your hosts will pamper you with wonderful extras like nightshirts and turn-down service.

Pridewell ✪
600 WEST 50TH STREET, KANSAS CITY, MISSOURI 64112

Tel: **(816) 931-1642**
Best Time to Call: **4–9 PM**
Hosts: **Edwin and Louann White**
No. of Rooms: **2**
No. of Private Baths: **1**
Double/pb: **$75**
Single/pb: **$70**

Open: **All year**
Breakfast: **Full**
Pets: **No**
Children: **Welcome**
Smoking: **No**
Social Drinking: **Permitted**

This fine Tudor residence is situated in a wooded residential area on the battlefield of the Civil War's Battle of Westport. The Nelson Art Gallery, the University of Missouri at Kansas City, and the Missouri Repertory Theatre are close by. It is adjacent to the Country Club Plaza shopping district, which includes several four-star restaurants, tennis courts, and a park.

The Dickey House Bed & Breakfast Inn ✪
331 SOUTH CLAY STREET, MARSHFIELD, MISSOURI 65706

Tel: **(417) 468-3000**
Hosts: **William and Dorothy Buesgen**
Location: **22 mi. NE of Springfield**
No. of Rooms: **6**
No. of Private Baths: **6**
Double/pb: **$60–$105**
Open: **All year**
Reduced Rates: **Available**

Breakfast: **Full**
Credit Cards: **DISC, MC, VISA**
Pets: **No**
Children: **Welcome, over 12**
Smoking: **No**
Social Drinking: **Permitted**
Airport Pickup: **Yes**
Foreign Languages: **German**

As you approach this lovely Greek Revival mansion, named for the prominent lawyer who built it in 1913, the Ionic columns, widow's walk, and front entrance with beveled glass will transport you to a by-gone era. Each bedroom is furnished with antiques and reproductions. Outside, oak trees and benches punctuate the lawns and gardens. An Amish settlement, the Buena Vista Exotic Animal Park, Laura Ingalls Wilder Museum, and Bass Pro Shop are among the nearby points of interest. Branson and Silver Dollar City are one hour to the south. To revive you after the day's activities, your hosts offer complimentary beverages and snacks.

Gramma's House
1105 HIGHWAY D, MARTHASVILLE, MISSOURI 63357

Tel: **(314) 433-2675**
Best Time to Call: **8 AM–5 PM**
Hosts: **Judy and Jim Jones**
Location: **50 mi. W of St. Louis**
No. of Rooms: **4**
No. of Private Baths: **4**
Double/pb: **$75**
Suite: **$105**

Guest Cottage: **$95**
Open: **All year**
Breakfast: **Full**
Credit Cards: **MC, VISA**
Pets: **No**
Children: **Welcome**
Smoking: **No**
Social Drinking: **Permitted**

At this romantic 150-year-old farmhouse, morning starts with a full, hearty breakfast like grandma used to make. You can relax and maybe hear the bobwhite's call, reminding you of special times you spent at your own grandparents' home. Accommodations range from bedrooms to snug cottages with their own fireplaces. There are antique shops in Marthasville and Washington, and wineries in Augusta, Dutzow, and

Hermann. Close by is the Missouri River hiking and biking trail. The historic Daniel Boone home and burial site are also in the area.

Dear's Rest B&B ✪

1408 CAPP HILL RANCH ROAD, OZARK, MISSOURI 65721
info@dearsrest.com

Tel: **(800) 588-2262; (417) 581-3839**
Best Time to Call: **Before 10:30 PM**

Hosts: **Linda and Allan Schilter**
Location: **10 mi. S of Ozark**

Suite: **$75**
Open: **All year**
Breakfast: **Full**
Credit Cards: **DISC, MC, VISA**

Pets: **No**
Children: **Welcome, crib**
Smoking: **No**
Social Drinking: **Permitted**

When was the last time you walked through a forest, saw wildlife, over 150 species of birds, wildflowers, explored the crystal-clear waters of a spring-fed creek, or relaxed in a hot tub surrounded by the natural beauty of the Ozark Hills? Dear's Rest makes it all a reality when you stay in this new rustic Amish-built home, decorated with a fireplace and family antiques that give guests a comfortable homey feeling. This B&B is located adjoining the Mark Twain National Forest, 45 minutes from Branson, Springfield, the famous Bass Pro Shops and Museum, and a major Civil War battlefield. Downtown Ozark is an antique shoppers' haven. A breakfast of simple country fare—often described as the "no lunch breakfast"—is served in the sunroom or on the deck. Linda and Allan entertain one party at a time, consisting of one through six people, to ensure your comfort and privacy.

Charlotte's Apple Blossom Inn ✪
200 WEST BROADWAY, PLATTSBURG, MISSOURI 64477

Tel: **(816) 930-3243**
Hosts: **Darrell and Charlotte Apple**
Location: **30 mi. N of Kansas City**
No. of Rooms: **3**
No. of Private Baths: **3**
Double/pb: **$55**

Open: **Feb.–Dec.**
Reduced Rates: **7th night free**
Breakfast: **Full**
Pets: **No**
Children: **By arrangement**
Smoking: **No**

Darrell and Charlotte lovingly restored this 1910 home with lighting, color, and a warm interior that says "welcome." After a day of exploring the Pony Express and Jesse James attractions or the Amish settlement, relax in their comfortable parlor with an evening apple dessert. In the morning enjoy a full breakfast consisting of an apple specialty with freshly ground coffee from a local shop and home-baked breads and muffins. For early risers, coffee is served upstairs. Each room's decor has a distinctive personality with antique wicker, claw-footed tub, or handmade quilts. Visit local shops for antiques and specialty gifts. Restaurants are within walking distance. Afterward, enjoy a stroll down the quiet tree-lined streets to see other period homes.

Lafayette House
2156 LAFAYETTE AVENUE, ST. LOUIS, MISSOURI 63104
http://www.bbonline.com/mo/lafaytte

Tel: **(314) 772-4429; (800) 641-8965**
Best Time to Call: **8 AM–5 PM**
Hosts: **Nancy Buhr and Anna Millét**

No. of Rooms: **6**
No. of Private Baths: **3**
Max. No. Sharing Bath: **3**

Double/pb: **$75–$140**
Double/sb: **$60**
Suite: **$90**
Open: **All year**
Breakfast: **Full**

Pets: **Sometimes**
Children: **Welcome**
Smoking: **No**
Social Drinking: **Permitted**

This 1876 Queen Anne mansion is located in historic Lafayette Square. Lafayette House is only minutes from downtown St. Louis. Attend a baseball or football game, shop historic Union Station, visit the St. Louis Arch, Science Center, zoo, or simply stroll through the lovely Lafayette Square Park. A gourmet breakfast will be a memorable treat. Anna's menu may consist of homemade breads, muffins, crab-stuffed quiche, or Belgian waffles with warm blueberry compote, just to name a few of her culinary delights. The house is furnished with antiques and traditional furniture. The suite can accommodate six and has a kitchen. For a romantic getaway, try the room with a fireplace and Jacuzzi. For business guests, this B&B offers a fax, in-room phones, and flexible breakfast hours.

Napoleon's Retreat ✪
1815 LAFAYETTE AVENUE, ST. LOUIS, MISSOURI 63104

Tel: **(314) 772-6979**
Best Time to Call: **8 AM–9 PM**
Hosts: **Michael Lance and Jeff Archuleta**
Location: **1 mi. SW of downtown**
No. of Rooms: **4**
No. of Private Baths: **4**
Double/pb: **$75–$85**
Single/pb: **$65–$75**
Suite: **$95**

Open: **All year**
Reduced Rates: **10% families; multiple nights, Dec.–Feb.**
Breakfast: **Full**
Credit Cards: **AMEX, MC, VISA**
Pets: **No**
Children: **Welcome, over 6**
Smoking: **No**
Social Drinking: **Permitted**

"Meet me in St. Louis" begins with your arrival at Napoleon's Retreat, an elegant Second French Empire Victorian located in the historic district of Lafayette Square, one mile from the Arch. This architectural gem combines today's modern comforts with traditional St. Louis charm. Guest rooms are furnished with European and American antiques and paintings, queen-size beds, telephones, and TV. Napoleon's Retreat is within 3 miles of the world-famous Botanical Gardens, St. Louis Cathedral, zoo, Forest Park, and Washington University. Breakfast includes the house blend of coffees, juice, fruit, and an entree. For pleasure or business, this is the perfect retreat.

Preston Place ✪
1835 LAFAYETTE AVENUE, ST. LOUIS, MISSOURI 63104

Tel: **(314) 664-3429; fax: (314) 664-6929**
Best Time to Call: **10 AM–11 PM**
Host: **Jenny Preston**
No. of Rooms: **2**
No. of Private Baths: **2**
Double/pb: **$70–$80**
Single/pb: **$60–$70**

Open: **All year**
Breakfast: **Full**
Credit Cards: **AMEX, DC, MC, VISA**
Pets: **No**
Children: **No**
Smoking: **No**
Social Drinking: **Permitted**
Station Pickup: **Yes**

Preston Place combines big-city convenience with historical ambiance in a beautiful Victorian town house. Located in Lafayette Square Historic District, and minutes from downtown St. Louis, this B&B provides easy access to businesses and most tourist attractions, including the Gateway Arch. Jenny restored the house, creating a calm and elegant oasis in the midst of the city. The parlors welcome you with rich Moroccan colors, while the bedrooms soothe with tranquil pastels. Heart-healthy breakfasts are the norm, but those who wish to indulge will be offered a selection of waffles, French toast, and other traditional dishes.

Soulard Inn ✪
1014 LAMI, ST. LOUIS, MISSOURI 63104

Tel: **(314) 773-3002**
Host: **Ray Ellerbeck**
Suites: **$55–$85**
Open: **All year**
Reduced Rates: **Available**

Breakfast: **Full**
Pets: **Sometimes**
Children: **Welcome**
Smoking: **No**
Social Drinking: **Permitted**

One of the oldest buildings in St. Louis, this recently renovated Inn is a showplace in the Soulard neighborhood, which takes its name from a French naval officer who disembarked here in 1796. Guests are only moments from the finest blues and jazz clubs, superb restaurants, and other entertainment. Your host promises to give you the highest level of service and one of the best breakfasts you've ever eaten.

The Winter House ✪
3522 ARSENAL STREET, ST. LOUIS, MISSOURI 63118

Tel: **(314) 664-4399**
Hosts: **Kendall and Sarah Winter**
Location: **1 mi. S of I-44; 1 mi. W of
 I-55**
No. of Rooms: **3**
No. of Private Baths: **3**
Double/pb: **$80–$95**
Single/pb: **$65–$80**
Suites: **$95 for 2**

Open: **All year**
Reduced Rates: **After 2nd night**
Breakfast: **Full**
Credit Cards: **AMEX, DC, MC, VISA**
Pets: **No**
Children: **Welcome**
Smoking: **No**
Social Drinking: **Permitted**

This ten-room Victorian, built in 1897, features a first-floor bedroom with a pressed-tin ceiling, and a second-floor suite with a balcony and decorative fireplace. Breakfast, served in the dining room on crystal and antique Wedgwood, always includes fresh-squeezed orange juice. Fruit, candy, and fresh flowers are provided in bedrooms; live piano is available by reservation. Nearby attractions include the Missouri Botanical Garden, which adjoins Tower Grove Park, a Victorian walking park on the National Register of Historic Places. The Arch, Busch Baseball Stadium, the zoo, the symphony, and Union Station are all within four miles, and fine dining is in walking distance. There is a $20 surcharge for one night stays.

The Schwegmann House B&B Inn ✪
438 WEST FRONT STREET, WASHINGTON, MISSOURI 63090

Tel: **(800) 949-2262**
Hosts: **Cathy and Bill Nagel**
Location: **50 mi. W of St. Louis**
No. of Rooms: **9**
No. of Private Baths: **9**
Double/pb: **$75–$95**
Suite: **$120–$150**

Open: **All year**
Breakfast: **Full**
Credit Cards: **MC, VISA**
Pets: **No**
Children: **Welcome, weekdays**
Smoking: **No**
Social Drinking: **Permitted**

This three-story 1861 Georgian brick home—listed on the National Register of Historic Places—overlooks the Missouri River in the historic district of Washington. Guest rooms are tastefully decorated with antiques and locally handmade quilts. The Miller's suite boasts a thermo-massage tub for two, a bottle of Missouri wine, and breakfast delivered to your door. This B&B is located in the heart of Missouri River Wine Country, where there is much for guests to enjoy, including eleven nearby wineries, biking, hiking, antique shops, historic sites, unique gift shops, and excellent cuisine. A bountiful breakfast of local fare is served each morning.

MONTANA

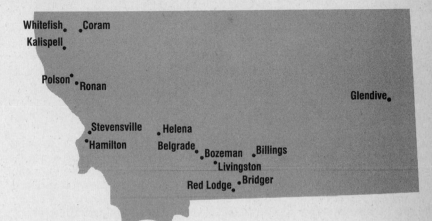

Heart Mountain Bed and Breakfast ✪
10920 CORBLY GULCH ROAD, BELGRADE, MONTANA 59714

Tel: **(406) 587-2004**
Best Time to Call: **6–9 PM**
Hosts: **Sam and Julie Wagner**
Location: **13 mi. N of Bozeman**
No. of Rooms: **2**
Max. No. Sharing Bath: **4**
Double/sb: **$65**
Single/sb: **$55**
Suite: **$55–$65**

Open: **All year**
Reduced Rates: **Available**
Breakfast: **Full**
Pets: **Sometimes**
Children: **Welcome, over 6**
Smoking: **No**
Social Drinking: **Permitted**
Airport/Station Pickup: **Yes**

Heart Mountain Bed and Breakfast is country comfort and privacy at its best. The suite includes two rooms with queen-size beds, kitchenette, lounge area, private entrance, and a piano for your enjoyment. A hearty breakfast featuring Montana country fare—sourdough pancakes, waffles, biscuits, or fresh-baked breads with homemade chokecherry syrup or apple butter—is served on the patio or in the dining room. Bring your binoculars for bird-watching and viewing the wildlife. Nearby attractions include blue-ribbon trout streams and the Museum of the Rockies. Yellowstone National Park is an hour and a half away.

The Josephine Bed & Breakfast ✪

514 NORTH 29TH STREET, BILLINGS, MONTANA 59101
josephine@imt.net

Tel: **(406) 248-5898**	Open: **All year**
Best Time to Call: **Anytime**	Reduced Rates: **Medical and extended**
Hosts: **Doug and Becky Taylor**	**stays**
No. of Rooms: **5**	Breakfast: **Full**
No. of Private Baths: **3**	Credit Cards: **AMEX, MC, VISA**
Max. No. Sharing Bath: **4**	Pets: **No**
Double/pb: **$68–$78**	Children: **Welcome, over 12**
Single/pb: **$58–$68**	Smoking: **No**
Double/sb: **$58**	Social Drinking: **Permitted**
Single/sb: **$48**	Airport Pickup: **Yes**

This lovely, historic home is comfortably elegant. The porch, with its swing and quaint seating, offers the ideal place for breakfast or relaxing. Charming picket fences, shade trees, and flowers take you back in time. Each room is individually decorated with antiques, collectibles, and old photographs. Doug, a Billings native, enjoys cooking and travel, Becky enjoys crafts and antiques, and both are knowledgeable about the area. The B&B is within walking distance of downtown's museums, galleries, theaters, and shopping. It's only minutes to the airport, horse-racing rodeos, golf courses, and historic attractions. Skiing and Little Big Horn (Custer) Battlefield are an hour away; Yellowstone National Park is a beautiful 3-hour drive via scenic Beartooth Pass.

Chokecherry House ✪

1233 STORYMILL ROAD, BOZEMAN, MONTANA 59715

Tel: **(406) 587-2657**	Breakfast: **Continental**
Best Time to Call: **Mornings, evening**	Pets: **No**
Hosts: **Rick and Kimberly Pope**	Children: **Welcome**
Location: **2 mi. N of Bozeman**	Smoking: **No**
Guesthouse: **$120**	Social Drinking: **Permitted**
Open: **All year**	Minimum Stay: **2 nights**
Reduced Rates: **10% seniors,**	Airport/Station Pickup: **Yes**
Oct.–Nov.; 5% families	

This quiet guesthouse is located in the southwestern part of the state, and has been restored to its original Americana style. Amenities include a private hot tub, phone, TV, VCR, and a fully equipped kitchen. The decor of this quonset house is that of the fifties diner look, with original art and Western memorabilia. Chokecherry House is 13 miles from Bridger Bowl ski area, and 4 miles from Montana State University, Museum of the Rockies, and historic downtown Bozeman. Yellowstone National Park and world-class trout fishing are two hours away.

Millers of Montana Bed & Breakfast Inn ✪
1002 ZACHARIA LANE, BOZEMAN, MONTANA 59715

Tel: **(406) 763-4102**	Single/sb: **$45**
Hosts: **Doug and Joyce Miller**	Open: **All year**
Location: **12 mi. SW of Bozeman**	Reduced Rates: **7th day free**
No. of Rooms: **4**	Breakfast: **Full**
No. of Private Baths: **2**	Pets: **Sometimes**
Max. No. Sharing Bath: **4**	Children: **Welcome**
Double/pb: **$60–$70**	Smoking: **No**
Double/sb: **$50**	Social Drinking: **Permitted**

This Cape Cod–style house is on a secluded 20-acre ranch, with breathtaking views of the Spanish Peaks and the Bridger Mountains. Quiet and comfortable, the B&B is furnished with country pieces and antiques. Yellowstone National Park is one hour away, and it's only 30 minutes to the Madison, Jefferson, and Yellowstone Rivers. For blueribbon trout fishing, walk over to the Gallatin River. Bozeman itself, home of Montana State University and the Museum of the Rockies, is worth visiting. Doug is in construction, and ranching, softball, and fishing are his hobbies. Joyce, a full-time hostess who retired from a culinary career, is interested in cooking, sewing, and crafts.

Torch and Toes B&B
309 SOUTH THIRD AVENUE, BOZEMAN, MONTANA 59715

Tel: **(406) 586-7285; (800) 446-2138**	Open: **All year**
Best Time to Call: **8 AM–noon**	Reduced Rates: **Government employees**
Hosts: **Ronald and Judy Hess**	Breakfast: **Full**
Location: **100 mi. SE of Helena**	Pets: **No**
No. of Rooms: **4**	Children: **Welcome**
No. of Private Baths: **4**	Smoking: **No**
Double/pb: **$80–$90**	Social Drinking: **Permitted**
Single/pb: **$70**	Airport/Station Pickup: **Yes**

Set back from the street, this Colonial Revival house is centrally located in the Bon Ton Historic District. Lace curtains, leaded glass windows, and period pieces remind one that this is a house with a past. Ron is a professor of architecture at nearby Montana State University; Judy is a weaver interested in historic preservation. Their home is furnished in a charming blend of nostalgic antiques, humorous collectibles, and fine furnishings. Breakfast always includes a special egg dish, fresh fruit, and muffins. Afterward, relax on the redwood deck in summer, or by a cozy fire in winter. Nearby attractions include blue-ribbon trout streams, hiking, skiing, and the Museum of the Rockies. Yellowstone National Park is one and a half hours away.

Voss Inn ✪

319 SOUTH WILLSON, BOZEMAN, MONTANA 59715

Tel: **(406) 587-0982; fax: (406) 585-2964**
Best Time to Call: **9:30 AM–9:30 PM**
Hosts: **Bruce and Frankee Muller**
Location: **3 mi. from I-90**
No. of Rooms: **6**
No. of Private Baths: **6**
Double/pb: **$85–$95**

Single/pb: **$75–$85**
Open: **All year**
Breakfast: **Full**
Credit Cards: **AMEX, MC, VISA**
Pets: **No**
Children: **Sometimes**
Smoking: **No**
Social Drinking: **Permitted**

This handsome 100-year-old brick mansion, flanked by Victorian gingerbread porches, is set like a gem on a tree-lined street in historic Bozeman. The bedrooms are elegantly wallpapered and furnished with brass and iron beds, ornate lighting, oriental throw rugs over polished hardwood floors—a perfect spot for a first or second honeymoon. The parlor has a good selection of books, as well as a chess set for your pleasure. It's north of Yellowstone, on the way to Glacier, with trout fishing, mountain lakes, and skiing within easy reach. Don't miss the Museum of the Rockies on the Montana State University campus ten blocks away.

Circle of Friends ✪

ROUTE 1, BOX 1250, BRIDGER, MONTANA 59014

Tel: **(406) 662-3264**
Best Time to Call: **Before 7 AM, after 6 PM**
Host: **Dorothy Sue Phillips**
Location: **45 mi. SW of Billings**
No. of Rooms: **3**
No. of Private Baths: **1**
Max. No. Sharing Bath: **4**
Double/pb: **$50**
Double/sb: **$45**

Single/sb: **$40**
Open: **All year**
Reduced Rates: **Weekly, groups**
Breakfast: **Full**
Other Meals: **Available**
Credit Cards: **MC, VISA**
Pets: **Sometimes**
Children: **Welcome**
Smoking: **No**
Social Drinking: **Permitted**

Circle of Friends is located across from the Clarks Fork River in an agricultural valley that produces wheat, barley, alfalfa, and sugar beets. On the other side of the farmland are rimrocks and dry rangeland that is home to cows and sheep. This B&B rests at the base of the Pryor Mountains to the southeast and the Beartooth Mountains to the west. The Pryors are home to wild mustangs, fossil remains, and ice caves. The Beartooth is snow-capped, allowing excellent winter skiing and hiking in the summer months. The Buffalo Bill Museum, Cody, Wyoming, and the gateway to Yellowstone Park are 60 miles away. Dorothy has 9 horses, 2 llamas, and 3 dogs. Arrive as a guest and leave as a friend.

A Wild Rose Bed and Breakfast ✪

10280 HIGHWAY 2 EAST, P.O. BOX 130396, CORAM, MONTANA 59913-0396

Tel: **(406) 387-4900**
Hosts: **Joseph and Brenda Mihalko**
Location: **6 mi. W of West Glacier**
No. of Rooms: **4**
No. of Private Baths: **3**
Max. No. Sharing Bath: **4**
Double/pb: **$85–$115**
Double/sb: **$75**
Open: **All year**

Reduced Rates: **Available**
Breakfast: **Full**
Other Meals: **Available**
Credit Cards: **MC, VISA**
Pets: **No**
Children: **Welcome, over 12**
Smoking: **No**
Social Drinking: **Permitted**

A Wild Rose offers luxurious accommodations in a peaceful mountain setting. Guest rooms are beautifully decorated in Victorian flair with deluxe mattresses, natural linens, and lavish amenities. One room has a whirlpool tub. Guests can explore the seven acres and enjoy fantastic views, unwind in the outdoor therapeutic spa, or indulge in a relaxing massage. A Wild Rose is located within ten minutes of hiking, biking, horseback riding, boat tours, golfing, skiing, and sightseeing. A hearty breakfast is served and includes the Mihalkos' own blend of freshly ground coffee.

The Hostetler House Bed & Breakfast ✪

113 NORTH DOUGLAS STREET, GLENDIVE, MONTANA 59330

Tel: **(406) 365-4505; (800) 965-8456**
Best Time to Call: **Anytime**
Hosts: **Craig and Dea Hostetler**
No. of Rooms: **2**
Max. No. Sharing Bath: **4**
Double/sb: **$50**
Single/sb: **$45**
Open: **All year**

Reduced Rates: **Weekly, seniors**
Breakfast: **Full**
Credit Cards: **DISC, MC, VISA**
Pets: **No**
Children: **Welcome, over 16**
Smoking: **No**
Social Drinking: **Permitted**
Airport/Station Pickup: **Yes**

Located one block from the Yellowstone River and two blocks from downtown shopping and restaurants, the Hostetler House is a charming 1912 historic home with two comfortable guest rooms done in casual country decor. Nearby are parks, a swimming pool, tennis courts, antique shops, churches, a golf course, a museum, Dawson Community College, fishing, hunting, and hiking. Guests may relax in the hot tub, sitting room, enclosed sunporch, or on the deck. Wake up to the smell of freshly ground gourmet coffee, tea, and homemade bread. A full breakfast is served on Grandma's china in the dining room, sunporch, or on the deck. Dea is an interior decorator who grew up on a nearby wheat farm, and Craig is a mechanical engineer, pilot, and avid outdoorsman.

Deer Crossing ✪
396 HAYES CREEK ROAD, HAMILTON, MONTANA 59840

Tel: **(406) 363-2232; (800) 763-2232**
Best Time to Call: **8 AM**
Host: **Mary Lynch**
Location: **45 mi. S of Missoula**
No. of Rooms: **5**
No. of Private Baths: **5**
Double/pb: **$70–$80**
Bunk House: **$100, sleeps 2–5**
Suites: **$95**
Open: **All year**

Reduced Rates: **5% seniors**
Breakfast: **Full**
Other Meals: **Available**
Credit Cards: **AMEX, MC, VISA**
Pets: **Horses**
Children: **Welcome**
Smoking: **No**
Social Drinking: **Permitted**
Airport/Station Pickup: **Yes**

Here is your invitation to experience Western hospitality at its finest. Deer Crossing is situated along the Lewis and Clark Trail on 24 acres of tall pines and pasture overlooking the Bitterroot Valley. Sit back and relax, or get involved in the ranch's daily activities. There are historic sites to visit, while athletic types can go swimming, rafting, fishing, skiing, hiking, and hunting. Accommodations include a large guest room, a suite with a spacious tub and a window overlooking the fields, and a bunkhouse that gives guests the feel of the Old West.

Appleton Inn Bed and Breakfast ✪
1999 EUCLID AVENUE, HIGHWAY 12 WEST, HELENA, MONTANA 59601

Tel: **(406) 449-7492; (800) 956-1999;**
    fax: (406) 449-1261
Hosts: **Cheryl Boid and Tom Woodall**
Location: **5 mi. W of I-15**
No. of Rooms: **5**

No. of Private Baths: **5**
Double/pb: **$75–$95**
Suites: **$85–$125**
Open: **All year**
Breakfast: **Full**

Credit Cards: **AMEX, DC, DISC, MC, VISA**
Pets: **Sometimes**
Children: **Welcome, over 8**

Smoking: **No**
Social Drinking: **Permitted**
Airport Pickup: **Yes**

Relax in the splendor of this beautiful Victorian built in 1890 by George Appleton and listed on the National Register of Historic Places. Guest rooms are individually decorated with antique and handcrafted furnishings and telephones. Wild rice quiche, huckleberry blintzes, or apple pancakes are breakfast favorites, served on antique Franciscan appleware and fine linens. Enjoy afternoon refreshments in one of the two parlors or in the perennial gardens. The Inn is close to hiking trails, golf courses, and a lake—mountain bikes are available. You'll be minutes from historic Last Chance Gulch, the state capitol, museums, restaurants, and specialty shops.

Creston Country Willows
70 CRESTON ROAD, KALISPELL, MONTANA 59901

Tel: **(800) 257-7517**
Best Time to Call: **8 AM–10 PM**
Hosts: **Ginger Lockner and Rick Mallock**
Location: **11 mi. E of Kalispell**
No. of Rooms: **4**
No. of Private Baths: **4**
Double/pb: **$80–$90**

Single/pb: **$65–$75**
Open: **May–Oct.**
Breakfast: **Full**
Credit Cards: **MC, VISA**
Pets: **No**
Children: **Welcome, over 12**
Smoking: **No**
Social Drinking: **Permitted**

Ginger and Rick welcome you to Creston Country Willows, a charming two-story farmhouse built in the 1920s. Guest rooms are decorated in old country style with oak and antique furniture. Relax on the porch or under golden willow trees while enjoying the view of the majestic mountains and the smell of the climbing sweet peas. Or take a leisurely stroll on the one-acre property. Awake to the aroma of freshly brewed coffee, then tuck into a hearty breakfast featuring a fresh fruit plate and all the huckleberry pancakes you can eat. Nearby attractions include Glacier National Park, Hungry Horse Dam, Gatiss Gardens, and Flathead Lake.

The River Inn ✪
4950 HIGHWAY 89 SOUTH, LIVINGSTON, MONTANA 59047

Tel: **(406) 222-2429**
Best Time to Call: **1–7 PM**
Hosts: **Dee Dee Van Zyl and Ursula Neese**
Location: **4 mi. S. of Livingston**
No. of Rooms: **3**
No. of Private Baths: **3**

Double/pb: **$70–$85**
Single/pb: **$60–$75**
Open: **Apr.–Oct.**
Reduced Rates: **$5 after 3rd night**
Breakfast: **Full**
Other Meals: **Available**
Credit Cards: **MC, VISA**

Pets: **Sometimes**
Children: **Welcome, over 9**
Smoking: **No**

Social Drinking: **Permitted**
Airport Pickup: **Yes**

Restored in 1995, this lovely one-hundred-year-old farmhouse is located 20 feet from the west bank of the Yellowstone River, with approximately 5 acres and 500 feet of riverfront for meandering or fishing. Guest rooms offer superb views of the Absaroka Mountains, the river, the islands, and the canyon. The dining room is large, with bookcases, leaded glass windows, and a window seat. French doors open onto a rock patio, where on the warmest of mornings breakfast is served. Hosts guide hiking, biking, and canoeing trips. Yellowstone Park is less than 50 miles away, Historical Livingston just minutes away.

Hawthorne House ✪
304 THIRD AVENUE, EAST, POLSON, MONTANA 59860

Tel: **(406) 883-2723; (800) 290-1345**
Best Time to Call: **After 5 PM, weekends**
Hosts: **Gerry and Karen Lenz**
Location: **70 mi. N of Missoula**
No. of Rooms: **4**
Max. No. Sharing Bath: **4**
Double/sb: **$50**

Single/sb: **$45**
Open: **All year**
Breakfast: **Full**
Pets: **No**
Children: **Welcome, over 12**
Smoking: **No**
Social Drinking: **No**

In the small western Montana town of Polson, at the foot of Flathead Lake, you'll find Hawthorne House, an English Tudor home on a quiet shady street. In summer, cheerful window boxes welcome the weary traveler. The house is furnished with antiques from Karen's grandparents. There are plate collections, Indian artifacts, and glassware. The kitchen has some interesting collections. Breakfast is always special, with something baked fresh each morning. Nearby attractions include Glacier National Park, the National Bison Range, Kerr Dam, and great scenic beauty. Golf abounds. There are always activities on the lake and river.

Willows Inn ✪
224 SOUTH PLATT AVENUE, RED LODGE, MONTANA 59068

Tel: **(406) 446-3913**
Best Time to Call: **8 AM–10 PM**
Hosts: **Elven, Kerry, and Carolyn Boggio**
Location: **60 mi. SW of Billings**
No. of Rooms: **5**
No. of Private Baths: **3**
Max. No. Sharing Bath: **4**
Double/pb: **$55–$75**
Double/sb: **$60**
Single/sb: **$50**
Guest Cottages: **$80 for 2**

Open: **All year**
Reduced Rates: **10% after 4th night; 10% seniors**
Breakfast: **Continental**
Credit Cards: **DISC, MC, VISA**
Pets: **No**
Children: **Welcome**
Smoking: **No**
Social Drinking: **Permitted**
Minimum Stay: **2 nights in cottage**

Tucked beneath the majestic Beartooth Mountains in the northern Rockies, the historic town of Red Lodge provides an ideal setting for this charming three-story Queen Anne. Flanked by giant evergreens and colorful flower beds, the Inn is reminiscent of a bygone age, complete with white picket fence, gingerbread trim, and front porch swing. Overstuffed sofas and wicker pieces complement the warm and cheerful decor. Delicious home-baked pastries are Elven's specialty—she uses her own Finnish recipes for these mouthwatering treats. Championship rodeos, excellent cross-country and downhill skiing, opportunities to hike, golf, and fish abound in this special area, still unspoiled by commercial progress. Yellowstone National Park is only 65 miles away.

The Timbers Bed and Breakfast ✪
1184 TIMBERLANE ROAD, RONAN, MONTANA 59864

Tel: **(406) 676-4373; (800) 775-4373**	Suites: **$75–$115; sleeps 4**
Best Time to Call: **9 AM–9 PM**	Open: **All year**
Hosts: **Doris and Leonard McCravey**	Breakfast: **Full, Continental**
Location: **52 mi. N of Missoula**	Credit Cards: **MC, VISA**
No. of Rooms: **2**	Pets: **Sometimes**
No. of Private Baths: **1**	Children: **Welcome, over 8**
Max. No. Sharing Bath: **4**	Smoking: **No**
Double/sb: **$65–$85**	Social Drinking: **Permitted**

The Timbers is situated at the base of the Rocky Mountain Mission Range on 21 secluded acres, midway between Glacier National Park and Missoula, Montana. The house has a wraparound deck, and is glassed in to provide a magnificent view of the Missions. Cathedral ceilings, hand-hewn beams, a barnwood dining area, and furnishings that Doris and Leonard collected give their home a sophisticated yet warm country feel. Leonard can tell you about his twenty-seven years on the professional rodeo circuit while you enjoy one of Doris's wonderful country breakfasts. Nearby attractions include Flathead Lake, National Bison Range, Glacier National Park, golf, water sports, fishing, horseback riding, skiing, white-water rafting, art galleries, local rodeos, and powwows.

Country Caboose ✪
852 WILLOUGHBY ROAD, STEVENSVILLE, MONTANA 59870

Tel: **(406) 777-3145**	Open: **May–Sept.**
Host: **Lisa Thompson**	Breakfast: **Full**
Location: **35 mi. S of Missoula**	Pets: **No**
No. of Rooms: **1**	Children: **Welcome**
No. of Private Baths: **1**	Smoking: **No**
Double/pb: **$59**	Social Drinking: **Permitted**
Single/pb: **$59**	

If you enjoy romantic train rides, why not spend the night in an authentic caboose? This one dates back to 1923, is made of wood, and is painted red, of course. It is set on real rails in the middle of the countryside. The caboose sleeps two and offers a spectacular view of the Bitter-root Mountains, right from your pillow. In the morning, breakfast is served at a table for two. Specialties include huckleberry pancakes, quiche, and strawberries in season. Local activities include touring St. Mary's Mission, hiking the mountain trails, fishing, and hunting.

Haus Rustika Bed and Breakfast ✪
396 DRY GULCH ROAD, STEVENSVILLE, MONTANA 59870
rustika@marsweb.com

Tel: **(406) 777-2291**	Reduced Rates: **7th night free; families 10–20%**
Best Time to Call: **8 AM–9 PM**	
Hosts: **Grace and Werner Will**	Breakfast: **Full**
Location: **26 mi. S of Missoula**	Other Meals: **Available**
No. of Rooms: **4**	Pets: **Sometimes**
Max. No. Sharing Bath: **4**	Children: **Welcome**
Double/sb: **$50**	Smoking: **No**
Single/sb: **$35**	Social Drinking: **Permitted**
Open: **All year**	

Haus Rustika is located near historic Stevensville in the Bitterroot Valley of western Montana. Nearby activities include a wildlife refuge, out-door sports, small-town entertainment, shopping, and restaurants. The use of wood and old barn boards in this Dutch Colonial house gives it a rustic charm and complements the antique furniture. All guest bed-rooms are accessible by a separate entrance. A mile-long nature trail is located behind the house and winds through the pine forest, the sage brush, and along the creek. Grace and Werner are retired teachers of special education and German. They love entertaining, gourmet cooking, and gardening. Their love of traveling is reflected in the guest bedrooms, where the decor of each typifies a different continent.

Good Medicine Lodge
537 WISCONSIN AVENUE, WHITEFISH, MONTANA 59937
http://www.wtp.net/go/goodrx

Tel: **(800) 860-5488**
Hosts: **Christopher and Susan Ridder**
Location: **½ mi. N of Whitefish**
No. of Rooms: **9**
No. of Private Baths: **9**
Double/pb: **$95**
Single/pb: **$85**
Suites: **$115–$170**
Open: **Dec. 15–Apr. 15, May 15– Oct. 15**

Reduced Rates: **$10 less Dec. 15– Apr. 15**
Breakfast: **Full**
Credit Cards: **AMEX, DISC, MC, VISA**
Pets: **No**
Children: **Welcome**
Smoking: **No**
Social Drinking: **Permitted**
Airport/Station Pickup: **Yes**
Foreign Languages: **French, German**

Good Medicine Lodge is a classic Montana getaway hewn from solid cedar timbers and decorated in a Western motif with fabrics influenced by Native American textiles. Guest rooms have vaulted ceilings and telephones; most have balconies with mountain views. One room is wheelchair accessible. The lodge features crackling fireplaces, an outdoor spa, guest laundry, and a ski room complete with boot and glove dryers. The Ridders' B&B is located minutes from skiing, golfing, skating, Glacier Park, shopping, and dining. Downtown Whitefish and the Amtrak station are one-half mile away. The lodge is 9 miles from Glacier International Airport, 24 miles from Glacier Park, and 60 miles from the Canadian border.

NEBRASKA

Oakland
Omaha
Gretna
Crete

The Parson's House ✪
638 FOREST AVENUE, CRETE, NEBRASKA 68333

Tel: **(402) 826-2634**
Hosts: **Harold and Sandy Richardson**
Location: **25 mi. SW of Lincoln**
No. of Rooms: **2**
Max. No. Sharing Bath: **4**
Double/sb: **$45**
Single/sb: **$35**

Open: **All year**
Breakfast: **Full**
Pets: **No**
Children: **No**
Smoking: **No**
Social Drinking: **No**
Airport/Station Pickup: **Yes**

Enjoy warm hospitality in this newly refinished, turn-of-the-century home tastefully decorated with antiques. Doane College lies one block away; the beautiful campus is just the place for a leisurely afternoon stroll. It's just a short drive to Lincoln, the state's capital and home of the University of Nebraska. Harold, a Baptist minister with the local U.C.C. church, runs a remodeling business while Sandy runs the bed and breakfast. After a day's activity, they invite you to relax in their modern whirlpool tub and make their home yours for the duration of your stay.

Bundy's Bed and Breakfast ✪
16906 SOUTH 255, GRETNA, NEBRASKA 68028

Tel: **(402) 332-3616**
Best Time to Call: **7 AM–9 PM**
Hosts: **Bob and Dee Bundy**
Location: **30 mi. S of Omaha**
No. of Rooms: **4**
Max. No. Sharing Bath: **4**
Double/sb: **$35**

Single/sb: **$20**
Open: **All year**
Breakfast: **Full**
Pets: **Sometimes**
Children: **No**
Smoking: **No**
Social Drinking: **No**

The Bundys have a pretty farmhouse painted white with black trim. Here you can enjoy country living just 30 minutes from downtown Lincoln and Omaha. The rooms are decorated with antiques, attractive wallpapers, and collectibles. In the morning, wake up to farm-fresh eggs and homemade breads. The house is just a short walk from a swimming lake, and is three miles from a ski lodge.

Benson Bed and Breakfast ✪
402 NORTH OAKLAND AVENUE, OAKLAND, NEBRASKA 68045-1135

Tel: **(402) 685-6051**
Hosts: **Stan and Norma Anderson**
Location: **58 mi. NW of Omaha**
No. of Rooms: **3**
Max. No. Sharing Bath: **4**

Double/sb: **$50–$55**
Single/sb: **$41.50**
Open: **All year**
Reduced Rates: **Available**
Breakfast: **Full**

Pets: **No**
Children: **Welcome, over 3**

Smoking: **No**
Social Drinking: **Permitted**

Once used as a rooming house, this B&B was built in 1905 with brick walls nearly one foot thick, and renovated in 1990. There is a common area of five beautifully decorated rooms for your relaxation; one is a new garden room featuring many plants and a picket fence on the wall. On the main floor there is a beauty, crafts, and gift shop. Nearby is the Swedish Heritage Center and an eighteen-hole golf course. Norma serves a huge breakfast and collects things from various soft drink companies, which are displayed in the family room.

The Offutt House ✪
140 NORTH 39TH STREET, OMAHA, NEBRASKA 68131

Tel: **(402) 553-0951**
Hosts: **Paul and Janet Koenig**
Location: **1 mi. from I-80**
No. of Rooms: **7**
No. of Private Baths: **7**
Double/pb: **$65–$90**
Single/pb: **$60–$85**
Suites: **$85–$105**

Open: **All year**
Reduced Rates: **After 5th night**
Breakfast: **Continental, weekday; Full, weekends**
Pets: **Sometimes**
Children: **By arrangement**
Smoking: **Restricted**
Social Drinking: **Permitted**

This comfortable mansion, circa 1894, is part of the city's Historic Gold Coast, a section of handsome homes built by Omaha's wealthiest residents. Offering peace and quiet, the rooms are air-conditioned, spacious, and furnished with antiques; some have fireplaces. Janet and Paul will direct you to nearby attractions such as the Joslyn Museum or the Old Market area, which abounds with many beautiful shops and fine restaurants.

NEVADA

Washoe • •Silver Springs   •East Ely

Steptoe Valley Inn ✪
P.O. BOX 151110, 220 EAST 11TH STREET, EAST ELY,
NEVADA 89315-1110

Tel: **(702) 289-8687 June–Sept.;**
   (702) 435-1196 Oct.–May
Hosts: **Jane and Norman Lindley**
Location: **70 mi. W of Great Basin**
   National Park
No. of Rooms: **5**
No. of Private Baths: **5**
Double/pb: **$84**
Single/pb: **$73**

Open: **June–Sept.**
Breakfast: **Full**
Credit Cards: **AMEX, MC, VISA**
Pets: **No**
Children: **By arrangement**
Smoking: **No**
Social Drinking: **Permitted**
Foreign Languages: **Spanish**

This Inn opened in July 1991 after major reconstruction. Located near
the Nevada Northern Railway Museum, it was originally Ely City Gro-
cery of 1907. The five second-floor rooms have country decor and private balconies, and the elegant Victorian dining room and library are
downstairs. The large yard has mature trees, a gazebo, and rose garden.

Norman is an airline captain and ex-rancher and Jane is a retired stewardess and local tour guide. Their guests can enjoy cool nights, scenic countryside, the "Ghost Train of Old Ely," the Great Basin National Park, and Cave Lake State Park, or just relax on the veranda!

A Secret Garden ✪
P.O. BOX 1150, SILVER SPRINGS, NEVADA 89429-1150

Tel: **(702) 577-0837**
Best Time to Call: **8 AM–9 PM**
Hosts: **Tom and Gail Wilson**
Location: **45 mi. SE of Reno**
No. of Rooms: **1**
No. of Private Baths: **1**
Double/pb: **$65**
Single/pb: **$55**

Open: **All year**
Breakfast: **Full**
Credit Cards: **VISA**
Pets: **Sometimes**
Children: **By arrangement**
Smoking: **No**
Social Drinking: **Permitted**
Airport/Station Pickup: **Yes**

In the sparsely populated Mountain View area of south Silver Springs, a tall fence shelters this freshly remodeled hacienda from the surrounding desert. Visitors will find shade trees and a wide verandah for summer afternoons and a cozy guest room for chilly nights. Breakfast time can be a surprise or guests can help with their menus. Tom and Gail cheerfully attempt to accommodate special menu requests when arranged at the time of your reservation. Within hiking or cycling distance are two state parks, Lake Lahontan and Fort Churchill. Also nearby are excellent restaurants and entertainment.

Deer Run Ranch Bed and Breakfast ✪
5440 EASTLAKE BOULEVARD, WASHOE VALLEY, CARSON CITY, NEVADA 89704

Tel: **(702) 882-3643**
Best Time to Call: **7 AM–8 PM**
Hosts: **David and Muffy Vhay**
Location: **8 mi. N of Carson City**

No. of Rooms: **2**
No. of Private Baths: **2**
Double/pb: **$80–$95**
Open: **All year**

Reduced Rates: **$10 less Mon.–Thurs.**
Breakfast: **Full**
Credit Cards: **AMEX, DISC, MC, VISA**
Pets: **No**
Children: **Welcome, over 12**

Smoking: **No**
Social Drinking: **Permitted**
Minimum Stay: **2 nights, holidays and special events weekends**

Deer Run Ranch, a working alfalfa farm, overlooks Washoe Lake and the Sierra Nevada Mountains. A private entry, Navajo rugs, old photographs, and paintings by well-known local artists grace the comfortable guest areas, lending Western ambience to this house designed and built by your host, who is an architect. Your hosts also have a pottery studio, woodshop, and large garden on the premises. Things to do in the area include skiing, biking, hiking, and hang gliding; Washoe Lake State Park is next door. For fine dining, casino hopping, and entertainment, Lake Tahoe, Reno, Virginia City, and Carson City are only minutes away.

For key to listings, see inside front or back cover.

✪ This star means that rates are guaranteed through December 31, 1998, to any guest making a reservation as a result of reading about the B&B in *Bed & Breakfast U.S.A.*—1998 edition.

Important! To avoid misunderstandings, always ask about cancellation policies when booking.

Please enclose a self-addressed, stamped, business-size envelope when contacting reservation services.

For more details on what you can expect in a B&B, see Chapter 1.

Always mention *Bed & Breakfast U.S.A.* when making reservations!

We want to hear from you! Use the form on page 625.

NEW HAMPSHIRE

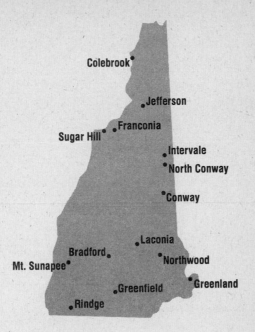

Candlelite Inn Bed and Breakfast ✪
5 GREENHOUSE LANE, BRADFORD,
NEW HAMPSHIRE 03221

Tel: **(603) 938-5571**
Best Time to Call: **Evenings**
Hosts: **Les and Marilyn Gordon**
Location: **20 mi. W of Concord**
No. of Rooms: **6**
No. of Private Baths: **6**
Double/pb: **$65–$85**
Open: **All year**

Reduced Rates: **Available**
Breakfast: **Full**
Credit Cards: **DISC, MC, VISA**
Pets: **No**
Children: **Welcome**
Smoking: **No**
Social Drinking: **Permitted**

Candlelite is an 1897 Victorian Inn nestled on three acres in the Lake
Sunapee region. True to this B&B's name, your hosts serve a candlelit
breakfast in the lovely dining room or in the sunroom overlooking the

pond. On a lazy summer day sip lemonade on the gazebo porch; on a chilly winter evening drink hot chocolate by a warm, cozy fire in the parlor. The Inn is just minutes from three ski areas, shopping, antiquing, and restaurants. Les enjoys woodworking and tole painting, while Marilyn pursues cross-stitching, quilting, and crafts.

Monadnock B&B ✪
1 MONADNOCK STREET, COLEBROOK, NEW HAMPSHIRE 03576

Tel: **(603) 237-8216**
Best Time to Call: **8 AM–9 PM**
Hosts: **Barbara and Wendell Woodard**
Location: **1 block from the junction of Rtes. 3 and 26**
No. of Rooms: **7**
Max. No. Sharing Bath: **4**
Double/sb: **$50–$60**
Single/sb: **$35**

Open: **All year**
Reduced Rates: **15% weekly**
Breakfast: **Full**
Pets: **Sometimes**
Children: **Welcome**
Smoking: **Permitted**
Social Drinking: **Permitted**
Airport/Station Pickup: **Yes**

When Wendell was in the Air Force, the Woodards lived all over the world, and their house is decorated with pieces collected in Europe and Asia. Now they have settled in New Hampshire's North Country, within walking distance of Vermont and only a 15-minute drive from Canada. Wendell cheerfully directs skiers, hunters, fishermen, and golfers to all his favorite haunts. But first, Barbara will ply guests with a hearty breakfast, featuring specialties such as sausage quiche, pancakes, and omelettes, accompanied by endless supplies of coffee and tea.

The Foothills Farm ✪
P.O. BOX 1368, CONWAY, NEW HAMPSHIRE 03818

Tel: **(207) 935-3799**
Best Time to Call: **Early evenings**

Hosts: **Kevin Early and Theresa Rovere**
Location: **10 mi. SE of Conway Village**

No. of Rooms: **5**
No. of Private Baths: **1**
Max. No. Sharing Bath: **4**
Double/pb: **$85**
Single/pb: **$85**
Double/sb: **$45–$50**
Single/sb: **$42**
Guest Cottage: **$85–$95**
Open: **All year**
Reduced Rates: **Available**

Breakfast: **Full**
Credit Cards: **AMEX, MC, VISA**
Pets: **Sometimes**
Children: **By arrangement**
Smoking: **No**
Social Drinking: **Permitted**
Minimum Stay: **2 nights weekends during fall foliage and holidays**
Airport/Station Pickup: **Yes**

This restored 1850s clapboard farmhouse is located on a quiet back road in the foothills of the White Mountains. The house is surrounded by gardens of flowers, vegetables, and herbs. The fifty-acre farm has a new stable to accommodate equine guests, a trout stream, and numerous trails for cross-country skiing, hiking, and mountain biking. You're welcome to feed the chickens and pet the horses. Guest rooms are furnished in period antiques; one has a fireplace. Relax in the den, where you will find a crackling fire, or in warmer weather, on the screened porch overlooking gardens and paddocks. Breakfast specialties include eggs Benedict with home fries and blueberry pancakes with sausage, served in a country kitchen that has an antique stove and pine paneling. Kevin and Theresa have bicycles to lend and can direct you to the less-traveled areas of this scenic region. Scores of restaurants, factory outlets, and antique shops are also nearby.

Blanche's B&B ✪

351 EASTON VALLEY ROAD, FRANCONIA, NEW HAMPSHIRE 03580
Shannon@ncia.net

Tel: **(603) 823-7061**
Best Time to Call: **Before 9 PM**
Host: **Brenda Shannon**
Location: **5 mi. SW of Franconia**
No. of Rooms: **5**
No. of Private Baths: **1**
Max. No. Sharing Bath: **4**
Double/pb: **$85–$95**
Double/sb: **$65**
Single/sb: **$40–$45**
Open: **All year**
Reduced Rates: **Weekly, groups**

Breakfast: **Full**
Credit Cards: **MC, VISA**
Other Meals: **Available to groups**
Pets: **No**
Children: **Welcome**
Smoking: **No**
Social Drinking: **Permitted**
Minimum Stay: **2 nights holiday weekends, Christmas vacation week, fall foliage season**
Airport/Station Pickup: **Yes**

Set in a meadow near the Appalachian Trail, this steep-gabled, Victorian farmhouse, circa 1887, is decorated with family pieces and auction finds. Brenda provides cotton linens on comfortable beds, a hearty breakfast, and good advice about the nearby hiking and cross-country ski trails. Franconia Notch and Cannon Mountain are a 10-minute drive. Your host will be happy to suggest the best spots for antiques, crafts, bird-watching, or help you discover the simple pleasures of life in the White Mountains. There is an artist's studio on the premises featuring colorful handmade floorcloths. The guest living room has a fireplace.

Bungay Jar Bed & Breakfast

**EASTON VALLEY ROAD, P.O. BOX 15, FRANCONIA,
NEW HAMPSHIRE 03580**

Tel: **(603) 823-7775**; fax: **(603) 444-0100**

Hosts: **Kate Kerivan and Lee Strimbeck, owners**

Location: **6 mi. from Rte. I-93, Exit 38**
No. of Rooms: **6**
No. of Private Baths: **4**
Max. No. Sharing Bath: **4**
Double/pb: **$75–$150**
Double/sb: **$75–$105**
Suite: **$150–$195**
Open: **All year**

Breakfast: **Full**
Credit Cards: **AMEX, DISC, MC, VISA**
Pets: **No**
Children: **Welcome, over 6**
Smoking: **No**
Social Drinking: **Permitted**
Minimum Stay: **2 nights foliage season, holiday weekends**

Built in 1969 from an 18th-century barn, this post-and-beam house is nestled among fifteen acres of woodland bounded by a river, forest, and spectacular mountain views. In winter, guests are greeted by a crackling fire and the aroma of mulled cider in the two-story living room reminiscent of a hayloft. Antique country furnishings enhance the decor. Apple pancakes served with local maple syrup are a specialty, as are homemade breads, preserves, fruit compotes, granola, and imaginative egg dishes. Refreshments of cider and cheese are served each afternoon. Your hosts are avid hikers and skiers, so you are sure to benefit from their expert knowledge. Guests can enjoy the flower and herb gardens, the water lily pond, and the view of the pastures and horses from the porches.

The Inn at Forest Hills

P.O. BOX 783, ROUTE 142, FRANCONIA, NEW HAMPSHIRE 03580
innfhills@connriver.com.net; http://www.innfhills.com

Tel: **(603) 823-9550; (800) 280-9550**
reservations only
Best Time to Call: **10 AM–10 PM**

Hosts: **Gordon and Joanne Haym**
Location: **150 mi. N of Boston**
No. of Rooms: **7**

No. of Private Baths: **7**
Double/pb: **$85–$145**
Suite: **$105–$145**
Open: **All year**
Reduced Rates: **Available**
Breakfast: **Full**
Other Meals: **Sometimes**
Credit Cards: **MC, VISA**

Pets: **No**
Children: **Welcome, over 12**
Smoking: **No**
Social Drinking: **Permitted**
Minimum Stay: **2 nights fall foliage and holiday weekends**
Station Pickup: **Yes**

Formerly part of the Forest Hills Hotel, this Tudor-style Inn was built in 1890 to accommodate social events and large families. In 1961 the building was donated to Franconia College and became the home of its president. Gordon and Joanne purchased the Inn in 1992 and began their bed and breakfast venture. Eighteen charming historic rooms showcase the majestic scenery and year-round attractions of the White Mountains. The Inn is located nearby to Cannon, Bretton Woods, and Loon. Guests can cross-country ski on the property or at nearby trails. Enjoy gracious hospitality and relax in country casualness in the sun-filled solarium or by the fireplaces in the living room or Alpine room. In the morning, savor a gourmet breakfast by the fireplace.

Greenfield Inn
BOX 400, FOREST ROAD, ROUTE 31N, GREENFIELD, NEW HAMPSHIRE 03047

Tel: **(800) 678-4144**
Best Time to Call: **Noon–9 PM**
Hosts: **Barbara and Vic Mangini**
Location: **90 min. from Boston**
No. of Rooms: **12**
No. of Private Baths: **9**
Max. No. Sharing Bath: **4**
Double/pb: **$69**
Double/sb: **$49**
Guest Cottage: **$59–$139**

Suites: **$79–$99**
Open: **All year**
Reduced Rates: **10% after 2 nights, 20% after 4 nights**
Breakfast: **Full**
Credit Cards: **AMEX, MC, VISA**
Pets: **No**
Children: **By arrangement**
Smoking: **Restricted**
Social Drinking: **Permitted**

Vic and Barbara purchased this Victorian mansion nine years ago with a bed and breakfast plan in mind. Guest rooms are decorated in Victorian style with antique furniture, lavish comforters, lace curtains and beautiful flowered wallpaper. Breakfast is a party at the Inn. Barbara's specialties include homemade muffins and granola, and a delicious ham and egg soufflé. Vic clears the tables while he socializes and helps guests plan their day. Specializing in romance and relaxation, your hosts make you feel comfortable and happy from the moment you arrive.

Ayres Homestead Bed & Breakfast ✪
47 PARK AVENUE, GREENLAND, NEW HAMPSHIRE 03840

Tel: **(603) 436-5992**
Hosts: **David and Priscilla Engel**

Location: **3 mi. W of Portsmouth**
No. of Rooms: **4**

No. of Private Baths: **1**
Max. No. Sharing Bath: **4**
Double/pb: **$55**
Single/pb: **$50**
Double/sb: **$50**
Single/sb: **$45**
Suites: **$95**

Open: **All year**
Breakfast: **Full**
Pets: **Sometimes**
Children: **Welcome**
Smoking: **No**
Social Drinking: **Permitted**

The Thomas Ayres House, begun in 1737 as a two-room post-and-beam structure, has been enlarged and remodeled many times in its 250-year history. Priscilla and Dave will tell you of the famous people, including Paul Revere, George Washington, and John Adams, who passed by its doors. Set on six acres on the historic village green, its nine rooms have wainscoting, exposed beams, and wide board floors; seven have fireplaces. The bedrooms are made cozy with antiques, braided rugs, afghans, and rockers. Breakfast is served in the dining room on an antique table set in front of a brick fireplace with artfully displayed pewterware and ironware.

The Forest—A Country Inn ✪
ROUTE 16A, P.O. BOX 37, INTERVALE, NEW HAMPSHIRE 03845
http://www.journeysnorth.com/mwv/forest.html

Tel: **(603) 356-9772; (800) 448-3534**
Hosts: **Lisa and Bill Guppy**
Location: **1½ m. from Rte. 16**
No. of Rooms: **11**
No. of Private Baths: **11**
Double/pb: **$70–$115**
Guest cottage: **$95–$169**
Open: **All year**
Reduced Rates: **May 1–June 30; Oct. 20–Dec. 13**

Breakfast: **Full**
Other Meals: **Available**
Credit Cards: **AMEX, DISC, MC, VISA**
Pets: **No**
Children: **Welcome, over 5**
Smoking: **No**
Social Drinking: **Permitted**

Located two miles north from North Conway Village and reigning over 25 acres in the White Mountains, this three-story Victorian Inn has been in operation since the late 1800s. As you enter the Inn, the warmth of a wood-burning fireplace and an oriental rug set the tone for a memorable stay. The stone cottage has a fireplace and is the favorite for honeymooners. The newly renovated Forest Cottage boasts a gas fireplace and a Jacuzzi tub. Relax by the garden-side pool or take advantage of all the recreational possibilities the valley has to offer, such as downhill and cross-country skiing, hiking, biking, canoeing, fishing, golfing, and much more. In the winter, enjoy cross-country trails that begin at the back door.

The Jefferson Inn ✪
ROUTE 2, RR1, BOX 68A, JEFFERSON, NEW HAMPSHIRE 03583

Tel: **(603) 586-7998; (800) 729-7908;** fax: **(603) 586-7808**

Hosts: **Marla Mason and Don Garretson**
No. of Rooms: **11**

No. of Private Baths: **11**
Double/pb: **$70–$120**
Single/pb: **$65–$100**
Suites: **$100–$150**
Open: **Dec.–Mar.; May–Oct.**
Reduced Rates: **Winter mid-week**
Breakfast: **Full**

Credit Cards: **AMEX, DISC, MC, VISA**
Pets: **No**
Children: **Welcome**
Smoking: **No**
Social Drinking: **Permitted**
Foreign Languages: **German**

Nestled in the foothills of the northern White Mountains near Mount Washington, this charming 1896 Victorian Inn offers spectacular views and outdoor adventures year-round. Bring your boots, binoculars, and bicycles for superb hiking, cycling, and sightseeing. Next to the Inn you'll find the trailhead to Mt. Starr King and Mt. Waumbek. Three of the best cycling trails start in the driveway. Tee off at the Waumbek, the oldest 18-hole championship golf course in New Hampshire, or take a dip in the spring-fed swimming pond. In the winter you can ski, ice skate, and snowmobile right outside the door. Antique shops, children's amusement parks, summer theater, and downhill skiing are nearby. The Inn is perfect for a private getaway or a family vacation. A delightful gourmet breakfast and afternoon tea with fresh baked goods are included.

Ferry Point House ✪

100 LOWER BAY ROAD, SANBORNTON, LACONIA, NEW HAMPSHIRE 03269
http://www.tial.net/users/berg

Tel: **(603) 524-0087**
Best Time to Call: **After 2 PM**
Hosts: **Diane and Joe Damato**
Location: **90 mi. N of Boston**
No. of Rooms: **5**
No. of Private Baths: **5**
Double/pb: **$75–$95**
Open: **May–Oct.**

Reduced Rates: **15% weekly**
Breakfast: **Full**
Pets: **No**
Children: **Welcome, over 10**
Social Drinking: **Permitted**
Airport/Station Pickup: **Yes**
Foreign Languages: **French**

New England's past is well preserved in this 150-year-old Victorian located on picturesque Lake Winnisquam. Enjoy breathtaking views of the water and the mountains from a 60-foot veranda. Of course, the view is even more enjoyable when you're sipping lemonade or the house blend of coffee. Guest rooms overlook the lake and are furnished with antiques, collectibles, and fresh flowers. Breakfast is served in a Victorian-style dining room, and your hosts take pride in offering unusual dishes, such as cheese baked apples, crepes, or Grand Marnier French toast. Ferry Point House is minutes from regional activities such as boating, skiing, dinner cruises, and a large selection of fine restaurants.

Rest Assured on Lake Winnisquam
47 LAIGHTON AVENUE, SOUTH, LACONIA, NEW HAMPSHIRE 03246

Tel: **(603) 524-9021**
Best Time to Call: **After 6 PM**
Hosts: **Maurice and Helene Gouin**
Location: **30 mi. N of Concord**
No. of Rooms: **3**
No. of Private Baths: **1**
Max. No. Sharing Bath: **2**
Double/pb: **$85**
Double/sb: **$70**
Single/sb: **$60**

Open: **All year**
Reduced Rates: **10% seniors**
Breakfast: **Full**
Pets: **Sometimes**
Children: **Welcome**
Smoking: **No**
Social Drinking: **Permitted**
Airport/Station Pickup: **Yes**
Foreign Languages: **French**

A private wooded road leads to Rest Assured, a cedar contemporary complemented by colorful flower gardens, evergreens and, behind a picket fence, a thriving vegetable and herb garden. After walking through the front door, guests are overwhelmed by the magnificent view of the mountains, and a crystal clear lake—the third largest in the state. The house has a cathedral ceiling and oak beams, floors, and trim; the sunny, open rooms are decorated with comfortable furniture and antiques, for homeyness. In warm weather, breakfast is served on the large covered deck off the kitchen. Guests are encouraged to walk down to the Gouins' private dock, where they'll find a canoe and rowboat, and chairs for lounging. For hikers, the White Mountains are 20 minutes away.

Blue Goose Inn B&B ✪
24 ROUTE 103B, P.O. BOX 2117, MT. SUNAPEE, NEW HAMPSHIRE 03255

Tel: **(603) 763-5519**
Best Time to Call: **Before noon**
Hosts: **Meryl and Ronald Caldwell**
Location: **10 mi. From I-89**
No. of Rooms: **5**
No. of Private Baths: **4**
Max. No. Sharing Bath: **3**
Double/pb: **$55**
Single/pb: **$45**
Double/sb: **$50**

Single/sb: **$41.50**
Open: **All year**
Breakfast: **Full**
Credit Cards: **MC, VISA**
Pets: **No**
Children: **Welcome**
Smoking: **No**
Social Drinking: **Permitted**
Airport/Station Pickup: **Yes**

This well-restored, early 19th-century Colonial farmhouse is located on 3$^1/_2$ acres along Lake Sunapee, at the base of Mt. Sunapee. The cozy, comfortable guest rooms are furnished in a quaint, country style. Make yourself at home in any of the common areas. The living room has a fireplace, TV, VCR, and book and video library; the card and game room has plenty of diversions; there's refrigerator space in the kitchen, and the porch, weather permitting, is ideal for breakfast and snacks. Kids will have fun in the summer playhouse. The Mt. Sunapee area is a mini-resort for vacationers of all ages, offering boating, swimming, hiking, downhill and cross-country skiing, snowmobiling, crafts fairs, antiquing, and much more.

The Buttonwood Inn
P.O. BOX 1817, MT. SURPRISE ROAD, NORTH CONWAY,
NEW HAMPSHIRE 03860

Tel: (603) 356-2625; (800) 258-2625
Hosts: Claudia and Peter Needham
Location: 1½ mi. from Rte. 16
No. of Rooms: 9
No. of Private Baths: 5
Max. No. Sharing Bath: 4
Double/pb: $80–$150
Single/pb: $70–$140
Double/sb: $70–$105
Single/sb: $60–$95
Open: All year

Reduced Rates: Available; families
Breakfast: Full
Other Meals: Available Jan., Feb.
Credit Cards: AMEX, DISC, MC, VISA
Pets: No
Children: Welcome, over 3
Smoking: No
Social Drinking: Permitted
Minimum Stay: 2 nights weekends Jan. and Feb.; 3 nights holiday weekends

Enjoy this 1820s cape in its secluded spot on Mt. Surprise, only two miles from North Conway. It has nine uniquely appointed guest rooms, fireplaced common rooms, gardens, pool, and cross-country skiing from the doorstep. Dinners are served in winter. The Inn is a spot for romantic getaways, families, groups, reunions, or weddings.

The Victorian Harvest Inn
28 LOCUST LANE, BOX 1763, NORTH CONWAY,
NEW HAMPSHIRE 03860-1763

Tel: (603) 356-3548; (800) 642-0749
Best Time to Call: 10 AM–8 PM
Hosts: Linda and Robert Dahlberg
Location: 140 mi. N of Boston, Mass.
No. of Rooms: 6
No. of Private Baths: 4
Max. No. Sharing Bath: 4
Double/pb: $80–$120
Single/pb: $65–$95
Double/sb: $55–$80
Single/sb: $45–$70

Open: All year
Reduced Rates: Available
Breakfast: Full
Credit Cards: AMEX, DISC, MC, VISA
Pets: No
Children: Welcome, over 6
Smoking: No
Social Drinking: Permitted
Minimum Stay: 2 days, foliage and holidays
Airport/Station Pickup: Yes

With its lush landscaped grounds and views of both the Moat and the nearby Presidential ranges, this multi-gabled 1853 Victorian is the perfect getaway. Start your day with a country breakfast which could consist of Belgian waffles, French toast, or Bob's apple cake. Guests can listen to music, read, play the piano, or relax by the pool. All rooms have air-conditioning and are decorated with antiques and homemade quilts. On each bed, you will find a teddy bear to adopt for the length of your stay.

Meadow Farm
JENNESS POND ROAD, NORTHWOOD, NEW HAMPSHIRE 03261

Tel: **(603) 942-8619**
Hosts: **Douglas and Janet Briggs**
Location: **18 mi. E of Concord**
No. of Rooms: **3**
Max. No. Sharing Bath: **4**
Double/sb: **$65**
Single/sb: **$45**
Open: **All year**

Reduced Rates: **Families**
Breakfast: **Full**
Credit Cards: **AMEX**
Pets: **Sometimes**
Children: **Welcome**
Smoking: **No**
Social Drinking: **Permitted**

Meadow Farm is set on 50 acres of quiet woods and horse pastures. The house is an authentic New England Colonial dating back to 1770, with wide-pine floors, beamed ceilings, and old fireplaces. In the morning, a country breakfast of homemade breads, seasonal fruit, and local syrup is served in the keeping room. Guests are invited to swim and canoe at the private beach. The property also has plenty of wooded trails for long walks or cross-country skiing. Meadow Farm is an ideal location for those en route to Concord, the seacoast, or the mountains.

Grassy Pond House
RINDGE, NEW HAMPSHIRE 03461

Tel: **(603) 899-5166, 899-5167**
Best Time to Call: **Mornings**
Hosts: **Carmen Linares and Robert Multer**
Location: **60 mi. NW of Boston**
No. of Rooms: **3**
No. of Private Baths: **2**
Max. No. Sharing Bath: **4**
Double/pb: **$70**

Single/pb: **$60**
Double/sb: **$60**
Single/sb: **$50**
Open: **All year**
Breakfast: **Full**
Pets: **No**
Children: **Welcome, over 14**
Smoking: **No**
Social Drinking: **Permitted**

This secluded 19th-century farmhouse is set among 150 acres of woods and fields. The house has been restored, enlarged, and decorated in period pieces. Guest quarters, overlooking the gardens and lake, feature a private entrance and a living room with fireplace. Breakfast specialties include pancakes with local maple syrup, fresh eggs and bacon, and plenty of good Colombian coffee. This setting, high in the Monadnock region, is perfect for hiking, skiing, boating, fishing, and swimming.

The Hilltop Inn ✪
SUGAR HILL, NEW HAMPSHIRE 03585
bb@hilltopinn.com

Tel: **(603) 823-5695; (800) 770-5695**
Hosts: **Mike and Meri Hern**
Location: **2¹/₂ mi. W of Franconia**
No. of Rooms: **6**
No. of Private Baths: **6**
Double/pb: **$70–$105**
Single/pb: **$60–$85**
Guest Cottage: **$200–$250**

Suites: **$90–$150**
Open: **All year**
Breakfast: **Full**
Pets: **Welcome**
Children: **No**
Smoking: **Restricted**
Social Drinking: **Permitted**
Airport/Station Pickup: **Yes**

The Hilltop Inn is a sprawling, 19th-century Victorian located in a small, friendly village. Inside, you'll find a warm, cozy atmosphere, comfortable furnishings, and lots of antiques. The kitchen is the heart of the house in more ways than one. In the morning, homemade muffins are served fresh from the old-fashioned Garland stove. Local attractions include Franconia Notch, White Mountain National Forest, North Conway, great skiing, and spectacular foliage. Enjoy lovely sunset views, strolls along the quiet country roads; read in porch rockers, or enjoy conversation by the fire. All guest rooms have handmade quilts and antiques.

NEW JERSEY

Stanhope
Glenwood
Princeton
Belmar
Jobstown
Ocean City
Cape May

Bed & Breakfast of Princeton—A Reservation Service

P.O. BOX 571, PRINCETON, NEW JERSEY 08542

71035.757 @ compuserve.com

Tel: **(609) 924-3189;**
   fax: **(609) 921-6271**
Coordinator: **John W. Hurley**
States/Regions Covered: **Princeton**

Rates (Single/Double):
   Average: **$40–$55 / $50–$65**
Credit Cards: **No**

Princeton is a lovely town; houses are set well back on carefully tended lawns, screened by towering trees. Some of John's hosts live within walking distance of Princeton University. Nassau Hall, circa 1756, is its oldest building; its chapel is the largest of any at an American university. Nearby corporate parks include national companies, such as Bristol Myers, Squibb, and the David Sarnoff Research Center. Restaurants feature every imaginable cuisine, and charming shops offer a wide variety of wares. Personal checks are accepted for deposit or total payment in advance; cash or traveler's checks are required for any balance due.

Down the Shore B&B ✪

201 SEVENTH AVENUE, BELMAR, NEW JERSEY 07719

Tel: **(908) 681-9023**
Best Time to Call: **Before noon**
Hosts: **Annette and Al Bergins**
Location: **1 block from ocean**
No. of rooms: **3**
No. of private baths: **1**
Max. No. Sharing Bath: **4**
Double/pb: **$90**
Double/sb: **$80**
Open: **All year**

Reduced Rates: **2-day specials, off-season, midweek, weekly**
Breakfast: **Full**
Pets: **Sometimes**
Smoking: **No**
Social Drinking: **Permitted**
Minimum Stay: **2 nights/weekends in season**
Station Pickup: **Yes**

Down the Shore's name couldn't be more appropriate—this B&B is located one block from the boardwalk and the beach. When you want to get out of the sun, rest up in your comfortable, air-conditioned room, read, play games on the shaded porch, or watch TV in the parlor. Racing fans can choose between the thoroughbreds at Monmouth Park and the trotters at Freehold Raceway, while the culturally inclined can catch world-class entertainment at the Garden State Arts Center. A complete breakfast is served each morning, including fresh fruit, juices, baked casseroles, and homemade granola.

Barnard-Good House ✪

238 PERRY STREET, CAPE MAY, NEW JERSEY 08204

Tel: **(609) 884-5381**
Best Time to Call: **9 AM–9 PM**
Hosts: **Nan and Tom Hawkins**
No. of Rooms: **5**
No. of Private Baths: **5**
Double/pb: **$90–$150**
Single/pb: **$76.50–$100**
Suites: **$125**
Open: **Apr.–Nov.**

Breakfast: **Full**
Credit Cards: **MC, VISA**
Pets: **No**
Children: **Welcome, over 14**
Smoking: **No**
Social Drinking: **Permitted**
Minimum Stay: **2 nights spring and fall; 3 nights summer**

Nan and Tom cordially invite you to their Second Empire Victorian cottage, circa 1865, just a five-minute walk from the beach and all tours, restaurants, and activities. They love antiques and continually add to their collection, using them to create a warm and comfortable atmosphere. Nan's breakfast is a four-course gourmet treat with everything made from scratch. It's touted as one of the best in New Jersey—Nan and Tom have been written up by many important publications. A typical morning repast could be strawberry-apple juice, chilled peach soup, shrimp and spinach roulade, tomato flan, three-grain wild rice bread, and walnut fudge tart. Many evening treats are served and iced tea is always available in the warm weather months.

Apple Valley Inn ✪

**P.O. BOX 302, CORNER OF ROUTES 517 AND 565, GLENWOOD,
NEW JERSEY 07418**

Tel: **(201) 764-3735**
Best Time to Call: **5–8 PM**
Hosts: **Mitzi and John Durham**
Location: **45 mi. NW of New York City**
No. of Rooms: **7**
No. of Private Baths: **2**
Max. No. Sharing Bath: **4**
Double/pb: **$90–$110**
Single/pb: **$90**

Double/sb: **$70–$80**
Single/sb: **$70**
Open: **All year**
Reduced Rates: **10% seniors midweek**
Breakfast: **Full**
Pets: **No**
Children: **Welcome, over 13**
Smoking: **Permitted**
Social Drinking: **Permitted**

Apple Valley Inn, a rustic 19th-century mansion with exposed beams, red brick chimneys, and hand-painted fire screens, takes its name from the fruit farms that used to dominate the area. Bedrooms are named for apples—Granny Smith, Jonathan, Yellow Delicious—and are furnished in Colonial style. Guests can stroll in an apple orchard, swim in a pool, and fish for river trout without leaving the property. Local recreational options include skiing and horseback riding. The Inn is located on the Appalachian Trail. Breakfasts feature ham-cheese dandy or Dutch baby pancakes, accompanied by fresh fruit and homemade breads, muffins, and jams.

Belle Springs Farm ✪
RD 1, BOX 420, JOBSTOWN, NEW JERSEY 08041

Tel: **(609) 723-5364**
Host: **Lyd Sudler**
Location: **5 miles from N.J. Tpke.,
  Exit 7**
No. of Rooms: **3**
Max. No. Sharing Bath: **4**
Double/sb: **$50**
Suites: **$85**

Open: **All year**
Breakfast: **Full**
Other Meals: **Available**
Pets: **No**
Children: **Welcome**
Smoking: **Permitted**
Social Drinking: **Permitted**

This spacious, contemporary farmhouse was built in 1961 and is attractively furnished with family heirlooms. The bedrooms are air-conditioned. From the porch, there's a spectacular view of the pastures with the cows grazing, and the deer that come out of the woods at dusk. It's situated in the heart of Burlington County, where every little town, including Burlington, Bordentown, and Mt. Holly, is a pre-Revolutionary gem. It is a half hour to Philadelphia or Princeton. Lyd enjoys music, gardening, and pampering her guests. If you want to bring your horse, there's a $10 charge for the turnout in the pasture.

Northwood Inn Bed & Breakfast
401 WESLEY AVENUE, OCEAN CITY, NEW JERSEY 08226

Tel: **(609) 399-6071**
Hosts: **Marj and John Loeper**
Location: **8 mi. S of Atlantic City**
No. of Rooms: **8**
No. of Private Baths: **8**
Double/pb: **$85–$105**
Single/pb: **$80–$90**
Suites: **$145; sleeps 4**
Open: **All year**

Breakfast: **Full**
Credit Cards: **MC, VISA**
Pets: **No**
Children: **Welcome, over 10**
Smoking: **No**
Social Drinking: **Permitted**
Minimum Stay: **Holiday weekends only**
Airport/Station Pickup: **Yes**

Antique and wicker furniture sets off the charm of this Queen Anne Victorian, with its sweeping staircase and oak and plank-pine floors. All guest rooms have custom-made bedspreads, ruffles, and window treatments in designer fabrics. Common space on the main floor consists of a parlor, a library and game room, a billiard room with a piano, and a dining room. Guests also have use of two porches and a rooftop deck. The location is ideal, since the beach, the boardwalk, stores, and restaurants are only three blocks away.

Serendipity Bed & Breakfast ✪
712 NINTH STREET, OCEAN CITY, NEW JERSEY 08226

Tel: **(609) 399-1554; (800) 842-8544;
  fax: (609) 399-1527**

Best Time to Call: **Mornings**
Hosts: **Clara and Bill Plowfield**

Location: **8 mi. S of Atlantic City**
No. of Rooms: **6**
No. of Private Baths: **4**
Max. No. Sharing Bath: **4**
Double/pb: **$85–$119**
Double/sb: **$75–$95**
Open: **All year**
Breakfast: **Full**

Other Meals: **Available, Oct.–May**
Credit Cards: **AMEX, DISC, MC, VISA**
Pets: **No**
Children: **Welcome, over 10**
Smoking: **No**
Social Drinking: **Permitted**
Minimum Stay: **2 nights weekends**

Like its name, Serendipity is delightfully unique. At this immaculate 1912 seashore inn, delicious, healthy natural food, spring drinking water, and air-conditioned rooms decorated with wicker and pastels make for a memorable getaway. Serendipity is located half a block from the beaches, boardwalk, and a shiatsu massage, and only 8 miles to Atlantic City's shows and casinos. Off-season, Clara—a first-rate natural food cook—will lovingly prepare dinner for you from the natural food menu. All rooms have color cable TV. Breakfast is served in the dining room or on the vine-shaded veranda.

Red Maple Farm
R.D. 4, RAYMOND ROAD, PRINCETON, NEW JERSEY 08540

Tel: **(908) 329-3821**
Best Time to Call: **Evenings**
Hosts: **Roberta and Lindsey Churchill**
Location: **1 hour from New York**

No. of Rooms: **3**
Max. No. Sharing Bath: **4**
Double/sb: **$58–$78**
Single/sb: **$48–$68**

Open: **All year**
Reduced Rates: **10% weekly**
Breakfast: **Full**
Credit Cards: **AMEX, MC, VISA**

Pets: **No**
Children: **Welcome, over 8**
Smoking: **No**
Social Drinking: **Permitted**

Roberta is a former chef who owned one of New Jersey's best restaurants; today she's a passionate gardener, reader, and political activist. Lindsey is a sociology professor. Their house, built between 1740 and 1820, has five working fireplaces, latched doors and, reportedly, a resident Hessian ghost. The grounds include a 1740 smokehouse, an 1850 barn whose cellar hid runaway slaves on the underground railroad, and the stone ruins of an older barn, which make a great backdrop for the modern swimming pool. The gates of Princeton University are four miles distant, and New York City, Philadelphia, and New Hope, Pennsylvania, are all about an hour away by car.

Whistling Swan Inn ✪
110 MAIN STREET, STANHOPE, NEW JERSEY 07874
wswan@worldnet.att.net; http://www.bbianj.com/whistlingswan

Tel: **(201) 347-6369**
Best Time to Call: **9 AM–6 PM**
Hosts: **Paula Williams and Joe Mulay**
Location: **45 mi. W of New York City**
No. of Rooms: **10**
No. of Private Baths: **10**
Double/pb: **$95–$140**
Open: **All year**
Reduced Rates: **Weekly; 10% seniors**

Breakfast: **Full**
Credit Cards: **AMEX, DISC, MC, VISA**
Pets: **No**
Children: **Welcome, over 12**
Smoking: **No**
Social Drinking: **Permitted**
Airport/Station Pickup: **Yes, by arrangement**

You'll feel like you're back in grandmother's house when you visit this lovely Queen Anne Victorian located in a small, historic village. The massive limestone wraparound porch leads to comfortable rooms filled with family antiques. Your hosts have labored tirelessly to make the ornate woodwork, large fireplaces, old-fashioned fixtures, and even the banister light look like new. Take a bubble bath in a claw-footed tub and then wrap yourself in a fluffy robe before retiring. Your room will be individually decorated in varying period motifs. Breakfast includes homemade muffins, breads, and fruit, along with a hot egg, cheese, or fruit dish. Special arrangements are easily made for corporate guests who need to eat early or require the use of a private telephone, copy service, or meeting room. The Inn is close to the International Trade Zone, Waterloo Village, Lake Musconetcong, restaurants, and state parks and forests.

NEW MEXICO

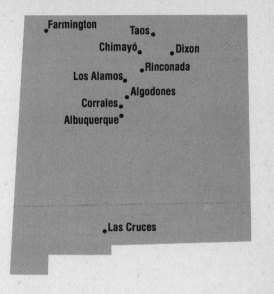

Bed & Breakfast Southwest Reservation Service— New Mexico ✪
2916 NORTH 70TH STREET, SCOTTSDALE, ARIZONA 85251
b&bsw@juno.com

Tel: **(602) 945-9704; (800) 762-9704;**
  fax: **(602) 874-1316**
Best Time to Call: **8 AM–8 PM**
Coordinators: **Jo Cummings and Joan Petersen**
States/Regions Covered: **Arizona, New Mexico, Southern Colorado, Southern California**

Descriptive Directory: **Free w/SASE**
Rates (Single/Double):
  Modest: **$40–$75**
  Average: **$80–$100**
  Luxury: **$105–up**

This service offers travelers unique homestays in suites, guesthouses, ranches, and inns. All host facilities are personally inspected and provide the three C's of bed and breakfasts: cleanliness, cordiality, and convenience. Jo and Joan's specialty is finding the perfect B&B for you.

They can plan your trip to include many of the historical and natural wonders of the great Southwest, such as the San Diego Zoo, Durango Historic Railroad, Scottsdale golf courses, Sedona's Red Rock formations and the Santa Fe opera. You will be awed by the spectacular scenic beauty and legendary Western hospitality.

Anderson's Victorian House ✪

11600 MODESTO AVENUE NORTHEAST, ALBUQUERQUE, NEW MEXICO 87122

Tel: **(505) 856-6211**	Single/sb: **$30**
Best Time to Call: **7–8:30 AM;**	Open: **All year**
4–9 PM	Reduced Rates: **10% families; weekly**
Hosts: **Judy and Jerris Anderson**	Breakfast: **Full**
Location: **3.8 mi. E from Rte. I-25N**	Other Meals: **Available**
No. of Rooms: **3**	Pets: **Sometimes**
No. of Private Baths: **1**	Children: **Welcome, over 4**
Max. No. Sharing Bath: **4**	Smoking: **No**
Double/pb: **$50–$70**	Social Drinking: **Permitted**
Single/pb: **$40**	Airport Pickup: **Yes**
Double/sb: **$35**	

Anderson's Victorian House is a newly constructed, two-story house on a one-acre tract with spectacular views. Guest rooms are decorated with antiques and pieces your hosts collected in their world travels. Horseback riding, skiing, hiking, and golf are available nearby. Judy and Jerris will gladly direct you to the Sandia Ski Area, Albuquerque's Old Town, Sante Fe, the Indian Cultural Center, and other points of interest. Prizewinning coffee cake, muffins, and more are breakfast delights. Cheese and wine or coffee, tea, and cookies are served in the evening.

Canyon Crest ✪

5804 CANYON CREST NORTHEAST, ALBUQUERQUE, NEW MEXICO 87111

Tel: **(505) 821-4898**	Double/sb: **$40–$60**
Best Time to Call: **7 AM–10 PM**	Single/sb: **$40**
Hosts: **Jan and Chip Mansure**	Open: **All year**
Location: **7 mi. NE of Albuquerque**	Breakfast: **Continental**
No. of Rooms: **2**	Pets: **No**
Max. No. Sharing Bath: **4**	Children: **Welcome, over 10**
Double/pb: **$50–$65**	Smoking: **No**
Single/pb: **$40**	Social Drinking: **No**

Warm hospitality awaits you upon entering this two-story contemporary home furnished in Southwestern decor. Enjoy the splash of color from the hosts' prize-winning batik pictures and floral arrangements, as well as antiques and collectibles from their teachings and travels in Africa. After a great day of skiing, hiking, ballooning, antiquing, visiting galleries and museums, exploring Indian pueblos or golfing, come home to a cup of coffee or tea and good conversation with Jan and Chip. Indulge in a quiet night's sleep and awaken to a hearty breakfast of cereal, muffins, and fresh fruit.

The Corner House ✪
9121 JAMES PLACE NORTHEAST, ALBUQUERQUE, NEW MEXICO 87111

Tel: **(505) 298-5800**
Host: **Jean Thompson**
Location: **4 mi. N of I-40**
No. of Rooms: **4**
No. of Private Baths: **2**
Max. No. Sharing Bath: **3**
Double/pb: **$45–$50**
Double/sb: **$40–$50**
Single/sb: **$30–$35**

Open: **All year**
Reduced Rates: **10% families, seniors**
Breakfast: **Full**
Other Meals: **Available**
Pets: **Sometimes**
Children: **Welcome (crib)**
Smoking: **No**
Social Drinking: **Permitted**

Jean welcomes you to her handsome Southwestern-style home decorated in a delightful mix of antiques and collectibles. Breakfast specialties include Jean's homemade muffins. The Corner House is located in a quiet residential neighborhood within view of the magnificent Sandia Mountains. It is convenient to Old Town Albuquerque, Santa Fe, many Indian pueblos, and the launch site for the International Balloon Fiesta.

The Ranchette B&B ✪
2329 LAKEVIEW ROAD SOUTHWEST, ALBUQUERQUE, NEW MEXICO 87105
http://www.viva.com/nm/ranchette/

Tel: **(505) 877-5140;**
  fax: **(505) 873-8274**
Best Time to Call: **After 4 PM**
Host: **Reverend Janis Hildebrand**
Location: **5 mi. SW of Albuquerque**
No. of Rooms: **2**
No. of Private Baths: **1**
Max. No. Sharing Bath: **3**
Double/pb: **$85**
Double/sb: **$65**
Open: **All year**

Reduced Rates: **Jan.–Mar.; 10% seniors; 20% families**
Breakfast: **Full**
Other Meals: **Available**
Credit Cards: **AMEX, DC, DISC, MC, VISA**
Pets: **Sometimes**
Children: **Welcome**
Smoking: **No**
Social Drinking: **No**

Enjoy vistas of mountains at sunrise and sunset in restful spiritual surroundings in this adobe-style home, complete with an Arabian horse. Accommodations inside and outside include a fireplace, grand piano, hot tub, swings, walking paths, terry robes, original art, antiques, and in-room phones. Gourmet vegetarian meals are served; breakfast is included with the room, dinner upon request for an additional fee.

Ranchette is located 10 minutes from downtown and Historic Old Town, 30 minutes from the Balloon Fiesta Park, and one hour from Santa Fe and Acoma Pueblo Sky City. Janis is a nondenominational minister, licensed marriage and family therapist, and licensed school counselor. A pianist and gourmet cook, she aspires to compete at dressage and hunter jumper events.

Rio Grande House ✪

3100 RIO GRANDE BOULEVARD NORTHWEST, ALBUQUERQUE, NEW MEXICO 87107

Tel: **(505) 345-0120**
Best Time to Call: **Anytime**
Hosts: **Richard Gray and James Hughes**
Location: **4 mi. N of Rte. I-40, Exit Rio Grande Blvd.**
No. of Rooms: **5**
No. of Private Baths: **5**
Double/pb: **$65–$85**

Single/pb: **$55–$65**
Open: **All year**
Breakfast: **Full**
Pets: **Sometimes**
Children: **Welcome**
Smoking: **Permitted**
Social Drinking: **Permitted**

This landmark white adobe residence is close to historic Old Town, major museums, Rio Grande Nature Center, and the International Balloon Fiesta launch site. Southwestern charm is reflected through the beamed ceilings, brick floors, and kiva fireplaces. Museum-quality antiques and collectibles from East Africa, Nepal, Yemen, and Pakistan are used to decorate each room. Jim, a college professor, writer, and actor, will be happy to relate their history.

Hacienda Vargas ✪

1431 EL CAMINO REAL, P.O. BOX 307, ALGODONES, NEW MEXICO 87001

Tel: **(505) 867-9115; (800) 261-0006**
Best Time to Call: **8:30 AM–9 PM**
Hosts: **Paul and Julie DeVargas**

Location: **22 mi. S of Santa Fe, 25 mi. N of Albuquerque**
No. of Rooms: **8**

No. of Private Baths: **8**
Double/pb: **$69–$89**
Suites: **$89–$139**
Open: **All year**
Reduced Rates: **Available**
Breakfast: **Full**
Credit Cards: **MC, VISA**

Pets: **No**
Children: **Welcome, over 12**
Smoking: **No**
Social Drinking: **Permitted**
Minimum Stay: **Balloon Fiesta,
    Christmas, Indian Market**
Foreign Languages: **Spanish, German**

Hacienda Vargas is a romantic hideaway in a historic old adobe hacienda, completely restored and elegantly decorated with antiques. The beautiful rooms have fireplaces and private entrances; four suites have Jacuzzi tubs. Golf, fishing, snow skiing, horseback riding, and hiking are nearby. This B&B is conveniently located south of Santa Fe and north of Albuquerque. Romance packages are available. Paul and Julie are ex-bankers who love history and have traveled extensively.

La Posada de Chimayó ✪
P.O. BOX 463, CHIMAYÓ, NEW MEXICO 87522

Tel: **(505) 351-4605**
Host: **Sue Farrington**
Location: **30 mi. N of Santa Fe**
No. of Rooms: **4**
No. of Private Baths: **4**
Double/pb: **$85**
Single/pb: **$75**
Open: **All year**

Reduced Rates: **Weekly in winter**
Breakfast: **Full**
Credit Cards: **MC, VISA (for deposits)**
Pets: **Sometimes**
Children: **Welcome, over 12**
Smoking: **No**
Social Drinking: **Permitted**
Foreign Languages: **Spanish**

Chimayó is known for its historic old church and its tradition of fine Spanish weaving. This is a typical adobe home with brick floors and *viga* ceilings. The suite is composed of a small bedroom and sitting room, and is made cozy with Mexican rugs, handwoven fabrics, comfortable furnishings, and traditional corner fireplaces. Sue's breakfasts are not for the fainthearted, and often feature stuffed French toast or chiles rellenos. Wine or sun tea are graciously offered after you return from exploring Bandelier National Monument Park, the Indian pueblos, cliff dwellings, and the "high road" to Taos.

Chocolate Turtle B&B ✪
1098 WEST MEADOWLARK LANE, CORRALES, NEW MEXICO 87048

Tel: **(505) 898-1800; (800) 898-1842;**
    fax: **(505) 898-5328**
Best Time to Call: **After 9 AM**
Host: **Carole Morgan**
Location: **4 mi. N of Albuquerque**
No. of Rooms: **4**
No. of Private Baths: **4**
Double/pb: **$70–$75**
Single/pb: **$55**

Suites: **$80–$85**
Open: **All year**
Reduced Rates: **Available**
Breakfast: **Full**
Credit Cards: **AMEX, DISC, MC, VISA**
Pets: **No**
Children: **Welcome, over 5**
Smoking: **No**
Social Drinking: **Permitted**

The Chocolate Turtle B&B is a refurbished Territorial located on the northern boundary of Albuquerque. It's a short drive to the Sandia Tram, Old Town Albuquerque, Rio Grande Zoo, the Indian Pueblo Cultural Center, the Petroglyphs, several golf courses, and the Kodak-Albuquerque Balloon Fiesta Park. Santa Fe is 45 minutes away. Guests have the main house to themselves, with its large room that offers views of the Sandia Mountains, TV, VCR, and dining room. Snacks and cold drinks are available at all times in the refrigerator. The decor is Southwestern, there is a spa, and in your room you will find the scrumptious handmade chocolates that give this B&B its name.

Sagebrush Circle Bed & Breakfast ✪
23 SAGEBRUSH CIRCLE, CORRALES, NEW MEXICO 87048

Tel/Fax: **(505) 898-5393**
Best Time to Call: **8:30 AM–9 PM**
Hosts: **Barbara and Victor Ferkiss**
Location: **10 mi. NW of Old Town Albuquerque**
No. of Rooms: **2**
No. of Private Baths: **2**
Double/pb: **$65–$85**
Single/pb: **$58–$77**
Open: **All year**

Reduced Rates: **Available**
Breakfast: **Continental, plus**
Other Meals: **Available**
Pets: **No**
Children: **Welcome, 12 and older**
Smoking: **No**
Social Drinking: **Permitted**
Minimum Stay: **2 nights**
Airport/Station Pickup: **Yes**

Sagebrush Circle is a dramatic pueblo-style home nestled in the hills of Corrales, a Spanish village settled in the 16th century. All rooms have magnificent views of the Sandia Mountains. During cooler mornings, freshly brewed coffee and homemade breads and muffins are served in the great room, which has a 16-foot beamed ceiling. In warmer weather, guests can eat outdoors. As you dine, you may hear the neighing of horses or see brilliantly colored balloons rise in the turquoise sky—they float over the house during Balloon Fiesta in October. Barbara and Victor are always delighted to give advice and information about the area.

The Sandhill Crane B&B ✪
389 CAMINO HERMOSA, CORRALES, NEW MEXICO 87048
thorpe@rt66.com

Tel: **(800) 375-2445; (505) 898-2445**
Best Time to Call: **8 AM–6 PM**
Hosts: **Carol Hogan and Phil Thorpe**
Location: **10 mi. NW of Albuquerque**
No. of Rooms: **3**
No. of Private Baths: **2**
Max. No. Sharing Bath: **4**
Double/pb: **$85**
Single/pb: **$75–$85**
Suites: **$125–$150, sleeps 4**

Open: **All year**
Reduced Rates: **Available**
Breakfast: **Full**
Other Meals: **Available**
Credit Cards: **AMEX, MC, VISA**
Pets: **No**
Children: **Welcome, over 8**
Smoking: **No**
Social Drinking: **Permitted**

Located near Rio Grande Bosque, this romantic adobe hacienda has spectacular mountain views. Enjoy memorable breakfasts and sunrises in this warm, friendly Southwestern-style B&B. Relax behind wisteria-draped walls or walk miles of trails in nearby Rio Grande Bosque. Tours, massages, and horseback riding can be arranged. Sandhill Crane is centrally located for exploring the enchantment of New Mexico.

La Casita Guesthouse ✪
P.O. BOX 103, DIXON, NEW MEXICO 87527

Tel: **(505) 579-4297**
Hosts: **Sara Pene and Celeste Miller**
Location: **25 mi. S of Taos**
Guest Cottage: **$75–$115, sleeps 2–4**
Open: **All year**
Breakfast: **Continental**

Pets: **No**
Children: **Welcome**
Smoking: **No**
Social Drinking: **Permitted**
Foreign Languages: **Spanish**

The rural mountain village of Dixon is home to many artists and crafts-people. La Casita is a traditional New Mexico adobe with *vigas*, *latillas*, and Mexican tile floors. Guests enjoy use of the living room, fully equipped kitchen, two bedrooms, one bath, and a lovely patio. It is a perfect spot for relaxing and is just minutes from the Rio Grande, river rafting, hiking, and cross-country skiing. Indian pueblos, ancient Anasazi ruins, museums, art galleries, horseback-riding ranches, and alpine skiing are within an hour's drive. Sara and Celeste are weavers.

Silver River Adobe Inn ✪
P.O. BOX 3411, FARMINGTON, NEW MEXICO 87499

Tel: **(505) 325-8219**
Best Time to Call: **Anytime**
Hosts: **Diana Ohlson and David Beers**

Location: **180 mi. NW of Albuquerque**
No. of Rooms: **3**
No. of Private Baths: **3**

Double/pb: **$75–$95**
Suite: **$85–$125**
Open: **All year**
Breakfast: **Continental**
Credit Cards: **MC, VISA**

Pets: **No**
Children: **Welcome, over 12**
Smoking: **No**
Social Drinking: **Permitted**
Airport/Station Pickup: **Yes**

Silver River Adobe Inn is a newly constructed, traditional New Mexican home with massive timber beams and exposed adobe. From its cliffside perch, it overlooks the fork of the San Juan and La Plata rivers. Indian reservations, Aztec ruins, and ski slopes are all within striking distance of this B&B.

T. R. H. Smith Mansion Bed & Breakfast
909 NORTH ALAMEDA BOULEVARD, LAS CRUCES, NEW MEXICO 88005

Tel: **(505) 525-2525**
Hosts: **Marlene and Jay Tebo**
Location: **45 mi. N of El Paso, Tex.**
No. of Rooms: **4**
No. of Private Baths: **2**
Max. No. Sharing Bath: **4**
Double/pb: **$70–$80**
Double/sb: **$60**
Open: **All year**
Reduced Rates: **Weekly; corporate, government**

Breakfast: **Full**
Credit Cards: **AMEX, MC, VISA**
Pets: **Sometimes**
Children: **Welcome, over 10**
Smoking: **No**
Social Drinking: **Permitted**
Airport pickup: **Yes**
Foreign Languages: **German**

This 1914 four-story brick and stucco mansion has all wood floors (even in the basement), high wood-beam ceilings, and several rooms all in wood. The house is surrounded by large gardens and fruit and pecan trees, all on one-half acre. Guest rooms are decorated and named after an area of the world where your hosts have traveled. A German-style breakfast is served, including fruits, homemade breads, cheeses, and a baked entree. Things to see include Mesilla Valley, Organ Mountains, Fort Selden, White Sands National Monument, White Sands Missile Range, Gila National Forest, and Gila Cliff Dwellings, as well as numerous festivals throughout the year.

Casa del Rey Bed & Breakfast
305 ROVER, LOS ALAMOS, NEW MEXICO 87544

Tel: **(505) 672-9401**	Open: **All year**
Best Time to Call: **After 5 PM**	Reduced Rates: **Weekly; families**
Host: **Virginia L. King**	Breakfast: **Continental, plus**
No. of Rooms: **2**	Pets: **No**
Max. No. Sharing Bath: **4**	Children: **Welcome, over 5**
Double/sb: **$45**	Smoking: **No**
Single/sb: **$35**	Social Drinking: **Permitted**

This adobe contemporary home is located in the quiet residential area of White Rock, and is situated in the Jemez Mountains with a view of Santa Fe across the valley. The surroundings are rich in Spanish and Indian history. Pueblos, museums, Bandelier National Monument, skiing, hiking trails, tennis, and golf are all within easy reach. Virginia is rightfully proud of her beautifully kept house, with its pretty flower gardens. In summer, her breakfast of granola, home-baked rolls and muffins, along with fruits and beverages, is served on the sunporch, where you can enjoy the lovely scenery.

Casa Rinconada del Rio ✪
BOX 10A, TAOS HIGHWAY 68, RINCONADA, NEW MEXICO 87531

Tel: **(505) 579-4466**	Breakfast: **Continental**
Host: **JoAnne Gladin**	Pets: **Sometimes**
Location: **20 mi. S of Taos; 45 mi. N. of Santa Fe**	Children: **Welcome**
	Smoking: **Yes**
Guest Houses: **$55–$130**	Social Drinking: **Permitted**
Open: **All year**	Foreign Languages: **Greek**

Casa Rinconada is nestled in the canyon of Sangre de Cristo Mountains, the spectacular backdrop for this historic northern village. Thirty-foot *vigas* adorned with skulls and lights border the entry to the guesthouses—two traditional tin-roofed adobes which are artfully decorated for your comfort and pleasure. The backyard is an orchard where guests are invited to enjoy seasonal fruit and stroll along the banks of the legendary Rio Grande. Indian pueblos, opera, galleries, rafting, historic churches and more are all within a short drive.

Bed & Breakfast of New Mexico ✪
P.O. BOX 2805, SANTA FE, NEW MEXICO 87504

Tel: **(505) 982-3332**
Best Time to Call: **9 AM–5 PM**
Coordinator: **Kathi Ackerman**
States/Regions Covered: **Statewide**

Descriptive Directory: **Free**
Rates (Single/Double):
  Average: **$90–$200**
  Luxury: **$90–$200**

Do come and enjoy the Santa Fe Opera in summer, the vibrant colors of the aspens in autumn, or skiing in winter. Don't miss the Indian pueblos and ancient cliff dwellings, the national forest areas, art colonies, museums, and Taos.

American Artist Gallery House Bed & Breakfast ✪
132 FRONTIER ROAD, P.O. BOX 584, TAOS, NEW MEXICO 87571
aagh@taos.newmex.com; http://www.taoswebb.com/hotel/artistshouse

Tel: **(800) 532-2041; (505) 758-4446**
Best Time to Call: **7 AM–9 PM**
Hosts: **LeAn and Charles Clamurro**
Location: **Less than 1 mi. from historic Taos Plaza**
No. of Rooms: **10**
No. of Private Baths: **10**
Double/pb: **$75–$150**

Guest Cottage: **$75–$115**
Suites: **$150**
Open: **All year**
Reduced Rates: **Available**
Breakfast: **Full**
Pets: **No**
Smoking: **No**

Step into the Clamurros' world and recreate at the American Artist Gallery House, tucked away on a secluded cul-de-sac. Adorning the walls throughout the inn is artwork of the three cultures that have come together at this charming hacienda. Enjoy unobstructed vistas of Taos Mountain, an outdoor hot tub, and kiva fireplaces crafted by renowned artist Carmen Velarde. From La Cocina enjoy a gourmet breakfast specially created by Charles. If it's romance you want, you'll want to stay in one of the new suites located in the old carriage house, complete with Jacuzzi tubs, oversized shower, wet bar, antique vigas, skylights, and kiva fireplaces.

La Posada de Taos ✪
309 JUANITA LANE, P.O. BOX 1118, TAOS, NEW MEXICO 87571

Tel: **(505) 758-8164**
Best Time to Call: **Before 9 PM**
Hosts: **Bill and Nancy Swan**
Location: **70 mi. N of Santa Fe**
No. of Rooms: **6**
No. of Private Baths: **6**
Double/pb: **$85–$120**
Single/pb: **$75–$110**
Open: **All year**

Reduced Rates: **10% Nov.–Jan., Apr.–May**
Breakfast: **Full**
Pets: **No**
Children: **Welcome, over 12**
Smoking: **No**
Minimum Stay: **2 nights**
Airport/Station Pickup: **Yes**

Escape to another world, to the warmth and serenity of northern New Mexico. La Posada is nestled in the heart of the historic district, just two-and-a-half blocks from the Taos Plaza, and is the first bed and breakfast in Taos. La Posada is within walking distance to galleries, museums, restaurants, and shops. After a busy day, return to casual elegance, country pine antiques, fireplaces, and tastefully decorated guest rooms with handmade quilts, local art, and attention to detail. A separate honeymoon house is available.

Touchstone Bed & Breakfast Inn ✪
110 MABEL DODGE LANE, P.O. BOX 2896, TAOS, NEW MEXICO 87571-2896
http://www.taoswebb.com/touchstone

Tel: **(505) 758-0192; (800) 758-0192;** fax: **(505) 758-3498**
Best Time to Call: **11 AM–2 PM**
Host: **Bren Price**
Location: **1 mi. N of Taos Plaza**
No. of Rooms: **8**
No. of Private Baths: **8**
Double/pb: **$85**

Suites: **$125–$150**
Reduced Rates: **10% seniors**
Breakfast: **Full**
Credit Cards: **MC, VISA**
Pets: **No**
Children: **Welcome, over 12**
Smoking: **No**
Social Drinking: **Permitted**

Situated on two acres bordering Pueblo lands, Touchstone Bed & Breakfast Inn offers a quiet ambiance. The property boasts full mountain views, towering cottonwoods, evergreens, wildflower gardens, a trout stream, and an impressive apple orchard. Antiques, kiva fireplaces, *viga* ceilings, fine art, oriental rugs, down pillows and comforters, and custom designed baths—some with Jacuzzis—complete the most luxurious accommodations. A gourmet breakfast is served each morning in an atrium that has a fireplace designed by Tony Luhan and overlooks the courtyard. Guests may use the video collection and cassette library as well as an outdoor hot tub. All rooms have cable TV, VCR, and phones.

NEW YORK

Thousand Islands Area

Lake Placid/ Adirondacks Area (Saranac Lake)

Finger Lakes/ Rochester-Syracuse Area

Niagra/ Buffalo Area

Lake George Area

Chautauqua/ Allegheny Area

Central New York/ Leatherstocking Area

Catskills

Hudson Valley/ Albany/ Kingston Area

New York City Area/ Westchester County

Long Island

CATSKILLS

Maplewood ✪
PARK ROAD, P.O. BOX 40, CHICHESTER, NEW YORK 12416

Tel: **(914) 688-5433**
Best Time to Call: **After 7 PM**
Host: **Nancy Parsons**
Location: **25 mi. NW of Kingston**
No. of Rooms: **4**
Max. No. Sharing Bath: **4**
Double/sb: **$55–$65**

Single/sb: **$40**
Open: **All year**
Breakfast: **Full**
Pets: **No**
Children: **Welcome**
Smoking: **No**
Social Drinking: **Permitted**

A Colonial manor on a quiet country lane, and nestled among stately maples, this is a charming B&B. Each spacious bedroom has a view of the Catskills. In summer, you can swim in the in-ground pool, or play badminton, croquet, or horseshoes. In winter, ski Belleayre, Hunter, and Cortina, all only 12 miles away. In any season, enjoy the art galleries, boutiques, great restaurants, and theater at Woodstock, 20 minutes away. After a great day outdoors, come home to a glass of wine and good conversation. After a good night's sleep, you'll enjoy freshly squeezed orange juice, homemade breads and pastries, and freshly ground coffee.

River Run ✪
MAIN STREET, FLEISCHMANNS, NEW YORK 12430

Tel: **(914) 254-4884**
Best Time to Call: **11 AM–11 PM**
Host: **Larry Miller**
Location: **2¹/₂ hrs from NYC; 35 mins. W of Woodstock**
No. of Rooms: **10**
No. of Private Baths: **6**
Max. No. Sharing Bath: **2**
Double/pb: **$70–$100**
Single/pb: **$63–$90**
Double/sb: **$55–$75**

Single/sb: **$50–$68**
Open: **All year**
Reduced Rates: **Groups; longer stays**
Breakfast: **Full**
Credit Cards: **MC, VISA**
Pets: **Welcome**
Children: **Welcome**
Smoking: **Restricted**
Social Drinking: **Permitted**
Minimum Stay: **2 nights peak seasons; 3 nights holiday weekends**

In 1887, at the confluence of the Bushkill and Little Red Kill trout streams, Addison Scott built a classic Victorian summer "cottage." Today, as River Run, this exquisite village landmark invites guests to enjoy the pleasures of every season. Tennis, swimming, theater, restaurants, a museum, antiques, and a weekly country auction are all within walking distance, while Belleayre skiing (downhill and cross-country), magnificent Forest Preserve hiking trails, fishing, golf, river float trips, and horseback riding are just minutes away. Rejuvenate on the delightful front porch or in the book-filled parlor, complete with piano and fireplace. Step into the oak-floored dining room, bathed in the colors of the inn's signature stained glass windows, and enjoy hearty, homemade breakfasts and refreshments. The bus from New York City stops right at the front door!

The Eggery Inn ✪
COUNTY ROAD 16, TANNERSVILLE, NEW YORK 12485

Tel: **(518) 589-5363; fax (518) 589-5774**
Best Time to Call: **10 AM–8 PM**
Hosts: **Julie and Abe Abramczyk**
No. of Rooms: **15**
No. of Private Baths: **15**
Double/pb: **$80–$110**
Open: **All year**
Reduced Rates: **Off-season**

Breakfast: **Full**
Credit Cards: **AMEX, MC, VISA**
Pets: **No**
Children: **Welcome**
Smoking: **Restricted**
Social Drinking: **Permitted; full liquor license**
Minimum Stay: **2 nights weekends; 3 nights holiday weekends**

This Dutch Colonial farmhouse, built circa 1900, is nestled in the northern Catskills at an elevation of 2,200 feet. Guest rooms, decorated in a country motif, have carpeting, color TV, phones, and comforters or spreads. Queen-size and two-bed accommodations are available, and six first-floor rooms are accessible to guests in wheelchairs. The public room's oak balustrade, Franklin stove, player piano, Mission Oak furniture, and panoramic views invite guests to relax. Breakfast selections include omelettes, fruit-filled hotcakes, and heart-smart entrees. The Inn is ideal for small groups. Hiking trails, scenic waterfalls, the famous Woodstock colony, and the alpine ski areas of Hunter and Windham mountains are nearby. A freshly prepared dinner is served for groups by prior arrangement.

CENTRAL NEW YORK/LEATHERSTOCKING AREA

Pickle Hill Bed and Breakfast ✪
795 CHENANGO STREET, BINGHAMTON, NEW YORK 13901

Tel: **(607) 723-0259**
Best Time to Call: **Anytime**
Hosts: **Leslie and Tom Rossi**
Location: **185 mi. NW of New York City**
No. of Rooms: **2**
Max. No. Sharing Bath: **4**
Double/sb: **$50**
Single/sb: **$40**
Open: **All year**

Reduced Rates: **On long stays**
Breakfast: **Full**
Credit Cards: **No**
Pets: **No**
Children: **Welcome**
Smoking: **Yes, area available**
Social Drinking: **Permitted**
Airport/Station Pickup: **Yes**

Make yourself comfortable at Pickle Hill, built more than 100 years ago. Read, listen to music, and play board games in the lounge, then rally around the living room piano for a songfest, or join your hosts in the family room for conversation. Sports lovers can play bocci, basketball, or badminton on the side lawn; baseball fields, tennis courts, golf courses, bike paths, and cross-country ski trails are all nearby. Mark Twain's Elmira home, the Farmer's Museum, and the Baseball Hall of Fame in Cooperstown are all within driving distance. Closer to home, Binghamton's Performing Arts Center supplies top-notch entertainment, and the Tri-Cities Opera Company features some of the nation's most promising young singers.

Chalet Waldheim ✪
RD 1, BOX 51-G-2, BURLINGTON FLATS, NEW YORK 13315

Tel: **(800) 654-8571; (607) 965-8803**
Hosts: **Franzi and Heinz Kuhne**
Location: **15 minutes W of Cooperstown**
Suite: **$160**
Open: **All year**
Reduced Rates: **15% seniors and 3-day stays**
Breakfast: **Continental, plus**

Pets: **No**
Children: **No**
Smoking: **No**
Social Drinking: **Permitted**
Minimum Stay: **Holidays and special events**
Station Pickup: **Yes**
Foreign Languages: **German**

Share the quiet seclusion of this very special hilltop setting amid seventy-five acres of forest and field. Built in 1990, this finely crafted chalet is molded in the age-old Black Forest style. It's the perfect hideaway, yet close enough to the village that offers lakes, museums, and opera. Come and enjoy a European country atmosphere—relax in the warmth of classic antique furnishings and abundant artwork. Breakfast is a bountiful Continental buffet that includes freshly baked breads and house specialties.

Creekside Bed & Breakfast ✪
RD 1, BOX 206, COOPERSTOWN, NEW YORK 13326

Tel: **(607) 547-8203**
Best Time to Call: **Anytime**
Hosts: **Fred and Gwen Ermlich**
Location: **2 mi. S of Cooperstown**
No. of Rooms: **6**
No. of Private Baths: **6**
Double/pb: **$80–$95**
Guest Cottage: **$135–$150; sleeps 2**
Suites: **$95–$150**
Open: **All year**

Breakfast: **Full**
Credit Cards: **AMEX, MC, VISA**
Pets: **No**
Children: **Welcome (crib)**
Smoking: **No**
Social Drinking: **Permitted**
Minimum Stay: **2 nights seasonal weekends; 3 nights holiday weekends**
Foreign Languages: **French, German**

This nationally renowned B&B offers beautiful furnishings in an elegant atmosphere. All rooms have private baths, queen-size beds, color TV, and HBO. The Bridal Suite, Penthouse Suite, and Honeymoon Cottage are ideal for newlyweds and other romantics. You can amble through the flower gardens and lawns, and fish or take a dip in the creek. Gwen and Fred, who perform with the Glimmerglass Opera, serve a full breakfast, catering to guests who are looking for something special.

Litco Farms Bed and Breakfast ✪
P.O. BOX 1048, COOPERSTOWN, NEW YORK 13326
wolffj@magnum.wpe.com

Tel: **(607) 547-2501**
Hosts: **Margaret and Jim Wolff**
Location: **2 mi. NW of Cooperstown**
No. of Rooms: **4**
Max. No. Sharing Bath: **4**
Double/sb: **$69–$99**
Suites: **$99–$119**

Open: **Apr.–Nov.**
Breakfast: **Full**
Pets: **No**
Children: **Welcome**
Smoking: **No**
Social Drinking: **Permitted**
Airport/Station Pickup: **Yes**

Seventy acres of unspoiled meadows and woodlands are yours to explore at Litco Farms. The day begins with fresh-baked breads, fresh eggs, milk, and local bacon, served in the dining room / library. You can canoe or fish on Canadarago Lake, which is stocked with freshwater salmon. You can also paddle or fish on the Glimmerglass, the lake made famous by James Fenimore Cooper. After spending a day at the Baseball Hall of Fame, guests may relax and unwind around the large in-ground pool. Heartworks, a charming quilt crafts shop, is on the premises.

The White Pillars Inn ✪
82 SECOND STREET, DEPOSIT, NEW YORK 13754

Tel: **(607) 467-4191**	Breakfast: **Full**
Best Time to Call: **8–10 AM; 5–10 PM**	Other Meals: **Dinner (reservations**
Host: **Najla Aswad**	**required)**
Location: **25 mi. SE of Binghamton**	Credit Cards: **AMEX, DC, DISC, MC,**
No. of Rooms: **4**	**VISA**
No. of Private Baths: **4**	Pets: **No**
Double/pb: **$85–$135**	Children: **Welcome**
Single/pb: **$85–$135**	Smoking: **No**
Open: **All year**	Social Drinking: **Permitted**
Reduced Rates: **10% AARP members**	Airport/Station Pickup: **Yes**

Here's the perfect place to do nothing but eat. With selections like Grand Marnier pecan cream cheese–stuffed French toast, fluffy omelettes filled with sun-dried tomatoes and fresh mozzarella, New York City bagels, home-baked muffins and coffee cakes, and robust, steaming coffee, five-course gourmet breakfasts are the highlight of your stay. The large guest rooms of this handsome Greek Revival mansion (circa 1820) are magnificently furnished with museum-quality antiques, inviting beds with fluffy comforters and pillows, concealed televisions and telephones, well-stocked refrigerators, and plenty of reading light. And Najla's cookies are always available in her trademark bottomless cookie jar.

Sunrise Farm ✪
RD 3, BOX 95, NEW BERLIN, NEW YORK 13411-9614

Tel: **(607) 847-9380**	Reduced Rates: **Families; weekly**
Hosts: **Janet and Fred Schmelzer**	Breakfast: **Full**
Location: **20 mi. from I-88**	Other Meals: **Available**
No. of Rooms: **1**	Pets: **No**
No. of Private Baths: **1**	Children: **Welcome**
Double/pb: **$55**	Smoking: **No**
Single/pb: **$40**	Social Drinking: **Permitted**
Open: **All year**	

Scottish Highland cattle are raised on this 80-acre organic farm about 20 miles from both Cooperstown and Oneonta. A restful night is assured in the large, comfortable second-floor guest room where, on clear nights, the stars can be seen through the skylight. Breakfast features home-baked goods, homemade preserves, and honey from the farm's hives. In winter, a wood stove keeps the house cozy. Several state parks lie a short distance away, and the local diversions include swimming, hiking, golf, horseback riding, cross-country skiing, ice skating, boating, and antiquing. Hunters welcome.

Country Spread Bed & Breakfast ✪
P.O. BOX 1863, 23 PROSPECT STREET, RICHFIELD SPRINGS, NEW YORK 13439

Tel: **(315) 858-1870**
Best Time to Call: **4–8 PM**
Hosts: **Karen and Bruce Watson**
Location: **20 mi. SE of Utica on Rte. 28; Cooperstown vicinity**
No. of Rooms: **2**
Max. No. Sharing Bath: **4**
Double/pb: **$60**
Single/pb: **$45**
Double/sb: **$50**
Single/sb: **$40**

Suites: **$80**
Open: **All year**
Breakfast: **Full**
Credit Cards: **MC, VISA**
Pets: **No**
Children: **Welcome (crib)**
Smoking: **No**
Social Drinking: **Permitted**
Minimum Stay: **Sometimes**
Airport/Station Pickup: **Yes**

Longtime area residents Karen and Bruce have restored their 1893 cozy home into a wonderful retreat, tastefully decorated in country style. Your day will start with warm muffins, homemade preserves, pancakes with pure maple syrup, fresh eggs, granola, and chilled juice. Relax on the deck with the newspaper, and then visit some of the area's attractions, including Cooperstown, museums, summer theater, opera, fine dining, antique and specialty shops, and small-town happenings. Nearby Canadarago and Otsego lakes offer excellent boating, fishing, and swimming.

CHAUTAUQUA/ALLEGHENY AREA

Brookside Manor Bed & Breakfast ✪
3728 ROUTE 83, FREDONIA, NEW YORK 14063-9740

Tel: **(716) 672-7721; (800) 929-7599**
Best Time to Call: **After noon**
Hosts: **Andrea Andrews and Dale Mirth**
Location: **42 mi. SW of Buffalo**
No. of Rooms: **3**
No. of Private Baths: **3**
Double/pb: **$69**
Single/pb: **$59**

Open: **All year**
Reduced Rates: **Available**
Breakfast: **Full**
Credit Cards: **MC, VISA**
Pets: **Sometimes**
Children: **Welcome**
Smoking: **No**
Social Drinking: **Permitted**

Situated on five and a half partially wooded acres, this brick Victorian manor, circa 1875, is only six minutes from historic Fredonia and the State University of New York campus there. Guest rooms feature air conditioners, queen-size beds, large windows with antique interior shutters, ceiling fans, hardwood floors, two-seated showers, and unique family heirlooms. Outside, a covered patio, woods, a meadow, and a spring-fed brook offer a relaxing atmosphere. Lily Dale Spiritualist Center and Lake Erie are ten minutes away. Andrea is a New England native and experienced caterer, Dale is a native and former research scientist. Both enjoy sharing their home and knowledge of the area with guests. Eight cats are in residence, but are permitted only in Andrea and Dale's private area.

FINGER LAKES/ROCHESTER/SYRACUSE AREA

Adventures Bed & Breakfast Reservation Service ✪
P.O. BOX 83, SCOTTSVILLE, NEW YORK 14546

Tel: **(716) 889-7190; (800) 724-1932**
Best Time to Call: **11:30 AM–7:30 PM**
Coordinator: **Andrea B. Barnhoorn**
States/Regions Covered: **Finger Lakes, Genesee Valley Area, Rochester**

Rates (Single/Double):
Modest: **$55–$65**
Average: **$75–$95**
Luxury: **$100–$195**

Adventures is more than a reservation service representing B&Bs in the Finger Lakes and Genesee Valley regions. Adventures can plan an exciting visit for you, whether it's cross-country skiing, fishing, hiking, a business meeting, a small retreat, or a wedding. Travel the country roads, hills, and velvet green vineyards. Stroll the path of history in a working Colonial village, take a hot-air balloon ride, spend the day antiquing, or hike along the Sea Way Trail. Visit the museums, planetarium, and theaters Rochester has to offer. Enjoy fun-filled festivals throughout the Finger Lakes and Rochester areas. All accommodations are within a few hours of Niagara Falls, Corning, Syracuse, and Toronto.

Addison Rose Bed & Breakfast ✪
37 MAPLE STREET, ADDISON, NEW YORK 14801

Tel: **(607) 359-4650**
Hosts: **Bill and Mary Ann Peters**
No. of Rooms: **3**
No. of Private Baths: **3**
Double/pb: **$65–$85**
Single/pb: **$65–$85**

Open: **All year**
Breakfast: **Full**
Pets: **No**
Children: **No**
Smoking: **No**
Social Drinking: **Permitted**

Warmth, friendliness, and hospitality characterize this bed and breakfast, which combines elegance and country charm. Built in 1892, this magnificent Queen Anne home has been painstakingly restored by the Peters family and furnished with period antiques to recapture the ambience of the Victorian age. Guest rooms, named for the original owners and other local personalities, suggest a bygone era. The city of Corning, museums, and Finger Lake wineries are just minutes away.

Pandora's Getaway ✪
83 OSWEGO STREET, BALDWINSVILLE, NEW YORK 13027

Tel: **(315) 635-9571; (888) 638-8668**
Best Time to Call: **Anytime**
Host: **Sandy Wheeler**
Location: **3 mi. from Route 90 Exit 90**
No. of Rooms: **4**
No. of Private Baths: **2**
Max. No. Sharing Bath: **2**
Double/pb: **$85**
Single/pb: **$70**
Double/sb: **$60**

Single/sb: **$50**
Open: **All year**
Reduced Rates: **Available**
Breakfast: **Full**
Credit Cards: **MC, VISA**
Pets: **No**
Children: **Welcome (crib)**
Smoking: **Restricted**
Social Drinking: **Permitted**
Airport Pickup: **Yes**

Standing on an imposing hill with lawns sloping to the street, Pandora's Getaway, an 1845 Greek Revival home, is a local landmark listed on the National Register of Historic Places. The stately trees sheltering the house add to its grandeur. Let Sandy show you upstate hospitality at its best. Guests are welcome to enjoy the entire B&B, including the front porch with rockers and the large living room with a fireplace. Rooms are furnished with interesting antiques, collectibles, and crafts, some of them for sale. Breakfast, served in the formal dining room with pieces drawn from Sandy's collection of colorful Depression glass, features specialties like quiche, homemade breads, and fresh fruit.

Roberts-Cameron House ✪
68 NORTH STREET, CALEDONIA, NEW YORK 14423

Tel: **(716) 538-6316**
Best Time to Call: **Evenings**
Hosts: **Elizabeth and Robert Wilcox**
Location: **12 mi. SW of Rochester**
No. of Rooms: **2**
Max. No. Sharing Bath: **4**
Double/sb: **$55**
Single/sb: **$45**

Open: **All year**
Breakfast: **Full**
Pets: **Sometimes**
Children: **Welcome**
Smoking: **Permitted (downstairs)**
Social Drinking: **Permitted**
Airport/Station Pickup: **Yes**

A clapboard farmhouse built in 1886 by William Roberts, a descendant of an early Scottish settler, this B&B is furnished with family antiques and collectibles from western New York. If you want to acquire some antiques of your own, the surrounding countryside is prime browsing territory, and Elizabeth runs her own antique and crafts shop. Just five minutes from the front door, the Genesee Country Museum lets visitors spend a day strolling through a re-created 19th-century hamlet; costumed villagers and craftspeople go about their daily chores May through October. Your hosts serve a generous country breakfast featuring New York maple syrup.

1865 White Birch Bed & Breakfast
69 EAST FIRST STREET, CORNING, NEW YORK 14830

Tel: (607) 962-6355	Single/sb: $55
Hosts: Kathy and Joe Donahue	Open: All year
Location: Off Rte. 17	Breakfast: Full
No. of Rooms: 4	Credit Cards: AMEX, MC, VISA
No. of Private Baths: 2	Pets: No
Max. No. Sharing Bath: 4	Children: Welcome
Double/pb: $75	Smoking: No
Single/pb: $60	Social Drinking: Permitted
Double/sb: $65	Airport/Station Pickup: Yes

The red-carpet treatment awaits you at this spacious 1865 Victorian home that has been restored to show off the beautifully crafted winding staircase and hardwood floors. Guests are welcome to choose a game or enjoy television by the fire in the common room. After a good night's sleep in a comfortable queen-size bed, you'll wake to the smell of home-made breads, muffins, and plenty of hot coffee. The White Birch is located in a residential area just two blocks from restored downtown Corning, and near such attractions as the Corning Glass Center, Rockwell Museum, and many fine wineries.

Fox Ridge Farm B&B
4786 FOSTER ROAD, ELBRIDGE, NEW YORK 13060
foxridge@dreamscape.com

Tel: (315) 673-4881	Single/sb: $40
Best Time to Call: 8 AM–9 PM	Open: All year
Hosts: Marge and Bob Sykes	Reduced Rates: Available
Location: 17 mi. SW of Syracuse	Breakfast: Full
No. of Rooms: 3	Credit Cards: MC, VISA
No. of Private Baths: 1	Pets: No
Max. No. Sharing Bath: 3	Children: Welcome, over 6
Double/pb: $65	Smoking: No
Single/pb: $50	Social Drinking: Permitted
Double/sb: $55	Airport Pickup: Yes

Fox Ridge Farm B&B is located on a quiet rural road surrounded by woods. Hiking trails wander through the 120 acres of woodlands, stately pines, and sparkling streams—a paradise for birders. These same trails are also used for cross-country skiing or snowshoeing in the winter. Stroll around the expansive lawns and flower gardens or kick off your shoes in the spacious family room, which has wood paneling, hardwood floors, a wood-burning stove, a TV, stereo, and reading library. Each guest room is individually decorated with floral wallpaper, handmade quilts, hardwood floors or carpeting, and in some cases, four-poster beds. One room, overlooking the flower garden, has both double and queen beds. Hearty breakfasts are served in the large country kitchen, with its stone fireplace.

Woods Edge ✪
151 BLUHM ROAD, FAIRPORT, NEW YORK 14450

Tel: **(716) 223-8877**
Best Time to Call: **8 AM–6 PM**
Hosts: **Betty and Bill Kinsman**
Location: **8 mi. SE of Rochester**
No. of Rooms: **3**
No. of Private Baths: **3**
Double/pb: **$70–$85**
Single/pb: **$55–$65**
Guest cabin: **$110–$120**

Open: **Not Feb., July, Aug.**
Reduced Rates: **Long stays; families**
Breakfast: **Full**
Pets: **No**
Children: **Welcome (crib, high chair)**
Smoking: **No**
Social Drinking: **Permitted**
Airport Pickup: **Yes**

Woods Edge is nestled among fragrant pines in a secluded location only 20 minutes from downtown Rochester. The hideaway cabin is a romantically decorated private lodge: a large living room with a fireplace and cathedral ceiling, a bedroom with a queen-size bed, full kitchen, and private bath. The main house has two additional bedrooms, one with king-size or twin beds, the other with a queen-size bed; each has a private bath. Both rooms are decorated with white walls, barn beams, and early country pine furnishings. Full breakfasts are served on the screened porch if weather permits. Cabin guests may have the refrigerator stocked or join everyone else in the main house for their morning meal.

Just a "Plane" Bed & Breakfast
RD 2, BOX 40, ROUTE 19A, FILLMORE, NEW YORK 14735

Tel: **(716) 567-8338**
Hosts: **Craig and Audrey Smith**
Location: **50 mi. S of Rochester**
No. of Rooms: **4**
No. of Private Baths: **4**

Double/pb: **$55**
Single/pb: **$42**
Open: **All year**
Reduced Rates: **10% seniors**
Breakfast: **Full**

Credit Cards: **AMEX, MC, VISA**	Smoking: **No**
Pets: **Sometimes**	Social Drinking: **Permitted**
Children: **Welcome**	Airport Pickup: **Yes**

A stay at Just a "Plane" Bed & Breakfast is anything but plain. This three-story Dutch Colonial was built in 1926 by Craig's grandparents, and has been well maintained with very few changes other than added bathrooms. Audrey's love of crafting, decorating, and baking are very noticeable. Breakfast is served in the sunroom and consists of fresh-baked muffins, bread, or waffles served with fresh fruit and jams. Craig's love for flying offers a special flair to your stay. He offers plane rides over the seventeen-mile gorge at Letchworth or a trip around beautiful Rushford Lake. Located seven miles south of the beautiful Grand Canyon of the East—Letchworth State Park—on an operating crop farm, this B&B offers a relaxing and enjoyable stay.

The Gorham House ✪
P.O. BOX 43, 4752 EAST SWAMP ROAD, GORHAM, NEW YORK 14461-0043

Tel: **(716) 526-4402**	Single/sb: **$60**
Hosts: **Nancy and Al Rebmann**	Open: **All year**
Location: **9 mi. SE of Canandaigua**	Reduced Rates: **Available**
No. of Rooms: **3**	Breakfast: **Full**
No. of Private Baths: **1**	Pets: **No**
Max. No. Sharing Bath: **4**	Children: **Welcome, over 12**
Double/pb: **$70**	Smoking: **No**
Single/pb: **$65**	Social Drinking: **Permitted**
Double/sb: **$65**	Minimum Stay: **2 nights peak season**

Built before the turn of the century, this 14-room country Colonial-style farmhouse is decorated with family treasures and special finds. You will never forget the two elegant common rooms and the intimate library with its cozy parlor, divided by large pocket doors. Spacious, beautifully appointed guest rooms have seating and reading areas. The kitchen contains a large collection of advertising tins; the eat-in pantry features framed Cream of Wheat advertisements from the 1900s. Warm yourself by the woodstove after skiing. Walk the five acres and explore the many different wildflowers, berry bushes, fruit trees, and Nancy's herb garden. Or just relax on one of three porches.

Sandy Creek Manor House ✪
1960 REDMAN ROAD, HAMLIN, NEW YORK 14464

Tel: **(716) 964-7528**	No. of Rooms: **3**
Best Time to Call: **Anytime**	Max. No. Sharing Bath: **4**
Hosts: **Shirley Hollink and James Krempasky**	Double/sb: **$70**
	Single/sb: **$60**
Location: **20 mi. W of Rochester**	Open: **All year**

Reduced Rates: **Weekly**
Breakfast: **Full**
Credit Cards: **AMEX, DISC, MC, VISA**
Pets: **Welcome**

Children: **Welcome, over 12**
Smoking: **No**
Social Drinking: **Permitted**

Six wooded acres and perennial gardens surround this 1910 English Tudor merely a stroll away from Sandy Creek. Natural woodwork, stained glass windows, feather pillows, and Amish quilts summon up thoughts of a bygone era, while an antique player piano adds to the nostalgic mood. Full breakfasts include fresh fruit and homemade breads. Hamlin Beach is only 5 minutes away; you can reach Rochester in 30 minutes and Niagara Falls in less than an hour and a half.

Blushing Rose B&B
11 WILLIAM STREET, HAMMONDSPORT, NEW YORK 14840

Tel: **(607) 569-3402; (800) 982-8818**
Best Time to Call: **10 AM–7 PM**
Hosts: **Ellen and Bucky Laufersweiler**
Location: **20 mi. W of Corning**
No. of Rooms: **4**
No. of Private Baths: **4**
Double/pb: **$75–$95**

Open: **All year**
Breakfast: **Full**
Pets: **No**
Smoking: **No**
Social Drinking: **Permitted**
Minimum Stay: **3 nights holiday weekends; 2 nights weekends**

Blushing Rose is like something right out of a country magazine, thanks to the quilts, wall hangings, wreaths, and candles that decorate this B&B. Hammondsport is located at the southern end of the Finger Lakes region, and it's a short walk to Keuka Lake. Watkins Glen, Corning, and the famous Finger Lakes wineries are all a short drive away. You'll look forward to breakfast: baked French toast, lemon poppy-seed waffles, and strawberry bread are among the house specialties.

Hanshaw House ✪
15 SAPSUCKER WOODS ROAD, ITHACA, NEW YORK 14850

Tel: **(800) 257–1437**
Best Time to Call: **Before 10 PM**
Host: **Helen Scoones**
No. of Rooms: **4**
No. of Private Baths: **4**
Double/pb: **$68–$120**
Single/pb: **$65–$90**
Suites: **$72–$135; sleeps 3**
Open: **All year**
Reduced Rates: **10% for 5 nights or**
more; **10–15% Dec. 1–Apr. 1;**
corporate/educational rate $60–$65
for a single
Breakfast: **Full**
Credit Cards: **AMEX, MC, VISA**
Pets: **No**
Children: **Welcome**
Smoking: **No**
Social Drinking: **Permitted**
Airport/Station Pickup: **Yes**

Not far from downtown Ithaca, this woodframe, elegantly restored farmhouse seems light-years away. Built in the 1830s, it has all the comforting country touches, from its white picket fence and dark blue shutters, to the down-filled quilts and pillows in the bedrooms. Bird-lovers should stroll down the road to Cornell's Laboratory of Ornithology and Sapsucker Woods, a bird sanctuary. Breakfasts include fresh fruit, juice, homemade muffins, and a hot entree such as pancakes or waffles.

Log Country Inn—B&B of Ithaca ✪
P.O. BOX 581, ITHACA, NEW YORK 14851

Tel: **(800) 274-4771**
Best Time to Call: **7 AM–11 PM**
Hosts: **Wanda and Slawomir Grunberg**
Location: **11 mi. S of Ithaca**
No. of Rooms: **3**
No. of Private Baths: **3**

Double/pb: **$65–$75**
Single/pb: **$55–$65**
Suites: **$130**
Open: **All year**
Reduced Rates: **Available**
Breakfast: **Full**
Credit Cards: **AMEX, MC, VISA**
Pets: **Sometimes**

Children: **Welcome**
Smoking: **No**
Social Drinking: **Permitted**
Minimum Stay: **During parents'
weekend, graduations, and reunions
at Cornell and Ithaca College**
Foreign Languages: **Polish, Russian**

Escape to the rustic charm of a log house located at the edge of a 7,000-acre state forest in the Finger Lakes region. Guests will enjoy modern accommodations provided in the spirit of international hospitality. You will wake up to the sound of birds and enjoy exploring the peaceful surroundings. A full European breakfast is served and might include blintzes or Russian pancakes. Your hosts offer afternoon tea and a sauna during the fall and winter months. Nearby, Cornell, Ithaca College, Corning Glass Center, wineries, and antique stores are just a few of the sites, and there is easy access to hiking and cross-country trails. Wanda is a former biologist and Slawomir is a documentary filmmaker.

Peregrine House ✪
140 COLLEGE AVENUE, ITHACA, NEW YORK 14850

Tel: **(607) 272-0919**
Best Time to Call: **8 AM–12 noon**
Host: **Susan Vance**
No. of Rooms: **8**
No. of Private Baths: **9**
Double/pb: **$69–$109**
Open: **All year**

Reduced Rates: **Nov. 20–Apr. 1; weekly**
Breakfast: **Full**
Credit Cards: **MC, VISA**
Pets: **No**
Children: **Welcome, over 8**
Social Drinking: **Permitted**

This three-story brick home, with mansard roof, dates back to 1874. Its faux-marble fireplaces and carved-wood ceilings have been beautifully preserved and are accented with Victorian oak furnishings. Pick a good book in the library and relax in a wing chair, or watch some television in your air-conditioned bedroom. Mexican, Italian, Greek, and Indian food can all be enjoyed within a short walk from here. Peregrine House is two blocks from the Cornell campus and only a few blocks from the Ithaca Commons. Cayuga Lake's wonderful boating and swimming, the wine country, biking, hiking, and cross-country skiing are all close by.

Allan's Hill Bed and Breakfast
2513 SAND HILL ROAD, MT. MORRIS, NEW YORK 14510

Tel: **(716) 658-4591; (800) 431-5580**
Best Time to Call: **After 5 PM**
Hosts: **George and Joyce Swanson**
Location: **35 mi. S of Rochester**
No. of Rooms: **3**

Max. No. Sharing Bath: **4**
Double/pb: **$80**
Double/sb: **$55–$65**
Open: **All year**
Breakfast: **Full**

Pets: **No**
Children: **Welcome**
Smoking: **No**

Social Drinking: **Permitted**
Airport/Station Pickup: **Yes**

Sixteen acres of land surround this restored 1830 country home, giving guests the chance to stroll through stately walnut groves, sit by the pond, picnic, and go bird-watching and cross-country skiing. Nearby Letchworth State Park offers a spectacular, 17-mile drive along the gorge of the Genesee River. The area's wineries will lure you with tours and tastings, and Rochester, with its museums, shops, concerts, and theaters, is within easy driving distance.

Finton's Landing Bed and Breakfast ✪
661 EAST LAKE ROAD, PENN YAN, NEW YORK 14527-9421

Tel: **(315) 536-3146**
Best Time to Call: **7 AM–9 PM**
Hosts: **Doug and Arianne Tepper**
Location: **53 mi. SE of Rochester**
No. of Rooms: **4**
No. of Private Baths: **4**
Double/pb: **$89**
Open: **All year**

Reduced Rates: **10% weekly**
Breakfast: **Full**
Credit Cards: **MC, VISA**
Pets: **No**
Children: **Welcome, over 10**
Smoking: **No**
Social Drinking: **Permitted**
Foreign Languages: **Dutch**

Finton's Landing, a historic steamboat landing on Keuka Lake, is known for its view of the Bluff, pristine water, and the 165-foot private cove. The Teppers' hammock defies anyone to stay awake while gazing into the evergreens. Artwork and murals add pure delight to this 1860 Victorian, while pine-plank floors and whimsical period pieces keep it casual. The parlor fireplace is a winter retreat. A luscious two-course breakfast is served on the porch, weather permitting, or in the dining room overlooking the wildflowers. Activities include nature walks, wine tastings, antiquing, Watkins Glen car races, Windmill Craft Market shopping, and relaxing at the beach.

The Wagener Estate Bed & Breakfast ✪
351 ELM STREET, PENN YAN, NEW YORK 14527

Tel: **(315) 536-4591**
Best Time to Call: **1–4 PM; 7–10 PM**
Hosts: **Joanne and Scott Murray**
Location: **20 mi. from NYS Thruway, Exit 42, Geneva**
No. of Rooms: **5**
No. of Private Baths: **3**
Max. No. Sharing Bath: **4**
Double/pb: **$80**
Single/pb: **$75**

Double/sb: **$70**
Single/sb: **$65**
Open: **All year**
Breakfast: **Full**
Credit Cards: **AMEX, DISC, MC, VISA**
Pets: **No**
Children: **Welcome, over 5**
Smoking: **No**
Social Drinking: **Permitted**

Once the home of Abraham Wagener, the founder of Penn Yan, this lovely fifteen-room estate is furnished with antiques and charm. This bed and breakfast sits on four scenic acres, with shaded lawns, apple trees, and gentle breezes. The pillared veranda offers you a perfect spot for reflection, conversation, and refreshments. Things to see include wineries, Keuka and Seneca Lakes, the Corning Glass Museum, Watkins Glen, public beaches, parks, Outlet Trail, and the well-known Windmill Farm and Crafts Market. Joanne and Scott serve a sumptuous breakfast as part of your relaxing stay.

HUDSON VALLEY/ALBANY/KINGSTON AREA

Battenkill Bed & Breakfast ✪
ROUTE 313, RD 1, BOX 143, CAMBRIDGE, NEW YORK 12816-9717

Tel: **(518) 677-8868; (800) 676-8768**
Hosts: **Veronica and Walt Piekarz**
Location: **30 mi. E of Saratoga**
No. of Rooms: **2**
Max. No. Sharing Bath: **4**
Double/sb: **$65**
Single/sb: **$50**
Open: **All year**

Breakfast: **Full**
Other Meals: **Available**
Credit Cards: **DISC, MC, VISA**
Pets: **No**
Children: **No**
Smoking: **No**
Social Drinking: **Permitted**

Relax and enjoy yourself at this post-and-beam home nestled in the Annaquassicoke Valley. Veronica delights in creative cooking while Walt, a jazz musician, is always ready to talk shop. Winter activities here include snowshoeing and cross-country skiing, with longer trails nearby. The rest of the year, guests can go fishing, canoeing, kayaking, tubing, and biking; the B&B's property borders the Battenkill River, and equipment may be rented from your hosts. Fly fishing instruction is available by reservation April–October.

Alexander Hamilton House ✪

49 VAN WYCK STREET, CROTON-ON-HUDSON, NEW YORK 10520

Tel: **(914) 271-6737**	Breakfast: **Full**
Best Time to Call: **8 AM–6 PM**	Credit Cards: **AMEX, DC, DISC, MC,**
Host: **Barbara Notarius**	**VISA**
Location: **30 mi. NW of New York City**	Pets: **No**
No. of Rooms: **7**	Children: **Welcome**
No. of Private Baths: **7**	Smoking: **No**
Double/pb: **$95–$125**	Social Drinking: **Permitted**
Single/pb: **$75–$85**	Minimum Stay: **2 nights weekends**
Suites: **$135–$250**	Airport/Station Pickup: **Yes**
Open: **All year**	Foreign Languages: **French**

No, Hamilton didn't live here; this beautiful Victorian home was built some eight decades after his death. The home, with its 35-foot in-ground swimming pool, and spectacular Hudson River views, would please even the most patrician lodgers. West Point, Van Cortlandt Manor, Boscobel, and Storm King Art Center are all nearby, and New York City is within striking distance. After sightseeing, relax in the large living room complete with fireplace, piano, and numerous antiques. Baby equipment is available for guests with small children. Five rooms have a fireplace and two have two-person Jacuzzis.

Hoosick Bed and Breakfast ✪

ROUTE 7 TROY-BENNINGTON ROAD, P.O. BOX 145, HOOSICK, NEW YORK 12089

Tel: **(518) 686-5875**	Reduced Rates: **5% families**
Hosts: **Maria and John Recco**	Breakfast: **Full**
Location: **8 mi. W of Bennington, Vt.**	Pets: **Yes**
No. of Rooms: **3**	Children: **Welcome**
Max. No. Sharing Bath: **4**	Smoking: **No**
Double/sb: **$45**	Social Drinking: **Permitted**
Single/sb: **$35**	Foreign Languages: **Greek, Spanish**
Open: **All year**	

This recently restored 1840 Greek Revival farmhouse is located fifteen miles from Williamstown, Massachusetts, forty miles from Saratoga Springs, a half hour from the ski slopes of Vermont and the Berkshires, and minutes from local antique centers. Right on site there are barnyard animals to feed and an open field for relaxing, walking, or cross-country skiing. Breakfast specialties might include fresh-baked Texas-size muffins, blueberry pancakes, eggs, coffee, and juice, which you can enjoy privately or with your hosts. Maria and John also offer guests evening tea and the use of a full kitchen.

Mallard Manor ✪
345 LAKEVIEW DRIVE, MAHOPAC, NEW YORK 10541

Tel: **(914) 628-3595**
Hosts: **Jean and Joe Costello**
Location: **50 mi. N of New York**
No. of Rooms: **2**
Max. No. Sharing Bath: **4**
Double/sb: **$70**
Open: **All year**

Reduced Rates: **10% seniors**
Breakfast: **Full**
Pets: **No**
Children: **Welcome, over 10**
Smoking: **No**
Social Drinking: **Permitted**

This warm and cozy Dutch Colonial is the perfect spot if you are looking to get away from the hectic pace of city life. Nestled among the rolling hills and reservoirs of the lower Hudson Valley, it lets guests unwind in comfortable surroundings. The house features wide-planked floors, faux finished and stenciled walls, and a mural depicting the history of Mahopac, painted by a local artist. Informal gardens continue the relaxed mood outdoors. Whether you are in town for business or pleasure, Jean and Joe will make your visit a memorable one.

Morgan House ✪
12 POWELTON ROAD, NEWBURGH, NEW YORK 12550
http://www.hudval.com/morgan

Tel: **(914) 561-0326**
Best Time to Call: **4:30 PM weekdays**
Hosts: **Pat and Richard Morgan**
Location: **60 mi. N of New York City**
No. of rooms: **2**
Max. No. Sharing Bath: **4**
Double/sb: **$75**
Single/sb: **$65**
Open: **All year**
Reduced Rates: **$10 less Nov. 1–
   Mar. 31, 10% seniors**

Breakfast: **Full**
Credit Cards: **AMEX, MC, VISA**
Other Meals: **Available**
Pets: **Sometimes**
Children: **Welcome, over 10**
Smoking: **No**
Social Drinking: **Permitted**
Airport/Station Pickup: **Yes, weekends
   only**

Warm hospitality awaits you in this lovely home nestled in a quiet wooded setting with perennial, herb, and "secret" gardens. Breakfast is served by candlelight in the dining room or on the deck. There are two rooms. The Heart Room is romantic and filled with touches of sweet sentiments, the Cottage Room is whimsical and enchanting. Each evening, beds are turned down and mints are placed on the pillows along with a slumber note. The bath, filled with luxuries and wonderful scents, is private or shared. Pat and Richard both work in nearby school districts. They enjoy gardening and warmly welcoming guests into their home.

Empty Nest B&B
423 LAKE ROAD, NEW WINDSOR, NEW YORK 12553

Tel: **(914) 496-9263**
Hosts: **Pat and Dick Coleman**
Location: **60 mi. N of New York City**
No. of Rooms: **3**
Max. No. Sharing Bath: **4**
Double/sb: **$65–$85**
Single/sb: **$55–$70**
Open: **Jan. 16–Nov. 14**

Breakfast: **Full**
Pets: **No**
Smoking: **No**
Social Drinking: **Permitted**
Minimum Stay: **2 nights holiday weekends, homecoming; 4 nights West Point graduation**
Airport/Station Pickup: **Yes**

Situated on a pretty country road, this traditional home is furnished with country charm and family antiques. Some of the most popular attractions are West Point Military Academy; Brotherhood Winery, the oldest in the U.S.; and Woodbury Commons, a beautiful outlet mall. Crestview Lake, Sugar Loaf Craft Village Museum, and Storm King Art Center are all nearby. For those of you who are energetic, swimming, fishing, hiking, horseback riding, golfing, antiquing, or cruising the Hudson are just a few of the many activities to choose from. After a peaceful night's sleep, spring through fall, guests can enjoy breakfast on the porch overlooking the rolling hills and meadows. In winter it's nice to gather around the wood-burning stove and enjoy the warmth. One guest commented, "The warmth and love in this house are infectious. It's restful for the soul as well as the body. It's wonderful to be so well cared for, so well fed."

The Milton Bull House ✪
1065 ROUTE 302, PINE BUSH, NEW YORK 12566

Tel: **(914) 361-4770**
Best Time to Call: **9 AM–9 PM**
Hosts: **Ellen and Graham Jamison**
Location: **75 mi. NW of New York City**
No. of Rooms: **2**
No. of Private Baths: **1**
Max. No. Sharing Bath: **4**
Double/sb: **$65**
Single/sb: **$54**

Open: **All year**
Reduced Rates: **Weekly**
Breakfast: **Full**
Pets: **No**
Children: **Welcome**
Smoking: **No**
Social Drinking: **Permitted**
Airport/Station Pickup: **Yes**
Foreign Languages: **French**

The Milton Bull House is a traditional bed and breakfast. The historic house has nine large rooms furnished with antiques. Part of the house dates to 1816 and is Federal in style. The two guest rooms share a full bath. The house is located in a lovely area of the Hudson Valley—in the foothills of the Shawangunk Mountain Ridge—which provides wonderful scenery as well as opportunities for hiking and rock climbing. Shopping malls, such as Woodbury Common, antique marts, and wineries are nearby. Although the area is rural, the Bull House is very close to Route 17, the NYS Thruway, and I-84. There are sixty acres of open farmland, lawns, gardens, orchards, and an in-ground swimming pool. Rates include an old-fashioned farm breakfast with home baking.

Maggie Towne's B&B ✪
PHILLIPS ROAD, PITTSTOWN, NEW YORK (MAILING ADDRESS: BOX 82, RD 2, VALLEY FALLS, NEW YORK 12185)

Tel: **(518) 663-8369; 686-7331**
Host: **Maggie Towne**
Location: **14 mi. E of Troy**
No. of Rooms: **3**
Max. No. Sharing Bath: **4**
Double/sb: **$45**
Single/sb: **$35**

Open: **All year**
Breakfast: **Full**
Pets: **Sometimes**
Children: **Welcome (crib)**
Smoking: **No**
Social Drinking: **Permitted**

This lovely old Colonial is located amid beautiful lawns and trees. Enjoy a cup of tea or glass of wine before the huge fireplace in the family room. Use the music room or curl up with a book on the screened-in porch. Mornings, your host serves home-baked goodies. She will gladly prepare a lunch for you to take on tour or enjoy at the house. It's 20 miles to historic Bennington, Vermont, and 30 to Saratoga.

Lee's Deer Run Bed & Breakfast ✪
411 COUNTY ROAD #71, STILLWATER, NEW YORK 12170

Tel: **(518) 584-7722, 587-0921**
Best Time to Call: **8 AM–8 PM**
Hosts: **Rose and Don Lee**
Location: **8 mi. SE of Saratoga Springs**
Suites: **$85–$200**
Open: **All year**

Breakfast: **Full**
Pets: **No**
Children: **Welcome, over 12**
Smoking: **No**
Social Drinking: **Permitted**
Minimum Stay: **2 nights racing season**

Lee's Deer Run is located on 65 acres of rolling countryside adjacent to Saratoga National Park and just ten minutes from the Saratoga Race Track, performing arts center, spa and mineral baths, Skidmore College, and historic Saratoga Springs. Rose and Don transformed a circa 1800 barn into an exquisite home. The two suites have king-size poster beds, comfortable sofas, easy chairs, and air-conditioning. Rose and Don will offer plenty of suggestions on area restaurants and information on current events.

Sharon Fern's Bed & Breakfast ✪
8 ETHIER DRIVE, TROY, NEW YORK 12180

Tel: **(518) 279-1966**
Best Time to Call: **Mornings**
Hosts: **Bill and Sharon Ernst**
Location: **10 mi. from NYS Thruway**
No. of Rooms: **2**
Max. No. Sharing Bath: **3**
Double/sb: **$55**
Single/sb: **$50**

Open: **All year**
Reduced Rates: **10% seniors**
Breakfast: **Full**
Pets: **No**
Children: **Welcome (crib)**
Smoking: **No**
Social Drinking: **Permitted**

Bill and Sharon's tri-level contemporary home rests on a quiet street in the country just 20 minutes outside of Albany, New York's capital. Enjoy spacious accommodations plus many extras, including an in-ground pool, a recreation room with a Ping-Pong table, and a beautiful backyard, where badminton and croquet will test your mettle. Skiers and hikers will find mountains in nearly every direction—the Adirondacks, Catskills, and Green Mountains are all a half hour away.

Boulevard House Bed and Breakfast ✪
1017 ROUTE 52, WALDEN, NEW YORK 12586

Tel: **(914) 778-1602**
Best Time to Call: **8 AM–10 PM**
Hosts: **Larry and Jean Winum**
Location: **60 mi. NW of New York City**
No. of Rooms: **1**
No. of Private Baths: **1**
Double/pb: **$75**
Open: **Jan. 11–Dec. 21**

Breakfast: **Full**
Other Meals: **Available**
Credit Cards: **DISC, MC, VISA**
Pets: **Sometimes**
Children: **Welcome, crib**
Smoking: **No**
Social Drinking: **Permitted**
Airport/Station Pickup: **Yes**

The Boulevard Bed and Breakfast is centrally located outside the village of Walden. The Winums live within a comfortable driving distance of golf courses, antique shops, wineries, West Point, Hudson River attractions, historic sites, and farmers markets. A three-course breakfast is served every morning, beginning with fresh fruit and ending with a sweet treat often made from local apples. Raising a large family made it easy for Larry and Jean to extend their hospitality to guests.

LAKE GEORGE AREA
Hilltop Cottage ✪
P.O. BOX 186, 6883 LAKESHORE DRIVE, BOLTON LANDING, NEW YORK 12814

Tel: **(518) 644-2492**
Best Time to Call: **Anytime**
Hosts: **Anita and Charlie Richards**

Location: **8 mi. from I-87**
No. of Rooms: **4**
No. of Private Baths: **2**

Max. No. Sharing Bath: **4**
Double/pb: **$75**
Double/sb: **$60**
Open: **All year**
Breakfast: **Full**

Credit Cards: **MC, VISA**
Children: **Welcome, over 4**
Smoking: **Restricted**
Social Drinking: **Permitted**
Foreign Languages: **German**

Hilltop Cottage is a clean, comfortable, renovated caretaker cottage in the beautiful Lake George–Eastern Adirondack region. You can walk to the beach, marinas, shops, and restaurants. Guests will enjoy the hearty breakfasts, homey atmosphere, helpful hosts, wood-burning stove, and fall foliage.

Crislip's Bed & Breakfast ✪
693 RIDGE ROAD, QUEENSBURY, NEW YORK 12804-9717

Tel: **(518) 793-6869**
Hosts: **Ned and Joyce Crislip**
Location: **20 mi. N of Saratoga Springs**
No. of Rooms: **4**
No. of Private Baths: **3**
Max. No. Sharing Bath: **3**
Double/pb: **$55–$75**
Single/pb: **$45–$65**
Single/sb: **$35**
Open: **All year**

Reduced Rates: **Over 3 nights**
Breakfast: **Full**
Credit Cards: **MC, VISA**
Pets: **Sometimes**
Children: **Welcome**
Smoking: **No**
Social Drinking: **Permitted**
Minimum Stay: **Major holiday weekends**
Airport/Station Pickup: **Yes**

Located between Saratoga Springs and Lake George, this Quaker-built Federal home provides spacious accommodations complete with period antiques, four-poster beds, down comforters, and private baths. The country breakfast menu features buttermilk pancakes, scrambled eggs, and sausages. Ned Crislip, a music teacher, and his wife, Joyce, invite you to enjoy the grounds surrounding their dwelling, which include nearly two acres of lawn and gardens, old stone walls, and mountain views of Vermont.

The Inn on Bacon Hill ✪
P.O. BOX 1462, SARATOGA SPRINGS, NEW YORK 12866

Tel: **(518) 695-3693**
Best Time to Call: **7–10 AM**
Host: **Andrea Collins-Breslin**
Location: **8 mi. E of Saratoga Springs**
No. of Rooms: **4**
No. of Private Baths: **2**
Max. No. Sharing Bath: **4**
Double/pb: **$85–$135**
Double/sb: **$75–$125**
Suites: **$95–$150; sleeps 2**

Open: **All year**
Reduced Rates: **Available**
Breakfast: **Full**
Credit Cards: **MC, VISA**
Pets: **No**
Children: **Welcome, over 13**
Smoking: **No**
Social Drinking: **Permitted**
Minimum Stay: **Weekends during racing season—2 days**

Experience the peace and quiet of elegant country living and the fun and excitement of nearby city life. Relax in this large, beautifully re-stored 1862 home, with its four air-conditioned bedrooms, original mar-ble fireplaces and wallcoverings, high ceilings, and finely crafted mold-ings and woodwork that take you back to Victorian times. A hearty country breakfast is served daily, with early morning coffee or after-noon beverages to be enjoyed in the screened-in gazebo surrounded by soothing rural settings and the distant hills of Vermont. Albany, Lake George, and Vermont are all within a 45-minute drive. Like many oth-ers, innkeeper Andrea Collins-Breslin left the corporate world to pursue a career in hospitality with no regrets!

Six Sisters Bed and Breakfast ✪

149 UNION AVENUE, SARATOGA SPRINGS, NEW YORK 12866

Tel: **(518) 583-1173;**
 fax: **(518) 587-2470**
Hosts: **Kate Benton and Steve Ramirez**
Location: **30 mi. N of Albany**
No. of Rooms: **4**
No. of Private Baths: **4**
Double/pb: **$75–$100**
Single/pb: **$65–$85**
Suites: **$85–$150**
Open: **All year**

Reduced Rates: **10%–15% Sun.–Thurs. Nov.–Mar.; 10% seniors; corporate, extended stays**
Breakfast: **Full**
Pets: **No**
Children: **Welcome, over 10**
Smoking: **No**
Social Drinking: **Permitted**
Minimum Stay: **Special weekends, racing season**

Some people visit this town for its naturally carbonated mineral waters, other people for its racetracks. Bathers and railbirds will both be de-lighted by Kate and Steve's 1890 Victorian, named for Kate's sisters. All rooms have air-conditioning and either king- or queen-size beds (except for the second-floor parlor suite, which has two double beds). After sampling one of Steve's mouth-watering breakfasts, guests are encouraged to take a mug of coffee, tea, or cider out to the veranda overlooking Saratoga's streets and racecourse. Then it's an easy walk to boutiques, antique shops, restaurants, and the National Museum of Racing.

LAKE PLACID/ADIRONDACKS AREA

Crown Point Bed & Breakfast ✪
P.O. BOX 490, MAIN STREET, ROUTE 9 N, CROWN POINT, NEW YORK 12928

Tel: (518) 597-3651
Best Time to Call: 10 AM–7 PM
Hosts: Hugh and Sandy Johnson, owners
Location: 7 mi. N of Ticonderoga
No. of Rooms: 5
No. of Private Baths: 5
Double/pb: $60–$75
Single/pb: $55–$75
Suites: $120, sleeps 4
Open: All year

Reduced Rates: 10% seniors
Breakfast: Continental, plus
Credit Cards: MC, VISA
Pets: No
Children: Welcome
Smoking: No
Social Drinking: Permitted
Minimum Stay: 2 nights on holiday weekends

Return to an era of stately Victorian elegance. Sleep in a hundred-year-old manor house graciously furnished with period antiques. The 18-room house, built in 1886 by Richard Wymann, a local banker, took three years to complete. It was designed by Witherbee and Sherman and constructed by an Italian craftsman. Six different kinds of paneled woodwork (oak, pine, chestnut, mahogany, cherry, and walnut), pocket doors, and four fireplaces grace the house. Enjoy a summer evening on one of the three porches, view the sunrise over the Green Mountains of Vermont, or experience the double rainbows of the Adirondack region.

Gatehouse Herbs Bed & Breakfast ✪
98 VAN BUREN STREET, DOLGEVILLE, NEW YORK 13329

Tel: (315) 429-8366
Best Time to Call: 5 PM–9 PM
Hosts: Carol and Kermit (Kerry) Gates
Location: 30 mi. E of Utica
No. of Rooms: 3
No. of Private Baths: 3
Double/pb: $75
Single/pb: $65
Suites: $85

Open: June thru Oct. 12th
Reduced Rates: 10% if longer than 15 days
Breakfast: Full
Pets: Sometimes
Children: Welcome
Smoking: No
Social Drinking: Permitted

Nestled in the Adirondack foothills and overlooking a lily pond in the charming village of Dolgeville, Gatehouse Herbs Bed & Breakfast is an exquisite example of Victorian architecture. Its twelve-acre grounds include English gardens, wooded walks, and a bubbling brook. There are three guest rooms decorated with family antiques. Fresh fruit and cold spring water are complimentary in each room. Enjoy bountiful breakfasts in the dining room or on the breakfast porch. Specialties include multigrain pancakes with fresh local maple syrup, omelettes, blueberry muffins, or scones. Saratoga Springs, Cooperstown, and the oldest Russian Orthodox Monastery in the U.S. are within an hour's drive. Hiking, biking, and canoeing in the Adirondack Park are just minutes away.

The Book & Blanket Bed & Breakfast ✪
ROUTE 9N (P.O. BOX 164), JAY, NEW YORK 12941

Tel: **(518) 946-8323**
Best Time to Call: **Anytime**
Hosts: **Kathy, Fred, Samuel, and Daisy the Basset Hound**
Location: **17 mi. E of Lake Placid**
No. of Rooms: **3**
No. of Private Baths: **1**
Max. No. Sharing Bath: **4**
Double/pb: **$75**

Single/pb: **$70**
Double/sb: **$55–$60**
Single/sb: **$40**
Open: **All year**
Breakfast: **Full**
Pets: **Sometimes**
Children: **Welcome**
Smoking: **No**
Social Drinking: **Permitted**

This 125-year-old Greek revival residence is situated on the east branch of the Ausable River in Jay, N.Y.—an Adirondack hamlet complete with covered bridge and village green. Filled with antiques and books for borrowing and browsing, this house boasts three guest bedrooms honoring Jane Austen, F. Scott Fitzgerald, and Jack London. In winter, guests can relax before a fire; in summer the porch swing is just the thing. Whiteface Ski Mountain is seven miles away, and Lake Placid a mere 17. Ausable Chasm, Fort Ticonderoga, and ferries to Vermont are easy day trips. The owners enjoy baking, juggling, and their adorable basset hound.

Brook's Sunshine Cottage ✪
6 MAPLE STREET, LAKE PLACID, NEW YORK 12946

Tel: **(518) 523-3661; fax: (518) 523-2331**
Best Time to Call: **9 AM–8 PM**
Hosts: **Bernadine and Joseph Brooks**
Location: **150 mi. N of Albany**
No. of Rooms: **4**
Max. No. Sharing Bath: **4**
Double/pb: **$75**
Double/sb: **$55–$60**
Single/sb: **$40**
Suites: **$75–$99; sleeps 4**

Open: **All year**
Reduced Rates: **Available**
Breakfast: **Full**
Credit Cards: **MC, VISA**
Pets: **No**
Children: **Welcome**
Smoking: **No**
Social Drinking: **Permitted**
Minimum Stay: **2 nights winter and summer, weekends**
Airport/Station Pickup: **Yes**

This century-old B&B is located one block from Main Street in the center of the Olympic Village. Skating, tobogganing, downhill and cross-country skiing, boating, biking, visiting Olympic venues, and hiking the forty-six majestic Adirondack peaks are just some of the activities to pursue during your stay. Brook's Sunshine Cottage offers guests four bedrooms, two fireplaces, TV, VCR, off-street parking, and a bountiful breakfast buffet. Also available are two suites, each equipped with a full kitchen, TV, and living room.

Fogarty's Bed and Breakfast ✪
37 RIVERSIDE DRIVE, SARANAC LAKE, NEW YORK 12983

Tel: **(518) 891-3755; (800) 525-3755**
Best Time to Call: **After 3 PM**
Hosts: **Jack and Emily Fogarty**
Location: **150 mi. N of Albany**
No. of Rooms: **5**
Max. No. Sharing Bath: **3**
Double/sb: **$55**
Single/sb: **$40**

Open: **All year**
Breakfast: **Full**
Pets: **No**
Children: **Welcome**
Smoking: **Permitted**
Social Drinking: **Permitted**
Airport Pickup: **Yes**

High on a hill overlooking Lake Flower and Mts. Baker, McKenzie, and Pisgah—but only three minutes from the center of town—you'll find Fogarty's. The B&B's porches, wide doors, and call buttons attest to its past as a cure cottage. The living and dining rooms are decorated with handsome woodwork, and the bathrooms have the original 1910 fixtures. Swimmers and boaters can use Fogarty's dock, and cross-country skiers will find trails within a mile. More ambitious athletes should take a brief drive to Lake Placid's Olympic courses or the slopes of Whiteface and Big Tupper. Emily and Jack are Adirondack natives, so feel free to ask them for suggestions.

Mountain Shadows Guesthouse ✪
50 OLD MILITARY ROAD, SARANAC LAKE, NEW YORK 12983

Tel: **(518) 891-0327**
Best Time to Call: **Evenings**
Host: **Tricia Sullivan Bixler**
Location: **140 mi. N of Albany**
No. of Rooms: **2**
Max. No. Sharing Bath: **4**
Double/sb: **$40–$50**
Single/sb: **$30–$40**

Suite: **$60–$110**
Open: **All year**
Reduced Rates: **10% seniors**
Breakfast: **Full**
Pets: **No**
Children: **Welcome**
Smoking: **No**
Social Drinking: **Permitted**

Mountain Shadows Guesthouse is located in the heart of the Adirondack Mountains of upstate New York, just seven miles from Lake Placid, site of the 1980 Winter Olympic Games. Although Mountain Shadows is within walking distance of the village center, this charming home is in the most prestigious neighborhood. With its unusual architectural design and hidden stairways, you'll find this a unique, out-of-the-way retreat. Relax on the porch or deck, or climb the mountain just outside your window. Nearby activities include bird-watching, hiking, swimming, boating, golfing, fishing, and, in the winter, downhill or Nordic skiing. When you leave you will feel as though you've been in the country visiting friends.

LONG ISLAND

A Reasonable Alternative, Inc. ✪
117 SPRING STREET, PORT JEFFERSON, NEW YORK 11777

Tel: **(516) 928-4034**
Best Time to Call: **Noon–5 PM**
Coordinator: **Kathleen Dexter**
States/Regions Covered: **East Quoque, Glen Cove, Long Beach, Miller Place, Montauk, Port Jefferson, Setauket, Southampton, Stony Brook, Syosset**

Rates (Single/Double):
  Modest: **$44/$52**
  Average: **$60/$68**
  Luxury: **$78/$150**
Credit Cards: **MC, VISA**
Minimum Stay: **2 nights weekends resort area, 3 nights holiday weekends resort areas**

Bounded by Long Island Sound and the Atlantic Ocean, from the New York City border to Montauk 100 miles to the east, the cream of host homes has been culled by Kathleen for you. There's much to see and do, from museums, historic homes, theater, and horse racing, to the famous beaches, including Jones Beach, Fire Island, Shelter Island, and the exclusive Hamptons. (The Hamptons require a two-day minimum stay in July and August.) Adelphi College, Hofstra University, C. W. Post, Stony Brook, and St. Joseph's are a few of the nearby schools.

Country Life B&B ✪
237 CATHEDRAL AVENUE, HEMPSTEAD, NEW YORK 11550

Tel: (516) 292-9219;
  fax: (516) 292-2393
Best Time to Call: 6–9 PM
Hosts: Wendy and Richard Duvall
Location: 20 mi. E of New York City, on
  the Garden City border
No. of Rooms: 4
No. of Private Baths: 3
Double/pb: $60–$85

Suite: $95–$150; sleeps 4–5
Open: All year
Breakfast: Full, weekends; Continental,
  weekdays
Pets: No
Children: Welcome (crib)
Smoking: No
Social Drinking: Permitted
Foreign Languages: German, Spanish

Guests feel right at home in this charming Dutch Colonial, with four-poster beds and antique reproductions. Soda and cheese are served on arrival, and breakfast features puff pancakes and French toast. Guests enjoy the garden or visiting nearby sights. Kennedy International Airport and La Guardia Airport are less than 40 minutes away; Adelphi and Hofstra universities and the Nassau Coliseum are one mile away.

Mainstay Bed & Breakfast ✪
579 HILL STREET, SOUTHAMPTON, NEW YORK 11968

Tel: (516) 283-4375
Best Time to Call: AM
Host: Elizabeth Main
Location: 80 mi. E of New York City
No. of Rooms: 8
No. of Private Baths: 3
Max. No. Sharing Bath: 4
Double/pb: $50–$165
Double/sb: $50–$120
Suite: $150–$215

Open: All year
Reduced Rates: Available
Breakfast: Continental
Credit Cards: MC, VISA
Pets: No
Children: Welcome
Smoking: No
Social Drinking: Permitted
Minimum Stay: 2 nights weekends
  June–Labor Day

This charmingly restored Colonial guesthouse was built in the 1870s. Once a country store, Mainstay now accommodates those looking for a cozy retreat where they can enjoy white sandy beaches, nature walks, sports, biking, and dining. Rooms are beautifully decorated with antique iron and brass beds. The large master suite has a fireplace, TV, and claw-footed tub. (If you fall in love with the furniture, you may be able to buy it—many of the antique and European country pieces are available for purchase.) Breakfast, typically including homemade muffins, cereals, fruit, juice, and coffee, is served in the dining room. The B&B is within walking distance of antique shops, other stores, galleries, and museums.

1880 Seafield House ✪
2 SEAFIELD LANE, WESTHAMPTON BEACH, NEW YORK 11978

Tel: (800) 346-3290
Best Time to Call: 9 AM–5 PM

Host: Elsie Collins
Location: 90 mi. E of New York City

No. of Rooms: **3 suites**
No. of Private Baths: **3**
Suites: **$175–$200**
Open: **All year**
Reduced Rates: **$95, Oct. 15–May 15**

Breakfast: **Full**
Pets: **No**
Children: **No**
Smoking: **No**
Social Drinking: **Permitted**

This 100-year-old home in posh Westhampton is five blocks from the beach, and boasts its own pool and tennis court. Victorian lounges, a caned rocker, piano, hurricane lamps, Shaker benches, Chinese porcelain all combine to create the casual, country inn atmosphere. When the sea air chills Westhampton Beach, the parlor fire keeps the house toasty warm. The aromas of freshly brewing coffee and Mrs. Collins' breads and rolls baking in the oven are likely to wake you in time for breakfast. You'll leave this hideaway relaxed, carrying one of Mrs. Collins' homemade goodies.

NEW YORK CITY AREA/WESTCHESTER COUNTY

Abode, Ltd. ✪
P.O. BOX 20022, NEW YORK, NEW YORK 10021

Tel: **(212) 472-2000; (800) 835-8880**
Best Time to Call: **Mon.–Fri., 9 AM–**
 5 PM; Sat., 11 AM–2 PM
Coordinator: **Shelli Leifer**

States/Regions Covered: **Manhattan**
Rates (Single/Double): **$100–$325**
Credit Cards: **AMEX**
Minimum Stay: **2 nights**

Shelli is a friendly, savvy New Yorker with sensitive insight as to where a guest would be most comfortable. Her roster grows steadily with accommodations in safe neighborhoods that are "East Side, West Side, and all around the town." Private brownstones boasting a country inn ambience and private luxury apartments are especially attractive for couples traveling together. Prices range from $100 for a studio to $325 for 3 bedrooms. Reduced rates are available for extended stays. Theaters, museums, galleries, restaurants, and shopping are within easy reach of all accommodations.

Bed & Breakfast (& Books)
35 WEST 92ND STREET, NEW YORK, NEW YORK 10025

Tel: **(212) 865-8740**
Best Time to Call: **10 AM–5 PM**
 Mon.–Fri.
Coordinator: **Judith Goldberg**
States/Regions Covered: **Manhattan**

Rates (Single/Double):
 Average: **$60–$75 / $85–$100**
Credit Cards: **AMEX**
Minimum Stay: **2 nights**

Accommodations are conveniently located in residential areas near transportation and within walking distance of many cultural attractions. Hosts are photographers, psychologists, lawyers, dancers, teachers, and artists. They are pleased to share their knowledge of fine shops, reasonable restaurants, galleries, theater, and bookstores. Unhosted apartments are $100 to $130 for two.

A Hospitality Co. ✪
315 EAST 86TH STREET, SUITE 8B EAST, NEW YORK, NEW YORK 10028

Tel: **(212) 213-8952; (212) 965-1102**	Rates (Single/Double):
Best Time to Call: **10 AM–6 PM**	Average: **$90–$115**
Coordinator: **Howard Pitter**	Luxury: **$110–$150**
States/Regions Covered: **New York City,**	Credit Cards: **DISC, MC, VISA**
Long Island, Westchester, New Jersey	

Locations on this service roster include the theater district, Lincoln Center, Greenwich Village, and many more. All locations are in doorman buildings and are equipped with cable TV and air-conditioning. Many are on high floors and have spectacular views of the city. Discounts are available for extended stays. Free airport pickup is available for most reservations, with the exception of tolls and parking, if necessary.

Manhattan Lodgings, Inc. ✪
61 EAST 8TH STREET, SUITE 332, NEW YORK, NEW YORK 10003

Tel: **(212) 475-2090;**	Rates (Single/Double):
fax: **(212) 477-0420**	Modest: **$60–$80**
Best Time to Call: **Anytime**	Average: **$70 / $85–$100**
Coordinator: **Mara Spiegel**	Luxury: **$100 / $150**
States/Regions Covered: **Manhattan**	Credit Cards: **AMEX, MC, VISA**
	Minimum Stay: **2 nights**

Manhattan Lodgings has accommodations in all New York City neighborhoods. From penthouse to town house, Mara provides the best hotel alternative. Accurate descriptions and photographs are available upon request. The New York host can provide information about local places, events, restaurants, and transportation that will make your stay more interesting.

The New York Bed and Breakfast Reservation Center ✪
331 WEST 57TH STREET, SUITE 221, NEW YORK, NEW YORK 10019

Tel: **(212) 977-3512**	Rates (Single/Double):
Coordinator: **Yann Gabriel**	Modest: **$60–$70**
States/Regions Covered: **New York City,**	Average: **$70–$80**
Southampton, New York; San	Luxury: **$75–$95**
Francisco; Paris, France	Credit Cards: **AMEX**
	Minimum Stay: **2 nights**

Yann has a wide range of bed and breakfast accommodations. Several are within a few blocks of major midtown hotels and theaters. As an ex-bed and breakfast host, Yann has insight on what travelers expect. Personal inspections and specific descriptions help guests and corporations trying to cut down on travel expenses. Yann can suggest reasonably priced airport pickups to facilitate getting into New York. Hosted and unhosted flats are also available in Paris.

The Bennett's
226 READ AVENUE, CRESTWOOD, NEW YORK 10707

Tel: **(914) 779-8559**
Host: **Françoise Bennett**
Location: **15 mi. N of New York City**
No. of Rooms: **1**
No. of Private Baths: **1**
Single/pb: **$40**
Open: **All year**

Breakfast: **Continental**
Other Meals: **Available**
Pets: **No**
Children: **No**
Smoking: **No**
Social Drinking: **Permitted**
Foreign Languages: **French**

Located in beautiful Westchester County, and owned by an artistic couple, this private home offers one single room with a twin bed. Nearby are Sarah Lawrence College, Bronxville, and Scarsdale. The B&B is only 35 minutes by train to Grand Central Station in New York City, with a three-minute walk to Crestwood Station.

Kroghs Nest ✪
4 HILLCREST ROAD, HARTSDALE, NEW YORK 10530

Tel: **(914) 946-3479**
Best Time to Call: **7 AM–10 PM**
Hosts: **Claudia and James P. Krogh**
Location: **21 mi. N of New York City's Grand Central Station**
No. of Rooms: **3**
No. of Private Baths: **2**
Max. No. Sharing Bath: **4**
Double/pb: **$65**
Single/pb: **$55**
Double/sb: **$55**

Single/sb: **$50**
Open: **All year**
Reduced Rates: **15% weekly; students**
Breakfast: **Full**
Credit Cards: **AMEX**
Pets: **No**
Children: **Welcome (crib & highchair)**
Smoking: **No**
Social Drinking: **Permitted**
Airport/Station Pickup: **Yes**

Built in 1896, this Center Hall Victorian sits on a hillside acre, enclosed by greenery and beautiful flowers. You'll admire the authentic Colonial decor: breakfast is served on a large antique table surrounded by pine cupboards and porcelain ornaments. The upstairs bedrooms are air-conditioned; two rooms have color TVs. Washing machines and dryers are available for guests' use. The location couldn't be more convenient, since New York City's stores, historic sites, museums, restaurants, and theaters are easily accessible. Educational institutions within 10 miles include Sarah Lawrence College, Pace Westchester University, the State University of New York at Purchase, and New York Medical College.

NIAGARA/BUFFALO AREA

Eden Inn Bed & Breakfast ✪
8362 NORTH MAIN STREET, EDEN, NEW YORK 14057

Tel: **(716) 992-4814**
Hosts: **Chris and Betsy Walits**
Location: **17 mi. SW of Buffalo**
No. of Rooms: **5**
No. of Private Baths: **4**
Max. No. Sharing Bath: **4**
Double/pb: **$69–$82**
Single/pb: **$69–$82**
Double/sb: **$59–$69**
Single/sb: **$59–$69**
Suites: **$79–$92**

Open: **All year**
Reduced Rates: **Corporate, after 3rd night**
Breakfast: **Full, weekends; Continental, weekdays**
Credit Cards: **AMEX, DISC**
Pets: **No**
Children: **Welcome**
Smoking: **No**
Social Drinking: **Permitted**

Each room at the Eden Inn is tastefully appointed, with a theme in mind. The Rose suite features roses, brass, wicker, and a whirlpool tub. The Bluhmen suite has a double whirlpool tub. The Vineyard features grapes and a claw-footed tub. Standard room themes include trains and the Garden of Eden. Located in the center of Eden, the inn is six miles from Hamburg and forty miles from Niagara Falls. Nearby is the Erie Country Fair and Eden's Corn Festival. There are three cats on the premises.

The Teepee ✪
14396 FOUR MILE LEVEL ROAD, GOWANDA, NEW YORK 14070-9796

Tel: **(716) 532-2168**
Hosts: **Max and Phyllis Lay**
Location: **30 mi. S of Buffalo**
No. of Rooms: **3**
Max. No. Sharing Bath: **3**
Double/sb: **$50**
Single/sb: **$40**

Open: **All year**
Breakfast: **Full**
Pets: **Sometimes**
Children: **Welcome (crib)**
Smoking: **No**
Social Drinking: **Permitted**
Airport/Station Pickup: **Yes**

Max and Phyllis Lay are Seneca Indians living on the Cattaraugus Indian Reservation. Their airy four-bedroom home is clean, modern, and decorated with family Indian articles, many of them crafted by hand. The reservation offers country living and the opportunity of seeing firsthand the customs of a Native American community. A fall festival with arts, crafts, and exhibition dancing is held in September. Canoeing, fishing, rafting, cross-country and downhill skiing, and a sport called snowsnake are among the local activities. Your hosts will gladly arrange tours of the Amish community and hot-air balloon rides over the beautiful rolling hills.

The Cameo Inn ✪
4710 LOWER RIVER ROAD, LEWISTON, NEW YORK 14092

Tel: **(716) 754-2075**
Best Time to Call: **9 AM–9 PM**
Hosts: **Gregory and Carolyn Fisher**
Location: **5 mi. N of Niagara Falls**
No. of Rooms: **4**
No. of Private Baths: **2**
Max. No. Sharing Bath: **4**
Double/pb: **$85**
Single/pb: **$80**
Double/sb: **$65**
Single/sb: **$60**
Suites: **$115**

Open: **All year**
Breakfast: **Full**
Credit Cards: **AMEX, DISC, MC, VISA**
Pets: **No**
Children: **Welcome, over 8**
Smoking: **No**
Social Drinking: **Permitted**
Minimum Stay: **2 nights holiday weekends, special events, and June–Sept. must include a Sat. July–Aug.**

Gregory and Carolyn's authentically furnished Queen Anne Victorian home commands a majestic view of the lower Niagara River. Located just 25 miles north of Buffalo and 5 miles north of Niagara Falls, The Cameo is conveniently situated for sightseeing, antiquing, fishing and boating, golfing, bicycling, or shopping at local factory outlets and malls. History buffs will want to travel 5 miles north to Old Fort Niagara, which dates from the American Revolution; the bridge to Canada is minutes away. A full country breakfast is served in the dining room each morning.

Manchester House
653 MAIN STREET, NIAGARA FALLS, NEW YORK 14301
71210.65@compuserve.com

Tel: **(716) 285-5717, 282-2144; (800) 489-3009**
Best Time to Call: **9 AM–6 PM**
Hosts: **Lis and Carl Slenk**
No. of Rooms: **3**
No. of Private Baths: **3**
Double/pb: **$75**
Single/pb: **$60**
Open: **All year**

Reduced Rates: **Available**
Breakfast: **Full**
Credit Cards: **MC, VISA**
Pets: **No**
Children: **Welcome**
Smoking: **No**
Social Drinking: **Permitted**
Foreign Languages: **German**

Before it was incorporated, Niagara Falls was known as Manchester—hence the name for this tastefully renovated B&B, which was a doctor's office for more than sixty years. Lis and Carl collected ideas and furniture for their home during the ten years they spent in England and Germany. Manchester House is conveniently located near the falls, with easy access to Canada. (Spacious off-street parking is provided.) The bright, cheerful guest rooms offer a choice of queen-size or single beds. Breakfast features home-baked specialties.

THOUSAND ISLANDS AREA

Battle Island Inn ✪
2167 STATE ROUTE 48 NORTH, FULTON, NEW YORK 13069

Tel: **(315) 593-3699**
Hosts: **Joyce and Richard Rice**
Location: **30 mi. N of Syracuse**
No. of Rooms: **6**
No. of Private Baths: **6**
Double/pb: **$60–$80**
Single/pb: **$50–$65**

Open: **All year**
Breakfast: **Full**
Pets: **No**
Children: **Welcome**
Smoking: **No**
Social Drinking: **Permitted**

The Rice family welcome you to their pre–Civil War estate, which they restored themselves with lots of love and hard work. The Inn is across the street from a golf course and is surrounded by fields and orchards. The rooms feature Victorian antiques and marble fireplaces. Guest bedrooms are spacious and elegant with imposing high-backed beds. Joyce is a full-time host, who will tempt your palate with homemade rolls, biscuits, and crepes. Richard is a systems analyst who oversees the challenges of an 1840s house. Whether you're enjoying the privacy of your room or socializing in the formal front parlor, you are sure to appreciate the friendly family atmosphere.

Way Back In Bed & Breakfast ✪
247 PROCTOR AVENUE, OGDENSBURG, NEW YORK 13669
http://www.1000islands.com/wayback/

Tel: **(315) 393-3844**
Best Time to Call: **Before 9 PM**
Hosts: **Rena and Milton Goldberg**
Location: **Minutes from 1000 Islands**
No. of Rooms: **2**
Max. No. Sharing Bath: **4**
Double/sb: **$60**

Open: **All year**
Breakfast: **Full**
Pets: **No**
Children: **Welcome, over 5**
Smoking: **No**
Social Drinking: **Permitted**
Airport Pickup: **Yes**

Situated on just over three acres, this bed and breakfast sits "way back in" from the road and offers quiet, friendly surroundings away from street noises. Both attractively appointed guest rooms have a view of the St. Lawrence River and assure you a pleasant night's sleep. Breakfast, served either in the dining room or the Florida room, opens with a mug of fresh-brewed coffee or tea to provide a wonderful start to the day's activities. Your hosts will gladly assist you in choosing restaurants and keep you informed of any special events, such as antique and horse shows, fishing derbies, and the Ogdensburg Seaway Festival Days.

For key to listings, see inside front or back cover.

✪ This star means that rates are guaranteed through December 31, 1998, to any guest making a reservation as a result of reading about the B&B in *Bed & Breakfast U.S.A.*—1998 edition.

Important! To avoid misunderstandings, always ask about cancellation policies when booking.

Please enclose a self-addressed, stamped, business-size envelope when contacting reservation services.

For more details on what you can expect in a B&B, see Chapter 1.

Always mention *Bed & Breakfast U.S.A.* when making reservations!

We want to hear from you! Use the form on page 625.

NORTH CAROLINA

Winston-Salem
Sparta
Germanton
Madison
Weldon
Banner Elk
Burnsville
Blowing Rock
Durham
Tarboro
Belhaven
Kill Devil Hills
Siler City
Lake Junaluska
Asheville
Washington
Waynesville
Statesville
Franklin
Hendersonville
Oriental
Highlands
Pigsah Forest
New Bern
Murphy
Charlotte
Mount Gilead
Beaufort
Swansboro
Wilmington
Tabor City
Shallote

A Bed of Roses ✪
135 CUMBERLAND AVENUE, ASHEVILLE, NORTH CAROLINA 28801
info@abedofroses.com

Tel: **(704) 258-8700; (800) 471-4182**
Best Time to Call: **10 AM–9 PM**
Host: **Caroline Logie**
Location: **½ mi. N of Asheville**
No. of Rooms: **5**
No. of Private Baths: **5**
Double/pb: **$90–$110**
Suites: **$125–$140 for 2**
Cottage: **$125–$135**
Open: **All year**

Reduced Rates: **Available**
Breakfast: **Full**
Credit Cards: **MC, VISA**
Pets: **No**
Children: **Welcome, over 10 main house, under 10 cottage**
Smoking: **Restricted**
Social Drinking: **Permitted**
Minimum Stay: **2 nights holidays; in-season weekends**

Styled after an English country cottage, this inn is a cheery Queen Anne Victorian, circa 1897, listed on the Register of Historic Homes. Each guest room is uniquely decorated, some with antique bath fixtures and claw-footed tubs. Guests are invited to enjoy a cool glass of lemonade or iced tea and cookies on the front porch rockers. There are a couple of bicycles available for you to use. Breakfast consists of homemade granola, muffins, seasonal fruit, waffles and crepes. Gourmet coffees and English teas are always available. Biltmore House and Gardens, the Thomas Wolfe Memorial, botanical gardens, and the Blue Ridge Parkway are just minutes from the inn.

Acorn Cottage
25 SAINT DUNSTANS CIRCLE, ASHEVILLE, NORTH CAROLINA 28803

Tel: **(704) 253-0609; (800) 699-0609**
Best Time to Call: **10 AM–9 PM**
Host: **Sharon Tabor**
Location: **1¼ mi. from Route I-40, exit 50/50B**
No. of Rooms: **4**
No. of Private Baths: **4**
Double/pb: **$80–$100**
Single/pb: **$75**

Open: **All year**
Breakfast: **Full**
Credit Cards: **DISC, MC, VISA**
Pets: **No**
Smoking: **No**
Social Drinking: **Permitted**
Minimum Stay: **2 nights weekends, March 15–Dec. 31**

An English country cottage in the woodsy heart of Asheville, Acorn is built of local granite; the interior boasts maple floors and a granite fireplace. The guest rooms feature queen-size beds, fine linens, air-conditioning, TV, and baths stocked with special soaps. A delicious full breakfast is served each morning with fresh fruit, varied entrees, juice, coffee or tea, and an assortment of breads. Then you're ready for the quarter-mile trip to the Biltmore Estate.

Carolina Bed & Breakfast ✪
177 CUMBERLAND AVENUE, ASHEVILLE, NORTH CAROLINA 28801

Tel: **(704) 254-3608; (888) 254-3608**
Best Time to Call: **10 AM–9 PM**
Hosts: **Sam and Karin Fain**
Location: **½ mi. from Route 240, Exit 4C**
No. of Rooms: **7**
No. of Private Baths: **7**
Double/pb: **$80–$150**
Open: **All year**

Breakfast: **Full**
Credit Cards: **DISC, MC, VISA**
Pets: **No**
Children: **Welcome, over 12**
Smoking: **No**
Social Drinking: **Permitted**
Minimum Stay: **2 nights holidays, in-season weekends**

This turn-of-the-century Colonial Revival home has been painstakingly restored; feel free to relax on the front and back porches, or just take in the view from the second-floor guest rooms, with their distinctive, twelve-over-one panes. In springtime, the grounds bloom with dogwoods and rhododendrons. On cooler days, you can curl up in front of one of the house's seven fireplaces. Your hosts serve a different full breakfast each day; the usual fare includes eggs or quiche and fresh bread and muffins.

The Colby House
230 PEARSON DRIVE, ASHEVILLE, NORTH CAROLINA 28801

Tel: **(704) 253-5644; (800) 982-2118**	Breakfast: **Full**
Hosts: **Everett and Ann Colby**	Credit Cards: **MC, VISA**
No. of Rooms: **4**	Pets: **No**
No. of Private Baths: **4**	Children: **Welcome, over 12**
Double/pb: **$80–$110**	Smoking: **Restricted**
Open: **All year**	Social Drinking: **Permitted**

This elegant Dutch-Tudor house in the Montford Historic District is a special place, thanks to its porch, beautiful gardens, and inviting fireplaces. Each guest room has its own individual decor and queen-size beds. Refreshments are available at all times, and wine and cheese are served in the evening. Breakfasts vary daily, but are always served on fine china, with heirloom crystal and silver. Southern hospitality abounds in your hosts' personal attention to every guest's needs.

Corner Oak Manor ✪
53 ST. DUNSTANS ROAD, ASHEVILLE, NORTH CAROLINA 28803

Tel: **(704) 253-3525**	Cottage: **$130–$145**
Best Time to Call: **9 AM–9 PM**	Open: **All year**
Hosts: **Karen and Andy Spradley**	Breakfast: **Full**
Location: **1¼ mi. from Rte. 40, Exit 50**	Credit Cards: **AMEX, DISC, MC, VISA**
No. of Rooms: **4**	Pets: **No**
No. of Private Baths: **4**	Children: **Welcome, over 12**
Double/pb: **$90–$115**	Smoking: **No**
Single/pb: **$75–$85**	Social Drinking: **Permitted**

Surrounded by maple, oak, and evergreen trees, this lovely English Tudor home is located minutes away from the famed Biltmore Estate and Gardens. The rooms have queen-size beds beautifully covered in fine linen. The window treatments and coordinated wall coverings could easily grace the pages of a decorating magazine. Handmade wreaths, weavings, and stitchery complement the furnishings. Breakfast specialties include orange French toast, blueberry-ricotta pancakes, or four-cheese-herb quiche. A living room fireplace, baby grand piano, outdoor deck, and Jacuzzi are among the gracious amenities.

Flint Street Inns ✪
100 & 116 FLINT STREET, ASHEVILLE, NORTH CAROLINA 28801

Tel: **(704) 253-6723**	Location: **¼ mi. from Rte. 240**
Hosts: **Rick, Lynne, and Marion Vogel**	No. of Rooms: **8**

No. of Private Baths: **8**
Double/pb: **$85**
Single/pb: **$70**
Open: **All year**
Breakfast: **Full**

Credit Cards: **AMEX, DISC, MC, VISA**
Pets: **No**
Children: **No**
Smoking: **Permitted**
Social Drinking: **Permitted**

These turn-of-the-century homes on an acre with century-old trees are listed in the National Register of Historic Places. Stained glass, pine floors, and a claw-footed bathtub are part of the Victorian decor. The Inns are air-conditioned for summer comfort; some have fireplaces for winter coziness. Guests are served coffee and soft drinks. The Blue Ridge Parkway is close by.

The Banner Elk Inn Bed & Breakfast ✪
407 MAIN STREET EAST, HIGHWAY 194 NORTH, BANNER ELK, NORTH CAROLINA 28604

Tel: **(704) 898-6223**
Best Time to Call: **9 AM–10 PM**
Host: **Beverly Lait**
Location: **17 mi. W of Boone**
No. of Rooms: **5**
No. of Private Baths: **4**
Double/pb: **$80–$110**
Single/pb: **$70–$110**
Suites: **$120–$150; sleeps 4**
Open: **All year**
Reduced Rates: **Available**

Breakfast: **Full**
Credit Cards: **MC, VISA**
Pets: **Yes**
Children: **Welcome, Sun.–Thurs.; over 6, weekends**
Smoking: **No**
Social Drinking: **Permitted**
Minimum Stay: **Mid-July; first 2 weeks of Oct.; ski season Dec. 25–Mar. 30; 2 nights weekends**
Foreign Languages: **Spanish, German**

Your host, Beverly, spent years with the Foreign Service, and original tapestries, artwork, and antiques from around the world fill her stunningly renovated historic home. The Inn is located halfway between the Sugar Resort and Beech Mountain ski slopes, near such major tourist attractions as Grandfather Mountain and Natural Habitat, Linville Falls, Valle Crucis, and the Blue Ridge Parkway. You'll have energy to visit all these places after Beverly's full breakfasts of homemade breads, eggs, fruit, juice, and coffee or tea.

Delamar Inn ✪
217 TURNER STREET, BEAUFORT, NORTH CAROLINA 28516

Tel: **(919) 728-4300; (800) 349-5823**
Best Time to Call: **Anytime**
Hosts: **Tom and Mabel Steepy**
Location: **140 mi. SE of Raleigh**
No. of Rooms: **4**
No. of Private Baths: **4**
Double/pb: **$94**
Single/pb: **$94**

Open: **All year**
Breakfast: **Continental, plus**
Credit Cards: **MC, VISA**
Pets: **No**
Children: **Welcome, over 10**
Smoking: **Restricted**
Social Drinking: **Permitted**
Airport/Station Pickup: **Yes**

The Delamar Inn, built in 1866, is located in historic Beaufort, North Carolina's third oldest town. The Inn offers four guest rooms furnished with antiques, each room with a private bath. After a delightful breakfast, stroll down to the historic restoration grounds, maritime museum, or the open-air bus, or browse in the waterfront specialty shops. Tom and Mabel, your hosts, can offer directions to local beaches for shell collecting, sunbathing, or fishing. Try a short ride to Fort Macon, Tryon Palace, or the ferry to the Outer Banks. The Inn was selected for the '95 historic homes tour.

Thistle Dew Inn ✪
325 EAST FRONT STREET, BELHAVEN, NORTH CAROLINA 27810

Tel: **(919) 943-6900**
Best Time to Call: **6–10 PM**
Hosts: **Karen and Risto Sairanen**
Location: **48 mi. E of Greenville**
No. of Rooms: 3
No. of Private Baths: 3
Double p/b: **$65**
Single p/b: **$60**
Open: **All year**

Reduced Rates: **15% less 4 nights or more**
Breakfast: **Full**
Pets: **No**
Children: **Welcome, over 12**
Smoking: **No**
Social Drinking: **Permitted**
Foreign Languages: **Finnish, Swedish, German**

Thistle Dew Inn is a lovely Queen Anne Victorian, about 100 years old. The Inn features gingerbread, stained glass, crown moldings, plantation shutters, beaded board ceilings, and a unique painted floor in the dining room. The guest rooms all face water and are beautifully furnished with European country antiques. There is a large sitting room that offers books, TV, games, and a fireplace. Also on the premises, antiques and local crafts are for sale. Things to do and see include a ferry to Ocracoke, Lake Mattamuskeet Wildlife Refuge, historic Bath, and Belhaven, which offers a museum, restaurants, galleries, and craft shops. The Pungo River offers fishing, boating, kayaking, and water sports.

Maple Lodge
P. O. BOX 1236, 152 SUNSET DRIVE, BLOWING ROCK, NORTH CAROLINA 28605

Tel: **(704) 295-3331**
Best Time to Call: **10 AM–4 PM**
Hosts: **Marilyn and David Bateman**
No. of Rooms: **11**
No. of Private Baths: **11**
Double/pb: **$82.57–$128.44**
Single/pb: **$73.39–$119.27**
Suites: **$128.44**
Open: **Mar. 1–Jan. 5**

Reduced Rates: **Available**
Breakfast: **Full**
Credit Cards: **AMEX, DISC, MC, VISA**
Pets: **No**
Children: **Welcome, over 12**
Smoking: **No**
Social Drinking: **Permitted**
Minimum Stay: **2 nights weekends and special occasions**

This charming inn reflects the simplicity and grace of the '30s and '40s. Guest rooms are furnished with antiques, handmade quilts, and goosedown comforters. Two parlors offer guests a homey atmosphere, complete thanks to the stone fireplace, old-timey pump organ, books, and games. Breakfast features fruits, cereals, home-baked breads and muffins, and a different main dish each day. Maple Lodge is within a short stroll to craft shops, art galleries, antiques, fine restaurants, and the Blowing Rock Stage Company, which performs during the summer.

Outside town is the Blue Ridge Parkway and the Moses Cone Park; nearby is Grandfather Mountain, golf, canoeing, and white-water rafting.

Estes Mountain Retreat ○
ROUTE 10, BOX 500, BURNSVILLE, NORTH CAROLINA 28714

Tel: **(704) 682-7264; (888) 272-9885**
Best Time to Call: **After 7 PM**
Hosts: **Bruce and Maryallen Estes**
Location: **37 mi. NE of Asheville**
No. of Rooms: **2**
No. of Private Baths: **2**
Double/pb: **$65**
Single/pb: **$55**
Open: **All year**

Reduced Rates: **15%** Jan.–May; **10% seniors**
Breakfast: **Full**
Pets: **No**
Children: **Welcome, over 3**
Smoking: **No**
Social Drinking: **Permitted**
Foreign Languages: **French**

Breathtaking mountain views await you at this three-level cedar log home with a rock chimney, fireplace, and porches. Because Burnsville is in Pisgah National Forest, you won't have to travel far to go rafting, fishing, hiking, and rock and gem hunting, and there's golfing. Mt. Mitchell, Linville Caverns, outdoor theater, the Biltmore Mansion, and the Carl Sandburg Home are all within an hour's drive.

Hamrick Inn ○
7787 HIGHWAY 80 SOUTH, BURNSVILLE, NORTH CAROLINA 28714

Tel: **(704) 675-5251**
Best Time to Call: **Mornings**
Hosts: **Neal and June Jerome**
Location: **55 mi. NE of Asheville; 16 mi. from I-40, Exit 72**
No. of Rooms: **4**
No. of Private Baths: **4**
Double/pb: **$70–$80**

Single/pb: **$65–$75**
Open: **Apr. 2–Oct. 31**
Reduced Rates: **Weekly**
Breakfast: **Full**
Pets: **No**
Children: **Welcome**
Smoking: **Permitted**
Social Drinking: **Permitted**

This charming three-story Colonial-style stone Inn is nestled at the foot of Mt. Mitchell, the highest mountain east of the Mississippi River. Much of the lovely furniture was built by Neal and June. The den has a fine selection of books as well as a TV set for your enjoyment. There is a private porch off each bedroom, where you may take in the view and the cool mountain breezes. Golfing, hiking, fishing, rock hounding, crafts shopping, and fall foliage wandering are local activities. Pisgah National Park, Linville Caverns, Crabtree Meadows, and the Parkway Playhouse are area diversions.

The Morse's Little South-Toe-Hold ✪
**873 SOUTH TOE RIVER ROAD, BURNSVILLE,
NORTH CAROLINA 28714**

Tel: **(704) 675-5036**
Best Time to Call: **10 AM–9 PM**
Hosts: **Ursula and Jay Morse**
Location: **55 mi. NE of Asheville**
No. of Rooms: **1**
No. of Private Baths: **1**
Double/pb: **$75**
Single/pb: **$70**
Suites: **$90**

Open: **May 1–Nov. 15**
Reduced Rates: **Weekly, 10% seniors**
Breakfast: **Full**
Pets: **No**
Children: **No**
Smoking: **No**
Social Drinking: **Permitted**
Foreign Languages: **German, Spanish,
French**

Set among rhododendrons and 80-foot pines, this lovely chalet home features a Great Room with a cathedral ceiling, 2-person Jacuzzi in the suite, antiques, objets d'art and paintings, and a library of books for your enjoyment. South-Toe-Hold is surrounded by two national parks, scenic South Toe River, and the Blue Ridge Parkway. You are invited to hike, swim, fish, water-tube, or gem-mine at Little Switzerland. Mt. Mitchell Golf Course is within walking distance. Nearby attractions include the Biltmore Estate, Penland Art School, Mt. Mitchell, and Grandfather Mountain with its Biosphere and bear habitat.

The Elizabeth Bed & Breakfast ✪
2145 EAST 5TH STREET, CHARLOTTE, NORTH CAROLINA 28204

Tel: **(704) 358-1368**
Best Time to Call: **Evening**

Host: **Joan Mastny**
Location: **3 mi. from Rte I-77, Exit 10B**

No. of Rooms: **4**
No. of Private Baths: **4**
Double/pb: **$69–$84**
Single/pb: **$60–$75**
Suite: **$80–$89**
Open: **All year**

Breakfast: **Full**
Credit Cards: **MC, VISA**
Pets: **No**
Children: **Welcome, over 12**
Smoking: **No**
Social Drinking: **Permitted**

This 1927 lavender "lady" is in historic Elizabeth, Charlotte's second oldest neighborhood. Rooms are decorated in European country style and are beautifully appointed with antiques, ceiling fans, decorator linens, and unique collections. All rooms have central air-conditioning; some have TV and phone. Guests may relax in the garden courtyard complete with a charming gazebo or stroll beneath giant oak trees to convenient restaurants and shopping.

The Homeplace
5901 SARDIS ROAD, CHARLOTTE, NORTH CAROLINA 28270

Tel: **(704) 365-1936; fax: (704) 366-2729**
Hosts: **Peggy and Frank Dearien**
Location: **10 mi. from I-77; I-85**
No. of Rooms: **3**
No. of Private Baths: **3**
Double/pb: **$98**
Single/pb: **$88**

Suite: **$115**
Open: **All year**
Breakfast: **Full**
Credit Cards: **AMEX, MC, VISA**
Pets: **No**
Children: **Welcome, over 10**
Smoking: **No**
Social Drinking: **No**

The warm and friendly atmosphere hasn't changed since 1902. The minute you arrive at this country Victorian and walk up to the wrap-around porch with its rockers, you'll feel you've "come home." The handcrafted staircase, 10-foot beaded ceilings, and heart-pine floors add to the interior's beauty. It's convenient to malls, furniture and textile outlets, and treasure-filled antique shops.

Still Waters ✪

6221 AMOS SMITH ROAD, CHARLOTTE, NORTH CAROLINA 28214

Tel: **(704) 399-6299**
Best Time to Call: **Evenings**
Hosts: **Janet and Rob Dyer**
Location: **3 mi. W of Charlotte**
No. of Rooms: **4**
No. of Private Baths: **4**
Double/pb: **$65–$85**
Open: **All year**

Reduced Rates: **Available**
Breakfast: **Full**
Credit Cards: **MC, VISA**
Pets: **No**
Children: **Welcome**
Smoking: **No**
Social Drinking: **Permitted**

Relax on the river just outside Charlotte city limits—only minutes away from downtown, the airport, or the interstates, but a world away from the bustle of everyday life. Visit this lakefront log home on two wooded acres. Enjoy the deck, garden, dock, and boat ramp, or play on the sport court. Guests stay in either of two large rooms or in a suite. Full breakfasts always feature homemade sourdough rolls and fresh-ground coffee.

The Blooming Garden Inn ✪
513 HOLLOWAY STREET, DURHAM, NORTH CAROLINA 27701

Tel: **(919) 687-0801; fax: (919) 688-1401**
Best Time to Call: **Evenings**
Hosts: **Frank and Dolly Pokrass**
Location: **Downtown Durham**
No. of Rooms: **5**
No. of Private Baths: **5**
Double/pb: **$90–$110**
Suites: **$145–$180**

Open: **All year**
Reduced Rates: **Corporate**
Breakfast: **Full**
Credit Cards: **AMEX, DC, DISC, MC, VISA**
Pets: **No**
Children: **Welcome**
Smoking: **No**
Social Drinking: **Permitted**

If you appreciate flowers—and who doesn't?—you'll love staying at this restored 1892 Victorian with glorious gardens at every turn. The house is handsome, too, with its gabled roof, beveled and stained glass windows, and wraparound porch supported by Tuscan columns. What's more, you're right in the center of Durham's historic Holloway District, just moments from shops, galleries, theaters, Duke University, and the University of North Carolina. For the ultimate in pampering, luxury suites with Jacuzzis are available. A big feature at Blooming Garden Inn is the gourmet breakfast. Guests are given a brief local tour by hosts.

Blaine House ✪

661 HARRISON AVENUE, HIGHWAY 28 NORTH, FRANKLIN, NORTH CAROLINA 28734
blainebb@dnet.net; http://www.intertekweb.com/blainebb/

Tel: **(704) 349-4230**
Best Time to Call: **10 AM–8 PM**
Hosts: **Suzy Chandler and Karin Gorboff**
Location: **65 mi. SW of Asheville**
No. of Rooms: **3**
No. of Private Baths: **3**
Double/pb: **$65–$79**
Single/pb: **$60–$74**
Suites: **$85**
Open: **All year**

Reduced Rates: **10% Nov. 15–March 15**
Breakfast: **Full, Continental**
Credit Cards: **MC, VISA**
Pets: **No**
Children: **Welcome, over 13**
Smoking: **No**
Social Drinking: **Permitted**
Minimum Stay: **2 nights in Oct.**
Foreign Languages: **French**

Blaine House reflects the grace and serenity reminiscent of days gone by. Built in 1910 by Charles Blaine, this house was transformed to a bed & breakfast in 1995 and furnished with period antiques, heirlooms, silk trees, and chandeliers. Gaze outside for gorgeous views of the Smokey Mountains. Guest rooms have been distinctively decorated to enhance their individuality and have cable TVs. The cottage is fully furnished, with full kitchen, living room, dining room, and cable TV. Awake to the aroma of a gourmet breakfast served by candlelight. Within minutes of the Blaine House you will find gem mines, shops, restaurants, a Cherokee casino, the Smokey Mountain Railway, and the Biltmore Estate.

Buttonwood Inn ✪
50 ADMIRAL DRIVE, FRANKLIN, NORTH CAROLINA 28734

Tel: **(704) 369-8985**
Best Time to Call: **After 5 PM**
Host: **Liz Oehser**
Location: **75 mi. SW of Asheville**
No. of Rooms: **4**
No. of Private Baths: **2**
Max. No. Sharing Bath: **4**
Double/pb: **$60–$85**
Single/pb: **$50**

Double/sb: **$55**
Single/sb: **$45**
Suites: **$95**
Open: **Apr. 15–Nov. 15**
Breakfast: **Full**
Pets: **No**
Children: **Welcome, over 10**
Smoking: **Permitted**
Social Drinking: **Permitted**

The Buttonwood is a small country inn surrounded by towering pines, a spacious lawn, and mountain views. The original residence was a small cottage built in the late 1920s adjacent to the greens of the Franklin golf course. Years later, a new wing was added with rustic, charming rooms. Guests may choose from comfortable bedrooms decorated with antiques, cozy quilts, and handcrafts, many of which are offered for sale. Breakfast selections include sausage-apple ring, eggs Benedict, or cheese frittata, with coffee cake and plenty of hot coffee or tea. Golfers will be glad to be so close to the beautiful fairways and Bermuda grass greens right next door. Nearby there are also crafts shops, hiking trails, the Blue Ridge Parkway, gem mines, and plenty of places to swim and ride.

Heritage Inn ✪
101 HERITAGE HOLLOW, FRANKLIN, NORTH CAROLINA 28734

Tel: **(704) 524-4150; (888) 524-4150**
Best Time to Call: **3–9 PM**
Host: **Sally Wade**
Location: **135 mi. NE Atlanta, Georgia**
No. of Rooms: **6**
No. of Private Baths: **6**
Double/pb: **$65–$85**
Single/pb: **$55–$75**
Cottage: **$95–$115, sleeps 4**

Open: **Apr.–Nov.**
Breakfast: **Full, Continental**
Pets: **No**
Children: **Welcome, over 14**
Smoking: **No**
Social Drinking: **Permitted**
Minimum Stay: **2 nights, holiday and October weekends**
Airport Pickup: **Yes**

Rocking on the veranda over a cascading waterfall is one of the favorite pastimes at this tin-roofed, in-town country inn. Nestled in the Smoky Mountains tall pines, it is close to gem mining, white-water rafting, hiking trails, and country auctions, within walking distance of museums and mountain crafts and antique shops. On the premises is a gallery of tribal art and artifacts that Sally collected in her world travels. Each immaculate, tastefully furnished room has its own entrance and porch for added privacy. Kitchenettes are available. A full breakfast and evening dessert are served. Complimentary beverages are offered throughout the day and evening at the lovely, creekside gazebo.

MeadowHaven Bed & Breakfast ✪
NC HIGHWAY 8, P.O. BOX 222, GERMANTON,
NORTH CAROLINA 27019

Tel: **(910) 593-3996**
Best Time to Call: **9 AM–9 PM**
Hosts: **Samuel and Darlene Fain**
Location: **16 mi. N of Winston-Salem**
No. of Rooms: **3**
No. of Private Baths: **3**
Double/pb: **$80–$105**
Cabins: **$150–$175**
Open: **All year**

Breakfast: **Full**
Pets: **No**
Children: **No**
Smoking: **No**
Social Drinking: **Permitted, in guest
rooms**
Minimum Stay: **2 nights weekends;
holidays and special event weeks**

MeadowHaven is a chalet-style retreat on 25 acres, with stunning mountain views from the B&B's large deck. Immerse yourself in the hot tub or the heated indoor pool, grab some snacks from the pantry, and test your skills in the game room or at the fishing pond. For honeymooners, the Lovebirds' Retreat, with its whirlpool tub and steam shower, is ideal. You won't have to travel far for horseback riding, canoeing, and golf; other local attractions include a winery, an art gallery, and Sauratown Mountain. Darlene, a former controller for the Marriott Corporation, runs her family's construction business, and Sam is a retail manager interested in greenhouse gardening, magic, and birds.

The Waverly Inn ✪
783 NORTH MAIN STREET, HENDERSONVILLE,
NORTH CAROLINA 28792
jsheiry@aol.com

Tel: **(800) 537-8195; (704) 693-9193;
fax: (704) 692-1010**
Best Time to Call: **9:30 AM–10 PM**
Hosts: **John and Diane Sheiry**
Location: **20 mi. S of Asheville**
No. of Rooms: **14**
No. of Private Baths: **14**
Double/pb: **$79–$149**
Single/pb: **$79**

Open: **All year**
Reduced Rates: **Off-season**
Breakfast: **Full**
Credit Cards: **AMEX, DISC, MC, VISA**
Pets: **No**
Children: **Welcome**
Smoking: **Restricted**
Social Drinking: **Permitted**

Built as a boardinghouse in 1898, the Waverly is distinguished by its handsome Eastlake staircase—a factor that earned the Inn a listing on the National Register of Historic Places. Furnishings like four-poster canopy beds and claw-footed tubs combine Victorian stateliness and Colonial Revival charm. You'll walk away sated from all-you-can-eat breakfasts of pancakes and French toast. Noteworthy local sites include the Biltmore Estate, the Carl Sandburg house, the Blue Ridge Parkway, and the Flat Rock Playhouse.

Colonial Pines Inn ✪
541 HICKORY STREET, HIGHLANDS, NORTH CAROLINA 28741

Tel: **(704) 526-2060**
Best Time to Call: **Afternoons**
Hosts: **Chris and Donna Alley**
Location: **80 mi. SW of Asheville**
No. of Rooms: **7**
No. of Private Baths: **7**
Double/pb: **$80–$105**
Single/pb: **$70–$95**
Suites: **$105–$200, sleeps 4**

Guest Cottages: **$85–$200; sleep 4–6**
Open: **All year**
Reduced Rates: **Winter**
Breakfast: **Full**
Credit Cards: **MC, VISA**
Pets: **No**
Children: **Welcome, in cottage only**
Smoking: **No**
Social Drinking: **Permitted**

Located in a charming, uncommercial mountain resort town, this white Colonial is flanked by tall columns and is surrounded by two acres. The scenic view may be enjoyed from comfortable rocking chairs on the wide veranda. Donna, a former interior decorator, has furnished the Inn with antiques, art, and interesting accessories. Chris is a classical guitarist, woodworker, and great cook. The hearty breakfast includes a variety of homemade breads.

The Guest House ✪
RT. 2, BOX 649E (HWY E 64), HIGHLANDS, NORTH CAROLINA 28741

Tel: **(704) 526-4536**
Best Time to Call: **9 AM–9 PM**
Host: **Juanita Hernandez**
Location: **100 mi. NE of Atlanta**
No. of Rooms: **4**
No. of Private Baths: **4**
Double/pb: **$68–$85**
Single/pb: **$60–$70**
Open: **All year**
Reduced Rates: **Available**

Breakfast: **Full**
Credit Cards: **MC, VISA**
Pets: **No**
Children: **Welcome**
Smoking: **No**
Social Drinking: **Permitted**
Minimum Stay: **Weekends July–Sept., holidays, and Oct.**
Foreign Languages: **Spanish, German**

A charming Alpine-style mountain chalet nestled among stately trees, this B&B is more ample than its compact looks suggest. Inside you'll admire the plush, cream-colored carpeting, chestnut paneling, light wallcoverings, teakwood furniture, and native stone fireplace. Deep contemporary seats invite guests to slip off their shoes and relax. Partake of the spectacular view from the open deck, with its sun umbrella and rocking chairs. After a restful night in your tastefully decorated room—accented with Juanita's artistic touches—you'll wake up to one of her superb breakfasts.

Lakeside Inn ✪
1921 FRANKLIN ROAD, HIGHLANDS, NORTH CAROLINA 28741

Tel: **(704) 526-4498**
Best Time to Call: **After 6 PM**

Hosts: **Cathy and Hank Ross**
Location: **120 mi. NE of Atlanta**

No. of Rooms: **4**
No. of Private Baths: **4**
Double/pb: **$75–$85**
Single/pb: **$70–$80**
Open: **All year**
Breakfast: **Full, Continental**
Credit Cards: **MC, VISA**

Pets: **No**
Children: **Welcome**
Smoking: **No**
Social Drinking: **Permitted**
Minimum Stay: **June–Oct. 2 nights, weekends**

Nestled among the oaks and hemlocks, Lakeside Inn has a lovely view of Lake Sequoyah and borders the Nantahala National Forest. You can enjoy the scenery from the patio of this restored 1930s lodge or use the canoe that is provided by your hosts for a leisurely ride. Lakeside Inn offers cozy rooms and has a common area with a fireplace, cable TV, books and games. Breakfast entrees include French toast, burritos, fresh fruits, and freshly baked muffins. Area activities range from hiking, horseback riding, mountain biking, fishing, rappelling, and white-water rafting to enjoying the quaint town of Highlands.

Ye Olde Stone House ✪

1337 SOUTH FOURTH STREET, HIGHLANDS, NORTH CAROLINA 28741

Tel: **(704) 526-5911**
Best Time to Call: **Afternoons; evenings**
Hosts: **Jim and Rene Ramsdell**
Location: **80 mi. SW of Asheville**
No. of Rooms: **4**
No. of Private Baths: **4**
Double/pb: **$70–$85**
Single/pb: **$65–$70**
Chalet: **$95–$115, sleeps 4**
Guest cabin: **$130–$180, sleeps 7**

Open: **All year**
Reduced Rates: **Available**
Breakfast: **Full**
Credit Cards: **MC, VISA**
Pets: **No**
Children: **Welcome**
Smoking: **No**
Social Drinking: **Permitted**
Minimum Stay: **2 nights holiday weekends**

Built of stones taken from a local river by mule and wagon, the house is less than a mile from the center of town, where you will find a nature center, museum, galleries, tennis courts, swimming pool, and shops offering antiques or mountain crafts. The rooms are bright, cheerful, and comfortably furnished. The sunroom and porch are perfect spots to catch up on that book you've wanted to read. On cool evenings, the Ramsdells invite you to gather round the fireplace for snacks and conversation.

Cherokee Inn Bed & Breakfast ✪
500 NORTH VIRGINIA DARE TRAIL, KILL DEVIL HILLS, NORTH CAROLINA 27948

Tel: **(919) 441-6127; (800) 554-2764**
Best Time to Call: **Evenings**
Hosts: **Bob and Kaye Combs**
Location: **75 mi. S of Norfolk**
No. of Rooms: **6**
No. of Private Baths: **6**
Double/pb: **$65–$95**
Open: **Apr. 1–Oct. 30**
Reduced Rates: **$5 less per night, seniors**
Breakfast: **Continental**
Credit Cards: **AMEX, MC, VISA**
Pets: **No**
Children: **No**
Smoking: **No**
Social Drinking: **Permitted**
Minimum Stay: **2 nights July–Aug.; 3 nights holidays**

Only 500 feet from the Atlantic Ocean you'll find this beach house with wraparound porches, soft cypress interiors, and white ruffled curtains. Cherokee Inn is near the historic Roanoke Island settlement, Cape Hatteras, and the Wright Brothers Memorial at Kitty Hawk. Of course, you may just want to spend the day at the beach. In the evening, curl up with a book or watch TV. You'll start the next day with coffee and pastries.

The Laurels ✪
P.O. BOX 1354, LAKE JUNALUSKA, NORTH CAROLINA 28745

Tel: **(704) 456-7186**
Hosts: **Mary and Roger Kayler**
Location: **20 mi. W of Asheville**
No. of Rooms: **3**
No. of Private Baths: **1**
Max. No. Sharing Bath: **4**
Double/pb: **$75**
Single/pb: **$70**
Double/sb: **$65**
Single/sb: **$60**
Open: **All year**
Breakfast: **Full**
Pets: **No**
Children: **Welcome, over 10**
Smoking: **No**
Social Drinking: **Permitted**
Airport/Station Pickup: **Yes**

This two-story, Foursquare house sits on 1.5 acres, shaded by lovely old hemlocks and stately white oaks, and surrounded by rhododendrons and laurels. Recently restored, The Laurels is furnished with treasured family antiques, many crafted with wood from local forests. It maintains the warmth and charm of a stately mountain home. Rock on the expansive side porch or relax in the parlor with a glass of sherry. Fine linens, down comforters and pillows, terry robes, flowers, and gourmet chocolates pamper guests. A full breakfast, casual in atmosphere, is served on fine china, crystal, and old family silver. The Laurels lies in the heart of the Blue Ridge Mountains near Waynesville, Maggie Valley, and adjacent to the Methodist Assembly at Lake Junaluska. This area offers many outdoor activities and shopping opportunities. Inquire about mystery weekends.

The Boxley Bed & Breakfast
117 EAST HUNTER STREET, MADISON, NORTH CAROLINA 27025

Tel: **(800) 429-3516**
Best Time to Call: **8 AM–8 PM**
Hosts: **JoAnn and Monte McIntosh**
Location: **22 mi. N of Greensboro**
No. of Rooms: **4**
No. of Private Baths: **4**
Double/pb: **$70**
Single/pb: **$60**

Open: **All year**
Reduced Rates: **10% seniors, weekly**
Breakfast: **Full**
Credit Cards: **AMEX, MC, VISA**
Pets: **No**
Children: **Welcome**
Smoking: **No**
Social Drinking: **Permitted**

This Greek Federal-style home was built in 1825 on over an acre, located in the historic district of Madison. Furnished with oriental rugs, antiques, fine linens and china, the house possesses an aura of simple elegance, charm, and grace. Guests will enjoy the peacefulness and serenity of this 19th-century setting. A gourmet breakfast is served in the country kitchen, dining room, or on the porch. JoAnn and Monte are full-time hosts; their interests are gardening and refinishing furniture. The Boxley is your home away from home.

The Pines Plantation Inn ✪
1570 LILLY'S BRIDGE ROAD, MOUNT GILEAD, NORTH CAROLINA 27306
http://www.bestinns.net/usa/nc/Pines.html

Tel: **(800) 711-1134; (910) 439-1894**
Hosts: **Carol and Don Day**
Location: **50 mi. E of Charlotte**
No. of Rooms: **5**
No. of Private Baths: **5**
Double/pb: **$55–$70**
Open: **All year**
Reduced Rates: **10% corporate, multiple rooms; 5th night free**

Breakfast: **Full**
Credit Cards: **MC, VISA**
Pets: **Sometimes**
Children: **Welcome, over 8**
Smoking: **No**
Social Drinking: **Permitted**

On beautiful, unspoiled Lake Tillery on the western edge of the Uwharrie National Forest, you'll find this 1878 antique-filled mansion house, once the center of a 1500-acre working plantation. The house has 14-

foot ceilings, an elegant staircase, and beautifully appointed guest rooms—most with fireplaces. Guests are invited to enjoy the sunroom, library, parlor, and dining room. Take a stroll on the beautiful grounds or relax on one of the quiet porches. Nearby attractions include Lake Tillery, Morrow Mountain State Park, Town Creek Indian Mounds, Reed Gold Mine, Charlotte Motor Speedway, and Seagrove pottery shops.

Huntington Hall Bed and Breakfast ✪
500 VALLEY RIVER AVENUE, MURPHY, NORTH CAROLINA 28906
hhallbnb@grove.net

Tel: **(704) 837-9567; (800) 824-6189;** fax: **(704) 837-2527**	Reduced Rates: **15% Dec.–Feb., based on availability**
Best Time to Call: **8 AM–9 PM**	Breakfast: **Full**
Hosts: **Bob and Kate DeLong**	Credit Cards: **AMEX, DC, DISC, MC, VISA**
Location: **100 mi. N of Atlanta, Georgia**	
No. of Rooms: **5**	Pets: **No**
No. of Private Baths: **5**	Children: **Welcome**
Double/pb: **$65–$95**	Smoking: **No**
Single/pb: **$65–$75**	Social Drinking: **Permitted**
Open: **All year**	Airport/Station Pickup: **Yes**

Two huge maple trees shade this pleasant clapboard home, circa 1881; tall columns accent the front porch, and English ivy and Virginia creeper climb the low stone wall surrounding the property. Each spacious bedroom blends the old-world charm of tall windows, wooden floors, and Victorian decor with such modern amenities as cable TV and private baths. Wonderful breakfasts served on the sunporch precede the day's explorations of the historical district in nearby Brasstown, or of the Valley River Valley—original home of the Cherokee Indians and site of their "Trail of Tears." Both Bob and Kate are outdoor enthusiasts, eager to help guests plan white-water rafting trips on the Nanathala and Ocoee Rivers and hikes in Great Smokey Mountain National Park.

New Berne House Bed and Breakfast Inn ✪
709 BROAD STREET, NEW BERN, NORTH CAROLINA 28560

Tel: **(919) 636-2250; (800) 842-7688**	Reduced Rates: **AAA, AARP**
Hosts: **Marcia Drum and Howard Bronson**	Breakfast: **Full**
Location: **1 mi. from Hwy. 70**	Credit Cards: **AMEX, MC, VISA**
No. of Rooms: **7**	Pets: **No**
No. of Private Baths: **7**	Children: **Welcome, over 12**
Double/pb: **$88**	Smoking: **No**
Single/pb: **$68**	Social Drinking: **Permitted**
Open: **All year**	Airport/Station Pickup: **Yes**

Located in the heart of New Bern's historic district, this brick Colonial is furnished in the style of an English country manor with a mixture of antiques, traditional pieces, and attic treasures. Guests are pampered with afternoon tea or coffee served in the parlor. A sweeping stairway leads upstairs to romantic bedchambers, one with a brass bed reportedly rescued in 1897 from a burning brothel. Breakfast specialties such as praline and cream waffles, honey-glazed ham, and homemade breads and muffins are served in the dining room. New Berne House is within walking distance of Tryon Palace, North Carolina's Colonial capitol, and the governor's mansion. Ask about the exciting Mystery Weekends.

The Tar Heel Inn ☉
508 CHURCH STREET, ORIENTAL, NORTH CAROLINA 28571

Tel: **(919) 249-1078; fax: (919) 249-0005**
Best Time to Call: **7 AM–9 PM**
Hosts: **Shawna and Robert Hyde**
Location: **24 mi. E of New Bern**
No. of Rooms: **8**
No. of Private Baths: **8**
Double/pb: **$70–$90**
Single/pb: **$60–$80**
Open: **All year**

Breakfast: **Full**
Credit Cards: **DISC, MC, VISA**
Pets: **No**
Children: **Prior arrangement**
Smoking: **No**
Social Drinking: **Permitted**
Minimum Stay: **2 nights holiday weekends**
Airport/Station Pickup: **Yes**

This circa-1800s guesthouse has been lovingly restored to capture the feeling of an English country inn. Rooms are individually decorated with four-poster or canopy beds, Laura Ashley wallpaper, and antique furnishings. Breakfast specialties may include southern pecan French toast with homemade syrup, blintzes with North Carolina blueberry sauce, and garden quiches. Located within walking distance are restaurants, shops, sailing, tennis, and fishing. Your hosts will be happy to help you plan your day, or assist with anything else that will make your day more enjoyable.

Key Falls Inn ☉
151 EVERETT ROAD, PISGAH FOREST, NORTH CAROLINA 28768

Tel: **(704) 884-7559**
Best Time to Call: **9 AM–9 PM**
Hosts: **Clark and Patricia Grosvenor, and Janet Fogleman**
No. of Rooms: **4**
No. of Private Baths: **4**
Double/pb: **$55–$75**
Single/pb: **$45–$65**

Suites: **$85**
Open: **All year**
Breakfast: **Full**
Credit Cards: **AMEX, DC, MC, VISA**
Pets: **No**
Children: **Welcome, over 12**
Smoking: **No**
Social Drinking: **Permitted**

Visitors to this B&B will be able to make the most of western North Carolina's natural and cultural attractions. Key Falls Inn is situated on a 28-acre estate with its own tennis court, pond, and outdoor barbecue. For quieter moments, sit on one of the porches and enjoy the mountain views. Music lovers will want to get tickets to the acclaimed Brevard Festival, an annual summer event.

Breakfast Creek ✪
4361 OCEAN BREEZE AVENUE SW, SHALLOTTE, NORTH CAROLINA 28470

Tel: **(888) 754-3614**	Suite: **$75**
Best Time to Call: **Mornings**	Open: **All year**
Hosts: **Tim Tryon and Diana Turtle**	Breakfast: **Full**
Location: **35 mi. S of Wilmington**	Pets: **No**
No. of Rooms: **3**	Children: **Welcome**
No. of Private Baths: **2**	Smoking: **No**
Max. No. Sharing Bath: **4**	Social Drinking: **Permitted**
Double/pb: **$60**	

Breakfast Creek is a modest white brick house filled with sunlight and antiques. It overlooks the Atlantic Ocean, Shallotte Inlet, Intracoastal Waterway, and acres of living wetlands. Diana is a devoted gardener, Tim is a musician and woodworker; both love sailing and the beach. The B&B is located fifteen minutes from Ocean Isle, and twenty minutes from Holden Beach, Calabash, Southport, Fort Fisher, Wilmington, and the Grand Strand. None of these are reachable without passing at least one golf course. During his first visit, a guest said, "It's like staying with friends at the beach without the sand."

Bed and Breakfast at Laurel Ridge ✪
3188 SILER CITY–SNOW CAMP ROAD, SILER CITY, NORTH CAROLINA 27344

Tel: **(800) 742-6049; (919) 742-6049**	Cottage: **$125**
Best Time to Call: **9 AM–9 PM**	Open: **All year**
Hosts: **David Simmons and**	Reduced Rates: **6th night free**
Lisa Reynolds	Breakfast: **Full**
Location: **35 mi. SE of Greensboro**	Credit Cards: **AMEX, MC, VISA**
No. of Rooms: **3**	Pets: **No**
No. of Private Baths: **4**	Children: **Welcome, over 10**
Double/pb: **$59–$69**	Smoking: **No**
Single/pb: **$59**	Social Drinking: **Permitted**
Suites: **$99**	

Bed and Breakfast at Laurel Ridge is a contemporary rustic post and beam home situated on 26 forested acres that border the Rocky River. Centrally located in the heart of North Carolina, between the Triad furniture markets, Research Triangle Park, North Carolina Zoo, and Seagrove Pottery, this guesthouse provides visitors with many choices of things to do. Some say David, a professional chef for over 25 years, prepares the best breakfast in North Carolina using locally grown, organic products. The menu may include soufflés, specialty pancakes, and stuffed French toast.

Turby Villa B&B ✪
2072 NC HIGHWAY 18 NORTH, SPARTA, NORTH CAROLINA 28675

Tel: **(910) 372-8490**	Open: **All year**
Host: **Mrs. Maybelline Turbiville**	Breakfast: **Full**
No. of Rooms: **3**	Pets: **No**
No. of Private Baths: **3**	Children: **Welcome**
Double/pb: **$50**	Smoking: **Permitted**
Single/pb: **$35**	Social Drinking: **Permitted**

At an altitude of 3000 feet, this contemporary two-story brick home is the centerpiece of a 20-acre farm. The house is surrounded by an acre of trees and manicured lawns, and the lovely views are of the scenic Blue Ridge Mountains. Breakfast is served either on the enclosed porch with its white wicker furnishings or in the more formal dining room with its Early American–style furnishings. Mrs. Turbiville takes justifiable pride in her attractive, well-maintained B&B.

Cedar Hill Farm B&B ✪
778 ELMWOOD ROAD, STATESVILLE, NORTH CAROLINA 28677

Tel: **(704) 873-4332; (800) 948-4423**	Guest Cottages: **$75–$95**
Best Time to Call: **Before 2 PM; after 5 PM**	Open: **All year**
	Breakfast: **Full**
Hosts: **Brenda and Jim Vernon**	Credit Cards: **MC, VISA**
Location: **45 mi. N of Charlotte**	Pets: **Sometimes**
No. of Rooms: **3**	Children: **Welcome**
No. of Private Baths: **3**	Smoking: **No**
Double/pb: **$60**	Social Drinking: **Permitted**

A three-story Federal farmhouse furnished with antique and country pieces, Cedar Hill is surrounded by 32 acres of rolling green, the better to feed the Vernons' sheep. Brenda and Jim sell fleece coverlets and crafts from their own hand-spun wool; they also make furniture and cure turkey and ham in a smokehouse on site. Stay in the farmhouse or in the private cottages. Either way you'll have an air-conditioned room with a telephone and cable TV. The country breakfasts will leave you full. You can work off calories swimming in your hosts' pool or playing badminton, but you might want to relax in a porch rocker or hammock first. The cottages now have working fireplaces.

Scott's Keep ✪
308 WALNUT STREET, SWANSBORO, NORTH CAROLINA 28584

Tel: **(910) 326-1257; (800) 348-1257**
Best Time to Call: **Anytime**
Hosts: **Frank and Norma Scott**
Location: **150 mi. SE of Raleigh**
No. of Rooms: **3**
Max. No. Sharing Bath: **4**
Double/pb: **$60**
Double/sb: **$50**
Open: **All year**

Reduced Rates: **15% weekly**
Breakfast: **Full**
Credit Cards: **AMEX, DISC, MC, VISA**
Pets: **No**
Children: **Welcome, over 6**
Smoking: **No**
Social Drinking: **Permitted**
Minimum Stay: **2 nights, May 15–Sept. 15**

This simple contemporary is located on a quiet street two blocks from the waterfront. Your hosts want you to feel right at home in the bright, spacious living room and comfortable guest rooms. The larger bedroom is decorated with wicker and features an antique trunk, queen-size bed, and colorful quilts. The smaller bedroom is furnished in classic maple with twin beds and grandmother's quilts. For breakfast, Norma serves blueberry or apple spice muffins with fruit and homemade jellies. This historic seaside village is filled with inviting shops and waterside seafood restaurants. Your hosts will point the way to beautiful beaches, waterskiing, sailing, and windsurfing.

Four Rooster Inn ✪
403 PIREWAY ROAD, ROUTE 904, TABOR CITY,
NORTH CAROLINA 28463

Tel: **(910) 653-3878; (800) 653-5008**
Hosts: **Gloria and Bob Rogers**
Location: **24 mi. NW of Myrtle Beach,**
  South Carolina; 45 min. from I-95
No. of Rooms: **4**
No. of Private Baths: **2**
Max. No. Sharing Bath: **4**
Double/pb: **$65–$75**
Single/pb: **$55–$65**
Double/sb: **$65**
Single/sb: **$55**

Open: **All year**
Reduced Rates: **Fifth night free**
Breakfast: **Full**
Credit Cards: **AMEX, DC, DISC, MC, VISA**
Pets: **No**
Children: **Welcome, by arrangement**
Smoking: **No**
Social Drinking: **Permitted**
Airport/Station Pickup: **Yes**

Experience the warm, gracious hospitality of the old South in the charm of a country setting. The Inn has been restored to a comfortable elegance with china, crystal, antiques, beautiful fabrics and fine linens. Amenities include afternoon tea, evening turn-down service accented with chocolates, and coffee or tea at your door when you awake. A full breakfast is served in the dining room and may include yam bread, French toast, or eggs Benedict. The Four Rooster Inn is located forty-five minutes from Interstate 95 and a short drive from Myrtle Beach golf courses, Waccamaw Pottery shopping, Brookgreen Gardens, and historic Wilmington. The Inn provides a comfortable haven whether you are traveling for business or pleasure. Gloria and Bob are dedicated to the art of service for their guests.

Little Warren ✪
304 EAST PARK AVENUE, TARBORO, NORTH CAROLINA 27886

Tel: **(919) 823-1314; (800) 309-1314**
Hosts: **Patsy and Tom Miller**
Location: **Easy access from I-95**
No. of Rooms: **3**
No. of Private Baths: **3**
Double/pb: **$65**
Single/pb: **$58**
Open: **All year**
Reduced Rates: **Corporate, upon request**

Breakfast: **Full**
Credit Cards: **AMEX, DISC, MC, VISA**
Pets: **No**
Children: **Welcome, over 6**
Smoking: **Permitted**
Social Drinking: **Permitted**
Foreign Languages: **Spanish**

Little Warren is actually a large and gracious family home built in 1913. It is located along the Albemarle Trail in Tarboro's historic district. The deeply set, wraparound porch overlooks one of the last originally chartered town commons still in existence. Inside, you'll find rooms of beautiful antiques from England and America. In the morning, choose from a full English, Southern, or expanded Continental breakfast.

Acadian House Bed & Breakfast ✪
129 VAN NORDEN STREET, WASHINGTON, NORTH CAROLINA 27889

Tel: **(919) 975-3967**
Best Time to Call: **Mornings and evenings**

Hosts: **Johanna and Leonard Huber**
Location: **105 mi. E of Raleigh**
No. of Rooms: **4**

No. of Private Baths: **4**
Double/pb: **$55–$65**
Suites: **$100**
Open: **Feb. 1–Dec. 14**
Breakfast: **Full**

Credit Cards: **AMEX, DISC, MC, VISA**
Pets: **No**
Children: **Welcome, over 12**
Smoking: **No**
Social Drinking: **Permitted**

Acadian House Bed & Breakfast, a 1900 home located in Colonial Washington, features a unique herringbone-patterned brick porch. It is decorated throughout with antiques and local crafts. A Victorian staircase leads to guest rooms and the library, where books and games are provided. Johanna and Leonard, transplanted New Orleanians, serve a full breakfast featuring southern Louisiana Acadian specialties such as beignets and café au lait along with traditional breakfast foods. Acadian House is one block from the scenic Pamlico River; museums and antique shops are nearby. The business traveler will find a writing table, telephone, and fax available. Copying facilities are also nearby.

Pamlico House ✪
400 EAST MAIN STREET, WASHINGTON, NORTH CAROLINA 27889

Tel: **(919) 946-7184; (800) 948-8507**
Best Time to Call: **9 AM–8 PM**
Hosts: **George and Jane Fields**
Location: **20 mi. E of Greenville**
No. of Rooms: **4**
No. of Private Baths: **4**
Double/pb: **$75–$85**
Single/pb: **$65–$75**

Open: **All year**
Breakfast: **Full**
Credit Cards: **AMEX, DISC, MC, VISA**
Pets: **No**
Children: **Welcome, over 6**
Smoking: **No**
Social Drinking: **Permitted**
Airport/Station Pickup: **Yes**

Located in the center of a small, historic town, this stately Colonial Revival home's large rooms are a perfect foil for the carefully chosen antique furnishings. Guests are drawn to the classic Victorian parlor or to the spacious wraparound porch for relaxing conversation. Take a self-guided walking tour of the historic district or a stroll along the quaint waterfront. Recreational pleasures abound. Nature enthusiasts enjoy the wildlife and exotic plants in nearby Goose Creek State Park. Should you get homesick for your favorite pet, Lawrence and Jeanne will share theirs.

Belle Meade Inn ✪
1534 SOUTH MAIN STREET, WAYNESVILLE, NORTH CAROLINA 28786

Tel: **(704) 456-3234**	Reduced Rates: **10% AARP; weekly**
Hosts: **Gloria and Al DiNofa**	Breakfast: **Full**
Location: **27 mi. W of Asheville**	Credit Cards: **DISC, MC, VISA**
No. of Rooms: **4**	Pets: **No**
No. of Private Baths: **4**	Children: **Welcome, over 6**
Double/pb: **$65–$70**	Smoking: **No**
Single/pb: **$55–$60**	Social Drinking: **Permitted**
Open: **All year**	

Nestled in the mountains, and within easy reach of the Great Smoky National Park, this elegant home is a frame dwelling built in the craftsman style popular in the early 1900s. The warm richness of the chestnut woodwork in the formal rooms and the large stone fireplace in the living room complement the appealing blend of antique and traditional furnishings. The friendly attention to guests' needs is exemplified in such thoughtful touches as "early bird" coffee brought to your door, complimentary refreshments on the veranda, and fresh flowers and mints in your room. Nearby attractions include Biltmore House, Catalooche Ski Slope, mountain art and crafts festivals, and white-water rafting and tubing.

Weldon Place Inn ✪
500 WASHINGTON AVENUE, WELDON, NORTH CAROLINA 27890

Tel: **(919) 536-4582; (800) 831-4470**	Open: **All year**
Best Time to Call: **Anytime**	Reduced Rates: **Available**
Hosts: **Angel and Andy Whitby**	Breakfast: **Full**
Location: **2 mi. E of I-95, exit 173**	Credit Cards: **AMEX, MC, VISA**
No. of Rooms: **4**	Pets: **No**
No. of Private Baths: **4**	Children: **Welcome, over 12**
Double/pb: **$60–$89**	Smoking: **Restricted**
Single/pb: **$55–$60**	Social Drinking: **No**

If you love antiques and country elegance, step back in time as you cross the threshold of Weldon Place Inn. Sleep in a canopy bed, wake to singing sparrows, and savor a gourmet breakfast. Then explore this historic neighborhood: the Inn, built in 1913, stands amid homes that date to the mid 1800s, and nearby, there is a canal system aqueduct that is two decades older. Breakfast specialties like sausage-and-cheese-stuffed French toast and strawberry bread will help to fuel your excursions.

Anderson Guest House ✪
520 ORANGE STREET, WILMINGTON, NORTH CAROLINA 28401

Tel: **(910) 343-8128**	Open: **All year**
Best Time to Call: **8 AM–5 PM**	Breakfast: **Full**
Hosts: **Landon and Connie Anderson**	Pets: **Sometimes**
No. of Rooms: **2**	Children: **Welcome**
No. of Private Baths: **2**	Smoking: **No**
Double/pb: **$85**	Social Drinking: **Permitted**
Single/pb: **$65**	Airport/Station Pickup: **Yes**

This 19th-century town house has a private guest house overlooking a garden. The bedrooms have ceiling fans, fireplaces, and air-conditioning. Enjoy cool drinks upon arrival and a liqueur before bed. Breakfast specialties are eggs Mornay, blueberry cobbler, and crepes. Your hosts can point out the sights of this historic town and direct you to the beaches.

Taylor House Inn ✪
14 NORTH SEVENTH STREET, WILMINGTON, NORTH CAROLINA 28401

Tel: **(910) 763-7581; (800) 382-9982**	Breakfast: **Full**
Best Time to Call: **After 9 AM**	Credit Cards: **AMEX, MC, VISA**
Hosts: **Karen and Scott Clark**	Pets: **No**
Location: **120 mi. SE of Raleigh**	Children: **Welcome, over 12**
No. of Rooms: **5**	Smoking: **No**
No. of Private Baths: **5**	Social Drinking: **Permitted**
Double/pb: **$95–$110**	Minimum Stay: **2 nights weekends May–Aug.**
Single/pb: **$80–$90**	
Open: **All year**	Airport/Station Pickup: **Yes**

Upon entering the foyer of the Taylor House Inn, one is in awe of its stately elegance and warmth. The golden oak staircase with two stained glass windows, high ceilings, and parquet floors provide a dramatic expression of a long-lost art. Guest rooms are decorated with period antiques, fresh flowers, and beautiful linens. A gourmet breakfast is served in the formal dining room, with bone china, crystal, and candlelight. Taylor House is located in the historic district, within walking distance to the riverfront, antique shops, and museums. Walking tours and horse-drawn tours are also available. Wonderful beaches are a 15-minute drive.

Mickle House ✪
**927 WEST FIFTH STREET, WINSTON-SALEM,
NORTH CAROLINA 27101**

Tel: **(910) 722-9045**
Best Time to Call: **9 AM–10 PM**
Host: **Barbara Garrison**
Location: **1 mi. from Rte. 40, Broad St.
  exit**
No. of Rooms: **2**
No. of Private Baths: **2**
Double/pb: **$85–$95**

Single/pb: **$85–$95**
Open: **All year**
Breakfast: **Full**
Credit Cards: **MC, VISA**
Pets: **No**
Children: **No**
Smoking: **No**
Social Drinking: **Permitted**

Step back in time to visit a quaint Victorian cottage painted a soft yellow, with dark green shutters and gingerbread trim. The fully restored home, located in the National Historic District of West End, is furnished with lovely antiques, such as the canopy and poster beds in the guest rooms. Dessert is served in the afternoon or evening, and a full breakfast, with fresh fruit and freshly baked breads and muffins, awaits you in the morning. Old Salem, the Medical Center, and the Convention Center are five minutes away; fine restaurants, parks, shops, and the library are within walking distance.

For key to listings, see inside front or back cover.

✪ This star means that rates are guaranteed through December 31, 1998, to any guest making a reservation as a result of reading about the B&B in *Bed & Breakfast U.S.A.*—1998 edition.

Important! To avoid misunderstandings, always ask about cancellation policies when booking.

Please enclose a self-addressed, stamped, business-size envelope when contacting reservation services.

For more details on what you can expect in a B&B, see Chapter 1.

Always mention *Bed & Breakfast U.S.A.* when making reservations!

We want to hear from you! Use the form on page 625.

NORTH DAKOTA

.Stanley

The Triple T Ranch ✪
93 TRIPLE T ROAD, STANLEY, NORTH DAKOTA 58784

Tel: **(701) 628-2418**
Best Time to Call: **Anytime**
Hosts: **Joyce and Fred Evans**
Location: **60 mi. W of Minot**
No. of Rooms: **2**
Max. No. Sharing Bath: **4**
Double/sb: **$50**
Single/sb: **$35**

Open: **All year**
Reduced Rates: **Available**
Breakfast: **Full**
Pets: **Sometimes**
Children: **Welcome (crib)**
Smoking: **No**
Social Drinking: **No**

You're warmly invited to come to Joyce and Fred's rustic ranch home, where you're welcome to take a seat in front of the stone fireplace, put your feet up, and relax. There's a lovely view of the hills and the valley, and their herd of cattle is an impressive sight. Lake Sakakawea, for seasonal recreation such as fishing and swimming, is 11 miles away. Indian powwows, area rodeos, and hunting for Indian artifacts are fun. The State Fair is held every July.

For key to listings, see inside front or back cover.

○ This star means that rates are guaranteed through December 31, 1998, to any guest making a reservation as a result of reading about the B&B in *Bed & Breakfast U.S.A.*—1998 edition.

Important! To avoid misunderstandings, always ask about cancellation policies when booking.

Please enclose a self-addressed, stamped, business-size envelope when contacting reservation services.

For more details on what you can expect in a B&B, see Chapter 1.

Always mention *Bed & Breakfast U.S.A.* when making reservations!

We want to hear from you! Use the form on page 625.

OHIO

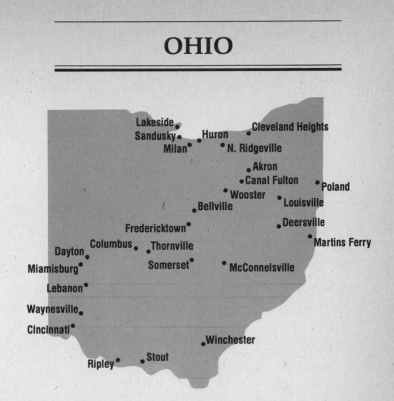

Lakeside
Sandusky · Huron · Cleveland Heights
Milan · · N. Ridgeville
· Akron
· Canal Fulton
· Poland
· Wooster
Bellville · · Louisville
Fredericktown · · Deersville
Columbus · Thornville · Martins Ferry
Dayton · · Somerset · McConnelsville
Miamisburg · · Somerset
Lebanon ·
Waynesville ·
Cincinnati ·
· Winchester
Ripley · · Stout

Helen's Hospitality House
1096 PALMETTO, AKRON, OHIO 44306

Tel: **(330) 724-7151; 724-3034**
Best Time to Call: **8 AM–11 PM**
Host: **Helen Claytor**
Location: **1 mi. from I-77 S, Exit 123B**
No. of Rooms: **2**
No. of Private Baths: **1**
Max. No. Sharing Bath: **4**
Double/pb: **$40**
Single/pb: **$35**
Double/sb: **$35**

Single/sb: **$30**
Open: **All year**
Reduced Rates: **Weekly**
Breakfast: **Full**
Pets: **No**
Children: **Welcome, over 10**
Smoking: **No**
Social Drinking: **Permitted**
Airport/Station Pickup: **Yes**

Located in a quiet neighborhood on a dead-end street, Helen's centrally air-conditioned house is a bit of country in the city. It is a renovated old farmhouse furnished with antiques and reproductions. On warm days, breakfast is served on the screened, glass-enclosed porch. Quaker Square, Akron University, the Firestone PGA, and Portage Lakes are just a few of the local attractions. Helen is a retired teacher who enjoys being a B&B hostess.

Portage House ✪
601 COPLEY ROAD, STATE ROUTE 162, AKRON, OHIO 44320

Tel: **(330) 535-1952**
Best Time to Call: **8 AM–11 PM**
Host: **Jeanne Pinnick**
Location: **2 mi. from I-77**
No. of Rooms: **4**
No. of Private Baths: **1**
Max. No. Sharing Bath: **3**
Double/pb: **$44**
Double/sb: **$36**

Single/sb: **$34**
Open: **Feb. 1–Nov. 30**
Reduced Rates: **$3 less after 1st night**
Breakfast: **Full**
Pets: **Restricted**
Children: **Welcome (crib)**
Smoking: **No**
Social Drinking: **Permitted**
Foreign Languages: **French, Spanish**

Steeped in history, this gracious Tudor home, nestled in a parklike setting, dates back to 1917. A stone wall down the street served as the western boundary of the United States in 1785. Jeanne and her late husband Harry, a physics professor at the nearby University of Akron, opened their B&B in 1982. Jeanne manages the B&B and has the coffeepot on with refreshments available for arriving guests. If bread is being baked, you'll be offered some hot out of the oven.

Pleasant Valley ✪
1226 HATHAWAY ROAD, BELLVILLE, OHIO 44813

Tel: **(419) 886-2366**
Hosts: **Dan and Antonia Reese**
Location: **60 mi. N of Columbus**
No. of Rooms: **5**
No. of Private Baths: **3**
Max. No. Sharing Bath: **4**
Double/pb: **$80**
Double/sb: **$60**
Suites: **$100–$140**

Open: **All year**
Breakfast: **Full**
Other Meals: **Available**
Credit Cards: **AMEX, MC, VISA**
Pets: **No**
Children: **Welcome, over 12**
Smoking: **No**
Social Drinking: **Permitted**

Enjoy the warmth and charm of Old World elegance with all the modern conveniences. The house is decorated with stained glass, oriental rugs, antiques, parquet floors, and art treasures collected from all over the world. Dan and Antonia own a landscaping business that is located on the premises. Guests will enjoy the beauty and variety of trees and shrubbery used for landscaping. You can enjoy relaxing in the privacy of your room, play croquet or badminton, swim in the pool, explore the forty acres of fields and woods, or browse in the Reeses' art- and antique-filled Castle Door Gallery. Breakfast is served in the dining area, around the pool, or on the screened porch.

Pleasant Hill—1845 ✪
451 EAST CHERRY STREET, CANAL FULTON, OHIO 44614

Tel: **(330) 854-0551**
Hosts: **Betty and Terry Stoffer**
Location: **15 mi. S of Akron**
No. of Rooms: **2**
Max. No. Sharing Bath: **4**
Double/sb: **$50–$60**
Single/sb: **$45–$55**

Open: **All year**
Reduced Rates: **10% after 3 nights**
Breakfast: **Full**
Credit Cards: **DISC, MC, VISA**
Pets: **No**
Children: **Welcome**
Smoking: **No**

Built in 1845 at the height of the canal era, Pleasant Hill provides a glimpse of an earlier time. Lovingly restored in 1993 and located in Canal Fulton's National Register Historic District, this Greek Revival home offers warm hospitality along with the comfort of air-conditioning and in-room color cable TV. Enjoy a walk around the village, visit the shops, ride the canal boat, see the museums, then relax with a glass of iced tea on the veranda. Breakfast includes juice, fruit, hearty main dishes, and home-baked breads and muffins.

Prospect Hill Bed and Breakfast
408 BOAL STREET, CINCINNATI, OHIO 45210

Tel: **(513) 421-4408**
Best Time to Call: **10 AM–8 PM**
Hosts: **Gary Hackney and Tony Jenkins**
Location: **Downtown**
No. of Rooms: **4**
No. of Private Baths: **2**

Max. No. Sharing Bath: **4**
Double/pb: **$99–$129**
Single/pb: **$99–$129**
Double/sb: **$89–$109**
Single/sb: **$89–$109**
Open: **All year**

Reduced Rates: **10% weekly**
Breakfast: **Full**
Pets: **No**

Children: **Welcome, over 10**
Smoking: **No**
Social Drinking: **Permitted**

This restored Italianate Victorian town house was built in 1867 on Prospect Hill, Cincinnati's first suburb, now a national historic district. The original woodwork, doors, hardware, and light fixtures remain intact—your hosts are interested in historic preservation. All the rooms have spectacular views, fireplaces, and period antique furniture. It's only a fifteen-minute walk from here to Fountain Square or the Ohio River. Mt. Adams, the University of Cincinnati, Playhouse in the Park, the Music Hall, Eden Park, the William Howard Taft Historic Site, and most area museums and hospitals are within a mile.

Notre Maison Inc. ✪
2557 NORTH PARK BOULEVARD, CLEVELAND HEIGHTS, OHIO 44106

Tel: **(216) 932-8769; (800) 216-8769**
Host: **Renee Lewis Van Cauwenberghe**
No. of Rooms: **4**
No. of Private Baths: **4**
Double/pb: **$72.50**
Single/pb: **$65**
Open: **All year**
Reduced Rates: **Available**

Breakfast: **Continental**
Children: **Welcome**
Smoking: **No**
Social Drinking: **No**
Airport/Station Pickup: **Yes**
Foreign Languages: **French, Russian, Spanish, Italian, German, Polish**

Notre Maison, a French manor situated on two acres of land, is surrounded by a black cast iron fence and nearly 300 pine, oak, and maple trees. The house has 21 rooms filled with antiques, Persian rugs, and paintings. Guest rooms have TVs and a phone is available. Notre Maison is safe, relaxing, and near everything. A staff of maids and maintenance people are here year-round and provide a clean, comfortable atmosphere. Breakfast includes coffee, croissants, fruit, juice, tea and coffee cake, served with jams and jellies made on the premises.

Shamrock B&B ✪
5657 SUNBURY ROAD, COLUMBUS, OHIO 43230

Tel: **(614) 337-9849**
Best Time to Call: **8 AM–10 PM**
Host: **Tom McLaughlin**
Location: **½ mi. from I-270 Exit 30B #161**
No. of Rooms: **2**
No. of Private Baths: **2**
Double/pb: **$60**
Single/pb: **$50**
Open: **All year**

Reduced Rates: **5% seniors; 10% over 4 days**
Breakfast: **Full**
Other meals: **Available**
Pets: **Sometimes**
Children: **Welcome, over 10**
Smoking: **No**
Social Drinking: **Permitted**
Airport Pickup: **Yes**

Shamrock B&B is situated on one and a quarter acres of woods in the northeastern Columbus area. A host of attractions lie nearby: shopping malls, cinemas, Hoover Dam, Inniswoods Botanical Gardens, Busch Brewery, Ohio Historical Village, Short North Gallery Hop, German Village, the Polaris Amphitheatre, and Ohio State University. Tom is a retired schoolteacher who loves gardening and travel, and his brick home is filled with 18th-century antiques and original art. Guest areas are on the first floor, so this B&B is wheelchair accessible.

Candlewick Bed & Breakfast ✪
4991 BATH ROAD, DAYTON, OHIO 45424

Tel: **(937) 233-9297**	Open: **All year**
Hosts: **George and Nancy Thompson**	Breakfast: **Full**
Location: **10 mi. NE of Dayton**	Pets: **No**
No. of Rooms: **2**	Children: **No**
Max. No. Sharing Bath: **4**	Smoking: **No**
Double/sb: **$55–$60**	Social Drinking: **No**
Single/sb: **$45**	Airport Pickup: **Yes**

This tranquil Dutch Colonial home sits atop a hill on five rolling acres. George, a retired engineer, and Nancy, a retired teacher, invite you to spend a quiet, restful night in comfortable rooms containing a charming blend of antiques and Colonial and country furnishings. A full breakfast includes fresh fruit and juice, choice homemade pastries, and freshly brewed coffee. Weather permitting, enjoy breakfast on the screened porch overlooking a large pond often visited by wild ducks and geese. Convenient to Wright-Patterson Air Force Base and Museum and two major universities, Candlewick is a peaceful retreat, perfect for either business or pleasure.

Mulberry Lane ✪
224 WEST MAIN STREET, P.O. BOX 61, DEERSVILLE, OHIO 44693

Tel: **(614) 922-0425**	Single/sb: **$55**
Best Time to Call: **9 AM–5 PM**	Open: **All year**
Hosts: **Dick and Ferrel Zeimer**	Breakfast: **Full**
Location: **90 mi. S of Cleveland**	Pets: **No**
No. of Rooms: **3**	Children: **No**
Max. No. Sharing Bath: **4**	Smoking: **No**
Double/sb: **$70**	Social Drinking: **Permitted**

Built in 1830, restored in 1989, and tastefully furnished with antiques and period pieces, Mulberry Lane is a great getaway place. Peaceful little Deersville lies between two large lakes where guests can go fishing and boating. Country auctions, antique shops, glass factories, the birthplaces of Clark Gable and General George Armstrong Custer, early Moravian settlements, and Amish country are all within reach. If you don't feel like touring, you're welcome to relax on the porch swing with a good book. Freshly baked muffins are always served at Dick and Ferrel's breakfasts in their country kitchen.

Heartland Country Resort ☉
2994 TOWNSHIP ROAD 190, FREDERICKTOWN, OHIO 43019

Tel: **(800) 230-7030; (419) 768-9300**	Reduced Rates: **10% seniors**
Best Time to Call: **Evenings**	Breakfast: **Continental, plus**
Host: **Dorene Henschen**	Other meals: **Available**
Location: **40 mi. NE of Columbus**	Credit Cards: **DISC, MC, VISA**
No. of Rooms: **7**	Children: **Welcome**
No. of Private Baths: **7**	Smoking: **No**
Double/pb: **$85–$155**	Social Drinking: **Permitted**
Open: **All year**	

At the Heartland Country Resort you can rent a horse, bring your own, or just watch others. The bed and breakfast is an inviting, restored 1878 farmhouse with a deck and screened porch. You will experience serenity in this 104-acre country setting with hills, streams, woods, wildlife, pastures, fields, and barns, which you can explore on foot or horseback. During every season, you can enjoy a petting zoo of farm animals and numerous recreation opportunities, both on and near the resort. The new log home suites have private Jacuzzi's.

Captain Montague's Bed & Breakfast ☉
229 CENTER STREET AT CLEVELAND ROAD, HURON, OHIO 44839
http://www.innsandouts.com/property/captain_montagues.html

Tel: **(800) 276-4756; (419) 433-4756**	Reduced Rates: **Nov. 1–Mar. 31**
Hosts: **Judy and Mike Tann**	Breakfast: **Continental, plus**
Location: **54 mi. W of Cleveland, 60 mi.**	Pets: **No**
E of Toledo	Children: **No**
No. of Rooms: **7**	Smoking: **No**
No. of Private Baths: **7**	Social Drinking: **Permitted**
Double/pb: **$68–$125**	Minimum Stay: **2 nights weekends,**
Suite: **Bridal $105–$135**	**Memorial Day–Labor Day**
Open: **All year**	

The Captain's is that perfect romantic retreat in a stately colonial manor that radiates Victorian charm. Experience a bygone era of lace, luster, and love. Nestled in the heart of Ohio's vacation land on the shores of Lake Erie, the Captain's is within minutes of golfing, nature preserves, boating, antiquing, Cedar Point Amusement Park, and the Lake Erie Islands. Enjoy the pool, latticed gazebo, and impeccable gardens. Discover the excitement of the Captain's themed weekends from November through March.

Idlewyld Bed & Breakfast ✪
350 WALNUT STREET, LAKESIDE, OHIO 43440 (MAILING ADDRESS:
13458 PARKWAY DRIVE, LAKEWOOD, OHIO 44107)

Tel: **(419) 798-4198; (216) 228-8168**
Hosts: **Dan and Joan Barris**
Location: **70 mi. W of Cleveland**
No. of Rooms: **14**
No. of Private Baths: **5**
Max. No. Sharing Bath: **3**
Double/pb: **$45–$65**
Double/sb: **$40–$50**

Open: **Mid May–Oct.**
Reduced Rates: **Available**
Breakfast: **Continental, plus**
Pets: **No**
Children: **Welcome**
Smoking: **No**
Social Drinking: **No**

A stay at Idlewyld is like visiting an era when life was uncomplicated by high tech. Nestled in a quaint Victorian community on the shore of Lake Erie, the house is newly decorated in a country antique style. Many rooms feature stenciling. Guests gather in the large dining room for a Continental buffet breakfast, which includes an uncommon assortment of fresh fruit and homemade breads and muffins. Afterward, you can relax on one of the two spacious porches or participate in a myriad family-oriented activities offered in the Lakeside community.

Hexagon House
419 CINCINNATI AVENUE, LEBANON, OHIO 45036

Tel: **(513) 932-9655**
Best Time to Call: **Anytime**
Hosts: **Ron and Lois Duncan Hart**
Location: **30 mi. N of Cincinnati**
No. of Rooms: **3**
No. of Private Baths: **2**
Max. No. Sharing Bath: **4**
Double/pb: **$65–$75**

Double/sb: **$60**
Single/sb: **$50**
Open: **All year**
Breakfast: **Full**
Pets: **No**
Children: **Welcome, over 12**
Smoking: **No**

Built in the mid-1850s on a large, well-landscaped lot, Hexagon House is listed on the National Register of Historic Places due to its unique six-sided exterior, its interesting interior floor plan, and history. Rooms are spacious, comfortable, and tastefully decorated. A full breakfast is served on a flexible schedule. The objective of your full-time hostess is to provide each guest with a pleasantly memorable experience. Hexagon House is easy to reach from interstates and convenient to local attractions.

White Tor ✪
1620 OREGONIA ROAD, LEBANON, OHIO 45036

Tel: **(513) 932-5892**
Best Time to Call: **Before 9 AM;
after 6 PM**

Hosts: **Eric and Margaret Johnson**
Location: **25 mi. N of Cincinnati**
No. of Rooms: **1 suite**

No. of Private Baths: **1**	Children: **No**
Suite: **$75**	Smoking: **No**
Open: **All year**	Social Drinking: **Permitted**
Breakfast: **Full**	Foreign Languages: **French**
Pets: **No**	

Just a half hour's drive from both Cincinnati and Dayton, this handsome farmhouse, built in 1862, crowns a hilltop on seven wooded acres. Margaret's full English breakfast will give you stamina for a day of antique shopping or viewing artful stitchery at local quilt shows. Area attractions range from Kings Island and the Beach Waterpark to the Honey and Sauerkraut festivals. Or, simply relax on the porch in view of the pretty Miami Valley, with a good book and cold drink.

The Mainstay ✪
1320 EAST MAIN STREET, LOUISVILLE, OHIO 44641

Tel: **(330) 875-1021**	Open: **All year**
Hosts: **Mary and Joe Shurilla**	Reduced Rates: **15% weekly**
Location: **7 mi. E of Canton**	Breakfast: **Full**
No. of Rooms: **3**	Pets: **No**
No. of Private Baths: **3**	Children: **Welcome, over 3**
Double/pb: **$50–$60**	Smoking: **No**
Single/pb: **$40–$50**	Social Drinking: **Permitted**
Suite: **$50; sleeps 3**	Airport/Station Pickup: **Yes**

Enjoy a step backward in time at this century-old Queen Anne Victorian with its richly carved oak woodwork, spacious rooms, original tin ceilings, and numerous antiques. Louisville was the home of Charles Juilliard, founder of the famous New York City music school that bears his name; his house, listed on the National Register of Historic Places, may be toured by arrangement. If you prefer halftime shows to string quartets, you'll probably want to visit the Pro Football Hall of Fame in nearby Canton. Mary and Joe, both educators, greet newly arrived guests with fruit, cheese, and a sparkling beverage. In the morning, have your choice of full or Continental breakfast, with specialties like quiche and home-baked bread.

Mulberry Inn ✪
53 NORTH FOURTH STREET, MARTINS FERRY, OHIO 43935

Tel: **(614) 633-6058; (800) 705-6171** **ext. 3136**	Single/sb: **$45**
	Open: **All year**
Hosts: **Charles and Shirley Probst**	Reduced Rates: **10% seniors**
Location: **5 mi. W of Wheeling, W. Va.**	Breakfast: **Continental, plus**
No. of Rooms: **3**	Credit Cards: **AMEX, DISC, MC, VISA**
Max. No. Sharing Bath: **4**	Pets: **No**
Double/pb: **$60**	Children: **Welcome, over 5**
Single/pb: **$50**	Smoking: **No**
Double/sb: **$55**	Social Drinking: **Permitted**

Built in 1880, this frame Victorian is on a tree-lined street within walking distance of a Civil War cemetery and the Sedgwick Museum. (Martins Ferry is the oldest settlement in Ohio.) Beautiful woodwork, antiques, and mantels grace the large rooms, and air-conditioning cools the house in summer. A retired medical secretary, Shirley devotes her time to making her guests feel comfortable and welcome, tempting them with her unusual French toast recipe. Dog races, recreational activities, the Fostoria Glass Outlet, the Jamboree-in-the-Hills, Ohio University, and Bethany College are less than 10 miles away.

The Outback Inn Bed & Breakfast ✪
171 EAST UNION AVENUE, McCONNELSVILLE, OHIO 43756

Tel: **(614) 962-2158; (800) 542-7171**	Open: **All year**
Best Time to Call: **9 AM–9 PM**	Breakfast: **Full**
Hosts: **Carol and Bob Belfance**	Pets: **No**
No. of Rooms: **3**	Children: **Sometimes**
No. of Private Baths: **3**	Smoking: **No**
Double/pb: **$62.50–$69.50**	Social Drinking: **Permitted**

This restored 1880s banker's home is located in the heart of a small historic village, midway between Zanesville and Marietta. You'll find original oak woodwork, antiques, memorabilia, and stained glass throughout the Inn and all three air-conditioned rooms. Works by local artists are also on display. Breakfast delicacies are served in the dining room or in the private fenced-in yard. Excellent restaurants, a restored 1890 Opera House (showing movies on weekends), covered bridges, and a wildlife preserve where rare and vanishing species are bred are just a few of the attractions in this historic area.

English Manor ✪
505 EAST LINDEN AVENUE, MIAMISBURG, OHIO 45342

Tel: **(937) 866-2288; (800) 676-9456**	Open: **All year**
Best Time to Call: **9 AM–11 PM**	Reduced Rates: **10% after 3 nights**
Hosts: **Marilyn and Jack Didrichsen**	Breakfast: **Full**
Location: **9 mi. SW of Dayton**	Other Meals: **Available**
No. of Rooms: **4**	Credit Cards: **AMEX, DC, DISC, MC,**
No. of Private Baths: **3**	**VISA**
Max. No. Sharing Bath: **2**	Pets: **No**
Double/pb: **$80**	Children: **Welcome**
Single/pb: **$75**	Smoking: **No**
Double/sb: **$70**	Social Drinking: **Permitted**
Single/sb: **$65**	Airport Pickup: **Yes**

Marilyn, a retired real estate investor, and Jack, a retired executive, welcome you to their antique-filled 1920s home in historic Miamisburg. Read by the fireplace, lounge in the hammock, sip lemonade on the wicker porch. Then wander past charming neighborhood homes, or head toward the Great Miami River walking and bike trail. Antique shops, ancient Indian mounds, golf courses, tennis courts, and fine restaurants are all nearby. To start your day, a sumptuous breakfast is served on antique china, silver, and linens.

Gastier Farm Bed & Breakfast ✪

1902 STRECKER ROAD, MILAN, OHIO 44846

Tel: **(419) 499-2985**
Best Time to Call: **After 5 PM**
Hosts: **Ted and Donna Gastier**
Location: **60 mi. W of Cleveland**
No. of Rooms: **3**
Max. No. Sharing Bath: **3**
Double/sb: **$50**
Single/sb: **$35**

Open: **All year**
Breakfast: **Continental**
Credit Cards: **MC, VISA**
Pets: **No**
Children: **Welcome**
Smoking: **No**
Social Drinking: **No**
Aiport/Station Pickup: **Yes**

Ted and Donna's working farm has been a family tradition for more than one hundred years, providing the local community with grain, fresh produce, cattle, and a variety of house plants. Now the farmhouse has become a bed and breakfast. The rooms have all been decorated in a homey country atmosphere. Nearby attractions include Edison Birthplace, Milan Museum, Lake Erie, Cedar Point Amusement Park, and antique shops.

St. George House ✪
33941 LORRAIN ROAD, NORTH RIDGEVILLE, OHIO 44039

Tel: **(440) 327-9354**
Best Time to Call: **Early mornings; evenings until 9 PM**
Hosts: **Helen Bernardine and Muriel Dodd**
Location: **22 mi N of Cleveland**
No. of Rooms: **4**
No. of Private Baths: **1**
Max. No. Sharing Bath: **4**
Double/pb: **$55**
Single/pb: **$50**
Double/sb: **$45**

Single/sb: **$40**
Open: **All year**
Reduced Rates: **Weekly**
Breakfast: **Continental**
Other Meals: **Available**
Pets: **Sometimes**
Children: **Welcome, over 12**
Smoking: **Permitted**
Social Drinking: **Permitted**
Minimum Stay: **2 nights**
Airport/Station Pickup: **Yes**

This spacious Colonial home sits on an acre of scenic country. You may want to enjoy the renaissance of nearby downtown Cleveland. For those of you who enjoy night life, a trip to the Flats, which boasts comedy halls, saloons, galleries, and microbreweries, is in order. Flats restaurants offer dockside service for boaters. Playhouse Square has top-shelf theater, and Gateway is the home of the Cleveland Indians and the Cavaliers. Also nearby are the Rock and Roll Hall of Fame, Case Western Reserve, Oberlin College, and University Circle (home of the Cleveland Orchestra, Museum of Art, Cleveland Playhouse, and Cleveland Clinic). Freeway access is within two minutes.

Inn at the Green ✪
500 SOUTH MAIN STREET, POLAND, OHIO 44514

Tel: **(330) 757-4688**
Best Time to Call: **After 12 PM**
Hosts: **Ginny and Steve Meloy**
Location: **7 mi. SE of Youngstown**
No. of Rooms: **4**
No. of Private Baths: **4**
Double/pb: **$60**
Single/pb: **$55**

Open: **All year**
Breakfast: **Continental**
Other Meals: **No**
Credit Cards: **DISC, MC, VISA**
Pets: **No**
Children: **Welcome, over 10**
Smoking: **Permitted**
Social Drinking: **Permitted**

The Inn at the Green is an 1876 Victorian town house located on the south end of the village green. The rooms have the grandeur of bygone days, with original moldings, 12-foot-high ceilings, and original poplar floors. There are five Italian marble fireplaces and extensive public rooms furnished with gracious antiques. Guests are welcome to relax in the parlor, greeting room, and enclosed porch. Sleeping quarters are air-conditioned, and are furnished with poster beds, Posturepedic mattresses, antiques, and working fireplaces. Coffee, croissants, muffins, and French jam are served in the greeting room in winter and on the wicker-furnished porch during moderate weather. Enjoy a glass of sherry on the porch overlooking the garden before dinner. Your hosts will gladly direct you to gourmet dining as well as cross-country ski trails, golf, tennis, and the Butler Institute, home of one of the nation's finest American art collections.

The Signal House ✪
234 NORTH FRONT STREET, RIPLEY, OHIO 45167

Tel: **(937) 392-1640**	Reduced Rates: **Available**
Best Time to Call: **Morning**	Breakfast: **Full**
Hosts: **Vic and Betsy Billingsley**	Credit Cards: **DISC, MC, VISA**
Location: **55 mi. E of Cincinnati**	Pets: **No**
No. of Rooms: **2**	Children: **No**
Max. No. Sharing Bath: **4**	Smoking: **Permitted**
Double/sb: **$65–$75**	Social Drinking: **Permitted**
Open: **All year**	

This stately 1830 historic home is located on the Ohio River, offering relaxing porches and beautiful sunsets for a romantic getaway. Legends tell of two Civil War officers who lived here and of the house's role in the Underground Railroad. The town of Ripley has 55 acres on the National Register of Historic Places. Guests can enjoy Ohio River fishing, boating, water- and jet skiing—marina pickup is available upon request. Things to do include antiquing, shopping, visiting three museums, enjoying the restaurants, and meeting a lot of friendly people.

The Red Gables B&B ✪
421 WAYNE STREET, SANDUSKY, OHIO 44870

Tel: **(419) 625-1189**	Reduced Rates: **Oct. 1–May 1 all rooms**
Best Time to Call: **9 AM–9 PM**	**are $50–$60**
Host: **Jo Ellen Cuthbertson**	Breakfast: **Continental, plus**
Location: **60 mi. W of Cleveland**	Credit Cards: **MC, VISA**
No. of Rooms: **4**	Pets: **No**
No. of Private Baths: **2**	Children: **By arrangement**
Max. No. Sharing Bath: **4**	Smoking: **No**
Double/pb: **$80–$95**	Social Drinking: **Permitted**
Double/sb: **$70–$85**	Station Pickup: **Yes**
Open: **Feb.–Dec.**	

A lovely old Tudor Revival home finished in 1907, The Red Gables is located in the historic Old Plat District. Guests are welcomed into the great room, which features a massive fireplace and large bay window where breakfast is served. The home's many interesting architectural details include lots of oak woodwork. The Red Gables is decorated in a very eclectic style, from Oriental artifacts in the great room to flowered chintz in the bedrooms. The innkeeper, a semi-retired costume maker, has filled the rooms with handmade slipcovers, curtains, and comforters. Guest rooms are light and airy, with easy access to a wicker-filled sitting room, a refrigerator, and coffeemaker or teakettle. Guests have said, "It's like going to grandma's house!" Guest rooms have air-conditioning.

Wagner's 1844 Inn ✪
230 EAST WASHINGTON STREET, SANDUSKY, OHIO 44870

Tel: **(419) 626-1726**
Hosts: **Walt and Barb Wagner**
Location: **8 mi. from Ohio Tpke., Exit 7**
No. of Rooms: **3**
No. of Private Baths: **3**
Double/pb: **$70–$100**
Single/pb: **$50–$90**
Open: **All year**

Reduced Rates: **Oct.–Apr.**
Breakfast: **Continental**
Credit Cards: **DISC, MC, VISA**
Pets: **Sometimes**
Children: **No**
Smoking: **No**
Social Drinking: **Permitted**
Airport/Station Pickup: **Yes**

This elegantly restored Italianate home, built in 1844, is listed on the National Register of Historic Places. The warm interior features old-fashioned amenities like a billiard room, an antique piano, and a wood-burning fireplace. The screened porch and enclosed courtyard provide tranquil settings for conversation with your hosts Walt, an attorney, and Barb, a registered nurse. Within easy walking distance are parks, tennis courts, antique shops, art galleries, and ferries to Cedar Point Amusement Park and the Lake Erie Islands.

Somer Tea B&B ✪
200 SOUTH COLUMBUS STREET, BOX 308, SOMERSET, OHIO 43783

Tel: **(614) 743-2909**
Hosts: **Richard and Mary Lou Murray**
Location: **40 mi. SE of Columbus**
No. of Rooms: **2**
Max. No. Sharing Bath: **4**
Double/sb: **$55**
Single/sb: **$45**

Open: **All year**
Breakfast: **Full**
Pets: **Welcome**
Children: **Welcome**
Smoking: **No**
Social Drinking: **Permitted**

Somerset was the boyhood home of the Civil War general Phil Sheridan. Two of his nieces lived in the Somer Tea, a stately brick residence listed on the National Register of Historic Places. And yes, tea is always available here; guests are encouraged to sit with a cup on the porch swing. Ask Mary Lou to show you her collection of more than 300 teapots. If you'd like to do some collecting yourself, she'll direct you to the region's numerous antique shops and crafts stores. Full country breakfasts, with an egg casserole, a fruit dish, home fries, and raisin bran muffins, are served in the elegant dining room.

100 Mile House Bed & Breakfast ✪
U.S. 52, BOX 4866D (PORTSMOUTH), STOUT, OHIO 45684

Tel: **(614) 858-2984; (800) 645-2051**
Best Time to Call: **Anytime before
   10 PM**
Hosts: **Jim and Barb Larter**
Location: **15 mi. W of Portsmouth**
No. of Rooms: **4**
No. of Private Baths: **2**
Max. No. Sharing Bath: **4**
Double/pb: **$70**
Double/sb: **$55**

Open: **All year**
Breakfast: **Full**
Other Meals: **Available**
Credit Cards: **AMEX, DISC, MC, VISA**
Pets: **No**
Children: **Welcome**
Smoking: **No**
Social Drinking: **Permitted**
Station Pickup: **Yes**

Perhaps the most noted of estates in southern Ohio, this majestic mansion has all anyone could ask for. Beautiful and breathtaking views of the Ohio River, the lush mature landscape, and the birds singing while you sit under your favorite tree give you the feeling of total relaxation. The 11 acres offer plenty of room for a nice walk, or you can bask in the sun and enjoy the junior Olympic-size pool. The riverfront stretches for over 600 feet for a gorgeous view. For sports enthusiasts, 100 Mile House is close to Shawnee State Forest golf course and marina.

Soloman Whitmer House ✪
13917 ZION ROAD, THORNVILLE, OHIO 43076

Tel: **(614) 246-5999**
Hosts: **Katherine Brown and Bud Potter**
Location: **35 mi. E of Columbus**
No. of Rooms: **2**
No. of Private Baths: **2**
Double/pb: **$75**
Single/pb: **$55**

Open: **All year**
Reduced Rates: **Seniors $55**
Breakfast: **Full**
Pets: **No**
Children: **No**
Smoking: **No**
Social Drinking: **Permitted**

The Soloman Whitmer House is one of the oldest homes in Ohio to be converted into a bed and breakfast. This beautifully restored circa 1830 Federal- and Greek Revival–style home is situated on two countryside acres. Guests are made to feel relaxed and very comfortable as they enjoy the many antiques and original pieces found throughout the house. If you would like to feel closer to nature, the teahouse is available for viewing the countryside. July through October, hundreds of black-eyed susans are in bloom—it's truly a stunning site. Breakfast is served on Katherine's aunt's china at a time requested by guests. You might enjoy French toast or fruit-filled biscuits while watching the birds feed outside the original, poured-glass windows.

Lakewood Farm Bed & Breakfast, Inc. ✪
8495 ROUTE 48, WAYNESVILLE, OHIO 45068

Tel: (937) 885-9850
Best Time to Call: 8 AM–11 AM
Hosts: Liz and Jay Jorling
Location: 15 mi. S of Dayton
No. of Rooms: 4
No. of Private Baths: 4
Double/pb: $75
Suites: $125

Open: Mar.1–Dec. 31
Reduced Rates: Available
Breakfast: Full
Credit Cards: MC, VISA
Pets: Sometimes
Children: Welcome, over 2
Smoking: No
Social Drinking: No

Lakewood Farm, built in the early 1830s, is a year-round 25-acre estate with a 5-acre lake, 17 acres of forest, a horse stable, several pastures, and plenty of wildlife. Guests are invited to experience breath-taking views, miles of hiking trails, fishing, sunbathing, tennis, croquet, horseshoes, sledding, and ice skating. The guest rooms are all furnished with turn-of-the-century decor, queen-size beds, telephone service within the rooms, and air-conditioning. Breakfast is served in the courtyard dining room, in the garden, or, if you wish, brought to your room.

Amish Country Log Cabin ✪
2658 COON HILL ROAD, WINCHESTER, OHIO 45697

Tel: (937) 386-3144
Best Time to Call: 9 AM–9 PM
Hosts: Donna and Glenn Sorrell
Location: 58 mi. E of Cincinnati
No. of Rooms: 2
No. of Private Baths: 2
Double/pb: $65
Single/pb: $60
Open: All year

Reduced Rates: 10% Nov.–Mar.,
  seniors, Mon.–Wed.
Breakfast: Full
Credit Cards: MC, VISA
Pets: No
Children: Welcome, over 6
Smoking: No
Social Drinking: No

Amish Country Log Cabin Bed & Breakfast was built in 1788, and was moved to its present location in 1988. Rooms are decorated with a mix of antiques and traditional furniture, queen-size beds, TV, and VCR. Guests are invited to walk on the well-trodden paths, which cover 27 acres of woods. Fish in the pond or have a barbecue in the picnic shelter. Places to visit include Serpent Mound, the Amish bakery and auction, Ohio River towns, Ohio Brush Creek, and the nature preserve.

Millennium Classic Bed & Breakfast ✪
1626 BEALL AVENUE, WOOSTER, OHIO 44691

Tel: (330) 264-6005
Best Time to Call: 8 AM–9 PM
Host: John Byler
Location: 50 mi. S of Cleveland

No. of Rooms: 5
No. of Private Baths: 3
Max. No. Sharing Bath: 4
Double/pb: $65–$75

Double/sb: **$60–$70**
Single/sb: **$45–$55**
Suites: **$75–$85**
Open: **All year**
Reduced Rates: **10% seniors, 10% less
Mon–Thurs**
Breakfast: **Continental**

Credit Cards: **AMEX, DISC, MC, VISA**
Pets: **No**
Children: **Welcome**
Smoking: **No**
Social Drinking: **No**
Airport/Station Pickup: **By arrangement**
Foreign Languages: **German**

Built in 1911, the Millennium Classic Bed & Breakfast is located in the heart of Wooster, one block from the college, hospital, and shopping center and three doors north of Friendly's Ice Cream. The world's largest Amish community and tourist center is twenty minutes away. Millennium's exterior is post-Victorian and the interior is traditional classic. Outside there are quiet sitting areas with a lot of shade trees and a second-story deck that overlooks the backyard.

For key to listings, see inside front or back cover.

❂ This star means that rates are guaranteed through December 31, 1998, to any guest making a reservation as a result of reading about the B&B in *Bed & Breakfast U.S.A.*—1998 edition.

Important! To avoid misunderstandings, always ask about cancellation policies when booking.

Please enclose a self-addressed, stamped, business-size envelope when contacting reservation services.

For more details on what you can expect in a B&B, see Chapter 1.

Always mention *Bed & Breakfast U.S.A.* when making reservations!

We want to hear from you! Use the form on page 625.

OKLAHOMA

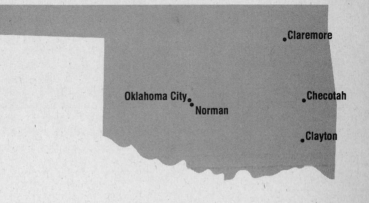

Claremore

Oklahoma City
Norman

Checotah

Clayton

Sharpe House ✪
301 NORTHWEST 2ND, CHECOTAH, OKLAHOMA 74426

Tel: **(918) 473-2832**
Best Time to Call: **After 4 PM**
Host: **Kay Kindt**
Location: **60 mi. SE of Tulsa**
No. of Rooms: **3**
No. of Private Baths: **3**
Double/pb: **$50**
Single/pb: **$35**

Suites: **$70**
Open: **All year**
Breakfast: **Full**
Pets: **Yes**
Children: **Welcome**
Smoking: **No**
Social Drinking: **Permitted**

Built in 1911, the Sharpe House has an antebellum look. The house is surrounded by huge old oak and magnolia trees, the front has "Southern mansion" columns, and there's a large screened-in porch in the back. The yard has a fish pond, secluded seating places for quiet conversation or contemplation, and blooming plants for every season. Inside, the house is decorated with antiques, family heirlooms, and collectibles that restore the ambiance of bygone days. Kay is semiretired and loves to read, garden, and do needlework.

Country Inn
ROUTE 3, BOX 1925, CLAREMORE, OKLAHOMA 74017

Tel: **(918) 342-1894**
Best Time to Call: **8 AM–8 PM**
Hosts: **Leland and Kay Jenkins**
Location: **25 mi. NE of Tulsa**
No. of Rooms: **3**
No. of Private Baths: **3**
Double/pb: **$52**
Single/pb: **$35**

Suite: **$65**
Open: **All year**
Reduced Rates: **10% seniors**
Breakfast: **Full**
Children: **No**
Smoking: **No**
Social Drinking: **Permitted**

Leland and Kay look forward to making you feel right at home in the charming barn-style guest quarters, separate from the main house. They invite you to enjoy the swimming pool, improve your suntan, or just sit back in the shade and enjoy a cool drink. The Will Rogers Memorial, the J. M. Davis Gun Museum, the 29,500-acre Oologah Lake, and Oral Roberts University are close by.

Clayton Country Inn ✪
ROUTE 1, BOX 8, HIGHWAY 271, CLAYTON, OKLAHOMA 74536

Tel: **(918) 569-4165, 747-1990**
Best Time to Call: **8 AM–9 PM**
Hosts: **Betty Lundgren, Eula and Al Taylor**
Location: **140 mi. SE of Tulsa**
No. of Rooms: **11**
No. of Private Baths: **11**
Double/pb: **$45**
Single/pb: **$39**

Guest Cottage: **$42; for 2**
Open: **All year**
Breakfast: **Continental**
Other Meals: **Available, dinner only**
Credit Cards: **AMEX, DISC, MC, VISA**
Pets: **No**
Children: **Welcome**
Smoking: **Permitted**
Social Drinking: **Permitted**

Perched on a hill amid 140 acres and surrounded by the Kiamichi Mountains is this 50-year-old, two-story, stone and wood inn. It's furnished in a simple, traditional style with a beamed ceiling and fireplace. The on-premises restaurant is noted for its fine cooking. Bass fishing at Lake Sardis is two miles away, and an 18,000-acre game preserve is just across the highway. Feel free to bring your horse and enjoy trail rides under the vast Western skies.

Holmberg House Bed & Breakfast ✪
766 DEBARR, NORMAN, OKLAHOMA 73069

Tel: **(405) 321-6221; (800) 646-6221**
Host: **Jo Meacham**
Location: **17 mi. S of Oklahoma City**
No. of Rooms: **4**
No. of Private Baths: **4**
Double/pb: **$65–$85**
Single/pb: **$55–$75**
Open: **All year**

Reduced Rates: **$10 less Sun.–Thurs.**
Breakfast: **Full**
Credit Cards: **AMEX, DISC, MC, VISA**
Pets: **No**
Children: **Welcome, over 12**
Smoking: **No**
Social Drinking: **Permitted**

Located in Norman's National Register Historic District and across the street from the University of Oklahoma's campus, this handsome 1914 Craftsman house was built by Professor Frederick Holmberg and his wife Signy. Jo bought the house in 1993 and it now accommodates many of the university's visiting scholars and parents. Guest rooms are individually decorated with antiques, private baths with claw-footed tubs, and color cable TVs. A parlor with a fireplace, porches with rockers, and gardens are for your pleasure. A hearty breakfast is served in the dining room.

Country House ✪
10101 OAKVIEW ROAD, OKLAHOMA CITY, OKLAHOMA 73165

Tel: **(405) 794-4008**
Best Time to Call: **8 AM–10 PM**
Hosts: **Dee and Nancy Ann Curnutt**
Location: **10 mi. SE of center of
    Oklahoma City**
No. of Rooms: **2**
No. of Private Baths: **2**
Double/pb: **$70–$90**

Single/pb: **$60–$80**
Open: **All year**
Breakfast: **Full**
Pets: **Sometimes**
Children: **Welcome**
Smoking: **Restricted**
Social Drinking: **Permitted**

At Country House you will find genuine, old-fashioned hospitality in a warm romantic setting. The house rests on five beautiful acres; the interior is tastefully furnished with 19th-century antiques and country collectibles. Nancy offers in-room color TV on request, as well as a scrumptious breakfast served on the balcony if you wish. For fishing, water sports, and horseback riding go to nearby Lake Draper, where Captain Dee, Nancy's husband, runs a charter boat service. Ask about the large red heart-shaped whirlpool suite.

For key to listings, see inside front or back cover.

✪ This star means that rates are guaranteed through December 31, 1998, to any guest making a reservation as a result of reading about the B&B in *Bed & Breakfast U.S.A.*—1998 edition.

Important! To avoid misunderstandings, always ask about cancellation policies when booking.

Please enclose a self-addressed, stamped, business-size envelope when contacting reservation services.

For more details on what you can expect in a B&B, see Chapter 1.

Always mention *Bed & Breakfast U.S.A.* when making reservations!

We want to hear from you! Use the form on page 625.

OREGON

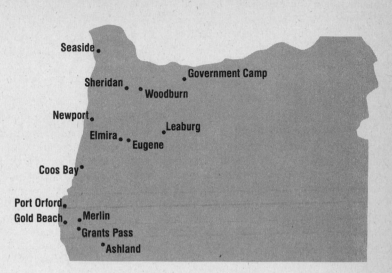

Northwest Bed and Breakfast Reservation Service
1067 HANOVER COURT SOUTH, SALEM, OREGON 97302-6002

Tel: **(503) 243-7616, 370-9033; fax:
(503) 316-9118**
Best Time to Call: **8 AM–5 PM**
Coordinator: **David and Betty
Hickerson**
States/Regions Covered: **Pacific
Northwest, British Columbia**

Rates (Single/Double):
  Modest: **$60–$80**
  Average: **$80–$100**
  Luxury: **$100–up**
Credit Cards: **AMEX, DISC, MC, VISA**

Northwest Bed and Breakfast Reservation Service is a network established in 1979. The Hickersons list hundreds of homes and inns throughout the Pacific Northwest, including British Columbia.

Cowslip's Belle Bed & Breakfast ✪

159 NORTH MAIN STREET, ASHLAND, OREGON 97520
stay@cowslip.com; http://www.cowslip.com/cowslip

Tel: **(800) 888-6819; (541) 488-2901;** fax: **(541) 482-6138**	Breakfast: **Full**
Hosts: **Jon and Carmen Reinhardt**	Credit Cards: **MC, VISA**
Location: **285 mi. S of Portland**	Pets: **No**
No. of Rooms: **4**	Children: **Welcome, over 10**
No. of Private Baths: **4**	Smoking: **No**
Double/pb: **$95–$130**	Social Drinking: **Permitted**
Single/pb: **$85–$125**	Minimum Stay: **2 nights weekends June–Sept.**
Open: **All year**	Airport/Station Pickup: **Yes**
Reduced Rates: **Available**	

From the moment you step inside this 1913 Craftsman bungalow or its adjacent carriage house, you will receive modern-day comfort sprinkled with old-fashioned hospitality. Snuggle up to one of the resident teddy bears. Guest rooms have luxurious queen beds, caressed by soft white linens, down comforters, and air-conditioning. Indulge your sweet tooth with a melt-in-your-mouth homemade chocolate truffle, placed on your pillow when your bed is turned down each evening. Daily fare includes a scrumptious breakfast with a hearty serving of lively conversation. Whether you wish to explore Ashland by foot or by car, Jon and Carmen will be happy to help you plan your itinerary and assist you with reservations for dinner, bike rentals, and raft trips.

The Woods House Bed & Breakfast Inn ✪

333 NORTH MAIN STREET, ASHLAND, OREGON 97520
woodshse@mind.net

Tel: **(541) 488-1598; (800) 435-8260;** fax: **(541) 482-8027**	Reduced Rates: **Available**
Best Time to Call: **10 AM–10 PM**	Breakfast: **Full**
Hosts: **Françoise and Lester Roddy**	Credit Cards: **MC, VISA**
Location: **4 blks. N of Downtown Plaza**	Pets: **No**
No. of Rooms: **6**	Children: **Welcome, over 12**
No. of Private Baths: **6**	Smoking: **No**
Double/pb: **$65–$118**	Social Drinking: **Permitted**
Single/pb: **$65–$113**	Minimum Stay: **2 days June–Oct.; weekends Nov.–May**
Open: **All year**	Station Pickup: **Yes**

The Woods House is located in Ashland's historic district four blocks from the Shakespearean theater, shops, restaurants, and 100-acre Lithia Park. The Inn, a 1908 Craftsman home renovated in 1984, has six sunny and spacious guest rooms. Simple furnishings, comprising warm woods, antique furniture and linens, watercolors, oriental carpets, and leather books, combine with high-quality amenities to create a sophisticated comfortable atmosphere. The terraced English gardens provide many areas for guests to relax and socialize. Françoise previously worked in human resources and event planning and is skilled in calligraphy, cooking, and needlecrafts. Lester has spent the past 25 years in business management and consulting. Their aim is to make each guest feel like a special friend, not just a paying customer. They strive to anticipate guests' needs and cheerfully accommodate the unexpected, always maintaining the highest standards of cleanliness, cordiality, and fine food.

Old Tower House B&B ✪
476 NEWMARK AVENUE, COOS BAY, OREGON 97420

Tel: **(541) 888-6058**; fax: **(541) 888-6058**
Hosts: **Don and Julia Spangler**
Location: **5 mi. W of Coos Bay**
No. of Rooms: **3**
Max. No. Sharing Bath: **4**
Double/sb: **$65–$85**
Guest Cottage: **$65**
Suites: **$85**

Open: **All year**
Breakfast: **Full**
Credit Cards: **DISC, MC, VISA**
Pets: **No**
Children: **Welcome, over 10, by arrangement**
Social Drinking: **No**
Airport Pickup: **Yes**

Built in 1872, this Victorian home is on the National Historic Register and is furnished with antiques throughout. All three guest rooms have pedestal sinks and share two full baths with clawfoot tubs. For relaxing, a spacious parlor is offered. For seclusion you might want to enjoy the Carriage House loft suite with a queen-size bed, clawfoot tub, kitchen, and sitting room with TV, or the Ivy Cottage with a double bed and a private bath.

McGillivray's Log Home Bed and Breakfast ✪
88680 EVERS ROAD, ELMIRA, OREGON 97437

Tel: **(541) 935-3564**
Best Time to Call: **8 AM–8 PM**
Host: **Evelyn McGillivray**
Location: **14 mi. W of Eugene**
No. of Rooms: **2**
No. of Private Baths: **2**
Double/pb: **$70–$80**
Single/pb: **$60–$70**

Open: **All year**
Breakfast: **Full**
Credit Cards: **MC, VISA**
Pets: **No**
Children: **By arrangement**
Smoking: **No**
Social Drinking: **Permitted**

This massive home is situated on five acres covered with pines and firs. The air-conditioned structure is designed with six types of wood, and features a split-log staircase. Guests may choose from a spacious, wheelchair accessible bedroom, or an upstairs room that can accommodate a family. All are beautifully decorated in a classic Americana motif. Evelyn usually prepares buttermilk pancakes using an antique griddle her mother used to use. She also offers fresh-squeezed juice from farm-grown apples and grapes, fresh bread, eggs, and all the trimmings. It's just three miles to a local vineyard; country roads for bicycling and a reservoir for fishing and boating are close by.

Maryellen's Guest House
1583 FIRCREST, EUGENE, OREGON 97403

Tel: **(541) 342-7375**
Best Time to Call: **9 AM–9 PM**
Hosts: **Maryellen and Bob Larson**
Location: **1 mi. off I-5, Exit 191-192**
No. of Rooms: **2**
No. of Private Baths: **2**
Double/pb: **$82**
Single/pb: **$72**
Open: **All year**

Reduced Rates: **10% weekly**
Breakfast: **Full**
Other Meals: **Available**
Credit Cards: **MC, VISA**
Pets: **No**
Children: **Welcome, over 12**
Smoking: **No**
Social Drinking: **Permitted**
Airport/Station Pickup: **Yes**

Maryellen's Guest House is a contemporary hillside home with casual elegance. This B&B is close to the University of Oregon, Hendrick's Park, and shopping. Each guest room is private and spacious with a sitting area, TV, and phone. A guest refrigerator, games, books, bicycles, and a pool and hot tub located on the spacious cedar decks are available for your enjoyment. A bountiful breakfast is served in the dining room, or you may request special room service.

The Oval Door ✪
988 LAWRENCE STREET, EUGENE, OREGON 97401

Tel: **(541) 683-3160; fax: (541) 485-5339; (800) 882-3160**
Hosts: **Judith McLane and Dianne Feist**
No. of Rooms: **4**
No. of Private Baths: **4**
Double/pb: **$70–$95**
Single/pb: **$60–$90**
Open: **All year**

Breakfast: **Full**
Credit Cards: **AMEX, DC, MC, VISA**
Pets: **No**
Children: **By arrangement**
Smoking: **No**
Social Drinking: **Permitted**
Minimum Stay: **2 nights during conventions, University functions**

This inviting 1920s-style farmhouse was built as a B&B in 1990. From its location in the heart of downtown Eugene, it's an easy walk to fine restaurants and the Hult Performing Arts Center. The University of Oregon campus is also nearby. Scrumptious breakfasts include a seasonal fruit dish, homemade breads, and a special entree, such as zucchini filbert waffles. You'll also find extra touches like terry robes, Perrier water, Frango Mints, and the Tub Room with its whirlpool bath for two, music, candles, and bubbles.

Pookie's Bed 'n' Breakfast on College Hill ✪
2013 CHARNELTON STREET, EUGENE, OREGON 97405

Tel: **(541) 343-0383; (800) 558-0383**
Hosts: **Pookie and Doug Walling**
Location: **110 mi. S of Portland**
No. of Rooms: **2**

No. of Private Baths: **1**
Max. No. Sharing Bath: **4**
Double/pb: **$80–$90**
Single/pb: **$70–$80**

Double/sb: **$65**
Single/sb: **$55**
Open: **All year**
Reduced Rates: **20% families**
Breakfast: **Full**

Pets: **No**
Children: **Welcome, over 6**
Smoking: **No**
Social Drinking: **Permitted**

Although it has been remodeled on the outside, this Craftsman-style house, built in 1918, retains much of its original interior charm. One room has antique mahogany furniture and a queen-size bed; the other has oak furnishings and either a king or twin beds. Pookie's is in a quiet older neighborhood just south of downtown, where you'll find great shopping, excellent dining, and access to the Hult Performing Arts Center. The University of Oregon campus is all of a mile away. Early morning coffee is served in the small sitting room upstairs. A full breakfast, with specialties like quiche and orange custard baked French toast, follows.

Endicott Gardens ✪
95768 JERRY'S FLAT ROAD, GOLD BEACH, OREGON 97444

Tel: **(541) 247-6513**
Best Time to Call: **10 AM–noon**
Hosts: **Beverly and Mary Endicott**
No. of Rooms: **4**
No. of Private Baths: **4**
Double/pb: **$55**
Single/pb: **$45**

Open: **All year**
Breakfast: **Continental, plus**
Pets: **No**
Children: **Welcome**
Smoking: **Restricted**
Social Drinking: **Permitted**

This classic contemporary B&B is across the road from Rogue River, famous for fishing and riverboat trips to white water. The guest rooms are located in a private wing of the house with decks overlooking the forest, mountains, and beautiful grounds. Homegrown strawberries, blueberries, apples, and plums are often featured in delicious breakfast treats served on the deck or in the dining room. In cool weather, the living room with its cozy fireplace is a favorite gathering spot. Beverly and Mary will be happy to share their collection of restaurant menus from nearby eating establishments with you.

Falcon's Crest Inn ✪
87287 GOVERNMENT CAMP LOOP HIGHWAY (MAILING ADDRESS: P.O. BOX 185, GOVERNMENT CAMP, OREGON 97028)

Tel: **(503) 272-3403; (800) 624-7384**
Hosts: **BJ and Melody Johnson**
Location: **54 mi. E of Portland**
No. of Rooms: **5**
No. of Private Baths: **5**
Double/pb: **$95–$99.50**
Suites: **$169–$179; sleeps 2**

Open: **All year**
Reduced Rates: **Nov.–Mar.; with ski package, multiple nights**
Breakfast: **Full**
Other Meals: **Available**
Credit Cards: **AMEX, DISC, MC, VISA**
Pets: **No**

Children: **Welcome, over 6**	Social Drinking: **Permitted**
Smoking: **No**	Airport/Station Pickup: **Yes**

Falcon's Crest Inn is nestled among the firs on the 4000-foot level of Mount Hood. The two-story glass front of this elegant, intimate B&B provides a spectacular view of Ski Bowl, a year-round recreational area. Duffers can head to the 27-hole championship course just 12 miles from the front door, and those who love water sports can occupy themselves with fishing, swimming, and white-water rafting. The bedrooms, which are decorated with family heirlooms and keepsakes, have forest or mountain views. In the morning, fresh muffins and a beverage are delivered to your door. Then you'll breakfast on hearty fare like buttermilk pancakes, waffles, or French toast.

Ahlf House Bed & Breakfast ✪
762 N.W. 6TH STREET, GRANTS PASS, OREGON 97526

Tel: **(541) 474-1374; (800) 863-1374**	Open: **All year**
Hosts: **Ken and Cathy Neuschafer**	Breakfast: **Full**
Location: **2 blocks from downtown**	Pets: **No**
Grants Pass	Children: **No**
No. of Rooms: **4**	Smoking: **No**
Double/pb: **$65–$95**	Social Drinking: **Permitted**
Single/pb: **$60–$90**	Airport/Station Pickup: **Yes**

Ahlf House is located on a main street on a hill overlooking the surrounding mountains. The house dates back to 1902, and is listed on the National Register of Historic Places. The rooms are beautifully appointed and furnished in fine antiques. Guest rooms feature fluffy comforters, down pillows, fresh flowers, and candles. Enjoy a cup of fresh coffee first thing in the morning in the quiet of your room or on the sunny front porch. Your coffee is followed by a full gourmet breakfast including fruit, fresh-baked muffins, and homemade jams and jellies. There is much to explore in Grants Pass, which is set on the Rogue River and is surrounded by the beautiful Cascade Mountains. Your hosts can direct you to guided fishing, raft trips, and jet boats. In the evening, return to this lovely Victorian for evening dessert.

Marjon Bed and Breakfast Inn ✪
44975 LEABURG DAM ROAD, LEABURG, OREGON 97489

Tel: **(541) 896-3145**	Open: **All year**
Host: **Marguerite Haas**	Breakfast: **Full**
Location: **24 mi. E of Eugene**	Pets: **No**
No. of Rooms: **2**	Children: **No**
No. of Private Baths: **2**	Smoking: **Permitted**
Double/pb: **$95**	Social Drinking: **Permitted**
Suites: **$125**	Airport/Station Pickup: **Yes**

This cedar chalet is located on the banks of the McKenzie River. The suite overlooks the river and a secluded Japanese garden, and features a sunken bath. The other has a fish bowl shower and a view of a 100-year-old apple tree. Relax in the living room with its wraparound seating and massive stone fireplace. One of the walls is made entirely of glass with sliding doors that lead to a terrace that faces the river. A multicourse breakfast is served there on balmy days. Waterfalls, trout fishing, white-water rafting, and skiing are all nearby.

Pine Meadow Inn B&B ✪
1000 CROW ROAD, MERLIN, OREGON 97532

Tel: **(541) 471-6277; (800) 554-0806**	Reduced Rates: **10% weekly**
Hosts: **Maloy and Nancy Murdock**	Breakfast: **Full**
Location: **10 mi. NW of Grants Pass**	Pets: **No**
No. of Rooms: **4**	Children: **Welcome, over 8**
No. of Private Baths: **4**	Smoking: **No**
Double/pb: **$80–$110**	Social Drinking: **Permitted**
Open: **All year**	Minimum Stay: **No**

Secluded on nine acres of meadow and woods, Pine Meadow Inn B&B is styled after Midwestern farmhouses, and features a wraparound porch with comfortable wicker furniture. There are many exciting choices of things to do: white-water rafting, walking, biking, jogging, visiting the California redwoods, Crater Lake, the Shakespeare Festival, or historic Jacksonville. When your day is complete you might want to read a book from the library in the quiet sitting room, which has a fireplace. Or take a dip in the hot tub. All guest rooms have queen-size beds with private baths, window seat, or sitting area. Awake in the morning to a healthful gourmet breakfast.

Oar House Bed & Breakfast ✪
520 SOUTHWEST 2ND STREET, NEWPORT, OREGON 97365

Tel: **(800) 252-2358; (541) 265-9571**
Best Time to Call: **10 AM–9 PM**
Host: **Jan LeBrun**
No. of Rooms: **5**
No. of Private Baths: **5**
Double/pb: **$90–$110**
Suites: **$120**
Open: **All year**
Reduced Rates: **$10 less Nov.–May; $5 less multiple nights Mon.–Thurs. off-season**

Breakfast: **Full**
Credit Cards: **DISC, MC, VISA**
Pets: **No**
Children: **No**
Smoking: **No**
Social Drinking: **Permitted**
Minimum Stay: **2 nights holidays and special events**

The Oar House Bed & Breakfast was built over 100 years ago, and was renovated in 1993 to provide modern amenities. Its location allows guests to walk to the beach, the historic bay front, performing and visual arts centers, and excellent restaurants. A spacious living room with a bar area for beverages and snacks and a sitting room with a fireplace and a music system provide guests with both comfort and ambience. Following early coffee, Jan serves a gourmet-inspired breakfast in the dining room. A unique feature of the inn is its lighthouse tower, from which guests have spectacular views.

Home by the Sea Bed & Breakfast
444 JACKSON STREET, PORT ORFORD, OREGON 97465-0606
http://www.homebythesea.com

Tel: **(541) 332-2855**
Best Time to Call: **8 AM–8 PM**
Hosts: **Alan and Brenda Mitchell**
Location: **54 mi. N of California border**
No. of Rooms: **2**
No. of Private Baths: **2**
Double/pb: **$85–$95**
Suite: **$95; sleeps 2**

Open: **All year**
Breakfast: **Full**
Credit Cards: **MC, VISA**
Pets: **No**
Children: **No**
Smoking: **No**
Social Drinking: **Permitted**

Alan and Brenda built this contemporary home overlooking a stretch of the Oregon coast that will take your breath away. Both guest rooms have queen Oregon myrtlewood beds and cable TV. It's a short walk to restaurants, public beaches, historic Battle Rock Park, and the town's harbor, the home port of Oregon's only crane-launched commercial fishing fleet.

Anderson's Boarding House Bed & Breakfast ❶
208 NORTH HOLLADAY DRIVE, SEASIDE, OREGON 97138

Tel: **(503) 738-9055; (800) 995-4013**
Host: **Barb Edwards**
Location: **¹/₂ mi. from Rte. 101**
No. of Rooms: **6**
No. of Private Baths: **6**
Double/pb: **$75–$85**
Single/pb: **$70–$80**
Guest Cottage: **$115; sleeps 6, $600 weekly**

Open: **All year**
Reduced Rates: **Available**
Breakfast: **Full**
Credit Cards: **MC, VISA**
Pets: **No**
Children: **Welcome**
Smoking: **No**
Social Drinking: **Permitted**
Airport/Station Pickup: **Yes**

Located on the banks of the Necanicum River, this rustic Victorian was built as a private residence in 1898. During World War I, the house became a boarding home. After an extensive renovation, the wood walls and beamed ceilings have been restored to their original charm. Guest rooms feature brass or white iron beds, down quilts, family heirlooms, wicker, and wood. Claw-footed tubs, window seats, antiques, and a picture of grandma make you feel as if this house is your own. A fire is often burning in the fir-paneled parlor, and an old melody sounds just right on the old-fashioned Victrola. A 100-year-old guest cottage with wood paneling, country furnishings, bedroom, loft, and river view is also available. Breakfast specialties such as cheese-and-egg strata, orange French toast, and blueberry scones are served in the dining room or outside on the wraparound porch. The house is just four blocks from the ocean and two blocks from downtown.

Brightridge Farm Bed & Breakfast
18575 BRIGHTRIDGE ROAD, SHERIDAN, OREGON 97378

Tel: **(503) 843-5230**
Best Time to Call: **After 2 PM**
Hosts: **Bettyanne and Dick Shoaff**
Location: **11 mi. W of McMinnville**
No. of Rooms: **2**
No. of Private Baths: **2**
Double/pb: **$80–$85**
Single/pb: **$75–$80**

Open: **All year**
Breakfast: **Full**
Pets: **No**
Children: **No**
Smoking: **No**
Social Drinking: **Permitted**
Minimum Stay: **2 nights holiday weekends**

Located in the heart of Oregon's wine country, this unique farmhouse is a wonderfully peaceful and relaxing place. Enjoy great views of the beautiful Willamette Valley and the Coast Range from your rocking chair on the front porch. Guest rooms are comfortably decorated with queen-size beds; both rooms have private decks. Brightridge Farm is convenient to many wineries of Yamhill and Polk counties, art galleries, excellent restaurants, and antique shops, as well as bicycle and auto touring on the back roads. There is lots of wildlife to see. Your hosts raise Shetland sheep, a small friendly breed sometimes known to wag their tails when scratched. Bettyanne and Dick are retired and are interested in art, architecture, and theater.

The Carriage House ✪
515 SOUTH PACIFIC HIGHWAY, WOODBURN, OREGON 97071

Tel: **(503) 982-6321**
Best Time to Call: **Before 9 AM; after 6 PM**
Hosts: **Lawrence and Marilyn Paradis**
Location: **30 mi. S of Portland**
No. of Rooms: **2**
Max. No. Sharing Bath: **4**
Double/sb: **$50**
Single/sb: **$45**

Open: **All year**
Breakfast: **Full**
Credit Cards: **MC, VISA**
Pets: **Sometimes**
Children: **Welcome**
Smoking: **No**
Social Drinking: **Permitted**
Airport/Station Pickup: **Yes**
Foreign Languages: **French**

The Carriage House is a 1906 Victorian known for its peaceful country elegance. Completely restored, it is furnished with family treasures and heirloom quilts. Lawrence and Marilyn keep horses and an antique buggy in a carriage house next to the inn. This is an excellent location for visiting the Enchanted Forest, the Oregon State Fair, the Octoberfest in Mt. Angel, the Bach Festival, historic Champoeg, and numerous antique shops and wineries.

PENNSYLVANIA

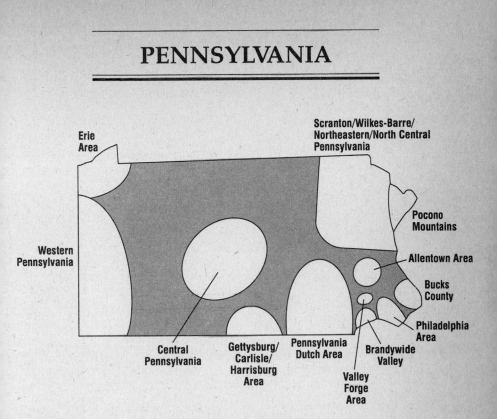

Erie Area

Scranton/Wilkes-Barre/Northeastern/North Central Pennsylvania

Pocono Mountains

Western Pennsylvania

Allentown Area

Bucks County

Philadelphia Area

Central Pennsylvania

Gettysburg/Carlisle/Harrisburg Area

Pennsylvania Dutch Area

Brandywide Valley

Valley Forge Area

Bed and Breakfast in Pennsylvania ✪
BOX 169, PINE GROVE MILLS, PENNSYLVANIA 16868

Tel: **(814) 861-6566; fax: (814) 234-9890**
Best Time to Call: **10 AM–2 PM Mon.–Fri.**

Coordinator: **Linda Feltman**
States/Regions Covered: **Pennsylvania Statewide**
Rates (Single/Double): **$50–$125**

Linda has been involved with Pennsylvania's bed and breakfasts since 1982, and has traveled extensively around the state. In 1995 she decided to share her knowledge of Pennsylvania's diverse bed and breakfasts and start her own reservation service, listing only those properties she has personally visited and, in most cases, stayed at overnight.

ALLENTOWN AREA

Brennans B&B ○

3827 LINDEN STREET, ALLENTOWN, PENNSYLVANIA 18104

Tel: **(610) 395-0869**
Best Time to Call: **7 AM–11 PM**
Hosts: **Lois and Edward Brennan**
Location: **1 mi. from 78 and 22**
No. of Rooms: **2**
No. of Private Baths: **1**
Max. No. Sharing Bath: **2**
Double/pb: **$40**
Single/pb: **$35**

Double/sb: **$30**
Single/sb: **$25**
Open: **Apr.–Dec.**
Breakfast: **Full**
Pets: **Sometimes**
Children: **Welcome**
Smoking: **Permitted**
Social Drinking: **Permitted**
Airport/Station Pickup: **Yes**

Furnished in Early American fashion, accented with lush plants and family treasures, this comfortable brick ranch-style house can be your home away from home. The Brennans are history buffs who, now that they're retired, enjoy traveling and entertaining travelers. Breakfast features bacon and eggs with home fries, or sausages and pancakes, or delicious muffins to go with the homemade jam. You can walk off the calories on your way to the Haines Mill, Dorney Park, or one of the area's many museums.

Around the World Bed & Breakfast ○

30 SOUTH WHITEOAK STREET, KUTZTOWN, PENNSYLVANIA 19530

Tel: **(610) 683-8885**
Hosts: **Jean and Joel Masiko**
Location: **15 mi. E/W of Allentown/
  Reading**
No. of Rooms: **2**
No. of Private Baths: **2**
Double/pb: **$79**
Single/pb: **$69**
Suites: **$75–$125**
Open: **All year**
Reduced Rates: **$10 less Dec.–March;
  10% seniors**

Breakfast: **Full**
Credit Cards: **DISC, MC, VISA**
Pets: **No**
Children: **Welcome, over 12**
Smoking: **No**
Social Drinking: **Permitted**
Minimum Stay: **2 nights Renninger's
  Antique Show, last week Apr., June,
  Sept.**
Airport/Station Pickup: **Yes**

Around the World Bed & Breakfast is located one half-block from Main Street, an antique lover's paradise in the heart of Pennsylvania Dutch countryside. Built in 1830, this brick Victorian still maintains the charm and character of a well-kept home. Rooms are authentically decorated with artifacts from around the world to suggest Australia, the Pacific Coast, western parts of North America, and the local Amish culture. All guest rooms have queen-size beds, phone, and air-conditioning. The suites have TV. Jean and Joel invite you to enjoy the landscaped gardens, complete with a lily pond and gazebo.

Longswamp Bed and Breakfast ✪
1605 STATE STREET, MERTZTOWN, PENNSYLVANIA 19539

Tel: **(610) 682-6197**
Hosts: **Elsa and Dean Dimick**
Location: **12 mi. SW of Allentown**
No. of Rooms: **10**
No. of Private Baths: **6**
Max. No. Sharing Bath: **4**
Double/pb: **$78–$83**
Single/pb: **$68**
Double/sb: **$78–$83**

Single/sb: **$68**
Open: **All year**
Breakfast: **Full**
Credit Cards: **AMEX, MC, VISA**
Pets: **No**
Children: **Welcome**
Smoking: **No**
Social Drinking: **Permitted**
Foreign Languages: **French**

This guesthouse was originally built around 1750 and served as the first post office in town. The main house, completed in 1863, was a stop on the Underground Railroad. Today, Longswamp is a comfortable place with high ceilings, antiques, large fireplaces, plants, and bookcases full of reading pleasure. Breakfast specialties include home-dried fruits, *pain perdu*, quiche, and homemade breads. Elsa offers wine, cheese, and coffee anytime. She will gladly direct you to antique shops, auction houses, Reading, and the Amish country.

Classic Victorian ✪
35 NORTH NEW STREET, NAZARETH, PENNSYLVANIA 18064

Tel: **(610) 759-8276**
Best time to call: **Morning–evenings**
Hosts: **Irene and Dan Sokolowski**
No. of Rooms: **3**
No. of Private Baths: **3**
Double/pb: **$80–$85**
Suite: **$105**
Open: **All year**
Reduced Rates: **10% weekly**

Breakfast: **Full**
Credit Cards: **AMEX, MC, VISA**
Pets: **No**
Children: **Welcome**
Smoking: **No**
Social Drinking: **Permitted**
Minimum Stay: **2 nights holiday weekends, special events**

Step into this circa 1908 brick Colonial Revival located in the historic district of Nazareth, the oldest Moravian settlement of North America. Classic Victorian offers a comfortable mix of antique and traditional furnishings coupled with a warm and relaxed atmosphere. Amenities include down-filled comforters, classical music, evening turn-down service, air-conditioning, TVs, and a three-course breakfast served on Wedgwood in the dining room, front veranda, or second-floor balcony. The Bach Festival in May and the Music Fest in August are 15 minutes away. Jacobsburg Environmental Education Center, within a ten-minute drive, offers hiking, bird-watching, nature photography, horseback riding, and 1166 acres of the great outdoors. Irene and Dan enjoy entertaining and restoring their Colonial Revival.

Reiff Farm Bed & Breakfast ✪
495 OLD STATE ROAD, OLEY, PENNSYLVANIA 19547

Tel: **(610) 987-6216**	Cabin: **$120**
Host: **John Moxon**	Open: **All year**
Location: **8 mi. E of Reading**	Reduced Rates: **10% seniors**
No. of Rooms: **5**	Breakfast: **Full**
No. of Private Baths: **2**	Pets: **No**
Max. No. Sharing Bath: **4**	Children: **Welcome**
Double/pb: **$60**	Smoking: **Permitted**
Double/sb: **$60**	Social Drinking: **Permitted**

Established in the early 1700s, this Pennsylvania Dutch homestead is listed on the National Register of Historic Places. Reiff Farm is nestled in the hills overlooking the Oley Valley, one mile from the center of town. The grounds feature over 200 acres of accessible foot and horse trails. The two-bedroom log cabin can be a family retreat or a honeymoon cottage. The main house has four bedrooms decorated with period antiques and lots of fireplaces. Guests are invited to spend a chilly evening in the library in front of the fire reading one of the many books on the history of Berks County; local artists are well-represented on the walls. To learn more about 18th-century life, a peek at the old forge, icehouse, spring, and smokehouse, as well as the summer kitchen and bake oven, is a must.

BRANDYWINE VALLEY

Bed & Breakfast at Walnut Hill ✪
541 CHANDLER'S MILL ROAD, AVONDALE, PENNSYLVANIA 19311

Tel: **(610) 444-3703**	Single/sb: **$70**
Best Time to Call: **Anytime**	Open: **All year**
Hosts: **Sandy and Tom Mills**	Breakfast: **Full**
Location: **2 mi. S of Kennett Square**	Pets: **No**
No. of Rooms: **2**	Children: **Welcome, over 2**
Max. No. Sharing Bath: **4**	Smoking: **Permitted**
Double/sb: **$85**	Social Drinking: **Permitted**

Sandy and Tom's 1844 mill house is in Kennett Square (despite the mailing address above) in the heart of the Brandywine Valley, midway between Philadelphia and Amish country. Longwood Gardens, Chadds Ford Winery, Winterthur, and other museums are all within an eight-mile radius. But nature lovers may want to stay on the B&B grounds, where horses graze in the meadow and a great blue heron fishes in the stream. Deer, Canada geese, and the occasional red fox also put in appearances. Guests enjoy walking along the country road, sitting on the wicker-filled porch, or relaxing in the hot tub. However you plan to spend your day, you'll begin it with breakfast specialties like cottage cheese pancakes with blueberry sauce, fresh mushroom omelettes, and

French toast. Sandy welcomes guests with lemonade, iced tea, hot cider, and homemade sweets.

Bankhouse Bed & Breakfast ❂
875 HILLSDALE ROAD, WEST CHESTER, PENNSYLVANIA 19382

Tel: (610) 344-7388
Best time to call: 2–10 PM
Hosts: Diana and Michael Bove
No. of Rooms: 2
No. of Private Baths: 1
Max. No. Sharing Bath: 4
Double/pb: $90
Double/sb: $70
Suite: $90

Open: All year
Reduced Rates: Available
Breakfast: Full
Pets: No
Children: Welcome, over 12
Smoking: No
Social Drinking: Permitted
Minimum Stay: 2 nights weekends
  May–Oct.

This 18th-century stuccoed stone bankhouse overlooks a 10-acre horse farm and pond. Bankhouse is conveniently located to Brandywine Valley attractions such as Longwood Gardens, Winterthur, and Brandywine River Museum. Philadelphia and Lancaster are only a 45-minute drive away. Guests have a private entrance, porch, and sitting room. The house is charmingly decorated with country antiques, folk art, stenciling, and a wall full of books and games. Michael is a production engineer in the media services department of a local college. Diana markets her cross-stitch and quilting projects, and prides herself on having more than 100 muffin recipes—you're sure to sample some of her homemade snacks.

BUCKS COUNTY

Plain & Fancy—Pennsylvania ❂
32 WILLIAMSBURG DRIVE, TOMS RIVER, NEW JERSEY 08755

Tel: (800) 374-STAY
Best Time to Call: 9 AM–5 PM
  Mon.–Sat.
Coordinator: Debbie Coccia
States/Regions Covered: Bird in Hand,
  Bucks County, Doylestown, Hershey,
  Lancaster, New Hope, Philadelphia,
  Poconos, Washington's Crossing

Descriptive Directory: Free
Rates (Single/Double):
  Modest: $50–$70
  Average: $75–$90
  Luxury: $95–$185
Credit Cards: AMEX, MC, VISA

Discriminating travelers will delight in the choices of over 100 inspected B&B and country inns available by Plain & Fancy. You will find a unique welcome tucked into the countryside or in one of the quaint towns. The service covers Lancaster, New Hope, and the Poconos in Pennsylvania as well as New Jersey, Vermont, and Key West, Florida. Whatever your selection, your visit will include a Continental or full country breakfast. Experience festivals, antique shops, and quaint restaurants.

Maplewood Farm Bed & Breakfast O
5090 DURHAM ROAD, P.O. BOX 239, GARDENVILLE,
PENNSYLVANIA 18926

Tel: **(215) 766-0477**
Best Time to Call: **10 AM–9 PM**
Hosts: **Cindy and Dennis Marquis**
Location: **45 mi. NW of Philadelphia**
No. of Rooms: **6**
No. of Private Baths: **6**
Double/pb: **$85**
Suite: **$135**
Open: **All year**

Reduced Rates: **Mon.–Thurs.**
Breakfast: **Full**
Credit Cards: **AMEX, DISC, MC, VISA**
Pets: **No**
Children: **Welcome, Sun.–Thurs.**
Smoking: **No**
Social Drinking: **Permitted**
Minimum Stay: **2 nights weekends, 3 nights holidays**

Hundred-year-old maples shelter this fieldstone farmhouse, dated 1792. The five-acre property includes a tranquil stream, sheep-filled pastures, and a two-story bank barn that houses playful barnyard cats. Inn rooms feature local antiques, cozy comforters, and handmade quilts. Choose Victoria's Room, with a four-poster bed and ceiling fan, or the two-story loft suite, with its exposed beams and sitting room. Upon your arrival, Cindy and Dennis will offer you refreshments in the antique summer kitchen, which boasts a double walk-in fireplace. For year-round fun, your hosts will direct you to Peddler's Village, New Hope, and lots of charming river towns. In the morning, gather eggs fresh from the source and have them turned into fluffy omelettes, crisp waffles, fruit-filled pancakes, or Dennis's famous French toast. Breakfast is served in the country dining room with random-width floors, beamed ceilings, and an exposed stone wall. After dinner, return to the inn to enjoy conversation and a nightcap with your hosts, and exchange tales of your day with the other guests. For those of you who don't mind paying a higher rate, 3 rooms are available.

Aaron Burr House O
80 WEST BRIDGE STREET, NEW HOPE, PENNSYLVANIA 18938

Tel: **(215) 862-2343, 862-2570**
Best Time to Call: **10 AM–10 PM**
Hosts: **Jesse and Carl Glassman**
Location: **20 mi. N of Philadelphia**
No. of Rooms: **6**
No. of Private Baths: **6**
Double/pb: **$75**
Single/pb: **$70**
Suites: **$95–$195; sleeps 3**
Open: **All year**

Reduced Rates: **Mon.–Thurs., corporate guests**
Breakfast: **Continental, plus**
Pets: **Sometimes**
Children: **Welcome**
Smoking: **No**
Social Drinking: **Permitted**
Minimum Stay: **2 nights on weekends, 3 nights holidays**
Station Pickup: **Yes**

This 1874 Victorian is tucked onto a tree-lined street in the town's historic district, just steps from the village center. New Hope was founded in 1681, so visitors can absorb three centuries of architecture and American history, plus fine antique shops, excellent restaurants, and art galleries and crafts shops. At the end of the day, join your host in the parlor for reading, games, refreshments, and friendly conversation. After a peaceful night's rest in a canopy bed, you'll wake up to the aroma of fresh coffee and home-baked muffins.

Wedgwood Inn of New Hope ✪
111 WEST BRIDGE STREET, NEW HOPE, PENNSYLVANIA 18938-1401

Tel: **(215) 862-2520**
Best Time to Call: **10 AM–10 PM**
Hosts: **Carl Glassman and
   Nadine Silnutzer**
Location: **62 mi. SW of New York City**
No. of Rooms: **12**
No. of Private Baths: **12**
Double/pb: **$70–$125**
Single/pb: **$65–$115**
Double/sb: **$65–$85**
Single/sb: **$60–$80**
Suites: **$90–$185**
Open: **All year**

Reduced Rates: **Available**
Breakfast: **Continental, plus**
Credit Cards: **AMEX, MC, VISA**
Pets: **Sometimes**
Children: **Welcome**
Smoking: **No**
Social Drinking: **Permitted**
Minimum Stay: **3 holiday weekends, 2
   nights if stay includes Saturday**
Station Pickup: **Yes**
Foreign Languages: **French, Hebrew,
   Spanish**

Wedgwood pottery is displayed throughout this aptly named two-and-a-half-story home with lots of 19th-century details: a gabled roof, veranda, porte cochere, and gazebo. Rooms are decorated with antiques, original art, handmade quilts, and fresh flowers. You can breakfast on house specialties like lemon yogurt poppyseed bread and ricotta pineapple muffins on the sunporch, in the gazebo, or in the privacy of your room. Carl and Nadine are such accomplished hosts that they conduct workshops and seminars on innkeeping, and Carl has taught courses on buying and operating country inns.

CARLISLE/HARRISBURG AREA

Line Limousin Farmhouse B&B ✪

2070 RITNER HIGHWAY, CARLISLE, PENNSYLVANIA 17013

Tel: **(717) 243-1281**
Hosts: **Bob and Joan Line**
Location: **22 mi. W of Harrisburg**
No. of Rooms: **4**
No. of Private Baths: **2**
Max. No. Sharing Bath: **4**
Double/pb: **$75**
Single/pb: **$65**
Double/sb: **$65**

Single/sb: **$55**
Open: **All year**
Breakfast: **Full**
Pets: **No**
Children: **Welcome, over 8**
Smoking: **No**
Social Drinking: **Permitted**
Minimum Stay: **3 nights car shows**
Airport/Station Pickup: **Yes**

Bob's great-grandfather built this eleven-room stone and brick house in 1864, using walnut wood from the farm for all the woodwork. Rooms are furnished with family heirlooms—some older than the house—and have fresh flowers, air-conditioning, and cable TV. A hearty breakfast is served in an antique-filled dining room on Limoges china. A refrigerator for guest use is stocked with juice and soft drinks. Bob and Joan raise Limousin beef cattle from Limoges, France. If you're tired of artificial, mass-produced country decor, come and experience the real thing.

CENTRAL PENNSYLVANIA

Rest & Repast Bed & Breakfast Service ✪
P.O. BOX 126, PINE GROVE MILLS, PENNSYLVANIA 16868

Tel: **(814) 238-1484**
Best Time to Call: **8:30–11:30 AM Mon.–Fri.**
Coordinators: **Linda and Brent Peters**
States/Regions Covered: **Aaronsburg, Bellefonte, Boalsburg, Clearfield,**

Phillipsburg, Potters Mills, Spruce Creek, State College, Tyrone
Rates (Single/Double):
  Average: **$50–$55 / $55–$65**
  Luxury: **$60–$75 / $75–$100**
Credit Cards: **No**

You will enjoy touring historic mansions, Penns Cave, Woodward Cave, and several Civil War museums in this lovely area. A two-day minimum stay is required for the second week in July, the time of the annual Central Pennsylvania Festival of the Arts, and for all Penn State University home games in autumn. Rates are increased during peak weekends to a maximum of $100 per night double. (No single rates on peak PSU weekends.) Pennsylvania State University is close by.

Christopher Kratzer House ✪
101 EAST CHERRY STREET, CLEARFIELD, PENNSYLVANIA 16830

Tel: **(814) 765-5024; (888) 252-2632**
Hosts: **Bruce and Ginny Baggett**
No. of Rooms: **3**
No. of Private Baths: **1**
Max. No. Sharing Bath: **4**
Double/pb: **$70**
Single/pb: **$55**
Double/sb: **$55**
Single/sb: **$45**

Open: **All year**
Reduced Rates: **10% after 3rd night**
Breakfast: **Full**
Credit Cards: **MC, VISA**
Pets: **No**
Children: **Welcome**
Smoking: **Permitted**
Social Drinking: **Permitted**
Airport/Station Pickup: **Yes**

This Classic Revival House, located in the Old Town Historic District, was built prior to 1840 by Christopher Kratzer, a noted lumberman, carpenter, architect, politician, and owner of the county's first newspaper. Bruce and Ginny have filled the rooms with an interesting mix of historical and contemporary pieces that reflect their interest in music and art. The house has views of the river and park, white picket fences, a spacious yard and large old trees. You'll be within walking distance of shops, an antique emporium, library, restaurants, movie theater, and the Clearfield County Historical Society Museum. Activities nearby include boating, fishing, and hiking; Penn State University football stadium is less than an hour away.

Victorian Loft Bed & Breakfast ✪
216 SOUTH FRONT STREET, CLEARFIELD, PENNSYLVANIA 16830

Tel: (814) 765-4805; (800) 798-0456
Best Time to Call: Evenings
Hosts: Tim and Peggy Durant
Location: 40 mi. NW of State College
No. of Rooms: 3
Max. No. Sharing Bath: 4
Double/pb: $65–$75
Single/pb: $60–$70
Double/sb: $50–$60
Single/sb: $45–$55
Suites: $85–$105

Cabin: $65–$100
Open: All year
Reduced Rates: 10% over 3 nights
Breakfast: Full
Credit Cards: AMEX, DISC, MC, VISA
Pets: Sometimes
Children: Welcome
Smoking: No
Social Drinking: No
Airport/Station Pickup: Yes

Victorian charm fills this elegant 1894 riverfront home in the historic district, from the double-decker gingerbread porches to the grand staircase and original stained glass windows. Yet it's only minutes to myriad outdoor recreational activities—the B&B is just three miles off Exit 19 on I-80. Amenities, in addition to warm hospitality, include a memorable full breakfast, air-conditioned rooms with skylights, a private kitchen and dining room, a guest entertainment center, and a whirlpool bath. For those interested in clothing and textile design, Peggy, a fiber enthusiast, gives spinning demonstrations on request.

North Bend Bed & Breakfast ✪
P.O. BOX 214, ROUTE 120, JOHN AVENUE, NORTH BEND, PENNSYLVANIA 17760

Tel: (717) 923-2927
Best Time to Call: 6 PM–10 PM
Hosts: Barbara and John Mastriania
Location: 24 mi. W of Lock Haven
No. of Rooms: 4
Max. No. Sharing Bath: 4
Double/sb: $56
Single/sb: $54

Open: All year
Reduced Rates: Jan.–Feb. 2 nights $99
Breakfast: Full
Credit Cards: AMEX, DISC, MC, VISA
Pets: No
Children: Welcome
Smoking: Permitted
Social Drinking: Permitted

Nestled in the heart of Pennsylvania's Keystone Mountain country, North Bend Bed & Breakfast offers a peaceful getaway. Barbara and John operate an antique shop located on the premises. Breakfast features homemade breads and is served in a large dining room. Guests are invited to have early morning coffee in the cozy kitchen featuring a radiator with a built-in warmer, or on the front porch in warm weather. This area is ideal for outdoor enthusiasts and those who love to visit the roads less traveled.

ERIE AREA

Raspberry House Bed & Breakfast ✪
118 ERIE STREET, ROUTE 99, EDINBORO, PENNSYLVANIA 16412

Tel: **(814) 734-8997**
Best Time to Call: **After 6 PM weekdays, anytime on weekends**
Hosts: **Betty and Hal Holmstrom**
Location: **20 mi. S of Erie**
No. of Rooms: **4**
No. of Private Baths: **4**
Double/pb: **$80**
Single/pb: **$55**
Open: **All year**

Reduced Rates: **Available**
Breakfast: **Full**
Pets: **No**
Children: **Welcome**
Smoking: **No**
Social Drinking: **Permitted**
Minimum Stay: **2 nights on Edinboro homecoming weekend**
Airport/Station Pickup: **Yes**

Raspberry House Bed & Breakfast is an 1860 Victorian home that has been restored to its original charm. Located in the heart of Edinboro, this B&B allows guests the opportunity to enjoy biking, skiing, boating, golf, historical attractions, shopping, and university activities. Breakfast is served daily, with accommodation for special dietary needs; wake-up coffee can be served in your room. A common room for guests is furnished with a TV, VCR, and telephone. All guest rooms are individually decorated and have a private bath.

GETTYSBURG AREA

Shultz Victorian Mansion Bed & Breakfast ✪
756 PHILADELPHIA AVENUE, CHAMBERSBURG, PENNSYLVANIA 17225

Tel: **(717) 263-3371**
Best Time to Call: **8 AM–9 PM**
Hosts: **Doris and Joe Shultz**
Location: **23 mi. W of Gettysburg**
No. of Rooms: **9**
No. of Private Baths: **9**
Double/pb: **$63–$85**
Single/pb: **$58–$80**
Suites: **$115**

Open: **All year**
Reduced Rates: **10% Jan.–Mar.; after 4th night**
Breakfast: **Full**
Credit Cards: **MC, VISA**
Pets: **No**
Children: **Welcome, over 10**
Smoking: **No**
Social Drinking: **Permitted**

Shultz Victorian Mansion Bed & Breakfast is located twenty-four miles north of Hagerstown, Maryland, along a tree-lined street in a charming neighborhood. This 1880 Victorian brick home has an onion-topped turret and elaborate wood carving throughout. Guests are invited to enjoy three common rooms, large porches and gardens, balcony, air-conditioning, and the family collection of antiques. Wilson College, Shippensburg University, two state parks, Mercersburg Academy, and Dickenson College and Law School are all within minutes of this bed and breakfast. Breakfast is served by candlelight.

The Brafferton Inn
44 YORK STREET, GETTYSBURG, PENNSYLVANIA 17325

Tel: **(717) 337-3423**
Best Time to Call: **9 AM–9 PM**
Hosts: **Jane and Sam Back**
Location: **90 mi. N of Washington, D.C.;**
  2 mi. from Rte 15 York Street exit
No. of Rooms: **10**
No. of Private Baths: **10**
Double/pb: **$80–$100**

Suites: **$110–$125**
Open: **All year**
Breakfast: **Full**
Credit Cards: **AMEX, DISC, MC, VISA**
Pets: **No**
Children: **Welcome, over 7**
Smoking: **No**
Social Drinking: **Permitted**

Listed on the National Register of Historic Places, the Brafferton Inn is a landmark in the historic town of Gettysburg. This 1786 fieldstone home has been fully restored and decorated with exquisite antiques and original artistry throughout. The Inn combines elegance and ease. Warm-colored oriental rugs, comfortable wingbacks, and a tall 1800 grandfather clock grace the living room. The dining room boasts a stunning folk art mural. A deck and an in-town garden provide guests with quiet getaway spots.

Country Escape ✪
275 OLD ROUTE 30, P.O. BOX 195, MCKNIGHTSTOWN, PENNSYLVANIA 17343

Tel: **(717) 338-0611**
Hosts: **Merry V. Bush and Ross Hetrick**
Location: **6 mi. W of Gettysburg**
No. of Rooms: **3**
No. of Private Baths: **1**
Max. No. Sharing Bath: **4**
Double/pb: **$75**
Double/sb: **$50**

Open: **All year**
Breakfast: **Full**
Credit Cards: **AMEX, DISC, MC, VISA**
Pets: **Sometimes**
Children: **Welcome**
Smoking: **No**
Social Drinking: **Permitted**

Country Escape Bed and Breakfast is located on the road the Confederates took to Gettysburg. The house was built in 1868, and is located 5 miles from the famous battlefield. Rooms are furnished in country decor with some antiques. Local crafts are displayed throughout and are for sale. The extensive gardens include a pond, and the mountains can be seen in the distance. Merry and Ross invite you to come and immerse yourself in history or relax in a quiet atmosphere. Merry runs a desktop publishing company, and Ross owns a used bookshop/coffee bar in Gettysburg.

Fox Run Inn ✪
14873 BAIN ROAD, MERCERSBURG, PENNSYLVANIA 17236

Tel: **(717) 328-3570**
Best Time to Call: **After 8 PM**
Hosts: **Dick and Elsie Secrest**

Location: **54 mi. NW of Washington, D.C.**
No. of Rooms: **4**

No. of Private Baths: **4**
Double/pb: **$65**
Open: **All year**
Breakfast: **Full**
Credit Cards: **MC, VISA**

Pets: **No**
Children: **Welcome, over 12**
Smoking: **No**
Social Drinking: **Permitted**

Built in 1786, this authentically restored farmhouse is surrounded by 170 acres of fields with walking trails. The Inn's views of the countryside and Tuscarora Mountain are spectacular. The kitchen and dining area have open beamed ceilings and an exposed log wall in the dining area. Each of the four bedrooms has private baths and three have queen-size beds. Guests have full use of the house including the always full cookie jar. Barbecue facilities are also provided. Whitetail Ski Resort, Mercersburg Academy, State Parks, Antietam Battlefield, country auctions and antique shops, and Fort Frederick are among the nearby attractions.

PENNSYLVANIA DUTCH AREA

Adamstown Inns ✪
62 WEST MAIN STREET, ADAMSTOWN, PENNSYLVANIA 19501

Tel: **(717) 484-0800; (800) 594-4808**
Hosts: **Tom and Wanda Berman**
Location: **10 mi. SW of Reading**
No. of Rooms: **7**
No. of Private Baths: **7**

Double/pb: **$70–$80**
Suite: **$105–$135**
Open: **All year**
Reduced Rates: **10% after 4th night**
Breakfast: **Continental, plus**

Credit Cards: **MC, VISA**
Pets: **No**
Children: **Welcome, over 12**

Smoking: **Restricted**
Social Drinking: **Permitted**

In the heart of Adamstown's antique district, and just a short drive from Pennsylvania Dutch country and Reading's factory outlets, you'll find Victorian B&B—the Adamstown Inn and the Amethyst Inn. Inside, lace and balloon curtains and oriental rugs complement the chestnut wood-work and leaded-glass doors. Five rooms feature two-person Jacuzzis. Three rooms also include gas log fireplaces. Your hosts are avid an-tiquers and will gladly direct you to their favorite haunts. Coffee or tea will be brought to your door in the morning; refills, as well as juice, fresh fruit, cheese, and home-baked goodies are served during a Conti-nental breakfast.

Mill Creek Homestead Bed & Breakfast ✪
2578 OLD PHILADELPHIA PIKE, BIRD-IN-HAND, PENNSYLVANIA 17505

Tel: **(717) 291-6419; (800) 771-2578**
Hosts: **Vicki and Frank Alfone**
Location: **5 mi. E of Lancaster**
No. of Rooms: **3**
No. of Private Baths: **3**
Double/pb: **$65–$80**
Single/pb: **$55–$70**
Suites: **$95–$130**
Open: **All year**

Reduced Rates: **Available**
Breakfast: **Full**
Credit Cards: **DISC, MC, VISA**
Pets: **No**
Children: **Welcome, over 10**
Smoking: **No**
Social Drinking: **Permitted**
Minimum Stay: **2 nights holidays**

Mill Creek Homestead is the second oldest home in Bird-In-Hand. This fieldstone farmhouse was built in the eighteenth century, but it has cen-tral air-conditioning, and is gracefully decorated with treasured family pieces and locally made Amish quilts. Before beginning your day of activities, enjoy a hearty breakfast served in the formal dining room. Upon returning, enjoy complimentary light refreshments and a dip in the pool on those hot summer days. Or pull up a rocking chair on the porch and watch the horse and buggies while sipping your first cup of coffee or that cool glass of iced tea. There are so many things to do and see that there will be no time for phones or TV.

The Enchanted Cottage ✪
RD 4, 22 DEER RUN ROAD, BOYERTOWN, PENNSYLVANIA 19512

Tel: **(610) 845-8845**
Hosts: **Peg and Richard Groff**
Location: **16 mi. S of Allentown**
No. of Private Baths: **1**
Double/pb: **$90**
Single/pb: **$80**
Open: **All year**

Reduced Rates: **$5 less Mon.–Thurs. except holidays and special events**
Breakfast: **Full**
Pets: **No**
Children: **Welcome, over 12**
Smoking: **Permitted**
Social Drinking: **Permitted**

Complete privacy awaits you in this cozy cottage nestled in a clearing in the woods. Downstairs, the exposed beams, wood-burning fireplace, quilts, and antique furniture lend themselves to quiet, romantic evenings. On the second floor you'll find an air-conditioned double bedroom and a Laura Ashley bathroom. Gourmet breakfasts are served in the main house in front of either the garden or a cheerful fire, depending on the season. While the cottage is a destination in itself, you'll have easy access to the Pennsylvania Dutch area, the Reading factory outlets, antique shops, historic sites, and country auctions. An excellent restaurant is within walking distance.

The Columbian ❂
360 CHESTNUT STREET, COLUMBIA, PENNSYLVANIA 17512
bedandb@aol.com; http://www.user.aol.com/bedandb

Tel: **(717) 684-5869**	Breakfast: **Full**
Hosts: **Chris and Becky Will**	Credit Cards: **MC, VISA**
Location: **8 mi. W of Lancaster**	Pets: **No**
No. of Rooms: **5**	Children: **Welcome**
No. of Private Baths: **5**	Smoking: **No**
Double/pb: **$65–$99**	Social Drinking: **Permitted**
Suites: **$99**	Minimum Stay: **2 nights June–Oct.,**
Open: **All year**	**holiday weekends**
Reduced Rates: **10% seniors; after 4th**	Airport/Station Pickup: **Yes**
night	

Built in 1896, this brick Colonial Revival mansion features an ornate stained glass window, tiered staircase, and unique wraparound porches. The Columbian is centrally located minutes from the local attractions in the historic river town of Columbia, a onetime stop on the Underground Railroad that came within two votes of becoming the capital of the United States. This is a porch-sitting town where you can still get a malted at the local drugstore. Come relax with Becky and Chris in their lovely bed and breakfast and browse through nearby antique shops, art galleries, museums, and enjoy ice cream from Chris and Becky's seasonal ice cream shop on the premises.

George Zahm House Bed & Breakfast ❂
6070 MAIN STREET, EAST PETERSBURG, PENNSYLVANIA 17520

Tel: **(717) 569-6026**	Breakfast: **Continental, plus**
Hosts: **Robyn Kemple-Keeports and Jeff**	Credit Cards: **MC, VISA**
Keeports	Pets: **No**
Location: **4 mi. N of Lancaster**	Children: **Welcome, over 12**
No. of Rooms: **4**	Smoking: **No**
No. of Private Baths: **4**	Social Drinking: **Permitted**
Double/pb: **$65**	Minimum Stay: **2 nights weekends and**
Suites: **$85**	**holidays**
Open: **All year**	
Reduced Rates: **10% seniors, weekly,**	
corporate	

A Federal home built in 1854 and restored, George Zahm House boasts ten-foot ceilings throughout and is richly furnished with an eclectic collection of family heirlooms and antiques. Three restaurants are within walking distance and Lancaster City is only a ten-minute drive away. Robyn, her mother Daneen, and Jeff all planned and worked on the renovations and decor of the inn and enjoy refinishing furniture, antiquing, and going to auctions. Breakfast is served on Blue Willow china in the formal dining room and includes homemade breads, jams, Belgian waffles, granolas, and seasonal fresh fruit.

Elm Country Inn Bed & Breakfast ✪
P.O. BOX 37, ELM AND NEWPORT ROADS, ELM, PENNSYLVANIA 17521

Tel: **(717) 664-3623; (800) 245-0532;**
   fax: **(717) 664-2734**
Best Time to Call: **After 4:30 PM**
Hosts: **Betty and Melvin Meck**
Location: **12 mi. N of Lancaster**
No. of Rooms: **2**
Max. No. Sharing Bath: **4**
Double/pb: **$65**
Double/sb: **$50–$55**
Single/sb: **$35**

Open: **All year**
Reduced Rates: **Families**
Breakfast: **Full**
Credit Cards: **MC, VISA**
Pets: **No**
Children: **Welcome**
Smoking: **No**
Social Drinking: **Permitted**
Airport/Station Pickup: **Yes**

Located in a small country village, this 1860 brick farmhouse overlooks beautiful farmland. The large, sunny rooms feature original wood trim and are furnished with a pleasing blend of antiques and collectibles. Antique shops, crafts shops, and opportunities to fish or canoe are available. Betty and Melvin thoroughly enjoy having visitors and do their best to make them feel instantly at home.

Gibson's Bed & Breakfast ✪

141 WEST CARACAS AVENUE, HERSHEY, PENNSYLVANIA 17033

Tel: **(717) 534-1305**	Open: **All year**
Hosts: **Frances and Bob Gibson**	Breakfast: **Full**
Location: **One block off Rte. 422**	Pets: **No**
No. of Rooms: **3**	Children: **Welcome, over 5**
Max. No. Sharing Bath: **3**	Smoking: **No**
Double/sb: **$50**	Social Drinking: **Permitted**
Single/sb: **$40**	Airport/Station Pickup: **Yes**

Bob and Frances Gibson have a 65-year-old Cape Cod, located in the center of Hershey, within walking distance to many local attractions. The house has been recently renovated to enhance the charm of the hardwood floors, wood trim, and original windows. The atmosphere is friendly and informal. The Gibsons will gladly help you find local sights such as Hershey Park, Chocolate World, Founders Hall, and the Amish country.

Walkabout Inn ✪

837 VILLAGE ROAD, LAMPETER (LANCASTER COUNTY), PENNSYLVANIA 17537

Tel: **(717) 464-0707**	Reduced Rates: **Available**
Hosts: **Richard and Maggie Mason**	Breakfast: **Full**
Location: **3 mi. S of Lancaster**	Other Meals: **Available**
No. of Rooms: **5**	Credit Cards: **AMEX, MC, VISA**
No. of Private Baths: **5**	Pets: **No**
Double/pb: **$99**	Children: **Welcome, over 10**
Single/pb: **$79**	Smoking: **No**
Honeymoon Suite: **$149**	Social Drinking: **Permitted**
Open: **All year**	

The Walkabout Inn takes its name from the Australian word, which means to go out and discover new places. Australian-born host Richard Mason and his wife, Maggie, will help you explore the Amish country that surrounds their brick Mennonite farmhouse. The 22-room house was built in 1925 and features wraparound porches, balconies, and chestnut woodwork. Guest rooms feature Maggie's hand stenciling and are decorated with antiques, oriental rugs, and Pennsylvania Dutch quilts. When it's time to say "good day," a candlelight gourmet breakfast is served on silver and crystal in the dining room. Homemade Australian bread, pastries, and tea imported from Down Under are always on the menu. You can choose a romantic honeymoon or anniversary suite that comes with a gift. Special packages include dinner with the Amish, three-hour scenic bus tour, and free maps and information.

Lincoln Haus Inn Bed & Breakfast ✪
1687 LINCOLN HIGHWAY EAST, LANCASTER, PENNSYLVANIA 17602

Tel: (717) 392-9412
Best Time to Call: Before 11 PM
Host: Mary K. Zook
Location: 2 mi. E of Lancaster
No. of Rooms: 5
No. of Private Baths: 5
Double/pb: $50–$65
Single/pb: $48–$62
Suites: $75–$80

Open: All year
Reduced Rates: Available
Breakfast: Full
Other Meals: Available
Pets: No
Children: Welcome
Smoking: No
Social Drinking: No

Ten minutes east of historic Lancaster and five minutes from Route 30 and the Pennsylvania Dutch Visitors Bureau in Lancaster County, you'll find this 1915 stucco home with distinctive hip roofs and black trim. Above the living room door, your host has hung a "Welcome" sign. Mary prides herself on giving guests a glimpse of the Amish life-style; the farmers market, horse auctions, buggy rides, quilt sales, and traditional Amish farmlands are all within ten to twenty minutes by car. But before you set out, you'll have a hearty family-style breakfast including juice, fruit, quiche, sausage, and different kinds of muffins.

The Loom Room ✪
1458 OLD BERNVILLE ROAD, LEESPORT, PENNSYLVANIA 19533

Tel: (610) 926-3217
Hosts: Mary and Gene Smith
Location: 4 mi. N of Reading
No. of Rooms: 3
No. of Private Baths: 1
Max. No. Sharing Bath: 4
Double/pb: $50
Single/pb: $50
Double/sb: $45

Single/sb: $45
Open: All year
Breakfast: Full
Reduced Rates: Weekly
Pets: No
Children: Welcome (crib)
Smoking: No
Social Drinking: Permitted
Airport/Station Pickup: Yes

The Loom Room is a stucco-covered stone farmhouse dating back more than 175 years. It is located in the countryside surrounded by shade trees, flowers, and herb gardens. Inside, the spacious rooms feature country antiques, open beams, fireplaces, and handwoven accessories. Mary invites you to her studio, where her work is on display. Her talents also extend to the kitchen, where she helps Gene cook up eggnog French toast, homemade jams, muffins, and chipped beef. Breakfast may be served in the sunny kitchen or outside in the gazebo. This lovely farm is near Reading's outlet complexes, Blue Marsh Lake Recreation Area, antique shops, and many historic sights.

Market Sleigh Bed & Breakfast ✪
BOX 99, 57 SOUTH MAIN STREET, LOGANVILLE, PENNSYLVANIA 17342-0099

Tel: **(717) 428-1440**
Best Time to Call: **3–6 PM**
Hosts: **Judy and Jerry Dietz**
Location: **7 mi. S of York**
No. of Rooms: **1**
No. of Private Baths: **1**
Suite: **$55–$100**
Open: **All year**
Reduced Rates: **Corporate travelers
   Mon.–Thurs.**

Breakfast: **Full**
Credit Cards: **MC, VISA**
Pets: **No**
Children: **Welcome, over 12**
Smoking: **No**
Social Drinking: **Permitted**
Minimum Stay: **2 nights convention
   weekends**

This bed and breakfast takes its name from the large 19th-century sleigh parked by the main entrance, as if stranded when the snow melted. Guests are encouraged to wander around the 22-acre property, or just sit with a book in the back porch swing. The many local attractions range from parks and wineries to museums and malls. Judy dishes out a hearty farmer's breakfast of fruit, homemade breads, eggs, cheese, bacon, and French toast or pancakes.

Cedar Hill Farm ✪
305 LONGENECKER ROAD, MOUNT JOY, PENNSYLVANIA 17552

Tel: **(717) 653-4655**
Best Time to Call: **Anytime**
Hosts: **Russel and Gladys Swarr**
Location: **10 mi. W of Lancaster**
No. of Rooms: **5**
No. of Private Baths: **5**
Double/pb: **$65–$75**
Single/pb: **$55–$65**
Open: **All year**

Reduced Rates: **Weekly**
Breakfast: **Continental, plus**
Credit Cards: **AMEX, DISC, MC, VISA**
Pets: **No**
Children: **Welcome (crib)**
Smoking: **No**
Social Drinking: **Permitted**
Airport/Station Pickup: **Yes**

Russel was born in this restored 1817 farmhouse and can tell you all about its history. It has an open, winding staircase, original pine floors, and an Indian door; breakfast is served beside a walk-in fireplace. Stroll the acreage or relax on the large porch overlooking a peaceful stream. Beautiful wallpapers and family heirlooms enhance the comfortable, air-conditioned bedrooms; the honeymoon suite has a private balcony. Quilt auctions and other attractions for collectors are plentiful year-round. Every Tuesday a farmers market and antiques auction take place just minutes away. Amish country, Hershey Park, and Chocolate World are nearby attractions.

Country Gardens Farm Bed & Breakfast
686 ROCK POINT ROAD, MOUNT JOY, PENNSYLVANIA 17552

Tel: **(717) 426-3316**
Best Time to Call: **Anytime**
Hosts: **Andy and Dottie Hess**
Location: **16 mi. W of Lancaster**
No. of Rooms: **3**
No. of Private Baths: **3**
Double/pb: **$60–$70**
Single/pb: **$50–$60**

Open: **All year**
Reduced Rates: **Available**
Breakfast: **Full**
Credit Cards: **AMEX, MC, VISA**
Pets: **No**
Children: **Welcome**
Smoking: **No**

Country Gardens offers the friendly down-home hospitality that made Lancaster County famous. Colorful flower gardens accent the 1860s brick farmhouse with large porches and spacious lawns. The farmhouse is graced with handmade crafts, houseplants, original oil paintings, and family heirlooms. The host and hostess spent most of their lives working on the farm and delight in sharing it with you. Relax in clean comfortable bedrooms, air-conditioning, electric heat, and private baths. There's easy access to farmers markets, quilt shops, antique shops, and historic sites, and other attractions are available year-round. Country Gardens is also close to Amish country and Hershey Park.

Hillside Farm B&B ✪
607 EBY CHIQUES ROAD, MOUNT JOY, PENNSYLVANIA 17552-8819

Tel: **(717) 653-6697**
Best Time to Call: **Anytime**
Hosts: **Gary and Deb Lintner**
Location: **10 mi. W of Lancaster**
No. of Rooms: **5**
No. of Private Baths: **3**
Max. No. Sharing Bath: **4**
Double/pb: **$70**
Single/pb: **$70**
Double/sb: **$55**

Single/sb: **$55**
Open: **All year**
Reduced Rates: **Available**
Breakfast: **Full**
Credit Cards: **MC, VISA**
Pets: **No**
Children: **Welcome, over 10**
Smoking: **No**
Social Drinking: **Permitted**

Quiet and secluded, this 1863 brick homestead overlooks Chickies Creek, a dam and waterfall. Amish country, Hershey Park, antique shops, flea markets, auctions, wineries, and hiking and biking trails are all nearby. (Bike trail maps are available.) Although it is not a working farm, the B&B is entirely surrounded by farmland. Guests can explore a large barn or watch milking at a neighborhood farm; dinner with an Amish family can be arranged. Hillside Farm is filled with cozy country furnishings, dairy antiques, and milk bottles. Gary, an electrical project superintendent, and Deb, an executive secretary, run this special inn.

Churchtown Inn B&B ✪
2100 MAIN STREET, ROUTE 23 W, NARVON, PENNSYLVANIA 17555

Tel: **(717) 445-7794**
Best Time to Call: **9 AM–9 PM**
Hosts: **Jim Kent Hermine and Stuart Smith**
Location: **4 mi. off Pennsylvania Turnpike, Exit 22**
No. of Rooms: **8**
No. of Private Baths: **8**
Double/pb: **$80–$95**
Single/pb: **$75–$85**

Open: **All year**
Reduced Rates: **Weekly**
Breakfast: **Full**
Other Meals: **Available**
Credit Cards: **MC, VISA**
Pets: **No**
Children: **Welcome, over 12**
Smoking: **No**
Social Drinking: **Permitted**
Foreign Languages: **German**

Churchtown Inn is a lovely fieldstone Federal Colonial mansion built in 1735. Located in the heart of Pennsylvania Dutch country, this B&B is close to Amish attractions, antique markets, and manufacturers' outlets. Rooms are decorated with the hosts' personal treasures: antique furniture, original art, and music boxes. Stuart (a former music director) and Jim (a former accountant who moonlighted as a ballroom dance instructor) stage events throughout the year. The schedule includes concerts, costume balls, carriage rides, walks, and holiday celebrations. Every Saturday, guests have the opportunity of joining Amish or Mennonite families for dinner at an additional fee. Of course, after a Churchtown Inn breakfast, you may not have room for any more meals; the table groans with English oatmeal custard, apple pancakes, Grand Marnier French toast, homemade coffee cake, and other delectables.

The "Hen-Apple" Bed and Breakfast ✪
409 SOUTH LINGLE AVENUE, PALMYRA, PENNSYLVANIA 17078

Tel: **(717) 838-8282**
Best Time to Call: **9 AM–9 PM**
Hosts: **Flo and Harold Eckert**
Location: **E of Hershey**
No. of Rooms: **6**
No. of Private Baths: **6**
Double/pb: **$75**
Single/pb: **$65**

Open: **All year**
Reduced Rates: **Available**
Breakfast: **Full**
Credit Cards: **AMEX, MC, VISA**
Pets: **No**
Children: **No**
Smoking: **No**

Wood floors, stenciling, antiques, and candlelit windows create a cozy country atmosphere at this 1825 farmhouse five minutes from Hershey. Home-baked breads and muffins, served on old china, make breakfast a treat, whether you enjoy it on the screened porch or in the dining room. In warm weather, guests may relax in the orchard on lawn furniture, a swing, and a hammock. The local attractions are many and varied: antique and crafts shops, horse racing and ice hockey, theaters and museums, even a winery and a bologna factory that welcome visitors.

The House on the Canal ✪
4020 RIVER ROAD, READING, PENNSYLVANIA 19605

Tel: **(610) 921-3015**
Best Time to Call: **Anytime**
Hosts: **Mr. and Mrs. Robert Yenser**
No. of Rooms: **3**
No. of Private Baths: **3**
Double/pb: **$85**
Suites: **$90**

Apartment: **$95**
Open: **All year**
Breakfast: **Full**
Pets: **Welcome**
Children: **Welcome**
Smoking: **Restricted**
Social Drinking: **Permitted**

This secluded enchanting old house was built back in the late 1700s and recently restored. The property's two-foot stone walls and 200-year-old trees are nestled along the banks of the Schuylkill River, and fishing, hiking, and biking are literally at your doorstep. Depending on the season, you might even catch a glimpse of the Canadian wild geese who have made their home by the old wooden dam nearby. Whatever your interests, you'll find something to do here. It's 5 minutes to Reading Airport and the Reading outlets; 10 minutes to the campuses of Albright, Alvernia, and Penn State; and 30 minutes to Redners Antique Market and Black Angus Beer Fest.

Hiwwelhaus ✪
R.D. #1 BOX 456, WOMELSDORF, PENNSYLVANIA 19567

Tel: **(610) 589-4660**
Best Time to Call: **8–10 AM; 6–9 PM**
Host: **Mary E. Keeler**

Location: **15 mi. NW of Reading**
No. of Rooms: **2**
No. of Private Baths: **2**

Double/pb: **$55**
Single/pb: **$45**
Open: **Apr.–Dec.**
Reduced Rates: **10% seniors**
Breakfast: **Full**
Pets: **No**

Children: **Welcome, over 6**
Smoking: **No**
Social Drinking: **No**
Station Pickup: **Yes**
Foreign Languages: **German**

In 1743 this area was part of a thousand-acre plantation purchased from the Penn family. On a corner of the original property stands a log home known as "Hiwwelhaus"—"house on a hill" in the local Pennsylvania German dialect. From its hilltop perch, this B&B overlooks a lovely rural landscape. After a country breakfast, relax on the spacious porch and plan your day. Reading outlets, Hershey Park, Lancaster County's Amish country, Hawk Mountain, the Appalachian Trail, and many other attractions are close by. The area also boasts an abundance of excellent restaurants. Attend a country auction, browse antique and crafts shops; the sports-minded can go fishing, boating, swimming, biking, hiking, or skiing. An easy drive takes you to a wildlife area with birds and deer in residence.

PHILADELPHIA AREA

A Bed and Breakfast Connection/Bed & Breakfast of Philadelphia ◉

P.O. BOX 21, DEVON, PENNSYLVANIA 19333
bnbphila@libertynet.org

Tel: **(610) 687-3565; (800) 448-3619;**
fax: **(610) 995-9524**
Best Time to Call: **9 AM–7 PM**
Mon.–Fri.; 9 AM–5 PM Sat.
Coordinators: **Peggy Gregg and Mary Alice Hamilton**
States/Regions Covered: **Amish country,**

Philadelphia and Main Line suburbs; Reading, Valley Forge, York County
Rates (Single/Double):
Modest: **$30 / $40**
Average: **$45 / $85**
Luxury: **$75 / $175**
Credit Cards: **AMEX, MC, VISA**

A Bed and Breakfast Connection/Bed & Breakfast of Philadelphia invites you to select a personally inspected host home in the greater Philadelphia area, from historic Center City to Revolutionary Valley Forge. It also serves the scenic Brandywine Valley and Pennsylvania Dutch country. While the locations range from country farmhouses to downtown high rises, they all offer an inviting atmosphere and dedicated, attentive hosts.

Association of Bed & Breakfasts in Philadelphia, Valley Forge, Brandywine ◉

P.O. BOX 562, VALLEY FORGE, PENNSYLVANIA 19481-0562

Tel: **(610) 783-7838; (800) 344-0123;**
fax: **(610) 783-7783**
Best Time to Call: **10 AM–9 PM**

Coordinator: **Carolyn J. Williams**
States/Regions Covered: **Philadelphia, Valley Forge, Main Line, Brandywine**

Valley, Bucks County, Lancaster County, West Chester
Rates (Single/Double):
  Modest: **$35–$45 / $45–$55**

Average: **$50–$65 / $60–$75**
Luxury: **$70–$85 / $85–up**
Credit Cards: **AMEX, DC, DISC, MC, VISA**

Even George Washington would applaud the manner in which Carolyn has brought the British tradition of bed and breakfast to his former headquarters. Choose from more than 130 sites in southeast Pennsylvania. Whether you are on vacation, business, personal getaway or using a gift certificate, Carolyn says, "There is a B&B for you!" Her roster includes modest homestays, city/country inns and town houses, historic and farm homes, guest cottages, carriage houses, and elegant, grand estates close to where you need to be. Free brochures include sample descriptions, rates, and locations.

POCONO MOUNTAINS

La Anna Guest House ✪
RD 2, BOX 1051, CRESCO, PENNSYLVANIA 18326

Tel: **(717) 676-4225**
Host: **Kay Swingle**
Location: **9 mi. from I-80 and I-84**
No. of Rooms: **4**
Max. No. Sharing Bath: **4**
Double/sb: **$40**
Single/sb: **$30**

Open: **All year**
Breakfast: **Continental**
Pets: **No**
Children: **Welcome (crib)**
Smoking: **Permitted**
Social Drinking: **Permitted**

This Victorian home has large rooms furnished with antiques; it is nestled on 25 acres of lush, wooded land, and has its own pond. Kay will happily direct you to fine dining spots that are kind to your wallet. Enjoy scenic walks, waterfalls, mountain vistas, Tobyhanna and Promised Land state parks; there's cross-country skiing right on the property. Lake Wallenpaupack is only 15 minutes away.

The Shepard House ❂

P.O. BOX 486, 108 SHEPARD AVENUE, DELAWARE WATER GAP, PENNSYLVANIA 18327

Tel: **(717) 424-9779**	Open: **All year**
Best Time to Call: **9 AM–9 PM**	Reduced Rates: **Available**
Host: **Jeanni Buonura**	Breakfast: **Full**
Location: **3 mi. E of Stroudsburg**	Pets: **No**
No. of Rooms: **7**	Children: **Welcome, over 8**
Max. No. Sharing Bath: **4**	Smoking: **No**
Double/sb: **$79–$110**	Social Drinking: **Permitted**
Single/sb: **$69–$79**	Minimum Stay: **2 nights holidays**

Originally called "The Far View House," this large Victorian operated as a summer vacation boardinghouse in the early 1900s. Today, from its site just off the Appalachian Trail, The Shepard House greets visitors year-round. Guest rooms are filled with antiques and special touches. Take a seat in the comfortable parlor or on the veranda that wraps around the entire house. Your host serves a four-course breakfast and offers afternoon tea and refreshments.

Morning Glories ❂

204 BELLEMONTE AVENUE, HAWLEY, PENNSYLVANIA 18428

Tel: **(717) 226-0644**	Single/sb: **$45**
Best Time to Call: **8–10 PM**	Open: **All year**
Hosts: **Becky and Roberta Holcomb**	Reduced Rates: **Weekly**
Location: **35 mi. E of Scranton**	Breakfast: **Full**
No. of Rooms: **3**	Credit Cards: **MC, VISA**
No. of Private Baths: **1**	Pets: **No**
Max. No. Sharing Bath: **4**	Children: **No**
Double/pb: **$55**	Smoking: **No**
Single/pb: **$55**	Social Drinking: **Permitted**
Double/sb: **$45**	

From this B&B's location in the small town of Hawley, you can walk to the downtown shopping area, summer theater, and several fine restaurants. Your own transportation will allow you to enjoy the area's attractions, such as Lake Wallenpaupack, the Delaware River, train rides, canoeing, rafting, skiing, horseback riding, antiquing, hunting, and fishing. The house has a front porch and a deck in the rear for relaxation, and the living room makes a nice gathering place. The oak staircase leads to the guest rooms on the second floor.

Bonny Bank ✪
P.O. BOX 481, MILLRIFT, PENNSYLVANIA 18340

Tel: (717) 491-2250	Open: May 15–Sept. 15
Best Time to Call: 9 AM–9 PM	Reduced Rates: 10% weekly
Hosts: Doug and Linda Hay	Breakfast: Full
Location: 5 mi. from I-84	Pets: No
No. of Rooms: 1	Children: No
No. of Private Baths: 1	Smoking: No
Double/pb: $50	Social Drinking: Permitted
Single/pb: $45	

Stay in a picture-book small town on a dead-end road. The sound of the rapids will lull you to sleep in this charming bungalow perched on the banks of the Delaware River. Doug and Linda invite you to use their private swimming area and will lend you inner tubes for float trips. Nearby attractions include the Zane Grey house, Minisink Battlefield, Grey Towers Historical Site, the Victorian village of Milford, and all the sports and variety of restaurants the Poconos are known for.

The Lampost Bed & Breakfast ✪
HCR BOX 154, ROUTE 507, PAUPACK, PENNSYLVANIA 18451

Tel: (717) 857-1738	Single/sb: $50
Best Time to Call: 6–9 PM	Open: Apr.–Nov. weekends only
Hosts: Karen and David Seagaard	Breakfast: Continental
Location: 9 mi. S of Hawley	Credit Cards: MC, VISA
No. of Rooms: 4	Pets: No
No. of Private Baths: 3	Children: Welcome, over 10
Max. No. Sharing Bath: 4	Smoking: No
Double/pb: $75	Social Drinking: Permitted
Double/sb: $60	

An assortment of lampposts line the driveway leading to this white Colonial home on two acres overlooking Lake Wallenpaupack. This is an ideal stopover for those who love waterfront activities—swimming, boating, fishing, and water skiing. If you'd rather stay high and dry, there are facilities for golfing, tennis, and horseback riding nearby. Other recreational options include scenic train excursions and balloon rides.

SCRANTON/WILKES-BARRE/NORTHEASTERN/ NORTH CENTRAL PENNSYLVANIA

Harts' Content ✪
P.O. BOX 97, HUNTINGTON MILLS, PENNSYLVANIA 18622

Tel: **(717) 864-2499**	Open: **All year**
Best Time to Call: **After 5 PM**	Breakfast: **Full**
Hosts: **Kenneth and Gerry Hart**	Pets: **No**
Location: **25 mi. SW of Wilkes-Barre**	Children: **Welcome**
No. of Rooms: **3**	Smoking: **No**
No. of Private Baths: **3**	Social Drinking: **Permitted**
Double/pb: **$50–$55**	Airport/Station Pickup: **Yes**

Harts' Content is nestled on twenty-seven wooded acres in the old 19th-century mill town of Huntington Mills. The area abounds in wildlife. Fish in the B&B's private pond or quietly wander through the woods to Huntington Mills Creek. Delight in a leisurely country breakfast with friendly conversation around an oak table. Nearby, enjoy golf, Rickett's Glen State Park, covered bridges, and antiquing. Gerry and Ken will gladly help you plan your stay.

The Bodine House ✪
307 SOUTH MAIN STREET, MUNCY, PENNSYLVANIA 17756

Tel: **(717) 546-8949**	Single/pb: **$50–$60**
Best Time to Call: **Evenings**	Open: **All year**
Hosts: **David and Marie Louise Smith**	Credit Cards: **AMEX, MC, VISA**
Location: **15 mi. S of Williamsport;**	Breakfast: **Full**
10 mi. from I-80, Exit 31B	Pets: **No**
No. of Rooms: **4**	Children: **Welcome, over 6**
No. of Private Baths: **4**	Smoking: **No**
Double/pb: **$60–$70**	Social Drinking: **Permitted**

This restored town house dates back to 1805. A baby grand piano, four fireplaces, and a candlelit living room add to its old-fashioned appeal. A full country breakfast and wine and cheese are on the house. Local attractions include the Susquehanna River, the Endless Mountains, and the fall foliage.

The Weeping Willow Inn ✪
RR 7, BOX 254, TUNKHANNOCK, PENNSYLVANIA 18657

Tel: **(717) 836-7257**	Single/pb: **$60–$70**
Best Time to Call: **6–9 PM**	Open: **All year**
Hosts: **Patty and Randy Ehrenzeller**	Breakfast: **Full**
Location: **25 mi. NW of Scranton**	Other Meals: **Available**
No. of Rooms: **3**	Pets: **No**
No. of Private Baths: **3**	Children: **Welcome**
Double/pb: **$65–$80**	Smoking: **No**

Patty and Randy have lovingly restored this charming Colonial home and cordially invite you to experience its warmth and rich history. Antiques can be seen throughout the house, and breakfast is served by candlelight each morning. The Susquehanna River offers opportunities for hiking, canoeing, and fishing. Or travel the Endless Mountains region of northeastern Pennsylvania and partake of the antique and craft shops along the way. A relaxing bed and breakfast experience awaits you at the Weeping Willow Inn.

VALLEY FORGE AREA

Association of Bed & Breakfasts in Philadelphia, Valley Forge, Brandywine ✪

P.O. BOX 562, VALLEY FORGE, PENNSYLVANIA 19481

Tel: **(610) 783-7838; (800) 344-0123;** fax: **(610) 783-7783**
Best Time to Call: **9 AM–9 PM**
Coordinator: **Carolyn J. Williams**
States/Regions Covered: **Philadelphia, Valley Forge, Main Line, Brandywine Valley, Bucks County, Lancaster County**

Descriptive Directory: **Free**
Rates (Single/Double):
  Modest: **$35–$45 / $45–$55**
  Average: **$50–$65 / $60–$75**
  Luxury: **$70–$85 / $85–up**
Credit Cards: **AMEX, DC, DISC, MC, VISA**

Even George Washington would applaud the manner in which Carolyn has brought the British tradition of bed and breakfast to his former headquarters. Choose from more than 130 sites in southeast Pennsylvania. Whether you are on vacation, business, personal getaway or using a gift certificate, Carolyn says, "There is a B&B for you!" Her roster includes modest homestays, city/country inns and town houses, historic and farm homes, ski lodges, guest cottages, carriage houses, and elegant, grand estates close to where you need to be.

WESTERN PENNSYLVANIA

Weatherbury Farm ✪
RR 1, BOX 250, AVELLA, PENNSYLVANIA 15312

Tel: **(412) 587-3763**	Breakfast: **Full**
Hosts: **Dale, Marcy, and Nigel Tudor**	Credit Cards: **AMEX, DISC, MC, VISA**
Location: **20 mi. SW of Pittsburgh**	Pets: **No**
No. of Rooms: **8**	Children: **Welcome, crib**
No. of Private Baths: **8**	Smoking: **No**
Double/pb: **$65–$70**	Social Drinking: **Permitted**
Single/pb: **$60–$65**	Airport Pickup: **Yes**
Suites: **$85–$90**	Foreign Languages: **German**
Open: **All year**	

One hundred acres of meadows, gardens, fields, and valleys create a tranquil setting at the Tudors' B&B, the perfect getaway from everyday pressures. Guest rooms at this 1860s farm have been lovingly furnished with an old-fashioned country charm. Awake to a bountiful farm breakfast, which might include apple cinnamon pancakes, garden vegetable eggs, or creamy peach-filled French toast. Later, get acquainted with the chickens, sheep, and cattle. Opportunities for golf, fishing, boating, and antiquing abound. Or visit the historic nineteenth-century Meadowcroft Village, Starlake Amphitheater, or West Virginia attractions nearby.

Mountain View Bed and Breakfast Inn ✪
MOUNTAIN VIEW ROAD, DONEGAL, PENNSYLVANIA 15628

Tel: **(412) 593-6349; (800) 392-7773**	Breakfast: **Full**
Hosts: **Lesley and Jerry O'Leary**	Credit Cards: **AMEX, DC, DISC, MC,**
Location: **1 mi. E of Pa. Tpke. Exit 9**	**VISA**
No. of Rooms: **7**	Pets: **No**
No. of Private Baths: **7**	Children: **Welcome, over 10**
Double/pb: **$115–$150**	Smoking: **No**
Open: **All year**	Social Drinking: **Permitted**

In a quiet pastoral setting in the heart of the Laurel Highlands, you can enjoy lodging and breakfast in a restored 1850s farmhouse and barn furnished with period American furniture. Mountain View is a Westmoreland County historic landmark which affords a magnificent view of the Laurel Ridge. This location is convenient to several mountain resorts, state parks, white-water rafting, and Frank Lloyd Wright's Fallingwater. Lesley's Tea Room is open daily 10 AM–5 PM.

The Lamberton House ○

1331 OTTER STREET, FRANKLIN, PENNSYLVANIA 16323-1530

Tel: **(814) 432-7908; (800) 481-0776**
Hosts: **Jack and Sally Clawson**
Location: **80 mi. N of Pittsburgh**
No. of Rooms: **6**
No. of Private Baths: **4**
Max. No. Sharing Bath: **4**
Double/pb: **$60–$75**
Double/sb: **$50–$65**

Open: **All year**
Reduced Rates: **Available**
Breakfast: **Full**
Pets: **Sometimes**
Children: **Welcome**
Smoking: **Restricted**
Social Drinking: **Permitted**

Named for its original occupant, this Queen Anne Victorian was built in 1874 and is listed in the National Register of Historic Places. The rooms feature beautiful glass, original brass chandeliers, and woodwork of old-world craftsmanship. When they aren't exploring nearby recreational and historic sites, guests can relax in the drawing room, watch TV, play the piano, read in the library, swing on the front porch, or walk in the flower garden. A full country breakfast is served in the elegant dining room each morning.

Lynnrose Bed & Breakfast ○

114 WEST MAIN STREET, GROVE CITY, PENNSYLVANIA 16127

Tel: **(412) 458-6425**
Hosts: **Dave and Susie Lynn**
Location: **60 mi. N of Pittsburgh**
No. of Rooms: **5**
No. of Private Baths: **5**
Double/pb: **$65–$75**
Single/pb: **$50**
Open: **All year**

Reduced Rates: **10% seniors**
Breakfast: **Full**
Credit Cards: **DISC, MC, VISA**
Pets: **Sometimes**
Children: **Welcome, over 12**
Smoking: **No**
Social Drinking: **Permitted**
Airport/Station Pickup: **Yes**

Lynnrose Bed & Breakfast is decorated in Victorian style, with beautiful antiques and lace curtains. The large foyer and living room, with beamed ceilings and hardwood floors, are tastefully furnished, so guests may relax in front of the fireplace or enjoy TV and the VCR. All guest rooms have air-conditioning. Dave and Susie offer afternoon tea and provide a bountiful, nutritious breakfast. Lynnrose is located within walking distance of Grove City College and the downtown area and only a short way from Slippery Rock University, outlet shops, and wonderful restaurants.

Snow Goose Inn ✪
112 EAST MAIN STREET, GROVE CITY, PENNSYLVANIA 16127

Tel: **(412) 458-4644; (800) 317-4644**	Open: **All year**
Best Time to Call: **10 AM–10 PM**	Breakfast: **Full**
Hosts: **Orvil and Dorothy McMillen**	Credit Cards: **MC, VISA**
Location: **60 mi. N of Pittsburgh**	Pets: **Sometimes**
No. of Rooms: **4**	Children: **Welcome**
No. of Private Baths: **4**	Smoking: **No**
Double/pb: **$65**	Social Drinking: **Permitted**
Single/pb: **$60**	Airport/Station Pickup: **Yes**

Formerly a country doctor's home and office, the Snow Goose Inn, built around 1895, has a large porch with an old-fashioned swing. Inside, you'll find tastefully furnished bedrooms with a cozy, warm atmosphere. Each morning, freshly brewed coffee and a complete breakfast, including homemade muffins and nut breads, await guests in the dining room. The Inn is conveniently located across from Grove City College, next door to a restaurant, and two blocks from the business district. Orvil and Dorothy will be glad to direct you to all the local points of interest.

Foursquare B&B ✪
250 SOUTH FIFTH STREET, INDIANA, PENNSYLVANIA 15701

Tel: **(412) 465-6412**	Open: **All year**
Best Time to Call: **Before 10 PM**	Breakfast: **Full**
Hosts: **Mary Ann and Walt Ballard**	Credit Cards: **MC, VISA**
Location: **60 mi. NE of Pittsburgh**	Pets: **No**
No. of Rooms: **3**	Children: **Welcome**
Max. No. Sharing Bath: **4**	Smoking: **Restricted**
Double/sb: **$50**	Social Drinking: **Permitted**
Single/sb: **$37**	

Come stay at this buff brick American Foursquare house, built in the 1920s. Children will adore Sam, the resident collie, adults will admire Mary Ann's handmade quilts, and everyone will enjoy Walt's breakfast specialties. Indiana, the "Christmas Tree Capital of the World," is also Jimmy Stewart's birthplace and the home of Indiana University of Pennsylvania. Local attractions include an Amish community and a fine winery. Indiana is now the home of a Jimmy Stewart museum.

Eagle's Mere Gardens B&B ✪
4518 EAST LAKE ROAD, JAMESTOWN, PENNSYLVANIA 16134

Tel: **(412) 932-3572**	Open: **Spring–Fall**
Best Time to Call: **8 AM–9 PM**	Reduced Rates: **10% seniors**
Hosts: **Richard and Doris Ostermeyer**	Breakfast: **Full**
No. of Rooms: **1**	Pets: **Sometimes**
No. of Private Baths: **1**	Smoking: **No**
Double/pb: **$55**	Social Drinking: **Permitted**
Single/pb: **$45**	

From the wraparound porch of this rustic home, you can look down on gardens, trees, and Pymatuning State Park Lake—the view is especially picturesque in autumn. Inside, the decor is primitive, with country motifs. Since the guest room is detached from the main house, you'll have complete privacy, but you can join your hosts for conversation and breakfast. Gardeners take note: both Dick and Doris love cultivating dahlias. For athletic sorts, fishing and nature trails are within walking distance, and five golf courses are nearby.

Woolley Fox ✪
61 LINCOLN HIGHWAY EAST, LIGONIER, PENNSYLVANIA 15658

Tel: **(412) 238-3004**	Breakfast: **Full**
Hosts: **Barbara and Wayne Carroll**	Pets: **No**
Location: **50 mi. E of Pittsburgh**	Children: **Welcome, over 12**
No. of Rooms: **2**	Smoking: **Restricted**
No. of Private Baths: **2**	Social Drinking: **Permitted**
Double/pb: **$80**	Minimum Stay: **2 nights holidays,**
Suites: **$125–$165**	**Highland Games, Fort Ligonier Days**
Open: **All year**	

The Woolley Fox is located on a wooded hillside in Pennsylvania's Laurel Highlands, one-and-a-half miles from historic Ligonier. The main house resembles an English stone cottage and features a cheerfully decorated bedroom with a queen-size bed and an adjacent sitting area with a TV. The guest house is Swiss chalet–style, with a queen-size bed, sitting room, fireplace, and balcony that overlooks the pool and the natural woodlands. Both houses are furnished with country antiques and crafts, including Barbara's primitive hooked rugs. The front porch of the main house offers guests a place to relax with a beverage, look at the stars, or watch the deer.

Mehard Manor ✪
146 NORTH PITT STREET, MERCER, PENNSYLVANIA 16137

Tel: **(412) 662-2489**
Best Time to Call: **8 AM–8 PM**
Hosts: **Jerry and Lucille Carlson**
Location: **60 mi. N of Pittsburgh**
No. of Rooms: **4**
No. of Private Baths: **4**
Double/pb: **$75–$85**
Open: **All year**

Reduced Rates: **Available**
Breakfast: **Full**
Credit Cards: **DISC, MC, VISA**
Pets: **No**
Children: **By arrangement**
Smoking: **No**
Social Drinking: **Permitted**

Mehard Manor is a 1913 vintage, sixteen-room Georgian Colonial located near the historic courthouse square. The house features turn-of-the-century architectural details, including rich moldings, wainscot paneling, molded plaster ceilings, balustrade, Doric columns, fireplaces, and a leaded-glass skylight. Guest rooms are uniquely decorated with antique beds, richly carved headboards, and other period pieces that blend warmth with the elegance of the structure itself. Breakfast is served in the formal dining room or in the sunlit solarium.

Beechwood Inn ✪
175 BEECHWOOD ROAD, NEW WILMINGTON, PENNSYLVANIA 16142

Tel: **(412) 946-2342**
Best Time to Call: **8 AM–10 PM**
Hosts: **Tom and Janet Hartwell**

Location: **60 mi. N of Pittsburgh**
No. of Rooms: **3**
No. of Private Baths: **3**

Double/pb: **$60**
Open: **All year**
Breakfast: **Full**
Credit Cards: **MC, VISA**

Pets: **No**
Children: **No**
Smoking: **No**
Social Drinking: **Permitted**

Beechwood Inn is centrally located between Pittsburgh and Erie. Built just after the Civil War, the house has retained its original charm. Guest rooms contain antiques, Victorian clothes, military memorabilia, collectibles, and quilts, and are cooled by central air. A common room is provided with a TV, small refrigerator, coffee and tea pots, dishes, daybed, and chairs. Three roofed porches offer a beautiful view of the area. After breakfast you can take a stroll in the park right across the street or around the quiet neighborhood. Then drive through the Amish community that surrounds the area, shop at Volant's and Leesburg's many antique shops, and pick up contemporary bargains at Grove City's Outlet Plaza, with over 125 brand-name stores. Nearby are several colleges, state parks, golfing, and great restaurants. Ask for details as Tom and Janet serve fresh cider or hot coffee upon your arrival.

Heather Hill Bed & Breakfast Inn ✪
268 RADER SCHOOL ROAD, RENFREW, PENNSYLVANIA 16053

Tel: **(412) 789-7911**
Best Time to Call: **Mornings**
Hosts: **Patricia and David Nicklas**
Location: **30 mi. N of Pittsburgh**
No. of Rooms: **6**
No. of Private Baths: **4**
Max. No. Sharing Bath: **4**
Double/pb: **$65**
Single/pb: **$60**

Double/sb: **$60**
Single/sb: **$55**
Suites: **$75**
Open: **All year**
Breakfast: **Full**
Pets: **No**
Children: **Welcome**
Smoking: **No**
Social Drinking: **No**

For those who want to experience country living on a 180-acre farm, consider this an invitation. Outdoor amenities include an in-ground pool, horseshoe pits, bocci court, volleyball net, shuffleboard, croquet, and a screened pavilion with picnic tables and electricity. Indoors, a spacious family room with a cathedral ceiling and wood-burning stove is a perfect setting for browsing through the extensive collection of old and new books, watching TV or a movie, or enjoying the beautiful view from the huge picture window. Patricia and David offer a day-after-the-wedding outdoor country picnic during late spring, summer, and early fall.

Zephyr Glen Bed and Breakfast ✪
205 DEXTER ROAD, SCOTTSDALE, PENNSYLVANIA 15683

Tel: **(412) 887-6577**
Best Time to Call: **8 AM–10 PM**
Hosts: **Noreen and Gil McGurl**

Location: **45 mi. SE of Pittsburgh**
No. of Rooms: **3**
No. of Private Baths: **3**

Double/pb: **$75**
Single/pb: **$65**
Open: **All year**
Breakfast: **Full**
Credit Cards: **DISC, MC, VISA**
Pets: **No**
Children: **Welcome, over 12**

Smoking: **No**
Social Drinking: **Permitted**
Minimum Stay: **2 nights Christmas,
  Easter, Labor Day and October
  weekends**
Airport/Station Pickup: **Yes**

Would a trip back to the mid-19th century appeal to you? If so, Zephyr Glen Bed and Breakfast is the place to stay. This Federal farmhouse was built in 1822 and has been restored to its original condition: oak floors and handsome woodwork period antiques, Noreen's stenciling, and fireplaces. The house sits on a hillside in the midst of mature maple, oak, linden, and fruit trees, herb gardens, and a fish pond. Breakfast may include fruit, juice, homemade granola, jams, baked goodies, yogurt, a cooked entree, coffee, and tea. Noreen and Gil enjoy meeting new people, making them feel at home and sharing experiences with them. Hiking, biking, skiing, and historic attractions are all within a thirty-minute drive.

Charbert Farm Bed and Breakfast ✪
RR 3, BOX 68, LAUREL ROAD, SHELOCTA, PENNSYLVANIA 15774

Tel: **(412) 726-8264**
Best Time to Call: **8–9 AM**
Hosts: **Barbara and Bob Rago**
Location: **7 mi. S of Indiana**
No. of Rooms: **4**
Max. No. Sharing Bath: **4**
Double/pb: **$75**
Single/pb: **$65**
Doubls/sb: **$70**

Single/sb: **$55**
Suites: **$85**
Open: **All year**
Reduced Rates: **Available**
Breakfast: **Full**
Pets: **Sometimes**
Children: **Welcome**
Smoking: **No**
Social Drinking: **Permitted**

A stay here is like coming to grandma's house. The rural mystique and nostalgic images begin as you approach this bed and breakfast. Built in the mid-1800s and restored, Charbert Farm has not eliminated the antiques or country atmosphere. Guests have full use of the house during their stay. Rooms are spacious, each with its own decor. Visit the music room and sing along with the player piano or relax in the cozy Country Western room with a fireplace, TV, and VCR. If you prefer the outdoors, there are 108 scenic acres with a gazebo and a newly stocked pond.

H.B.'s Cottage ✪
231 WEST CHURCH STREET, SOMERSET, PENNSYLVANIA 15501

Tel: **(814) 443-1204**
Best Time to Call: **Evenings**
Hosts: **Phyllis and Hank Vogt**
Location: **70 mi. E of Pittsburgh**

No. of Rooms: **2**
No. of Private Baths: **2**
Double/pb: **$75**
Open: **All year**

Breakfast: **Full**
Credit Cards: **MC, VISA**
Pets: **Sometimes**
Children: **No**
Smoking: **No**

Social Drinking: **Permitted**
Minimum Stay: **2 nights on holiday
weekends**
Airport Pickup: **Yes**

H.B.'s Cottage, an exclusive and elegant B&B located within the Borough of Somerset, is a 1920s stone and frame house with an oversized fireplace in the living room. Pieces acquired in the Vogts' overseas travels—Hank is a retired naval officer—and teddy bears from Phyllis's extensive collection accent the traditional furnishings. The warm, romantic guest room has a private porch. Downhill and cross-country skiing, mountain biking, and tennis are the hosts' specialties. Fortunately for them and their guests, H.B.'s Cottage is close to 7 Springs Mountain Resort, Fallingwater, Hidden Valley Resort, biking and hiking trails, and white-water sports.

Dodson's Valentine House ✪
99 OLD NATIONAL PIKE, WEST ALEXANDER, PENNSYLVANIA 15376

Tel: **(412) 484-7843**
Best Time to Call: **8 AM–9 PM**
Hosts: **Bryce and Pam Dodson**
Location: **45 mi. W of Pittsburgh**
No. of Rooms: **2**
No. of Private Baths: **2**
Double/pb: **$60**

Single/pb: **$50**
Open: **All year**
Breakfast:**Full**
Pets: **No**
Children: **Welcome, over 10**
Smoking: **No**
Social Drinking: **Permitted**

Step into one of the most popular stopping places along the Old National Park. Built in 1810, the house served as an inn, and has been restored and furnished with antiques from various periods of American history. Each guest has a chance to experience the aura of the days of stagecoaches and Conestoga wagons. Located one mile off Interstate 70, Dodson's is just minutes from Wheeling's Festival of Lights, Oglebay Park, Jamboree U.S.A., and Washington's Trolley Museum. You are welcome to spend time relaxing in the Colonial living room, family TV room, or perhaps spot a deer or a wild turkey while on a nature walk around the ten-acre estate. Every morning, you'll awaken to the aroma of homemade muffins and breads.

The Inn on Grandview ✪
**310 EAST GRANDVIEW AVENUE, ZELIENOPLE,
PENNSYLVANIA 16063**

Tel: **(412) 452-0469**
Best Time to Call: **Mornings, evenings**
Hosts: **Richard and Juanita Eppinger**
Location: **30 mi. N of Pittsburgh**
No. of Rooms: **4**

No. of Private Baths: **4**
Double/pb: **$85–105**
Open: **All year**
Breakfast: **Full**
Credit Cards: **DISC, MC, VISA**

Pets: **No**

Children: **Welcome**

Smoking: **No**

Social Drinking: **No**

Airport Pickup: **Yes**

Built in the early 19th century, when it was known as the Zimmerman Hotel, The Inn on Grandview is now beautifully restored. Furnished with antiques and reproductions, each room has a different feel. But the feeling is that of elegance and warmth. Guest rooms have cable TV, computer hook-up, and telephones. Wake up to a large breakfast of sweet rolls, pancakes, fresh fruit, and sausage from the local smokehouse. What makes the Inn so successful is the warmth of your hosts. Rich is a barber and enjoys golfing. Juanita has an interior design shop, and enjoys showing hospitality to her guests. You will leave feeling refreshed, satisfied, and wanting to return.

For key to listings, see inside front or back cover.

✪ This star means that rates are guaranteed through December 31, 1998, to any guest making a reservation as a result of reading about the B&B in *Bed & Breakfast U.S.A.*—1998 edition.

Important! To avoid misunderstandings, always ask about cancellation policies when booking.

Please enclose a self-addressed, stamped, business-size envelope when contacting reservation services.

For more details on what you can expect in a B&B, see Chapter 1.

Always mention *Bed & Breakfast U.S.A.* when making reservations!

We want to hear from you! Use the form on page 625.

RHODE ISLAND

Providence

Bristol

Wyoming

Newport

Wakefield

Westerly

Rockwell House Inn ✪
610 HOPE STREET, BRISTOL, RHODE ISLAND 02809-1945

Tel: **(401) 253-0040; (800) 815-0040**
Hosts: **Debra and Steve Krohn**
Location: **15 mi. SE of Providence; 12 mi. NE of Newport, 60 mi. S of Boston**
No. of Rooms: **4**
No. of Private Baths: **4**
Double/pb: **$75–$110**
Open: **All year**
Reduced Rates: **Weekly; off-season, corporate**

Breakfast: **Full**
Credit Cards: **AMEX, DISC, MC, VISA**
Pets: **No**
Children: **Welcome, over 12**
Smoking: **No**
Social Drinking: **Permitted**
Minimum Stay: **Major holidays, weekends**
Foreign Languages: **Spanish**

This beautifully restored Federal-style home, built in 1809, is located in the heart of Bristol's historic waterfront district, 20 minutes from Newport and within walking distance of museums and antique shops. Rooms feature fireplaces, king-size beds, terrycloth robes, hair dryers,

English bath amenities, and a casual elegance that will immediately put you at ease. Enjoy afternoon tea in the garden, read in one of the parlors, and meet new friends over evening sherry. Your hosts Steve and Debra will share their passion for wines, cooking, and entertaining.

William's Grant Inn ✪
154 HIGH STREET, BRISTOL, RHODE ISLAND 02809

Tel: **(401) 253-4222; (800) 596-4222**
Best Time to Call: **8 AM–9 PM**
Hosts: **Mary and Michael Rose**
Location: **15 mi. SE of Providence**
No. of Rooms: **5**
No. of Private Baths: **3**
Max. No. Sharing Bath: **4**
Double/pb: **$65–$105**
Double/sb: **$55–$95**
Suites: **$85**
Open: **All year**

Reduced Rates: **Off-season**
Breakfast: **Full**
Credit Cards: **AMEX, DISC, DC, MC, VISA**
Pets: **No**
Children: **Welcome, over 12**
Smoking: **No**
Social Drinking: **Permitted**
Minimum Stay: **2 nights, holidays and graduation**

Just two blocks from Bristol's unspoiled harbor you'll find the sea captain's house that Deputy Governor William Bradford granted to his grandson in 1808. Mary and Mike restored and remodeled the five-bay Federal house, turning it into a gracious, beautifully appointed Inn decorated with traditional and folk art. Breakfasts are always a treat, with home-baked goodies, granola, and perhaps Mike's huevos rancheros or Mary's pesto omelettes. Each guest room has a firm queen-size bed, a comfortable chair to read in, and a fireplace. Within a 3-mile radius you'll find seven museums and a 30-mile bike/walking path. Your hosts are Mary, a development coordinator with the Nature Conservancy and part-time innkeeper, and Mike, a full-time innkeeper. They enjoy kayaking, exercise, gardening, and many other activities too numerous to mention.

The Melville House ✪

39 CLARKE STREET, NEWPORT, RHODE ISLAND 02840

Tel: **(401) 847-0640**
Hosts: **Vince DeRico and David Horan**
Location: **35 mi. from I-95, Exit 3**
No. of Rooms: **7**
No. of Private Baths: **5**
Max. No. Sharing Bath: **4**
Double/pb: **$85–$135**
Double/sb: **$60–$110**
Suite: **$150 (winter only)**

Open: **All year**
Breakfast: **Full**
Credit Cards: **AMEX, DISC, MC, VISA**
Pets: **No**
Children: **Welcome, over 12**
Smoking: **No**
Social Drinking: **Permitted**
Minimum Stay: **2 nights weekends; 3 nights holidays**

The Melville House is a 1750s shingled home set in Newport's historic Hill section. This quiet street is just one block from the Brick Market and wharfs, and around the corner from Touro Synagogue and Trinity Church. Vince and Dave welcome you to guest rooms decorated with oak furnishings, braided rugs, and lace curtains, with special touches such as fresh flowers and a bowl of fruit. Your hosts will start your day off with homemade muffins, granola, and other home-baked items served at polished wood tables in the sunny breakfast room. When you want to relax, the country parlor with its collection of old grinders and gadgets and comfortable wing chairs awaits. Vince and Dave will be glad to provide sightseeing advice, and when the day is at a close, you can enjoy a 4 o'clock sherry at the house.

Cady House ✪
127 POWER STREET, PROVIDENCE, RHODE ISLAND 02906

Tel: **(401) 273-5398**
Hosts: **Anna and Bill Colaiace**
Location: **1 mi. from Rte. 195 E, Exit 2**
No. of Rooms: **3**
No. of Private Baths: **3**
Double/pb: **$80**
Single/pb: **$70**

Open: **All year**
Breakfast: **Continental**
Pets: **Sometimes**
Children: **Welcome**
Smoking: **No**
Social Drinking: **Permitted**

Cady House is a beautiful Classical Revival house (circa 1839) on College Hill, in the heart of the Brown University campus and within walking distance of the Rhode Island School of Design and Johnson and Wales University. The interior is decorated with antique furnishings, oriental carpets, and the owners' extensive collection of American and international folk art. A screened veranda overlooks a large landscaped garden and patio for warm weather relaxation. The hosts are health professionals, cooks, and musicians. They enjoy helping guests discover the attractions of Providence and Rhode Island.

Green Shadows Bed and Breakfast ✪
803 GREEN HILL BEACH ROAD, WAKEFIELD, RHODE ISLAND 02879

Tel: **(401) 783-9752**
Hosts: **Don and Mercedes Kratz**
Location: **40 mi. S of Providence**
No. of Rooms: **2**
No. of Private Baths: **2**
Double/pb: **$85–$95**
Open: **All year**
Reduced Rates: **Available**
Breakfast: **Full**

Pets: **No**
Children: **Welcome, over 15**
Smoking: **No**
Social Drinking: **Permitted**
Minimum Stay: **2 nights weekends July 1–Labor Day; 3 nights summer holiday weekends**
Station Pickup: **Yes**

Set on one wooded acre, on the south coast of Rhode Island near Green Hill Pond, you will find Green Shadows Bed and Breakfast. Don and Mercedes offer privacy and seclusion with all the benefits of the seaside climate. The beach is only one half-mile away. Rooms are spacious and airy, with king-size beds. Guests can relax in the cozy TV room or on the screened-in porch. Nearby are wildlife preserves, art galleries, flea markets, restaurants, and summer theater, and it's a short drive to historic Mystic, Connecticut, Newport, or the Foxwoods Casino.

Woody Hill B&B ✪
149 SOUTH WOODY HILL ROAD, WESTERLY, RHODE ISLAND 02891

Tel: **(401) 322-0452**
Best Time to Call: **After 5 PM during school year**

Host: **Ellen L. Madison**
Location: **¾ mi. from Rte. 1**
No. of Rooms: **3**

No. of Private Baths: **3**
Double/pb: **$85–$110**
Open: **All year**
Reduced Rates: **Off-season**
Breakfast: **Full**

Pets: **No**
Children: **Welcome**
Smoking: **No**
Social Drinking: **Permitted**

This Colonial reproduction is set on a hilltop among informal gardens and fields. Antiques, wide-board floors, and handmade quilts create an Early American atmosphere. Your hostess may serve homemade jams, muffins, and fresh raspberries in the morning. She can direct you to Mystic Seaport, Block Island, and historic areas. Watch Hill and Westerly beaches are two miles away. She now has an in-ground 40-foot pool.

The Cookie Jar B&B ✪
64 KINGSTOWN ROAD, ROUTE 138, WYOMING, RHODE ISLAND 02898

Tel: **(401) 539-2680; (800) 767-4262**
Best Time to Call: **After 5 PM**
Hosts: **Dick and Madelein Sohl**
Location: **7/10 mi. off I-95, Exit 3A**
No. of Rooms: **3**
No. of Private Baths: **3**
Double/pb: **$75**
Single/pb: **$67.50**

Open: **All year**
Reduced Rates: **20% Nov. 15–Apr. 15, 7th night free**
Breakfast: **Full**
Pets: **No**
Children: **Welcome**
Smoking: **No**
Social Drinking: **Permitted**

The heart of this house, the living room, was a blacksmith's shop built in 1732; the original ceiling, hand-hewn beams, and granite walls are still in use. Fittingly, Dick and Madelein have furnished their home with a mixture of antique, country, and contemporary pieces. You'll enjoy strolling around their property, which includes a barn, flower garden, and lots of fruit trees, berry bushes, and grapevines. Despite the rural setting, you'll have only a short drive to the University of Rhode Island, the beaches, and cities like Mystic, Newport, and Providence. Golfing, horseback riding, bicycling, and waterfront sports are all close at hand. All guest rooms have color TV, air-conditioning, and a private sitting room.

SOUTH CAROLINA

Landrum

Hartsville
Camden

Myrtle Beach

Georgetown

McClellanville
Mt. Pleasant
Charleston

Hilton Head

Candlelight Inn ✪
1904 BROAD STREET, CAMDEN, SOUTH CAROLINA 29020

Tel: **(803) 424-1057**
Hosts: **George and JoAnn Celani**
Location: **30 mi. N of Columbia**
No. of Rooms: **3**
No. of Private Baths: **3**
Double/pb: **$75–$125**
Open: **All year**
Breakfast: **Full**

Credit Cards: **DISC, MC, VISA**
Pets: **No**
Children: **Welcome, over 12**
Smoking: **No**
Social Drinking: **Permitted**
Minimum Stay: **2 nights Carolina and Colonial Cup Steeplechase**

Located in Camden's Historic District, Candlelight Inn stands on two
acres, surrounded by azaleas and camellias and shaded by a canopy of
grand old oaks. A brick drive will guide you to the Inn where the glow
of candles illuminates the windows. The warm and inviting interior

reflects George and JoAnn's interest in needlework, quilts, and antiques. Nearby, guests can enjoy antique shops, Steeplechase facilities, golf courses, and fine restaurants. One description by a guest says it all: "Candlelight, comfort, camellias, charm, cookies, conversation, and cooking all add up to the Candlelight Inn."

Historic Charleston Bed & Breakfast
57 BROAD STREET, CHARLESTON, SOUTH CAROLINA 29401

Tel: **(803) 722-6606; (800) 743-3583**
Best Time to Call: **9 AM–5 PM**
  Mon.–Fri.
Coordinator: **Jo Bacon, manager**
States/Regions Covered: **South Carolina**
Descriptive Directory: **Free**

Rates (Single/Double):
  Modest: **$65 / $75**
  Average: **$80 / $95**
  Luxury: **$120 / $225**
Credit Cards: **MC, VISA**
Minimum Stay: **2 nights Mar. 15–June 15, Oct.**

This port city is one of the most historic in the United States. Through the auspices of this service, you will enjoy your stay in a private home, carriage house, or mansion in a neighborhood of enchanting walled gardens, cobblestoned streets, and moss-draped oak trees. Each home is unique, yet each has a warm and friendly atmosphere provided by a host who sincerely enjoys making guests welcome. All are historic properties dating from 1720 to 1890, yet all are up to date with air-conditioning, phones, and television. Reduced rates may be available for weekly stays. There is a one-time $15 reservation fee charged with each reservation.

Ann Harper's Bed & Breakfast
56 SMITH STREET, CHARLESTON, SOUTH CAROLINA 29401

Tel: **(803) 723-3947**
Best Time to Call: **Before 10 AM; after 6 PM**
Host: **Ann D. Harper**
Location: **1 mi. from I-26**
No. of Rooms: **2**
Max. No. Sharing Bath: **3**
Double/pb: **$70–$85**

Single/pb: **$65–$70**
Open: **All year**
Breakfast: **Full**
Pets: **No**
Children: **Welcome, over 10**
Smoking: **Restricted**
Social Drinking: **Permitted**

This attractive home, circa 1870, is located in Charleston's historic district. The rooms, ideally suited for two friends traveling together, are decorated with wicker pieces and family treasures. Take a moment to relax on the porch or in the intimate walled garden out back. Ann serves a hot, Southern-style breakfast each morning featuring homemade bread and hominy grits. She will gladly direct you to the interesting sights of this historic area. There is a $5 surcharge for one-night stays; no single rates March 15 to June 15.

Country Victorian Bed and Breakfast ✪
105 TRADD STREET, CHARLESTON, SOUTH CAROLINA 29401

Tel: **(803) 577-0682**
Host: **Diane Deardurff Weed**
Location: **96 mi. S of Myrtle Beach**
No. of Rooms: **2**
No. of Private Baths: **2**
Double/pb: **$75–$100**
Single/pb: **$75–$100**

Suites: **$100–$140**
Open: **All year**
Breakfast: **Continental**
Pets: **No**
Children: **Welcome, over 8**
Smoking: **No**
Social Drinking: **Permitted**

As tourists pass in horse-drawn carriages, their eyes are drawn to the beautiful screen doors of this Victorianized house, built in 1820. Rooms have private entrances and are comfortably decorated with antique iron and brass beds, old quilts, and antique oak and wicker furniture. You'll find homemade cookies waiting for you when you arrive. Coffee and tea can be prepared in your room at any time, and snacks are served in the afternoon. Restaurants, churches, antique shops, museums, and art galleries are all within walking distance.

Johnson's Six Orange Street B&B
6 ORANGE STREET, CHARLESTON, SOUTH CAROLINA 29401

Tel: **(803) 722-6122**
Hosts: **Becky and Bill Johnson**
Location: **Located in historic district of Charleston**
No. of Rooms: **1**
No. of Private Baths: **1**
Apartment: **$100**
Open: **All year**

Breakfast: **Continental**
Credit Cards: **No**
Pets: **No**
Children: **Welcome (crib)**
Smoking: **No**
Social Drinking: **Permitted**
Foreign Languages: **French, German**

Within Charleston's historical district, Becky and Bill maintain an attached guesthouse complete with sitting room, efficiency kitchen, upstairs bedroom, and private bath and entrance. The bedroom sleeps three and features an antique sleigh bed plus an iron and brass single bed. A crib is also available for families with an infant. Enjoy scrumptious home-baked coffee cakes, pastries, and breads before you explore the numerous sights and attractions this city has to offer.

1790 House ✪
630 HIGHMARKET STREET, GEORGETOWN, SOUTH CAROLINA 29440

Tel: **(803) 546-4821; (800) 890-7432**
Best Time to Call: **9 AM–9 PM**
Hosts: **Patricia and John Wiley**
Location: **60 mi. N of Charleston; 35 mi. S of Myrtle Beach**

No. of Rooms: **6**
No. of Private Baths: **6**
Double/pb: **$80–$95**
Guest Cottage: **$125**
Suites: **$95**

Open: **All year**
Reduced Rates: **Nov.–Feb. 10% less
Sun.–Thurs., 10% seniors**
Breakfast: **Full**
Credit Cards: **AMEX, DISC, MC, VISA**

Pets: **No**
Children: **Welcome**
Smoking: **No**
Social Drinking: **Permitted**
Minimum Stay: **Holiday weekends**

This meticulously restored, 200-year-old Colonial plantation-style inn in Georgetown's historic district has spacious, luxurious rooms, 11-foot ceilings, and seven fireplaces. Slaves once slept in the Slave Quarters, while the elegant Rice Planters and Indigo Rooms have four-poster beds, sitting areas, and fireplaces. Your other options include the Prince George Suite, a hideaway under the eaves; Gabrielle's Library, with built-in bookcases and a fireplace; and the Dependency Cottage, with its private entrance, patio, and spacious bath with a Jacuzzi. Whichever you pick, you can walk to shops, restaurants, and historic sites. Or take a short drive to Myrtle Beach, golfing on the Grand Strand, the Brookgreen Gardens, Pawleys Island, and downtown Charleston.

Missouri Inn B&B ❂

314 EAST HOME AVENUE, HARTSVILLE, SOUTH CAROLINA 29550

Tel: **(803) 383-9553**
Best Time to Call: **Noon–9 PM**
Hosts: **Kyle and Kenny Segars, and Lucy Brown**
Location: **28 mi. NW of Florence**
No. of Rooms: **5**
No. of Private Baths: **5**
Double/pb: **$85**
Single/pb: **$75**

Open: **All year**
Reduced Rates: **Corporate**
Breakfast: **Full**
Credit Cards: **AMEX, MC, VISA**
Pets: **No**
Children: **Welcome, over 10**
Smoking: **Permitted**
Social Drinking: **Permitted**

An elegant Southern mansion built around the turn of the century and completely renovated in 1990, the Missouri Inn offers discriminating guests exceptional peace, quiet, and privacy in a small, luxurious setting. Located in Hartsville's official historic district, the Inn stands opposite the lovely Coker College campus, on about five acres landscaped with stately trees and flowering shrubs. The distinctively furnished rooms not only have telephones and TVs, but terry robes, bath sheets, towel warmers, hair dryers, and fresh floral arrangements. Amenities include afternoon tea and complimentary beverages at all times.

Ambiance Bed & Breakfast

8 WREN DRIVE, HILTON HEAD, SOUTH CAROLINA 29928

Tel: **(803) 671-4981**
Host: **Marny Kridel Daubenspeck**
Location: **40 mi. from I-95, Exit 28**
No. of Rooms: **2**
No. of Private Baths: **2**

Double/pb: **$75**
Single/pb: **$70**
Open: **All year**
Breakfast: **Continental**
Pets: **No**

Children: **Welcome, over 12**   Social Drinking: **Permitted**
Smoking: **No**

Marny welcomes guests to sunny Hilton Head Island. This cypress home, nestled in subtropical surroundings, is in Sea Pines Plantation. Ambiance reflects the hostess's interior decorating business by the same name. All the amenities of Hilton Head are offered in a contemporary, congenial atmosphere. The climate is favorable year-round for all sports. Ambiance is across the street from a beautiful beach and the Atlantic Ocean.

The Red Horse Inn ✪
310 NORTH CAMPBELL ROAD, LANDRUM, SOUTH CAROLINA 29356

Tel: **(864) 895-4968**
Best Time to Call: **After 6:30 PM**
Hosts: **Roger and Mary Wolters**
Location: **8 mi. S of Landrum**
Guest Cottages: **$85–$105**
Open: **All year**
Reduced Rates: **Jan.–Feb.; 10% seniors**

Breakfast: **Continental**
Pets: **Sometimes**
Children: **Welcome**
Smoking: **No**
Social Drinking: **Permitted**
Airport Pickup: **Yes**

Located on 190 mountain-view acres, the Red Horse Inn offers five romantic Victorian-style cottages. Each has a kitchen, living room with fireplace, decks or patios, color TV, and air-conditioning. Three have sleeping lofts and Jacuzzis. The equestrian sport of fox hunting takes place in the fall to early spring, and golfing, tennis, hiking, antiquing, sporting clays, hunting, and parks beckon year-round. The Flatrock Playhouse and the Peace Center offer professional performing arts productions. Or guests can simply relax and consume the mountain views from the rocking porch. Breakfast is served in baskets containing muffins or croissants, fruit or juice, and coffee.

Laurel Hill Plantation ✪
8913 NORTH HIGHWAY 17, P.O. BOX 190, McCLELLANVILLE, SOUTH CAROLINA 29458

Tel: **(803) 887-3708**
Best Time to Call: **Before 9 PM**
Hosts: **Jackie and Lee Morrison**
Location: **30 mi. N of Charleston**
No. of Rooms: **4**
No. of Private Baths: **4**
Double/pb: **$65–$95**

Single/pb: **$75**
Open: **All year**
Breakfast: **Full**
Pets: **No**
Children: **Welcome, over 6**
Smoking: **No**
Social Drinking: **Permitted**

The original Laurel Hill, an 1850s plantation house listed on the National Register of Historic Places, was destroyed by Hurricane Hugo in 1989. Nestled in a nook by a picturesque tidal creek, the spacious reconstruction retains the romance of the past while affording the convenience of the contemporary. Wraparound porches provide a sweeping panorama of the Atlantic Ocean and Cape Romain's salt marshes, islands, and waterways. Four charming guest rooms feature fascinating views of the landscape and are furnished with carefully chosen primitives and antiques reflecting the renowned hospitality of South Carolina's low country.

Sunny Meadows ✪
1459 VENNING ROAD, MT. PLEASANT, SOUTH CAROLINA 29464

Tel: **(803) 884-7062**
Best Time to Call: **11 AM–10 PM**
Hosts: **Charles and Agnes Houston**
Location: **5 mi. E of Charleston**
No. of Rooms: **2**
No. of Private Baths: **2**
Double/pb: **$75–$85**

Open: **All year**
Breakfast: **Full**
Pets: **No**
Children: **Welcome, over 8**
Smoking: **No**
Social Drinking: **Permitted**

Enjoy Southern hospitality at its best, where elegance blends with the charm of country living. This two-story Southern Colonial, situated on three acres of beautifully landscaped grounds, is located fifteen minutes from Historic Charleston and five minutes from Charleston's finest beaches. Guest rooms are located away from the family living area, ensuring full privacy. Each room is decorated with 18th-century antiques and reproductions. One room has a king and a double bed. The other has a four-poster bed, TV, and telephone. Weather permitting, you can enjoy breakfast on the back porch and read the paper on the swing. Breakfast specialties include stratta and cheese-stuffed French toast.

Brustman House
400 25TH AVENUE SOUTH, MYRTLE BEACH,
SOUTH CAROLINA 29577

Tel: (803) 448-7699; (800) 448-7699;
  fax: (803) 626-2478
Best Time to Call: **Early evening**
Host: **Dr. Wendell C. Brustman**
Location: **90 mi. N of Charleston**
No. of Rooms: **5**
No. of Private Baths: **5**
Double/pb: **$59–$85**
Single/pb: **$54–$80**
Suites: **$89–$135**

Open: **All year**
Reduced Rates: **Extended stay; Oct.**
  1–Mar. 31
Breakfast: **Full**
Pets: **No**
Children: **Welcome, over 10**
Smoking: **No**
Social Drinking: **Permitted**
Airport/Station Pickup: **Yes**

Maybe you can't have it all, but Brustman House comes close. This Georgian-style home is two short blocks from the beach, and without leaving the almost 2-acre, tree-studded property you can admire the fresh herb garden or have a tête-à-tête on the glider in the rose garden gazebo. Located nearby are golf courses, seafront restaurants, discount shops, and country music theaters. Afternoon tea includes wines, waters, and sweets served on exquisite Scandinavian dinnerware. Sleep late in your quiet room, its snug bed warmed by a down comforter. The Rosewood Room has a Jacuzzi tub for two. The breakfast menu includes healthful specialties, such as ten-grain buttermilk pancakes.

Serendipity, An Inn ✪
**407 71ST AVENUE NORTH, MYRTLE BEACH,
SOUTH CAROLINA 29572**

Tel: **(803) 449-5268; (800) 762-3229**
Best Time to Call: **8 AM–10 PM**
Hosts: **Terry and Sheila Johnson**
Location: **60 mi. from Rte. 95**
No. of Rooms: **14**
No. of Private Baths: **14**
Double/pb: **$67–$92**
Suites: **$78–$110**

Open: **Jan.–Nov.**
Breakfast: **Continental**
Credit Cards: **MC, VISA**
Pets: **No**
Children: **Welcome**
Smoking: **Permitted**
Social Drinking: **Permitted**

Serendipity is a Spanish Mission–style inn surrounded by lush tropical plants and flowers. The setting is peaceful, the street is quiet, and the ocean is less than 300 yards away. Bedrooms are highlighted with antiques drawing from Art Deco, Oriental, wicker, and pine motifs. The Garden Room is the place for a generous breakfast of homemade breads, fresh fruit, eggs, and cereal. Your hosts invite you to use the heated pool and spa, play shuffleboard, Ping-Pong, or just share a quiet moment beside the patio fountain. Myrtle Beach is known for its fine restaurants, but the Johnsons have a gas grill if you want to do your own cooking. Terry and Sheila will gladly direct you to nearby shops, fishing villages, golf courses, miles of beaches, and music theaters.

SOUTH DAKOTA

Custer Mansion Bed & Breakfast ✪
35 CENTENNIAL DRIVE, CUSTER, SOUTH DAKOTA 57730

Tel: **(605) 673-3333**
Hosts: **Millard and Carole Seaman**
Location: **42 mi. W of Rapid City**
No. of Rooms: **5**
No. of Private Baths: **5**
Double/pb: **$65–$95**
Suite: **$110, sleeps 4**
Open: **All year**
Reduced Rates: **Off-season, extended stays**

Breakfast: **Full**
Pets: **No**
Children: **Welcome**
Smoking: **No**
Social Drinking: **No**
Minimum Stay: **2 nights, holidays, peak season**
Foreign Languages: **Spanish**

Built in 1891, this Victorian Gothic home is listed on the National Register of Historic Places and features a blend of Victorian elegance, country charm, and Western hospitality. Guests enjoy clean quiet accommodations and a delicious home-cooked breakfast. Custer Mansion is centrally located to all Black Hills attractions including Mt. Rushmore, Custer State Park, Crazy Horse Memorial, and much more. Afternoon tea is served between 4 and 5 PM.

Cheyenne Crossing B&B ✪
HC 37, BOX 1220, LEAD, SOUTH DAKOTA 57754

Tel: **(605) 584-3510, 584-2636;** **(800) 400-7722**	Reduced Rates: **Families; groups**
	Breakfast: **Full**
Hosts: **Jim and Bonnie LeMar**	Other Meals: **Available**
Location: **Junction Hwys. 85 and 14A**	Credit Cards: **DISC, MC, VISA**
No. of Rooms: 3	Pets: **By arrangement**
Max. No. Sharing Bath: **4**	Children: **Welcome, over 6**
Double /pb: **$89**	Smoking: **No**
Open: **All year**	Social Drinking: **Permitted**

This two-story frame building with its facade of rough-sawed pine is situated in the heart of Spearfish Canyon. The main floor houses a typical country general store and cafe; the guest quarters are upstairs. From 1876 to 1885 the original building was a stop for the Deadwood–Cheyenne stagecoach. After it burned down in 1960, the present building was built to replace it. Jim and Bonnie will be delighted to map out special trips tailored to your interests. Spend the day visiting Mt. Rushmore and Crazy Horse Monument, pan for gold, hike, or fish for trout on Spearfish Creek, which flows behind the store. It's also close to the Black Hills Passion Play. Sourdough pancakes are a frequent breakfast treat. A new two-bedroom creekside cabin with fireplace and whirlpool bath is now available.

Abend Haus Cottages & Audrie's
Bed & Breakfast ✪
23029 THUNDERHEAD FALLS ROAD, RAPID CITY, SOUTH DAKOTA 57702-8524

Tel: **(605) 342-7788**	Suites: **$95**
Best Time to Call: **9 AM–9 PM MST**	Open: **All year**
Hosts: **Hank and Audrie Kuhnhauser**	Breakfast: **Full**
Location: **¼ mi. from Hwy. 44**	Pets: **No**
No. of Rooms: 9	Children: **No**
No. of Private Baths: 9	Smoking: **No**
Double/pb: **$95**	Social Drinking: **Permitted**
Guest Cottages: **$145**	

At this country home and 5-acre estate in a secluded Black Hills setting just 30 miles from Mt. Rushmore and 7 miles from Rapid City, you can experience charm and old-world hospitality. There are free trout fishing, biking, and hiking on the property, which is surrounded by thousands of acres of national forest land. Each suite and cottage has a private entrance, bath, hot tub, patio, cable TV, VCR, coffee pot, microwave, and refrigerator. Full breakfast is provided for you to heat and serve at your convenience.

Bed and Breakfast Domivara ☉
2760 DOMIVARA ROAD, RAPID CITY, SOUTH DAKOTA 57702-6008

Tel: **(605) 574-4207**	Open: **All year**
Best Time to Call: **Mornings; 6–8 PM**	Breakfast: **Full**
Host: **Betty Blount**	Pets: **Sometimes**
Location: **26 mi. SW of Rapid City**	Children: **Welcome**
No. of Rooms: **4**	Smoking: **No**
No. of Private Baths: **4**	Social Drinking: **Permitted**
Double/pb: **$70–$75**	Minimum Stay: **2 nights**
Single/pb: **$60–$65**	

Enjoy Western hospitality in a unique log home located in the picturesque Black Hills of South Dakota. The homey wood interior is decorated with comfortable antiques and accents of stained glass. A large picture window overlooks the countryside where you may see an occasional wild turkey or deer. Betty Blount offers complimentary snacks served with coffee. She prepares a variety of special breakfast dishes including sourdough pancakes, egg soufflés, fresh trout, and homemade blueberry muffins. There are good restaurants nearby. Domivara is conveniently located just 20 minutes from Mt. Rushmore and the Crazy Horse Memorial.

Lakeside Farm ☉
RR 2, BOX 52, WEBSTER, SOUTH DAKOTA 57274

Tel: **(605) 486-4430**	Single/sb: **$35**
Hosts: **Joy and Glenn Hagen**	Open: **All year**
Location: **60 mi. E of Aberdeen on Hwy. 12**	Breakfast: **Full**
	Pets: **No**
No. of Rooms: **2**	Children: **Welcome**
Maximum No. Sharing Bath: **4**	Smoking: **No**
Double/sb: **$45**	Social Drinking: **No**

This 750-acre farm where Joy and Glenn raise oats and corn is located in the Lake Region where recreational activities abound. You are certain to be comfortable in their farmhouse, built in 1970 and furnished in a simple, informal style. You will awaken to the delicious aroma of Joy's heavenly cinnamon rolls or bread and enjoy breakfast served on the enclosed porch. Nearby attractions include Fort Sisseton and the June festival that recounts Sam Brown's historic ride. You will also enjoy the Blue Dog fish hatchery and the Game Reserve. Dakotah, Inc., manufacturers of linens and wall hangings, is located in Webster. It has an outlet shop where great buys may be found.

Rockinghorse Bed & Breakfast ✪
RR 1, BOX 133, WHITEWOOD, SOUTH DAKOTA 57793

Tel: **(605) 269-2625**
Hosts: **Sharleen and Jerry Bergum**
Location: **30 mi. NW of Rapid City**
No. of Rooms: **3**
No. of Private Baths: **3**
Double/pb: **$45–$65**
Guest Cottage: **$100–$250**
Open: **All year**

Reduced Rates: **Available**
Breakfast: **Full**
Credit Cards: **MC, VISA**
Pets: **Sometimes**
Children: **Welcome**
Smoking: **No**
Social Drinking: **No**
Airport/Station Pickup: **Yes**

A cedar clapboard–sided house, built in 1914 to accommodate local timber teams, Rockinghorse was moved from its first site by Jerry and Sharleen, who have lovingly restored the interior. Handsome wood floors, columns, and trims grace the living and dining areas, and the original stairway is still usable. Antiques, lace, and country delights complement the homey atmosphere. Rockinghorse is situated at the base of the rustic Black Hills, where deer graze in nearby fields and wild turkeys strut across the valley below the house. Nature walks and panoramic views will appeal to the artist/photographer. Domestic animals abound—after a rooster's crow awakens you, you may pet a bunny in the petting zoo, visit the horses, take a buggy ride, or watch the art of wool spinning.

TENNESSEE

Bed & Breakfast—About Tennessee ✪
P.O. BOX 110227, NASHVILLE, TENNESSEE 37222-0227

Tel: **(615) 331-5244 for information;**
  (800) 458-2421 for reservations; fax:
  (615) 833-7701
Coordinator: **Fredda Odom**
States/Regions Covered: **Statewide**

Descriptive Directory of B&Bs: **$5**
Rates (Single/Double):
  Average: **$40–$50 / $65**
  Luxury: **$80–$100 / $80–$150**
Credit Cards: **AMEX, DISC, MC, VISA**

From the Great Smoky Mountains to the Mississippi, here are diverse attractions that include fabulous scenery, Tennessee's Grand Ole Opry and Opryland, universities, Civil War sites, horse farms, and much more. Fredda will arrange sightseeing tours, car rentals, tickets to events, and everything she can to assure you a pleasant stay. There is a $5 booking fee.

Chadwick House ✪

2766 MICHIGAN AVENUE, RD NORTH EAST, CLEVELAND, TENNESSEE 37323

Tel: **(423) 339-2407**
Host: **Winnie A. Chadwick**
Location: **35 mi. N of Chattanooga**
No. of Rooms: **3**
No. of Private Baths: **1**
Max. No. Sharing Bath: **4**
Double/pb: **$52**
Double/sb: **$47**
Single/sb: **$35**

Open: **All year**
Reduced Rates: **10% seniors**
Breakfast: **Full**
Other Meals: **Available**
Pets: **No**
Children: **Welcome**
Smoking: **Permitted**
Social Drinking: **Permitted**
Airport/Station Pickup: **Yes**

White shutters and trim accent the multicolored bricks of this handsome ranch home just a half hour from Chattanooga. White-water rafting, Red Clay's historic Indian meeting grounds, and Cherokee National Forest are close by, and golfing and tennis are available right in Cleveland. In their spare moments B&B guests can watch the squirrels and birds in the back garden or relax by the fireplace with a glass of locally made wine. Winnie's full country breakfasts include homemade rolls and muffins.

Butcher House in the Mountains ✪

1520 GARRETT LANE, GATLINBURG, TENNESSEE 37738

Tel: **(423) 436-9457**
Best Time to Call: **10 AM–9 PM**
Hosts: **Hugh and Gloria Butcher**
Location: **50 mi. SE of Knoxville**
No. of Rooms: **5**
No. of Private Baths: **5**
Double/pb: **$79–$119**
Open: **All year**
Reduced Rates: **$10 less after 2nd night,**
  Mon.–Thurs.

Breakfast: **Full**
Credit Cards: **AMEX, MC, VISA**
Pets: **No**
Children: **Welcome, over 12**
Smoking: **No**
Social Drinking: **Permitted**
Minimum Stay: **Weekends**
Foreign Languages: **Italian**

The ambiance at Butcher House is one of elegance, warmth, and beauty. Hugh and Gloria's years of collecting have resulted in a home filled with one-of-a-kind antique treasures. Guest rooms are decorated with unique linens and furniture from various eras. Nearby attractions include Pigeon Forge, Dollywood, and Great Smoky Mountains National Park. Guests can enjoy hiking, fishing, skiing, golfing, or visiting the many crafts shops. Your hosts will send you on your way after a gourmet breakfast that may consist of eggs Sebastian, Italian crepes, or eggs cardamom.

Olde English Tudor Inn ✪
135 WEST HOLLY RIDGE ROAD, GATLINBURG, TENNESSEE 37738

Tel: **(423) 436-7760; (800) 541-3798**
Best Time to Call: **11 AM–9 PM**
Hosts: **Kathy and Larry Schuh**
Location: **45 mi. SE of Knoxville**
No. of Rooms: **7**
No. of Private Baths: **7**
Double/pb: **$75–$85**
Single/pb: **$65**
Suites: **$95–$105**

Open: **All year**
Reduced Rates: **10% seniors**
Breakfast: **Full**
Credit Cards: **MC, VISA**
Pets: **No**
Children: **Welcome**
Smoking: **No**
Social Drinking: **Permitted**
Airport Pickup: **Yes**

From the Olde English Tudor Inn's ideal downtown location, it's just a few minutes' walk to the attractions of Gatlinburg, and only a brief drive to Dollywood, Craft Community, outlet malls, and Great Smoky National Park. Handsomely decorated bedrooms have cable TV with HBO. Guests are invited to relax in the large, comfortably furnished community room with a TV/VCR and free-standing wood burning stove, or enjoy the peaceful seclusion of the rear patio. Generous breakfasts typically include fresh fruit, pancakes, or French toast, and eggs, bacon, sausage, or ham. Make sure to save room for freshly baked breads with jams and jellies. Kathy and Larry want your visit to be memorable and will be happy to assist you with your touring, dining, and shopping questions.

Woodshire B&B ✪
600 WOODSHIRE DRIVE, GOODLETTSVILLE, TENNESSEE 37072

Tel: **(615) 859-7369**
Best Time to Call: **Before 9 AM; after 6 PM**
Hosts: **Beverly and John Grayson**
Location: **11 mi. N of Nashville**
No. of Rooms: **2**
No. of Private Baths: **2**
Double/pb: **$60**
Single/pb: **$50**

Guest Cabin: **$55–$65**
Open: **Feb. 1–Dec. 31**
Breakfast: **Continental**
Pets: **No**
Children: **Welcome**
Smoking: **No**
Social Drinking: **No**
Airport/Station Pickup: **Yes**

A blue clapboard house inspired by New England saltboxes, Woodshire B&B is 20 minutes from downtown Nashville and its attractions—Opryland Park, Andrew Jackson's Hermitage, and the homes and museums of country music stars. Beverly will gladly tell you the stories behind the antique family furniture. She's a retired art teacher, and as you look around you'll see her paintings and weavings, and John's woodcrafts. Continental breakfast features homemade preserves, breads, and waffles.

Hilltop House Bed and Breakfast Inn ✪
6 SANFORD CIRCLE, GREENEVILLE, TENNESSEE 37743

Tel: **(423) 639-8202**
Best Time to Call: **5 PM–7 PM**
Host: **Denise M. Ashworth**
Location: **7 mi. S. of Greeneville**
No. of Rooms: **3**
No. of Private Baths: **3**
Double/pb: **$80**
Single/pb: **$75**
Open: **All year**

Reduced Rates: **Available**
Breakfast: **Full**
Other Meals: **Available**
Credit Cards: **AMEX, MC, VISA**
Pets: **No**
Children: **Welcome, over 3 years**
Smoking: **No**
Social Drinking: **Permitted**
Airport/Station Pickup: **Yes**

Hilltop House is a 1920s manor house on a hillside above the Noli-chucky River Valley, with the Appalachian Mountains in the background. All the guest rooms, which are furnished in 18th-century English antiques and period reproductions, have mountain views; two have verandas. In keeping with her British birth, the innkeeper sets out a proper English tea every afternoon. The family-style breakfast consists of fruit, cereal, egg dishes, and homemade biscuits or muffins. Then it's time to explore the great outdoors: white-water rafting, hiking, biking, trout fishing, golfing, hunting, and bird-watching are among your options. Cherokee National Forest is within striking distance, as are the Great Smoky Mountains and the Blue Ridge Parkway.

Natchez Trace B&B Reservation Service
P.O. BOX 193, HAMPSHIRE, TENNESSEE 38461

Tel: **(800) 377-2770; (615) 285-2777**
Best Time to Call: **Evening; weekends**
Coordinator: **Kay Jones**
States/Regions Covered:
  Alabama—Florence, Cherokee;
  Mississippi—Church Hill, Corinth,
  French Camp, Jackson, Kosciusko,
  Lorman, Natchez, New Albany, Port
  Gibson, Vicksburg; Tennessee—

Columbia, Mt. Pleasant, Culleoka,
Fairview, Franklin, Hohenwald,
Leiper's Fork, Nashville
Descriptive Directory of B&Bs: **Free**
Rates (Single/Double):
  Modest: **$55 / $65**
  Average: **$70 / $80**
  Luxury: **$90 / $175**
Credit Cards: **MC, VISA**

Kay's reservation service is unique in that the homes are all convenient to the Natchez Trace National Parkway, the historic Nashville-to-Natchez route that was first designated by President Thomas Jefferson. The parkway is known for both its natural beauty and the charming Southern towns along the way. Kay can help you plan your trip and give you access to homes ranging from rustic, woodsy sites to fine antebellum mansions. Call her for a free list of homes, as well as literature about the Natchez Trace.

Hart House Bed and Breakfast ◑
207 EAST HOLSTON AVENUE, JOHNSON CITY, TENNESSEE 37601

Tel: **(423) 926-3147**
Hosts: **Francis and Vanessa Gingras**
Location: **90 mi. NE of Knoxville**
No. of Rooms: **3**
No. of Private Baths: **3**

Double/pb: **$65**
Single/pb: **$55**
Open: **All year**
Reduced Rates: **10% seniors**
Breakfast: **Full**

Credit Cards: **AMEX, DISC, MC, VISA**
Pets: **Sometimes**
Children: **Welcome**

Smoking: **No**
Social Drinking: **Permitted**

Hart House is named after the original owner of this 1910 Dutch Colonial, which Francis and Vanessa have filled with antiques and collectibles. Johnson City is located in the heart of upper northeast Tennessee, an area brimming with both notable sites and scenic beauty. For history buffs, Jonesborough, the oldest town in the state, is five miles away, and those who love the great outdoors—camping, hiking, fishing, whitewater rafting—will find plenty to do here. Each morning, guests wake up to an elegant breakfast of fresh fruit, homemade muffins, eggs, and fresh brewed coffee.

The Jam N Jelly Inn Bed and Breakfast ✪
1310 INDIAN RIDGE ROAD, JOHNSON CITY, TENNESSEE 37604

Tel: **(423) 929-0039; fax: (423) 929-9026**
Best Time to Call: **After 5 PM**
Host: **Walter D. Kidner**
Location: **5 mi. SW of I-181, Exit 35**
No. of Rooms: **6**
No. of Private Baths: **6**
Double/pb: **$65**
Single/pb: **$55**
Suites: **$75**
Open: **All year**

Reduced Rates: **Available**
Breakfast: **Full**
Credit Cards: **AMEX, DISC, MC, VISA**
Pets: **No**
Children: **By arrangement**
Smoking: **No**
Social Drinking: **Permitted**
Minimum Stay: **2 nights special events weekends**
Airport Pickup: **Yes**

The Jam N Jelly Inn, Johnson City's newest bed & breakfast, offers a unique lodging experience. The Inn is a custom-built log home that offers comfort and privacy to guests. The decor is a tasteful blend of casual elegance in a homelike atmosphere. Guest rooms all have queen beds and reproduction antiques. Amenities include a well-stocked book and video library, snacks and beverages, an eight- to ten-person hot tub, a spacious front porch, and a rear covered deck for quiet reflection. Inside, you'll find a centrally located VCR, fax machine, air-conditioning, and TV; three rooms have private telephones. One room is accessible to disabled visitors.

"Mitchell's" ✪
1031 WEST PARK DRIVE, KNOXVILLE, TENNESSEE 37909

Tel: **(423) 690-1488**
Host: **Mary M. Mitchell**
Location: **1.6 mi. from I-75-40, Exit 380**
No. of Rooms: **1**
No. of Private Baths: **1**
Double/pb: **$40**
Single/pb: **$35**

Open: **All year**
Breakfast: **Continental**
Pets: **Sometimes**
Children: **Welcome**
Smoking: **Permitted**
Social Drinking: **Permitted**
Airport/Station Pickup: **Yes**

Located in a pleasant, quiet neighborhood with numerous shade trees, Mary's B&B is air-conditioned and has a private entrance with no steps to climb. There's a double bed, and a rollaway is available. Breakfast features homemade muffins or cinnamon rolls with coffee. Windy Hill is convenient to the University of Tennessee; Oak Ridge is only a 15-minute drive while Great Smoky Mountains National Park is an hour away.

Snapp Inn B&B ○

1990 DAVY CROCKETT PARK ROAD, LIMESTONE, TENNESSEE 37681

Tel: **(423) 257-2482**
Best Time to Call: **Before 10 AM;**
    after 7 PM
Hosts: **Dan and Ruth Dorgan**
Location: **4 mi. from Rte. 11 E**
No. of Rooms: **2**
No. of Private Baths: **2**
Double/pb: **$65**

Single/pb: **$55**
Open: **All year**
Breakfast: **Full**
Pets: **Welcome**
Children: **Welcome (one at a time)**
Smoking: **No**
Social Drinking: **Permitted**
Airport/Station Pickup: **Yes**

Built in 1815 and situated in farm country, this Federal brick home has lovely mountain views. The house is decorated with antiques, including a Victorian reed organ. Now retired, Ruth and Dan have the time to pursue their interests in antiques restoration, history, needlework, and bluegrass music. It is an easy walk to Davy Crockett Birthplace State Park, and 15 minutes to historic Jonesboro or the Andrew Johnson Home in Greeneville. A swimming pool, golf, and fishing are close by. You are welcome to use the laundry facilities, television, and pool table.

Cedar Lane Bed and Breakfast ○

ROUTE 3, BOX 155E, LYNCHBURG, TENNESSEE 37352

Tel: **(615) 759-6891**
Best Time to Call: **After 4 PM**
Hosts: **Elaine and Chuck Quinn**
Location: **45 mi. N of Huntsville,**
    Alabama
No. of Rooms: **4**
No. of Private Baths: **4**
Double/pb: **$70–$75**
Single/pb: **$65**
Open: **All year**

Reduced Rates: **10% weekly**
Breakfast: **Continental, plus**
Other Meals: **Available**
Credit Cards: **AMEX, MC, VISA**
Pets: **No**
Children: **Welcome, over 10**
Smoking: **No**
Social Drinking: **Permitted**
Foreign Languages: **Hungarian**

On the outskirts of historic Lynchburg, home of the Jack Daniel's Distillery, this newly built farmhouse offers guests comfort and relaxation. Whether it be a weekend or a week's stay, guests can spend time antiquing in nearby shops or reading a book in the sunroom. Rooms are beautifully decorated in rose, blue, peach, and green, with queen- and twin-size beds. Dinner is available by reservation.

Historic Falcon Manor✪

2645 FAULKNER SPRINGS ROAD, McMINNVILLE, TENNESSEE 37110
falconmanor@falconmanor.com; http://www.falconmanor.com

Tel: **(931) 668-4444**
Best Time to Call: **Anytime**
Hosts: **George and Charlien McGlothin**
Location: **72 mi. SE of Nashville**
No. of Rooms: **7**
No. of Private Baths: **3**
Max. No. Sharing Bath: **4**
Double/pb: **$85–$105**
Single/pb: **$85**
Double/sb: **$75**

Single/sb: **$75**
Open: **All year**
Reduced Rates: **$5 off per day, 3 days or more**
Breakfast: **Full**
Credit Cards: **MC, VISA**
Pets: **No**
Children: **Welcome, over 12**
Smoking: **No**
Social Drinking: **Permitted**

This historic Victorian mansion re-creates the romance of the 1890s. Relax in the friendly warmth of this fine old house and savor the luxury of its museum-quality antiques. The huge gingerbread veranda is well stocked with rocking chairs and shaded by giant trees. Falcon Manor is a favorite for couples celebrating anniversaries. It's also the ideal base for a middle Tennessee vacation—halfway between Nashville and Chattanooga and just thirty minutes from four state parks. McMinnville is "the nursery capital of the world" and the home of America's second largest cave. George left a career in retail management to spend four years restoring the house, while Charlien pitched in during time off from her job as a NASA public affairs writer. They love sharing stories about Falcon Manor's history and their adventures, bringing it back to life.

The Home Place
132 CHURCH LANE, MOORESBURG, TENNESSEE 37811

Tel: **(800) 521-8424; (423) 921-8424;**
   fax: **(423) 921-8003**
Host: **Priscilla Rogers**
Location: **50 mi. NE of Knoxville**
No. of Rooms: **4**
Max. No. Sharing Bath: **4**
Double/pb: **$65**
Single/pb: **$45**
Double s/b: **$55**

Suites: **$100**
Open: **All year**
Reduced Rates: **10% seniors, 3 nights or
   more**
Breakfast: **Continental**
Pets: **No**
Children: **Welcome, crib**
Smoking: **No**

Built as a log cabin, The Home Place has been in the family since the 1850s. Located in a private setting adjacent to Cherokee Lake, The Home Place offers four guest rooms; suites are available, one with a Jacuzzi tub. The first floor is suitable for guests with disabilities and has a TDD, accessible bath, and other features. Amenities include phone jacks in every room, a television located in the family room, and use of a microwave and refrigerator. The breakfast menu varies, offering everything from fresh fruit and cereal to country ham and biscuits.

Clardy's Guest House ✪
435 EAST MAIN STREET, MURFREESBORO, TENNESSEE 37130

Tel: **(615) 893-6030**
Best Time to Call: **After 10 AM**
Hosts: **Robert and Barbara Deaton**
Location: **2 mi. from I-24**
No. of Rooms: **3**
No. of Private Baths: **2**
Max. No. Sharing Bath: **4**
Double/pb: **$49**
Single/pb: **$39**

Double/sb: **$39**
Single/sb: **$32**
Open: **All year**
Breakfast: **Continental**
Pets: **Sometimes**
Children: **Welcome (crib)**
Smoking: **Restricted**
Social Drinking: **Permitted**

This Romanesque-style Victorian dates back to 1898. The 20 rooms are filled with antiques; with 40 antique dealers in town, you can guess what Murfreesboro is best known for. The world championship horse show at Shelbyville is 30 minutes away. Your hosts will be glad to advise on local tours and can direct you to the home of the Grand Ole Opry, one hour away in Nashville, and fine eating places. Middle Tennessee State University is close by.

Fall Creek Falls Bed & Breakfast ✪
ROUTE 3, BOX 298B, PIKEVILLE, TENNESSEE 37367

Tel: **(423) 881-5494**
Hosts: **Doug and Rita Pruett**
Location: **50 mi. N of Chattanooga**

No. of Rooms: **7**
No. of Private Baths: **7**
Double/pb: **$75–$105**

Single/pb: **$65**
Suite: **$118**
Open: **All year (except Jan.)**
Breakfast: **Full**
Pets: **No**

Children: **Welcome, over 10**
Smoking: **No**
Social Drinking: **Permitted**
Minimum Stay: **2 nights, weekends in October and holidays**

Enjoy the relaxing atmosphere of a new country manor home on forty acres of rolling hillside one mile from the nationally acclaimed Fall Creek Falls State Resort Park. Beautiful guest rooms have pickled oak floors and antique furniture with two common sitting areas. Lodging includes a full breakfast served in a cozy country kitchen or an elegant dining room. Doug enjoys grouse hunting and trout fishing and is a licensed Tennessee building contractor. Rita is an insurance executive who enjoys bargain hunting and antique auctions. Touring, dining, and shopping information is always available.

Ross House Bed and Breakfast ✪
504 MAIN STREET, P.O. BOX 398, SAVANNAH, TENNESSEE 38372

Tel: **(901) 925-3974; (800) 467-3174**
Best Time to Call: **9 AM–5 PM**
Hosts: **John and Harriet Ross**
Location: **110 mi. E of Memphis**
Suites: **$75–$150**
Open: **All year**
Breakfast: **Full**

Credit Cards: **AMEX, DISC, MC, VISA**
Pets: **No**
Children: **Welcome, over 10**
Smoking: **No**
Social Drinking: **Permitted**
Foreign Languages: **French, Spanish**

Part of Savannah's National Register Historic District, which contains residences from the late 1860s to the 1920s, this B&B is a Neoclassical brick house built in 1908 by John's grandparents. Inside you'll see the original owners' furniture, books, paintings, and photographs. It is a short walk to the Cherry Mansion and Tennessee River and a short drive to Shiloh National Military Park and Pickwick Lake, for fishing and boating. If you'd rather paddle your canoe, take the 45-minute drive to the Buffalo River. John practices law next door where his grandfather once did, but when time permits, he accompanies guests on bicycle tours. Harriet is an English teacher in a local public school.

Blue Mountain Mist Country Inn & Cottages ✪
1811 PULLEN ROAD, SEVIERVILLE, TENNESSEE 37862

Tel: **(800) 497-2335; (423) 428-2335**
Best Time to Call: **10 AM–9 PM**
Hosts: **Norman and Sarah Ball**
Location: **4 mi. E of Pigeon Forge**
No. of Rooms: **12**
No. of Private Baths: **12**
Double/pb: **$95**
Guest Cottage: **$135**

Suites: **$105–$125**
Open: **All year**
Breakfast: **Full**
Pets: **No**
Children: **Welcome (2 rooms)**
Smoking: **No**
Social Drinking: **Permitted**

This Victorian-style farmhouse inn with country cottages is located on 60 acres in the foothills of the Great Smoky Mountains. Away from the congestion you can enjoy beautiful views of rolling meadows and mountains while rocking on the huge front porch. The Inn is filled with country antiques, handmade quilts, and local art. In the morning awake to a hearty Tennessee breakfast, in the evening indulge in a delicious homemade dessert. Each cottage has a large Jacuzzi and a fireplace designed for a peaceful romantic getaway. Nearby attractions include Gatlinburg, the Crafts Community, Pigeon Forge, and Dollywood.

Calico Inn ✪
757 RANCH WAY, SEVIERVILLE, TENNESSEE 37862

Tel: **(423) 428-3833; (800) 235-1054**
Best Time to Call: **11 AM–9 PM**
Hosts: **Lill and Jim Katzbeck**
Location: **35 mi. N of Knoxville**
No. of Rooms: **3**
No. of Private Baths: **3**
Double/pb: **$85–$95**
Open: **All year**

Reduced Rates: **Jan.–Feb.**
Breakfast: **Full**
Pets: **No**
Children: **Welcome, over 6**
Smoking: **No**
Social Drinking: **Permitted**
Minimum Stay: **2 nights holidays and special events**

Nestled among trees atop a peaceful ridge, Calico Inn offers guests a serene panoramic view of the Smoky Mountains. Lill and Jim invite you to start your day with a delightful breakfast that may include juice, fresh fruit, homemade bread or muffins, hash browns, biscuits and gravy. The Katzbecks are only minutes from Dollywood, shopping, fishing, golfing, and hiking in the mountains. Best of all, you can take pleasure in knowing that the quiet Calico Inn awaits you each evening.

Little Greenbrier Lodge ✪
3685 LYON SPRINGS ROAD, SEVIERVILLE, TENNESSEE 37862

Tel: **(423) 429-2500; (800) 277-8100**
Best Time to Call: **Anytime**
Hosts: **Charles and Susan LeBon**
No. of Rooms: **10**
No. of Private Baths: **8**
Max. No. Sharing Bath: **4**
Double/pb: **$95–$110**
Double/sb: **$75**
Single/sb: **$55–$65**
Open: **All year**

Reduced Rates: **10% seniors**
Breakfast: **Full**
Credit Cards: **DISC, MC, VISA**
Pets: **No**
Children: **Welcome, over 12; under 12 by arrangement**
Smoking: **No**
Social Drinking: **Permitted**
Airport Pickup: **Yes**

Nestled in the hills of the Great Smoky Mountains, Little Greenbrier Lodge was built in 1939 and renovated in 1993. All rooms offer guests modern comforts with the Victorian decor. The view of the valley provides a perfect backdrop for a delicious country breakfast. Cades Cove, Dollywood, outlet malls, and numerous antique and craft shops are all within 30 minutes. If you enjoy hiking, the lodge is located right next to a park and just 150 yards from Little Greenbrier Trailhead, which will connect you to other interesting paths in the park.

For key to listings, see inside front or back cover.

✪ This star means that rates are guaranteed through December 31, 1998, to any guest making a reservation as a result of reading about the B&B in *Bed & Breakfast U.S.A.*—1998 edition.

Important! To avoid misunderstandings, always ask about cancellation policies when booking.

Please enclose a self-addressed, stamped, business-size envelope when contacting reservation services.

For more details on what you can expect in a B&B, see Chapter 1.

Always mention *Bed & Breakfast U.S.A.* when making reservations!

We want to hear from you! Use the form on page 625.

TEXAS

Bed & Breakfast Texas Style ✪
4224 WEST RED BIRD LANE, DALLAS, TEXAS 75237

Tel: **(972) 298-8586; (800) 899-4538**
Best Time to Call: **9 AM–4:30 PM CST**
Coordinator: **Ruth Wilson**
States/Regions Covered: **Austin, Dallas, Houston, Lake Travis, San Antonio, Tyler**

Descriptive Directory: **$8**
Rates (Single/Double):
  Modest: **$60 / $70**
  Average: **$70 / $90**
  Luxury: **$100 / $150**
Credit Cards: **AMEX, DISC, MC, VISA**

The above cities are only a small sample of the locations of hosts waiting to give you plenty of warm hospitality. Ruth's register includes comfortable accommodations in condos, restored Victorians, lakeside cottages, and ranches. Texas University, Southern Methodist University, Baylor University, Rice University, and Texas Christian University are convenient to many B&Bs.

Bolin's Prairie House Bed & Breakfast ✪
508 MULBERRY, ABILENE, TEXAS 79601

Tel: **(915) 675-5855; (800) 673-5855**
Best Time to Call: **8AM–8 PM**
  Mon.–Sat.
Hosts: **Sam and Ginny Bolin**
Location: **180 mi. W of Dallas**
No. of Rooms: **4**
No. of Private Baths: **2**
Max. No. Sharing Bath: **4**

Double/pb: **$65**
Double/sb: **$55**
Open: **All year**
Breakfast: **Full**
Credit Cards: **AMEX, MC, VISA**
Children: **Welcome, over 12**
Smoking: **No**

Tucked into the heart of this famous frontier town is Bolin's Prairie House, a 1902 house furnished with antiques and modern luxuries. The warm, homey atmosphere puts guests at their ease. Relax in the living room with its wood-burning stove, or settle in the den for a little TV. Each of the four bedrooms—named Love, Joy, Peace, and Patience—has its own special charm. Breakfast features Ginny's delicious baked egg dishes, fresh fruit, and homemade bread, all lovingly served in the dining room, where fine china and cobalt Depression glass are displayed.

Parkview House ✪
1311 SOUTH JEFFERSON STREET, AMARILLO, TEXAS 79101
dia1311@aol.com; http://www.members.aol.com/dia/311

Tel: **(806) 373-9464; fax: (806) 373-3166**
Hosts: **Carol and Nabil Dia**
Location: **½ mi. from I-40**
No. of Rooms: **5**
No. of Private Baths: **3**
Max. No. Sharing Bath: **4**
Double/pb: **$75**
Double/sb: **$65**
Suite: **$85**

Open: **All year**
Breakfast: **Continental**
Credit Cards: **AMEX, MC, VISA**
Pets: **No**
Children: **By arrangement**
Smoking: **No**
Social Drinking: **Permitted**
Airport/Station Pickup: **Yes**
Foreign Languages: **Arabic**

This circa 1908 Prairie Victorian is located at the edge of the Historic District, and just minutes from I-27, I-40, and Old Route 66. Guest rooms are warm and inviting, with romantic draped beds, cozy reading areas, and antiques and Victoriana throughout. A gourmet breakfast is served in the dining room or the eclectic country kitchen with a view of the rose garden. The large columned porch is a wonderful place to relax and engage in conversation, or you could enjoy the hot tub and the bicycles that are available. Nabil, an engineer, and Carol, a lab technician, enjoy having guests join them for a social hour. Nearby is Palo Duro Canyon, West Texas A&M University, and city tennis.

Austin's Wildflower Inn ✪
1200 WEST 22½ STREET, AUSTIN, TEXAS 78705

Tel: **(512) 477-9639; fax: (512) 474-4188**
Best Time to Call: **Anytime**
Host: **Kay Jackson**
Location: **2 mi. from Rte. IH35, Exit MLK**
No. of Rooms: **4**
No. of Private Baths: **2**
Max. No. Sharing Bath: **4**
Double/pb: **$84–$89**

Single/pb: **$74–$79**
Double/sb: **$69**
Single/sb: **$60**
Open: **All year**
Reduced Rates: **10% seniors**
Breakfast: **Full**
Credit Cards: **AMEX, MC, VISA**
Pets: **No**
Smoking: **No**
Social Drinking: **Permitted**

Built in the early 1930s and nestled on a quiet, tree-lined street, this central Austin home is within a few blocks of the University of Texas and within minutes of the State Capitol complex. Outdoor enthusiasts will love the hike and bike trails at Shoal Creek or tennis at Caswell Courts. Kay prides herself on her warm Texas hospitality and delights in serving you her hearty gourmet specialties each morning.

The McCallum House ✪
613 WEST 32ND, AUSTIN, TEXAS 78705
mccallum@austintx.net

Tel: **(512) 451-6744; fax: (512) 451-4752**
Best Time to Call: **10 AM–9 PM**
Hosts: **Roger and Nancy Danley**
Location: **1 mi. W of I-35**
No. of Rooms: **5**
No. of Private Baths: **5**
Double/pb: **$89–$99**
Single/pb: **$75–$85**
Suites: **$89–$119**

Open: **All year**
Reduced Rates: **Weekdays, $10 one night, $20 2 nights or more**
Breakfast: **Full**
Credit Cards: **MC, VISA**
Pets: **No**
Children: **Welcome, over 11**
Smoking: **No**
Social Drinking: **Permitted**

This late Victorian home is just 10 blocks north of the University of Texas and 20 blocks north of the capitol and downtown. Air-conditioned and furnished with antiques, all five guest rooms have private verandas. All facilities have phones, color TVs, sitting areas, and kitchens or mini-kitchens, irons, ironing boards, lighted mirrors, hair dryers. The garden apartment suite has a whirlpool tub and shower. McCallum House has a Texas historic marker, an Austin landmark designation and a preservation award from the Austin Heritage Society and is listed on the Register of Historic Places. Guests breakfast daily on fresh fruits and homemade egg dishes, muffins, and coffee cakes.

B & G's ✪
15869 NEDRA WAY, DALLAS, TEXAS 75248

Tel: **(917) 386-4323**
Best Time to Call: **Before 8 AM**
Hosts: **George and Betty Hyde**
No. of Rooms: **2**
No. of Private Baths: **2**
Double/pb: **$60**
Single/pb: **$50**
Open: **All year**

Reduced Rates: **Available**
Breakfast: **Full**
Other Meals: **Available**
Pets: **No**
Children: **Welcome**
Smoking: **No**
Social Drinking: **Permitted**
Airport/Station Pickup: **Yes**

Betty and George are retirees who have had visitors from around the world since 1980. They want you to think of their home—furnished with "an eclectic collection of family heirlooms and junk"—as your own. Upon your arrival, they'll pour you something to drink, ascertain your interests, and direct you to appropriate activities in the Dallas–Fort Worth area. This B&B is close to prestigious shopping malls, the University of Texas at Dallas, Southern Methodist University, and the sights of downtown Dallas, such as the Kennedy Assassination Museum and the new Arts District. You'll start the day with conversation and a three-course breakfast at a lovely table set with grandma's antique silver and good crystal.

Bergmann Inn ✪
10009 TRINIDAD DRIVE, EL PASO, TEXAS 79925

Tel: **(915) 599-1398**
Host: **David Bergmann**
No. of Rooms: **2**
Max. No. Sharing Bath: **4**
Double/sb: **$50**
Single/sb: **$35**
Open: **All year**

Breakfast: **Continental**
Other Meals: **Available**
Pets: **No**
Smoking: **No**
Social Drinking: **Permitted**
Airport Pickup: **Yes**

David has a spacious, two-story home with two large bedrooms, a sizable living room, a den with a fireplace, and air-conditioning. Guests will enjoy the back patio overlooking a yard with flower beds and fruit trees that provide shade in the summertime. Bergmann Inn offers easy access to the east–west freeway and the northbound highways leaving El Paso.

The Texas White House ✪
1417 8TH AVENUE, FORT WORTH, TEXAS 76104

Tel: **(817) 923-3597; (800) 279-6491**
Best Time to Call: **7 AM–10:30 PM**
Host: **Jamie Sexton**
Location: **2 mi. SW of downtown Fort Worth**
No. of Rooms: **3**

No. of Private Baths: **3**
Double/pb: **$105**
Open: **All year**
Reduced Rates: **Available**
Breakfast: **Full**
Other Meals: **Available**

Credit Cards: **AMEX, DISC, MC, VISA**
Pets: **No**
Children: **Welcome**

Smoking: **Restricted**
Social Drinking: **Permitted**
Airport/Station Pickup: **Yes**

Texas White House is a 1910 Colonial Revival home with a large wrap-around porch on the first floor. The parlor, living room with a fireplace, and formal dining room may be rented for business conferences and luncheons. Secretarial and notary services can also be arranged. Each guest room features a queen-size bed, desk, and chair, and sitting area. You'll receive keys both to your room and the front door, so you can come and go at your leisure. Full breakfasts are served; you may eat either in your bedroom or in the dining room. Architecture buffs will want to tour the area's historical districts and landmark homes, while flora and fauna fans may prefer the Botanical Gardens and the Fort Worth Zoo.

La Casita Bed and Breakfast ✪
1908 REDWOOD DRIVE, GRANITE SHOALS, TEXAS 78654

Tel: **(830) 598-6443**
Best Time to Call: **9 AM–9 PM**
Hosts: **Joanne and Roger Scarborough**
Location: **56 mi. NW of Austin**
Guest Cottage: **$70**
Open: **All year**
Reduced Rates: **$5 less per day weekly**

Breakfast: **Full**
Pets: **No**
Children: **Welcome**
Smoking: **No**
Social Drinking: **Permitted**
Minimum Stay: **2 nights holiday weekends**

La Casita is a private guest cottage in the Highland Lakes area of the popular Texas Hill Country. The cottage is rustic outside but thoroughly modern inside, with Persian rugs, artwork, and mementos collected from around the world by your hosts. Guests are free to enjoy the grounds, flowers, gardens, and wildlife. You can choose breakfast from a varied menu and dine in the main house with your hosts. Joanne and Roger, a retired Navy couple, are native Texans and can recommend restaurants, state parks, winery tours, lake recreation, and other activities.

The Lovett Inn ✪
501 LOVETT BOULEVARD, HOUSTON, TEXAS 77006

Tel: **(713) 522-5224; (800) 779-5224;** fax: **(713) 528-6708**
Best Time to Call: **10 AM–6 PM**
Host: **Tom Fricke**
Location: **Downtown Houston**
No. of Rooms: **8**
No. of Private Baths: **8**
Double/pb: **$75–$95**
Single/pb: **$75–$95**
Town House: **$75–$150**

Suites: **$75–$125**
Open: **All year**
Reduced Rates: **Weekly**
Breakfast: **Continental**
Credit Cards: **AMEX, DISC, MC, VISA**
Pets: **Sometimes**
Children: **By arrangement**
Smoking: **Restricted**
Social Drinking: **Permitted**

It's easy to be fooled by the Lovett Inn: although it looks far older, this stately Federalist-style mansion, attractively furnished with 19th-century reproductions, was actually built in 1924. Its convenient museum-district location puts visitors within easy striking distance of downtown Houston, the Galleria, and the Houston Medical Center. After spending the day in the city, guests are sure to appreciate a dip in the pool. Each room has a color TV.

Trails End Bed & Breakfast ✪
12223 TRAILS END ROAD #7, LEANDER, TEXAS 78641

Tel: **(512) 267-2901**
Best Time to Call: **10 AM–10 PM**
Hosts: **JoAnn and Tom Patty**
Location: **10 min. from Austin and Lake Travis**
No. of Rooms: **2**
No. of Private Baths: **2**
Double/pb: **$68.90**
Single/pb: **$58.30**
Guesthouse: **$79.50–$180.20, sleeps 6**
Open: **All year**
Reduced Rates: **Over 2 nights**
Breakfast: **Full**
Pets: **No**
Children: **Welcome**
Smoking: **No**
Social Drinking: **Permitted**

JoAnn designed this Colonial Texas–style home with the intention of opening a B&B. The main house has two guest rooms furnished with mahogany pieces. For greater privacy, stay in the guesthouse and save money by preparing your own meals in the fully furnished kitchen. Banana pancakes and cheese-and-bacon biscuits are among the highlights of breakfast, served in the main house. After your morning meal, walk around the six-acre property or visit local points of interest, such as Zilker Gardens, Texas Memorial Museum, and Erwin Special Events Center. Golfers are urged to go to Lago Vista, while fans of water sports can swim, ski, fish, or sail on Lake Travis. For your enjoyment a pool and bicycles are available.

Aunt Nora's Bed and Breakfast ✪
120 NAKED INDIAN TRAIL, NEW BRAUNFELS, TEXAS 78132-1865

Tel: **(830) 905-3989; (800) 687-2887**
Best Time to Call: **9 AM–5 PM**
Hosts: **Iralee and Alton Haley**
Location: **15 mi. NW of New Braunfels**
Guest Cottages: **$95–$125**
Open: **All year**
Reduced Rates: **Available**
Breakfast: **Full, Continental**
Pets: **No**
Children: **Welcome**
Smoking: **No**
Social Drinking: **Permitted**

In the Texas hill country at Canyon Lake, just minutes from New Braunfels and Guadalupe River, is a country house with old-time Victorian charm, nestled on four tree-covered acres with a meadow. Walk to the top of the hill to view Canyon Lake, or breathe the fresh country air from the front porch swing. Relax amid handmade furnishings, antiques, a woodstove, and natural wood floors. Tastefully decorated queen rooms have handmade quilts. The cottages have private decks, kitchens, beautiful decor, private baths, and a view.

River Haus Bed & Breakfast ✪
817 EAST ZIPP ROAD, NEW BRAUNFELS, TEXAS 78130

Tel: **(830) 625-6411**
Hosts: **Dick and Arlene Buhl**
Location: **25 mi. NE of San Antonio**
No. of Rooms: **1**
No. of Private Baths: **1**
Double/pb: **$75**
Single/pb: **$70**

Open: **All year**
Breakfast: **Full**
Pets: **Sometimes**
Children: **No**
Smoking: **No**
Social Drinking: **No**
Foreign Languages: **German**

Historic New Braunfels, a major tourist destination, offers museums, antique shopping, and unparalleled canoeing and river sports, all in the charming setting of the German Hill Country. River Haus is a delightful hill country–style home located on the Guadalupe River at Lake Dunlap. Watch the sun set over the lake from your spacious bedroom or sitting room. On the enclosed porch, with its deck overlooking the lake, you can sip a cool drink or enjoy the warmth of a wood-stove fire. The complete gourmet breakfasts include local specialties and homemade bread and preserves.

The Rose Garden ✪
195 SOUTH ACADEMY, NEW BRAUNFELS, TEXAS 78130

Tel: **(800) 569-3296**
Best Time to Call: **Before 8 PM**
Host: **Dawn Mann**
Location: **1½ mi. from I-35, Exit 187**
No. of Rooms: **2**
Double/pb: **$65–$105**
Open: **All year**

Reduced Rates: **Available**
Breakfast: **Full**
Pets: **No**
Children: **No**
Smoking: **No**
Social Drinking: **Permitted**
Foreign Languages: **German**

This half-century-old white brick Colonial is located one block from historic downtown New Braunfels. Enjoy a movie, browse the antique shops, or stroll along the Comal Springs. Then relax by the fireplace in the parlor, or in the formal dining room with a flavored cup of coffee. The Royal Rose Room features a four-poster bed; you'll also find English and German books, pictures, and magazines concerning the royal family. The Romantic Country Rose Room has a Victorian wrought-iron and brass bed, and an antique English dresser.

The White House
217 MITTMAN CIRCLE, NEW BRAUNFELS, TEXAS 78132

Tel: **(830) 629-9354**
Best Time to Call: **9 AM–9 PM**
Hosts: **Beverly and Jerry White**

Location: **20 mi. N of San Antonio**
No. of Rooms: **3**
Max. No. Sharing Bath: **4**

Double/pb: **$60–$70**
Single/pb: **$55–$65**
Double/sb: **$45–$50**
Single/sb: **$40–$45**
Open: **All year, except Thanksgiving
and Christmas**

Breakfast: **Full**
Pets: **No**
Children: **Welcome (crib)**
Smoking: **No**
Social Drinking: **Permitted**

This Spanish-style white brick home is nestled among cedar and oaks in Texas Hill Country. Guests are welcomed here with tea and pastries and shown to comfortable rooms with antique beds and oak dressers. A large fishing pond is located on the premises, and a few miles away you may enjoy a refreshing tube or raft ride down the Guadalupe River. Other attractions include the Alamo, the Riverwalk, and the many old missions located nearby in San Antonio.

Beckmann Inn and Carriage House ✪
222 EAST GUENTHER STREET, SAN ANTONIO, TEXAS 78204

Tel: **(210) 229-1449; (800) 945-1449**
Best Time to Call: **8 AM–10 PM**
Hosts: **Betty Jo and Don Schwartz**
Location: **¾ mi. S of downtown San Antonio**
No. of Rooms: **5**
No. of Private Baths: **5**
Double/pb: **$95–$130**
Single/pb: **$90–$120**
Open: **All year**

Reduced Rates: **Available**
Breakfast: **Full**
Credit Cards: **AMEX, DC, DISC, MC, VISA**
Pets: **No**
Children: **Welcome, over 12**
Smoking: **No**
Social Drinking: **Permitted**
Minimum Stay: **2 nights, weekends**

Enjoy gracious hospitality in an elegant Victorian inn located in San Antonio's King William historic district. The beautiful wraparound porch welcomes guests. Inside, rooms are colorfully decorated, with high-back, queen-size, antique Victorian beds. Gourmet breakfast, complete with dessert, is served in the formal dining room on a table set with china, crystal, and silver. Then guests may stroll over to the Riverwalk or ride the trolley to the sights of San Antonio.

A Yellow Rose Bed & Breakfast ✪
229 MADISON, SAN ANTONIO, TEXAS 78204

Tel: **(800) 950-9903; (210) 229-9903**
Best Time to Call: **10 AM–8 PM**
Hosts: **Deb Field and Justin Walker**
Location: **Downtown San Antonio**
No. of Rooms: **5**
No. of Private Baths: **5**
Double/pb: **$90–$135**
Open: **All year**

Reduced Rates: **Available**
Breakfast: **Full**
Credit Cards: **AMEX, DISC, MC, VISA**
Pets: **No**
Children: **Welcome, over 12**
Smoking: **No**
Social Drinking: **Permitted**
Minimum Stay: **2 nights weekends**

A Yellow Rose Bed & Breakfast is an 1878 Victorian home in the King William Historic District of San Antonio. The guest rooms are appointed with turn-of-the-century antiques, cable TV, and queen-size beds. Off-street covered parking is also provided. Breakfast is served in the 18th-century dining room, and afterward you are invited to enjoy relaxing on one of the B&B's comfortable porches. Your hosts have an art gallery that includes many of their favorite artists. The Riverwalk and the trolley are only two blocks away.

Rosevine Inn Bed and Breakfast ✪
415 SOUTH VINE AVENUE, TYLER, TEXAS 75702

Tel: **(903) 592-2221**
Best Time to Call: **After 9:30 AM**
Hosts: **Bert and Rebecca Powell**
Location: **100 mi. E of Dallas**
No. of Rooms: **7**
No. of Private Baths: **7**
Double/pb: **$85**
Suites: **$150**
Open: **All year**
Reduced Rates: **Available**

Breakfast: **Full**
Other Meals: **Available**
Credit Cards: **AMEX, DC, DISC, MC, VISA**
Pets: **No**
Children: **Welcome, over 3**
Smoking: **No**
Social Drinking: **Permitted**
Airport/Station Pickup: **Yes**

Rosevine Inn combines the best qualities of a bed & breakfast, offering hospitality, comfort, convenience, and a sense of history. The house sits on a hill and overlooks the Historic Brick Street District that has become a favorite of tourists because of the specialty shops and restored homes. You may also want to visit the Azalea District, where homes are notable for architectural styles representing many periods in Tyler's past. Guest rooms are cheerfully decorated with antiques and country collectibles. Guests are invited to use the living room, a denlike room upstairs with couches and a TV, the game room in the barn, or the hot tub. Breakfast is a grand affair of homemade delights served in the dining room.

UTAH

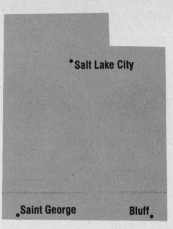

• Salt Lake City

• Saint George   Bluff •

Bluff Bed and Breakfast ✪
BOX 158, BLUFF, UTAH 84512

Tel: **(801) 672-2220**
Host: **Rosalie Goldman**
Location: **At intersection of 163 and 191**
No. of Rooms: **2**
No. of Private Baths: **2**
Double/pb: **$75**
Single/pb: **$70**
Open: **All year**

Breakfast: **Full**
Other Meals: **Available**
Pets: **No**
Children: **Welcome**
Smoking: **No**
Social Drinking: **Permitted**
Airport/Station Pickup: **Yes**
Foreign Languages: **French**

Close to the Four Corners (the junction of Colorado, New Mexico, Arizona, and Utah), this Frank Lloyd Wright–style home is nestled among huge boulders at the foot of redrock cliffs, near the San Juan River. On the main highway between Grand Canyon and Mesa Verde, it is secluded on seventeen desert acres. Across the river is the Navajo Reservation, and prehistoric ruins have been discovered nearby. Simply furnished, it is bright and tidy; large picture windows frame four different spectacular views. Rosalie prepares your breakfast of choice, from oatmeal to steak.

Seven Wives Inn ✪
217 NORTH 100 WEST, ST. GEORGE, UTAH 84770

Tel: **(801) 628-3737; (800) 600-3737**
Best Time to Call: **After 9 AM**
Hosts: **Jay and Donna Curtis**
Location: **125 mi. NE of Las Vegas**
No. of Rooms: **13**
No. of Private Baths: **13**
Double/pb: **$55–$85**
Single/pb: **$55–$85**
Suites: **$125**

Open: **All year**
Reduced Rates: **Special business rate (single occupancy) $50**
Breakfast: **Full**
Credit Cards: **AMEX, DC, MC, VISA**
Children: **By arrangement**
Smoking: **No**
Social Drinking: **Permitted**

This delightful Inn is featured on the walking tour of St. George; it is just across from the Brigham Young home and two blocks from the historic Washington County Court House. Your hosts offer traditional Western hospitality. Their home is decorated with antiques collected in America and Europe. Bedrooms are named after some of the seven wives of Donna's polygamous great-grandfather. A gourmet breakfast is served in the elegant dining room that will give you a hint of the past. St. George is located near Zion and Bryce national parks, boasts eight golf courses, and is noted for its mild winters. Dixie College is nearby. There's a swimming pool for your pleasure.

The Log Cabin on the Hill B&B ✪
2275 EAST 6200 SOUTH, SALT LAKE CITY, UTAH 84121

Tel: **(888) 639-2969; (801) 272-2969**
Best Time to Call: **9 AM–9 PM**
Host: **Geri M. Symes**
No. of Rooms: **4**
No. of Private Baths: **4**
Double/pb: **$75–$95**
Open: **All year**
Reduced Rates: **Available**

Breakfast: **Full**
Credit Cards: **AMEX, MC, VISA**
Pets: **No**
Children: **Welcome**
Smoking: **No**
Social Drinking: **Permitted**
Minimum Stay: **4 nights Dec. 20–Apr. 15**

Nestled in a natural hollow of the canyon foothills, this B&B is located just minutes from every major ski resort and area attraction. Guest rooms have down-filled comforters, fresh flowers, and terrycloth robes. Mornings begin with a hearty breakfast. After a day of skiing, sightseeing, or shopping, you're invited to sit by the fire and visit with other guests, curl up with a good book, or soak in the hot tub under the stars.

VERMONT

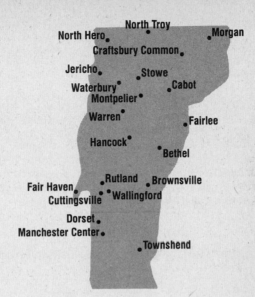

Vermont Center Point ✪
P.O. BOX 8513, ESSEX, VERMONT 05451

Tel: **(800) 449-2745; fax: (802) 872-2745**
Best Time to Call: **9 AM–6 PM**
Coordinator: **Denise L. Perraudin**
States/Regions Covered: **Vermont statewide**
Descriptive Directory of B&Bs: **$5**

Rates (Single/Double):
   Modest: **$45–$60**
   Average: **$60–$100**
   Luxury: **$100–$200**
Credit Cards: **AMEX, MC, VISA**
Minimum Stay: **2 nights seasonally**

Vermont Center Point is a meticulous and attentive reservation service dedicated to the bed and breakfast traveler. Denise has knowledge of every home listed and offers a variety of styles, sizes, and rates. You are assured of receiving gracious hospitality, breakfast, and a host who is familiar with the area.

Greenhurst Inn
RIVER STREET, BETHEL, VERMONT 05032

Tel: **(802) 234-9474**
Hosts: **Lyle and Claire Wolf**
Location: **30 mi. E of Rutland**
No. of Rooms: **13**
No. of Private Baths: **7**
Max. No. Sharing Bath: **4**
Double/pb: **$75–$95**
Single/pb: **$65–$85**
Double/sb: **$50–$65**

Single/sb: **$40–$55**
Open: **All year**
Breakfast: **Continental**
Credit Cards: **DISC, MC, VISA**
Pets: **Welcome (no cats)**
Children: **Welcome (crib)**
Smoking: **Permitted**
Social Drinking: **Permitted**

Located 100 yards from the White River, this elegant Queen Anne mansion, built in 1890, is listed on the National Register of Historic Places. The heavy brass hinges, embossed floral brass doorknobs, and etched windows at the entry have withstood the test of time. The cut-crystal collection is magnificent, and the stereoscope and old Victrola add to the old-fashioned atmosphere. The mansion is close to many points of historic interest, and seasonal recreational activities are abundant. Vermont Law School is close by.

The Pond House at Shattuck Hill Farm
SHATTUCK HILL ROAD, BROWNSVILLE, VERMONT 05037
http://www.windsor.K12.vt.us/pondhse.html

Tel: **(802) 484-0011**
Best Time to Call: **5–9 PM**
Hosts: **David Raymond and Gretel Schuck**
Location: **10 mi. S of Woodstock**
No. of Rooms: **3**
No. of Private Baths: **2**
Max. No. Sharing Bath: **4**
Double/pb: **$85–$125**
Double/sb: **$85–$100**
Open: **All year**

Breakfast: **Full**
Other Meals: **Dinner included with rate**
Credit Cards: **MC, VISA**
Pets: **Sometimes**
Children: **Welcome, over 6**
Smoking: **No**
Social Drinking: **Permitted**
Minimum Stay: **2 nights holiday weekends**
Airport/Station Pickup: **Yes**
Foreign languages: **French**

Miles of stone walls surround this 1830s Cape with a pond, croquet lawn, gardens, and meadows. Winter brings down comforters and fireside dinners with a Continental flair, such as wild mushroom risotto with roast chicken and apple tart with caramel sauce. Ascutney, Okemo, and Killington skiing are all within easy access. Return from the day's outing to cheese, fresh fruit, and wine. Summer features candlelit dinners al fresco overlooking the mountains. Hike the Long Trail or Appalachian Trail, bike one of the routes designed for the casual rider, or just relax with a good read in a garden or by the pond.

Creamery Inn Bed & Breakfast ✪
P.O. BOX 187, CABOT, VERMONT 05647

Tel: **(802) 563-2819**
Hosts: **Dan and Judy Lloyd**
Location: **18 mi. NE of Montpelier**
No. of Rooms: **3**
No. of Private Baths: **1**
Max. No. Sharing Bath: **4**
Double/pb: **$65**
Single/pb: **$45**
Double/sb: **$60**
Single/sb: **$40**

Suites: **$75**
Open: **All year**
Reduced Rates: **Families, Nov.–June**
Breakfast: **Full**
Other Meals: **Available**
Pets: **Sometimes**
Children: **Welcome**
Smoking: **No**
Social Drinking: **Permitted**

Enjoy lovely year-round accommodations in this Federal-style home, circa 1835. Guest rooms are tastefully decorated, with stenciling, old-fashioned wallpaper, a canopy bed, and old trunks. Located one mile from Cabot Creamery, the Inn is on two acres in a country setting beautiful in any season. New lambs each spring attract many visitors. It's a great area for joggers, hikers, bicyclists, and nature lovers—walk up the road and delight in ponds and waterfalls along the way. Full breakfasts include Finnish pancakes and other homemade fare. Candlelight dinner is available by advance reservation.

Craftsbury Bed & Breakfast on Wylie Hill ✪
CRAFTSBURY COMMON, VERMONT 05827

Tel: **(802) 586-2206**
Best Time to Call: **Mornings; evenings**

Host: **Margaret Ramsdell**
Location: **40 mi. N of Montpelier**

No. of Rooms: **6**
Max. No. Sharing Bath: **4**
Double/sb: **$60–$75**
Single/sb: **$50**
Open: **All year**
Breakfast: **Full**

Pets: **No**
Children: **Welcome (crib)**
Smoking: **No**
Social Drinking: **Permitted**
Foreign Languages: **French**

This 1860 Georgian hilltop farmhouse has beautiful views. The homey guest rooms adjoin the living room with its wood stove, where you are welcome to relax and visit. You may use Margaret's kitchen, barbecue, and picnic table should the crisp mountain air stoke your appetite. You're sure to enjoy the bountiful breakfast that often features cinnamon apple pancakes with fresh maple syrup. Dinner is served only by prior arrangement. The ski slopes of Stowe are 30 miles away, and lakes and rivers are within a two-mile radius. Cross-country skiing starts at the door.

Buckmaster Inn ✪
LINCOLN HILL ROAD, CUTTINGSVILLE, VERMONT 05738

Tel: **(802) 492-3485**
Best Time to Call: **8 AM–8 PM**
Hosts: **Sam and Grace Husselman**
Location: **8 mi. SE of Rutland**
No. of Rooms: **3**
No. of Private Baths: **2**
Max. No. Sharing Bath: **4**
Double/pb: **$55–$65**
Single/pb: **$55–$65**
Double/sb: **$55**

Single/sb: **$40–$50**
Open: **All year**
Reduced Rates: **Weekly**
Breakfast: **Full**
Pets: **No**
Children: **Welcome, over 8**
Smoking: **No**
Social Drinking: **Permitted**
Airport/Station Pickup: **Yes**
Foreign Languages: **Dutch**

The Buckmaster Inn, located near Cuttingsville in the Green Mountains, is a Federal clapboard Colonial overlooking a picturesque valley. Its center hall, grand staircase, and wide-plank pine floors are typical of 19th-century style. This is New England relaxation at its best: fireplaces, wood-burning stove, library, and two porches. Homemade muffins, casseroles, and jams are among the specialties served in the country kitchen each morning. Ski slopes, hiking trails, and craft shops are nearby.

The Little Lodge at Dorset ✪
ROUTE 30, BOX 673, DORSET, VERMONT 05251

Tel: **(802) 867-4040; (800) 378-7505**
Best Time to Call: **Anytime**
Hosts: **Allan and Nancy Norris**
Location: **6 mi. N of Manchester**
No. of Rooms: **5**
No. of Private Baths: **5**
Double/pb: **$85–$105**
Single/pb: **$75–$95**

Open: **All year**
Breakfast: **Continental, plus**
Credit Cards: **AMEX, DISC**
Pets: **No**
Children: **Welcome**
Smoking: **No**
Social Drinking: **Permitted**

Situated in one of the prettiest little towns in Vermont, this delightful 1820 Colonial house, on the Historic Register, is perched on a hillside way back from the road, overlooking the mountains and its own trout pond that's used for skating in winter or swimming in summer. The original paneling and wide floorboards set off the splendid antiques. After skiing at nearby Stratton or Bromley, toast your feet by the fireplace while sipping hot chocolate. If you prefer, bring your own liquor, and Nancy and Allan will provide Vermont cheese and crackers.

Maplewood Inn

ROUTE 22A SOUTH, FAIR HAVEN, VERMONT 05743
http://www.sover.net/~maplewd

Tel: **(802) 265-8039; (800) 253-7729**
Best Time to Call: **9 AM–9 PM**
Hosts: **Cindy and Doug Baird**
Location: **18 mi. W of Rutland**
No. of Rooms: **5**
No. of Private Baths: **5**
Double/pb: **$75–$95**
Suites: **$115–$130**
Open: **All year**
Reduced Rates: **After 5th night**

Breakfast: **Continental, plus**
Credit Cards: **AMEX, CB, DC, DISC, MC, VISA**
Pets: **No**
Children: **Welcome, over 5**
Smoking: **Restricted**
Social Drinking: **Permitted**
Minimum Stay: **Parents college weekends, holidays, foliage**

The Inn is a beautifully restored Greek Revival–style home, built in 1843, with lovely country views from every window. Chippendale furnishings, original pine floors polished to a warm glow, four-poster or brass beds, wingback chairs, and carefully chosen accessories provide a soothing backdrop for a relaxing visit. Cindy and Doug have added air-conditioning, TVs, and phones, and four out of the five rooms have fireplaces. After a multicourse breakfast, enjoy a walk in the historic village or participate in the recreational activities at nearby Lakes Bomoseen and St. Catherine, or take a short drive to ski the slopes of Killington or Pico. Linger on the porch, play croquet on the lawn, enjoy a board game or a book in the parlor. The gourmet restaurants and shops of Rutland are close by. Reserve early for the fall foliage season.

Silver Maple Lodge and Cottages ✪

SOUTH MAIN STREET, RR1, BOX 8, FAIRLEE, VERMONT 05045

Tel: **(802) 333-4326; (800) 666-1946**
Hosts: **Scott and Sharon Wright**
Location: **20 mi. N of White River Junction**
No. of Rooms: **14**
No. of Private Baths: **12**
Max. No. Sharing Bath: **4**
Double/pb: **$62–$79**
Single/pb: **$58–$75**
Double/sb: **$54**

Single/sb: **$50**
Open: **All year**
Reduced Rates: **10% seniors, AAA**
Breakfast: **Continental**
Credit Cards: **AMEX, MC, VISA**
Pets: **Sometimes**
Children: **Welcome**
Smoking: **Permitted**
Social Drinking: **Permitted**
Airport/Station Pickup:. **Yes**

Built as a farmhouse in 1855, Silver Maple Lodge became an inn some seventy years later. To accommodate extra guests, several cottages were added, constructed from lumber cut on the property. It's easy to see why this B&B remains popular. There's swimming, boating, and fishing at two local lakes. Other outdoor activities in the area include golf, tennis, horseback riding, canoeing, hiking, and skiing. If you're tired of feeling earthbound, Post Mills Airport, seven miles away, offers flights in a hot-air balloon and gliding rides. (Special packages, combining a flight in a hot-air balloon and other activities of your choice, can be arranged.) And for concerts, theater, and art exhibits, it's an easy drive to Dartmouth College, in Hanover, New Hampshire.

Sweet Onion Inn ✪

ROUTE 100, P.O. BOX 66, HANCOCK, VERMONT 05748

Tel: **(802) 767-3734; fax: (802) 767-9227**
Best Time to Call: **9 AM–4 PM**
Hosts: **Ron and Kathy Heatley; Chuck and Pat Merithew**
Location: **75 mi. SE of Burlington**
No. of Rooms: **4**
No. of Private Baths: **2**
Max. No. Sharing Bath: **4**
Double/pb: **$75**
Single/pb: **$65**
Double/sb: **$65**

Single/sb: **$55**
Open: **All year**
Reduced Rates: **Available**
Breakfast: **Full**
Other Meals: **Available**
Credit Cards: **AMEX, DISC, MC, VISA**
Pets: **No**
Children: **Welcome**
Smoking: **No**
Social Drinking: **Permitted**
Station Pickup: **Yes**

The simplicity of this peaceful rural country Inn is complemented by its location on scenic Route 100, along the White River. From its setting in the middle of the Green Mountains, Sweet Onion is close to all Vermont has to offer. Established in the early 1800s, this former homestead is freshly decorated yet retains its charm with old, wide-plank floors. There is a spacious backyard where guests can enjoy majestic mountain and river views after a day of hiking, biking, or sightseeing. The dining room serves wonderfully delicious vegetarian meals that are made from scratch with only the best ingredients.

Milliken's ✪

RD 2, BOX 397, JERICHO, VERMONT 05465
maha11@aol.com

Tel: **(802) 899-3993**
Best Time to Call: **Mornings; evenings**
Hosts: **Rick and Jean Milliken**
Location: **12 mi. E of Burlington**
No. of Rooms: **2**
Max. No. Sharing Bath: **4**
Double/sb: **$45**
Single/sb: **$35**

Suites: **$60**
Open: **All year**
Breakfast: **Full**
Pets: **No**
Children: **Welcome**
Smoking: **No**
Social Drinking: **Permitted**
Airport/Station Pickup: **Yes**

This Second Empire early Victorian was built in 1867 by a lumber magnate. The house has a graceful mansard roof, original woodwork, and floors of alternating cherry and white maple. The spaciousness of the rooms is enhanced by high ceilings, large windows, and gracious decor. Rick is a hotel manager and Jean is a choreographer and host. She prepares such breakfast specialties as French toast with maple syrup and hot mulled cider. In the evening, a good-night brandy and snack are offered. Your family is sure to enjoy its stay with the Millikens, their son Patrick, and two friendly dogs named Bailey and Barnum. Nearby attractions are hiking trails on Mt. Mansfield, skiing, and fabulous fall foliage.

Brook 'n' Hearth ✪
STATE ROAD 11/30, BOX 508, MANCHESTER CENTER,
VERMONT 05255

Tel: **(802) 362-3604**
Best Time to Call: **10 AM–10 PM**
Hosts: **Larry and Terry Greene**
Location: **1 mi. E of US 7**
No. of Rooms: **3**
No. of Private Baths: **3**
Double/pb: **$70**
Single/pb: **$46**
Suites: **$80 for 2**

Open: **May 22–Oct. 30; Nov. 20–**
Apr. 17
Reduced Rates: **Available**
Breakfast: **Full**
Credit Cards: **AMEX, DISC, MC, VISA**
Pets: **No**
Children: **Welcome (crib)**
Smoking: **No**
Social Drinking: **Permitted**

True to its name, a brook runs through the property and a fire warms the living room of this country home. Terry and Larry offer setups and happy-hour snacks for your self-supplied cocktails. You're within five miles of the ski slopes at Bromley and Stratton; it is also convenient to art centers, summer theater, restaurants, and a score of sports that include hiking on the Long Trail. The B&B is air-conditioned in summer, and you can enjoy the pool, lawn games, and barbecue. The game room, with its VCR, pocket billiards, and Ping-Pong, is always available.

Betsy's B&B ✪
74 EAST STATE STREET, MONTPELIER, VERMONT 05602

Tel: **(802) 229-0466**
Hosts: **Jon and Betsy Anderson**
Location: **Downtown Montpelier**
No. of Rooms: **10**
No. of Private Baths: **10**
Double/pb: **$50–$90**
Single/pb: **$45–$85**
Suites: **$120–$150**
Open: **All year**

Reduced Rates: **Available**
Breakfast: **Full, Continental**
Credit Cards: **AMEX, DISC, MC, VISA**
Pets: **No**
Children: **Welcome**
Smoking: **No**
Social Drinking: **Permitted**
Airport/Station Pickup: **Yes**

This fancy Queen Anne B&B in the historic district near downtown, Statehouse, Vermont College, and history and art museums is a real find. It is lavishly furnished with period antiques. Great restaurants and interesting book, crafts, and sporting goods shops are nearby. Walk or run in nearby parks or neighborhoods with Victorian homes, then relax on the porch or decks. Betsy's boasts award-winning building restoration and landscaping. Amenities include in-room cable TV and telephone, exercise room, hot tub, and fax. Your hosts are interested in historic preservation, gardening, antiques, law, and politics.

Hunt's Hideaway ✪
RR 1, BOX 570, WEST CHARLESTON, MORGAN, VERMONT 05872

Tel: **(802) 895-4432, 334-8322**
Best Time to Call: **7 AM–11 PM**

Host: **Pat Hunt**
Location: **6 mi. from I-91**

No. of Rooms: **3**
Max. No. Sharing Bath: **4**
Double/sb: **$35**
Single/sb: **$25**
Open: **All year**
Reduced Rates: **Available**

Breakfast: **Full**
Pets: **Sometimes**
Children: **Welcome**
Smoking: **Restricted**
Social Drinking: **Permitted**

This modern, split-level home is located on 100 acres of woods and fields, with a brook, pond, and large swimming pool. Pancakes with Vermont maple syrup are featured at breakfast. Ski Jay Peak and Burke, or fish and boat on Lake Seymour, two miles away. Visiting antique shops or taking a trip to nearby Canada are other local possibilities.

Charlie's Northland Lodge ✪
BOX 88, NORTH HERO, VERMONT 05474

Tel: **(802) 372-8822**
Best Time to Call: **Before 8 PM**
Hosts: **Charles and Dorice Clark**
Location: **60 mi. S of Montreal, Canada**
No. of Rooms: **3**
Max. No. Sharing Bath: **4**
Double/sb: **$65**
Guest Cottage: **$400–$600 weekly;**
  sleeps 6

Open: **All year**
Breakfast: **Continental**
Pets: **No**
Children: **Welcome, over 5**
Smoking: **Permitted**
Social Drinking: **Permitted**

The lodge is a restored Colonial, circa 1850, located on Lake Champlain, where bass and walleye abound. A sport and tackle shop is on the premises. Fall and winter fishing should appeal to all anglers. In summer, hiking, biking, fishing, boating, kayaking, or relaxing in the reading room are pleasant activities.

Rose Apple Acres Farm ✪
RR 2, BOX 300, EAST HILL ROAD, NORTH TROY, VERMONT 05859

Tel: **(802) 988-4300**
Best Time to Call: **Evenings**
Hosts: **Jay, Camilla, and Courtney Mead**
Location: **30 minutes from I-91, Exit 26**
No. of Rooms: **3**
No. of Private Baths: **1**
Max. No. Sharing Bath: **4**
Double/pb: **$60**

Double/sb: **$50**
Single/sb: **$45**
Open: **All year**
Breakfast: **Continental, plus**
Pets: **No**
Children: **Welcome, over 6**
Smoking: **No**

Situated on fifty-two acres of fields, woods, gardens, and ponds, Rose Apple Acres Farm is located on the Vermont–Canada line, only four hours north of Boston and two hours from Montreal. The atmosphere is peaceful and quiet, with panoramic views that are especially spectacular during the fall foliage. In addition to the B&B, the farm is home to Alpine goats, Lincoln sheep, Belgian horses, and of course, the collies.

Hiking, cross-country skiing, and snowshoeing can be enjoyed on the premises; horse-drawn sleigh or wagon rides are also offered. Downhill skiing is only twenty minutes away. Also on the premises is Henderson Forge, with wrought-iron creations by Courtney, and Camilla's Porcelain Doll Studio.

Hillcrest Guest House ✪
RR 1, BOX 4459, RUTLAND, VERMONT 05701
Pegdombro@aol.com

Tel: **(802) 775-1670**	Open: **All year**
Hosts: **Bob and Peg Dombro**	Breakfast: **Continental**
Location: **³/₁₀ mi. from Rte. 7**	Pets: **No**
No. of Rooms: **3**	Children: **Welcome, over 5**
Max. No. Sharing Bath: **5**	Smoking: **No**
Double/sb: **$50**	Social Drinking: **Permitted**
Single/sb: **$45**	Airport/Station Pickup: **Yes**

This 150-year-old farmhouse, with a comfortable screened porch for warm-weather relaxing, is furnished with country antiques. Pico and Killington ski areas are 7 and 16 miles away, respectively. Summer brings the opportunity to explore charming villages, covered bridges, and antiques and crafts centers. Country auctions, marble quarries, trout streams, and Sunday-evening band concerts are pleasant pastimes. Bob and Peg always offer something in the way of between-meal refreshments.

Bittersweet Inn
692 SOUTH MAIN STREET, STOWE, VERMONT 05672

Tel: **(802) 253-7787; (800) 387-8789**	Suites: **$140–$175**
Best Time to Call: **7 AM–10 PM**	Open: **All year**
Hosts: **Barbara and Paul Hansel**	Reduced Rates: **5-night stays**
Location: **36 mi. E of Burlington**	Breakfast: **Continental, plus**
No. of Rooms: **8**	Credit Cards: **AMEX, DISC, MC, VISA**
No. of Private Baths: **5**	Children: **Welcome (play area)**
Max. No. Sharing Bath: **4**	Smoking: **No**
Double/pb: **$66–$84**	Social Drinking: **Permitted**
Double/sb: **$42–$74**	

Bittersweet Inn is a brick Cape with converted clapboard carriage house, dating back to 1835. The house is set on eleven and a half acres, overlooking Camel's Hump Mountain. Inside you'll find comfortable rooms decorated with a combination of antiques and family pieces. It's just a half mile to the center of town and minutes to ski lifts and a cross-country touring center. A good-size swimming pool is located out back with plenty of room for laps or just taking it easy. In the winter season, hot soup and the indoor hydro-spa will·be waiting after your last ski run. Your hosts, Barbara and Paul, invite you to relax in the game room with BYOB bar and will help you plan your evening.

Ski Inn ○
ROUTE 108, STOWE, VERMONT 05672

Tel: **(802) 253-4050**	Single/sb: **$30–$45**
Best Time to Call: **Before 10 AM; after 7:30 PM**	Open: **All year**
	Reduced Rates: **Off-season**
Hosts: **The Heyer Family**	Breakfast: **Continental**
Location: **47 mi. NE of Burlington**	Other Meals: **In winter, full breakfast and dinner (additional fee)**
No. of Rooms: **10**	
No. of Private Baths: **5**	Pets: **Sometimes**
Max. No. Sharing Bath: **5**	Children: **Welcome**
Double/pb: **$50–$65**	Smoking: **No**
Double/sb: **$45–$50**	Social Drinking: **Permitted**

This traditional New England inn, set back from the highway among evergreens on a gentle sloping hillside, is a quiet place to relax and sleep soundly. In winter, it's a skier's delight, close to Mt. Mansfield's downhill and cross-country trails. In summer, the rates drop and include just Continental breakfast. The Heyer family offers warm hospitality in all seasons.

Boardman House Bed & Breakfast ○
P.O. BOX 112, TOWNSHEND, VERMONT 05353

Tel: **(802) 365-4086**	Open: **All year**
Hosts: **Sarah Messenger and Paul Weber**	Reduced Rates: **10–15% seniors; off-season; weekly**
Location: **125 mi. N of Boston**	
No. of Rooms: **6**	Breakfast: **Full**
No. of Private Baths: **5**	Pets: **Sometimes**
Max. No. Sharing Bath: **4**	Children: **Welcome**
Double/pb: **$70–$80**	Smoking: **No**
Single/pb: **$65–$75**	Social Drinking: **Permitted**
Suites: **$90–$100**	

If you tried to imagine an idealized New England home, it would resemble this white 19th-century farmhouse set on Townshend's Village Green. This is a prime foliage and antiquing area. Direct access to State Routes 30 and 35 allows you to pursue other interests, from skiing at Stratton to canoeing on the West River. Gourmet breakfasts feature pear pancakes, individual soufflés, hot fruit compotes, and more.

White Rocks Inn ○
RR 1, BOX 297, ROUTE 7, WALLINGFORD, VERMONT 05773

Tel: **(802) 446-2077**	Hosts: **June and Alfred Matthews**
Best Time to Call: **Mornings; evenings**	Location: **20 mi. N of Manchester**

No. of Rooms: **5**
No. of Private Baths: **5**
Double/pb: **$75–$110**
Single/pb: **$70–$100**
Guest Cottage: **$130–$140**
Open: **Dec. 1–Oct. 31**
Breakfast: **Full**
Credit Cards: **MC, VISA**

Pets: **No**
Children: **Welcome, over 10**
Smoking: **No**
Social Drinking: **Permitted**
Minimum Stay: **2 nights holidays, fall foliage season**
Foreign Languages: **French, Spanish**

If your idea of paradise is a pasture, a creek stocked with trout, an old-fashioned swimming hole, and a peaceful valley surrounded by mountains, then reserve a room here. June and Alfred have renovated their vintage 1800 farmhouse with care, preserving the charm of wide-board floors, wainscoting, ornate moldings, and high ceilings, while enhancing it with antiques, oriental rugs, and canopied beds. In summer, such breakfast delights as banana pancakes or raisin bread French toast is served on the large veranda overlooking the meadows. In cooler weather, this feast is presented in the dining room. Five downhill ski areas are a short drive away, and miles of cross-country ski trails are adjacent to the Inn.

West Hill House ✪

RR1, BOX 292, WEST HILL ROAD, WARREN, VERMONT 05674
dotty@westhillhouse.com; http://www.westhillhouse.com

Tel: **(802) 496-7162; (800) 898-1427**
Best Time to Call: **7 AM–10 PM**
Hosts: **Dotty Kyle and Eric Brattstrom**
Location: **25 mi. SW of Montpelier**
No. of Rooms: **7**
No. of Private Baths: **7**
Double/pb: **$95–$145**
Single/pb: **$85–$135**
Open: **All year**

Reduced Rates: **Available**
Breakfast: **Full**
Credit Cards: **AMEX, MC, VISA**
Pets: **No**
Children: **Welcome, over 10**
Smoking: **No**
Social Drinking: **Permitted**
Minimum Stay: **2 nights weekends**

Up a quiet country lane, on nine wooded and open acres with stunning mountain views, gardens, pond and apple orchard, this 1860s farmhouse is one mile from Sugarbush Ski Resort, adjacent to its golf course and cross-country ski trails. Take advantage of an outdoor sports paradise near fine restaurants, quaint villages, covered bridges, and unique shops. After a busy day, enjoy the comfortable front porch or a roaring fire, eclectic library, oriental rugs, art, antiques, and the interesting company of other guests. Bedrooms feature premium linens, down comforters, and good reading lights. The guest pantry has a wet bar and fridge. Dotty and Eric pride themselves on their memorable breakfasts and afternoon and bedtime snacks.

Grünberg Haus B&B and Cabins ✪
RR2, BOX 1595, BU ROUTE 100 SOUTH, WATERBURY, VERMONT 05676

Tel: **(802) 244-7726; (800) 800-7760**
Hosts: **Christopher Sellers and Mark Frohman**
Location: **25 mi. E of Burlington**
No. of Rooms: **15**
Max. No. Sharing Bath: **4**
Double/pb: **$80–$150**
Single/pb: **$55–$105**
Double/sb: **$55–$75**
Single/sb: **$35–$55**

Open: **All year**
Reduced Rates: **10% after 3rd night**
Breakfast: **Full**
Credit Cards: **DISC, MC, VISA**
Pets: **No**
Children: **Welcome**
Smoking: **No**
Social Drinking: **Permitted**
Airport/Station Pickup: **Yes**

You'll think you're in the Alps when you see this hand-built Tyrolean chalet perched on a secluded hillside. The living room features an eight-foot grand piano, a massive fieldstone fireplace, and a long breakfast table overlooking the valley and distant forest. All eleven guest rooms open onto the quaint balcony that surrounds the chalet. There are two secluded bedroom cabins with wood stoves hidden along the walking trails. The BYOB rathskeller features hand-stenciled booths; the formal dining room is furnished with antiques. Outside, cleared logging trails provide cross-country skiing and hiking access to hundreds of acres of meadows and woodlands. And Waterbury's central location makes it easy to get to ski resorts like Stowe and Sugarbush. Whatever you plan to do, bring an appetite; Grünberg Haus serves memorable gourmet breakfasts, and other meals can be arranged.

Inn at Blush Hill ✪
BOX 1266, BLUSH HILL ROAD, WATERBURY, VERMONT 05676

Tel: **(802) 244-7529; (800) 736-7522**
Hosts: **Gary and Pam Gosselin**
Location: **22 mi. E. of Burlington**
No. of Rooms: **5**
No. of Private Baths: **5**
Double/pb: **$59–$130**
Open: **All year**
Reduced Rates: **Available**

Breakfast: **Full**
Credit Cards: **AMEX, DISC, MC, VISA**
Pets: **No**
Children: **Welcome, over 6**
Smoking: **No**
Social Drinking: **Permitted**
Airport/Station Pickup: **Yes**

This 1790 brick farmhouse, the oldest Inn in Waterbury, is located half-way between the Stowe and Sugarbush ski areas. The atmosphere is warm and homey, with antiques, old-time rockers, books, and lots of fireplaces. Your host Pam is a gourmet cook and enjoys making her own bread and muffins each morning. A huge lake with boating, swimming, and fishing is located just one and a half miles from the house, and a nine-hole golf course is located directly across the street. The Inn is back to back to Ben & Jerry's Ice Cream Factory. At the end of the day, sit back and enjoy the surroundings, relaxing on the large, old-fashioned porch. Afternoon and evening refreshments are served. One room has a fireplace, another has a canopy queen-size bed with a 13-foot-wide window view of the sunrise over the mountains. The newest room has a queen-size bed with a sitting room and Jacuzzi tub.

For key to listings, see inside front or back cover.

✪ This star means that rates are guaranteed through December 31, 1998, to any guest making a reservation as a result of reading about the B&B in *Bed & Breakfast U.S.A.*—1998 edition.

Important! To avoid misunderstandings, always ask about cancellation policies when booking.

Please enclose a self-addressed, stamped, business-size envelope when contacting reservation services.

For more details on what you can expect in a B&B, see Chapter 1.

Always mention *Bed & Breakfast U.S.A.* when making reservations!

We want to hear from you! Use the form on page 625.

VIRGINIA

Woodstock
New Market
Harrisonburg
Flint Hill
Luray
Manassas
Fredricksburg
Chincoteague Island
Staunton
Goshen
Waynesboro
Rockville
Montross
Urbana
Onancock
Lexington
Lynchburg
Williamsburg
Cape Charles
Blacksburg
Smith Mountain Lake
Pulaski
Capron
Abingdon
Cluster Springs
Virginia Beach

River Garden ✪
19080 NORTH FORK, RIVER ROAD, ABINGDON, VIRGINIA 24210

Tel: **(540) 676-0335; (800) 952-4296**
Best Time to Call: **Evenings and weekends**
Hosts: **Bill Crump and Carol Schoenherr-Crump**
Location: **9 mi. NE of Abingdon**
No. of Rooms: **4**
No. of Private Baths: **4**

Double/pb: **$60–$65**
Open: **All year**
Breakfast: **Full**
Pets: **Caged only**
Children: **Welcome, infants, over 4**
Smoking: **No**
Social Drinking: **Permitted**

River Garden is tucked into the foothills of the Clinch Mountains, on the bank of the Holston River's North Fork. Each room has its own riverside deck, private entrance, and a king- or queen-size bed. Guests are encouraged to try their hand at weaving on the antique loom. More contemporary challenges can be had in the recreation room, which is equipped with a Ping-Pong table, board games, and exercise equipment. Fishing equipment, a picnic table, and inner tubes are also at your disposal. The center of Abingdon, fifteen minutes away, is home to the historic Barter Theater, as well as many eateries. Lovers of the outdoors will want to head for the Virginia Creeper Trail—34 miles of scenic mountain trails for hikers, bikers, and horseback riders.

Alexandria and Arlington Bed and Breakfast Network ✪
P.O. BOX 25319, ARLINGTON, VIRGINIA 22202-9319

Tel: **(703) 549-3415**
Best Time to Call: **10 AM–2 PM**
  Mon.–Fri.
Coordinator: **Leslie C. and Ann L.**
  Garrison
States/Regions Covered: **Alexandria, Arlington, Falls Church, Fairfax; D.C.; Maryland—Patuxent River;**

Pennsylvania—**Gettysburg, Hanover;**
West Virginia—**Moorefield**
Rates (Single/Double):
  Modest: **$65 / $75**
  Average: **$75 / $85**
  Luxury: **$250**
Credit Cards: **AMEX, MC, VISA**

The range of listings in the Alexandria and Arlington Bed & Breakfast Network is breathtaking and can be well described as eclectic. Homes range from Colonial town houses of Old Towne Alexandria to modern, high-rise urban dwellings. Locations outside the D.C. metro area allow travelers to experience the quiet civility of the countryside and expand sightseeing possibilities to nearby areas of historic interest. Hosts are equally eclectic, including civil servants, political activists, veterans, diplomats, and yuppies.

Princely B&B Ltd. ✪
HCR 69, BOX 17215, MATHEWS, VIRGINIA 23109

Tel: **(800) 470-5588**
Best Time to Call: **10 AM–6 PM**
  Mon.–Fri.
Coordinator: **Betsy Henderson**

States/Regions Covered: **Alexandria**
Rates (Single/Double):
  Modest: **$75 / $125**
Minimum Stay: **2 nights**

This reservation service lists more than thirty privately owned historic homes, circa 1750 to 1890, many furnished with fine antiques, located in the heart of the Old Town area of Alexandria. All are within eight miles of the White House or Mount Vernon and afford easy access to shopping, dining, and monuments in and around Washington, D.C.

Clay Corner Inn ✪
401 CLAY STREET SOUTHWEST, BLACKSBURG, VIRGINIA 24060
claycorner@aol.com

Tel: **(540) 953-2604; fax: (540) 951-0541**
Best Time to Call: **9 AM–9 PM**
Hosts: **John and Joanne Anderson**

Location: **35 mi. SW of Roanoke**
No. of Rooms: **8**
No. of Private Baths: **8**
Double/pb: **$75–$85**

Single/pb: **$68–$85**
Open: **All year**
Breakfast: **Full**
Credit Cards: **AMEX, MC, VISA**

Pets: **No**
Children: **Welcome, over 12**
Smoking: **No**
Social Drinking: **Permitted**

Clay Corner Inn is a cluster of houses on a corner a few blocks from downtown and the Virginia Tech campus. The main house is decorated with a mix of traditional and Southwestern decors. The Huckleberry House next door, circa 1913, has four guest rooms, each with a fireplace. Each of the two Cape-style guesthouses has a kitchen, dining area, living room, and two guest rooms. A heated swimming pool is located in the center of the complex and is open May through September. Wood decks with benches and rockers provide wonderful places to relax, read, visit, and enjoy coffee, tea, or breakfast.

Bay Avenue's Sunset Bed & Breakfast ✪
108 BAY AVENUE, CAPE CHARLES, VIRGINIA 23310

Tel: **(757) 331-2424; 888-4BAYAVE for reservations; fax: (757) 331-4877**
Hosts: **Al Longo and Joyce Tribble**
Location: **35 mi. N of Norfolk**
No of Rooms: **4**
No. of Private Baths: **4**
Double/pb: **$75–$95**
Single/pb: **$70–$90**
Open: **All year**
Reduced Rates: **Available**

Breakfast: **Full**
Credit Cards: **DISC, MC, VISA**
Pets: **No**
Children: **Welcome, over 10**
Smoking: **Restricted**
Social Drinking: **Permitted**
Minimum Stay: **2 nights, holiday weekends**
Airport Pickup: **Yes**

Enjoy a waterfront getaway on the unspoiled Eastern Shore. Cape Charles is directly on the Chesapeake Bay, at the southernmost part of the Delmarva Peninsula; this picturesque town has no traffic lights or parking meters. You'll be able to watch spectacular unobstructed sunsets from the Inn's breezy porch or common area. Sun, swim, and relax. Two rooms have Vermont casting fireplaces for cozy winter nights. Then walk the beach, explore the historic district, or take a bike ride. Bird-watching and charter fishing are nearby. A hearty full breakfast features homemade baked goods and fresh fruit, and delicious hot entrees.

Nottingham Ridge

28184 NOTTINGHAM RIDGE LANE, CAPE CHARLES, VIRGINIA 23310
notridge@pilot.infi.net

Tel: **(757) 331-1010**
Best Time to Call: **Anytime**
Hosts: **Bonnie Nottingham and M. S. Scott**
Location: **20 mi. N of Norfolk**
No. of Rooms: **4**
No. of Private Baths: **4**
Double/pb: **$85**
Single/pb: **$80**

Open: **All year**
Breakfast: **Full**
Other Meals: **No**
Pets: **No**
Children: **Welcome, over 7**
Smoking: **No**
Social Drinking: **Permitted**
Airport/Station Pickup: **Yes**

Reflecting the beauty and charm of Virginia's historic Eastern Shore, this lovely home boasts a private secluded beach on the Chesapeake Bay, bordered by tall trees, sand dunes, and abundant wildlife. Guests can savor breakfast on the porch while watching boats and birds; at day's end, the sunsets are spectacular. Cooler times can be spent in the den by a crackling fire. Biking, fishing, tennis, golf, running, bird-watching, crabbing, swimming, and sightseeing are just a few pastimes guests can enjoy. Visitors to Nottingham Ridge can look forward to an informal, relaxed atmosphere with emphasis on the small details that create a memorable stay.

Sandy Hill Farm B&B ✪
11307 RIVERS MILL ROAD, CAPRON, VIRGINIA 23829

Tel: **(804) 658-4381**
Best Time to Call: **6:30–8 AM;**
  7:30–11:30 PM
Host: **Anne Kitchen**
Location: **11 mi. from I-95**
No. of Rooms: **2**
Double/pb: **$50**
Single/pb: **$40**

Open: **Mar. 20–Dec. 5**
Reduced Rates: **Families; 5 nights**
Breakfast: **Full**
Other Meals: **Available**
Pets: **Welcome**
Children: **Welcome**
Smoking: **Permitted**
Social Drinking: **Permitted**

Experience the pleasures of an unspoiled rural setting at this ranch-style farmhouse. There are animals to visit, quiet places to stroll, and a lighted tennis court on the grounds. This is an ideal hub from which to tour southeastern and central Virginia. Day trips to Williamsburg, Norfolk, and Richmond are possibilities. Fresh fruits and homemade breads are served at breakfast.

Guesthouses Reservation Service ✪
P.O. BOX 5737, CHARLOTTESVILLE, VIRGINIA 22905

Tel: **(804) 979-7264**
Best Time to Call: **12–5 PM Mon.–Fri.**
Coordinator: **Mary Hill Caperton**
States/Regions Covered: **Albemarle**
  County, Charlottesville
Descriptive Directory: **$1**

Rates (Single/Double):
  Modest: **$52 / $60**
  Average: **$68 / $80**
  Luxury: **$100 / $150**
  Estate Cottages: **$100 up**
Credit Cards: **AMEX, MC, VISA**

Charlottesville is a gracious town. The hosts in Mary's hospitality file offer you a genuine taste of Southern hospitality. All places are close to Thomas Jefferson's Monticello and James Madison's Ash Lawn, as well as the University of Virginia. Unusual local activities include ballooning, steeplechasing, and wine festivals. Reduced rates are available for extended stays, and most hosts offer a full breakfast.

Miss Molly's Inn ✪
4141 MAIN STREET, CHINCOTEAGUE ISLAND, VIRGINIA 23336

Tel: **(757) 336-6686; (800) 221-5620**
Best Time to Call: **10 AM–10 PM**
Hosts: **Barbara and David Wiedenheft**
Location: **50 mi. S of Salisbury,**
  Maryland
No. of Rooms: **7**
No. of Private Baths: **5**

Max. No. Sharing Bath: **4**
Double/pb: **$69–$145**
Single/pb: **$59–$109**
Double/sb: **$75–$109**
Single/sb: **$65–$99**
Open: **Mar. 1–New Year**

Reduced Rates: **10% seniors; Oct. 1–Memorial Weekend**
Breakfast: **Full**
Other Meals: **Available**
Pets: **No**
Children: **Welcome, over 8**

Smoking: **No**
Social Drinking: **Permitted**
Minimum Stay: **2 days, weekends**
Airport/Station Pickup: **Yes**
Foreign Languages: **French, Dutch, German**

This bayside Victorian Inn has been lovingly restored to its 19th-century charm; lace curtains, stained glass windows, and period pieces add to the ambience. While writing her book *Misty of Chincoteague,* Marguerite Henry stayed here. The ponies celebrated by that story roam wild at the nearby National Wildlife Refuge close to the unspoiled beaches of Assateague Island. You, too, may find Miss Molly's cool breezes, five porches, and traditional English tea—complete with superlative scones—worth writing about.

The Watson House ○

4240 MAIN STREET, CHINCOTEAGUE, VIRGINIA 23336

Tel: **(757) 336-1564; (800) 336-6787**
Hosts: **Tom and Jacque Derrickson, David and Joanne Snead**
Location: **180 mi. SE of Washington, D.C.**
No. of Rooms: **6**
No. of Private Baths: **6**
Double/pb: **$59–$85**
Suites: **$79–$99**
Open: **Apr.–Nov.**

Reduced Rates: **Available**
Breakfast: **Full**
Credit Cards: **MC, VISA**
Pets: **No**
Children: **Welcome, over 10**
Smoking: **No**
Social Drinking: **Permitted**
Minimum Stay: **2 nights, weekends; 3 nights, holidays**

Friendly hosts and Southern hospitality await you at this newly restored country Victorian home. Guest rooms are tastefully decorated with antiques, wicker, and nostalgic pieces; each room has a ceiling fan and air-conditioning. Watson House is within biking distance of Assateague National Wildlife Refuge, where you can enjoy numerous nature trails, guided tours, crabbing, fishing, clamming, or swimming. Your hosts will equip you with bicycles, beach chairs, and towels. In the mornings, you can mingle with other guests over a hearty breakfast, which includes fruit, eggs, breads, pastries, and aromatic coffee and tea.

Oak Grove Plantation Bed & Breakfast ✪
P.O. BOX 45, 1245 CLUSTER ROAD, CLUSTER SPRINGS, VIRGINIA 24535

Tel: **(804) 575-7137**	Breakfast: **Full**
Host: **Pickett Craddock**	Other Meals: **Available**
Location: **60 mi. N of Durham, N.C.**	Pets: **No**
No. of Rooms: **3**	Children: **Welcome**
Max. No. Sharing Bath: **4**	Smoking: **No**
Double/sb: **$60**	Social Drinking: **Permitted**
Single/sb: **$55**	Airport/Station Pickup: **Yes**
Open: **May and Sept. weekends, full-time June–Aug.**	Foreign Languages: **Spanish**

Thomas Easley, a prominent Virginia legislator, built this estate in 1820 and it has remained in the family ever since. Pickett, the director of a preschool in Washington, D.C., is a fifth-generation descendant. She encourages guests to hike, bike, and look at the wildlife on the 400-acre grounds. All bedrooms have fireplaces and are decorated with comfortable period pieces and family heirlooms. Guests will enjoy reading or chatting in the elegant parlor or on the cheerful sunporch. Breakfast is served in the Victorian dining room. Historic Danville, last capital of the Confederacy, and Buggs Island Lake, are within a half-hour drive. Appomattox is one hour away.

Caledonia Farm—1812 ✪
47 DEARING ROAD, FLINT HILL, VIRGINIA 22627
http://www.bnb-m-va.com/cale1812.html

Tel: **(540) 675-3693; (800) BNB-1812**	Suite: **$140**
Best Time to Call: **10 AM–6 PM**	Open: **All year**
Host: **Phil Irwin**	Breakfast: **Full**
Location: **68 mi. SW of Washington, D.C.; 4 mi. N of Washington, Va.**	Credit Cards: **DISC, MC, VISA**
	Pets: **No**
No. of Rooms: **3**	Children: **Welcome, over 12**
Max. No. Sharing Bath: **4**	Smoking: **No**
Double/sb: **$80**	Social Drinking: **Permitted**

This charming 1812 stone manor house and its companion "summer kitchen" are located on a working beef cattle farm adjacent to Shenandoah National Park. Each accommodation has a fireplace, period furnishings, individual temperature controls for heat or air-conditioning, and spectacular views of the Blue Ridge Mountains. A candlelight breakfast is served from a menu that offers a choice of omelette, smoked salmon, or eggs Benedict. The Skyline Drive, fine dining, caves, wineries, hayrides, hot tub, antiquing, historic sites, and sporting activities are a few of the possible diversions. Caledonia Farm is a Virginia Historic Landmark and on the National Register of Historic Places.

La Vista Plantation ✪

4420 GUINEA STATION ROAD, FREDERICKSBURG, VIRGINIA 22408

Tel: **(540) 898-8444; (800) 529-2823**
Best Time to Call: **Before 9:30 PM**
Hosts: **Michele and Edward Schiesser**
Location: **60 mi. S of Washington, D.C.;**
   4.5 mi. from I-95
No. of Rooms: **2**
No. of Private Baths: **2**
Double/pb: **$95**
Single/pb: **$75**

Guest Apartment: **$95; sleeps 6**
Open: **All year**
Reduced Rates: **7th night free; families**
Breakfast: **Full**
Credit Cards: **MC, VISA**
Pets: **No**
Children: **Welcome**
Smoking: **No**
Social Drinking: **Permitted**

Built in 1838, this Classical Revival country home is nestled amidst ancient tulip poplars, cedars, and hollies, and surrounded by pastures, woods, and fields. The site is close to historic Fredericksburg, but in a quiet rural area. The house retains its original charm, with intricate acorn and oak leaf moldings, high ceilings, wide pine floors and a two-story front portico. Guest rooms have private baths, air-conditioning, working fireplaces, TV, radio, and refrigerator. Enjoy brown egg breakfasts from resident hens. The Schiessers also have a stocked pond.

The Hummingbird Inn

30 WOOD LANE, P.O. BOX 147, GOSHEN, VIRGINIA 24439
hmgbird@cfw.com; http://www.hummingbirdinn.com

Tel: **(540) 997-9065; (800) 397-3214**
Best Time to Call: **8 AM–5 PM**
Hosts: **Jeremy and Diana Robinson**
Location: **23 mi. NW of Lexington**
No. of Rooms: **5**
No. of Private Baths: **5**
Double/pb: **$85–$125**
Open: **All year**

Reduced Rates: **10% seniors;**
  Nov. 1–Mar. 31
Breakfast: **Full**
Other Meals: **Available**
Credit Cards: **AMEX, DISC, MC, VISA**
Pets: **Sometimes**
Children: **Welcome, over 12**
Smoking: **No**
Social Drinking: **Permitted**

Located on an acre of landscaped grounds in the Shenandoah Valley, this Victorian Carpenter Gothic villa has accommodated Eleanor Roosevelt and Efrem Zimbalist, Sr. Wraparound verandas, original pine floors, a rustic den and a solarium give Hummingbird Inn an old-fashioned ambiance. In keeping with its architecture, the B&B is decorated in an early Victorian style and furnished with antiques. Nearby recreational facilities offer golf, swimming, hiking, skiing, canoeing, tubing, fishing, and hunting. Head out in your car for scenic routes like the Blue Ridge Parkway and Skyline Drive. Or visit the Garth Newell Music Center, historic Staunton, the Museum of American Frontier Culture, Virginia Military Institute, and Washington and Lee University. Rates for MAP double: $140–$170.

Kingsway Bed & Breakfast ✪
3581 SINGERS GLEN ROAD, HARRISONBURG, VIRGINIA 22801

Tel: **(540) 867-9696**
Hosts: **Chester and Verna Leaman**
Location: **2.5 mi. NW of Harrisonburg**
No. of Rooms: **3**
No. of Private Baths: **1**
Max. No. Sharing Bath: **4**
Double/pb: **$55–$60**
Single/pb: **$45**
Double/sb: **$50**

Single/sb: **$40**
Open: **All year**
Reduced Rates: **Available**
Breakfast: **Full**
Pets: **Yes**
Children: **Welcome**
Smoking: **No**
Social Drinking: **No**
Airport Pickup: **Yes**

This modern country home reveals the carpentry and decorating skills of Chester, a cabinet builder, and Verna, a full-time homemaker. Enjoy the gardens or take a dip in the pool. If you're up for an excursion, visit George Washington National Forest, Shenandoah National Park with picturesque Skyline Drive, Thomas Jefferson's home at Monticello, or New Market Battlefield and caverns. Local sports range from hiking and skiing to pricing the wares at the antique shops, flea markets, and the Valley Mall.

A B&B at Llewellyn Lodge ✪
603 SOUTH MAIN STREET, LEXINGTON, VIRGINIA 24450
LLL@rockbridge.net

Tel: **(800) 882-1145; (540) 463-3235;**
    fax: (540) 464-3122
Best Time to Call: **8 AM–10 PM**
Hosts: **Ellen and John Roberts**
Location: **50 mi. N of Roanoke**
No. of Rooms: **6**
No. of Private Baths: **6**
Double/pb: **$70–$98**
Single/pb: **$55–$88**

Open: **All year**
Breakfast: **Full**
Credit Cards: **AMEX, DISC, MC, VISA**
Pets: **No**
Children: **Welcome, over 10**
Smoking: **Restricted**
Social Drinking: **Permitted**
Airport/Station Pickup: **Yes**

The location of this brick Colonial makes it the perfect home base for exploring historic Lexington and the beautiful surrounding areas. A warm friendly atmosphere, combining country charm with a touch of class, awaits your arrival. Your comfort and satisfaction are the main concern of your hosts. Ellen's fabulous breakfasts may include omelettes, Belgian waffles, Virginia maple syrup, sausage, bacon, ham, and her famous blueberry muffins, which bring many repeat visitors. John, a Lexington native, takes special delight in sharing his knowledge of the local area and invites you to try one of his top ten hikes as detailed in his new hiking and outdoor guide. The lodge is an easy walk from the Robert E. Lee Chapel, Stonewall Jackson's house, George Marshall Museum, Washington and Lee University, and Virginia Military Institute.

Brierley Hill
RT 2, BOX 21A BORDEN ROAD, LEXINGTON, VIRGINIA 24450

Tel: **(540) 464-8421; (800) 422-4925**
Best Time to Call: **8 AM–8 PM**
Hosts: **Barry and Carole Speton**
Location: **50 mi. N of Roanoke**
No. of Rooms: **6**
No. of Private Baths: **6**
Double/pb: **$85–$145**
Open: **All year**

Reduced Rates: **Available**
Breakfast: **Full**
Other Meals: **Available**
Credit Cards: **MC, VISA**
Pets: **No**
Children: **Welcome, over 14**
Smoking: **No**
Social Drinking: **Permitted**

This charming B&B sits on eight acres of farmland. Guests are sure to appreciate the spectacular views of the Blue Ridge Mountains and the Shenandoah Valley. Located nearby are Blue Ridge Parkway, the Natural Bridge area, and historic Lexington. All rooms are furnished with antique brass or canopy beds, plus Laura Ashley wall coverings and linens. A TV room and a sitting room with a fireplace are at your disposal, and the dining room also has a fireplace. Barry, a retired Canadian lawyer, is interested in antique prints and refinishing furniture. Carole likes cooking, gardening, and quilting. Together, they offer relaxed comfort, wonderful food, and friendly hospitality.

Lavender Hill Farm B&B ✪
ROUTE 1, BOX 515, LEXINGTON, VIRGINIA 24450

Tel: **(540) 464-5877; (800) 446-4240**
Best Time to Call: **9 AM–9 PM**
Hosts: **Sarah and John Burleson**
Location: **50 mi. N of Roanoke**
No. of Rooms: **3**
No. of Private Baths: **3**
Double/pb: **$69–$74**
Single/pb: **$59–$64**
Suites: **$105–$115**
Open: **All year**

Reduced Rates: **Available**
Breakfast: **Full**
Other Meals: **Available**
Credit Cards: **MC, VISA**
Pets: **No**
Children: **Welcome**
Smoking: **No**
Social Drinking: **Permitted**
Minimum Stay: **2 nights on holidays or
special events**

Situated on a 20-acre working farm in the beautiful Shenandoah Valley, this restored farmhouse (circa 1790) is located five miles from historic Lexington. It has been carefully renovated to blend old and new for your comfort and relaxation. Enjoy the large front porch, fishing, hiking, bird-watching, panoramic mountain views, and lambs frolicking on the hillside. Breakfast specialties include homemade bread, stuffed French toast, fresh farm eggs, and much more. Dinner, served to guests by advance reservation, is highly recommended. John is the chef whose specialties involve fresh herbs and vegetables from the garden. Sarah will be glad to direct you to nearby attractions, introduce you to farm animals, or arrange a horseback riding package for you.

The Woodruff House Bed & Breakfast ✪
330 MECHANIC STREET, LURAY, VIRGINIA 22835

Tel: **(540) 743-1494**
Hosts: **Lucas and Deborah Woodruff**
Location: **89 mi. W of Washington, D.C.**
No. of Rooms: **3**
No. of Private Baths: **3**
Double/pb: **$98–$125**
Suites: **$115–$145**
Open: **All year**
Reduced Rates: **20% Mon.–Thurs.,**
  5% after 3 nights

Breakfast: **Full**
Other meals: **Dinner, included with**
  room rate
Credit Cards: **DISC, MC, VISA**
Pets: **No**
Children: **Welcome, Mon.–Thurs. only**
Smoking: **No**
Social Drinking: **Permitted**
Minimum Stay: **2 nights weekends**

jim joggins

This fairy-tale Victorian, beautifully appointed with period antiques, hallmarked silver and fine china, is chef-owned and -operated. Escape from reality and come into this fairy tale, where the ambiance never ends. Awaken to your choice of freshly brewed coffees delivered to your door; a gourmet candlelit breakfast follows. A sumptuous candlelit high-tea buffet dinner is also included. You may want to relax in the fireside candlelit garden spa, or enjoy the canoes and bicycles provided by your hosts. Each guest room has a working fireplace and a private bath. The Woodruff House is located in the beautiful Shenandoah Valley of Virginia.

Federal Crest Inn B&B ✪
1101 FEDERAL STREET, LYNCHBURG, VIRGINIA 24504

Tel: **(804) 845-6155; (800) 818-6155**
Best Time to Call: **10 AM–10 PM**
Hosts: **Phil and Ann Ripley**
Location: **50 mi. E of Roanoke**

No. of Rooms: **5**
No. of Private Baths: **4**
Max. No. Sharing Bath: **4**
Double/pb: **$85**

Single/pb: **$80**
Double/sb: **$55**
Suites: **$100–$115**
Open: **All year**
Reduced Rates: **10% Sun.–Thurs.,
business rates, seniors**
Breakfast: **Full**
Other Meals: **Available**

Credit Cards: **AMEX, DISC, MC, VISA**
Pets: **No**
Children: **Welcome, over 10**
Smoking: **No**
Social Drinking: **Permitted**
Minimum Stay: **May–Oct. 2 nights
weekends**
Airport/Station Pickup: **Yes**

This elegant 1909 Georgian Revival home has over 8000 square feet and is located in the Federal Hill Historic District. The original charm is seen in the woodwork and the interior columns that lead to the grand central staircase in the front foyer. Guests are invited to enjoy the antiques, the unique mantels of the seven fireplaces and the '50s cafe which offers delightful surprises. Perhaps there will be a special visitation to the third floor, where the original owner constructed a stage for his children to give plays. All rooms have queen beds, down comforters, plush robes and towels, snack baskets, and clock radios. In one room, atmosphere is meant to be shared in the romantic Jacuzzi tub, as the lights dim on a painted mural of Virginia's Blue Ridge Mountains. Federal Crest lies within walking distance to many attractions.

Lynchburg Mansion Inn B&B ✪
405 MADISON STREET, LYNCHBURG, VIRGINIA 24504

Tel: **(804) 528-5400; (800) 352-1199**
Hosts: **Bob and Mauranna Sherman**
Location: **65 mi. S of Charlottesville**
No. of Rooms: **5**
No. of Private Baths: **5**
Double/pb: **$95–$114**
Suites: **$129**
Open: **All year**

Reduced Rates: **Available**
Breakfast: **Full**
Credit Cards: **AMEX, DC, MC, VISA**
Pets: **No**
Children: **Welcome**
Smoking: **No**
Social Drinking: **Permitted**

Restored with your every comfort in mind, this Spanish Georgian mansion has pretty gardens, a spacious veranda, oak floors, tall ceilings, pocket doors, and cherry woodwork. Bedrooms are lavish, with either king- or queen-size beds, luxurious linens, fireplaces, TVs, and turn-down service. Bob and Mauranna have also added an outdoor hot tub for guests to use. Fine china, silver, and crystal complement the sump-tuous full breakfasts. The mansion surveys a half-acre in downtown Lynchburg's Garland Hill Historic District, which is listed on the Na-tional Register of Historic Places; impressive Federal and Victorian homes line Madison Street, still paved in its turn-of-the-century brick. Plus there are Civil War sites, antique shops, art galleries, and countless programs offered by the city's colleges and universities.

Sunrise Hill Farm ✪
5590 OLD FARM LANE, MANASSAS, VIRGINIA 20109

Tel: **(703) 754-8309**
Best Time to Call: **Anytime**
Hosts: **Frank and Sue Boberek**
Location: **35 minutes W of Washington, D.C.**
No. of Rooms: **2**
No. of Private Baths: **1**
Max. No. Sharing Bath: **4**
Double/pb: **$90**
Double/sb: **$78**

Open: **All year**
Reduced Rates: **15% families using both rooms**
Breakfast: **Full**
Credit Cards: **MC, VISA**
Pets: **Horses boarded**
Children: **Welcome, over 10**
Smoking: **No**
Social Drinking: **Permitted**

Standing in the heart of the 6000-acre Manassas National Battlefields, this Civil War treasure overlooks Bull Run Creek. Sunrise Hill Farm is an uncommonly charming, Federal-era country home furnished in pe-riod style. This B&B is a haven for Civil War buffs and guests visiting northern Virginia and the nation's capital. Situated within the re-nowned Virginia hunt country, it is just 35 minutes from Washington, D.C., and close to Harpers Ferry, Antietam, Skyline Drive, Luray Cav-erns, and numerous historic sites and antique-filled towns.

Porterville Bed & Breakfast ✪
ROUTE 3, BOX 1002, MONTROSS, VIRGINIA 22520

Tel: **(804) 493-9394**
Best Time to Call: **7–8 AM; evenings**
Host: **Mary P. Hall**
No. of Rooms: **2**
Max. No. Sharing Bath: **4**
Double/sb: **$55**
Single/sb: **$45**
Open: **All year**

Reduced Rates: **10% seniors (Tues. only)**
Breakfast: **Full**
Pets: **No**
Children: **Welcome, over 8**
Smoking: **No**
Social Drinking: **Permitted**
Airport Pickup: **Yes**

Porterville Bed & Breakfast is a brick home nestled behind lovely shade trees near Chandler's mill pond. The property was originally owned by two Baptist churches and the house was built as a parsonage. Mary offers your choice of two guest rooms. The Cornelia room has a double bed, and the Juanita room has twin beds. Nearby attractions include Stratford Hall Plantation, Popes Creek Plantation, and Colonial Beach. Historic Fredericksburg and the battlegrounds are only 45 minutes away. A country breakfast is served either on the porch or in the dining area.

The Jacob Swartz House ✪
574 JIGGADY ROAD, NEW MARKET, VIRGINIA 22844

Tel: **(540) 740-9208**
Best Time to Call: **Before 9 PM**
Host: **Virginia Harris-Selby**
Location: **110 SW of Washington, D.C.**
Guesthouse: **$125–$215**
Open: **Mar.–Dec.**
Reduced Rates: **Available**
Breakfast: **Full**

Other Meals: **Available**
Pets: **No**
Children: **Welcome**
Smoking: **No**
Social Drinking: **Permitted**
Minimum Stay: **2 nights holidays, weekends, special events**

Perched on a bluff overlooking the Shenandoah River, the Jacob Swartz House is the perfect place for the angler, nature lover, or history buff. This 1852 clapboard farmhouse and adjacent cobbler shop survived the Battle of New Market and raid by General Custer in 1864. The converted shop, tastefully appointed in a blend of antique and traditional furnishings, features a living room with a wood-burning stove, sunroom, full kitchen, screened porch, and terrace. The B&B makes an ideal hub for those who want to explore the many splendors of Virginia's valley of the Shenandoah. A lavish breakfast is served in the main house. A picnic, perfect for your afternoon excursion, may be arranged.

A Touch of Country Bed & Breakfast ✪
9329 CONGRESS STREET, NEW MARKET, VIRGINIA 22844

Tel: **(540) 740-8030**
Hosts: **Jean Schoellig and Dawn Kasow**
Location: **18 mi. N of Harrisonburg**
No. of Rooms: **6**
No. of Private Baths: **6**
Double/pb: **$60–$75**
Single/pb: **$50–$65**

Open: **All year**
Breakfast: **Full**
Credit Cards: **DISC, MC, VISA**
Pets: **No**
Children: **Welcome, over 12**
Smoking: **No**
Social Drinking: **Permitted**

This restored 1870s home is located in a historic town in the beautiful Shenandoah Valley. It displays the original hardwood floors and is decorated with antiques and collectibles in a country motif. You'll start your day with a hearty breakfast of pancakes, meats, gravy, and biscuits. Daydream on the porch swings or stroll through town with its charming shops, dine at a variety of restaurants or visit the legendary New Market Battlefield and Park. Close by are Skyline Drive, George Washington National Forest, caverns, and vineyards.

The Spinning Wheel Bed & Breakfast ✪
31 NORTH STREET, ONANCOCK, VIRGINIA 23417

Tel: **(804) 787-7311;** Nov. 1–March 31
  (703) 684-0067
Hosts: **David and Karen Tweedie**
Location: **60 mi. N of Virginia Beach**
No. of Rooms: **5**
No. of Private Baths: **5**
Double/pb: **$85–$95**
Open: **Apr. 1–Oct. 31**

Reduced Rates: **Over 4 nights**
Breakfast: **Full**
Credit Cards: **MC, VISA**
Pets: **No**
Children: **Welcome, over 12**
Smoking: **No**
Social Drinking: **Permitted**
Minimum Stay: **2 nights, weekends**

This 1890s folk Victorian home is in the historic waterfront town of Onancock, on the Eastern Shore peninsula separating the Chesapeake Bay from the Atlantic Ocean. The B&B is decorated with antiques and, true to its name, spinning wheels. Guest rooms have queen-size beds and air-conditioning. Kerr Place (a 1799 museum), restaurants, shops, the town wharf, and the ferry to Tangier Island are all within walking distance. David is a college professor and Karen is a teacher of the deaf. Their guests are greeted by Nelly, the resident old English sheepdog.

Count Pulaski Bed & Breakfast and Gardens ✪
821 NORTH JEFFERSON AVENUE, PULASKI, VIRGINIA 24301

Tel: **(540) 980-1163**
Host: **Dr. Flo Stevenson**
Location: **55 mi. S of Roanoke**
No. of Rooms: **3**
No. of Private Baths: **3**
Double/pb: **$95**
Single/pb: **$75**

Open: **All year**
Breakfast: **Full**
Credit Cards: **MC, VISA**
Pets: **Sometimes**
Children: **Welcome, over 15**
Smoking: **No**
Social Drinking: **No**

In a mountain village in southwest Virginia, you'll find this spacious eighty-year-old house furnished with family antiques, paintings, and pieces your host collected around the world. Guest rooms have carpeting, air-conditioning, and king- or queen-size beds; one room has a fireplace. A television, beverage center, and games and books are inside, while garden sitting areas beckon you outside. Breakfast is served by candlelight on a 150-year-old table set with china, crystal, and silver. From its quiet hillside perch, this B&B overlooks the town and mountains below, yet Main Street's restaurants and antique shops are only a few blocks away. A fifty-mile bike trail originates in Pulaski; other recreational options include rafting, canoeing, and golf.

Woodlawn ✪
2211 WILTSHIRE ROAD, ROCKVILLE, VIRGINIA 23146

Tel: **(804) 749-3759**
Best Time to Call: **3–10 PM**
Host: **Ann Nuckols**
Location: **20 mi. W of Richmond**
No. of Rooms: **2**
No. of Private Baths: **2**
Double/pb: **$75**

Open: **All year**
Breakfast: **Full**
Pets: **No**
Children: **No**
Smoking: **No**
Social Drinking: **Permitted**

An ideal hub from which to tour many historic points of interest in the area, this circa 1813 farmhouse is set on 40 acres of peaceful, grassy slopes, just 3 miles from the interstate. The interior has been completely restored, tastefully decorated, and furnished with antiques. The house has central air-conditioning for summer comfort. Each of the two guest rooms has its own fireplace. Both guest rooms are furnished with majestic hand-carved double beds and down pillows and comforters. Breakfasts with sourdough rolls, bran muffins, homemade jellies, and juice are served on the screened porch or in the dining area in the English basement.

The Manor at Taylor's Store B&B Country Inn ✪
P.O. BOX 510, SMITH MOUNTAIN LAKE, VIRGINIA 24184

Tel: **(540) 721-3951; (800) 248-6267**
Hosts: **Lee and Mary Lynn Tucker**
Location: **20 mi. E of Roanoke**
No. of Rooms: **10**
No. of Private Baths: **8**
Double/pb: **$90–$185**
Guest Cottage: **$95–$190; sleeps 2–6**
Open: **All year**
Reduced Rates: **$300–up weekly for cottage**

Breakfast: **Full**
Credit Cards: **MC, VISA**
Pets: **No**
Children: **Welcome in cottage**
Smoking: **Cottage only**
Social Drinking: **Permitted**
Airport/Station Pickup: **Yes**

Situated on 120 acres in the foothills of the Blue Ridge Mountains, this elegant manor house, circa 1799, was the focus of a prosperous tobacco plantation. It has been restored and refurbished, and you'll experience the elegance of the past combined with the comfort of tasteful modernization. The estate invites hiking, swimming, and fishing. The sunroom, parlor, and hot tub are special spots for relaxing. Smith Mountain Lake, with its seasonal sporting activity, is five miles away. Breakfast, designed for the health-conscious, features a variety of fresh gourmet selections.

Frederick House ✪
28 NORTH NEW STREET, STAUNTON, VIRGINIA 24401

Tel: (540) 885-4220; (800) 334-5575
Best Time to Call: 7 AM–10 PM
Hosts: Joe and Evy Harman
Location: 2.7 mi. from I-81 exit 222; on 250 W
No. of Rooms: 14
No. of Private Baths: 14
Double/pb: $65–$150
Single/pb: $65–$135
Suites: $95–$150

Open: All year
Reduced Rates: Available
Breakfast: Full
Credit Cards: AMEX, DC, DISC, MC, VISA
Pets: No
Children: Welcome
Smoking: No
Social Drinking: Permitted
Station Pickup: Yes

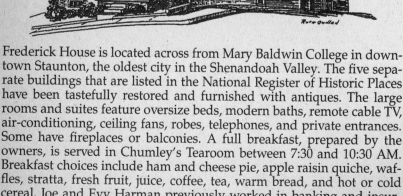

Frederick House is located across from Mary Baldwin College in downtown Staunton, the oldest city in the Shenandoah Valley. The five separate buildings that are listed in the National Register of Historic Places have been tastefully restored and furnished with antiques. The large rooms and suites feature oversize beds, modern baths, remote cable TV, air-conditioning, ceiling fans, robes, telephones, and private entrances. Some have fireplaces or balconies. A full breakfast, prepared by the owners, is served in Chumley's Tearoom between 7:30 and 10:30 AM. Breakfast choices include ham and cheese pie, apple raisin quiche, waffles, stratta, fresh fruit, juice, coffee, tea, warm bread, and hot or cold cereal. Joe and Evy Harman previously worked in banking and insurance. Since 1984 they have enjoyed informing guests about the area and suggesting trips to many nearby interesting sights.

Kenwood ✪

235 EAST BEVERLEY STREET, STAUNTON, VIRGINIA 24401

Tel: **(540) 886-0524**
Hosts: **Liz and Ed Kennedy**
Location: **30 mi. W of Charlottesville**
No. of Rooms: **3**
No. of Private Baths: **3**
Double/pb: **$80**
Single/pb: **$70**
Open: **All year**

Breakfast: **Full**
Credit Cards: **MC, VISA**
Pets: **No**
Children: **Welcome, over 8**
Smoking: **No**
Social Drinking: **Permitted**
Airport/Station Pickup: **Yes**

Kenwood, a stately brick Colonial revival home built in 1910, has been restored and decorated with floral wallpapers and antique furniture. The Woodrow Wilson Birthplace—and its museum and research library—are next door. Staunton boasts several other museums and numerous antique shops, and it's only a half-hour drive to attractions like Monticello and the Virginia Horse Center. Select your destinations over such breakfast fare as fresh seasonal fruit and homemade baked goods.

The Sampson Eagon Inn ✪

238 EAST BEVERLEY STREET, STAUNTON, VIRGINIA 24401

Tel: **(540) 886-8200; (800) 597-9722**
Best Time to Call: **10 AM–9 PM**
Hosts: **Laura and Frank Mattingly**
Location: **35 mi. W of Charlottesville**
No. of Rooms: **5**
No. of Private Baths: **5**
Double/pb: **$89**
Suites: **$109**

Open: **All year**
Breakfast: **Full**
Pets: **No**
Children: **Welcome, over 12**
Smoking: **No**
Social Drinking: **Permitted**
Minimum Stay: **Weekends in Oct. and May**

This circa 1840 in-town Greek Revival mansion provides affordable luxury accommodations in a preservation award–winning setting. Comfort and hospitality are key. Guest rooms are spacious, air-conditioned, and have modern ensuite baths. Canopied beds and antique furnishings reflect various periods of this elegant building's past. Scrumptious, gourmet breakfasts are served daily. Within two blocks of shops and restaurants, the Inn is adjacent to the Woodrow Wilson Birthplace and Mary Baldwin College. Nearby, guests can enjoy the natural and historic attractions and recreational activities of the central Shenandoah Valley. Charlottesville and Lexington are within a 40-minute drive.

Thornrose House at Gypsy Hill ✪

531 THORNROSE AVENUE, STAUNTON, VIRGINIA 24401

Tel: **(540) 885-7026; (800) 861-4338**
Best Time to Call: **9 AM–9 PM**
Hosts: **Suzanne and Otis Huston**

Location: **3^1/$_2$ mi. from Rte. I-81, Exit 222**
No. of Rooms: **5**

No. of Private Baths: **5**
Double/pb: **$60–$80**
Single/pb: **$50–$70**
Open: **All year**
Reduced Rates: **Available**
Breakfast: **Full**

Pets: **No**
Children: **Welcome, over 5**
Smoking: **No**
Social Drinking: **Permitted**
Minimum Stay: **Apr.–Oct. weekends**
Airport/Station Pickup: **Yes**

This 1912 Georgian Revival home is six blocks from the center of Victorian Staunton and adjacent to 300-acre Gypsy Hill Park, which has facilities for golf, tennis, swimming, and summer concerts. A wraparound veranda and Greek colonnades grace the exterior of the house. Inside, there's a cozy parlor with a fireplace and a grand piano. A relaxed, leisurely breakfast is set out in the dining room, which offers the comfort of a fireplace on chilly mornings. Local attractions include Blue Ridge National Park, Natural Chimneys, Skyline Drive, Woodrow Wilson's birthplace, and the Museum of American Frontier Culture.

The Duck Farm Inn ✪

P.O. BOX 787, RTES. 227 AND 639, URBANNA, VIRGINIA 23175

Tel: **(804) 758-5685**
Host: **Fleming Godden**
Location: **55 mi. E of Richmond**
No. of Rooms: **6**
No. of Private Baths: **2**
Max. No. Sharing Bath: **4**
Double/pb: **$85**
Single/pb: **$70**
Double/sb: **$75**

Single/sb: **$60**
Open: **All year**
Reduced Rates: **After first visit**
Breakfast: **Full**
Pets: **No**
Children: **Welcome**
Smoking: **No**
Social Drinking: **Permitted**
Airport/Station Pickup: **Yes**

This elegant, contemporary Inn is situated on Virginia's middle peninsula, surrounded by 800 secluded acres and bordered by the Rappahannock River. Guests are welcome to hike along the shore or through the woods, fish in the river, sunbathe on the private beach, lounge on the deck, or retire to the cozy library with a good book. Fleming has traveled all over the world and thoroughly enjoys her role as full-time innkeeper. One of her breakfast menus consists of seasonal fresh fruit, jumbo blueberry muffins, cheese-and-egg scramble served with spiced sausage, and a variety of hot beverages.

Angie's Guest Cottage ✪

302 24TH STREET, VIRGINIA BEACH, VIRGINIA 23451

Tel: **(757) 428-4690**
Best Time to Call: **10 AM–9 PM**
Host: **Barbara G. Yates**
Location: **20 mi. E of Norfolk**
No. of Rooms: **6**
No. of Private Baths: **1**
Max. No. Sharing Bath: **4**

Double/pb: **$78**
Single/pb: **$68**
Double/sb: **$52–$72**
Single/sb: **$44–$62**
Guest Cottage: **$450–$575 weekly;**
 sleeps 2–6
Open: **Apr. 1–Oct. 1**

Reduced Rates: **Off-season**	Smoking: **No**
Breakfast: **Continental, plus**	Social Drinking: **Permitted**
Pets: **Sometimes**	Minimum Stay: **2 nights**
Children: **Welcome**	

Just a block from the beach, shops, and restaurants is this bright and comfortable beach house. Former guests describe it as "cozy, cute, and clean." Deep-sea fishing, nature trails, and harbor tours are but a few things to keep you busy. Freshly baked croissants in various flavors are a breakfast delight. You are welcome to use the sundeck, barbecue, and picnic tables.

Barclay Cottage ✪
400 16TH STREET, VIRGINIA BEACH, VIRGINIA 23451

Tel: **(757) 422-1956**	Reduced Rates: **10% seniors**
Hosts: **Peter and Claire**	Breakfast: **Full**
Location: **20 mi. E of Norfolk**	Credit Cards: **AMEX, MC, VISA**
No. of Rooms: **5**	Pets: **No**
No. of Private Baths: **3**	Children: **No**
Max. No. Sharing Bath: **2**	Smoking: **No**
Double/pb: **$80–$90**	Social Drinking: **Permitted**
Double/sb: **$65–$75**	Minimum Stay: **2 nights**
Open: **Apr.–Oct.; special holidays**	

The Barclay is a historic building designed in turn-of-the-century, Southern Colonial style. Your hosts bring you casual sophistication in a warm, innlike atmosphere two blocks from the beach and fishing pier. The inn has been completely restored to add the feeling of yesterday to the comfort of today. Peter and Claire look forward to welcoming you to their B&B, where the theme is, "We go where our dreams lead us."

The Iris Inn ○

191 CHINQUAPIN DRIVE, WAYNESBORO, VIRGINIA 22980

Tel: **(540) 943-1991**	Reduced Rates: **Corporate, Sun.–Thurs.**
Best Time to Call: **10 AM–8 PM**	Breakfast: **Full**
Hosts: **Wayne and Iris Karl**	Credit Cards: **AMEX, MC, VISA**
Location: **25 mi. W of Charlottesville**	Pets: **No**
No. of Rooms: **9**	Children: **Welcome, over 10**
No. of Private Baths: **9**	Smoking: **No**
Double/pb: **$80–$140**	Social Drinking: **Permitted**
Single/pb: **$75**	Minimum Stay: **2 nights weekends**
Open: **All year**	Airport: **Yes**

The charm and grace of Southern living in a totally modern facility, nestled in a wooded tract on the western slope of the Blue Ridge overlooking the historic Shenandoah Valley—that's what awaits you at the Iris Inn in Waynesboro. It's ideal for a weekend retreat, a refreshing change for the business traveler, and a tranquil spot for the tourist to spend a night or a week. Guest rooms are spacious, comfortably furnished, and delightfully decorated in nature and wildlife motifs. Each room has a private bath and individual temperature control.

Blue Bird Haven B&B ○

8691 BARHAMSVILLE ROAD, WILLIAMSBURG-TOANO, VIRGINIA 23168

Tel: **(757) 566-0177**	Suites: **$76**
Host: **June Cottle**	Open: **All year**
Location: **9 mi. N of Williamsburg**	Breakfast: **Full**
No. of Rooms: **3**	Pets: **Sometimes**
No. of Private Baths: **2**	Children: **Welcome**
Max. No. Sharing Bath: **4**	Smoking: **No**
Double/pb: **$65**	Social Drinking: **Permitted**

June welcomes you to her ranch-style home, located 20 minutes from Colonial Williamsburg. Guest accommodations, located in a private wing, feature traditional furnishings. June is interested in many kinds of handcrafts and has decorated the rooms with one-of-a-kind quilts, spreads, rugs, and pictures. Breakfast includes a Southern-style assortment of Virginia ham, spoon bread, red-eye gravy, blueberry pancakes, fresh fruits, home-baked biscuits, and granola. Blue Bird Haven is convenient to Busch Gardens, James River Plantations, and Civil War battlefields. After a full day of seeing the sights, you are welcome to enjoy some of June's evening desserts.

Candlewick Inn B&B ○

800 JAMESTOWN ROAD, WILLIAMSBURG, VIRGINIA 23185

Tel: **(804) 253-8693; (800) 418-4949**	Location: **2 miles from Route 64, Exit 242A**
Best Time to Call: **Anytime**	
Host: **Mary L. Peters**	No. of Rooms: **3**

No. of Private Baths: **3**
Double/pb: **$90–$115**
Single/pb: **$90–$95**
Open: **All year**
Reduced Rates: **Available**
Breakfast: **Full**
Credit Cards: **MC, VISA**

Pets: **No**
Children: **Welcome, over 12**
Smoking: **No**
Social Drinking: **Permitted**
Minimum Stay: **2 nights**
Station Pickup: **Yes**
Foreign Languages: **German**

Mary restored and redecorated this 1946 two-story frame house so that it looks like a farmhouse from the previous century, with beam ceilings, chair rails, and beautiful canopy beds. She also sets out wonderful country breakfasts featuring home-baked bread and muffins. Then it's an easy four-block walk or bike ride to the historic area; first stop is William and Mary College, just across the way.

Colonial Capital Bed & Breakfast ✪
501 RICHMOND ROAD, WILLIAMSBURG, VIRGINIA 23185
ccbb@widomaker.com; http://www.ccbb.com

Tel: **(800) 776-0570; (757) 229-0233;**
  fax: **(757) 253-7667**
Hosts: **Barbara and Phil Craig**
Location: **2.5 mi. from I-64, Exit 238**
No. of Rooms: **5**
No. of Private Baths: **5**
Double/pb: **$76–$125**
Suites: **$108–$140**

Open: **All year**
Breakfast: **Full**
Credit Cards: **AMEX, DISC, MC, VISA**
Pets: **No**
Children: **Welcome, over 8**
Smoking: **Restricted**
Social Drinking: **Permitted**
Airport/Station Pickup: **Yes**

Barbara and Phil offer a warm welcome to guests in their three-story Colonial revival (c.1926) home only three blocks from the historic area. The B&B is decorated with period antiques, oriental rugs, and many of the original lighting and plumbing fixtures; all guest rooms feature four-poster beds crowned with charming canopies. In the morning you can look forward to such treats as a soufflé, French toast, fluffy omelette, or yeast waffles complemented with a choice of juices, fresh fruits, and specially blended coffees and tea. The sunny solarium or formal dining room invite guests to linger over breakfast and get to know one another as does the plantation parlor, where tea and wine are served during afternoons and evenings. Games, books, and puzzles are provided for your pleasure. Jamestown, Yorktown, some of the state's finest plantations, Busch Gardens, and Water Country USA are only a few minutes away. Personalized gift certificates are available.

For Cant Hill Guest Home
4 CANTERBURY LANE, WILLIAMSBURG, VIRGINIA 23185-3410

Tel: **(757) 229-6623; fax: (757) 229-1863**
Best Time to Call: **Anytime**

Hosts: **Martha and Hugh Easler**
No. of Rooms: **2**
No. of Private Baths: **2**

Double/pb: **$75–$85**
Open: **All year**
Breakfast: **Continental**
Credit Cards: **MC, VISA**
Pets: **No**

Children: **Welcome, over 10**
Smoking: **No**
Social Drinking: **Permitted**
Minimum Stay: **2 nights weekends Mar. 15–Dec. 31**

Situated in the heart of town, overlooking Lake Matoaka, a part of the campus of the College of William and Mary, the home is only a few blocks from the restored area of Colonial Williamsburg, yet very secluded and quiet in a lovely wooded setting. Both rooms are tastefully decorated, accented in winter with homemade quilts. Each room has a TV and a hearty Continental breakfast is served in the room. The hosts are happy to make dinner reservations for guests and provide very helpful information on the many attractions in the entire area.

Fox & Grape Bed & Breakfast ✪
701 MONUMENTAL AVENUE, WILLIAMSBURG, VIRGINIA 23185

Tel: **(757) 229-6914; (800) 292-3699**
Best Time to Call: **9 AM–9 PM**
Hosts: **Bob and Pat Orendorff**
Location: **2 mi. from I-64, Exit 238**
No. of Rooms: **4**
No. of Private Baths: **4**
Double/pb: **$84**
Open: **All year**

Reduced Rates: **Jan. 1–Mar. 26 for 2 nights**
Breakfast: **Continental, plus**
Pets: **No**
Children: **Welcome**
Smoking: **No**
Social Drinking: **Permitted**
Station Pickup: **Yes**

Fox & Grape is located five blocks north of Virginia's restored Colonial capital. This two-story Colonial has a spacious wraparound porch that is a perfect place for guests to enjoy morning coffee, plan their day, or just relax with a favorite book. The decor inside includes antiques, counted cross-stitch, duck decoys, and folk-art Noah's Arks made by your host.

Governor's Trace ✪
303 CAPITOL LANDING ROAD, WILLIAMSBURG, VIRGINIA 23185

Tel: **(757) 229-7552; (800) 303-7552; fax: (757) 220-2767**
Best Time to Call: **9 AM–10 PM**
Hosts: **Sue and Dick Lake**
Location: **2 mi. from I-64, exit 238**
No. of Rooms: **3**
No. of Private Baths: **3**
Double/pb: **$75–$125**

Suites: **$105–$125**
Open: **All year**
Breakfast: **Full**
Credit Cards: **MC, VISA**
Pets: **No**
Children: **No**
Smoking: **No**
Social Drinking: **Permitted**

This Georgian brick home featured on the back cover of the 1992 edition of *Bed & Breakfast U.S.A.* is Colonial Williamsburg's closest B&B neighbor, just one door away. Hardy patriot, loyal royalist, or plantation gentry travelers would have found the rooms here comfortably familiar but with modern exceptions, king- and queen-size beds, and private baths. Special amenities include a fireplace in one bedroom and a screened-in porch off another. Private romantic candlelit breakfast is served in each room. Sue and Dick provide refuge from the modern world's hectic pace to let you discover unexpected treasures in an 18th-century atmosphere. Make "take away" memories at the Governor's Trace.

The Homestay Bed & Breakfast ✪
517 RICHMOND ROAD, WILLIAMSBURG, VIRGINIA 23185

Tel: **(757) 229-7468; (800) 836-7468**	Breakfast: **Full**
Best Time to Call: **10 AM–9 PM**	Credit Cards: **MC, VISA**
Hosts: **Barbara and Jim Thomassen**	Pets: **No**
Location: **3 mi. from Rte. I-64, Exit 238**	Children: **Welcome, over 10**
No. of Rooms: **3**	Smoking: **No**
No. of Private Baths: **3**	Social Drinking: **Permitted**
Double/pb: **$80–$100**	Minimum Stay: **2 nights, weekends,**
Single/pb: **$70–$90**	**holidays, and special events**
Open: **All year**	Airport/Station Pickup: **Yes**
Reduced Rates: **20% less Jan. 2–**	
Mar. 15	

Cozy and convenient! Enjoy the comfort of a lovely Colonial Revival home furnished with turn-of-the-century family antiques and country charm. Rooms with a queen- or king-size bed are available. The rooms are accented with an attention to detail. You may relax in the second floor sitting room or by the fire in the living room. A full breakfast, served in the formal dining room, features homemade breads, herb jellies (made with herbs from the garden), and delicious hot dishes. You are just four blocks from Williamsburg's famed historic area, adjacent to the College of William and Mary campus, alumni house, and football stadium, and minutes away from Jamestown, Yorktown, and Busch Gardens.

War Hill ✪
4560 LONG HILL ROAD, WILLIAMSBURG, VIRGINIA 23188

Tel: **(757) 565-0248; (800) 743-0248**	Cottage: **$115–$160; sleeps 2–5**
Best Time to Call: **9 AM–9 PM**	Open: **All year**
Hosts: **Shirley, Bill, and Will Lee**	Breakfast: **Full**
Location: **2 mi. from Williamsburg**	Credit Cards: **MC, VISA**
No. of Rooms: **5**	Pets: **No**
No. of Private Baths: **5**	Children: **Welcome**
Double/pb: **$75–$95**	Smoking: **No**
Suite: **$100–$145; sleeps 2–5**	Social Drinking: **Permitted**

War Hill is situated in the center of a 32-acre working farm, just three miles from the tourist attractions. Built in 1968, this Colonial replica couples the charm of yesteryear with today's contemporary conveniences. The suite is composed of two bedrooms and a bath. The wide heart-pine floors came from an old school, the stairs from a church, the overhead beams from a barn; the oak mantel is over 200 years old. Fruits from a variety of trees in the orchard are yours to pick in season. In autumn, Shirley and Bill serve delicious homemade applesauce and cider. Angus show cattle graze in the pasture, and the sounds you'll hear are crickets, frogs, owls, and the morning crowing of the rooster.

Williamsburg Sampler Bed and Breakfast ✪
922 JAMESTOWN ROAD, WILLIAMSBURG, VIRGINIA 23185

Tel: **(800) 722-1169; (757) 253-0398;**
  fax: (757) 253-2669
Best Time to Call: **7:30 AM–10:30 PM**
Hosts: **Helen and Ike Sisane**
Location: **Heart of Williamsburg**
No. of Rooms: **4**
No. of Private Baths: **4**
Double/pb: **$95–$140**

Open: **All year**
Breakfast: **Full**
Pets: **No**
Children: **Welcome, over 12**
Smoking: **No**
Social Drinking: **Permitted**
Airport/Station Pickup: **Yes**

Welcome to one of Williamsburg's finest 18th-century plantation-style homes. The three-story brick Colonial B&B is richly furnished throughout with antiques, pewter, and samplers. This elegant home complements those located in the restored area and is within walking distance to historic Colonial Williamsburg. Lovely accommodations include two suites, four-poster beds in king and queen sizes, television, fireplaces, and your hosts' famous "skip lunch" breakfast. Personalized gift certificates are available.

Azalea House

551 SOUTH MAIN STREET, WOODSTOCK, VIRGINIA 22664

Tel: **(540) 459-3500**
Hosts: **Margaret and Price McDonald**
Location: **35 mi. N of Harrisonburg**
No. of Rooms: **4**
No. of Private Baths: **4**
Double/pb: **$55–$75**
Open: **All year**

Breakfast: **Full**
Credit Cards: **AMEX, MC, VISA**
Pets: **No**
Children: **Welcome, over 6**
Smoking: **No**
Social Drinking: **Permitted**

This spacious home, built in the early 1890s, served as a parsonage for 70 years. It has been restored following its Victorian tradition and has porches, bay windows, and a white picket fence—in spring, one hundred blooming azaleas enhance its beauty. The interior is made particularly lovely with family heirlooms and pretty color schemes. Azalea House is within walking distance of a fine restaurant. It is convenient to antique shops, wineries, orchards, trails, horseback riding, and fishing. Air-conditioning assures your summer comfort.

For key to listings, see inside front or back cover.

✪ This star means that rates are guaranteed through December 31, 1998, to any guest making a reservation as a result of reading about the B&B in *Bed & Breakfast U.S.A.*—1998 edition.

Important! To avoid misunderstandings, always ask about cancellation policies when booking.

Please enclose a self-addressed, stamped, business-size envelope when contacting reservation services.

For more details on what you can expect in a B&B, see Chapter 1.

Always mention *Bed & Breakfast U.S.A.* when making reservations!

We want to hear from you! Use the form on page 625.

WASHINGTON

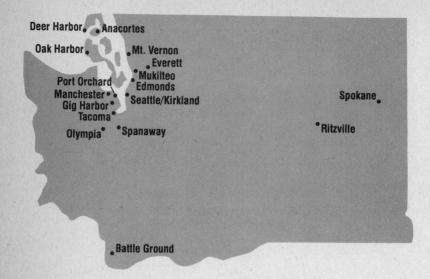

Deer Harbor • Anacortes
Oak Harbor •
• Mt. Vernon
• Everett
Port Orchard • • Mukilteo
Manchester • • Edmonds
Gig Harbor • • Seattle/Kirkland
Tacoma •
Olympia • • Spanaway
Spokane •
• Ritzville
• Battle Ground

Pacific Bed & Breakfast Agency ✪
701 NORTHWEST 60TH STREET, SEATTLE, WASHINGTON 98107

Tel: **(206) 439-7677, 784-0539; fax:**
  (206) 431-0932
Best Time to Call: **9 AM–5 PM**
Coordinator: **Greg Kaminski**
States/Regions Covered: **Statewide;**
  Canada—Vancouver, Victoria
Descriptive Directory: **$5**

Rates (Single/Double):
  Modest: **$45 / $55**
  Average: **$55 / $85**
  Luxury: **$85 / $200**
Credit Cards: **AMEX, MC, VISA**
Minimum Stay: **2 nights in Seattle**

Victorians, contemporaries, and private suites, apartments, and condos
are available. Most are close to downtown areas, near bus lines, in fine
residential neighborhoods. Many are near water, some with views and
near beaches.

A Burrow's Bay B&B ✪
4911 MACBETH DRIVE, ANACORTES, WASHINGTON 98221

Tel: **(360) 293-4792**
Hosts: **Beverly and Winfred Stocker**
Location: **92 mi. N of Seattle**
Suites: **$95; sleep 2–4**
Open: **All year**
Breakfast: **Continental, plus**

Credit Cards: **MC, VISA**
Pets: **Sometimes**
Children: **Welcome**
Smoking: **No**
Social Drinking: **Permitted**
Airport/Station Pickup: **Yes**

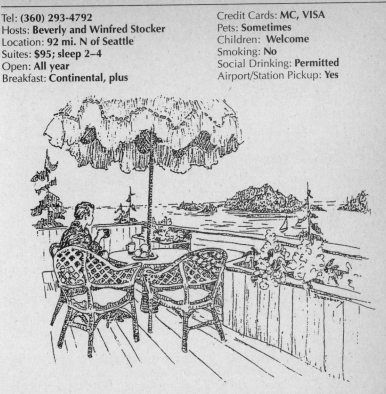

Enjoy sweeping views of the San Juan Islands from this lovely contemporary Northwest home. The guest suite consists of a large sitting room with a view and a comfortable bedroom with a blue-and-tan motif and wall-to-wall carpeting. You are sure to enjoy the privacy and relaxation of having your own private deck, fireplace, TV, and a separate entrance. Beverly and Winfred offer Continental-plus breakfast. The B&B is located within walking distance of Washington Park, restaurants, and ferry rides to the nearby islands. Your hosts will be glad to provide touring advice for day trips to Victoria, B.C., Deception Pass, and Port Townsend.

The Channel House
2902 OAKES AVENUE, ANACORTES, WASHINGTON 98221
beds@sos.net; http://www.Channel-house.com

Tel: **(360) 293-9382; (800) 238-4353;**
   fax: (360) 299-9208
Hosts: **Dennis and Patricia McIntyre**

Location: **65 mi. N of Seattle; 18 mi. W**
   of I-5, Exit 230
No. of Rooms: **6**

No. of Private Baths: **6**	Credit Cards: **AMEX, DISC, MC, VISA**
Double/pb: **$69–$95**	Pets: **No**
Cottage: **$105**	Children: **Welcome, over 12**
Open: **All year**	Smoking: **No**
Breakfast: **Full**	Social Drinking: **Permitted**

Built in 1902 by an Italian count, this three-story Victorian house has stained glass windows, rare antiques, gracious ambience, and is in mint condition. The guest rooms have beautiful views of Puget Sound and the San Juan Islands. It's an ideal getaway for relaxing in the "cleanest corner of the country." Your hosts serve gourmet breakfasts in front of the fireplace. The communal hot tub is a treat after salmon fishing, tennis, or golf. And it's only minutes from the ferry for visiting Victoria, British Columbia.

Sunset Beach B&B ✪

100 SUNSET BEACH, ANACORTES, WASHINGTON 98221

Tel: **(360) 293-5428; (800) 359-3448**	Reduced Rates: **Available**
Best Time to Call: **8 AM–10 PM**	Breakfast: **Full**
Hosts: **Joann and Hal Harker**	Credit Cards: **MC, VISA**
Location: **80 mi. NW of Seattle**	Pets: **No**
No. of Rooms: **3**	Children: **Welcome, over 12**
No. of Private Baths: **3**	Smoking: **No**
Double/pb: **$79–$89**	Social Drinking: **Permitted**
Open: **All year**	

This B&B is located on exciting Rosario Straits. Relax and enjoy the view of seven major islands from every room and deck. Stroll on the beach or walk in beautiful Washington Park, adjacent to the private gardens.

Guest rooms all have private baths with a Jacuzzi shower. A hot tub is available upon request. This guest house is five minutes from San Juan Ferry, fine restaurants, marina, and convenience store. The sunsets are outstanding.

Teddy Bear House ✪
18404 NORTHEAST 109 AVENUE, BATTLE GROUND, WASHINGTON 98604
bdasher@worldaccess.com

Tel: (360) 687-4328
Hosts: **Bertha and Bill Dasher**
Location: **20 mi. NE of Portland, Oregon**
No. of Rooms: **2**
Max. No. Sharing Bath: **4**
Double/sb: **$60**

Open: **All year**
Breakfast: **Full**
Pets: **Sometimes**
Children: **Welcome, over 12**
Smoking: **No**
Social Drinking: **No**

Located in southwest Washington, the heart of the beautiful Pacific Northwest, this home can be your hub for exploring the Columbia Gorge National Scenic Area, Mt. St. Helens National Monument, and the historic Fort Vancouver Restoration. A working grist mill is a few miles away and the Lewis and Clark Railroad excursion train station is nearby. Teddy Bear House is named for Bertha's large collection of teddy bears and teddy bear memorabilia, which are used in the decor throughout the house. You will enjoy this quiet secluded country home surrounded by flowers, lawn, and large fir, dogwood, and maple trees.

Palmer's Chart House ✪
P.O. BOX 51, ORCAS ISLAND, DEER HARBOR, WASHINGTON 98243

Tel: (360) 376-4231
Hosts: **Majean and Don Palmer**
Location: **50 mi. N of Seattle**
No. of Rooms: **2**
No. of Private Baths: **2**
Double/pb: **$60–$70**
Single/pb: **$45–$50**

Open: **All year**
Breakfast: **Full**
Pets: **No**
Children: **Welcome, over 10**
Smoking: **No**
Social Drinking: **Permitted**
Foreign Languages: **Spanish**

It's just an hour's ride on the Washington State ferry from Anacortes to Orcas Island. Seasoned travelers, Majean and Don know how to make your stay special. Each guest room has a private deck from which to view the harbor scene. Blueberry pancakes are a breakfast specialty. *Amante*, the 33-foot sloop, is available for sailing with Don, the skipper.

The Harrison House ✪
210 SUNSET AVENUE, EDMONDS, WASHINGTON 98020

Tel: (206) 776-4748
Hosts: **Jody and Harve Harrison**

Location: **15 mi. N of Seattle**
No. of Rooms: **2**

No. of Private Baths: **2**
Double/pb: **$55–$65**
Single/pb: **$45–$55**
Open: **All year**
Breakfast: **Continental**

Pets: **No**
Children: **No**
Smoking: **No**
Social Drinking: **Permitted**

This new, informal, waterfront home has a sweeping view of Puget Sound and the Olympic Mountains. It is a block north of the ferry dock and two blocks from the center of this historic town. Many fine restaurants are within walking distance. Your spacious room has a private deck, TV, wet bar, telephone, and king-size bed. The University of Washington is nearby.

Hudgens Haven ✪
9313 190 SOUTH WEST, EDMONDS, WASHINGTON 98020

Tel: **(206) 776-2202**
Best Time to Call: **4–8 PM**
Hosts: **Lorna and Edward Hudgens**
Location: **20 min. from downtown Seattle**
No. of Rooms: **1**
No. of Private Baths: **1**
Double/pb: **$58**

Single/pb: **$54**
Open: **All year**
Breakfast: **Full**
Pets: **No**
Children: **Welcome, over 10**
Smoking: **No**
Social Drinking: **Permitted**

Hudgens Haven is located in a picture postcard town on Puget Sound. Windows on the west side boast a lovely view of the waterfront. The guest room is furnished with antiques as well as a queen-size bed, rocker, and plenty of drawer space. Edmonds, located 20 minutes from downtown Seattle, is a former lumber town with interesting old houses and an abundance of small shops and excellent restaurants.

The Maple Tree ✪
18313 OLYMPIC VIEW DRIVE, EDMONDS, WASHINGTON 98020

Tel: **(425) 774-8420**
Hosts: **Marion and Hellon Wilkerson**
Location: **15 mi. N of Seattle**
No. of Rooms: **1**
No. of Private Baths: **1**
Double/pb: **$60**
Single/pb: **$55**

Open: **All year**
Breakfast: **Continental**
Pets: **No**
Children: **Welcome, over 5**
Smoking: **No**
Social Drinking: **Permitted**

The Maple Tree is a beautifully restored older home with landscaped grounds. Located across the street from Puget Sound, it commands a stunning view of the Olympic Mountains. You're welcome to watch the activity on Puget Sound through the telescope in the solarium. Lounge on the brick patio or watch the sun set over the snowcapped mountains as you sip a glass of Washington State wine. Hellon and Marion enjoy having guests and exchanging travel experiences with them. Hellon loves to cook; both like to work in their rose garden.

East Everett Tea Rose B&B ✪
2825 SOUTH LAKE STEVENS ROAD, EVERETT, WASHINGTON 98205

Tel: **(206) 334-3428**
Best Time to Call: **Mornings**
Hosts: **Helen and Arden Hilmo**
Location: **5 mi. E of Everett**
No. of Rooms: **3**
No. of Private Baths: **1**
Max. No. Sharing Bath: **4**
Double/pb: **$75**

Double/sb: **$60**
Open: **All year**
Breakfast: **Full**
Pets: **No**
Children: **Welcome**
Smoking: **No**
Social Drinking: **No**

East Everett Tea Rose is located ten minutes away from Lake Stevens and historic Snohomish, where you can go antiquing as well as take a hot-air balloon ride. Nearby you can enjoy scenic hiking, beaches, and ferry rides, and explore or view the mountains. When you return to the East Everett Tea Rose B&B, settle back on the front porch, where you will find food for the soul and rest for your body, surrounded by flower gardens and trees. You may want to do a little bird-watching! The house is a potpourri of country, lace, and flowers, with some antiques and touches of Victorian splendor.

Olde Glencove Hotel ✪
9418 GLENCOVE ROAD, GIG HARBOR, WASHINGTON 98329

Tel: **(206) 884-2835**
Hosts: **Lawrence and Luciann Nadeau**
No. of Rooms: **4**
No. of Private Baths: **2**
Max. No. Sharing Bath: **4**
Double/sb: **$65**
Suites: **$85**

Open: **All year**
Breakfast: **Full**
Pets: **No**
Children: **Welcome**
Smoking: **No**
Social Drinking: **Permitted**

Built in 1897, this historic landmark is a perfect location for honeymoons, anniversaries, or any romantic weekend. Located on the water, the Olde Glencove Hotel offers guests a lovely view and a unique peaceful atmosphere. Lawrence and Luciann have painstakingly restored their lovely home to its authentic 1890s ambiance, complete with antiques of the period, wood-burning stoves, velvet chairs, and stained glass windows and lamps. They want to share their home with experienced world travelers, interesting local folks, and gentle people who appreciate antiques and fine accommodations.

Peacock Hill Guest House ✪

9520 PEACOCK HILL AVENUE, GIG HARBOR, WASHINGTON 98332

Tel: **(206) 858-3322; (800) 863-2318**
Best Time to Call: **10 AM–8 PM**
Hosts: **Steven and Suzanne Savlov**
Location: **50 mi. S of Seattle**
No. of Rooms: **2**
No. of Private Baths: **2**
Double/pb: **$85**
Suites: **$115**

Open: **All year**
Breakfast: **Full**
Pets: **No**
Children: **Welcome, over 10**
Smoking: **No**
Social Drinking: **Permitted**
Minimum Stay: **2 nights weekends**
Station Pickup: **Yes**

As you descend toward the quaint fishing village of Gig Harbor you take in a panoramic view of majestic Mount Rainier towering over ship masts, galleries, restaurants, and a potpourri of shops. This contemporary home sits on a wooded hilltop and has large picture windows that offer a postcard view of the harbor. In the morning you'll awaken to the aroma of a gourmet breakfast; it will give you the energy you need for a picturesque walk around the marina, or a drive to the nearby museums, gardens, zoo, and aquarium. The Scandinavian village of Poulsbo is 40 minutes away. It's a little bit farther to the Bainbridge Island Ferry, which takes you to Seattle's Pike Place Market where you can sample the sights and smells of a large open market. Summit Winter Sports Area is one hour away and has excellent skiing.

Shumway Mansion

11410-99 PLACE NORTH EAST, KIRKLAND, WASHINGTON 98033

Tel: **(206) 823-2303; fax: (206) 822-0421**
Best Time to Call: **9 AM–7 PM**
Hosts: **Richard and Sallie Harris, and Julie and Marshall Blakemore**
Location: **5 mi. NE of Seattle**
No. of Rooms: **8**
No. of Private Baths: **8**
Double/pb: **$70–$95**

Suites: **$105 for 2**
Open: **All year**
Breakfast: **Full**
Credit Cards: **AMEX, MC, VISA**
Pets: **No**
Children: **Welcome, over 12**
Smoking: **No**
Social Drinking: **Permitted**

This stately 24-room mansion, built in 1909, has a regal presence overlooking Lake Washington. The eight antique-filled guest rooms, including a charming corner suite, pair today's comforts with intricately carved pieces from yesteryear. Richard and Sallie will indulge your palate with variety-filled breakfasts that always feature homemade scones and jams. Within a short distance are water and snow recreation, an athletic club, downtown Seattle, and lots of shopping. After a busy day, return "home" and relax in front of the fire with a seasonal treat.

Laurel Inn ✪
7914 BEACH DRIVE EAST, P.O. BOX 677, MANCHESTER, WASHINGTON 98353

Tel: **(360) 769-9544; (888) 888-9661**	Open: **All year**
Host: **Judy McQueen**	Reduced Rates: **10% after 3 nights**
Location: **35 mi. N of Tacoma**	Breakfast: **Full**
No. of Rooms: **3**	Credit Cards: **DISC, MC, VISA**
No. of Private Baths: **1**	Pets: **No**
Max. No. Sharing Bath: **4**	Children: **Welcome, over 12**
Double/pb: **$75**	Smoking: **No**
Single/pb: **$70**	Social Drinking: **Permitted**
Double/sb: **$55–$65**	Minimum Stay: **2 nights holidays**
Single/sb: **$50–$60**	Airport/Station Pickup: **Yes**

Located across the Puget Sound from West Seattle, this contemporary home is furnished with family heirlooms and needlework from three generations. Large windows frame the view of Mt. Rainier and Blake Island. Ocean-bound vessels, local sailboats, and ferries dot the seascape of Manchester. This charming community northeast of Port Orchard is on a popular bicycle route from the Southworth Ferry north to Bremerton, and Laurel Inn is just two miles from Manchester State Park. Wake to the aroma of a gourmet breakfast, which may include poached eggs with salmon cakes and lemon sauce, or cinnamon French toast with bananas and coconut syrup.

The White Swan Guest House ✪
1388 MOORE ROAD, MT. VERNON, WASHINGTON 98273

Tel: **(360) 445-6805**	Location: **60 mi. N of Seattle, 6 mi. SE of La Conner**
Best Time to Call: **Mornings; evenings**	
Host: **Peter Goldfarb**	No. of Rooms: **3**

Max. No. Sharing Bath: **3**
Double/sb: **$80**
Single/sb: **$65**
Guest Cottage: **$125–$165; sleeps 4**
Open: **All year**
Reduced Rates: **Weekly in cottage**

Breakfast: **Continental**
Credit Cards: **MC, VISA**
Pets: **No**
Children: **Welcome (in cottage)**
Smoking: **No**
Social Drinking: **Permitted**

Surrounded by farmland and country roads, this storybook Victorian farmhouse, built in 1898, is painted crayon yellow and framed by English-style gardens. There's a wood stove in the parlor, wicker chairs on the porch, books for browsing, and a unique collection of old samplers. A platter of homemade chocolate chip cookies is waiting for you on the sideboard. It's only 6 miles to LaConner, a delightful fishing village brimful of interesting art galleries, shops, waterfront restaurants, and antique stores. The San Juan ferries are a half hour away.

By the Bay Bed & Breakfast
821 FOURTH STREET, MUKILTEO, WASHINGTON 98275

Tel: **(206) 347-4997**
Hosts: **Jerry and Mary Epps**
Location: **30 mi. N of Seattle, 5 mi. S of Everett**
No. of Rooms: **2**
No. of Private Baths: **2**
Double/pb: **$65**

Guest Cottage: **$75 for two**
Open: **All year**
Breakfast: **Continental**
Pets: **No**
Children: **Welcome**
Smoking: **No**
Social Drinking: **Permitted**

This handsome 1914 Craftsman-style home has a lovely yard with flowers and flowering shrubs. Listed on the Mukilteo Historical Register, the house is light, charming, and decorated with some antiques. The windows look upon the Puget Sound and several islands. By the Bay is within walking distance of shopping, restaurants, the ferry to Whidbey Island, and a beautiful state park with a working lighthouse. The San Juan Islands are nearby and you can take an easy day trip to the mountains, or a 30-minute ride into Seattle.

North Island B&B ✪
1589 NORTH WEST BEACH ROAD, OAK HARBOR, WASHINGTON 98277

Tel: **(360) 675-7080**
Best Time to Call: **Weekdays**
Hosts: **Jim and Maryvern Loomis**
Location: **65 mi. NW of Seattle**
No. of Rooms: **2**
No. of Private Baths: **2**
Double/pb: **$95**
Single/pb: **$90**

Open: **All year**
Breakfast: **Continental**
Credit Cards: **AMEX, DISC, MC, VISA**
Pets: **No**
Children: **No**
Smoking: **No**
Social Drinking: **No**

Ships of all kinds sail by as the sound of ocean waves lulls you to sleep at night at North Island B&B. Located on the west shore of historic and picturesque Whidbey Island, this is a newly constructed home on 175 feet of private beach. Ample parking, king-size beds, and a fireplace combine to give guests the very best in accommodations. Guests have access to the beach, yard, and living room. Breakfast, served between 8:30 and 9:30 AM, features fresh fruit in season, juice, homemade breads and muffins, cereals, and freshly ground coffee or tea.

Puget View Guesthouse ☻

7924 61ST NORTHEAST, OLYMPIA, WASHINGTON 98516

Tel: **(360) 459-1676**
Best Time to Call: **Evenings**
Hosts: **Dick and Barbara Yunker**
Location: **4¹/₂ mi. from I-5, Exit 111**
No. of Rooms: **1 cottage**
No. of Private Baths: **1**
Guest Cottage: **$89–$102; sleeps 4**
Open: **All year**

Reduced Rates: **Families; weekly; off-season**
Breakfast: **Continental, plus**
Credit Cards: **MC, VISA**
Pets: **Sometimes**
Children: **Welcome**
Smoking: **No**
Social Drinking: **Permitted**

This charming waterfront guest cottage is located next to Tolmie State Park and adjacent to Dick and Barbara's log home. The panoramic Puget Sound setting makes it a popular, romantic getaway. You are apt to discover simple pleasures such as beachcombing or bird-watching and activities such as kayaking or scuba diving. Your breakfast, an elegant repast, is brought to the cottage. You are welcome to use the beachside campfire for an evening cookout or to barbecue on your deck.

Swantown Bed and Breakfast Inn

1431 11TH AVENUE SOUTHEAST, OLYMPIA, WASHINGTON 98501

Tel: **(360) 753-9123**
Best Time to Call: **Evenings**
Hosts: **Lillian and Ed Peeples**
Location: **¹/₂ mi. from I-5 Exit 105 (Port of Olympia)**
No. of Rooms: **4**
No. of Private Baths: **4**
Double/pb: **$65–$115**
Single/pb: **$75–$125**

Open: **All year**
Reduced Rates: **Weekly**
Breakfast: **Full**
Credit Cards: **MC, VISA**
Pets: **No**
Children: **Welcome, over 12**
Smoking: **No**
Social Drinking: **Permitted**

Built in 1893, this stately Queen Anne/Eastlake mansion is an Olympia landmark, listed on both the state and city historical registers. Guests are invited to relax with a hot beverage in the drawing room or stroll among the Inn's half-acre gardens and orchard. It is conveniently located near the State Capitol campus, Farmers Market, downtown shops, restaurants, and waterfront boardwalk. The Inn has a great location for day trips to the Olympic peninsula, Mount St. Helens, Mount Rainier, and the city of Seattle. Accommodations include queen-size beds, and most rooms have a view of the Capitol dome. Breakfast entrees may include German apple pancakes, crepes benedict, and cream cheese French toast with homemade syrups.

"Reflections"—A Bed and Breakfast Inn ✪
3878 REFLECTION LANE EAST, PORT ORCHARD, WASHINGTON 98366

Tel: **(360) 871-5582**
Best Time to Call: **Anytime**
Hosts: **Jim and Cathy Hall**
Location: **1 hour from ferry ride**
No. of Rooms: **4**
No. of Private Baths: **2**
Max. No. Sharing Bath: **4**
Double/pb: **$70**
Single/pb: **$70**
Double/sb: **$60**

Single/sb: **$60**
Suites: **$95**
Open: **All year**
Breakfast: **Full**
Credit Cards: **MC, VISA**
Pets: **No**
Children: **Welcome, over 15**
Smoking: **No**
Social Drinking: **Permitted**

This sprawling Colonial home stands majestically on a bluff overlooking Puget Sound and Bainbridge Island. Each cheerful guest room, furnished with New England antiques, affords superb views of the water and ever-changing scenery. Port Orchard offers a variety of diversions, from small shops filled with antiques and crafts, to marinas, parks, and boat excursions around the peninsula.

The Portico, Victorian Bed & Breakfast ✪
502 SOUTH ADAMS STREET, RITZVILLE, WASHINGTON 99169

Tel: **(509) 659-0800**
Best Time to Call: **Day or evening**
Hosts: **Mary Anne and Bill Phipps**
Location: **60 mi. SW of Spokane**
No. of Rooms: **2**
No. of Private Baths: **2**
Double/pb: **$59–$79**
Single/pb: **$53–$73**

Open: **All year**
Breakfast: **Full**
Other Meals: **Available**
Credit Cards: **AMEX, DISC, MC, VISA**
Pets: **No**
Children: **Welcome**
Smoking: **No**
Social Drinking: **Permitted**

The Portico is regarded as one of the finest bed and breakfast experiences in the region, where cordial hospitality, delectable food, and tastefully appointed accommodations offer superior ease and comfort in Victorian style. The historic 1902 mansion combines Classical Revival and Queen Anne architecture. The interior displays gleaming oak woodwork, inglenooks, columns, spindled screens, and a grand entry. Victorian wallpapers, furnishings, and lighting will delight antique lovers. Rooms have exceptionally comfortable beds and discreetly hidden TVs. This B&B is set in a rural community with easy access to I-90 and Highway 395.

Chelsea Station on the Park ✪

4915 LINDEN AVENUE NORTH, SEATTLE, WASHINGTON 98103

Tel: **(206) 547-6077; (800) 400-6077**
Best Time to Call: **10 AM–6 PM**
Hosts: **John Griffin and
    Karen Carbonneau**
Location: **Seattle's North End**
No. of Rooms: **8**
No. of Private Baths: **8**
Double/pb: **$89–$119**
Open: **All year**

Reduced Rates: **Off-season, weekly**
Breakfast: **Full**
Credit Cards: **AMEX, DC, DISC, MC,
    VISA**
Pets: **No**
Children: **Welcome, over 12**
Smoking: **No**
Social Drinking: **Permitted**

Chelsea Station on the Park, circa 1929, is nestled between the Fremont neighborhood and Woodland Park. Largely decorated in Mission style, the house features antiques throughout. Guest rooms have king- or queen-size beds complete with soft down comforters. Awake to the aroma of fresh coffee, followed by a hearty breakfast including delicious selections such as orange French toast or ginger pancakes. Freshly baked cookies are always available. Take in the Seattle Rose Garden, the famous Fremont Troll, or just go for a leisurely stroll through the neighborhood. Enjoy the warm and casual mood at Chelsea Station on the Park, a place to refresh your spirit.

Mildred's Bed & Breakfast ✪

1202 15TH AVENUE EAST, SEATTLE, WASHINGTON 98112

Tel: **(206) 325-6072**
Best Time to Call: **Mornings**

Hosts: **Mildred and Melodee Sarver**
Location: **3 mi. NE of City Center**

No. of Rooms: **3**
No. of Private Baths: **3**
Double/pb: **$95–$120**
Single/pb: **$85–$105**
Open: **All year**
Breakfast: **Full**

Credit Cards: **AMEX, DC, MC, VISA**
Pets: **No**
Children: **Welcome**
Smoking: **No**
Social Drinking: **Permitted**

Mildred's is the ultimate trip-to-grandmother's fantasy come true. A large white 1890 Victorian, it's the perfect setting for traditional, caring B&B hospitality. Guest rooms on the second floor have sitting alcoves, lace curtains, and antiques. Mildred's special touches, like coffee and juice delivered to your room one-half hour before breakfast, and tea and cookies on arrival, make her guests feel truly pampered. Across the street is historic 44-acre Volunteer Park with its art museum, flower conservatory, and tennis courts. An electric trolley stops at the front door and there is ample street parking. It is just minutes to the city center, freeways, and all points of interest.

Prince of Wales

133 THIRTEENTH AVENUE EAST, SEATTLE, WASHINGTON 98102

Tel: **(206) 325-9692; (800) 327-9692;**
   fax: **(206) 322-6402**
Best Time to Call: **10 AM–9 PM**
Host: **Carol Norton**
Location: **In heart of Seattle**
No. of Rooms: **4**
No. of Private Baths: **4**
Double/sb: **$70–$90**
Suites: **$90–$110**

Open: **All year**
Reduced Rates: **10% weekly Nov.–Mar.**
Breakfast: **Full**
Credit Cards: **AMEX, DISC, MC, VISA**
Pets: **No**
Children: **Welcome**
Smoking: **No**
Social Drinking: **Permitted**
Foreign Languages: **Italian, Spanish**

From this convenient address, it's just a brief walk to the Convention Center and a short bus ride to the Space Needle, Pikes Place Market, and downtown Seattle's many other attractions. In the evening, you're sure to be tempted by the menus of neighborhood restaurants. Carol serves a delicious breakfast. All rooms have queen beds, private baths, and great views.

Roberta's Bed and Breakfast

1147 SIXTEENTH AVENUE EAST, SEATTLE, WASHINGTON 98112
robertasbb@aol.com

Tel: **(206) 329-3326;**
   fax: **(206) 324-2149**
Host: **Roberta Barry**
No. of Rooms: **5**
No. of Private Baths: **5**
Double/pb: **$90–$120**
Single/pb: **$85–$105**

Open: **All year**
Breakfast: **Full**
Credit Cards: **MC, VISA**
Pets: **No**
Children: **Welcome, over 12**
Smoking: **No**
Social Drinking: **Permitted**

Roberta's is a 1903 frame Victorian with a large, old-fashioned front porch. The house is located in a quiet, historic neighborhood near the heart of the city. The cheerful rooms all boast queen-size beds. The Peach Room has bay windows, oak furniture, and Grandma's fancy desk; the Rosewood Room has a window seat and built-in oak bookcase; all five rooms are filled with books. In the morning you'll smell a pot of coffee right beside your door. That's just a warm-up for the large breakfast to come. The specialty of the house is Dutch Babies, a local dish, served with powdered sugar or fresh berries. For your convenience the *New York Times* and local newspapers are available every morning.

Seattle Guest Suite ✪
701 NORTHWEST 60TH STREET, SEATTLE, WASHINGTON 98107

Tel: **(206) 783-2169**	Breakfast: **Continental**
Host: **Inge Pokrandt**	Pets: **No**
Location: **1 mi. from I-5**	Smoking: **No**
No. of Rooms: **1**	Social Drinking: **Permitted**
No. of Private Baths: **1**	Minimum Stay: **2 nights**
Double/pb: **$55**	Foreign Languages: **German**
Open: **All year**	

This private garden-level guest suite offers everything a traveler may need: a quiet neighborhood, privacy, nearby parks, beaches, and the University of Washington. Guests enjoy many special touches such as fresh flowers, a fully stocked refrigerator, chocolates on their pillow, daily maid service, and much more. One guest from Florida wrote, "This must be the best value we ever experienced in all our travels."

English Gardens B&B ✪

8305-201ST STREET EAST, SPANAWAY, WASHINGTON 98387

Tel: **(800) 505-5612; (206) 846-5220**
Best Time to Call: **10 AM–10 PM**
Hosts: **Earl and Emy Atchley**
No. of Rooms: **1**
Double/pb: **$60**
Open: **May–Sept.**

Breakfast: **Full**
Pets: **Sometimes**
Children: **Welcome**
Smoking: **No**
Airport/Station Pickup: **Yes**

Stress and tension melt away in the peaceful surroundings of English Gardens B&B. During the day guests can enjoy the many sights, including Mount Rainier, located just minutes away. At the end of the day unwind in the large living room. Depending on your appetite, Emy will serve you a full country breakfast or a lighter Continental fare.

Marianna Stoltz House ✪

427 EAST INDIANA, SPOKANE, WASHINGTON 99207

Tel: **(509) 483-4316; (800) 978-6587;**
   fax: **(509) 483-6773**
Hosts: **James and Phyllis Maguire**
No. of Rooms: **4**
No. of Private Baths: **2**
Max. No. Sharing Bath: **4**
Double/pb: **$65–$85**
Single/pb: **$55–$75**
Open: **All year**

Breakfast: **Full**
Credit Cards: **AMEX, DC, DISC, MC,**
   VISA
Pets: **No**
Children: **Welcome, over 4**
Smoking: **No**
Social Drinking: **Permitted**
Airport/Station Pickup: **Yes**

The Marianna Stoltz House, a Spokane landmark, is a classic American Foursquare home built in 1908. Period furnishings complement the house's woodwork, tile fireplace, and leaded glass bookshelves and cupboards. The bedroom quilts are heirlooms from Phyllis's mother, the B&B's namesake. The Maguires are Spokane natives—Phyllis grew up in this very house—and can tell you about local theaters, museums, and parks. Full breakfasts consist of juice, fruit, muffins, and main dishes such as sausage-cheese strata and puffy Dutch pancakes with homemade syrup.

A Greater Tacoma B&B Reservations Service ✪
3312 NORTH UNION AVENUE, TACOMA, WASHINGTON 98407
tacomabnbs@aol.com; http://www.tacoma.net/bandb.html

Tel: **(253) 759-4088; fax: (253) 759-4025; (800) 406-4088**
Best Time to Call: **9 AM–9 PM**
Coordinator: **Sharon Kaufmann**
States/Regions Covered: **Auburn, Fox Island, Gig Harbor, Mt. Rainier, Olalla, Puyallup, Tacoma**

Descriptive Directory: **Free**
Rates (Single/Double):
  Modest: **$55–$70**
  Average: **$75 / $90**
  Luxury: **$95 / $135**
Credit Cards: **AMEX, DISC, MC, VISA**

Greater Tacoma B&B Reservations Service offers more than twenty-five inspected and licensed accommodations. Prefer full or Continental breakfast? Shared or private bath? Have your choice of homes that range from a cozy cottage to a historic waterfront mansion. Some sites have extra amenities like hot tubs and romantic Jacuzzis.

Commencement Bay B&B ✪
3312 NORTH UNION AVENUE, TACOMA, WASHINGTON 98407
greatviews@aol.com; http://www.bbonline.com/wa/cbay

Tel: **(253) 752-8175; fax: (253) 759-4025**
Best Time to Call: **9 AM–9 PM**
Hosts: **Bill and Sheri Kaufmann**
Location: **1 mi. N of Tacoma**
No. of Rooms: **3**
No. of Private Baths: **3**
Double/pb: **$75–$115**
Open: **All year**

Reduced Rates: **Available**
Breakfast: **Full**
Credit Cards: **AMEX, DISC, MC, VISA**
Pets: **No**
Children: **Welcome, over 12**
Smoking: **Restricted**
Social Drinking: **Permitted**
Airport/Station Pickup: **Yes**

An elegantly decorated Colonial home overlooking scenic north end Tacoma, this B&B has dramatic bay and mountain views from both the rooms and the common areas. Guests can enjoy a quiet, relaxing fireside reading area, an outdoor hot tub in a lovely garden, weight room, bicycles, covered outdoor smoking deck, a casual game room with TV, VCR, microwave, and refrigerator—even an office for business travelers (with a fax/modem available). The B&B offers guests cable TV, VCR, or telephone in rooms, an early businessman's breakfast on weekdays, and transportation to nearby universities or downtown business areas. It is close to several waterfront parks, jogging/hiking trails, great restaurants, quaint shops (including antiques), and easy freeway access. A delicious breakfast and different gourmet coffees and teas are served daily.

Inge's Place ✪
6809 LAKE GROVE SW, TACOMA, WASHINGTON 98499

Tel: **(206) 584-4514**	Suites: **$60**
Host: **Ingeborg Deatherage**	Open: **All year**
Location: **3 mi. from I-5**	Reduced Rates: **Available**
No. of Rooms: **3**	Breakfast: **Full**
No. of Private Baths: **1**	Pets: **No**
Max. No. Sharing Bath: **4**	Children: **Welcome**
Double/pb: **$50**	Smoking: **No**
Single/pb: **$40**	Social Drinking: **Permitted**
Double/sb: **$45**	Airport/Station Pickup: **Yes**
Single/sb: **$40**	Foreign Languages: **German**

This spic-and-span home is in a lovely Tacoma suburb called Lakewood. Feel welcome to use the hot tub, large backyard, and patio. There are many restaurants and shopping centers within walking distance, and several nearby lakes where fishing is excellent. Tacoma is the gateway to Mount Rainier. Inge is a world traveler, teacher, and enthusiast about B&Bs.

WEST VIRGINIA

Hedgeville

Martinsburg

Romney

Charles Town

Elkins

Huttonsville

Charleston

Historic Charleston Bed & Breakfast ✪
114 ELIZABETH STREET, CHARLESTON, WEST VIRGINIA 25311

Tel: **(304) 345-8156; (800) CALL-WVA;**
  fax: **(304) 342-1572**
Best Time to Call: **8 AM–11 PM**
Hosts: **Bob and Jean Lambert**
Location: **1/2 mi. from I-77, I-64, Exit 99**
No. of Rooms: **3**
No. of Private Baths: **3**
Double/pb: **$75**

Single/pb: **$65**
Open: **All year**
Reduced Rates: **Available**
Breakfast: **Full**
Credit Cards: **AMEX, MC, VISA**
Children: **By arrangement**
Smoking: **No**

The exterior of this 1905 American Foursquare home is painted gray
clapboard with white trim. Most of the interior woodwork is the original natural oak. Guest accommodations are spacious—each room has a
fireplace, private sitting area, and central heating and air-conditioning.
The entrance hall is furnished with a Victorian loveseat, candle table,
and a claw-footed desk, setting the tone for the rest of the house, which

is decorated with antiques, collectibles, and handicrafts. Breakfast is served in the dining room, on an early 1930s dining suite. Then you can explore the area, starting with the state capitol and cultural center one block away.

Washington House Inn ✪
216 SOUTH GEORGE STREET, CHARLES TOWN,
WEST VIRGINIA 25414
mnvogel@intrepid.net; http://www.intrepid.net/whib&b

Tel: (304) 725-7923; (800) 297-6957	Reduced Rates: Available
Best Time to Call: 8 AM–10 PM	Breakfast: Full
Hosts: Nina and Mel Vogel	Credit Cards: AMEX, DISC, MC, VISA
Location: 60 mi. NW of Washington,	Pets: No
D.C., and Baltimore	Children: Welcome, over 10
No. of Rooms: 6	Smoking: No
No. of Private Baths: 6	Social Drinking: Permitted
Double/pb: $70–$125	Airport/Station Pickup: Yes
Open: All year	

George Washington didn't sleep here—but his relatives did. Built in 1899 by descendants of the president's brothers, John Augustine and Samuel, Washington House Inn is a wonderful example of Late Victorian architecture. From the three-story turret and wraparound porch to the carved oak mantels, this home echoes a bygone era. As you enter the main foyer, period antiques help you step back in time. In the morning, a hearty full breakfast is served in the dining room. Located in West Virginia's eastern gateway, the Inn is convenient to a host of activities. Within a ten-minute drive you will find Harpers Ferry National Park, white-water rafting, biking, and hiking on the restored C&O Canal towpath, thoroughbred horse racing, and Grand Prix–style sports car racing.

The Post House Bed and Breakfast ✪
306 ROBERT E. LEE AVENUE, ELKINS, WEST VIRGINIA 26241

Tel: (304) 636-1792	Double/sb: $60
Hosts: Toni Eddy, innkeeper; JoAnn Post	Single/sb: 55
Barlow, owner	Open: All year
Location: 120 mi. S of Pittsburgh, Pa.	Breakfast: Continental
No. of Rooms: 5	Pets: No
No. of Private Baths: 2	Children: Welcome
Max. No. Sharing Bath: 4	Smoking: No
Double/pb: $65	Social Drinking: Permitted
Single/pb: $55	Airport Pickup: Yes

Located in the heart of the mountains, the Post House Bed and Breakfast offers individual or group accommodations. Guests are invited to relax on the front porch, the lounge, or in the spacious backyard complete with a children's playhouse. To really unwind, enjoy a massage by a certified masseuse. Handmade quilts are available for purchase. Nearby attractions include Monongahela Forest, Seneca Rocks, and Blackwater Falls. Cultural events are offered by Davis and Elkins College, including the world-famous six-week instruction at the Augusta Heritage Arts Center.

The Warfield House
318 BUFFALO STREET, ELKINS, WEST VIRGINIA 26241

Tel: **(304) 636-4555**	Single/sb: **$55**
Best Time to Call: **7 AM–noon**	Open: **All year**
Hosts: **Connie and Paul Garnett**	Reduced Rates: **Available**
No. of Rooms: **4**	Breakfast: **Full**
No. of Private Baths: **2**	Pets: **No**
Max No. Sharing Bath: **4**	Children: **Welcome, over 12**
Double/pb: **$65**	Smoking: **No**
Single/pb: **$55**	Social Drinking: **Permitted**
Double/sb: **$65**	

Nestled on a corner in a small scenic town, The Warfield House faces the forested City Park. Restaurants, shops, and theaters are within walking distance. Built in 1901 of shingle and brick, the house has been restored with turn-of-the-century reproduction carpets and wallpaper, and boasts spectacular woodwork and stained glass. Guest rooms provide comfort and privacy. You will awaken to a hearty breakfast before you begin your day of hiking, biking, rafting, bird-watching, photography, mountain climbing, downhill and cross-country skiing, antiquing, and much more. Your hosts, both musicians, are waiting to share the beauty of the mountains and their home with you.

The Farmhouse on Tomahawk Run ☉
1 TOMAHAWK RUN PLACE, HEDGESVILLE, WEST VIRGINIA 25427

Tel: **(304) 754-7350**	Reduced Rates: **10% March**
Best Time to Call: **10 AM–noon, 6–9 PM**	Breakfast: **Full**
Hosts: **Hugh and Judy Erskine**	Credit Cards: **DISC, MC, VISA**
Location: **12 mi. W of Martinsburg**	Pets: **No**
No. of Rooms: **5**	Children: **Welcome, by arrangement**
No. of Private Baths: **5**	Smoking: **No**
Double/pb: **$65–$75**	Social Drinking: **Permitted**
Guest Cottage: **$140**	Minimum Stay: **2 nights weekends**
Open: **Mar.–Dec.**	

Nestled in a quiet valley next to the historic Tomahawk-shaped spring for which the area was named, the farmhouse was built by Judy's great-grandfather during the Civil War. The land itself has been occupied by her ancestors since 1740. Two of the guest rooms inside the farmhouse have balconies. The self-contained carriage house sleeps five to seven and is available for weekend or week-long stays. A peaceful, bubbling brook winds its way through the 280 acres of woods and meadows, where walking paths are maintained for your pleasure. A Jacuzzi on the back porch of the farmhouse will ensure a restful visit.

The Hutton House ✪
ROUTES 219 AND 250, HUTTONSVILLE, WEST VIRGINIA 26273

Tel: (304) 335-6701
Best Time to Call: Anytime
Hosts: Dean and Loretta Murray
Location: 17 mi. S of Elkins
No. of Rooms: 6
No. of Private Baths: 6
Double/pb: $70–$75
Single/pb: $60–$65
Open: All year

Reduced Rates: Available
Breakfast: Full
Other Meals: Available
Credit Cards: MC, VISA
Pets: No
Children: Welcome
Smoking: No
Social Drinking: Permitted
Airport/Station Pickup: Yes

Built in 1899 by a scion of Huttonsville's founder, Hutton House commands a broad view of the Tygart Valley and Laurel Mountain ridges. This ornate Queen Anne mansion, with its extraordinary woodwork and windows, is listed on the National Register of Historic Places. Travelers come here to ski at Snowshoe, visit Cass Railroad, and hike in the Monongahela National Forest. Civil War buffs will find plenty of battle sites to study, and the Augusta Heritage Arts Festival, in nearby Elkins, also merits a detour. For breakfast, your hosts dish out cantaloupe sorbet and whole wheat pancakes drizzled with maple syrup made from their own trees.

Pulpit & Palette Inn ✪
516 WEST JOHN STREET, MARTINSBURG, WEST VIRGINIA 25401

Tel: (304) 263-7012
Hosts: Bill and Janet Starr
Location: 20 mi. S of Hagerstown
No. of Rooms: 2
Max. No. Sharing Bath: 4
Double/sb: $75
Single/sb: $60
Open: Mar.–Dec.

Breakfast: Full
Credit Cards: DISC, MC, VISA
Pets: No
Children: Welcome, over 12
Smoking: No
Social Drinking: Permitted
Station Pickup: Yes

Built in 1870, this Italianate Victorian is furnished with American antiques, Oriental objets d'art, Tibetan rugs, paintings, and stained glass work done by the hostess. Bill and Janet's objective is to give personalized attention to guests with afternoon tea, complimentary evening drinks and hors d'oeuvres, a morning bed tray, and a full gourmet breakfast. Bill and Janet are retired educators; their interests include drama production, stained glass work, art appreciation, travel, and community service. The Pulpit & Palette Inn is located 30 minutes from

Harpers Ferry National Park and the Antietam National Battlefield, and 80 minutes from historic Gettysburg.

Hampshire House 1884 ✪
165 NORTH GRAFTON STREET, ROMNEY, WEST VIRGINIA 26757

Tel: **(304) 822-7171**
Hosts: **Jane and Scott Simmons**
Location: **35 mi. W of Winchester, Va.**
No. of Rooms: **5**
No. of Private Baths: **5**
Double/pb: **$70–$95**
Single/pb: **$55–$75**
Open: **All year**
Reduced Rates: **Available**

Breakfast: **Full**
Credit Cards: **AMEX, DC, DISC, MC, VISA**
Pets: **No**
Children: **Welcome**
Smoking: **No**
Social Drinking: **Permitted**
Airport/Station Pickup: **Yes**

Only two and a half hours west of Washington, D.C., via Route 50, lies Romney, the oldest town in West Virginia. Surrounded by beautiful rolling hills, Hampshire House is conveniently located to the downtown area. You will enjoy touring the town, with its quaint shops and historic buildings, and winery tours are nearby. The bedrooms are attractively furnished with old-fashioned furniture and wallpapers and kept comfortable with central heating and air-conditioning. Jane and Scott graciously offer complimentary snacks and invite you to enjoy the old pump organ, television, VCR, or a variety of games.

WISCONSIN

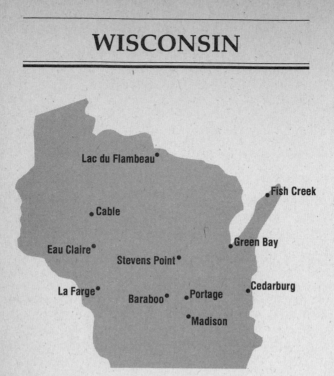

Lac du Flambeau

Fish Creek

Cable

Eau Claire

Green Bay

Stevens Point

La Farge

Baraboo

Portage

Cedarburg

Madison

The Gollmar Guest House B&B ✪
422 3RD STREET, BARABOO, WISCONSIN 53913

Tel: **(608) 356-9432**
Best Time to Call: **6–10 PM**
Hosts: **Linda and Thomas Luck**
Location: **200 mi. NW of Chicago**
No. of Rooms: **3**
No. of Private Baths: **3**
Double/pb: **$75**
Open: **All year**

Breakfast: **Full**
Credit Cards: **MC, VISA**
Pets: **No**
Children: **Welcome, over 7**
Smoking: **No**
Social Drinking: **Permitted**
Station Pickup: **Yes**

Welcome to the Gollmar Guest House B&B, an exquisite Victorian circus home laden with charming treasures, unique features, and a wealth of history. Original hand-painted ceiling frescoes, beveled glass, chandeliers, furniture, and antiques will delight antique connoisseurs. Guest rooms all have queen beds and are named after the exceptional Gollmar women. Isabell's room is pristine and elegant in white and periwinkle.

Leora's Country Meadow Room is soft and romantic, with hearts and flowers. Viola's Attic Room is peachy and private with French Impressionist prints. Guests may relax in the parlor or sit on the porch and enjoy the view. Breakfast may include apple pancakes, French toast, pastries, and fruit. The Inn is located within four blocks of downtown Baraboo. Your hosts will be happy to supply you with maps and acquaint you with the area.

Pinehaven ✪
E13083 STATE HIGHWAY 33, BARABOO, WISCONSIN 53913

Tel: (608) 356-3489
Best Time to Call: Before 10 PM
Hosts: Lyle and Marge Getschman
Location: 10 mi. from I-90
No. of Rooms: 4
No. of Private Baths: 4
Double/pb: $75–$85
Single/pb: $60–$70

Open: All year
Breakfast: Full
Credit Cards: MC, VISA
Pets: No
Children: Welcome, over 5
Smoking: No
Social Drinking: Permitted

Lyle and Marge's home is nestled in a pine grove with a beautiful view of the Baraboo Bluffs and a small private lake. Guest rooms have air-conditioning. The full breakfast may include fresh-baked muffins, coffee cakes, egg dishes, meat, fruit, and juice. Eat in the dining room, on the deck, or on the screened-in porch. Play the baby grand piano. Feel free to take a leisurely stroll in these inviting surroundings. A tour to see your hosts' Belgian draft horses and antique wagons and sleighs on the farm side of the highway, and wagon or sleigh rides pulled by the Belgians, may be arranged. Fine restaurants and numerous activities abound in the area. A guest cottage is now available.

The Victorian Rose ✪
423 THIRD AVENUE, BARABOO, WISCONSIN 53913

Tel: (608) 356-7828
Hosts: Bob and Carolyn Stearns
Location: 40 mi. N of Madison
No. of Rooms: 3
No. of Private Baths: 3
Double/pb: $70–$90

Open: All year
Breakfast: Full
Pets: No
Children: No
Smoking: No
Social Drinking: Permitted

The Victorian Rose is located on a large corner lot, surrounded by sugar maples and pine trees, within walking distance of Baraboo's historical sites, specialty shops, and galleries. The Stearns family welcomes you to their beautifully restored 19th-century "Painted Lady," furnished with roses, lace, antiques, and heirloom collectibles. Guests can enjoy a game or book in the library parlor or watch old classic movies by the fireplace with a cup of tea and sweet treats. Appropriately enough, guest rooms are decorated in Victorian style. A full gourmet candlelight breakfast awaits guests in the morning.

Connors Bed & Breakfast ✪
ROUTE 1, BOX 255, CABLE, WISCONSIN 54821

Tel: **(715) 798-3661; (800) 848-3932**	Open: **All year**
Hosts: **Alex and Mona Connors**	Breakfast: **Full**
Location: **1.7 mi. N of Cable**	Credit Cards: **MC, VISA**
No. of Rooms: **4**	Pets: **No**
No. of Private Baths: **2**	Children: **Welcome**
Max. No. Sharing Bath: **4**	Smoking: **No**
Double/sb: **$50**	Social Drinking: **Permitted**
Cabin: **$70 for 2**	Minimum Stay: **2 nights cabin**
Suites: **$85**	Airport/Station Pickup: **Yes**

Once a 77-acre farm, Connors Bed & Breakfast lies approximately 40 miles south of Lake Superior, surrounded by the Chequamegon National Forest. This central location gives guests easy access to nearby lakes, golf, casinos, numerous day trips, and downhill and cross-country skiing—there is a private trail on the property. A 107-year-old cabin, located in the apple orchard, is perfect for an unusual honeymoon getaway, or can accommodate up to six people. It has a kitchenette, wood-burning stove, gas heater, and a claw-footed tub in the master bedroom. The second floor has one room with a full bed and one with two singles.

Stagecoach Inn Bed & Breakfast ✪
W61 N520 WASHINGTON AVENUE, CEDARBURG, WISCONSIN 53012

Tel: **(414) 375-0208; (888) 375-0208;** fax: **(414) 375-6170**	Open: **All year**
	Breakfast: **Continental**
Hosts: **Brook and Liz Brown**	Credit Cards: **AMEX, DISC, MC, VISA**
Location: **20 mi. N of Milwaukee**	Pets: **No**
No. of Rooms: **12**	Children: **Welcome, over 12**
No. of Private Baths: **12**	Smoking: **No**
Double/pb: **$70**	Social Drinking: **Permitted**
Suites: **$105–$130**	

The Inn, listed on the National Register of Historic Places, is housed in a completely restored 1853 stone building in downtown historic Cedarburg. The rooms, air-conditioned for summer comfort, combine antique charm with modern conveniences. Each bedroom is decorated with antiques and trimmed with wall stenciling. A candy shop and a pub that is a popular gathering place for guests occupy the first floor. Specialty stores, antique shops, a winery, a woolen mill, and a variety of fine restaurants are within walking distance.

The Atrium Bed & Breakfast ✪
5572 PRILL ROAD, EAU CLAIRE, WISCONSIN 54701

Tel: **(715) 833-9045**
Best Time to Call: **8 AM–8 PM**
Hosts: **Celia and Dick Stoltz**
Location: **90 mi. E of Minneapolis**
No. of Rooms: **4**
No. of Private Baths: **2**
Max. No. Sharing Bath: **4**
Double/pb: **$85**
Single/pb: **$75**
Double/sb: **$70**

Single/sb: **$65**
Open: **All year**
Reduced Rates: **$10 less Sun.–Thurs.**
Breakfast: **Full**
Credit Cards: **MC, VISA**
Pets: **No**
Children: **Welcome, over 12**
Smoking: **No**
Social Drinking: **Permitted**

Named for its most unusual feature, this contemporary bed and breakfast is built around a 20 × 20-foot atrium where guests enjoy a leisurely breakfast in a natural setting. Exotic trees and plants reach toward the windowed ceiling and the sound of the fountain's trickling water brings the outdoors in to complete the ambiance. The Atrium is nestled on 15 wooded acres on Otter Creek that beckon the explorer. Follow the winding trails into the woods or watch the many varieties of wildlife right from the living room. Guests are always welcome to read by the fire, watch TV, or gather around the pump organ for a sing-along. Enjoy the best of both worlds at a woodland hideaway only minutes from shopping malls, restaurants, and the University of Wisconsin, Eau Claire.

Thorp House Inn & Cottages
4135 BLUFF LANE, P.O. BOX 490, FISH CREEK, WISCONSIN 54212

Tel: **(414) 868-2444**
Best Time to Call: **8 AM–10 PM**
Hosts: **Christine and
    Sverre Falck-Pedersen**
No. of Rooms: **3**
No. of Private Baths: **3**
Double/pb: **$75–$95**
Cottages: **$80–$135**
Open: **All year**

Reduced Rates: **Weekly**
Breakfast: **Continental**
Pets: **No**
Children: **Welcome, in cottages**
Smoking: **Yes, in cottages**
Social Drinking: **Permitted**
Minimum Stay: **3 nights summer and
    holiday weekends**
Foreign Languages: **Norwegian**

Thorp House is a turn-of-the-century country Victorian inn perched on a wooded hill overlooking Green Bay. The beach, shops, restaurants, and Peninsula State Park are just a stroll away. Four elegant guest rooms re-create romantic periods of the past with fine antiques and accessories, documentary wall coverings, and European lace. Each room has a private bath (one with a whirlpool), central air-conditioning, and ceiling fans. Guests have their own parlor with its original granite fireplace. A delicious home-baked breakfast is included. Also available: country cottages with wood-burning fireplaces, full kitchens and baths (some with whirlpools), decks, and views of the bay. For those of you who don't mind paying a higher rate, 1 room is available.

The Astor House ✪
637 SOUTH MONROE AVENUE, GREEN BAY, WISCONSIN 54301

Tel: **(920) 432-3585**
Best Time to Call: **8 AM–8 PM**
Host: **Doug Landwehr**
Location: **In Green Bay**

No. of Rooms: **5**
No. of Private Baths: **5**
Double/pb: **$79–$129**
Suites: **$89–$149**

Open: **All year**
Reduced Rates: **Business travelers,**
  multi-night
Breakfast: **Continental**
Credit Cards: **AMEX, DISC, MC, VISA**
Pets: **No**

Children: **No**
Smoking: **No**
Social Drinking: **Permitted**
Minimum Stay: **2 nights holiday**
  weekends

Welcome to the 1888 Astor House, where gracious seclusion, peace, and personal attention are yours from the time you enter the Astor Historic Neighborhood, near Green Bay's City Center. The five distinctive guest suites are incredibly decorated and equipped with queen or king beds, private shower or whirlpool bath, telephones, cable TV, VCR, CD and tape decks, refrigerators, and air-conditioning. Breakfast includes homemade baked goods, fruit, and gourmet coffee. Enjoy the public and private gardens, luxuriate in a gentle whirlpool for two, bask before a roaring fire, or sample the many shops, restaurants, theaters, events, and activities in the Green Bay area. The Astor House is designed for either the vacationer or the business visitor.

Trillium ✪

**E-10596, EAST SALEM RIDGE ROAD, LA FARGE,
WISCONSIN 54639-8015**

Tel: **(608) 625-4492**
Best Time to Call: **Mornings; evenings**
Hosts: **Joe Swanson and
  Rosanne Boyett**
Location: **40 mi. SE of La Crosse**
Guest Cottage: **$75 for 2**
Open: **All year**

Breakfast: **Full**
Reduced Rates: **Single guest; weekly;
  winter, after first night**
Pets: **No**
Children: **Welcome (crib)**
Smoking: **Restricted**
Social Drinking: **Permitted**

This private cottage is on a working farm located in the heart of a thriving Amish community. It has a large porch and is surrounded by an orchard, garden, and a lovely tree-shaded yard. There's a path beside the stream that winds through woods and fields. The cottage is light and airy, with comfortable wicker furniture. Nearby attractions include the Elroy-Sparta Bike Trail, Mississippi River, trout streams, and cheese factories.

Ty Bach B&B ✪

3104 SIMPSON LANE, LAC DU FLAMBEAU, WISCONSIN 54538

Tel: **(715) 588-7851**
Best Time to Call: **8 AM–10 PM**
Hosts: **Janet and Kermit Bekkum**
Location: **70 mi. N of Wausau**
No. of Rooms: **2**
No. of Private Baths: **2**
Double/pb: **$60–$70**

Single/pb: **$60–$70**
Open: **All year**
Breakfast: **Full**
Pets: **Sometimes**
Children: **No**
Smoking: **No**
Social Drinking: **Permitted**

In Welsh, *ty-bach* means "little house." Located on an Indian reservation in Lac du Flambeau, this modern little house overlooks a small, picturesque Northwoods lake. Sit back on the deck and enjoy the beautiful fall colors, the call of the loons, and the tranquility of this out-of-the-way spot. Choose from two comfortable rooms: one features a brass bed, the other opens onto a private deck. Your hosts offer oven-fresh coffee cakes, homemade jams, and plenty of fresh coffee along with hearty main entrees.

Annie's Bed & Breakfast

2117 SHERIDAN DRIVE, MADISON, WISCONSIN 53704

Tel: **(608) 244-2224**
Hosts: **Anne and Larry Stuart**
No. of Rooms: **2 suites**
No. of Private Baths: **2**
Suites: **$93–$124 for 2; $153–$204
  for 4**
Open: **All year**
Reduced Rates: **4th night free weekdays
  only**

Breakfast: **Full**
Credit Cards: **AMEX, MC, VISA**
Pets: **No**
Children: **Welcome, over 12**
Smoking: **No**
Social Drinking: **Permitted**
Minimum Stay: **2 nights**
Airport/Station Pickup: **Yes**

When you want the world to go away, come to Annie's, a quiet inn with a beautiful view of meadows, water, and woods. This charming, fully air-conditioned cedar shake home has been a getaway for travelers since 1985. The house is a block from a large lake and directly adjoining Warner Park, allowing guests a broad selection of activities, including swimming, boating, tennis, hiking, and biking during summer, and cross-country skiing and skating in winter. The four antique-filled guest rooms are full of surprises and unusual amenities. There is a great-hall dining room, a pine-paneled library with a well-stocked wood stove, and a soothing double whirlpool surrounded by plants. The unusually lovely gardens, with romantic gazebo and pond, have been selected for the annual Madison Garden Tours.

Country Aire ✪
N4452 COUNTY U, BOX 175, PORTAGE, WISCONSIN 53901

Tel: (608) 742-5716	Suites: $75
Best Time to Call: Evenings	Open: All year
Hosts: Bob and Rita Reif	Breakfast: Continental
Location: 37 mi. N of Madison	Pets: No
No. of Rooms: 3	Children: Welcome
No. of Private Baths: 2	Smoking: No
Double/pb: $60	Social Drinking: Permitted
Single/pb: $50	

Forty acres of woods and meadows surround this spacious country home, built into a hillside overlooking the Wisconsin River. The house has open cathedral ceilings and a beautiful view from every room. Choose from comfortable bedrooms with queen-size or twin beds; the kids will enjoy the room with bunk beds. Guests are welcome to use the tennis court or go canoeing on the river. In the winter, skating can be enjoyed on the pond, and the area is perfect for cross-country skiing. Devil's Head and Cascade Mountain are close by for downhill skiing. Bob and Rita are minutes away from the Wisconsin Dells, Baraboo, and Devil's Lake State Park. Relax at the end of the day in the serenity of this beautiful country setting.

Dreams of Yesteryear Bed & Breakfast ✪
1100 BRAWLEY STREET, STEVENS POINT, WISCONSIN 54481

Tel: (715) 341-4525	Open: All year
Best Time to Call: After 4 PM	Breakfast: Full
Hosts: Bonnie and Bill Maher	Credit Cards: AMEX, DISC, MC, VISA
Location: 30 mi. S of Wausau	Pets: No
No. of Rooms: 6	Children: Welcome, over 12
No. of Private Baths: 4	Smoking: No
Double/pb: $55–$129	Social Drinking: Permitted
Single/pb: $50–$120	Airport/Station Pickup: Yes

Dreams, listed on the National Register of Historic Places and featured in *Victorian Homes* magazine, was designed by architect J. H. Jeffers, who also designed the Wisconsin Building at the St. Louis World's Fair of 1904. Lavish in Victorian detail, the home is handsomely decorated, with floral wallpapers, and period furniture. One bathroom has a claw-footed tub and a pedestal sink. Bonnie, a University of Wisconsin secretary, and Bill, owner of a water-conditioning business, love to talk about the house and its furnishings. Skiing, canoeing, shopping, and university theater, among other activities, are in close proximity.

For key to listings, see inside front or back cover.

✪ This star means that rates are guaranteed through December 31, 1998, to any guest making a reservation as a result of reading about the B&B in *Bed & Breakfast U.S.A.*—1998 edition.

Important! To avoid misunderstandings, always ask about cancellation policies when booking.

Please enclose a self-addressed, stamped, business-size envelope when contacting reservation services.

For more details on what you can expect in a B&B, see Chapter 1.

Always mention *Bed & Breakfast U.S.A.* when making reservations!

We want to hear from you! Use the form on page 625.

WYOMING

Buffalo

Pinedale

Cloud Peak Inn ✪
590 NORTH BURRITT AVENUE, BUFFALO, WYOMING 82834

Tel: **(307) 684-5794; (800) 715-5794**
Best Time to Call: **Anytime**
Hosts: **Rick and Kathy Brus**
Location: **115 mi. N of Casper**
No. of Rooms: **5**
No. of Private Baths: **3**
Max. No. Sharing Bath: **4**
Double/pb: **$55–$80**
Single/pb: **$50–$65**
Double/sb: **$45–$60**
Single/sb: **$40–$50**

Open: **All year**
Reduced Rates: **Available**
Breakfast: **Full**
Other Meals: **Available**
Credit Cards: **AMEX, MC, VISA**
Pets: **No**
Children: **Welcome**
Smoking: **No**
Social Drinking: **Permitted**
Airport/Station Pickup: **Yes**

Built in 1912, this home is an expanded bungalow with a generous front porch. The grand curved staircase leads to spacious guest rooms decorated with period antiques. In the parlor and dining room, ten-foot wood-beamed ceilings enhance the feeling of luxury. Guests are encouraged to relax by the fossilized fireplace or in the Jacuzzi sunroom. You'll wake up to a three-course breakfast ranging from full country entrees to gourmet delights. The Big Horn Mountains offer something for everyone, including fishing, hiking, sightseeing, horseback riding, and boating. During spring, the wildflower display is unrivaled. Come and see what the West is all about.

Window on the Winds ✪
10151 HIGHWAY 191, P.O. BOX 996, PINEDALE, WYOMING 82941

Tel: **(307) 367-2600**	Reduced Rates: **Available**
Host: **Leanne McKay**	Breakfast: **Full**
Location: **75 mi. S of Jackson**	Other Meals: **Available**
No. of Rooms: **4**	Credit Cards: **MC, VISA**
Max. No. Sharing Bath: **4**	Pets: **Welcome**
Double/sb: **$75**	Children: **Welcome**
Single/sb: **$50**	Smoking: **No**
Open: **All year**	Social Drinking: **Permitted**

Pinedale, at the base of the Wind River Mountains in western Wyoming, is on one of the major routes to Grand Teton and Yellowstone National Parks. The Winds offers world-class hiking and fishing in the summer and snowmobiling and Nordic skiing in the winter. Or, go exploring with your hosts' self-guided driving tour of historic Sublette County and Oregon Trail sites. The comfortable log home, decorated in striking Western and Plains Indians themes, is a rustic retreat—the perfect base for your Wyoming vacation. There is room for pets and kids and a large garage to store extra gear. Host Leanne is an archaeologist who enjoys sharing her unique perspective on the cultural heritage of the area.

6

Canada

ALBERTA

Note: All prices listed in this section are quoted in Canadian dollars.

B&B at Harrison's ✪
6016 THORNBURN DRIVE NW, CALGARY, ALBERTA, CANADA T2K 3P7

Tel: **(403) 274-7281, 531-0065;**
   fax: **(403) 531-0069**
Best Time to Call: **7–8 AM; 4–7 PM**
Host: **Susan Harrison**
Location: **In Calgary**
No. of Rooms: **3**
Max. No. Sharing Bath: **2**
Double/pb: **$75**

Single/pb: **$50**
Single/sb: $35
Open: **All year**
Breakfast: **Full**
Pets: **No**
Children: **Welcome, over 10**
Smoking: **No**
Social Drinking: **Permitted**

Situated in a quiet residential area, B&B at Harrison's is a cozy bungalow located ten minutes from the city center and fifteen minutes from Calgary International Airport. Spend a peaceful afternoon walking to the nearby 1090-hectare, natural prairie Nose Hill Park, where you can view the distant Canadian Rockies, or eat at one of the many restaurants. One room features twin beds with a 1940s-style decor. Modern decor and a queen-size bed set the tone for the second room. And for the single traveler, a third room is located on the lower level. Guests share a lounge with a TV and library, and a sheltered patio with their host. The Calgary Exhibition and Stampede, the Calgary Zoo and Prehistoric Park, and the University of Calgary are within six miles. Banff and Kananaskis Country are a one-hour drive west.

Brink Bed and Breakfast ✪
79 SINCLAIR CRESCENT S.W., CALGARY, ALBERTA, CANADA T2W 0M1

Tel: **(403) 255-4523**
Best Time to Call: **Mornings**
Host: **Helen G. Scrimgeour-Brink**
Location: **In Calgary**
No. of Rooms: **3**
No. of Private Baths: **1**
Max. No. Sharing Bath: **4**
Double/pb: **$65**
Double/sb: **$55**
Single/sb: **$45**

Suite: **$70**
Open: **All year**
Breakfast: **Full**
Other Meals: **Available**
Pets: **Sometimes**
Children: **Welcome**
Smoking: **Permitted**
Social Drinking: **Permitted**
Airport/Station Pickup: **Yes**

Helen is a native Calgarian and a retired registered nurse who decided to open a bed and breakfast. Each bedroom is tastefully decorated. The suite "Sarah's Garden" is a private retreat with a queen-size bed, TV, loveseat, and complete bath. The "Teddy Bear" room is a single room across the hall from a full bathroom. The "Bed of Roses" room, on another level, has a comfortable double bed and is adjacent to a half-bath and a family room with a TV and a wide collection of books. Breakfast, served in a sunny dining room, features specialties like homemade scones, muffins, French toast, pancakes, fruit compote, and freshly squeezed juice. There is a large deck and well-landscaped private backyard. A traditional British afternoon tea, picnic baskets, or an evening meal are offered at an additional cost. There is a $5 surcharge for one-night stays.

BRITISH COLUMBIA

Note: All prices listed in this section are quoted in Canadian dollars.

Canada-West Accommodations ✪
P.O. BOX 86607, NORTH VANCOUVER, BRITISH COLUMBIA, CANADA V7L 4L2
reservations@b-b.com; http://www.b-b.com

Tel: **(604) 929-1424; (800) 561-3223;**
  fax: **(604) 929-6692**
Best Time to Call: **Daily to 10 PM**
Coordinator: **Ellison Massey**

Regions Covered: **Greater Vancouver, Victoria, Kelowna, Whistler**
Rates (Single/Double):
  Average: **$65–$95 / $85–$135**
Credit Cards: **AMEX, MC, VISA**

This registry has over 100 hosts with comfortable bed-and-breakfast accommodations. All serve a full breakfast, and most have a private bath for guest use. When traveling through British Columbia, visitors should note that B&Bs are available within a day's drive of one another. Canada-West features friendly host families eager to share their knowledge of cultural and scenic attractions.

Moonshadows Guest House
771 GEORGESON BAY ROAD, S16, C16, RR1, GALIANO ISLAND, BRITISH COLUMBIA, CANADA V0N 1P0
moonshadows@gulfnet.pinc.com

Tel/Fax: **(250) 539-5544; (888) 666-6742**
Hosts: **Pat Goodwin and Dave Muir**
No. of Rooms: **2**
No. of Private Baths: **2**
Double/pb: **$100–$110**
Single/pb: **$90–$95**
Suites: **$135**
Open: **All year**

Reduced Rates: **Winter, extended stays**
Breakfast: **Full**
Credit Cards: **MC, VISA**
Pets: **No**
Children: **Welcome, over 12**
Smoking: **No**
Social Drinking: **Permitted**
Minimum Stay: **2 nights holidays, Suite—2 nights**

This modern architect-designed home is welcoming, with plenty of natural light on its oak floors, paneled ceilings, and massive stone fireplace. The two-acre property is nestled in the center of tranquil Galiano Island, allowing easy access to hiking, cycling, kayaking, beaches, shops, and restaurants. Each guest room is individually decorated, featuring queen beds, complete privacy, and plenty of space to relax. The suite has a private entrance, indoor Jacuzzi tub, and walk-in shower. Breakfasts are an event to be anticipated, with fresh fruit and baked goods, followed by a frittata, soufflé, French toast, or perhaps feather-light pancakes. Guests can pamper themselves outdoors by soaking in the hot tub, or inside, snuggled in a chair next to the wood-burning fireplace with a good book.

Deep Cove Bed & Breakfast ○
2590 SHELLEY ROAD, NORTH VANCOUVER, BRITISH COLUMBIA, CANADA V7H 1J9
deepcove@istar.ca

Tel: **(604) 929-3932; fax: (604) 929-9330**
Hosts: **Diane and Wayne Moore**
Location: **8 mi. NE of Vancouver**
No. of Rooms: **2**
No. of Private Baths: **2**
Double/pb: **$90**
Single/pb: **$80**

Open: **All year**
Reduced Rates: **Available**
Breakfast: **Full**
Credit Cards: **MC, VISA**
Pets: **No**
Smoking: **No**
Social Drinking: **Permitted**

Only fifteen minutes from downtown Vancouver, Deep Cove Bed & Breakfast combines the privacy of a large secluded property with easy access to all major points of interest. The separate guest cottage is ideally suited for honeymoons and getaways. Guest rooms in the cottage have private baths, entrances, parking, and TV. Guests are invited to relax in the garden and in the outdoor cedar hot tub. Breakfast is served in the morning room or on the patio. Diane will be happy to direct you to all the special places that make Vancouver so exciting.

Poole's Bed & Breakfast ✪
421 WEST ST. JAMES ROAD, NORTH VANCOUVER, BRITISH COLUMBIA, CANADA V7N 2P6

Tel: **(604) 987-4594**; fax: **(604) 987-4283**	Single/sb: **$45**
Best Time to Call: **9 AM–9 PM**	Open: **All year**
Hosts: **Doreen and Arthur Poole**	Reduced Rates: **Available**
Location: **5 mi. N of Vancouver**	Breakfast: **Full**
No. of Rooms: **3**	Pets: **No**
Max. No. Sharing Bath: **4**	Children: **Welcome**
Double/sb: **$60**	Smoking: **No**
	Social Drinking: **Permitted**

On a lovely tree-lined street near the North Shore Mountains sits this quiet, Colonial home. The Pooles' residential neighborhood is close to the bus, restaurants, downtown Vancouver, Stanley Park, Capilano Suspension Bridge, Grouse Mountain Skyride, and Vancouver Island Ferry. Doreen and Arthur are retirees who are happy to assist you with information and directions. They'll serve you an abundant candlelight breakfast in the dining room.

Borthwick Country Manor B&B ✪
9750 ARDMORE DRIVE, SIDNEY, BRITISH COLUMBIA, CANADA V8L 5H5

Tel: **(250) 656-9498**; fax: **(250) 655-0715**	Reduced Rates: **Available**
Best Time to Call: **After 11 AM**	Breakfast: **Full**
Host: **Susan Siems**	Credit Cards: **AMEX, DC, MC, VISA**
Location: **15 mi. N of Victoria**	Pets: **No**
No. of Rooms: **4**	Children: **Welcome, over 12**
No. of Private Baths: **4**	Smoking: **No**
Double/pb: **$110–$130**	Social Drinking: **No**
Open: **All year**	Airport Pickup: **Yes**

This English Tudor is set on gorgeous landscaped gardens edged by ancient oak trees. Linger in the gardens, relax in the outdoor hot tub, or stroll on the nearby beach. Guests are welcome to use the large sitting room and library. Enjoy the most peaceful night's sleep in this quiet countryside manor; in the morning you will be treated to a delicious gourmet breakfast prepared by your English hosts and served outside on the covered patio. Borthwick is located minutes from Butchart Gardens, the town of Sidney, pubs, restaurants, fishing, sailing, scuba diving, golf, and beaches. This B&B also offers easy access to the Vancouver and U.S.A. Anacortes ferries as well as Victoria International Airport.

"Mandeville" Tudor Cottage by the Sea ✪
1064 LANDSEND ROAD, SIDNEY, BRITISH COLUMBIA, CANADA V8L 5L3

Tel: **(250) 655-1587**	Open: **All year**
Best Time to Call: **8 AM–10 PM**	Reduced Rates: **Oct.–Apr. $75 double**
Hosts: **Averil and Maurice Clegg**	Breakfast: **Full**
Location: **20 mi. N of Victoria**	Pets: **No**
No. of Rooms: **2**	Children: **Welcome**
No. of Private Baths: **2**	Smoking: **No**
Double/pb: **$95**	Social Drinking: **Permitted**
Single/pb: **$75**	Airport/Station Pickup: **Yes**
Suites: **$95**	

"Mandeville" Tudor Cottage, located at the north end of the Saanich Peninsula on Vancouver Island, is nestled in one acre of forest. Beautiful lawns and gardens lead to the beach. "Mandeville" is just minutes from British Columbia, Washington State ferry terminals, and Victoria International Airport. The capital city of Victoria is twenty miles away. The suites have private entrances, queen-size beds, large sitting rooms, and cable TV.

Beautiful Bed & Breakfast
428 WEST 40 AVENUE, VANCOUVER, BRITISH COLUMBIA, CANADA V5Y 2R4

Tel: **(604) 327-1102; fax: (604) 327-2299**	Single/sb: **$115–$210**
	Open: **All year**
Best Time to Call: **Evenings**	Reduced Rates: **10% less weekly**
Hosts: **Corinne and Ian Sanderson**	Breakfast: **Full, Continental**
Location: **In Vancouver**	Pets: **No**
No. of Rooms: **4**	Children: **Welcome, over 14**
No. of Private Baths: **1**	Smoking: **No**
Max. No. Sharing Bath: **4**	Social Drinking: **Permitted**
Double/sb: **$115–$210**	Foreign Languages: **French**

Relax in elegance in a gorgeous new Colonial home furnished with antiques, views, and fresh flowers. This is a great central location on a quiet residential street, just five minutes from downtown and within walking distance of Queen Elizabeth Park, Van Dusen Gardens, tennis, golf, three cinemas, wonderful restaurants, swimming, and a major shopping center. It's one block from bus to downtown, ferries, airport, and United British Columbia. Enjoy a view of the north shore mountain peaks or Vancouver Island and Mount Baker, comfortable beds, a large attractive backyard—and friendly helpful hosts who will assist you with your travel plans.

Johnson House Bed & Breakfast ✪
2278 WEST 34TH AVENUE, VANCOUVER, BRITISH COLUMBIA, CANADA V6M 1G6

Tel/Fax: **(604) 266-4175**
Best Time to Call: **10:30 AM–9:30 PM**
Hosts: **Sandy and Ron Johnson**

Location: **1½ mi. from Rte. 99, Oak St. Exit**
No. of Rooms: **3**

No. of Private Baths: **1**
Max. No. Sharing Bath: **4**
Double/pb: **$105–$155**
Single/pb: **$100–$145**
Double/sb: **$75–$95**
Single/sb: **$65–$85**
Open: **All year**

Reduced Rates: **Long stays, in winter**
Breakfast: **Full**
Pets: **No**
Children: **Welcome, over 12**
Smoking: **No**
Social Drinking: **Permitted**

Sandy and Ron invite you to their charming home on a quiet tree-lined avenue in Vancouver's lovely Kerrisdale district. Outside, a rock garden and sculpture catch the visitor's eye; inside, wooden carousel animals add to the homey decor. After a good night's rest on brass beds, you'll be treated to homemade muffins, breads, and jams. Then it's time to explore downtown Vancouver—a good selection of shops, restaurants, and city bus stops are only a few blocks away.

Kenya Court Ocean Front Guest House ✪
2230 CORNWALL AVENUE, VANCOUVER, BRITISH COLUMBIA, CANADA V6K 1B5

Tel: **(604) 738-7085**
Hosts: **Dr. and Mrs. H. Williams**
Location: **20 mi. from the U.S. border**
Suites: **$85 up**
Open: **All year**
Breakfast: **Full**

Pets: **No**
Children: **Welcome, over 8**
Smoking: **No**
Social Drinking: **Permitted**
Foreign Languages: **French, German, Italian**

There is an unobstructed view of the park, ocean, mountains, and downtown Vancouver from this heritage building on the waterfront. Across the street are tennis courts, a large heated outdoor saltwater pool, and walking and jogging paths along the water's edge. Just minutes from downtown, it's an easy walk to Granville Market, the Planetarium, and interesting shops and restaurants. All the suites are large and tastefully furnished. Breakfast is served in a glass solarium with a spectacular view of English Bay.

Town & Country Bed & Breakfast Reservation Service
BOX 74542, 2803 WEST 4TH AVENUE, VANCOUVER, BRITISH COLUMBIA V6K 1K2

Tel: **(604) 731-5942**
Coordinator: **Helen Burich**
States/Regions Covered: **Vancouver, Vancouver Island, Victoria**

Rates (Single/Double):
   Modest: **$35–$45 / $45–$55**
   Average: **$55–$75 / $75–$105**
   Luxury: **$75–$125 / $125–$225**
Minimum Stay: **2 nights**

Helen has the oldest reservation service in British Columbia. She has dozens of host homes, many of which have been accommodating guests for ten years. Ranging from modest homes to lovely heritage homes, they are a 15- to 20-minute drive to Stanley Park, beaches, Capilano and Lynn Canyons, Grouse Mountain Skyride, museums, and galleries; neighborhood restaurants and shopping areas are usually within walking distance. There are also a couple of cottages and self-contained suites. There is a $5 surcharge for Victoria and Vancouver Island reservations. In addition to normal business hours, Helen is often available evenings and weekends.

An Ocean View B&B ✪

715 SUFFOLK STREET, VICTORIA, BRITISH COLUMBIA, CANADA V9A 3J5

Tel: **(250) 386-7330**	Reduced Rates: **Available**
Hosts: **Yvette and Ralf Craig**	Breakfast: **Full**
No. of Rooms: **6**	Credit Cards: **AMEX, MC, VISA**
No. of Private Baths: **6**	Pets: **No**
Double/pb: **$110–$135**	Children: **Welcome, over 4**
Single/pb: **$105–$130**	Social Drinking: **Permitted**
Open: **All year**	Foreign Languages: **French, German**

An Ocean View B&B is located six blocks from downtown Victoria. The house is a modern Mediterranean-style home with a high-tech kitchen, 22-foot dining room, living room, sunroom, and large deck all overlooking the Strait of Juan de Fuca and the Olympic Mountains. Guest rooms, decorated in bright whimsical themes, have a private entrance, bar fridge, microwave, dishes, and queen- or king-size beds. Some have an outdoor garden patio, fireplace, and TV.

Beachside Bed and Breakfast

4208 EVERGREEN AVENUE, WEST VANCOUVER, BRITISH COLUMBIA, CANADA V7V 1H1

Tel: **(604) 922-7773; (800) 563-3311;**	Open: **All year**
fax: **(604) 926-8073**	Breakfast: **Full**
Hosts: **Gordon and Joan Gibbs**	Credit Cards: **MC, VISA**
Location: **4 mi. NW of Vancouver Ctr.**	Pets: **No**
No. of Rooms: **3**	Children: **By arrangement**
No. of Private Baths: **3**	Smoking: **No**
Double/pb: **$110–$200**	Social Drinking: **Permitted**

Guests are welcomed to this beautiful waterfront home with a fruit basket and fresh flowers. The house is a Spanish-style structure, with stained glass windows, located at the end of a quiet cul-de-sac. Its southern exposure affords a panoramic view of Vancouver. A sandy beach is just steps from the door. You can watch the waves from the patio or spend the afternoon fishing or sailing. The hearty breakfast features homemade muffins, French toast, and Canadian maple syrup.

Gordon and Joan are knowledgeable about local history and can gladly direct you to Stanley Park, hiking, skiing, and much more.

Dorrington B&B ✪
13851 19A AVENUE, WHITE ROCK, BRITISH COLUMBIA, CANADA V4A 9M2
http://www.bbcanada.com/508.html

Tel: **(604) 535-4408; fax: (604) 535-4409**	Reduced Rates: **Oct.–Apr., 5th night free**
Best Time to Call: **7 PM**	Breakfast: **Full**
Hosts: **Pat and Helen Gray**	Credit Cards: **VISA**
Location: **20 mi. S of Vancouver**	Pets: **No**
No. of Rooms: **2**	Children: **No**
No. of Private Baths: **2**	Smoking: **No**
Double/pb: **$65**	Social Drinking: **Permitted**
Single/pb: **$65**	Minimum Stay: **2 nights**
Open: **All year**	

Dorrington B&B is a magnificent brick and stone estate set on one half-acre of ponds and gardens featuring an outdoor hot tub, tennis court, and game room for guests to enjoy. A four-poster double bed graces the Victorian room with an *en suite* bathroom. The St. Andrews has a unique queen bed hewn from maple branches; the private bath is next door. Breakfast is served in the hunt salon or on the patio overlooking the gardens. Dorrington B&B is located close to the U.S. border, and 20 minutes from the ferry terminal to Victoria.

NEWFOUNDLAND

Note: All prices listed in this section are quoted in Canadian dollars.

Terra Nova Hospitality Home & Cottages ✪
PORT BLANDFORD, NEWFOUNDLAND, CANADA A0C 2G0

Tel: **(709) 543-2260; fax: (709) 543-2241**	Double/sb: **$55**
	Single/sb: **$45**
Host: **Rhoda Parsons**	Guest Cottage: **$75–$100**
Location: **130 mi. W of St. Johns**	Suites: **$65**
No of Rooms: **3**	Open: **All year**
Max. No. Sharing Bath: **5**	Reduced Rates: **Available**
Double/pb: **$55**	Breakfast: **Full**
Single/pb: **$45**	Other Meals: **Available**

Credit Cards: **MC, VISA**
Pets: **Yes, in cottage only**
Children: **Welcome, under 12 free**

Smoking: **Permitted**
Social Drinking: **Permitted**

Terra Nova is located three miles east of Terra Nova National Park and seventy miles east of Gander. Nearby there are three salmon rivers, a golf course, and hiking trails. Guide service is available for skidooing, hiking, and fishing. Kitchen and barbecue facilities are available, as well as a satellite TV, laundromat, sauna, and exercise equipment. For relaxing, there is a large room with cathedral ceiling, hardwood floor, and a fireplace, or a large deck that overlooks the ocean. Children will enjoy the play area and swings. Rhoda provides home-cooked meals with fresh-baked muffins, bread, and homemade jam.

NOVA SCOTIA

Note: All prices listed in this section are quoted in Canadian dollars.

Fairfield Farm Inn ✪
10 MAIN STREET, BOX 1287, MIDDLETON, NOVA SCOTIA, CANADA B0S 1P0

Tel: **(902) 825-6989; (800) 237-9896**
Best Time to Call: **9 AM–9 PM**
Hosts: **Richard and Shae Griffith**
Location: **90 mi. W of Halifax**
No. of Rooms: **5**
No. of Private Baths: **5**
Double/pb: **$50–$65**
Single/pb: **$45–$60**
Open: **All year**

Breakfast: **Full, Continental**
Credit Cards: **AMEX, DC, DISC, ER, MC, VISA**
Pets: **No**
Children: **Welcome, over 16**
Smoking: **No**
Social Drinking: **Permitted**
Airport/Station Pickup: **Yes**

This restored 1886 Victorian farmhouse features antique furnishings, air-conditioning, and king- or queen-size beds. One hundred and ten acres of garden, meadow, and woodland surround the Inn, yet it is a five-minute walk to restaurants, museums, and boutiques. The Annapolis River and Slocum Brook are on the property, as are birding and walking trails. Richard and Shae take pride in offering maritime hospitality and a wholesome country breakfast.

ONTARIO

Note: All prices listed in this section are quoted in Canadian dollars.

Cozy Corner ✪
2 MORTON CRESCENT, BARRIE, ONTARIO, CANADA L4N 7T3

Tel: **(705) 739-0157**
Best Time to Call: **10 AM–9 PM**
Hosts: **Charita and Harry Kirby**
Location: **36 mi. N of Toronto**
No. of Rooms: **3**
No. of Private Baths: **2**
Max. No. Sharing Bath: **3**
Double/sb: **$60**
Single/sb: **$50**
Suites: **$95**
Open: **All year**

Breakfast: **Full**
Other Meals: **Available**
Credit Cards: **VISA**
Pets: **No**
Children: **No**
Smoking: **No**
Social Drinking: **Permitted**
Minimum Stay: **2 nights**
Airport/Station Pickup: **Yes**
Foreign Languages: **Spanish, German**

A warm welcome awaits you at this contemporary two-story brick home. Choose from three lavishly appointed rooms. Amenities include a Jacuzzi, central air-conditioning, TV, and a sunny greenhouse. Charita, a former schoolteacher, spent four years as governess to Julio Iglesias's three children prior to moving to Canada; her English-born husband completed three years of culinary training in Germany before working at the Savoy Hotel London. Thanks to Harry's expertise, you'll wake to a superb British-style breakfast featuring imported Lincolnshire pork, sausage, bacon, grilled tomato, fried bread, and scrambled eggs. German coffee cake, muffins, or toast with marmalade will appeal to the guest with a sweet tooth.

Glen Mhor Guesthouse ✪
5381 RIVER ROAD, NIAGARA FALLS, ONTARIO, CANADA L2E 3H1

Tel: **(905) 354-2600; fax: (905) 354-2600**
Host: **Vi Moncur**
Location: **Between Rainbow and Whirlpool Bridges to USA**
No. of Rooms: **4**
No. of Private Baths: **2**
Max. No. Sharing Bath: **5**
Double/pb: **$75**
Single/pb: **$65**
Double/sb: **$55–$59**

Single/sb: **$45**
Open: **All year**
Reduced Rates: **Jan. 4–Apr. 30**
Breakfast: **Full**
Credit Cards: **MC, VISA**
Pets: **No**
Children: **Welcome, infants and over 7**
Smoking: **Restricted**
Social Drinking: **Permitted**
Station Pickup: **Yes**

You can expect a friendly welcome at this turn-of-the-century home. Glen Mhor Guesthouse is situated on the lovely Niagara River, only a short drive from Niagara-on-the-Lake, home of the Shaw Theatre. A leisurely walk takes you to the falls; cyclists may bring bicycles or rent them for a ride on the riverfront path. At all times you can relax in comfortable wicker chairs on the restored veranda overlooking the Niagara's awesome gorge. A hearty breakfast is served on the sunporch or in the antique-furnished dining room. For light snacks, a refrigerator is available.

Gretna Green ✪
5077 RIVER ROAD, NIAGARA FALLS, ONTARIO, CANADA L2E 3G7

Tel: **(905) 357-2081**
Hosts: **Stan and Marg Gardiner**
Location: **25 mi. NE of Buffalo, N.Y.**
No. of Rooms: **4**
No. of Private Baths: **4**
Double/pb: **$60–$70**
Single/pb: **$45–$50**

Open: **All year**
Reduced Rates: **10% Oct. 1–Apr. 30**
Breakfast: **Full**
Pets: **No**
Children: **Welcome**
Smoking: **Restricted**
Social Drinking: **No**

Gretna Green is an easy stroll from the falls—the front porch of this 90-year-old brick home overlooks Niagara Gorge. With Marineland, the Imax Theatre, the local museums, and year-round festivals, this area is rich in diversions. But you won't miss out on your favorite shows because each bedroom has a TV. Marg loves to bake, and prides herself on the homemade muffins and scones she serves at breakfast.

Almar House Bed & Breakfast ✪
339 MARY STREET, BOX 1103, NIAGARA-ON-THE-LAKE, ONTARIO, CANADA L0S 1J0

Tel: **(905) 468-1368**
Hosts: **Marie-Jane and Alan Johnson**
Location: **15 mi. N of Niagara Falls**
No. of Rooms: **3**
No. of Private Baths: **3**
Double/pb: **$60–$80**
Single/pb: **$55–$75**
Open: **All year**

Reduced Rates: **Winter**
Breakfast: **Full**
Pets: **No**
Children: **Welcome, prior arrangement**
Smoking: **No**
Social Drinking: **Permitted**
Station pickup: **Yes**
Foreign Languages: **French, German**

Situated in a peaceful part of a historic town, this Georgian-style home is within walking distance of shopping, restaurants, and the renowned Shaw Festival Theatres. Nearby you can visit Niagara Falls, battlefields, forts of the 1812 war, wineries, and the Welland Ship Canal. Breakfast is gourmet, served in the dining room. A guest lounge is available on the bedroom level, and the house is air conditioned. Relax and meet new friends in the elegant living room or mingle in the beautifully landscaped garden. Enjoy Marie-Jane and Alan's hospitality in your home away from home when visiting the Niagara region.

Hiebert's Guest House ✪
BOX 1371, 275 JOHN STREET, NIAGARA-ON-THE-LAKE, ONTARIO, CANADA L0S 1J0

Tel: **(905) 468-3687**
Hosts: **Otto and Marlene Hiebert**
Location: **10 mi. N of Niagara Falls**
No. of Rooms: **3**
No. of Private Baths: **3**
Double/pb: **$75–$85**
Double/sb: **$60–$65**
Single/sb: **$55–$60**

Open: **All year**
Reduced Rates: **10% Dec.–Mar.**
Breakfast: **Full**
Pets: **No**
Children: **Welcome**
Smoking: **No**
Social Drinking: **No**

The hosts wish they could share with you the many letters of reference attesting to "the cleanliness," "the warm Mennonite hospitality," "the delicious food," "the friendliness of the Hieberts." Their air-conditioned home is 10 miles from Niagara Falls, Ontario, and the U.S. border. The Shaw Festival Theatre and all of the area's points of interest are within walking distance. The breakfast muffins, served with homemade jams, are a special treat.

The Turner House ✪
P.O. BOX 1509, 293 REGENT STREET, NIAGARA-ON-THE-LAKE, ONTARIO, CANADA L0S 1J0

Tel: **(905) 468-4440**
Best Time to Call: **9 AM–9 PM**
Hosts: **Donna and Larry Turner**

Location: **20 mi. N of Niagara Falls**
No. of Rooms: **3**
No. of Private Baths: **1**

Max. No. Sharing Bath: **4**
Double/pb: **$90**
Double/sb: **$80**
Open: **All year**
Reduced Rates: **Jan.–Apr.**

Breakfast: **Full**
Pets: **No**
Children: **Welcome, over 12**
Smoking: **No**
Social Drinking: **No**

Located in a historic town near Niagara Falls, this 1880s Victorian home provides a quiet base for your tour of the battlefields and forts of the War of 1812, Niagara Falls, the Welland Ship canal, and local vineyards and wineries. Then attend one of the many plays at the Shaw Festival Theatre. Turner House is within walking distance of shops, dining, and three theaters. Enjoy your hosts' fine home, full breakfast, and knowledge of the area. Sit in the parlor, the upstairs sitting room, by the pool, or on the porch and relax before your next activity in this scenic and historic area.

Ottawa Bed & Breakfast ✪

488 COOPER STREET, OTTAWA, ONTARIO, CANADA K1R 5H9

Tel: **(613) 563-0161; (800) 461-7889**
Best Time to Call: **10 AM–10 PM**
Coordinators: **Robert Rivoire and R. G.
   Simmens**

Regions Covered: **Ontario—Ottawa**
Rates (Single/Double):
   Average: **$49 / $59**
Credit Cards: **No**

If you are seeking an interesting but inexpensive holiday, then Canada's capital, Ottawa, is the place for you. The city is packed with free activities including museums, the House of Parliament, art galleries, and historic sites. You can skate on the Rideau Canal or bike on miles of parkways and trails.

Australis Guest House ✪

35 MARLBOROUGH AVENUE, OTTAWA, ONTARIO, CANADA K1N 8E6

Tel/Fax: **(613) 235-8461**
Best Time to Call: **After 4 PM**
Hosts: **Brian, Carol, and Olivia Waters**
Location: **1 mi. from Parliament**
No. of Rooms: **3**
No. of Private Baths: **1**
Max. No. Sharing Bath: **4**
Double/pb: **$75**
Single/pb: **$62**
Double/sb: **$63**
Single/sb: **$52**

Open: **All year**
Reduced Rates: **10% seniors; 10% less
   Nov.–Mar.**
Breakfast: **Full**
Pets: **No**
Children: **Welcome, over 6**
Smoking: **Yes**
Social Drinking: **No**
Station Pickup: **Yes**
Foreign Languages: **French**

Located on a quiet tree-lined street in Sandy Hill, one of Ottawa's first residential areas, Australis House is next to the Rideau River and Strathcona Park. It is but a twenty-minute walk to the Parliament buildings, museums, and the art gallery. This handsome brick house boasts leaded windows, fireplaces, oak floors, and eight-foot stained glass windows overlooking the hall. Your hosts have lived in Africa, Asia, and Latin America, and mementos from their travels are displayed throughout. Hearty, delicious breakfasts, with fruit salads and home-baked breads and pastries, ensure that guests start the day in the right way.

Bed and Breakfast Homes of Toronto ✪
P.O. BOX 46093, COLLEGE PARK POST OFFICE, TORONTO, ONTARIO, CANADA M5B 2L8

Tel: **(416) 363-6362**
Best Time to Call: **8 AM–11 PM**
Coordinator: **May Jarvie**
States/Regions Covered: **Toronto**
Descriptive Directory of B&Bs: **Free**

Rates (Single/Double):
Modest: **$45–$55**
Average: **$60–$75**
Luxury: **$80–$125**

Bed and Breakfast Homes of Toronto is a friendly cooperative of eighteen homes located in various downtown and surrounding neighborhoods, all serviced by safe public transportation. Hosts offer individual rooms or private suites at about half the cost of hotels. Each bed and breakfast has its own unique ambience and decor, a high standard of cleanliness, comfort, and, in most cases, free parking.

The Downtown Toronto Association of B&B Guest Houses ✪
P.O. BOX 190, STATION B, TORONTO, ONTARIO, CANADA M5T 2W1

Tel: **(416) 368-1420; fax: (416) 368-1653**
Best Time to Call: **9 AM–8 PM Mon.–Fri.; 9 AM–noon Sat.–Sun.**
Coordinator: **Linda Lippa**
Region Covered: **Toronto**

Rates (Single/Double):
Modest: **$45–$55**
Average: **$65–$85**
Luxury: **$95–$110**
Credit Cards: **VISA**
Minimum Stay: **2 nights**

Quality, charm, and safety are the three main elements of the roster, which includes accommodations in more than twenty-five restored older homes throughout Toronto. A free brochure contains a map listing each neighborhood where the homes are located. All provide ample parking and are within 10 minutes of Eaton Centre, theaters, fine restaurants, and 24-hour public transit lines.

Toronto Bed & Breakfast (1987) Inc. ✪
21 KINGSWOOD ROAD, TORONTO, ONTARIO, CANADA M4E 3N4
beds@torontobandb.com

Tel: **(416) 588-8800; fax: (416) 927-0838**
Best Time to Call: **9 AM–7 PM, Mon.–Fri.**

Coordinator: **Marcie Getgood**
Region Covered: **Toronto**

Rates (Single/Double):
Modest: **$41 / $51**
Average: **$51 / $56**
Luxury: **$61 / $85**

Credit Cards: **AMEX, DC, MC, VISA**
Minimum Stay: **2 nights, holiday weekends**

Toronto's oldest professional reservation service represents twenty-five high-quality homes throughout metropolitan Toronto. All are close to the safe, efficient public transit system; most are situated in charming downtown neighborhoods, within walking distance of many attractions. Marcie matches your needs as closely as possible to the right home or guesthouse, where hosts share advice on local sights, dining, or shopping. A free brochure is available upon request.

Amblecote ✪

109 WALMER ROAD, TORONTO, ONTARIO, CANADA M54 2X8
beds@torontobandb.com

Tel: **(416) 927-1713; (416) 588-8800; fax: (416) 927-0838**
Hosts: **Dave and Marcie Getgood**
No. of Rooms: **4**
Max. No. Sharing Bath: **4**
Double/sb: **$65–$70**
Single/sb: **$55–$60**

Open: **All year**
Breakfast: **Full, Continental**
Pets: **No**
Children: **Welcome, over 12**
Smoking: **No**
Social Drinking: **Permitted**

An award-winning historical home built in the rambling English cottage style, Amblecote is located near tourist attractions, shopping, theaters, restaurants, cafes, and galleries. The B&B is just steps away from the subway line that takes you into Toronto. Yet you will return to a peaceful neighborhood of stately homes.

Beaconsfield B&B ✪

38 BEACONSFIELD AVENUE, TORONTO, ONTARIO, CANADA M6J 3H9
beacon@idirect.com

Tel: **(416) 535-3338; fax: (416) 535-3338**
Best Time to Call: **Anytime**
Hosts: **Bernie and Katya McLoughlin**
No. of Rooms: **4**
No. of Private Baths: **1**
Max. No. Sharing Bath: **4**
Double/pb: **$99**
Single/pb: **$89**
Double/sb: **$69**

Single/sb: **$59**
Suites: **$99**
Open: **All year**
Breakfast: **Full**
Pets: **No**
Children: **Welcome**
Smoking: **No**
Social Drinking: **Permitted**
Foreign Languages: **Spanish, Russian**

Bernie and Katya, an artist-actress couple, invite you to their colorful 1882 Victorian home full of fun and sun, art and heart. Beaconsfield is in a quiet, multicultural downtown neighborhood just beyond the commercial center. A short trolley ride takes you to major theaters, CN

Tower, SkyDome, Chinatown, and Eaton Centre. Choose between imaginatively decorated rooms or the very private Mexican honeymoon suite with its treetop terrace. All come with top-of-the-line beds and full, creative breakfasts presented musically in an eclectic dining room. Parking, TV, air-conditioning, sundecks, refrigerator, and microwave are among the amenities at guests' disposal.

Orchard View ☉
92 ORCHARD VIEW BOULEVARD, TORONTO, ONTARIO, CANADA M4R 1C2

Tel: (416) 488-6826
Hosts: Donna and Ken Ketchen
Location: In Toronto
No. of Rooms: 2
No. of Private Baths: 1
Max. No. Sharing Bath: 3
Double/pb: $75
Single/pb: $60

Double/sb: $70
Single/sb: $60
Open: All year
Breakfast: Full
Pets: Cats only
Children: No
Smoking: No
Social Drinking: Permitted

Donna and Ken's home is located in the Yonge-Eglinton area, a five-minute walk from the Eglinton subway station, your portal to all the major city attractions. Of course, right in the neighborhood, there are many fine shops to investigate and streets to explore. Choose between Orchard View's queen bedroom, decorated in shades of blue, and the room with twin beds, decorated in rose tones. If weather permits, breakfast is served on the deck; specialties include apple puff pancakes, omelettes, and waffles.

Vanderkooy Bed & Breakfast ☉
53 WALKER AVENUE, TORONTO, ONTARIO, CANADA M4V 1G3

Tel: (416) 925-8765
Best Time to Call: 7 AM–11 PM
Host: Joan Vanderkooy
Location: In Toronto
No. of Rooms: 3
No. of Private Baths: 1
Max. No. Sharing Bath: 4
Double/pb: $75
Single/pb: $60

Double/sb: $65
Single/sb: $50
Open: All year
Reduced Rates: Available
Breakfast: Full
Pets: No
Children: Welcome, over 12
Smoking: No
Social Drinking: Permitted

Joan and the resident cat, Jazz, welcome you to this charming home where you will enjoy comfortable guest rooms and breakfast served in an open dining room overlooking the garden. A short walk to Summerhill station on the Yonge subway line allows easy access to downtown attractions, including Harbourfront, Skydome, the Eaton Centre, and theaters. Restaurants and shopping districts are all within walking distance. Feel free to watch TV by the fire, enjoy the waterfall and pond in the garden, or relax on the flower-filled deck in the summer.

QUEBEC

Note: All prices listed in this section are quoted in Canadian dollars.

Bed & Breakfast à Montréal
P.O. BOX 575, SNOWDON STATION, MONTREAL, QUEBEC, CANADA H3X 3T8

Tel: **(514) 738-9410; (800) 738-4338;**
 fax **(514) 735-7493**
Coordinator: **Marian Kahn**
Regions Covered: **Montreal, Quebec City**

Rates (Single/Double):
 Modest: **$40 / $55**
 Average: **$45 / $65**
 Luxury: **$55 / $75**
Credit Cards: **AMEX, MC, VISA**

Marian established the province's first reservation service in 1980. Most of the fifty hosts in her group have been welcoming guests ever since and have seen many travelers return for repeat visits. Homes are located downtown, in the Latin Quarter, in fashionable Westmount, and in other attractive neighborhoods. Accommodations are in Victorian rowhouses, condo apartments, and even a contemporary ranch-style house overlooking a golf course. The standard of gracious hospitality is assured in all. Gift certificates are available.

Bed & Breakfast—A Downtown Network ✪
3458 LAVAL AVENUE, MONTREAL, QUEBEC, CANADA H2X 3C8

Tel: **(514) 289-9749; (800) 267-5180**
Best Time to Call: **8:30 AM–6 PM**
Coordinator: **Robert Finkelstein**
Regions Covered: **Montreal, Outremont, Quebec City, Westmount**

Rates (Single/Double):
 Modest: **$25 / $35**
 Average: **$30–$40 / $45–$55**
 Luxury: **$55–$65 / $65–$75**
Credit Cards: **AMEX, MC, VISA**
Foreign Languages: **Japanese**

Bob specializes in downtown accommodations with hosts ready to introduce you to good shopping, diverse restaurants, and places of special interest with an experienced eye on good value. After your day of hectic activity that might include a *calèche* ride through the cobbled streets of the Old Quarter, or a visit to the futuristic high-fashion urban area, and samples of excellent cuisine from all over the world, your hosts look forward to having you return to relax in their homes.

A Montreal Oasis ✪
3000 DE BRESLAY ROAD, MONTREAL, QUEBEC, CANADA H3Y 2G7

Tel: **(514) 935-2312**
Host: **Lena Blondel**
No. of Rooms: **3**
Max. No. Sharing Bath: **3**
Double/sb: **$60–$90**
Single/sb: **$50–$70**
Guest Cottage: **$80–$85; sleeps 3**

Open: **All year**
Breakfast: **Full**
Pets: **No**
Children: **Welcome, over 10**
Smoking: **No**
Social Drinking: **Permitted**
Minimum Stay: **June–Sept.**

This spacious home is located in the Priest Farm district. According to the Canadian Center for Architecture, this is the only 1920s residential development of interest in downtown Montreal. In downtown's select West End you can enjoy the Fine Art Museum and Crescent and St. Catherine's streets. The bed and breakfast is decorated with Quebec and Swedish furniture, and the art is African, Asian, and Swedish. Lena is Swedish and lives in Montreal by choice, although she has lived in many other parts of the world. She also operates a small network of homes in downtown Montreal, including the Latin Quarter and the Old City.

Bay View Farm/La Ferme Bay View ✪
P.O. BOX 21, 337 MAIN HIGHWAY ROUTE 132, NEW CARLISLE WEST, QUEBEC, CANADA G0C 1Z0

Tel: **(418) 752-2725, 752-6718**
Best Time to Call: **7–8 AM**
Host: **Helen Sawyer**
No. of Rooms: **5**

No. of Private Baths: **1**
Max. No. Sharing Bath: **4**
Double/pb: **$35**
Double/sb: **$35**

Single/sb: **$25**
Guest Cottage: **$350 weekly; sleeps 10**
Open: **All year**
Breakfast: **Full**
Other Meals: **Available**
Pets: **No**

Children: **Welcome**
Smoking: **No**
Social Drinking: **No**
Airport/Station Pickup: **Yes**
Foreign Languages: **French**

A spacious wooden home on the rugged Gaspé Peninsula coast, Bay View Farm is a mecca for folk music fans: there are concerts throughout the year, and an annual festival the second weekend of August. If you choose to exercise your body as well as your voice, the local options include golf, tennis, and waterfront sports. Your host serves generous breakfasts of bacon, farm-fresh eggs, toast, coffee, homemade muffins and jam, and fresh seasonal fruit from her own gardens and orchards. Additional light meals are offered at moderate cost.

Gîte de Campagne ✪
1028 PRINCIPALE, PRÉVOST, QUÉBEC, CANADA J0R 1T0

Tel: **(514) 224-7631**
Best Time to Call: **Days and evenings**
Hosts: **François Laroche**
Location: **35 mi. N of Montreal**
No. of Rooms: **4**
Max. No. Sharing Bath: **4**
Double/sb: **$47**
Single/sb: **$35**
Open: **All year**

Reduced Rates: **10% 3 nights and longer**
Breakfast: **Full**
Pets: **Sometimes**
Children: **Welcome**
Smoking: **Permitted**
Social Drinking: **Permitted**
Foreign Languages: **French**

Experience the warmth of France without crossing the ocean. The Gîte de Campagne, a hundred-year-old manor, offers it. Hiking, bicycling, cross-country skiing, horseback riding, golfing, canoeing, and nature await your arrival. This B&B is situated in the historic section of a small village. François, a young retired analyst, is available to help you understand the French way of living in North America. He welcomes you, cooks for you, and will often accompany you to outside activities.

Appendix:
UNITED STATES AND CANADIAN TOURIST OFFICES

Listed here are the addresses and telephone numbers for the tourist offices of every U.S. state and Canadian province. When you write or call one of these offices, be sure to request a map of the state and a calendar of events. If you will be visiting a particular city or region, or if you have any special interests, be sure to specify them as well.

State Tourist Offices

Alabama Bureau of Tourism
Box 4309, 401 Adams Avenue
Montgomery, Alabama 36103-4309
(334) 242-4169; (800) ALABAMA [252-2262]; fax (334) 264-7060

Alaska Division of Tourism
P.O. Box 110801
Juneau, Alaska 99811-0801
http://www.java.state.ak/tourism/
(907) 465-2010

Arizona Office of Tourism
2702 N 3rd Street
Suite 4015
Phoenix, Arizona 85009
(800) 842-8257

Arkansas Department of Park and Tourism
1 Capitol Mall
Little Rock, Arkansas 72201
(501) 682-7777 or (800) NATURAL

California Office of Tourism
P.O. Box 1499
Sacramento, California 95812
(800) 862-2543 or (916) 322-2881

Colorado Dept. of Tourism
P.O. Box 3524
Englewood, Colorado 80155
(303) 296-3384 or (800) COLORADO

Connecticut Department of Economic Development—Vacations
865 Brook Street
Rocky Hill, Connecticut 06067-3405
(203) 258-4355 or (800) CT-BOUND [282-6863]

Delaware Tourism Office
99 Kings Highway, P.O. Box 1401
Dover, Delaware 19903
http://www.state.de.us/tourism/intro.htm
(302) 736-4271 or (800) 441-8846

Washington, D.C. Convention and Visitors' Association
1212 New York Avenue N.W.
Suite 600
Washington, D.C. 20005
(202) 789-7000; (800) 422-8644 in USA

Florida Division of Tourism
126 W. Van Buren Street
Tallahassee, Florida 32399-2000
(904) 487-1462

Georgia Tourist Division
Box 1776
Atlanta, Georgia 30301
http://www.georgia-on-my-mind.org/
(404) 656-3590 or (800) 847-4842 in USA

Hawaii Visitors Bureau
2270 Kalakaua Avenue
Suite 801
Honolulu, Hawaii 96815
http://www.visit.hawaii.org/
(808) 923-1811; (800) 353-5846 in USA

Idaho Travel Council
700 W. State Street
Boise, Idaho 83720-2700
(800) 635-7820 in USA or (208) 334-2470

Illinois Office of Tourism
100 W Randolph Street
Suite 3-400
Chicago, Illinois 60602
(800) 223-0121

Indiana Tourism Development
 Division
1 North Capitol, Suite 100
Indianapolis, Indiana 46204-2288
(317) 232-8860 or (800) 291-8844 in USA

Iowa Tourism Office
200 East Grand Avenue
Des Moines, Iowa 50309
(515) 242-4705 or (800) 345-IOWA
 [4692] in USA

Kansas Travel and Tourism Division
700 SW Harrison Street, Suite 1300
Topeka, Kansas 66603-3712
(913) 296-2009 or (800) 252-6727 in USA

Kentucky Department of Travel
 Development
P.O. Box 2011
Frankfort, Kentucky 40602
(800) 225-8747 in USA
TDD-equipped

Louisiana Office of Tourism
P.O. Box 94291
Baton Rouge, Louisiana 70804-9291
(504) 342-8119 (within Louisiana) or
 (800) 677-4082 in USA

Maine Publicity Bureau
P.O. Box 2300
325-B Water Street
Hallowell, Maine 04347
(207) 623-0363 or (800) 533-9595 in USA

Maryland Office of Tourist
 Development
217 E. Redwood Street
Baltimore, Maryland 21202
http://www.mdisfun.org/
(410) 767-3400 or (800) MD-IS-FUN
 [634-7386]

Massachusetts Office of Tourism
100 Cambridge Street—13th Floor
Boston, Massachusetts 02202
(617) 727-3201 or (800) 447-MASS
 [6277] in USA

Michigan Travel Bureau
Department of Commerce
P.O. Box 30226
Lansing, Michigan 48909
atwoodt@state.mi.us
(517) 373-0670 or (800) 543-2YES [2937]
 in USA

Minnesota Tourist Information Center
121 7th Place East
#100 Metro Square
St. Paul, Minnesota 55101-2112
http://www.tccn.com/mn.tourism/
 mnhome.html
(612) 296-5029 or (800) 657-3700
 (out of state)

Mississippi Division of Tourism
Box 22825
Jackson, Mississippi 39205
(601) 364-2163 or (800) 927-6378 in USA

Missouri Division of Tourism
P.O. Box 1055
Jefferson City, Missouri 65102
(314) 751-4133 or (800) 877-1234 in USA

Travel Montana
P.O. Box 7549
Missoula, Montana 59807
(800) 548-3390

Nebraska Division of Travel and
 Tourism
P.O. Box 94666
Lincoln, Nebraska 68509-4666
http://www.ded.state.ne.us/
 tourism.html
(800) 228-4307 in USA

Nevada Commission on Tourism
Capitol Complex
Carson City, Nevada 89710
http://www.travelnevada.com/
(702) 687-4322 or (800) NEVADA 8
 [638-2328] in USA

New Hampshire Office of Travel and
 Tourism Development
P.O. Box 1856
Concord, New Hampshire 03302-1856
http://www.visitnh.gov
(800) FUN-IN-NH [386-4664] or (603)
 271-2666

New Jersey Division of Travel and
  Tourism
C.N. 826
Trenton, New Jersey 08625-0826
(609) 292-2470 or (800) JERSEY-7 [537-
  7397]

New Mexico Department of Tourism
491 Old Santa Fe Trail
Santa Fe, New Mexico 87503
(505) 827-7400, (800) 545-2040, or (800)
  545-2040 (out of state), (505) 827-
  7402 (FAX)

New York State Division of Tourism
1 Commerce Plaza
Albany, New York 12245
(518) 474-4116 or (800) CALL-NYS
  [225-5697]

North Carolina Travel and Tourism
  Division
301 North Wilmington Street
Raleigh, North Carolina 27626
(919) 733-4171 or (800) VISIT NC
  [847-4862] in USA

North Dakota Tourism Promotion
Liberty Memorial Building
604 E. Boulevard
Bismarck, North Dakota 58505
(701) 328-2525 or (800) HELLO ND
  [435-5663]

Ohio Division of Travel and Tourism
P.O. Box 1001
Columbus, Ohio 43266-0101
http://www.travel.state.oh.us
(800) BUCKEYE [282-5393]

Oklahoma Division of Tourism
500 Will Rogers Bldg.
Oklahoma City, Oklahoma 73105
(405) 521-3981 or (800) 652-OKLA
  [6552]

Oregon Economic Development
  Tourism Division
775 Summer Street N.E.
Salem, Oregon 97310
(503) 373-1270 or (800) 547-7842

Pennsylvania Bureau of Travel
  Marketing
Department of Commerce
400 Forum Building
Harrisburg, Pennsylvania 17120
(717) 232-8880 or (800) VISIT-PA [847-
  4872]

Puerto Rico Tourism Company
23rd Floor
575 Fifth Avenue
New York, New York 10017
(212) 599-6262 or (800) 223-6530
  or (800) 866-STAR [7827]

Rhode Island Department of Economic
  Development
Tourism Division
1 W Exchange St.
Providence, Rhode Island 02903
http://www.visitrhodeisland.com/
  (401) 277-2601 or (800) 556-2484

South Carolina Division of Tourism
1205 Pendleton Street
Columbia, South Carolina 29201-0071
(803) 734-0122; (800) 868-2492

South Dakota Division of Tourism
Capitol Lake Plaza
711 East Wells Avenue
Pierre, South Dakota 57501-3369
http://www.state.sd.us/state/
  executive/tourism/tourism.html
(605) 773-3301 or (800) 732-5682

Tennessee Tourist Development
P.O. Box 23170
320 6th Avenue N
Racheal Jackson Bldg., 5th Floor
Nashville, Tennessee 37202-3170
(615) 741-2158; (800) 836-6200

Texas Dept. of Commerce
Division of Tourism
P.O. Box 12728
Austin, Texas 78711-2728
(512) 462-9191 or (800) 8888-TEX [888-
  8839]

Utah Travel Council
Council Hall
Capitol Hill
Salt Lake City, Utah 84114
http://www.utah.com/
(801) 538-1030 or (800) 200-1160

Vermont Department of Travel and
  Tourism
134 State Street
Montpelier, Vermont 05602
(802) 828-3236 or (800) VERMONT
  [837-6668]

Virginia Division of Tourism
1021 E. Cary Street 14th Floor #500
Richmond, Virginia 23219
(804) 786-4484 or (800) VISIT-VA [847-4882]

Washington State Tourism
  Development Division
P.O. Box 42500
101 General Administration Building
Olympia, Washington 98504
(206) 586-2088 or (800) 544-1800 (out
  of state)

Travel West Virginia
Capital Complex, Bldg. 17
Charleston, West Virginia 25305-0312
(800) CALL WVA [225-5982] or
  (304) 558-2766

Wisconsin Division of Tourism
P.O. Box 7606
Madison, Wisconsin 53707-7606
(608) 266-2161; (800) 432-8747

Wyoming Travel Commission
I-25 and College Drive
Cheyenne, Wyoming 82002
(307) 777-7777 or (800) CALL-WYO
  [225-5996]

Canadian Province Tourist Offices

Alberta Tourism, Parks, and Recreation
City Center Building
P.O. Box 2400
Edmonton, Alberta, Canada T5J 2Z4
(403) 427-4321 (from Edmonton area)
  or (800) 661-8888 (from the U.S. and
  Canada)

Tourism British Columbia
Parliament Bldgs.
Victoria, British Columbia, Canada
  V8V 1X4
(604) 663-6000 or (800) 663-6000

Travel Manitoba
Department 6020
7th Floor
155 Carlton Street
Winnipeg, Manitoba, Canada
  R3C 3H8
http://www.gov.mb.ca/itt/travel/
  explore/
(204) 945-3777 or (800) 665-0040 (from
  mainland U.S. and Canada)

New Brunswick Tourism
P.O. Box 12345
Fredericton, New Brunswick, Canada
  E3B 5C3
(506) 453-8745 or (800) 561-0123 (from
  mainland U.S. and Canada)

Newfoundland/Labrador Tourism
  Branch
Department of Tourism & Culture
P.O. Box 8730
St. John's, Newfoundland, Canada
  A1B 4K2
info@tourism.gov.nf.ca
(709) 729-2830 (from St. John's area)
  or (800) 563-6353 (from mainland
  U.S. and Canada)

Northwest Territories Tourism
Box 1320, Yellowknife
http://www.edt.gov.nt.ca/guide/
  index.html
(403) 873-7200 or (800) 661-0788

Tourisme Quebec
C.P. 979
Montreal, Quebec H3C 2W3
(800) 363-7777 or (514) 873-2015

Tourism Saskatchewan
500-1900 Albert St.
Regina, Saskatchewan, Canada
  S4P 4L9
http://www.sasktourism.sk.ca/
(306) 787-2300 or (800) 667-7191

Tourism Yukon
P.O. Box 2703
Whitehorse, Yukon, Canada Y1A 2C6
http://www.touryukon.com/
(403) 667-5340

BED AND BREAKFAST RESERVATION REQUEST FORM

Dear _____
   Host's Name

I read about your home in *Bed & Breakfast U.S.A. 1998*, and would be interested in making reservations to stay with you.

My name: _____

Address: _____
   street

_____
   city   state   zip

Telephone: _____
   area code

Business address/telephone: _____

_____

Number of adult guests: _____

Number and ages of children: _____

Desired date and time of arrival: _____

Desired length of stay: _____

Mode of transportation: _____
(car, bus, train, plane)

Additional information/special requests/allergies: _____

_____

_____

_____

_____

_____

_____

I look forward to hearing from you soon.

Sincerely,

APPLICATION FOR MEMBERSHIP

(Please type or print)
(Please refer to Preface, pages xvii–xviii, for our membership criteria.)

Name of Bed & Breakfast: _____

Address: _____

City: _____ State: _____ Zip: _____ Phone: ( ) _____

Best Time to Call: _____

Host(s): _____

Located: No. of miles _____ compass direction _____ of Major

City _____ Geographic region _____

No. of miles _____ from major route _____ Exit: _____

No. of guest bedrooms with private bath: _____
No. of guest bedrooms that share a bath: _____
How many people (including *your* family) must use the shared
bath? _____
How many bedrooms, if any, have a sink in them? _____

Room Rates:
$ _____ Double—private bath $ _____ Double—shared bath
$ _____ Single—private bath $ _____ Single—shared bath
$ _____ Suites
Separate Guest Cottage $ _____ Sleeps _____

Are you open year-round? ☐ Yes ☐ No
If "No," specify when you are open: _____

How many rooms are wheelchair accessible? _____

Do you require a minimum stay? _____

Do you discount rates at any time? ☐ No ☐ Yes

If "yes," specify when you discount rates: _____

Do you offer a discount to senior citizens? ☐ No ☐ Yes: _____ %

Do you offer a discount for families? ☐ No ☐ Yes: _____ %

Breakfast: Type of breakfast included in rate:
☐ Full ☐ Continental

Describe breakfast specialties: _____
_____

Are any other meals provided? ☐ No   ☐ Yes
   Lunch ☐ cost: $ _____ Dinner ☐ cost: $ _____

Do you accept credit cards? ☐ No   ☐ Yes:
☐ AMEX ☐ DINERS ☐ DISCOVER ☐ MASTERCARD ☐ VISA

Will you GUARANTEE your rates from January through December
   1999? ☐ Yes   ☐ No

Note: This Guarantee applies only to those guests making reservations having read about you in *Bed & Breakfast U.S.A. 1999*.

If you have household pets, specify how many:
   ☐ Dog(s)   ☐ Cat(s)   ☐ Other

Can you accommodate a guest's pet?
   ☐ No   ☐ Yes   ☐ Sometimes

Are children welcome? ☐ No   ☐ Yes   If "Yes," specify age
   restriction _____

Do you permit smoking somewhere inside your house?
   ☐ No   ☐ Yes

Do you permit social drinking? ☐ No   ☐ Yes

Guests can be met at ☐ Airport ____ ☐ Train ____ ☐ Bus ____

Can you speak a foreign language fluently? ☐ No   ☐ Yes
Describe: _____

GENERAL AREA OF YOUR B&B (e.g., Boston historic district; 20 minutes from Chicago Loop):

GENERAL DESCRIPTION OF YOUR B&B (e.g., brick Colonial with white shutters; Victorian mansion with stained glass windows):

AMBIENCE OF YOUR B&B (e.g., furnished with rare antiques; lots of wood and glass):

THE QUALITIES THAT MAKE YOUR B&B SPECIAL ARE:

THINGS OF HISTORIC, SCENIC, CULTURAL, OR GENERAL INTEREST NEARBY (e.g., one mile from the San Diego Zoo; walking distance to the Lincoln Memorial):

YOUR OCCUPATION and SPECIAL INTERESTS (e.g., a retired teacher of Latin interested in woodworking; full-time host interested in quilting):

If you do welcome children, are there any special provisions for them (e.g., crib, playpen, high-chair, play area, baby-sitter)?

Do you offer snacks (e.g., complimentary wine and cheese; pretzels and chips but BYOB)?

Can guests use your kitchen for light snacks? ☐ No   ☐ Yes

Do you offer the following amenities? ☐ Guest refrigerator
   ☐ Air-conditioning ☐ TV ☐ Piano ☐ Washing machine
   ☐ Dryer ☐ Hot tub ☐ Pool ☐ Tennis court
   Other _____

What major college or university is within 10 miles?
_____

Please supply the name, address, and phone number of three personal references from people not related to you (please use a separate sheet).

Please enclose a copy of your brochure along with color photos including exterior, guest bedrooms, baths, and breakfast area. Bedroom photos should include view of the headboard(s), bedside lamps, and night tables. Please show us a typical breakfast setting. Use a label to identify the name of your B&B *on each*. If you have a black-and-white line drawing, send it along. If you have an original breakfast recipe that you'd like to share, send it along, too. (Of course, credit will be given to your B&B.) **Nobody can describe your B&B better than you. Limit your description to 100 words and submit it typed, double-spaced, on a separate sheet of paper. We will of course reserve the right to edit.** As a member of the Tourist House Association of America, your B&B will be described in the next edition of our book, *Bed & Breakfast U.S.A.*, published by Plume, an imprint of Dutton Signet, a member of Penguin Putnam Inc., and distributed to bookstores and libraries throughout the U.S. The book is also used as a reference for B&Bs in our country by major offices of tourism throughout the world.

Note: The following will NOT be considered for inclusion in *Bed & Breakfast U.S.A.:* Rental properties or properties where a host doesn't reside on the premises. B&Bs having more than fifteen guest rooms. Rates exceeding $35 where six people share a bath. Rates exceeding $45 where five people share a bath. Applications received after March 31, 1998. Incomplete applications, no photos, etc. Applications received in states that are overcrowded; this is due to space limitations. Higher-priced B&Bs and inns will only be included according to space availability.

Note: If the publisher or author receives negative reports from your guests regarding a deficiency in our standards of CLEANLINESS, COMFORT, and CORDIALITY, and/or failure to honor the rate guarantee, we reserve the right to cancel your membership.

This membership application has been prepared by:

_____
(Signature)

Please enclose your $40 membership dues.   Date: _____

I am insured by _____ .

Return to:
Tourist House Association of America, Inc.
RD 1, Box 12A
Greentown, Pennsylvania 18426

To ensure that your listing will be considered for the 1999 edition of *Bed & Breakfast U.S.A.*, we MUST receive your completed application by March 31, 1998. Thereafter, listings will be considered only for the 2000 edition.

APPLICATION FOR MEMBERSHIP FOR A
BED & BREAKFAST RESERVATION SERVICE

NAME OF BED & BREAKFAST SERVICE: _____

ADDRESS: _____

CITY: _____ STATE: _____ ZIP: _____ PHONE:(   ) _____

COORDINATOR: _____

BEST TIME TO CALL: _____

Do you have a telephone answering ☐ machine?   ☐ service?

Names of state(s), cities, and towns where you have hosts (in alphabetical order, please, and limit to 10):

Number of hosts on your roster: _____

THINGS OF HISTORIC, SCENIC, CULTURAL, OR GENERAL INTEREST IN THE AREA(S) YOU SERVE:

Range of Rates:
   Modest: Single $ _____   Double $ _____
   Average: Single $ _____   Double $ _____
   Luxury: Single $ _____   Double $ _____

Will you GUARANTEE your rates through December 1999?
☐ Yes   ☐ No

How often do you reinspect listings? _____
Do you require a minimum stay? _____
Surcharges for one-night stay? _____
Do you accept credit cards? ☐ No   ☐ Yes:
☐ AMEX ☐ DINERS ☐ DISCOVER ☐ MASTERCARD
☐ VISA

Is the guest required to pay a fee to use your service?
☐ No   ☐ Yes—The fee is $ _____

Do you publish a directory of your B&B listings?
☐ No   ☐ Yes—The fee is $ _____

Are any of your B&Bs within 10 miles of a university? Which? ____

Briefly describe a sample host home in each of the previous categories: e.g., a cozy farmhouse where the host weaves rugs; a restored 1800 Victorian where the host is a retired general; a contemporary mansion with a sauna and swimming pool.

Please supply the name, address, and phone number of three personal references from people not related to you (please use a separate sheet of paper). Please enclose a copy of your brochure.

This membership application has been prepared by:

_____
(Signature)

Please enclose your $40 membership dues.   Date: _____

If you have a special breakfast recipe that you'd like to share, send it along. (Of course, credit will be given to your B&B agency.) As a member of the Tourist House Association of America, Inc., your B&B agency will be described in the next edition of our book, *Bed & Breakfast U.S.A.*, published by Plume, an imprint of Dutton Signet, a member of Penguin Putnam Inc. Return to: Tourist House Association of America, Inc., Greentown, PA 18426.

To ensure that your listing will be considered for the 1999 edition, we must receive your completed application by March 31, 1998. Thereafter, listings will be considered only for the 2000 edition.

INFORMATION ORDER FORM

We are constantly expanding our roster to include new members in the Tourist House Association of America, Inc. Their facilities will be fully described in the next edition of *Bed & Breakfast U.S.A.* In the meantime, we will be happy to send you a list including the name, address, telephone number, etc.

For those of you who would like to order additional copies of the book, and perhaps send one to a friend as a gift, we will be happy to fill mail orders. If it is a gift, let us know and we'll enclose a special gift card from you.

ORDER FORM

To:
Tourist House
Association of
America, Inc.
Book Dept.
Greentown, PA
18426

From: _____
(Print your name)

Address: _____

_____
City   State   Zip

Date: _____

Please send:

☐ _____ copies of *Bed & Breakfast U.S.A.* @ $14.50 each (includes 4th class mail)

Send to: _____

Address: _____

_____
City   State   Zip

☐ Enclose a gift card from:

Please make check or money order payable to Tourist House Association of America, Inc.

WE WANT TO HEAR FROM YOU!

Name: _____

Address: _____
        street

_____
        city   state   zip

Please contact the following B&Bs; I think that they would be great additions to the next edition of *Bed & Breakfast U.S.A.*

Name of B&B: _____

Address: _____
        street

_____
        city   state   zip

Comments:

Name of B&B: _____

Address: _____
        street

_____
        city   state   zip

Comments:

_____

The following is our report on our visit to the home of:

Name of B&B: _____ Date of visit: _____

Address: _____ I was pleased. ☐

_____ I was disappointed. ☐

Comments:

Just tear out this page and mail it to us. It won't ruin your book!

Return to:
Tourist House Association of America, Inc.
Greentown, Pennsylvania 18426